Colour and Citizenship

Colour and Citizenship

A Report on British Race Relations

E. J. B. Rose
in association with Nicholas Deakin
and
Mark Abrams
Valerie Jackson
Maurice Peston
A. H. Vanags
Brian Cohen
Julia Gaitskell
Paul Ward

Published for the
Institute of Race Relations, London
OXFORD UNIVERSITY PRESS
LONDON NEW YORK TORONTO
1969

Oxford University Press, Ely House, London W.1

GLASGOW NEW YORK TORONTO MELBOURNE WELLINGTON
CAPE TOWN SALISBURY IBADAN NAIROBI LUSAKA ADDIS ABABA
BOMBAY CALCUTTA MADRAS KARACHI LAHORE DACCA
KUALA LUMPUR SINGAPORE HONG KONG TOKYO

Printed in Great Britain by
The Camelot Press Ltd., London and Southampton

To Pamela and Rose

All I have is a voice
To undo the folded lie,
The romantic lie in the brain
Of the sensual man-in-the-street
And the lie of Authority
Whose buildings grope the sky:
There is no such thing as the State
And no one exists alone;
Hunger allows no choice
To the citizen or the police;
We must love one another or die.

W. H. Auden

CONTENTS

Foreword   xix

PART I   INTRODUCTION   I

Chapter 1   A Map in the Making   I
The emergence of a race relations problem in Britain—the example of
Gunnar Myrdal's *An American Dilemma*—focus on the response of the
British—the self-confidence of post-war Britain—ten years after—the
assumptions of the Survey of Race Relations—the changing situation—
decision to publish a summary report—ingredients and character of the
Report—structure and outline—the genesis of the Survey

Chapter 2   The Liberal Hour and After   10
The liberal hour—the bankruptcy of idealistic themes—disillusion and
'realism'—the concept of citizenship

1 *Migration and Citizenship*   16
(*a*) The American Experience—European immigrants—the Negro's
predicament—(*b*) The British Experience—the Irish—Eastern European Jews—Polish and Eastern European migrants since the Second
World War—(*c*) Black Migrants—the multi-racial Commonwealth—
British Nationality Act 1948—the welfare period—*civis Britannicus
sum*—equal status—control modifies civil rights—the White Paper
and separate status

2 *Permutations : a Glossary*   23
Assimilation—integration—pluralism—accommodation

Chapter 3   England, Whose England?   27
The meaning of citizenship—extension of social rights—obligations of
the state—factors of diversity, conflict, and unity—British values and
beliefs—social changes in post-war Britain

Chapter 4   Race: Some Myths and Realities   34
Introduction—theories of race—history of the term 'race'—mankind
as one species—race and 'racial purity', racial superiority—the absence
of clear racial demarcation lines—the antiquity of different racial
groups—intelligence—intermarriage—conclusion

PART II   COLOURED IMMIGRATION TO
          BRITAIN   43

Chapter 5   The Sending Societies   43

1 *The Migrations from the West Indies and Guyana*   43
   The British cultural background—Christianity—education—the
   legacy of slavery—skill and occupational background of emigrants

2 *The Migrations from India and Pakistan*   52
   The limited areas from which migrants come—the Sikhs—the effects
   of Partition—the advantages of migration—Sikhism and the caste
   system—emigration and the caste system—education—the Gujaratis—differences between East and West Pakistan—Mirpur—
   Campbellpur—occupational background of Pakistani emigrants—
   education—Islam—the family

Chapter 6   How the Migration Developed   65
   The consequences of the Second World War—West Indians in the
   R.A.F.—Overseas Volunteers in industry—Jamaican emigration
   1948–51—the effect of the McCarran–Walter Act—West Indian
   migration and the British labour market—relatives in Britain—post-
   war migration from India and Pakistan—travel agents and the effects
   of controls—predominance of men in the Asian migration—the coloured
   population in 1951 and 1961

Chapter 7   The Dynamics of the Migration   74
   Labour demand and the changing flow before 1962—the effect of the
   Commonwealth Immigrants Act 1962

   The Immigrant and Labour Demand   78
   Labour shortages and the alternative to migration

Chapter 8   After Control   82
   The shift from the Caribbean to Asia—distribution of immigrants
   1955–67 and of voucher-holders 1962–7—the shift to skills—B vouchers
   1965–7—the shift from wage-earners to dependants 1962–7

PART III   THE EVIDENCE FROM THE TWO
           CENSUSES   91

Chapter 9   Introduction   91
   The 1966 10% Sample Census—analysis of the London and West
   Midlands conurbations—difficulties in using census data

Chapter 10 The Number and Distribution of Coloured Persons in England and Wales, 1966   96

1 *Numbers*   96
Number born overseas—number born in the U.K.

2 *Distribution and Concentration*   100
Distribution in conurbations 1961 and 1966—concentration in local authority areas

Chapter 11 The Changing Demographic Scene, 1961 to 1966   104

1 *Male Dominance among Immigrants*   104

2 *Marital Status*   106

3 *Age Structure*   108

4 *Fertility*   112
In England and compared with countries of origin—additional evidence from Birmingham

5 *Family Structure*   116
Summary   119

Chapter 12 Housing   120

1 *The Housing Conditions of Immigrants*   120
Introduction—(*a*) Housing Density—persons per room—the relationship of household size to size of dwelling—(*b*) Sharing Households—sharing and density—(*c*) Housing Facilities—sharing and facilities—access to facilities—variations in areas—(*d*) Housing Tenure—owner-occupation

2 *Changes in Immigrant Housing Conditions, 1961 to 1966*   138
Introduction—(*a*) Housing Density and Shared Accommodation—changes in seven London boroughs—tenure—(*b*) Who Benefits Most?—the comparative progress of different groups

Chapter 13 Employment   149
Introduction

1 *Economic Activity*   150

2 *Industrial Status*   152

3 *Occupations*   155
Concentrations—over-representation—'white-collar' analysis—change over time—evidence of discrimination

4 *Industry*   166
Concentrations—distribution in manufacturing and service industries

5 *Socio-Economic Status*   172
6 *Unemployment*   177
7 *Conclusions*   180

Chapter 14   The Household Expenditure of Immigrants   182
Introduction
1 *Immigrant Households*   183
The Birmingham sample of households for the survey of income and
expenditure
2 *Immigrant Incomes*   184
Net incomes—differentials in income between coloured and white
workers
3 *Immigrant Housing*   187
Type of accommodation by income—rents
4 *Savings and Remittances*   193
Household expenditure
5 *Conclusions*   195

PART IV   POLICIES AND PRACTICES   199

**Chapter 15   The Genesis of Official Policy: On the
Procrustean Bed**   199
Characteristics of the British system of government—general intro-
duction to Part IV—the transition from *laissez-faire* to planned equality

**Chapter 16   The Decline and Fall of Laissez-Faire:
Politics and Race Relations, 1955-65**   206
Definitions of race relations—the problems as seen in the 1940s and
early 1950s—the rejection of immigration control in 1955—the subsequent debate—reaction to Nottingham and Notting Dale disturbances
—Conservative policy 1959–62—the Commonwealth Immigrants Bill
1961–2—Labour and Conservative policies after control—Labour and
Conservative policies after 1964—the 1965 Race Relations Bill—the
White Paper on immigration policy, August 1965—significant features
of the period: the role of public opinion, the decline of the Commonwealth ideal, and the position of the Home Office

Chapter 17   Policies and Practices I: Housing   232
The White Paper on housing—housing resources and policies in the
1940s and 1950s—the fall in private rented accommodation—maldistribution—local authority powers and attitudes—failure to deal with
the twilight zone—evidence of the Milner Holland Committee—

Lambeth—house purchase and property values—Birmingham—Wolverhampton—Bradford—Bristol—rejection of positive action—N.C.C.I. Housing Panel's proposals—the concept of priority areas and the Urban Programme—housing associations—summary and conclusions

Chapter 18   Policies and Practices II: Education — 264

1 *Background* — 264
The education system

2 *The Dispersal Policy* — 265
The Second Report of the Commonwealth Immigrants Advisory Council—the Southall crisis—Circular 7/65 and the White Paper—the lack of statistics—standards of native children—Spring Grove—reactions to the dispersal policy

3 *Local Education Authorities* — 273
Language teaching—the problem of resources—administrative policies

4 *A.T.E.P.O.s, the N.C.C.I., and the Leeds Project* — 278

5 *West Indian Children* — 281
Lack of understanding—the Birmingham project—teachers' descriptions—some problems facing West Indian pupils—the use of the remedial service

6 *Achievement* — 286

7 *Conclusions* — 287
The lessons of the Schools Council reports—the failure to deal with twilight areas—structural weaknesses—the amount of integration—some discussion of 'all black' and 'all immigrant' schools

Chapter 19   Policies and Practices III: Industrial Relations — 296

Introduction — 296
The interrelationship between employment and housing and education

1 *The Pattern of Discrimination* — 297
The evidence of discrimination—the framework of discrimination

2 *Official Policy* — 301
(*a*) Government—general policy—labour exchanges—statistics—central government as an employer (Armed Forces, Civil Service, N.H.S.)—nationalized industries (London Transport, British Rail)—local government and municipal undertakings—(*b*) Trade Unions—policy—communication of policy—trade union membership—immigrant views of trade unions—trade unionist fears—'racial' strikes—leadership—(*c*) Employers' Associations—role—belief in extent of problems—reaction to legislation

3 *The Coloured Worker*   319
   Skill levels—assessment—selection—stereotypes—conflict of evidence

4 *The Industrial Relations System*   323
   Analytical framework

Conclusions   324
   The social role of industry

Chapter 20   Policies and Practices IV: Two Aspects
              of Social Control   330

1 *Health and Welfare Services*   330
   (a)Health Controls—(b) Tuberculosis and Venereal Diseases—(c)
   Demands on Hospital Services—maternity and child welfare—
   geriatric patients—mental health—(d) The Failure to Provide for
   Cultural Diversity—difficulties affecting the social worker—implications for social work training—(e) Specific Requirements—health
   education—day-care for pre-school children—(f) Evolution of
   Policy—no funds for local authorities until 1966—the Urban Programme and central intervention

2 *The Police and Law Enforcement*   349
   Introduction—(a) The Life and Labour of the Police—conflict of
   roles—relations with the public—sources of tension—delegation of
   authority—discretionary powers—investigation of complaints—
   police and immigrants—regulatory role—source of intelligence—
   deterioration of relationships—complaints of discrimination—low
   incidence of crime among immigrants—(b) The Police and Integration—change in concept of role since 1966—liaison officers—
   recruitment of coloured policemen—inadequacy of training—
   conclusions

Chapter 21   The Volunteer in the Vacuum   370

1 *The Churches and the Newcomers*   370
   The church in the inner city—different interpretations of integration
   —decline in West Indians' church attendance—community-based
   activities—attitudes to Pentecostal sects—attitudes to Asian migrants
   —publications and pronouncements—under-use of church buildings
   —children of immigrants in denominational schools

2 *Volunteers for Integration*   380
   Local effort—Government reliance on the volunteer—the complement of *laissez-faire*—early voluntary organization in the 1950s—
   paternalism and welfare—public education—indifference of local
   authorities—aim to preserve racial harmony—ambiguous attitude
   to racial discrimination—after 1965—co-ordination by N.C.C.I.—
   advice, information, and referral—the voluntary liaison committee
   and its influence on the local authority—the pattern of community
   work in Sparkbrook and Notting Hill—popular participation—

protest action—provision of services to immigrants—the role of the
paid liaison officer—relationship of the N.C.C.I. and its committees

3 *The Anti-Immigration Lobby*   393
Opposition to integration—the older extremist organizations—
newer groups formed in the 1960s—tactics—tenants and residents'
associations—analysis of propaganda—impact of the newer groups

**Chapter 22   Some Conclusions: The Lessons of the
P.E.P. Report**   403

The newcomer as catalyst—the varying responses of government—
weak universalism followed by weak selectivity—the burden on
voluntarism—the lessons of the P.E.P. Report

The Evidence of the P.E.P. Report   407
(a) Employment—(b) Housing—the factor of colour and racial
difference

PART V   THE IMMIGRANT RESPONSE   417

Chapter 23   Adaptation or Withdrawal   417
Introduction   417
1 *West Indians*   419
(a) Expectations and Illusions—(b) The Two Cultures—(c) The
Realities—Housing—(i) Dispersal at Bristol—(d) Adapting to
Change—conformity—Puritan standards for children—joining British
institutions—low crime record—attitudes to authority—demographic
evidence of change—emigration nearly complete—(e) Disillusion

2 *Pakistanis*   440
The predominance of men—sponsorship—the economics of life in
Britain—the effects of the 1965 White Paper—attitudes to authority
—attitudes towards contact with other migrant groups and the
English—the entrepreneurs and the professionals—the advantages
of the migration

3 *Indians*   452
(a) Sikhs—background—the educated and the illiterate—employment: the role of Woolf's rubber factory—housing—religious observance—the strike at Woolf's—the Indian Workers' Association—
caste, marriage, and the *gurdwara*—visitors from India—wives and
families—English hostility to the Sikhs—leadership—the Sikhs in
Canada—(b) Hindus—the Gujaratis—family, kinship, and caste

Chapter 24   The Second Generation   476
The increasing numbers of British-born children of immigrants—first-
generation teen-agers—child-minding and the shortage of day nurseries
—qualified pessimism

1 *Education*   479
Under-representation in selective schools—studies of attainment

2 *Employment*   481
The Youth Employment Service—frustration

3 *Social Contact*   484
Social distance after school—the evidence of the Hunt Report—
family influences

4 *Deliquency*   486
Lambert's Birmingham study—children in care

5 *Older Settlements*   487
Cardiff—Liverpool

Chapter 25   Leadership   492
Fragmented and unrepresentative—leaders without organizations—
coloured leadership before the Second World War—dilemma of the
West Indian middle class in the post-war migration—the effect of 1958
—West Indians fail to combine—the Indian Workers' Association—
Punjabi solidarity—contribution of Communists—relations with
Indian High Commission—the Migrant Services Division and the
West Indian Standing Conference—break-up of the Federation,
immigration control, and disillusion—splits within I.W.A.—relations
with Communist party of Great Britain—local pacts with the Labour
party—fissures in the Pakistani communities—no effective leadership—
the consequences of the 1964 general election—the Campaign Against
Racial Discrimination

**PART VI   ROY JENKINS AND LEGISLATION
AGAINST   DISCRIMINATION: A
CASE STUDY**   511

Chapter 26   Clearing the Way   511
Maurice Foley's one-man pressure group—public education—the
appointment of Roy Jenkins as Home Secretary—his political background—the appointment of Mark Bonham Carter as Chairman of the
Race Relations Board—the extension of the Race Relations Act 1965—
other issues in second place—timing—the strategy of the campaign—
the role of the Race Relations Board—the National Committee for
Commonwealth Immigrants—the P.E.P. and the Street Reports
commissioned—C.A.R.D.—opposition from the C.B.I. and the T.U.C.
—Oscar Hahn's proposals

Chapter 27   Sisyphus' Stone   534
The first Report of the Race Relations Board and the publication of the
P.E.P. Report—negotiations—the effects of domestic and international
developments—failures of communication—the N.C.C.I.—C.A.R.D.—
the Kenya Asian issue—exit Jenkins—some conclusions

PART VII ATTITUDES OF THE BRITISH PUBLIC 551

Chapter 28 The Incidence of Race Prejudice in Britain 551

1 *The Survey of Attitudes* 551
(a) The Analysis—(b) The Findings—(i) The Extent of Tolerance—by sex—by age—by social class—by length of education—by voting intention—by Party membership—by type of housing tenure—by type of employment—by trade union membership—by overseas travel—by social mobility—by degree of political activism—by authoritarianism—(ii) Elements of Prejudice—superiority/inferiority—similarity/difference—perception of class of immigrants—beliefs about the size of the coloured population in Britain—beliefs about immigrants and the social services—sympathy—(iii) Contact with Newcomers: its Form and Context—(iv) Competition and Allocation: Newcomers in Jobs and Housing—attitudes about discriminatory treatment in relation to dismissal, promotion, council housing, private rented housing—percentage of coloured immigrants in the five boroughs, by national origin—(v) Clues for Attitude Change—the importance attached to the presence of coloured people—(c) Conclusions

2 *The Findings in Perspective* 588
Changing attitudes on race relations 1958–68

PART VIII THE BALANCE SHEET 605

Chapter 29 The Descending Spiral 605
The style of debate changes—renewed pressure for immigration control—legislation in Kenya—increase in the numbers of Asians entering U.K.—belongers and non-belongers—the debates on the 1968 Commonwealth Immigrants Bill—British equals white—the coalition is scattered—Enoch Powell sees an opening—the Race Relations Bill under a cloud—analysis of the Bill—passage through Parliament—Government forfeits confidence—disillusion among immigrants and protest—critics of Race Relations Bill—still no effective leadership—the Urban Programme identified with 'the immigrant problem'—Edward Heath returns to the issue of control—the consequences of the Kenya Asian episode

Chapter 30 The Future Coloured Population of England and Wales 629

1 *The Method of Projection and the Assumptions* 630
(a) Assumptions about Fertility and Mortality—(b) The Flow of Dependants—(c) Future Voucher-Holders and their Dependants

2 *Projections* 633
Numbers—age structure

Chapter 31 Effects on the Economy   639

A discussion of the economic effects of immigration on the economy—immigration and unemployment—immigration and economic growth—immigration and technical progress—immigration and the balance of payments—immigration and inflation—gains and losses to the domestic population—some conclusions

Chapter 32 Society as a Whole   657

The discussion summarized—the consequences of migration—two sides of the balance sheet—economic gain and social stress—politicians reinforce anxiety—considerations for national policy—the notion of cultural amalgamation—one-sided social contract—the prospects for pluralism—the basic structure of society—a wider perspective—the social rights of minority groups—the rediscovery of poverty—the coloured immigrant as scapegoat—universal or selective provision—the principle of territorial welfare justice—rights and obligations of Black Britons—the limited case for special programmes within a policy of redistribution

PART IX CONCLUSIONS   675

Chapter 33 Findings and Recommendations   675

Introduction   675
  Dispersal

1 *The Machinery of Government*   683

2 *The Law*   686
  General—Race Relations Act 1965 : section 6

3 *Housing*   688
  The role of central government—local authorities—the problems of coloured immigrants and the private sector—the local authority and the immigrant—housing associations—some broader perspectives

4 *Education*   698
  General—a major limitation of the education service—the Department of Education and Science (the Inspectorate—training)—local education authorities—colleges and university departments of education—nursery education—primary education (infant schools—junior schools and the problems of transfer—middle schools)—secondary education—remedial groups—further education—parents and the link with the home—the school psychological and child guidance service—reports—Schools Council Project in English for Immigrant Children—the problems of West Indian children—Church schools

5 *Employment*   710
General—record-keeping—Government (contracts—employment exchanges—Youth Employment Service)—workshop bargaining—management—trade unions—training

6 *Social Welfare*   717
Training—day care—local authority care—social work in schools—the school as a community centre

7 *The Police*   722
The training of police—recruitment—community relations—complaints procedure—information and research—rights and obligations of the citizen

8 *Community Relations*   727
The Community Relations Commission—civil rights and immigrant leadership—the role of the Churches—the neighbourhood project and the individual—a national community service

9 *Public Education*   736
The mass media

10 *Immigration Policy*   744

Conclusion   755

APPENDIXES   757

Appendixes to Part I   757
Appendix I.1   A Note on the Survey of Race Relations in Britain   757
Research completed—research in progress, or completed and awaiting publication—the finances of the Survey

Appendix I.2   Acknowledgements   764

Appendixes to Part III   767
Appendix III.1   The Seven Inner London Boroughs   767
Appendix III.2   Selected Midlands Wards   768
Appendix III.3   Adjustments to Census Estimates   769
(a) The White Indians and White Pakistanis—(b) Coloured Children Born in the Host Community—(c) Census Under-Enumeration

Appendix III.4   Details of Aspects of the Procedure to Estimate the Total Coloured Population of England and Wales   776

Appendix III.5   The Percentages of the Population (15 and over) Retired and Students from Selected Birthplace Groups and Total Population, 1966   780

Appendix III.6   The Distribution in Major Industries for Selected Birthplace Groups by Percentage, by Sex, 1966   781

B

Appendixes to Part VII   785

Appendix VII.1   *Method of Sampling*   785

Appendix VII.2   *The Five-Borough Survey*   786

Appendix VII.3   *The Prejudice-Tolerance Scale*   790

Appendix VII.4   *The Questionnaire*   792

Appendix VII.5   *The Composition of Authoritarian and Non-Authori-* 793
tarian Groups

Appendix to Part VIII   795

Appendix VIII.1   *The Arrival of Further Dependants to Immigrants* 795
already in the U.K. by mid-1968

Bibliography   797

Index   807

FOREWORD

This book is the result of events which began in 1962. In the summer of that year, the Institute of Race Relations decided to sponsor a wide and penetrating survey of the existing state of race relations in Britain. The Notting Hill episode had shown how dangerous the situation might become, but it was still fluid; the general public and the leaders of political parties, assailed by small vociferous groups from either flank, were puzzled and uncertain. A searching analysis at this juncture might throw light on the whole scene and mould opinion.

A quarter of a century earlier, the Carnegie Corporation of New York, convinced of the growing importance of race in the United States, had conceived the idea of calling in a fresh mind to look at this obstinate problem. Gunnar Myrdal's great book *An American Dilemma* had been the result. It assembled a vast mass of information and set the whole in a new and illuminating perspective. Might not we in Britain do something at a much earlier stage, before attitudes hardened and were embodied in institutions? 'A Myrdal for Britain while there is still time' was the phrase into which the idea crystallized.

The proposal was put to the Nuffield Foundation in general terms in the autumn of 1962. At that stage, the Institute asked only for an expression of interest in principle. Such a project always presents the dilemma that its success depends on the man chosen, who will want to make his own plan of attack. But this will need thought and study which he cannot be expected to give without some indication that funds are likely to be forthcoming. He may need some months before he can formulate his plan exactly and this demands an act of faith on the part of all concerned. The Institute's first application to the Nuffield Foundation suggested that the Director of the Survey should 'be asked [as the Carnegie Corporation asked Gunnar Myrdal] largely to construct his own terms of reference'. With great imagination and foresight, the Nuffield Foundation recognized that this latitude in the scheme was inevitable and encouraged us to plan the project and look for

the man; for this we owe a special debt to the Director, Dr. Leslie
Farrer-Brown.

At first, we looked for someone not British, possibly Canadian
or Scandinavian; detachment from preconceived ideas about the
British scene seemed of paramount importance. The proposal was
discussed with a wide variety of people in Britain, Sweden, and
the United States. It was in the United States that powerful
arguments were put forward against the idea of a Director who
would not be British. Officers of the Carnegie Corporation and the
Rockefeller and Ford Foundations were unanimous in their advice;
they saw no need to bring in an outsider to look at a problem
which for us was new; theirs had been one on which they had grown
stale. Further, they doubted whether anyone not brought up in
England fully understood English society and they added,
politely but quite firmly, that they were not sure that the English
would take advice kindly from a foreigner.

There is no need here to repeat the history of that year of searching and planning. It is enough to say that in Mr. E. J. B. Rose we
had the good fortune to find a man who, though fully acquainted
with the English scene, had for more than ten years been Director
of the International Press Institute at Zurich and came to the
task with an international outlook and a freedom from previous
commitment. He was prepared to give the five years which we
had throughout assumed were necessary. We put to the Nuffield
Foundation an outline plan and the proposal to appoint Mr.
Rose; they accepted our proposals, making us a most generous
grant, which was supplemented a year later when detailed planning showed the need. Rose soon found as an Assistant, Nicholas
Deakin, who had decided to leave a career in the Civil Service for
independent work on social issues.

When Jim Rose came to write his own terms of reference and
formulate his approach in greater detail, he emphasized the profound difference of his task from Myrdal's; in the United States
there was too much information, in Britain nothing like enough.
In the United States, there was a vast literature and, as one of Dr.
Myrdal's associates told me, 'at least forty' distinguished socio-
logists well-versed in the subject. Here in Britain, there was the
pioneer work of Dr. Kenneth Little and Dr. Michael Banton,
Dr. Anthony Richmond, and others from the Department of
Social Anthropology at Edinburgh, but most of this dated from
before the arrival of immigrants in large numbers; in particular,

the scene had changed since the coming of Indians and Pakistanis. There was also the valuable work of Mrs. Glass. But there were vast areas of ignorance. It was necessary to commission a great deal of new work, but quite clearly neither the financial nor the human resources were available to consider every question to which an answer was desirable. A plan was drawn up and effort directed to the questions which could be answered most usefully in the time available.

This was refreshing. As we had hoped, Mr. Rose was approaching the subject as a national problem; his task, as he saw it, was to assemble a body of knowledge, to analyse it, and to suggest the aims to be borne in mind in framing policy. This had been emphasized in our application to the Nuffield Foundation. 'The inquiry', we had written, 'will aim at analysing the relationships between minorities in Britain and the wider community of which they form part. It will not consist of analysis for its own sake, but will aim at positive results. In particular, it will endeavour to identify and account for sources of friction and, when appropriate, will suggest means of eliminating these.' In short, funds had been made available for something to be carried out more in the spirit of a Royal Commission's report than is usual in an academic inquiry. This distinction, I am glad to say, was never lost from sight.

I do not wish to come between Mr. Rose and his audience. My main purpose is to explain the circumstances in which the Survey was undertaken and its purpose. But there are certain points I must emphasize. First, this is the only research in this subject which has been planned as a programme, the constituent parts supporting each other, and the whole intended to be summed up and assessed in a report. It has been evident for years that this was to become a national issue of the first importance; if there had been any doubts, they should have cleared by the time of the incidents in Notting Hill in 1958. But when the Survey began its work, we knew of no work in progress in Britain that was not sponsored by the Institute.

Secondly, the results (quite apart from the present book) form an impressive body of work. There are nineteen larger-scale research projects and twenty-two smaller projects. In his report after four years, the Director of the Survey remarked that 'the work of administering so many research projects and of helping to repair casualties has been a surprisingly heavy burden', when added to personal work and other commitments. But it is not surprising when one bears in mind that each project had to be linked to an overall plan, that the right person had then to be found for the project, that the relationship to the main plan had to be preserved throughout and results in writing achieved. Appendix I.1 of this Report shows the projects carried through to a result; it does not show the work that went into 'repairing casualties', that is, finding someone else to do the work when the first choice has had to give up—through marriage or ill-health, a change of circumstances or loss of nerve. Nor does it show the strain on someone working to a timetable and a budget of those inexhaustible postponements in search of an impossible perfection which are so frequent in this kind of work; there are those before whom research stretches as a happy eternity, a desert in which to travel is bliss, to talk of arrival a vulgarity. None the less, I believe that in addition to the solid work achieved, there has been an intangible benefit to thought on this subject; this was the first time that there had been a centre for research in race relations in Britain with power to commission work; it is too early to estimate the total effect.

There is a third point which is not the least important. The Institute has a very small central staff and has undertaken most of its work through contracts with writers who have undertaken to perform a specific task. In October 1963, when the Survey came into being, we had no member of the staff whose work was wholly centred on race relations in Britain. Nor was there any other body in Britain concerned to collect and disseminate information on this subject. A year later, in 1964, there was a startling increase in the scale of interest in race relations; quite suddenly, press, radio, and television began to emphasize what had so long been neglected. Quite apart, then, from its main task, the Survey produced an invaluable by-product; it provided a centre for explanation and information. Today, we have the Race Relations Board and the Community Relations Commission, both Government institutions with resources which no independent body can attempt to rival, and also the Runnymede Trust, whose task is specifically to educate and inform public opinion. None of these existed. The Survey at that stage performed a service of the first importance not only in stimulating research but in giving results to the public.

This enterprise arose from three convictions. First, that it is a cause of profound ill-health for a nation to include two kinds of citizen, of whom one is regarded and treated as inferior. Misery, resentment, and waste are the symptoms of the disease. Secondly, that social evils are extremely complex and are more likely to be improved if there is a body of accurate information available for those who frame policy and also a body of persons who make it their business to think about that information and interpret it. Thirdly, that ideas generated in the study by long thought will in time seep upward into the Cabinet offices as well as downward into the popular mind. This book will appear in 1969, not quite seven years after its conception. The scene has changed profoundly in those seven years but the three convictions have been strengthened. We have seen hasty legislation, belated and grudging recognition of the importance of a growing crisis, worried concessions to extremist clamour, conventional genuflexions to principles quickly rejected. But it is not too late to hope that this Report will focus attention and influence opinion as we hoped.

Seven years is a tenth of what till lately has been reckoned man's life. To say good-bye to this tenth part of one's life even with a consciousness of what it has achieved, must also mean loss. I cannot end this brief foreword without expressing my sense of the Institute's good fortune in finding such men as Rose and Deakin to carry out the Survey and my personal debt to them as colleagues.

February 1969   PHILIP MASON

PART I INTRODUCTION

1 A Map in the Making

When I was first asked if I would direct a survey of race relations in Britain I had just returned to England after an absence of more than ten years. It was perhaps natural to hesitate before undertaking a task that was to extend over five years in a field about which I knew almost nothing. Among the people whom I consulted was the author of one of the best studies of West Indians in this country who told me that the subject of race relations was a peripheral one in Britain and that it was doubtful if it was worth devoting five years of one's life to studying it. That was in the summer of 1963. Five years earlier there had been racial disturbances in London and the Midlands, but the stern sentences imposed by Mr. Justice Salmon on the young hooligans who had invaded Notting Hill seemed to have had a deterrent effect. The political passions that had been aroused by the debates on the Commonwealth Immigrants Bill had apparently died away, and now that coloured immigration was controlled the issue seemed to have lost much of its importance.

Philip Mason, the Council of the Institute of Race Relations, and the Nuffield Foundation clearly thought otherwise. And if I had doubts, they were not about the importance of the subject but of my fitness to undertake a task of such magnitude. I needed no convincing that for the first time for over fifty years there was a danger of the emergence of a minority problem in these islands and that the danger was more acute because the minorities were coloured. It was a situation which had grave implications for our society and for our position in the eyes of the world. What proved decisive for me was that the Survey was to aim at positive results. The outcome would be a number of independent studies and there would be an overall report in which we would make our own analysis based on the findings from this research and put forward recommendations for policy.

Philip Mason has explained in his foreword that the precedent for this Survey was set by Gunnar Myrdal's comprehensive study of the Negro in America. But Myrdal's influence on our work went beyond the mere conception of a similar survey in Britain; it continued to operate when we began to make the plan for our study. For Myrdal had seen that in the United States the Negro problem was in reality the white man's problem and that it was the white man's behaviour towards the Negro which had created and perpetuated the problem. It was one of the strengths of his study that he did not treat the Negro problem in isolation but focused his attention on American society at large, both because this was where power resided and because he assumed that the Negro's problem existed and was modified by the forces operating in the larger American society. Twenty-five years later this was also to be the conclusion of the National Advisory Commission on Civil Disorders (the Kerner Commission), which was appointed by President Johnson following the riots which took place in the summer of 1967.

The pivot of Myrdal's analysis was his perception of an inner contradiction between the American Creed, the profession of faith in the equality and the right to liberty of all Americans enshrined in the Declaration of Independence, and the American practice of according unequal treatment to one section of the population. He saw that this contradiction between belief and practice posed an acute moral problem for white Americans, which he called *An American Dilemma*. It was his great contribution that throughout his survey he kept recalling the American reader to the values underlying the American Creed in order to expose the rationalizations required to justify the unequal treatment of the Negro.

Myrdal was dealing with a familiar problem in a country where attitudes and positions were largely fixed. We were to consider a very recent phenomenon, the presence of coloured immigrants who had been in England for less than ten years; and yet it seemed to us that Myrdal's approach was in many ways also appropriate for us. It is true that Myrdal found an enormous literature on the Negro, while little was known about our immigrant communities: we should certainly need to commission separate studies of these groups. But whatever the influences of their origins and cultures on their adaptation to our society, the behaviour of the British would in the end be decisive and so the main focus of our inquiry was to be on the response of the British. British society and British policies would be the subject of inquiry at least as much as the immigrant communities. Our study would have to be concerned with the social life of the nation.

The England which I had left in 1951 was still, in Churchill's phrase, wearing hardship as a garment; the austerity of the war years had continued into the peace; there were shortages and food was still rationed. But the morale of the people was high. They had been fortified by the carrying through of the social and educational reforms that had been proposed as part of the country's war aims; they had seen the emergence of the Welfare State, which seemed likely to redress the balance that had for so long been weighted against the poor. Their society now appeared likely to become far more just than it had been in the pre-war years with its vast army of unemployed and its apparent indifference to the fate of the families who had made up nearly a quarter of the population and had been virtually left to rot on the dole. England had had to wait for a war to give it its New Deal; during the waiting period it had been gradually demoralized by the canker of unemployment and the appeasement of the dictators. The War had changed everything. Service in the Armed Forces, the War effort on the home front, the blitz, and the evacuation of children had broken down social and regional barriers and had brought the British people together in a camaraderie that had begun to mix up the classes. It was felt that the Welfare State would continue the process. Great Britain, conscious that for a time it had stood alone against tyranny, austere and dedicated to the principles of fairness and equality, seemed, for all the miscarriage of its economic plans, to be founding a just society.

There were other reasons too for self-respect. India had been given independence and the idea of a multi-racial Commonwealth and Empire was taking shape and was a source of liberal optimism, although independence for the African and West Indian colonies seemed to lie far in the future. Europe, emerging from the wreckage of war and discarding its illusions about sovereignty and national boundaries, looked to Britain for leadership and responded to Churchill's call for European unity.

Ten years later, it appeared to a stranger returning to this country that the mood had changed and much else had changed as well. I had heard that years of full employment had raised the standard of living of the mass of the people and that working-class youth for the first time had money to spend and was being courted as an important source of purchasing power. The electorate had been told that they had never had it so good and they were ready to believe it. There was a spirit of self-indulgence which was encouraged by the mass media and which had resulted in a loosening of traditional social controls. 'I'm all right, Jack', was said to typify a general mood. At the same time, there had been a resurgence of nationalism, which had found expression in the disastrous Anglo-French adventure at Suez and in the consequent disillusion with the United Nations. England had turned her back on Europe and her belated attempts to seek an entry had been rebuffed. There was a growing disenchantment with the coloured Commonwealth which had opposed the action at Suez and a growing realization of the decline in Britain's position as a world power.

If this were a true picture, if the country were indeed turning in on itself, if a loss of confidence was accompanied by an increasing nationalism, and if apparent affluence were engendering selfishness, then the climate might be unhealthy for the growth of a multi-racial society.

But there seemed to me much else that needed to be tested which might affect the prospects of successfully absorbing coloured newcomers. There had been signs of a renaissance of regional cultures; if this society was no longer so unitary as it had appeared before the War and did not impose a uniform pattern of behaviour, it might be easier for newcomers to fit in. Apart from the importance of regional variations there would almost certainly be significant differences between the experience of the different generations. At least half the adult population had been born since 1930 and had grown up in a very different society from their parents and grandparents; they had had virtually no experience of unemployment and no memories of Empire and of the White Man's Burden. Many of them would have benefited from the extension of secondary education under the 1944 Act and would be better educated than their parents. These and other differences in the experience of the pre-war and post-war generations must surely affect the quality of the response to newcomers and to colour.

These were some of the questions which would need to be tested in our inquiry. But whatever the variations between regions or classes or generations, could we assume a British dilemma? Could we postulate, as Clarence Senior had suggested, that there migh be a moral conflict between the British ideals of fair play and of equality before the law, on one side, and possible discrimination against groups of citizens distinguished by the colour of their skin, on the other? Great Britain too had owned slaves and had freed them, but her slaves had lived 3,000 miles away across the seas.

When 100 years after emancipation their descendants came here to seek a living, they came as immigrants and it might therefore be assumed that because they were immigrants they would not be on the conscience of the country in the way that the Negro had for generations been on the conscience of Americans. There might however be some feeling of obligation towards these immigrants because they were members of the Commonwealth, but this would have less force if there were different attitudes towards the coloured Commonwealth and the white Dominions.

Underlying these assumptions, that immigrants despite the possession of a common citizenship would not be felt to have a claim to equal treatment, there lay yet a further assumption about the importance of colour in determining the response of the British. This assumption was crucial and ran counter to prevailing theory. The ideas that had held the field were first, that in our class-conscious society colour is seen as a facet of class and a coloured man is perceived as occupying a position at the bottom of the class spectrum; this was the so-called colour-class theory. Another school held that colour should be equated with foreignness and that the coloured man is perceived as a stranger whose colour makes him appear more strange than other foreigners. He is in fact the archetypal stranger. On either of these theories the coloured immigrant would find barriers erected against him which would spring from class-consciousness or from xenophobia: but it is implicit in both theories that these barriers can be overcome as coloured people rise in the social scale or become familiar with British norms of behaviour and adopt them. Both theories had much force, but we felt that neither could wholly account for a phenomenon familiar elsewhere. European immigrants to the United States had overcome barriers of this kind and had dispersed into the general population, where Negroes had failed to do so. This phenomenon was due not to any inherent incapacity on the part of the black minority deriving from purely racial criteria (the notion that such criteria have any objective existence is now virtually extinct), but to the effects of discrimination past and present on the part of the white majority and to the progressively narrowing opportunities for those without skills in a changing economic situation. Without wanting to draw too close a parallel between the two situations, we could not exclude the possibility that something similar might occur here.

We therefore took the decision to concentrate on the factor of colour in most of the commissioned research. Our discussions with social scientists, who agreed to undertake research for us, convinced us that we must break away from the focus of an immigrant-host relationship and turn instead to a study of the relationships between groups within a society in which one of the groups was distinguished by the factor of colour. We felt that we must consider the possibility that colour generates a response which cannot be satisfactorily explained in terms of class or the fact of strangeness. For comparative purposes some of the research has included studies of other immigrants, but the emphasis has been on the differential response of the British to the factor of colour. This decision has also had vital implications for this Report, which concentrates on the three main immigrant groups from the West Indies, India, and Pakistan and on the British response to these groups, and has little to say about the aliens, the Irish, or the non-English speaking immigrants from the Commonwealth who are white.

These then were the assumptions with which we began the Survey. They would have to be tested against the evidence and in a rapidly developing situation they were also to be tested by events which took place during the course of our study. We were not conducting research in a vacuum. The situation which we were studying was changing all the time. It is sometimes difficult to realize the extent of the change that has taken place in the last five years.

The landmarks in this short period include the 1964 General Election in which the issues of race and immigration for the first time played an important part and threw the Labour party on to the defensive. Then, within a year the Labour Government issued a White Paper which imposed further restrictions on immigration. 1965 also saw the passing into law of the first Race Relations Act and the creation of the Race Relations Board. The political temperature then appeared to be lowered during the next two years, until the arrival of several thousand Asians from Kenya, entitled to entry as citizens of the U.K. and Colonies, revived the agitation about numbers entering the country. This led the Government early in 1968 to break its pledge to these citizens and to change the rules governing their entry, an action that was doubly dishonourable, both because it distinguished between citizens on the grounds of their colour and because it repudiated a solemn obligation. The confidence of coloured immigrants already in this country was shaken; it was not long before they were deeply disturbed by Mr. Enoch Powell's Birmingham speech and the expression of prejudice which followed in some parts of the country.

It was at this point, when the situation appeared to be deteriorating disastrously, that we decided to abandon our original intention and to produce a summary report of our findings.

Within the original plan of the Survey, which is described in Appendix I.1, we had commissioned or assisted nineteen major and twenty-two minor research projects in the universities or elsewhere. The timetable for the Survey envisaged the individual projects being completed—and in many cases published—before we produced our final Report, but by the spring of 1968 it became clear that this original concept of a final study based on completed research covering the whole field would not materialize, nor would it satisfy current requirements. Some of the projects have been published, some are completed and awaiting publication, and the remainder are on their way towards completion. Thus, there was a rich store of material which was of very great relevance to the current situation in which up-to-date information was at a premium. We therefore decided as a matter of urgency to produce a Report which would draw on the findings of the various research projects and make this information available while it was fresh and relevant. The Report has thus been enriched by this body of research, but it does not in any way pre-empt separate publication of these studies which have a depth that no overall work can possibly achieve.

The Report which we now present is the product of a number of hands.* First, there is a synthesis of the material obtained from the commissioned research, which is drawn on extensively throughout the Report, particularly for information on the various immigrant communities and on the development of group relations in areas of immigrant settlement. Secondly, there is original research which is incorporated in the Report and which consists of a full analysis of the data from the 1966 Census and the detailed findings of a survey of attitudes to colour. Thirdly, there is an examination of the evidence on the economic effects of immigration based in part on original material obtained for the Survey.

* A detailed account of the authorship is given in Appendix I.2, which also contains acknowledgements to all those who agreed to be consulted during the drafting of the Report.

Fourthly, there is a historical account of the course of events and a critical analysis of the changes in Government policy on immigration and race relations throughout the whole period of the immigration. Fifthly, and perhaps most important, there is a rigorous analysis of policies and practices in the main areas which affect the lives of immigrants, in housing, education, and employment, in health and welfare, and in the work of the police. This is followed by an examination of the contribution of voluntary organizations and the Churches. This examination is based to a large extent on investigations carried out for the Survey, for the Institute, and by other organizations.

The Report is thus partly descriptive and partly analytical. The analysis proceeds from the description and at times assumes the character of a diagnosis. From the analysis we draw certain conclusions and on the basis of the diagnosis we devote the final section of the Report to our findings and recommendations which have been drawn up in consultation with a number of specialists in the various fields.

Although the Report owes its present form to the changing political circumstances which led us to accelerate its production, the structure closely follows the original plan which was devised at the outset of the Survey. The Report falls into four main divisions. First, there is an account of the British society which the coloured immigrants were to enter (Part I). We then describe the sending societies, the history of the migrations and their development within this country (Parts II and III). The central section of the Report deals with the interaction of the native British and the immigrant communities. This is a study of challenge and response (Parts IV to VII). Finally, we assess the implications of our findings and make our recommendations (Parts VIII and IX).

The conception of a Survey of Race Relations in Britain owes everything to Philip Mason, the Director of the Institute of Race Relations. In 1958, immediately following the outbreaks of violence in Nottingham and Notting Hill, he launched an investigation which was published as *Coloured Immigrants in Britain*. This valuable symposium assembled what was known about the immigration at that time, reviewed the literature on race relations in Britain, summarized the statements of political parties about immigration, and with some prescience advocated an administrative agency to enforce a law against discrimination, using conciliation as a first resort. This was pioneer work and it convinced Mason that something on a much larger scale was needed. With great energy and persistence he canvassed opinion and gathered support for the project which he then successfully proposed to the Nuffield Foundation. Philip Mason not only inspired the idea of the Survey but he has supported us with advice and help throughout. I owe him a great debt of gratitude.

The Trustees of the Nuffield Foundation, which has made the Survey possible, have all along been the most benevolent and trusting of patrons. Their interest in the Survey was very properly critical in the initial stages when we were making our plan and again when we applied for further support, but throughout the life of the Survey the Foundation has never sought to influence our ideas or our approach and we are grateful for a relationship which on our side has been most rewarding.

The debt to Philip Mason and to the Nuffield Foundation is obvious and can be expressed in very clear terms. It is far harder to convey what I owe to Nicholas Deakin who has been my collaborator for five years. At every stage we have shared our ideas and discussed our plans and we have seldom disagreed. Together, we have maintained the complex relationship with all those who agreed to undertake research for us. Many research workers, whether they were collaborating with us or working independently, have sought his advice and acknowledged their debt to him. Similarly, his contribution to this Report goes far beyond the many chapters which he has written. During the last five years we have faced many vicissitudes and many pressures in a situation which was constantly developing and often seemed to be irremediably deteriorating. Neither of us has been able to live in an ivory tower and we have both been called upon to advise and help and sometimes to persuade. Anyone who works in the field of race relations finds his principles constantly put to the test. It is at such times that I have learnt to appreciate most fully my association with Nicholas Deakin.

A word about footnotes. Where they appear at the foot of the page they are required to amplify a point in the text. Numbered references which appear at the end of each chapter are primarily for reference and are not meant to detain the reader.

2 The Liberal Hour and After

It was the late Adlai Stevenson who first formulated the doctrine of 'the Liberal Hour'. This is the moment when public men of all shades of opinion, from radical to conservative, accept the necessity of a movement in policy on a social problem issue, in the liberal direction.[1] For race relations in Britain the liberal hour has already passed. It lasted at most two years. 1968, the year in which it ended, was what the French call *année zéro* for those who believe that there are solutions to be found to problems arising from inter-racial contact and that the way to achieve them is through the traditional devices of discussion, bargaining, and legislation.

One characteristic of the liberal hour, while it lasts, is that response to idealistic themes is general, even among those who normally reject an appeal to them as impractical or emotionally dishonest. At least four such themes can be distinguished in the appeal to action on race relations. First, a belief that the claim of ethnic groups, suffering disabilities deriving from colour, to a greater share in the rights and benefits enjoyed by white majorities is a natural subject for sympathy and concern. ('Am I not a man and a brother?') Secondly, the view that the significance of those issues transcends purely national interests and must be considered in a broader perspective—that of international morality, incarnated in international organizations, or of the supranational interests of a class, or that of a bridge-building multi-racial organization, the Commonwealth. Thirdly, the Christian view of the overriding importance of the brotherhood of man has often appeared important; so, finally, has the straightforward belief that human suffering, whatever its cause, urgently demands alleviation through formal intervention by the State.

Once, all these themes could evoke a clear response. Some of them have deep roots in our culture and, severally or together, provide the momentum for such diverse episodes as the anti-slavery movement, the response of the Nonconformist conscience to the exploitation of Africa, and the radical critique of imperialism. Two years ago, they commanded sufficient sympathy to underpin Roy Jenkins' attempt to translate liberal attitudes into practice. Now, even the relevance of the last is questioned. Honourable men shrug their shoulders and turn aside from a situation whose implications in terms of human misery are better known than ever before. The international perspective has for some time past produced mounting evidence of the inevitability of racial conflict, vastly magnified by the electronic revolution which brings televised violence from all quarters of the globe to every sitting-room. The image projected by this process is of mankind threatened with an apocalyptic rendezvous at some future super-Detroit. At the same time, there has been a progressive process of disillusionment, with the Commonwealth and with black Africa: for a country struggling with apparently intractable domestic problems, the easiest moral to draw is that we should opt out of our residual responsibilities.

But disillusion has gone further than this. There are now those who cannot by any stretch of the imagination be dismissed as racialist, who begin to wonder if the whole problem can be most effectively eliminated by exporting it. The appeal from the sufferings of minorities is stood on its head to provide support for the thesis that the liberal least of all men can accept—that if a problem is out of sight it can be out of mind as well.

A Rubicon was finally crossed in the spring of 1968. This was when the British Government decided, on grounds which were quite openly those of expediency rather than principle, that it could no longer accept responsibility for certain of its citizens because of the colour of their skins. Unlike the Dutch, we were not prepared to accept the responsibility for winding up our past imperial role. At that moment, the liberal rhetoric with which ministers clothed their policies finally ceased to convince. The credibility gap opened; and through it walked those who defined their objective in terms of 'realism'. That is to say, the wholesale rejection of all idealism in favour of a calculation based solely on what are perceived as British interests.

In this atmosphere, the British dilemma first identified by Clarence Senior—the tension between the ethic of fairness embedded in our culture and system of law and the failure to live up to those standards in practice[2]—has never been easier to resolve, because the relevance of the ethic to this particular situation is no longer accepted.

The implication for this Report is that appeals to idealism are no longer in order. Any proposals for the amelioration of relationships

between minorities and majority—and this Report is intended
principally as a constructive contribution towards policy making in
this field—must be justified in purely practical terms. That is, they
must be seen to have an application to the real problems of the
adjustment process, and relate to the short run as well as the long
term, the backstreets as well as Whitehall. That such an approach
can make a substantial contribution to resolving tensions without
forfeiting the strengths of a liberal perspective can be seen in the
impact made by the President's National Advisory Commission on
Civil Disorders (the Kerner Commission[3]) in the American situation. We have been deeply influenced by the Commission's approach
at all stages of the preparation of this Report.

In adopting this approach there are two preliminary issues
which we would like to resolve. First, that in rejecting the liberal's
approach from ideology, we do not wish to be understood to be
rejecting the liberals. The English, as George Orwell once pointed
out, take a peculiar pleasure in detecting hypocrisy, which has
been elevated in our culture almost to the status of a Deadly Sin.
But whatever the cultural imperatives, nothing can excuse the
disgraceful way in which the liberals are now being treated, particularly by those who at the height of the liberal hour subscribed
most fervently to the liberal orthodoxy—in other words, those
whom Robert Merton describes as 'fair-weather liberals'. Their
task has been made easier by the confusion produced by the
ambiguity of the term 'liberal'. In the race relations field, this has
a special meaning, deriving from the American situation. But the
parallel between the liberal position there and liberal attitudes in
our own society is a false one and needs to be vigorously rejected.
There, the liberals are accomplices to the process of exploitation;
here, they have been its earliest and still most effective opponents.
In fact, there is good evidence to show that the middle-class intellectuals have had more personal contact with the ordinary immigrant than the working class in whose name they are ritually
belaboured.[4] The fact that the means that they have chosen to
adopt in this situation—occasionally, it is true, the sherry glass,
more often the letter, the pamphlet, or the open meeting—were
pitifully inadequate and too soon abandoned is not ultimately
their fault. The failure of the rhetoric cut the ground from under
their feet. Unlike their critics, at least they tried—even if they did
not understand.

Nor do we accept the nihilism that has replaced liberalism as the fashionable orthodoxy. The twin doctrines of the necessity of violence and the impossibility of any solution short of sweeping all the pieces off the board and setting the game up afresh now command very wide support, and find strange bed-fellows among the believers. Although parallel events in other multi-racial societies (their significance enormously enhanced by the manner in which they are presented by the mass media) are important, we do not accept that they are decisive evidence of the inevitability of violent conflict. But neither do we wish to rest our case on the success stories of those other more fortunate societies (and there are authentic examples) which have achieved a solution to such problems.

For ultimately, the determining element will be not the factor of ethnic and cultural difference as such but the character of British society and the manner in which it responds to the stresses set up during the process of adaptation and change. To the extent that our society and its values are unique, so will the response be unique. And, in our view, there are still good grounds for arguing that present difficulties can be resolved without compromising either the cultural integrity of our society or the values and principles which animate it.

We have referred to the importance of the values held in common in our society: the problem is to capture the significance of these values in terms of the ordinary citizen and his everyday life. Attempts to chart the assumptions with which he approaches those problems that face him have generally revealed a number of misty preconceptions, whose substance dissolves on closer analysis. Or alternatively, investigators find that values whose significance has been taken for granted, like the American Creed—the pivot of Myrdal's analysis—have only intermittent and sometimes distant relevance for some citizens. For these reasons we have preferred to employ a concept which has a concrete reference through its function of binding society together—the concept of citizenship. It is this term that we intend to explore a little further, as a means of placing our analysis in perspective.

Definitions of citizenship are simple enough to produce: they are part of a lawyer's stock-in-trade. But the term citizenship, as we propose to employ it here, also implies something broader— the nexus that in any State links society and the individual. In other words, we conceive of citizenship more in the terms in which classical political philosophers discussed it and less in relation to practical issues of citizenship and nationality law, like the right to a passport. Not that this is a purely technical matter, as William Joyce (who was hanged for possessing one)[5] and British citizens in East Africa (who found theirs devalued overnight) discovered.

The key issue in assessing the real significance of citizenship in the broader sense is the terms on which the rights conferred by the relationship between State and citizen are guaranteed, and the manner and extent of access to them. And the test case which, more than any other, helps to resolve this issue is that of the individual who falls into one of the various groups classed as outsiders and the processes through which he has to pass to obtain these rights and then to exercise them.

The minority with which we are concerned here, coloured immigrants from the Commonwealth, enter society from outside in the strictly geographical sense. The majority of them originally came to this country equipped with the status of 'citizen of the United Kingdom and Colonies'; the latent rights attached to that citizenship sprang to life, so to speak, at the moment of their entry. The discrepancy between this ideal concept, in law, and reality, in terms of the social situation, caused a reaction to take place. We deal with the political aspects of this reaction later; but one of its implications is important here. For, in its extreme form, this takes the form of asserting that neither the newcomers nor their descendants can ever become full members of society because of the presence of the visible factor of colour. And this in turn evokes the response on the part of the minority that membership of a society in which distinctions of this kind are drawn is no longer desirable. Since the countries from which the minorities originally came have obtained independence, this response takes the form of stressing a separate status based on citizenship of those countries.

Both these reactions are as unrealistic as the original doctrine of the indivisible citizenship linking metropolitan country and colony—a lawyer's attempt to give substance to the fading shadow of the imperial connexion. What is called, in a famous definition of nationality, the 'connection of existence, interests and sentiments' does exist in a limited form from the outset—for example, in common economic interests. But the relationship is a dynamic one. It will develop over time to the substance of full citizenship (equality before the law and the franchise, on one side, and allegiance and readiness to perform military service, on the other, if underpinned from the start by unimpeded access to the rights and

acceptance of the duties secured by citizenship in the legal definition). And by full citizenship we mean the unfettered enjoyment of
social rights and the opportunity for full participation in public
affairs. With the descendants of the newcomers the two concepts
should converge and the rights deriving from birth in this country
be fully exercised.

In this process of evolution to full citizenship differences of
colour should not constitute an insuperable obstacle any more
than differences of class or foreign birth have done in the past.
Still more important, the elimination of cultural or religious differences is not a pre-condition of such citizenship: it has not been
exacted in the past from minorities such as the Jews. Or, to take
another example, women were not expected to change their sex
in order to obtain the vote. The balance was eventually tipped by
the contribution they made during the First World War, which
was rewarded by the franchise. Similarly, differences in skin
colour—which are as immutable as sexual differences—or of
culture and religion—whose legitimacy has been accepted in the
past—need not prevent this new minority from satisfying similar
tests.

But to speculate about the future is to run ahead of our argument: if we are to establish the relevance of the concept of citizenship to the realities of the present situation we shall have to do so
by other means. We will try to do this in two ways; first, by
analogy with the experiences of the United States, and secondly,
by examining the past experience of our own society, both in
relation to the entry of previous groups of outsiders, and the
internal processes of social change which have progressively
widened the circle of those who are accepted as full citizens. By
looking at the issue in these different perspectives we hope to
bring it into focus in some depth.

Although we have deprecated the placing of too much weight
on the experience of the United States, many of the values and
the legal system of that society and our own derive from a common
source. Talcott Parsons has analysed the American experience in
terms of citizenship and the rights derived from it and we shall
lean heavily on this analysis in our own discussion.[6] The significance of the fate of past migrations to this country should be clear:
that of the changing composition of our own society is perhaps
greater still. There is a sense in which all studies of minorities must
logically imply a concern with the majority. No analysis which

starts with the concept of the 'immigrant problem' can be complete: for what is at stake is the outcome of one further debate in a long series of disputes about who belongs inside the sheltering walls of our society.

1. MIGRATION AND CITIZENSHIP

(a) The American Experience

Immigration, as the American social historian Oscar Handlin puts it, has in the past always meant the entry into society of future citizens. In no case has this been more true than for the United States, a country which derives much of its character from the great migrations of the nineteenth century from Western Europe and the British Isles, and subsequently from Eastern and Southern Europe. In a well-known phrase, which the late President Kennedy used for the title of his last book, America is a nation of immigrants.[7]

In his essay on the situation of the American Negro, Talcott Parsons isolates various factors in the American situation which have had important consequences for successive minorities seeking 'inclusion' in what he calls the 'societal community'.[8] An open and pluralistic structure, in which diversity (for example, in the practice of religion) is explicitly recognized in the Constitution, and a separation of powers between the branches of government and the centre and periphery has created a situation in which minorities have in the past found it relatively easy to obtain inclusion. In order to gain entry, the group, in Parsons' concept, have had to obtain a 'fit'—that is, they have had to mobilize resources in terms of economic and political power and activate values and loyalties not only in the minority itself but in the majority society. Having done this, they are then able to obtain entry into the host society. Previous groups of immigrants of European origin have been able in turn to achieve this: even the Southern Europeans and the East European Jews, whom many observers dismissed as inassimilable, obtained entry on those terms. But for the Negro, bereft in the past of resources, this has not proved possible; the universalistic ideals of the American Creed (the Declaration of Independence deriving equal rights, in the first draft at least, from the equal creation of all men) have not in practice been susceptible to mobilization on the Negro's behalf.

In this analysis of the Negro's predicament, Parsons employs the definition of citizenship used by T. H. Marshall in his study, *Citizenship and Social Class.*[9] Marshall argues that citizenship confers rights under at least three heads: civil rights, political rights, and social rights—the last including access to social and economic resources on an equal footing.

In the past, the Negro had at best limited access to inadequately defined rights. But after the Second World War what Parsons calls an 'effervescence' began; the Supreme Court decision on segregated education in 1954 was followed by a series of other judgments and the enactment by Congress of Civil Rights Acts in 1960 and 1964. Political rights, lost only a few years after they had been gained by emancipation and the Civil Rights legislation of the Reconstruction Congress, have been gradually regained. Only in the direction of social rights has the Negro failed to gain sufficient ground; but failure here has been crucial to the success of the whole process, since it deprives him of the resources (especially in economic terms) necessary to obtain a 'fit' and enter American society on an equal footing. This failure may eventually lead to a situation when values and loyalties inside the Negro community will have become generally hostile to entry.

(b) The British Experience

Great Britain, by contrast, has in the past not been generally regarded as a country of immigration. Movement of population affecting this country has taken place on a large scale, but in an outward direction—at first, predominantly to the United States, but from the beginning of this century, to what are still sometimes called 'the white Dominions'. However, both in the nineteenth century and since, counter-currents of immigration have run, at times strongly. For present purposes the most interesting of the incoming migrant groups is the Irish.

The Great Famine, the grisly apotheosis of *laissez-faire* dogma, drove huge numbers of the Irish peasantry out of Ireland both to the United States and to the rest of the British Isles. It is a common observation that the hostility directed towards these refugees from economic and political exploitation was expressed in very similar terms to those employed in the case of their successors a century later. Both employed rationalizations based on primitive 'racial' concepts (the Irishman as 'milesian'), and similar stereotypes passed into circulation ('Paddy'—brutal, unreliable, and childlike—has many features in common with 'Sambo'). To this extent, the label of 'Toasted Irish' stuck on contemporary West Indians has a grain of logic in it. There is another parallel too. 'To the English and Scots and especially their middle-class', says Hobsbawm, 'they were merely dirty and feckless, undesirable semi-aliens subject to some discrimination. But their contribution to nineteenth-century Britain is capital.'[10] Yet for Marx, who saw the Irish situation as the archetype of the exploitation of a colonial country by capitalism, the Irish immigration was undesirable, because it struck a fatal blow at the unity of the working class in England. He wrote to Engels:

Every industrial and commercial centre in England possesses a working class divided into two camps, English proletarians and Irish proletarians. The ordinary English worker hates the Irishman as a competitor who lowers his standard of life. In relation to the Irish worker he feels himself a member of the *ruling* nation and so turns himself into a tool of the aristocrats and capitalists of his country against Ireland, thus strengthening their dominion over himself. He cherishes religious, social and national prejudices against the Irish worker. This attitude towards him is much the same as that of the 'Poor Whites' to the 'Niggers' in the former slave states of the U.S.A.[11]

Marx's remedy for this impasse was—as for the other groups in this significant comparison—for proletarians to recognize a common interest in their common exploitation which, he argues elsewhere, has essentially stripped them of all national characteristics. No such process actually took place; yet the Irish were duly accommodated within the social structure of twentieth-century England without any drastic modification of that structure. As E. P. Thompson puts it, 'It is not the friction but the relative ease with which the Irish were absorbed into the working class community which is remarkable.'[12]

At first sight this is surprising, because at least two obstacles in the way of such an adjustment existed. The major one was their Catholic religion, since one of the touchstones for inclusion had in the past been Protestantism. But neither religion nor political dissension over Home Rule, although this was the principal divisive issue of British politics in the late nineteenth century and culminated in open rebellion and civil war, were sufficient to prevent assimilation taking place. The system, although it came under considerable strain, proved capable of adjusting to a degree of cultural separatism. With their religion gaining acceptance and their political involvement reduced to a (none the less highly significant) reinforcement to the Labour vote, which symbolizes neatly the 'fit' achieved in class terms, the Irish were by the Second World War largely accepted. And their full participation in the extension of rights in the Welfare State was unquestioned.

The next case is more complex. The Eastern European Jews who arrived in Britain at the end of the nineteenth century as a result of pogroms in Russia and Russian Poland were not the first Jews to enter this country in significant numbers. The mid-nineteenth century Jewish community had established itself on a secure basis, partly by a process of self-segregation and informal communal control over the composition of the Jewish settlement. Like the Catholics, they had achieved political and civil rights. The Ashkenazy immigrants of the end of the century could be perceived as a threat not only to the host society but to this established community. The former reacted, as Paul Foot has shown, in a way not dissimilar to the contemporary response to coloured entry. Propagandists, of whom Arnold White may be taken as typical, argued that this group was biologically and culturally so sharply distinct as to be quite inassimilable. Evidence to support this was adduced from the geographical concentration of newcomers on arrival, and a distinguished economic historian, Archdeacon Cunningham, produced chapter and verse to destroy the analogy which some defenders of the migrants had been making with earlier, successfully absorbed, migrations.[18] These arguments were based not so much on the religious differences (which were constantly—and self-righteously—played down) as on cultural ones. Finally, although it was virtuously foresworn by all those involved, as colour prejudice is virtuously renounced by their successors, there was the element of endemic anti-Semitism common to all western Christian societies on which to draw.

Yet in two generations from the arrival of the refugees from Eastern Europe a form of accommodation had been reached; and this despite the Depression and an open and explicit attempt to harness anti-Semitism as a scapegoating device for the economic misfortune of the country to provide the motive power for a native Fascist movement on the European model.

The success of this process can partly be put down to sponsorship: that is, the mobilization of resources by the existing Anglo-Jewish community to minimize friction at the early stages. And also, the newcomers proved capable of meeting the demands of the host community in terms of values and loyalties, despite the scepticism of the Arnold Whites, and of obtaining the economic resources necessary to obtain a 'fit' (in the Parsonian vocabulary) into the class structure at the level of the middle-class. Discrimination, though never negligible, proved soluble when economic inducements were applied. The area of friction and perceived hostility has dwindled to the point where it is best described, in Dr. Percy Cohen's words, as a 'Golf Club Syndrome'.[14] The Six Days War of 1967 illustrated, rather paradoxically, the degree of acceptance achieved by the English community in the self-confidence with which Jews, especially middle-class ones, were prepared to display their separate loyalty to the State of Israel.

Then there is the almost equally interesting case of the Polish and Eastern European migrants since the Second World War. Between 1946 and 1950 this country experienced immigration on a scale not matched either previously or at the height of the entry from the Commonwealth ten years later. Many of the migrants spoke little or no English and did not possess relevant skills; but the main distinction that must be made between these migrants and their predecessors lies in the restrictive nature of the rights initially conceded to them. The civil rights of these minorities were restricted—grossly so in the state of the European Volunteer Workers—and their access to social rights limited.[15] This was partly because of a reluctance, felt perhaps most strongly in the Trade Union movement, to accept that the newcomers might legitimately be included in the circle of those to whom benefits conferred within the new Welfare State (especially those of full employment) could be conceded. But in this instance too, sponsorship was forthcoming and sufficient resources deployed to overcome the reluctance of the large part of the majority society to accept the newcomers entering this country. Twenty years later, the very existence of this migration is almost forgotten and the term 'immigrant' automatically suggests colour—although now, as before, coloured faces are in a minority among newcomers.

Yet it is this minority that has put the values embodied in the broader concept of citizenship to the most stringent test of all.

(c) Black Migrants

The case of the coloured minorities is more complex than that of their predecessors. Partly because of the factor of colour itself, with its unique capacity both to exclude reason and wipe out human individuality and substitute stereotypes of black and white, each as misleadingly monolithic as the other—creating, as Fanon puts it, a Manichean world in which the forces of light and darkness struggle perpetually together. Partly, also, because of a complex of political and historical factors embedded in British culture which were brought into play in the course of this migration. An example of considerable practical and symbolic significance which evoked some of these responses was the attempt made after the Second World War to revise the basis of British citizenship, in the legal definition of the term, to meet the changing needs of the new multi-racial Commonwealth.

In law, the citizenship provisions of what had been the British Empire were re-codified by the British Nationality Act of 1948. This immensely complex legislation in essence divided British citizenship (hitherto assumed to be a common possession of all the King-Emperor's subjects) into two broad categories—citizenship of independent Commonwealth countries and citizenship of the remainder of what had been the Empire, described for the purpose as a unified citizenship 'of the United Kingdom and Colonies'. During the first of the four broad phases into which the evolution of official policy on this issue can be divided, the immigrants entered the country from the West Indies as citizens of the U.K. and Colonies. In this capacity they continued to enjoy the pre-scriptive right of free entry they had possessed in the past—as the Colonial Secretary told the Commons when the first migrant ship arrived at Southampton in the year of the British Nationality Act. As citizens they were assumed to possess full civil rights: it being a dogma—though in fact, as Bob Hepple has shown,[16] a false one—that all British citizens have always enjoyed full equality of rights before the law regardless of colour. The question of political rights did not arise; although such migrants automatically acquired the vote, the political context in which they conceived themselves—and, more important, were conceived of participating—was the colonial situation. Their possession of political rights in relation to our own society was simply an irrelevance. Moreover, since the reference made was to the colonial situation (in which coloured people were still, broadly, in a subordinate and dependent situation), it was possible for the Colonial Office to assume a limited degree of responsibility and initiate and operate a welfare system for the benefit of newcomers without entrenching on their status as equal citizens. This period, which might be termed the welfare period, ended in 1955, the year in which it became clear that the Government of Sir Anthony Eden would not control immigration from the Colonies and Commonwealth. (This whole process is analysed in detail in Part IV.)

In the second period, which we will term the status period, the boundaries of citizenship shifted. Civil rights continued to be assumed and enjoyed *de facto*: but the successive acquisition of independence by a series of countries from the 'New' Commonwealth changed the status of the newcomers by reference to the new situation in the Commonwealth. The status conferred on them by the movement towards independence by their countries of origin reinforced their situation in terms of political rights and led to the creation of new welfare services set up by the authorities of those sending countries. But simultaneously, a deterioration took place in relation to social rights. No distinction of any kind could be made between equal citizens: separate services, apart from those provided by the separate institutions sanctioned by the evolution of the Commonwealth, could not exist without damaging that equality. Thus, the frequently quoted proposition '*Civis Britannicus Sum*', came to mean in practice 'I am a second-class (but equal status) citizen'.

The third period, which we have termed the period of diminished responsibility, opened when the Conservative Government decided in 1961 to modify the definition of citizenship applied to Commonwealth and colonial subjects. By placing control over entry both of citizens of independent Commonwealth countries and (more important) those citizens of the U.K. and Colonies whose passports were issued locally (i.e., not by the United Kingdom Government or its representatives), an inroad was made into the civil rights of the newcomers. For example, they became liable to deportation from the United Kingdom if convicted of an offence within five years of arrival—a form of double jeopardy; the separation of families by law also became under certain circumstances possible. A natural counterweight to these admittedly not very substantial modifications of equal civil rights would have been to carry the recognition of separate status within British citizenship over into the field of social rights. Separate provision could be made for specific difficulties arising from the process of immigration along the lines of other controlled and planned population movements within Europe, or colonial-metropolitan migrations like Indonesian repatriation to Holland. This was not done. It would in theory have been possible for migrants to mobilize the resources available to them in the shape of their hitherto unused political rights; but although there were efforts to use the Labour party for this purpose, a failure of involvement on both sides precluded the conclusion of a successful alliance and no such attempt was made.

This period ended in 1965 when the new Labour Government, shedding its temporarily assumed concern for the restoration of those civil rights lost in 1962, issued a White Paper outlining very much more stringent restrictions on the rights of citizens of the U.K. and Colonies and Commonwealth countries entering this country.[17] These proposals placed considerable emphasis on the desirability of defining new and restricted terms on which new-comers could reside here and be permitted to bring their families to this country. But the White Paper proposals also implied that the recognition of separate status involved accepting the necessity for separate measures to enable the newcomers to adapt to British circumstances. The proposals actually made in the White Paper were not in fact well adapted to that end. But the new Home Secretary, Roy Jenkins, subsequently embarked on a series of measures designed to promote integration in his definition of that term. The tension between the universalistic idea of common citizenship, implying common access to rights, and the distinctions increasingly made in practice in different directions had compelled the Government to redefine the objectives of policy in a pluralistic sense.

2. PERMUTATIONS: A GLOSSARY[18]

At this point it might be useful to consider the alternative processes through which a minority approaching our society and seeking to enter it can be expected to pass. A pluralistic solution is one; others have been illustrated by the fate of the various past migrations discussed above.

The end product of a process of migration may be assimilation. This term implies that the group has adapted itself so completely to the host society and has been so completely accepted that it has merged into the whole and lost its separate identity. Assimilation almost always involves or is preceded by inter-marriage, and the process may take generations. To say of a group or a member of a group that it has assimilating tendencies implies that there is a willingness to adopt the culture of the majority and to become completely identified with it. The term has recently fallen into disrepute because it has sometimes been associated with one-way political pressures and misleading biological associations. It is found polemical and offensive by certain minority groups; nevertheless, there are many instances of full assimilation, of groups as well as of individuals, in Britain, of which perhaps the most notable is the Huguenots, who have lost all identification except their names.

Integration is used in popular speech and in the press with a variety of meanings: there is the rather narrow and precise connotation of a part fitting into a whole, whether the fit is deliberately planned or the result of a gradual process. This is the sense in which it has been used throughout this book. But it is often used to denote the opposite of segregation; thus, in the United States, integrated schools are schools in which white and Negro pupils are mixed. It is sometimes used loosely as a synonym for assimilation. Whatever the meanings popularly attached to this over-used word, integration is regarded as both a process and a desirable goal to be achieved in promoting harmonious group relations, without anyone being very clear about the end-product or whether it would suit the cultural needs of the receiving society or the immigrant groups.

Integration has recently been used by social scientists who are students of immigration and race relations to denote a process whereby a minority group, while retaining its own culture and religion, adapts itself to and is accepted as a permanent member of the majority society in all the external aspects of association. Its members enjoy full political, civil, and social rights and perform all their obligations to society as equal citizens, but may remain members of separate communities with close links between themselves, preserving their own language within the home and retaining certain group institutions. This form of integration—in the sense of a part being integrated into the whole while retaining its separate identity—is sometimes called cultural pluralism or 'pluralism' and, as the name implies, it involves the co-existence and mutual tolerance of several cultures within one society. It is analogous to but should not be confused with the preservation of their cultural identity by groups that have a territorial base within one realm, as, for example, in federal societies like Switzerland, or even in Britain where the Scottish, Welsh, and Irish are integrated within the U.K. The integration or pluralism that we are speaking of is of minority groups which have separate cultures but no separate territorial base. Integration in this sense may be a seemingly final phase or it may lead on to full assimilation. As a goal to be achieved in this country, integration was defined by Roy Jenkins as 'not a flattening process of assimilation but as equal opportunity accompanied by cultural diversity, in an atmosphere of mutual tolerance'.[19] To avoid confusion, we have preferred the term pluralism to describe this type of pluralistic integration and it is in this sense that we use the term in this Report.

To achieve this type of pluralism may take one or more generations; but in the early stages of an economic migration, where the newcomer is striving to establish himself, the process of adaptation may be slow and the degree of adaptation may be the minimum required to get employment and shelter; it may be met by a minimal amount of acceptance. This minimum *modus vivendi* between host and immigrant has been termed a state of 'accommodation'. It implies that the immigrant has taken the first steps towards fitting in but may wish to remain encapsulated within his own group; he may be said to be seeking accommodation through self-segregation; or he may seek to adapt himself more fully to the ways of the receiving society but may experience rejection. This is the phase of more or less peaceful co-existence. While the newcomers begin to adapt themselves to the roles required of them to gain their existence and to have access to the social services, they are enabled to retain, rebuild, or re-orient their own patterns and values in other spheres. This process will differ as between groups that are potentially self-segregating, integrating, or assimilating. It is a two-way process of mutual adjustment and adaptation. Once begun, it is not by any means irreversible. The process may be retarded or halted by hostility on either side. The pace at which it proceeds will differ for different groups and will not be uniform for all the members of a group.

To the extent that the events of the past ten years are any clear guide, they suggest that the root causes of success or failure in mutual adjustment lies neither in the minority nor in the majority, but in the interaction of the two. The structure of our society derives much of its character from a dialectical process: a constant series of challenges produces responses, and their resolution determines where the boundary lines are drawn and who is included. And this process extends not merely to those entering society from the outside but to groups within it who attempt to obtain access to the sources of power, material possessions, and status.

D

NOTES TO CHAPTER 2

1. Quoted by J. Galbraith as the epigraph to *The Liberal Hour* (London, Hamish Hamilton, 1960).

2. C. Senior, 'Race Relations and Labour Supply in Great Britain', *Social Problems* (Vol. IV, no. 4, April 1957), p. 308.

3. *Report of The National Advisory Commission on Civil Disorders* (Kerner Report), (New York, Bantam Books, 1968).

4. Evidence from survey of attitudes (reported in Chapter 28).

5. William Joyce ('Lord Haw-Haw') was captured at the end of the Second World War, convicted of treason in respect of the broadcasts he had made for the German authorities, and executed—though not a British subject—because, it was held, he had implicitly accepted allegiance to the Crown by applying for a British passport.

6. Talcott Parsons, 'Full Citizenship for the Negro American?', in Talcott Parsons and Kenneth B. Clark, *The Negro American* (Boston, Houghton Mifflin, 1966), pp. 709–51.

7. John F. Kennedy, *A Nation of Immigrants* (London, Hamish Hamilton, 1964).

8. Parsons, op. cit.

9. T. H. Marshall, *Citizenship and Social Class* (Cambridge, Cambridge University Press, 1950).

10. E. J. Hobsbawm, *Industry and Empire* (London, Weidenfeld & Nicolson, 1968), p. 266.

11. K. Marx in *Marx–Engels on Britain* (Moscow, Foreign Languages Publishing House, 1954), p. 506.

12. E. P. Thompson, *The Making of the English Working Class* (London, Gollancz, 1963).

13. W. Cunningham, *Alien Immigrants to England* (London, Swann Sonnenschein, 1897).

14. Percy S. Cohen, 'The Jews in Modern Britain', Institute of Race Relations *Newsletter* (January 1965).

15. For European Volunteer Workers, see J. A. Tannahill, *European Volunteer Workers in Britain* (Manchester, Manchester University Press, 1958); and for Poles, J. Zubrzycki, *Polish Immigrants in Britain: a study of adjustment* (The Hague, Nijhoff, 1956).

16. Bob Hepple, *Race, Jobs and the Law* (London, Allen Lane, the Penguin Press, 1968).

17. Cmnd. 2379, *Immigration from the Commonwealth* (London, H.M.S.O., 1965).

18. Discussion in this section is based chiefly on Charles Price's introduction to *Australian Immigration* (Canberra, the Australian National University, 1966), and on the writings of Sheila Patterson.

19. Address given by the Home Secretary, the Rt. Hon. Roy Jenkins, M.P., on 23 May 1966 to a meeting of Voluntary Liaison Committees (London, N.C.C.I., 1966).

3 England, Whose England?

We have already quoted T. H. Marshall's definition of citizenship, in *Citizenship and Social Class*. It includes at least three components: civil rights (that is, rights under law to personal liberty, freedom of speech, association, religious toleration, and freedom from censorship), political rights (that is, rights to participation in the political processes), and social rights. The last involves access to social benefits and resources as a right: education, economic security, and all the range of services associated with the Welfare State. Marshall argues that in Britain the basic structure of civil rights had been completed by 1832, and that by the middle of the century it extended to all recognized minorities (except women). Equally, belief in equality before the law had become a permanent portable item in the educated Englishman's cultural baggage. Moreover, as the century advanced, the imperatives of the process of adaptation from a predominantly rural society with a complex social system based on inherited status through the stages of industrialization to a predominantly urban one with a simplified class system demanded the concession of a degree of political rights to the majority.

So Niagara was shot in 1867 in the Second Reform Act, which enfranchized a proportion of the urban working class; and when the extravagant fears of open tyranny by 'the least intelligent' proved ill-founded, the Third Reform Bill of 1884–5 took the process near to its conclusion—although sharp male resistance had to be overcome before the franchise was eventually extended to women. And in turn, at the end of the nineteenth century, the pressure for social rights which had made somewhat uneven progress as the century proceeded began to make further headway. The constitutional historian Dicey saw in the concessions to the trade unions made by the Liberal Government of 1906 the destruction of the Constitution by the creation of specially privileged groups. The collectivism in whose name this policy was justified was based partly on the drawing apart of the classes that had taken place as the nineteenth century progressed: Hobsbawm dates the evolution of a distinctive working-class culture to the late nineteenth century, and the accounts of poverty that investigators brought back from 'Darkest London' in the eighties and nineties have an unbelieving ring about them which signals virtual apartheid. Some physical anthropologists actually thought that the working class were a separate race. In his interestingly-titled study, *Colour and Race* (1903), Dr. J. Beddoe observed:

I regret the deterioration of the old Black Lympho-Sanguine stock, it has served Britain well in many ways but is apparently destined to give way to a darker and more mobile type, largely the offspring of the proletariat, and now adapted to . . . the great cities. The higher type of Scotchman in particular, confessedly the dominant breed of our islands, are rapidly being expended in the service of Empire or are melting away in the fatal atmosphere of great cities. Will the coming race be able to retain what these men died to win?[1]

And indeed, poor diet and living conditions had created a situation where life expectancy was far lower and physical growth retarded—a substantial height difference was recorded between army recruits of different social class. To this extent different physical types could almost be said to exist. But when the First World War threw the separated classes into each other's arms and the working class (with a few conspicuous exceptions) foreswore their internationalism, it must be said the similarities turned out to override these differences. The symbols of Passchendaele and Vimy Ridge (evoked on behalf of the Commonwealth by Hugh Gaitskell on a famous occasion) entered a pantheon possessed in common by all classes. The slower spread of other common values through universal education and the symbolic acceptance by the governing classes of the first Labour Government were further milestones along this road; the General Strike was an aberration in the age of Baldwin and Macdonald. As E. H. Carr put it: 'The socialisation of the nation has as its natural corollary the national-isation of socialism.'

By the twenties, the anthropologists had completely swung round; the British, Sir Arthur Keith thought, were racially probably the most homogeneous of all the European nations. He made a possible exception for the Welsh; in their case—and in the person of Lloyd George, with whom he was much obsessed—he thought he detected echoes of tribal separatism.[2] But anxieties about the population were now on a different footing; the British middle classes were failing to replace their population at the same rate as the working class. In a remarkable essay published in 1913, Sidney Webb had commented that 'This can hardly resolve in anything but national deterioration; or, as an alternative, in this country gradually falling to the Irish and the Jews. Finally, there are signs that even these races are being influenced. The ultimate future of these islands may be to the Chinese.'[3] These fears were still current in the twenties; but two intensive investigations in Scotland eventually disposed of the anxiety that the intellectual level of the population would be bound to decline as a result of differential fertility by class.

The Second World War had cemented a unity which the Depression had not substantially damaged; the apparatus of planning and centralized provision of welfare provided for by the Coalition Government and extended and passed into law by their successors completed the process of inclusion by the range of social rights it conferred. Asa Briggs, looking back at the Welfare State in historical perspective, points not only to the structural changes reflected in this process, but also to a basic change of attitude in which a key concept is the one of fairness and of tolerance and sympathy towards poverty, replacing the idea that to be poor is to have committed a social crime punishable by starvation or formal deprivation of rights in the workhouse. Unemployment is seen increasingly as a misfortune for which, like other social contingencies, it is the duty of the State to provide.

Of course it is possible to invert so over-simplified an outline and to present the picture in terms of unresolved conflict. It would be ludicrous to assert that social rights were gracefully conceded as part of a smooth process; the struggle to achieve them occupied the centre of the political stage for thirty years and was the *raison d'être* of the Labour party. Nor was this process of inclusion necessarily comprehensive; at all stages there have been those who drew, in Malthus's terrible phrase, 'a blank in the lottery of life'. There were many blanks drawn in the thirties, and some, perhaps less ostentatiously, since. Nor, finally, has the institutionalization of conflict within a system of parliamentary democracy meant that the consequences of conflict have been merely of ritual significance. Yet, as Hobsbawm points out, violence has not so far been a feature of the English political scene in the twentieth century; the point about Tonypandy is surely that the stubbornness of the myth—about Churchill's suppression of a strike by military force —illustrates the absence of genuine instances of open class war.

The historical evidence suggests that a marked degree of adaptability exists in the developing 'societal community'; successive groups have been effectively incorporated and the whole system modified to legitimate the process. With the result that, in Bonham's frequently quoted phrase, post-war British politics have been until the sixties 'almost wholly innocent of those issues which cross the class lines in other lands, for example race, nationality, religion, town and country interests, regional interests or the conflict between authoritarian and parliamentary methods'.[4]

Yet this placid surface is deceptive: it reflects not passivity but forces in balance. Beneath it, a series of tenaciously held beliefs can be glimpsed, widely diffused among all classes, which are susceptible of being translated into action under the stimulus of events—for example, by the appearance of a substantial group of newcomers, or (to take more extreme cases) by disaster or national emergency. Any attempt to describe national character and define national views is by definition inadequate, because no such clear-cut categories exist: but at the most general level it is possible to trace a series of beliefs which, when held in common, can be described as distinctively British. Some are favourable to newcomers, and can in the right circumstances produce favourable responses. Ideas of fairness, for example; respect for law and the acceptance of the legitimacy of authority; the rejection of violence. Others militate against their acceptance. Most of these are bound up with the rejection of outsiders; either directly—the xenophobia most foreign observers have found among the English, especially in the urban working class—or indirectly, in a shrinking away from contact with strangers. One side of this coin is the retreat into the private world of the contracting family unit: the other is the selfish lack of concern for those with whom no human contact has been established.

All these are characteristics mapped out by George Orwell in his seminal essay, *England, Your England*, and which he claims, half-seriously, to find crystallized in the seaside postcard:

Their old-fashioned outlook, their guarded snobberies, their mixture of bawdiness and hypocrisy, their extreme gentleness, their deeply moral attitude to life, all are mirrored here.[5]

Geoffrey Gorer has added to this picture, in his study of English character,[6] the acceptance of authority incarnated in the policeman as a key feature in the development of that character, and a detailed exposition of the pattern of restraints the English impose on themselves. Taken together, these seem to us still to provide the clearest explanation of the attitudes and behaviour of Englishmen of a certain generation, especially in the 'traditional' working class. But it needs to be modified in the light of various developments since the Second World War. One such development is the changing position of this country in relation to the outside world, perhaps most clearly reflected in the abandonment of the imperial role. Orwell refers in his essay to the habitual hypocrisy of the Englishman, who totally ignores the significance of the Empire in his evaluation of the state of the nation; and he half-answers himself by referring to the working classes' inability to grasp that the Empire even existed. What we have said so far is open to the same reproach; it is clear that—quite apart from its economic consequences—the experience of imperialism permanently marked and affected the attitudes of generations of Englishmen of the upper and middle class—perhaps especially the latter, in view of their crucial role in managing the gigantic confidence trick by which the lesser breeds were kept within the law. For those directly concerned in this way, the effects of the passing of Empire have been considerable; and the indirect consequences—reflected, for example, in the changing attitudes inculcated through the educational system—have not been negligible. But this has been to a surprising extent a passing phenomenon, a question of generations; the direct influence of imperialism seems to have been remarkably transitory.

The second important modifying factor has been the rapid social changes brought about by the wider diffusion of prosperity since the War, and the establishment of the Welfare State. The lessening of inequality that has taken place as a result has proceeded at a pace accepted as reasonable (broadly speaking) by all those who have been party to it—given that for all but a very small minority some inequality based on class differences is validated by consent. The result might have been expected to be a further reduction of tensions within society: instead it has had the opposite effect; the balance—or what Orwell calls 'the subtle network of compromise' which maintains it—has been disturbed. Runciman, in his analysis of the perception of deprivation,[7] suggests one reason for this. He argues that degrees of inequality persist in various different dimensions, but 'the relationship between inequality and grievance only intermittently corresponds with either the extent and degree of actual inequality, or the magnitude and frequency of relative deprivation which an appeal to social justice would vindicate'.

In the first of his dimensions, power, Runciman suggests that inequality has diminished and is seen to have diminished; in purely class terms, measured on an economic basis, inequality persists, but the sense of relative deprivation is low because each stratum chooses as a reference group a near neighbour in the scale. But in the status dimension, a steady advance towards equality co-exists with an increasing sense of deprivation—since only complete equality can ever be satisfactory. It is here that one potential source of conflict exists: the threat posed by the arrival of newcomers to a resource not the less prized for being intangible, the supply of which is perpetually inadequate.

These findings need to be set against the background of the profoundly significant material changes that have taken place in our society since the Second World War.

Mark Abrams, in his analysis of these changes, describes Britain at the beginning of the fifties, in sharp contrast to ten years later, as still bearing 'the stubborn imprints of the nineteenth century'.[8] The most important amenities of life were in short supply, housing in particular, and restricted educational opportunities and limited access to the consumer durables which were yet to become part of the citizen's common expectations (only 11% of householders owned a washing-machine in 1952, 10% a car, 9% a television set, and 5% a refrigerator). Leisure activities were virtually identical to those that had flourished in the thirties (and by extension to those 'distinctive' elements in working-class culture which Hobsbawm dates from the 1880s—dog tracks, music halls turned Odeons, pubs). By contrast, in the early sixties, sixteen million young people born after the death of Hitler confronted the twelve and a half million whose experience stretches back to before the First World War. Educational opportunities have expanded substantially and with it opportunities for social mobility. Housing conditions have also improved and alongside this improvement there has been a substantial shift in the pattern of tenure, involving a sharp increase in home ownership, and in location of dwellings; Abrams comments that 'if by urbanization is meant big city life then since the early 1950s Britain has almost ceased to be a predominantly urban society and has become a nation where nearly half the people live in small towns, suburbs and villages'. The comparative figures for consumer durables in 1963 were 85%

owning television, 52% a washing-machine, 37% a refrigerator, and 40% a car. Tastes have changed; foreign travel is a commonplace and the availability of cheap and well-designed clothes has meant that a visual identification by class is no longer possible. The other side of the coin is the growing disparity between the prosperous majority and the diminishing minority who have been left behind as standards rise. Fissures have opened not only between rich and poor but in relation to age and to stages in the family life cycle. Geographical segregation has become an increasingly common phenomenon; to those trapped in the shrinking private-rented sector, with rising rents and poor facilities, their underprivileged black neighbours trapped in the same sticky web are simultaneously perpetual symbols of their deprivation and potential scapegoats. In these ways, the movement has been not towards homogeneity but away from it: in this situation, a uniform response towards newcomers is less likely than a fragmented one.

Depending on material circumstances and psychological factors this fragmentation may help or hinder mutual adjustment. The common social handicaps suffered by newcomer and indigenous population alike may be the decisive factor; poverty can be the thread that leads to the lair of the Minotaur of prejudice. In a divided society the newcomer's function may be to show up the weaknesses in the structure of the societal community, and it is in this sense that he ultimately earns our attention, as the focus for the Condition of England question for this generation.

NOTES TO CHAPTER 3

1. J. Beddoe, *Colour and Race* (London, Anthropological Institute of Great Britain and Ireland, 1903), p. 237.

2. Sir A. Keith, *Nationality and Race* (London, Humphrey Milford, 1919), p. 28.

3. Sidney Webb, quoted by Bernard Semmel in *Imperialism and Social Reform* (London, George Allen & Unwin, 1960), p. 51.

4. J. Bonham, *The Middle Class Vote* (London, Faber & Faber, 1954).

5. George Orwell, *England Your England and Other Essays* (London, Secker & Warburg, 1953).

6. G. Gorer, *Exploring English Character* (London, Cresset Press, 1955).

7. W. G. Runciman, *Relative Deprivation and Social Justice* (London, Routledge & Kegan Paul, 1966).

8. Mark Abrams, *The Newspaper Reading Public of Tomorrow* (London, Odhams Press, 1964), p. 8.

4 Race: Some Myths and Realities*

Before proceeding to outline in detail the source of the migration from the New Commonwealth to this country, it might be helpful to deal with the basic objections often raised that this migration is so different in kind from all others as to create an entirely new situation. And certainly, although the experience of previous migrations is particularly useful in illuminating the different responses of our society to newcomers over time, it does not necessarily follow that the response which previous migrations encountered would be repeated in the case of the coloured newcomers entering this country from the New Commonwealth. It is true that some of the objections voiced to their arrival were phrased in an astonishingly similar way to those raised against their predecessors. But to say that these objections have turned out in past cases to be ill-founded does not necessarily dispose of their relevance to the present situation. The Flemings and the Huguenots have all too often been employed as a polemical device to stifle the doubts of those who feel instinctively that this migration differs basically from the previous ones, by virtue of the racial factor alone. As the survey of opinion which is described later in this Report shows, this view that there is an uncrossable gulf fixed between black and white is very widespread and plays an important part in determining the reaction of individuals to coloured strangers. Because uncertainties about the significance of race are so widespread and because the myths about racial differences are so tenaciously held and are invoked to legitimate prejudice and discrimination, we think it right to deal at some length in this Report with the basic questions of the objective significance of racial characteristics.

Theories which attribute immutable characteristics to individuals by virtue of belonging to a group are a common phenomenon in human history and have frequently been used to justify various patterns of interaction—hostility, segregation, or conflict. The most primitive theory of this kind concerns racial differences

* For this chapter we have drawn on and adapted what Philip Mason has written in *Common-Sense about Race* (Gollancz) and in his forthcoming book, *Patterns of Dominance* (O.U.P., for I.R.R.).

and the consequences that are alleged to flow from them. After some decades of scientific work, which has produced almost uniformly negative results, the view still commonly persists that the human species is divided into several 'races' which can be identified on the basis of readily visible differences and that these 'races' also differ markedly in intelligence and temperament.

It may be useful to start with a brief examination of what is reliably known about racial differences and the real as opposed to the alleged consequences of such differences.

Historically, the word 'race' has been used with the widest variety of meanings. Poets in the nineteenth century wrote of 'the feathered race', and we still speak of 'the human race'. Victorians of all shades of political and social persuasion used the term, often to denote what we should now call nationality and sometimes even of an ancient family. Until quite recently in South Africa 'the race question' meant relations between Afrikaans-speakers and English-speakers; relations between white and black were 'the native question'. We shall use the word to describe a category which has, or is thought to have, some biological significance, and we shall be interested chiefly in the social significances which these categories are alleged to possess.

We must note, first, that the term 'race' is itself unsatisfactory from a scientific point of view. It is used by biologists of plant and animal populations which belong to the same species but have been isolated long enough to have developed characteristic differences. This would seem at first sight easy enough to apply to human beings, but in fact there are considerable difficulties.

There is no longer any serious dispute that human beings are all of one species. Attempts at defining this term usually take account of the ability to breed together and produce fertile offspring. Thus a horse and a donkey may successfully breed together, but the offspring, a mule, will be infertile. Another aspect of the species which a definition would take into account is the possibility of demarcation: can it be precisely distinguished from any other group? On both counts, mankind must be judged one species. Men do of course breed together and produce fertile offspring, and there is no difficulty in distinguishing them from any other living group (though there is controversy about extinct forms).

But the question of demarcation does present difficulties when the word 'race' is used of human beings, among whom borderline cases are frequent. This is because human beings are the most widely distributed and mobile of animals. They have seldom been isolated for so long as is common in the case of plants.

Consequently some biologists have argued that 'race' is a term that cannot be used scientifically of human beings because human groups are too mixed to allow of such a classification. Their history has been a long record of migration, conquest, and trade contacts, interspersed in some cases with periods of isolation, but always followed by mixing.

The majority of biologists agree, however, that in spite of the difficulty of demarcation, the differences between, say, a typical population from the West Coast of Africa and a typical population from the Swedish countryside are so considerable that some term must be used to distinguish them. 'Race' is thus a term which has a biological meaning though it must be used with caution.

What is implied by this qualification? First, that the concept of 'racial purity' has little meaning. Since Columbus crossed the Atlantic in 1492, none of the major divisions of mankind have been isolated from contact with others; where small populations have been isolated for some time, they tend to show congenital defects. Secondly, it is not in accordance with the known facts to speak of one 'race' or 'breed' as superior in general to another. We have ceased to talk of 'race' as a group with a set of constant characteristics. To say of an individual that he belongs to a certain racial group has no uniquely predictive value: we cannot determine whether that person is taller or shorter, darker or lighter, more or less intelligent, than an individual belonging to some other 'race'. Individuals from one population will have more or fewer of some characteristics than individuals from others. But it does not follow that every individual in one group will be marked off from every individual in the other group in terms of these characteristics.

We used the term 'superior in general'. It is clearly possible to say that in some particular respect a typical population from one rural area will be better adapted to life in a particular environment than another; one can even sometimes say that a higher percentage of one racial group can be trained to excellence in one particular skill than from another group. For example, more Negroes than whites seem to make first-class sprinters over 100 metres. But it is not possible to deduce from this that A, who is a Negro, will necessarily beat B, who is white, over that distance.

There is, then, no 'pure' race to be found. The processes of mixing (or hybridization) have meant that every racial group shades off into some other group. Thus, although there is very general agreement on a broad division of most of mankind into three main streams—Mongolian, Negro, and White or Caucasian —there are puzzles about classification which preclude the use of 'race' as in any sense providing any clear lines of demarcation. The Caucasian stream, for example, will include South Indians who are dark-skinned, and the Australian aboriginal is thought by at least one authority to be 'archaic White'. In the South Pacific, the Polynesians show characteristics typical of all three great stocks. One authority classes them as predominantly 'White': there is no general agreement as to how they reached their islands or whether they were mixed before they came or later.

What we can conclude, then, is that the attempt to justify differential treatment of people on the grounds that they belong to one racial group rather than another will always founder on the fact that there will be many individuals who do not share those distinguishing characteristics of their group which are supposed to justify differential treatment. If there are no 'pure' races, it is misleading to talk of groups of people as though they approximated to some idea of racial purity. West Indians and West Africans may look alike to some eyes, but the differences between them are as great as (if not greater than) those between, say, a Lithuanian and a Geordie. A Chinese waiter, in a recent case reported in the press, was unable to pick out his assailants in an identification parade because 'they all looked alike'. The fact that people 'look alike' to us may say more about what we are used to than about what people really look like.

Linked to this reliance on visible characteristics is the popular belief that Negroid peoples are 'one step removed from the monkey'. There is still a good deal of controversy as to the stage of evolution at which racial differences arose and our knowledge is hampered by the fact that many distinguishing characteristics are perishable. We cannot always determine the skin-colour of a skeleton. At present, human remains that are distinctively Negroid have not been found which are comparable in antiquity with those which seem to be of Caucasoid or Mongoloid type. There is, therefore, no ground for regarding the Negroid type of man as biologically primitive. It seems, on the contrary, more likely that it is the most recent.

It is impossible to range the different stocks of man in an order of biological primitiveness. All one can say with certainty is that there are some traits or characteristics which are more ape-like than others, but that these are fairly evenly distributed among the major races or divisions of mankind. Hair on the body is more ape-like than smooth skin, and the so-called White race is more hairy than either Mongolians or Negroes. Apes have virtually no lips, and here the Mongolians are their nearest neighbours, and the Negroes furthest removed. The Negro ear is in general more developed than the White, and the Negro form of hair is quite remote from the ape's. On the other hand, the chin is a distinctively human feature, and the White chin is usually more pronounced than in the other main races. The teeth are also usually of a type that is evolutionally more advanced. But, once again, a pinko-grey man is rather more likely than a Negro to have traces of the ridges above the eyes which are so prominent in the gorilla and the extinct Neanderthal man. There are some grounds, then, for regarding the 'White' race as the oldest, but, as one authority puts it, 'no physical anthropologist can rank the existing races of man within an evolutionary hierarchy in the order of their distances of departure from the anthropoid apes, because each race shows its own combination of anthropoidal, primitive human and advanced specialized characters'.[1]

The question of who is 'closest to the ape' is an unprofitable and meaningless inquiry. What is of importance is not the antiquity of a distinct biological type but the stage any population has reached in the specifically human quality of ability to master the environment. It would be of real significance if there was any scientific indication of a relation between different racial types and different levels of intelligence.

On this question, the consensus of opinion is that it is extremely difficult to measure genetic aptitude for learning. What can be measured is skill already acquired, ability in displaying it, and, to some extent, the skill so far acquired in the art of acquiring more skill. But this is not at all the same as genetic aptitude for learning.

In fact, performance in intelligence tests is governed partly by environment and partly by inherited aptitude. It is not possible to say precisely how much is inherited and how much acquired. The difficulty arises from the fact that with human beings there can be no completely controlled experiments. We can find out something of what a child has learnt, but nothing precise about what he might have learnt in different circumstances. That is why it is impossible to compare the genetic aptitude of people from quite different backgrounds. What has emerged from much research and discussion is a majority opinion on two points.

First, within any human population of a fairly homogeneous background, the distribution of aptitude for learning is likely to follow roughly the same pattern, that is to say, there will be an average level near which many of the population will register scores, while above and below there will be a diminishing number in each grade, until extremes are reached some way above and below the average.

Secondly, the nearer two populations are to a common background, *whatever their racial origin*, the nearer the *averages* of intelligence are likely to be. Thus, tests in the United States have shown that there were marked differences in the results of intelligence tests for white and Negro children in the Deep South, where there were separate schools and where much less has been spent on Negro schools than on white. But the differences between Negro children in the Deep South and Negro children in the North were equally marked, and where in the Northern cities conditions between Negro and white were much nearer being equal, tests on children in state schools showed a much reduced average racial difference and that difference directly related to economic class and home background.

Educational research in Britain in the last two decades has shown the crucial influence on measured intelligence and educational performance of such factors as social class, the home environment, the educational attainment of the parents, and the character of the school itself. And a recent experiment in the United States has shown that when teachers were told that one particular group of children (selected at random) was about to do exceptionally well, the attainment of those children increased rapidly and significantly. In fact, the expectations of teachers plays a key role in the performance of the children whom they teach. And the less that is demanded of the child, the less he performs. And what we measure at the end of the process is not the genetic aptitude of the children concerned, whether they be working-class children or coloured children. We measure simply the efficacy with which we have imposed our beliefs upon the children.

One further point needs to be made about intelligence. Intelligence, in the sense of the ability to cope with the environment, will obviously depend upon familiarity with the particular environment involved. What is more, behaviour which is intelligent in one environment, say, a rural society, may well betoken the lack of intelligence in another, for example, an urban society, and vice versa. Much of what passes for 'racial differences' are in reality social and cultural differences. Furthermore, there is no scientific way of describing these social and cultural differences of behaviour as being 'superior' or 'inferior'. The most that can be said is that behaviour which is useful in one context or culture may become useless or even harmful in another.

Differences in the behaviour of human groups are more easily accounted for by history, by reaction to environment, by tradition, and by the skills handed down by ancestors, than by any inherited differences of intelligence or temperament. What biologists and anthropologists have to tell us is that 'racial purity' is an illusory concept and a delusive ideal, and that 'racial differences' (in the strictly qualified sense of the term 'race') cannot form the basis of selective social policies. No differences between different racial groups can justify the denial of economic, social, and political rights to individuals or to groups of people. Whatever the significance of the concept of 'racial differences', it does not possess that kind of significance.

Finally, there is a commonly held belief that marriages between members of different racial groups are undesirable because such a 'genetic mixture' has a deleterious effect on the offspring. For this belief there is no scientific evidence whatever. What is probably true is that in a society where racial intermarriage is frowned upon, the children of such a marriage have greater obstacles to surmount. But the point is that these obstacles are social and man-made. They are not inherent in the genes of the parents, nor in the 'genetic mixture' of the child. And if genetics provides no arguments against intermarriage, the fact of social difficulties provides none either. To say that intermarriage is undesirable because the children are liable to encounter racial prejudice is like saying that it is desirable not to have children since children are specially vulnerable to mumps.

To conclude: no group of men can intelligibly be said to be 'purer' than any other or innately superior to any other. What the study of anthropology impresses upon us is chiefly the diversity of human beings. Diversity does not imply superiority or inferiority. 'Superior' and 'inferior' in this context are social concepts—they are what we make of men, not what they are. In Part II of this Report we proceed to describe the diversity of the migrations which flowed to Britain from the coloured Commonwealth in the period following the Second World War.

NOTE TO CHAPTER 4

1. E. A. Hooton, *Up from the Ape* (New York, Macmillan, 1958).

5 The Sending Societies

In the last 500 years a great variety of peoples have come to settle in these islands; there have been Flemings and Huguenots; Irishmen; Jews from Spain, from the Pale and from Germany; Poles, Italians, and Hungarians; and the families cast up by the Second World War who were brought over from the refugee camps in Germany and Austria. They were moved by the classical forces that cause migration, some seeking asylum from political or religious persecution, some to escape from hunger and poverty. But their variety pales to the sameness of a monochrome print when they are compared with the immigrants from the tropical Commonwealth who have arrived here in the last twenty years. The differences between the latter are as great as the distances that separate their homelands. Yet the label of Commonwealth immigrant that has been attached to them, and which for most people is synonymous with colour, has tended to mask these differences and to disguise the nature of the influences that play upon them and affect the quality of their response to their environment as they settle in a new country.

Part II, which is confined to the West Indians, Indians, and Pakistanis, who have formed the bulk of the immigration, describes the kind of people they are, the life which they left behind them, the variety of their cultures, and the lands which gave them birth. It then traces the progress of the migrations in the period when the only restrictions on entry were the ability to pay the fare and the prospect of finding employment. There follows a discussion of the economic forces that played upon the migrants: the push of poverty, the pressure of population on the land, and the attractive power of a market hungry for labour. Finally it describes the kind of industries in which they found employment and the economic role which they were called on to play.

1. THE MIGRATIONS FROM THE WEST INDIES AND GUYANA

By far the largest of the migrations has come from the West Indies and Guyana. Jamaica contributed rather more than half this number and the remainder was drawn from a group of islands

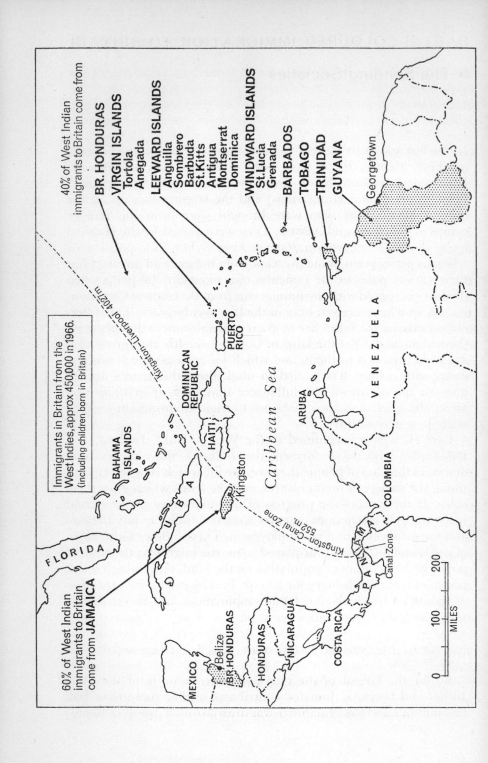

40% of West Indian immigrants to Britain come from

BR. HONDURAS
VIRGIN ISLANDS
  Tortola
  Anegada
LEEWARD ISLANDS
  Anguilla
  Sombrero
  Barbuda
  St.Kitts
  Antigua
  Montserrat
  Dominica
WINDWARD ISLANDS
  St.Lucia
  Grenada
BARBADOS
TOBAGO
TRINIDAD
GUYANA

Georgetown

Immigrants in Britain from the
West Indies, approx 450,000 in 1966.
(including children born in Britain)

Kingston—Liverpool 4021m

PUERTO
RICO

DOMINICAN
REPUBLIC

HAITI

BAHAMA
ISLANDS

C U B A

Kingston

Caribbean Sea

VENEZUELA

ARUBA

COLOMBIA

FLORIDA

60% of West Indian immigrants to Britain come from JAMAICA

Kingston—Canal Zone
552 m.

PANAMA

Canal Zone

MEXICO

Belize
BR. HONDURAS

HONDURAS

NICARAGUA

COSTA RICA

0   100   200
MILES

nearly 1,000 miles to the east, which extend in an arc from the
Virgins to Trinidad. The distance between Jamaica and the
Eastern Caribbean is often maintained by the immigrants, for the
small islanders have their own patriotisms which are rooted in their
nurture and their history. All the islands except Barbados were at
one time the possessions of European powers other than the British,
and some, like St. Lucia, have been shuttled between European
masters as they were captured and recaptured by the French and
the British in the eighteenth century. Some of the islands still carry
traces of Spanish culture, in others the native patois is French;
Barbados alone was continuously a British possession for 350 years
before it gained its independence in 1966.

Whatever may remain in the islands of other European cultures,
the men, women, and children who have come to Britain in the
last twenty years were brought up within a British culture, were
taught in English-speaking schools by teachers with English
middle-class values. The English taught in the schools was very
different from the English spoken in the home and in some of the
islands it was virtually a second language. But in their schools
West Indian children were taught from English textbooks about
the history of the Mother Country and learned as loyal subjects of
the Crown to sing 'Rule Britannia' and 'God Save the King'. Their
African origins had been overlaid by this colonial culture and by
the religion of Christian missionaries.

The Churches played an important part in the struggle for
Emancipation just over 100 years before the first shipload of
Jamaicans arrived in England after the War, and today play an
important part in the lives of the people throughout the British
Caribbean, for many of whom Christianity is a living faith; there
are members of all the major denominations of the church in
England, and in some of the islands the Roman Catholic faith is
preponderant. Church attendance is high, as is the number of
communicant church members.[1]

But not all West Indians belong to orthodox denominations.
In Jamaica particularly, the poorest peasants have evolved for
themselves over the years religious forms which are based ostensibly on Christianity, sometimes on a small number of selected
Biblical texts, sometimes including elements which seem to be
linked with African magical or religious practices. More important, there has recently been an extraordinary increase in the
number of adherents to the Pentecostal sects, of which several

originated in the Southern States of the U.S.A. Their faith is a form of Christian fundamentalism based on the Biblical texts: in their worship they seek the gift of tongues and the attainment through ecstasy of possession by the Spirit. At the last census the followers of the Church of God had become the third largest denomination in Jamaica.

The opportunities for education vary greatly with the comparative wealth or poverty of the islands. The level of literacy is highest in Barbados, and it is in Barbados, Antigua, and Trinidad that there is the greatest provision of secondary education. In most of the islands less than one in ten of the adult population has gone beyond an elementary education, but this kind of statistic can be misleading, as in some of the islands, for example in Jamaica, there are many all-age schools which provide elementary education up to the age of 15. While levels of education vary between islands, there are also great contrasts within the islands between the town and country schools. In country districts it is quite common to find classes of sixty or seventy children being taught in one open-plan building with as many as five and even six other classes under the same roof, often without a blackboard to separate them.[2] The children seated at the outer edge of one class may well be hearing the neighbouring teacher better than their own. In these conditions teachers, who are often not highly trained, have to rely on old-fashioned teaching methods and strict discipline: too much participation by the children would reduce the system to chaos. Until recently, secondary education has been available mainly for the middle classes who could pay for it, but this is no longer the case in the larger islands where free places, grants, and competitive entry have opened opportunities to a much wider field. Many of the secondary schools have a high standard but many teachers are burdened with large classes. There may be as many as 110 in a class in country schools, though with a high rate of absenteeism, particularly at the beginning or the end of the week when the children are required to help at home, or when it rains. For many teachers the children's loss is their gain.[3]

The variety between the islands is too great to describe in such a short treatment, but perhaps one or two references need to be made. After Emancipation the position of the freed slaves varied in different areas. In Trinidad and British Guiana the arrival of indentured Indian labour in large numbers radically altered the Creole's dependence on the plantation owner, but while in Trinidad there was plenty of land, in British Guiana the Creoles, unless they moved to the town, were confined to a cultivated strip along the coast where they lived in villages near the Indian barracks and continued to work on the sugar plantations. In Jamaica there was sufficient Crown land for many of the ex-slaves to escape from the plantations and from direct subservience. With the help of the missionaries some were able to obtain small holdings, but many hacked out a clearing in the mountains on waste lands which technically belonged to the Crown, where they squatted and eked out an existence in extreme poverty. In Barbados the position was different. This was not a Crown Colony and all the land was in private hands and in cultivation. There were no mountains and there was therefore nowhere for the emancipated slave to go; he remained closely bound to his previous owner, who gave him housing that was tied to part-time employment on the estate.

These initial variations in the effects of Emancipation have had deep influences on colour and class relationships. In the plural societies of Trinidad and Guyana the position of the Creole has been more dominant than in Jamaica, where society has been stratified along a colour spectrum. Barbados provides a further contrast, where the close patron–client relationship has brought the advantage of a high level of education which paternalism bestows (there were a large number of elementary schools from 1841 and a free lending library was opened as early as 1848), and has made the Barbadian more of an Englishman in his attitudes to law and authority than probably any of the other West Indian islanders. It has also left a more clear cut division between white and black than in other islands.

There are still people to be found in the islands whose grand-parents were brought over as slaves. Edith Clarke found instances of landowners whose grandparents came from Africa and who were given land by their mistress when they were free. They held their land, about one acre, in trust for all members of the family and could never sell it. 'They had the African tradition.'[4] Actual memories of Africa are dim and have little to do with the pictures of Africa drawn by poets and millennial sects who celebrate their African origins and long for a return to Africa. But the Africa of their dreams is Ethiopia and not the West Coast of their ancestors.[5]

Whatever the imprint of a British Christian culture may have been, the legacy of slavery remains in all these island societies in its effect on the family system and on the way society is stratified. Few slaves were allowed to marry and it was made impossible for a man to assume the responsibilities of the head of a family as he had no legal rights or duties towards his child. The male slave was further deprived of his manhood as families were frequently broken up and their members dispersed. Women were taken by their owners or overseers for their sexual pleasure, and they found in this form of concubinage an escape from hardship and a hope for their children, who were often treated with affection by their planter fathers, and might even be given their freedom. From their descendants were to spring the coloured middle and upper classes of the islands.

Today, West Indian family life still bears traces of slavery, in a very high illegitimacy rate and the instability of many unions. Among peasants and the urban working classes it is common to marry late, generally when the woman is past childbearing age and when there is enough economic security to undertake the obligations of a legal union. Marriage is thus solemnized among the middle aged and is not related to the rearing of children within the family and the home. Young girls have early sexual experience and remain at home after the birth of the first child, which is often left in the care of mother or sisters. A girl is likely to have borne one or two children before she leaves home and sets up a more or less stable union, but if this breaks down she returns to her family. By the time they are 30 most women are living in stable unions, sometimes called common law marriages, although the partners are not bound by any civil or religious sanctions. It is these unions which lead on to marriage. The irresponsibility of the father is part of the legacy of slavery: although a man will support the children of earlier unions while he is living with their mother and will often show great affection for these stepchildren, few men contribute to the care of their children once a union is broken. It follows that with so much instability the man's authority passes to the woman, and the role of the mother and the grandmother is by far the strongest in the West Indian family system.[6] The fact that women from an early age are used to managing their own lives and to leaving their children to the care of others explains the presence of so many women in the early years of the West Indian migration to Britain. Very often they came on their own to earn money for the support of their children, who were left in the care of their grandmothers.[7]

While the proportion of women in the West Indian migration was high, men were, of course, in the majority throughout the period of uncontrolled entry. What kind of people came and what education and skills did they possess? Davison has reported the serious concern felt by responsible leaders in the small islands of Dominica, St. Kitts, and St. Lucia at the loss of the most productive and skilled elements in the labour force. There seems no doubt that in the early stages the migration contained a very high proportion of skilled men, far higher than in the West Indian population as a whole. This high level of skills was maintained throughout the 1950s, although as the numbers grew the proportion of agricultural workers increased and the literacy rate, which had been high, declined.

However, it would be false to think that as time went by this became a migration of predominantly rural unskilled workers. As late as 1962 there were still more Jamaicans coming to England from Kingston and St. Andrew than from the rural parishes.[8] A number of them, it is true, had been born in a country parish but this is consistent with the great movement of population away from the countryside that had taken place in the previous forty years and brought nearly a quarter of a million people to the metropolitan area.[9] It seems clear also that the level of education of these Jamaicans in 1962 was higher than that of the general population: and half of them had had some form of vocational training.[10]

A considerable amount of detailed information has been collected about the occupational structure of the migrants from the West Indies to Britain up to 1962 (see Table 5.1). Roberts and Mills's study of 17,373 Jamaican emigrants covers the period 1953 to 1955, when migration to Britain reached significant numbers;[11] Mrs. Ruth Glass's analysis of a sample of West Indian immigrants drawn from the records of the Migrant Services Division includes those who arrived between 1956 and 1958 as well as earlier arrivals;[12] and a study of a sample of Jamaican emigrants in 1962 by Francis brings us up to the period just before control, when very large numbers of immigrants were entering Britain.[13] The main gap is 1960, when economic 'pull' factors in Britain were stimulating the migration, and when there was a high proportion of men among all immigrants from the West Indies. A survey conducted by the Economist Intelligence Unit in the summer of 1961 partly fills the gap, but unfortunately no figures are given about the date of arrival of West Indian immigrants.[14]

In each of these studies a majority of the men emigrating to Britain from the West Indies are shown to have been skilled or semi-skilled workers. This does not mean that a skilled worker in, for example, Jamaica, has the same training and expertise as a skilled man in the same trade in Britain (for further discussion about the assessment of skills of immigrants see below in Chapter 19), but it does mean that on the whole those who migrated were successful in their own societies. Only a small number were drawn from the ranks of the unemployed. The Economist Intelligence Unit Survey in 1961 found that 12% of a sample of 603 West Indians had been unemployed before leaving the West Indies. Francis, in his study of Jamaican emigrants leaving in 1962 during the 'beat the ban' rush, found that only 3% of wage earners had worked for three months or less during the year prior to their departure, and 73% of wage earners had worked for more than nine months. It cost £75 or £85 for a single ticket to the United Kingdom—the equivalent of half a year's wages for unskilled workers; it was therefore likely to be the most enterprising who decided to make the journey.

Table 5.1 shows that, compared with the occupational distribution of the population at the previous census, skilled workers were considerably over-represented and unskilled labourers, farmers, fishermen, and farm labourers considerably under-represented in the early years of migration. A study by Cumper, of 384 emigrants leaving Barbados in October 1955, reached similar conclusions to those of Roberts and Mills in Jamaica.[15] Seventy per cent of the Barbadian emigrants were skilled workers. This was more than double the proportion of such skills in the population of Barbados as a whole. Roberts and Mills noticed the rise in the numbers and in the proportion of unskilled workers during the three years of their study and wondered if the balance might be tilting the other way as more unskilled rural dwellers joined the migration.[16] The proportion of farm workers recorded in the different studies varies. While Cumper found only 5% in his 1955 Barbadian sample, Roberts and Mills found a steady increase between 1953 and 1955, from 12% to 14% to 24%. (1955 is also the year when the predominant mode of travel for emigrants changed from air to sea. The lower cost of emigration to Britain and the growth of travel agencies may be responsible for the increase in the numbers and the proportion of rural workers.) In 1962 Francis found that 375 out of a sample of 1,622 men had

Table 5.1. The occupational distribution of a sample of male emigrants from Jamaica (1953–5) compared with the occupations of males in Jamaica at the 1943 Census

	1953	1954	1955	1943 Census
Total number in each year	1,284	5,179	10,911	
Skilled workers	840 (65%)	3,430 (66%)	6,280 (61%)	18%
masons, carpenters, mechanics, etc., other skilled, tailors				
Unskilled workers (including farm workers)*	260 (20%)	1,120 (22%)	3,600 (33%)	69%
Non-manual and not stated	180 (15%)	630 (12%)	1,050 (6%)	13%

Sources:
G. W. Roberts and D. O. Mills, 'Study of External Migration affecting Jamaica 1953–55'; and based on Maunder's re-classification of Census data (*Social and Economic Studies*, Vol. IV, no. 1).

* Percentage of farm workers in total of all workers: 12%, 14%, 24%, 55%.

worked in agriculture. Mrs. Glass's analysis in 1958–9, which included those arriving throughout the previous period, recorded 12% of agricultural workers.

Roberts and Mills also give a detailed analysis of the occupations of women emigrants before they left Jamaica. The majority of the women were part of the labour force—only 14% in 1953, 13% in 1954, and 19% in 1955 were classed as outside the labour force. Seven years later Francis found that 69·5% of women were part of the labour force, and 20% were classified as 'homemakers'. The main occupations among women migrants, both between 1953–5 and in the 1962 sample, were dressmaking and domestic or personal service work. But there were also a minority of non-manual workers, for example, 630 clerical workers, 210 teachers, and 162 nurses, in Francis's sample.

2. THE MIGRATIONS FROM INDIA AND PAKISTAN

One of the most striking features of the migrations from both India and Pakistan is the limited extent of the areas from which they originate. When one considers the size of the two countries it is surprising that emigration has been confined to the Punjab and Gujarat and to half a dozen areas in the two wings of Pakistan.

The Sikhs, who constitute four-fifths of the Indian migration to Britain,[17] come mainly from two districts in Eastern Punjab, Jullundur and Hoshiarpur, in an area known as the Doaba, a Mesopotamia that lies between the two rivers Beas and Sutlej. They are men of the plains, which are among the most fertile in India.

The Sikhs are perhaps the most mobile and versatile people in the whole of India and are to be found in many of the large Indian cities, where they are conspicuous as drivers of taxis. They have contributed nearly one-quarter of the Indian armed forces, although they represent less than 2% of the total population. They are great wanderers and in the last hundred years have settled as far afield as Shanghai, Singapore, Honolulu, Australia, New Zealand, Fiji, Vancouver, California, and throughout East Africa. The Sikhs, unlike Hindus, have no caste inhibitions to prevent them from travelling. They are frontiersmen and pioneers: it was they who opened up the Western Punjab when the British built a canal system towards the end of the last century, and they turned these arid tracts into rich wheat producing farmland. But they were not to enjoy them for long; in 1947, after the Partition of India, they and the Hindus were driven out of their farms across the new frontier.

In the exchange of populations over four million refugees flooded into the Eastern Punjab where they took over the generally smaller and sometimes poorer Muslim holdings.[18] Most of the refugees went to Malwas, south of the Jullundur Doaba, but the migrations had their effect throughout East Punjab as all land-holdings were reduced by legislation to a ceiling of thirty acres.[19] As there is no system of primogeniture among the Sikhs, the land becomes fragmented through inheritance and the migrations after Partition greatly added to the already existing pressure of population on the land. Jullundur district, where one-quarter of all land-holdings are less than one acre, has the highest percentage of uneconomic landowners and also the highest population density in the Punjab.[20]

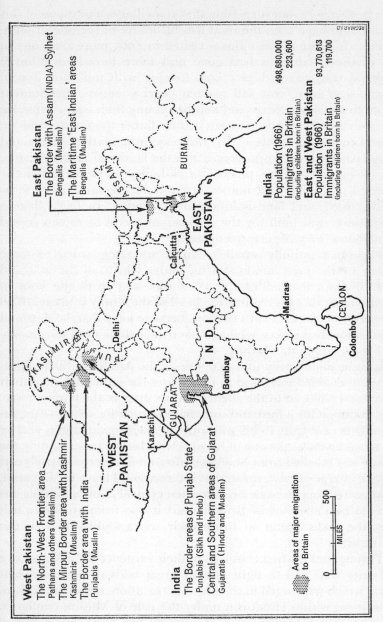

West Pakistan

The North-West Frontier area
Pathans and others (Muslim)
The Mirpur Border area with Kashmir
Kashmiris (Muslim)
The Border area with India
Punjabis (Muslim)

India

The Border areas of Punjab State
Punjabis (Sikh and Hindu)
Central and Southern areas of Gujarat
Gujaratis (Hindu and Muslim)

East Pakistan

The Border with Assam (INDIA)–Sylhet
Bengalis (Muslim)
The Maritime 'East Indian' areas
Bengalis (Muslim)

India
Population (1966)   498,680,000
Immigrants in Britain   223,600
(including children born in Britain)

East and West Pakistan
Population (1966)   93,770,613
Immigrants in Britain   119,700
(including children born in Britain)

BURMA

ASSAM

EAST PAKISTAN

Calcutta

KASHMIR

Delhi

PUNJAB

WEST PAKISTAN

Karachi

GUJARAT

INDIA

Bombay

Madras

CEYLON

Colombo

Areas of major emigration
to Britain

0   500
MILES

REGMARAD

Map 5.2. India and Pakistan: showing the areas from which Indians and Pakistanis have emigrated to the United Kingdom

It is, therefore, not surprising that the villages and towns of this area should have been the most fruitful source of the migration to Britain. In some of the villages visited in 1965 more than one in ten of the inhabitants had gone and more hoped to follow.[21] England was regarded as a land flowing with milk and honey. 'Come over here, you will get ten years younger', one student wrote to his headmaster, and another young Sikh who started his life in England as a labourer advised his father to join him and 'go to heaven in your life-time'. Remittances from relatives in England have brought great improvements to the land and to the villages. Everywhere there are pukka (brick-built) houses, colloquially referred to as 'England houses'; tube-wells are sunk, more fertilizer is used, and land-holdings are extended. In one village a clock tower was built for the *gurdwara* at a cost of 12,000 rupees contributed by villagers in England.

The often pitifully small holdings are safeguarded to some extent by the joint family system, under which all the sons and their families live under the same roof and work the land in common. During his lifetime the head of the family is master of all property, but at his death the sons become joint shareholders and trustees for their sisters, who also have their share until they marry and move to another family.

It is the joint family that determined the pattern of Sikh migration and enabled sons, and in some cases the father, to leave their wives and children to the shelter and security of the family home. It is common for a husband to remain abroad for many years, returning occasionally to his wife, only to leave again after a year or so, when he may take one of his sons with him.[22] In one family the father was recalled from Shanghai after an absence of thirty years to take charge of the farm so that his sons could leave for England. This pattern began to be broken when control of immigration was seen to be imminent in Britain: and it was from 1958 onwards that the Sikhs began to bring their wives and families to this country.[23]

Throughout the first centuries of their existence the Sikhs were a minority that had to fight against great odds to survive. Their faith, which was forged in the fire of persecution, began as a reform movement within Hinduism under the rule of Muslim emperors. The founder, Guru Nanak (1469–1539), preached the oneness of God and the equality of all men, and thus the movement was one of dissent not only from the ritualism and idolatry of the Hindu religion, but also against the burden of caste which imposes a social hierarchy ordained from birth. The faith taught by Nanak and by the nine gurus (teachers) who followed him in the next 200 years was eclectic and borrowed from both Hinduism and Islam. Nanak proclaimed 'there is no Hindu, there is no Mussulman', and the Holy Scripture, the *Granth Sahib*, incorporates the writings of both Hindu and Muslim saints. Nevertheless, it was the persecutions of non-Muslims under the Mogul emperors that led the later gurus to turn their pacifist followers into a militant sect. The work was completed by the tenth and last of the gurus, Gobind Singh, who founded the *Khalsa* or brotherhood of the pure. At the initiation of baptism all drank from the same bowl whatever their caste and were given new names with the suffix Singh, which Sikhs carry to this day and which served to remove the caste distinction revealed in the family name. The initiates swore to observe the five K's, namely to wear their hair and beard unshorn (*Kesh*), to wear a comb (*Kangha*), a pair of shorts (*Kāchhā*), a steel bangle on the wrist (*Kărā*), and to carry a sword (*Kirpān*). This observance is still the mark of a religious Sikh and the wearing of long hair plays a very important part in the cohesion of the Sikh community in the Punjab as it serves to mark them off as a religious community separate from the Hindus. However, many young Sikhs shave off their beards before they leave for England, and even some of the older Sikhs do not retain long hair in the emigration, though Aurora says that this is a matter of 'unavoidable shame' for them.[24] The orthodox Sikh will also abstain from tobacco, alchohol, and the eating of beef or of any meat that has been killed by bleeding. In practice, though most Sikhs refuse tobacco, only the most pious will refuse alcohol.

Although the gurus set their faces resolutely against caste, Sikhism has not succeeded in breaking the system. It is still of great importance in the choice of a partner in marriage. Yet it has been modified and weakened with time, and the rigid concept of pollution has disappeared. In fact, the *Gurha langar*, the free kitchen attached to the place of worship (*gurdwara*) at which all may cook and all may eat, strikes at the root of caste distinction. But within the villages there is an occupational hierarchy of caste in which the dominant and most numerous group are the Jats, the earliest converts to Sikhism, who became the backbone of the Sikh armies and owners of most of the land in the short but glorious period of the Sikh ascendancy under Ranjit Singh. It is the Jat peasant proprietors who probably form the majority in the Sikh emigration to Britain.

But Punjabi society is in the process of transition from a 'caste' to an open society, and the position of the artisan and craftsman is changing as industry comes to the villages and frees them from their traditional dependence on the agricultural castes. Craftsmen have also moved to relatives in the towns where their children receive a better education and they can escape from their traditional caste occupation. Many of the carpenter and blacksmith castes emigrated to East Africa and many more took the chance to seek their fortune in Britain. While Jats predominated in the emigration because they could raise a mortgage on their property to pay their passage, other families sold all their gold ornaments to launch a brother on the great adventure. Most of the other castes are also represented in the emigration, including some former untouchables.[25]

Another fundamental change is the gradual breaking up of the joint family which, for all the economic security it affords, has many disadvantages, particularly for women. Living at such close quarters leads to jealousies between the wives and there is often antagonism between the mother of the house and her daughters-in-law. Emigration is contributing to this change as with increasing prosperity from remittances women begin to assert their independence; quarrels may often lead to a brother and his family leaving the parental home. Thus transition is taking place in the small nuclear family which will more and more resemble the pattern of family life in the emigration.

While the man is the undisputed head of the Sikh household, women have a considerable freedom. They worship with the men in the *gurdwara* and have never been required to wear the veil. The girls receive the same education as boys and are even required to stay one year longer in school. Women work in groups in the fields and some work as domestic servants in the families for which their husbands work as labourers on a hereditary basis. Jat women, because of their caste claims, will not work for others but they do help on their husbands' land. A woman may retain her earnings and is not required to contribute any part of them to the expenses of the joint family. She exercises a great influence in family affairs.

The village schools are simple structures with few classrooms, but for most of the year lessons are taken out of doors, the children grouped around the teacher wherever there is a patch of shade. Primary education is free and in theory compulsory. A child enters at 5 and passes by examination to the middle school from 11 years upward, leaving at 14. English is taught in the last year of the primary school, but because of the very low pay there is a shortage of qualified teachers.[26] There is much learning by rote and it is not to be expected that children will leave school able to understand spoken English. Many more children now attend middle school, where a small fee has to be paid, another effect of the prosperity brought by the remittances. Aurora found in 1958 that of the 1,200 immigrants in his study 20% were fluent in English and about half were unable to speak any English at all. The literacy figure in the Punjab is 9% and literacy in English 1·5%, so it is clear that literates and those literate in English were over-represented in the emigration.

Not all the Punjabis who have come to England are Sikhs, but the number of Hindus is comparatively small and, unlike the Sikhs, who came mainly from the districts where they were born, many Hindus had already been uprooted once before when they fled from West Punjab at the time of Partition. Travelling across the sea involves ritual impurity and this may still inhibit some Hindus from migrating, but it does not seem to have proved an obstacle to the Hindus of Gujarat, the second area in India from which immigrants have come to this country. Gujaratis, like the Sikhs, have a long tradition of migration and for centuries have been trading with East Africa where they settled to become the traders and merchants of the country. According to Desai the Hindus from Gujarat who have settled in England belong mainly to the agricultural castes and the remainder are usually village craftsmen. Pressure on the land and unemployment have been the motive forces behind the emigration, which was drawn mainly from the central and southern parts of Gujarat, particularly from the district of Surat and Charottar.[27]

The Gujaratis who have emigrated appear to be a highly literate group. Desai did not come across one illiterate Gujarati in the five years in which he was working among them and all the 191 men in his sample had had a high school education, while sixteen had been to a university. There was always a significant minority of educated and professional people among the post-war Indian migrants. These not only included the doctors and university students but also those who came from a middle-class background in India and now perform manual jobs in Britain.

F

The Gujarati emigration also contains a minority of Muslims who appear to have come from the three administrative districts of Baroda, Surat, and Broach, drawn from some twenty villages, and from the towns of Baroda, Broach, Surat, and Bardoli, all within a distance of not much more than one hundred miles, and many within the coastal area, which is well known for its commerce and wealth. Michael Lyon in a study of Gujarati Muslims in East Lancashire found that many had relatives in East Africa;[28] they had grown up with an awareness of the trade routes which had borne settlers to other countries and had a certain sophistication in their approach to migration; many had come to England as complete families. Gujaratis and Punjabis are of different ethnic origin and, while both their languages are Sanskritic, they are mutually unintelligible, though simple Hindi which is connected with both might serve as a medium of communication. The two main elements in the Indian emigration are thus separated by custom, and in most cases by religion, and can probably best communicate with one another through the medium of English.

The two wings of Pakistan are separated by more than 1,000 miles and except at the official level and among businessmen there is very little communication between them. Migrants from East and West Pakistan have little in common except their religion and some sense of belonging to the same nation. Language is as great a barrier as distance, for although Urdu has been made an additional language it has not gained much currency in East Pakistan, where Bengali is the mother tongue, and is understood only by an educated minority in the Western wing, not by the majority of the migrants, who speak various dialects of Punjabi. The two peoples differ from one another in physique, the West Pakistani being on the whole taller and fairer than the Bengalis. There are great differences in the climate of the two regions which are reflected in differences in their diets: rice, fish and vegetables being the staples in East Pakistan; wheat, maize, milk products, and meat in the West. East Pakistan is an alluvial country lying within the deltas of two great rivers, the Ganges and the Brahmaputra; it is a tropical rice-producing area. By contrast, West Pakistan is a dry country and no part of it lies in the tropical zone. From the high mountains in the north this vast country stretches through hill districts down to the irrigated fertile plain that merges into large tracts of desert extending almost to the sea.

It is from the hill districts in both wings of the country, from Mirpur in the west and Sylhet in the east, that most of the Pakistanis have come to Britain. Poor soil which yields a bare subsistence drove many farmers' sons to the towns in search of employment; others took service in the Merchant Navy in the days of British rule and later settled in port towns of England and Wales. There was thus a traditional link between these areas and England which had its influence on the migrations in the 1950s.

The district of Mirpur was formerly part of the State of Jammu and Kashmir, and since 1947 it has been one of the three districts of Azad ('Free') Kashmir held by Pakistan. Under the Maharajas' rule taxation was heavy and crops used to be seized while standing in the fields. The whole area was 'shamefully neglected' and contained hardly any schools.[29] Partition and Independence have brought changes particularly in the spread of primary education, but there is a limit to progress in this developing country; unemployment is high (it was estimated to be 7·5 million at the end of 1964) and half the population may be under-employed;[30] according to President Ayub Khan, the per capita income is as low as £30 per annum.[31]

To the poverty of the region and the general tradition of emigration there was added a further impulse from the decision of the Pakistan Government, announced in 1960, to build a dam at Mangla, which was to submerge 250 villages in the Mirpur district.[32]

Most of the emigrants from Mirpur came from families connected with the land, whether as small peasant proprietors or landless labourers. It is villagers working on the land who also comprise the majority of the Campbellpuris, who form another large group from West Pakistan.[33] According to the 1961 Census less than 2,000 acres in the sub-district of Campbellpur were under cultivation and there was only one tube-well in the whole area. With an average rainfall of thirteen inches and the majority of the people depending on agriculture for their living, it is no wonder that the young men emigrate, or join the armed forces. Other poor farming districts around Rawalpindi and Jhelum have contributed to the emigration which has also come from the plains of West Punjab, particularly from around Lyallpur. Among the East Pakistanis in Britain Sylhetis predominate, but fairly large numbers have also come from the port town of Chittagong and from Camilla.

There are no detailed analyses of the occupations of Pakistanis prior to migration, but a sample of 300 West Pakistanis examined by Dahya showed that two-thirds had been helping to farm their family lands and of the rest nearly one-half had been in the Armed Forces or merchant navy and so presumably originated from the villages.[34] John Goodall found that most of the Pakistanis in Huddersfield came from land-owning castes but their holdings were so small as to make them virtually landless.[35] There is an urban-educated middle class in the emigration but it has always been a very small fraction of the whole.

The poverty of Pakistan is reflected in the low literacy rate (15%) and the poor provision of schools: little money is spent on primary education, teachers are very poorly paid and not always well qualified.[36] School attendance is irregular for many parents cannot afford to buy the slates and textbooks, which are not provided by the State, and there is a temptation to use the children to supplement the family income. Very few children enter secondary school and less than half stay to the age of 15. It is not surprising that so many of the Pakistani emigrants are illiterate. (A distinction must be made between Sylhetis, who were Assamese before Partition and have a low literacy rate, and emigrants from East Bengal, where there is a long tradition of literacy.)

All Muslims acknowledge five imperative religious duties: the profession of faith ('there is but one God, Mohammed is his prophet'), daily prayers, almsgiving, fasting during the month of Ramadan, and pilgrimage to Mecca. These are the pillars of Islam, and to these most Muslims add a dietary prohibition against eating the pig and drinking alcohol. But Islam is more than a set of ritual acts and a body of religious belief. Like Judaism it is a way of life in which there is no separation between the spiritual and the temporal, between religious and secular activities. 'For Muslims society exists so that men may live correctly and have a proper relationship with God in the ways revealed by the prophet and the interpreters of his revelation as embodied in the religious law or Sharia.'[37] This Canon law defines and governs rules of descent and kinship, inheritance and succession, marriage and divorce, as well as social, economic, and political relations among the believers. Thus, for a Muslim religion, law and social organization form an inseparable whole, governing not only religious practice and morality but social relationships, diet and hygiene, and those areas of conduct which in Western society are regulated by secular law and the civil authority.

Pakistan is an Islamic state which owes its existence and separate identity to the practice of Islam. For Pakistanis, therefore, Islam is an expression of patriotism as well as a religion and this duality in their outlook is reflected in the significance of their religion to them in the emigration. Emphasis on the external features of religious observance may be as much a mark of outward national identity as an inward spiritual exercise.

In their early phases migrations are predominantly male, but the imbalance between the sexes in the Pakistani emigration and the preponderance of boys among the children brought over to all-male households was determined by the cultural patterns in a Muslim community, the seclusion of women and their subordination within the home.

The Pakistani family consists of a man, his wife, his unmarried sons and daughters, and his married sons and their wives and children. In this extended family, authority is vested in the father and passes on his death to his eldest son. From the age of puberty all girls are secluded from men who are not related; this seclusion is far more rigidly enforced among the Sylhetis than in either Mirpur or Campbellpur and accounts for the very small numbers of wives who have come from East Pakistan. In the West, all but women of the large land-owning families may work together in groups in the fields, but their lives are spent with the other women in the family and on visits to the women of other families. When a woman marries she enters her husband's family as a subordinate and an outsider; she subordinates her will not only to her husband and his father but also to her husband's mother; her closest ties are with her own family.

In Pakistan the birth of a son is greeted with great rejoicing while a girl's generally goes unnoticed. He will work in the fields, when he marries his wife will bring a dowry, and he will support his parents in their old age. A girl is considered a debt to the family; she has to be protected in adolescence and much money is needed for her marriage and her dowry. This pre-eminence of the male is reflected not only in his authority within the family but in the early separation of boys from girls inside the home. After a certain age boys sleep in separate quarters and spend their days in the fields with the men. Women never eat with their husbands but only after they have served their meals. Men spend their leisure not with their wives but in the company of other men and so are absent from their homes during most of their waking hours.

This close relationship with their male kin and with other villagers is carried through into the emigration in England, and its influence on the pattern of settlement in this country is examined in Chapter 23.

NOTES TO CHAPTER 5

1. Clifford Hill gives the following figures for the West Indies, including British Guiana. Anglicans 897,000, Roman Catholics (who are in the majority in Trinidad and Tobago, and the Leeward and Windward Islands), 808,000, Baptists 156,000, Methodists 156,000, Congregationalists 30,000, Presbyterians 30,000. After the Anglicans and Roman Catholics the largest number, 390,000, are listed under Other Denominations, which embrace a number of Christian sects unknown in England (*West Indian Migrants and the London Churches*, London, Oxford University Press, for Institute of Race Relations, 1963). By far the largest are those who claim affiliation to the Church of God, a Pentecostal Sect which has in recent years attracted a great many believers, particularly in Jamaica, where at the 1960 Census it had become the third largest of the Churches (O. C. Francis, *The People of Modern Jamaica*, Kingston, Department of Statistics, 1963).

2. These conditions obtained in many English grammar schools until late in the nineteenth century, e.g. Bristol Grammar School, with a reputation second only to Manchester Grammar School.

3. G. W. Roberts and N. Abdulah, 'Some Observations on the Educational Position of the Caribbean', *Social and Economic Studies* (Vol. XIV, no. 1, March 1965).

4. Edith Clarke, *My Mother Who Fathered Me* (2nd ed.), (London, Allen & Unwin, 1966), p. 43.

5. For a fictionalized account of the Ras Tafarians, see O. Patterson, *The Children of Sisyphus* (London, Hutchinson, 1964).

6. M. G. Smith, introduction to *My Mother Who Fathered Me* (2nd ed.) by E. Clarke.

7. Davison found in 1961 (*West Indian Migrants*, London, Oxford University Press, for Institute of Race Relations, 1963), that 98% of the children in his sample had been left behind in Jamaica. In Francis's sample taken in 1962 70% of all those who were married or in common law unions were leaving all their children behind. The proportion of women in the emigration which was 40% in 1953 had risen to 46% in 1962 ('The Characteristics of Emigrants just prior to changes in British Commonwealth Immigration Policies', in *The Caribbean in Transition*, University of Puerto Rico, Institute of Caribbean Studies, 1965).

8. O. C. Francis, 'The Characteristics of Emigrants just prior to changes in British Commonwealth Immigration Policies'.

9. O. C. Francis, *The People of Modern Jamaica*. Evidence from the 1943 and 1960 Censuses shows a net gain of population into the Kingston Metropolitan area amounting to 233,000.

10. In Francis's sample 2·5% had never attended school: the figure for the population as a whole is 16%.

11. G. W. Roberts and D. O. Mills, 'Study of External Migration affecting Jamaica, 1953–55', *Social and Economic Studies* (Vol. VII, no. 2, Supplement, 1958).

12. Ruth Glass, *The Newcomers* (London, Allen & Unwin, for Centre for Urban Studies, 1960).

13. Francis, 'The Characteristics of Emigrants just prior to changes in British Commonwealth Immigration Policies'.

14. Economist Intelligence Unit, *Studies on Immigration from the Commonwealth, I. Basic Statistics* (London, E.I.U., 1961).

15. G. E. Cumper, 'Working Class Emigration from Barbados to the U.K. October 1955', *Social and Economic Studies* (Vol. VI, no. 1, 1957).

16. Farmers and fishermen were included by Roberts and Mills in a general category 'unskilled' which increased as a proportion of the total numbers of men emigrants from 20% in 1953 to 33% in 1955. Mrs. Glass recorded 13% unskilled workers, 9% farmers, and 3% farm labourers and fishermen, making 25% 'unskilled' in Roberts and Mills terms. The Economist Intelligence Unit Survey in 1961 found that of Manual Workers 42% had been in skilled jobs, 45% in unskilled jobs, including agriculture and fishing, and 13% had been in semi-skilled jobs.

17. R. Desai, *Indian Immigrants in Britain* (London, Oxford University Press, for Institute of Race Relations, 1963).

18. Kushwant Singh, *A History of the Sikhs*, Vol. 2, 1839–1964 (Princeton, Princeton U.P., 1966), p. 234, gives the following figures: 4,351,477 Hindus and Sikhs came from the N.W. Frontier Province and West Punjab against 4,286,755 Muslims who left East Punjab. The Hindus and Sikhs left behind 67 lac acres of the best agricultural land; the Muslims of East Punjab left behind 47 lac acres of comparatively poor soil.

19. K. Singh, op. cit., p. 285. The immigrations were not the sole reason for the ceiling which was also meant to break up the Zamindari estates.

20. G. S. Aurora, *The New Frontiersmen* (Popular Prakashan, Bombay, 1967).

21. From the village of Jandiala (population 10,000) 1,000 were said to be in the United Kingdom. In the neighbouring village of Samrai, one mile away, 700 out of 7,000 had gone.

22. Some typical cases from the village of Kala Singa, population 6,500: A teacher, J.S., has forty relatives in the U.K. His father emigrated to England 25 years ago and ran a clothing business in Nottingham. Now he is retired and has an income of £12 a week from the rent of a house which he has bought. He left behind in the joint family two brothers, two sisters, and his mother. Among J.S.'s forty relatives is an uncle with five children who lives in Dudley. He and two of his sons work in a factory and have a Hillman car. One son is married and has a daughter. There is a second uncle in Dudley with four sons there. One son is married and his wife is waiting to join him. The second son had married two months previously in the village. His father and mother came over for the wedding. This son will build a home in the village in which his mother will live and also the widow of the fifth brother and another sister-in-law. He also has four more cousins in Dudley, of whom one had just returned to marry and take his wife back to England. Out of these forty relatives none got married in the U.K. but all came back to find their wives in the Punjab.

23. A. Patnaik, 'Study of Sikhs in Southall' (for the Institute's 'Survey of Race Relations in Britain', 1968); Desai, op. cit., p. 7; and information given to the writer in the Punjab.

24. G. S. Aurora, op. cit., pp. 94, 111. Desai, op. cit., p. 10.

25. In the village of Mehru the writer heard of a Harijan who had gone to England and had prospered. His wife was building a beautiful home and had given 100 rupees to the Defence Fund during the short war between India and Pakistan. In most villages there is a quarter reserved for untouchables, generally outside the walls, easily distinguished by the very poor quality of their mud huts.

In a sample of eighty families taken in Southall, Narindar Uberoi found that occupations in India had been farming (25), military and police service (11), small business (8), carpentry (5), and other skilled crafts (5). There were twelve students in the sample and the rest had been in unskilled manual work or unemployed.

26. A fully qualified teacher with two degrees earns no more than £150 a year.

27. Desai, op. cit., pp. 13, 14.

28. Michael Lyon, 'Study of Gujarati settlement in S.E. Lancashire' (for the Institute's 'Survey of Race Relations in Britain', 1968).

29. L. F. Rushbrook Williams, *The State of Pakistan* (rev. ed) (London, Faber, 1955), p. 90.

30. Economist Intelligence Unit, *Quarterly Economic Review of Pakistan*, E.I.U., 1966.

31. President Ayub Khan in an address to the Royal Institute of International Affairs, 1966.

32. The dam was inaugurated on 23 November 1967.

33. Dahya estimated in 1965 that of 10,500 West Pakistanis in Bradford, 5,400 were Mirpuris and 3,000 Campbellpuris. These groups all have a rural background. He also estimated that 1,800 came from the larger cities ('Study of Pakistanis in Bradford', for Institute's 'Survey of Race Relations in Britain', 1968).

34. Of the remainder of the sample the largest numbers were: clerical (21), semi-skilled (9), teachers (8), and railway workers (5).

35. John Goodall, 'Huddersfield', Institute of Race Relations *Newsletter* (Supplement, October, 1966).

36. John Goodall in *New Backgrounds* edited by R. Oakley (Oxford University Press, for Institute of Race Relations, 1968) gives the following statistics. The average salary for primary school teachers is £4 10s. per month in East Pakistan and £7 10s. in West Pakistan. For every 100 children enrolled in Class I only fifteen in East and thirty-eight in West Pakistan survive to Class V. Only 20% of 11-year-olds go to secondary school and of these less than half remain in school up to the age of 15.

37. H. S. Morris, *The Indians in Uganda* (Weidenfeld & Nicolson, 1968), p. 64.

6 How the Migration Developed

We begin our account of the development of the migration from what eventually became known as the New Commonwealth with the Second World War. Not that this was the first occasion on which the British confronted black newcomers in any numbers: as we have shown in Part I, contact goes back to far earlier periods. But that great cataclysm which, it is now clear, had such important consequences in promoting the acceleration of social and structural change in our society and the shaking-up of obsolescent attitudes, also precipitated as one of its side effects (though on an infinitesimally smaller scale) a change in attitudes towards coloured people. The sensation of solidarity in the face of common danger, which acted as such a remarkable—if often temporary—solvent of class differences, also functioned to modify the approach generally adopted towards the very greatly increased number of coloured people who entered this country during the wartime years. The combination of curiosity and patronage previously prevalent was replaced by something approaching acceptance.

Troops from all of the Empire were stationed in Britain during the War; in particular, 7,000 West Indians enlisted in the Royal Air Force and were stationed in the United Kingdom. The troops which attracted most attention, however, and who, initially at least, gained more from the favourable inclinations of the British towards coloured newcomers, were American Negro G.I.'s. This partly accounted for the uncertain policy adopted towards them by their own commanding officers. On several occasions local inhabitants made a point of demonstrating their preference for Negroes over white G.I.'s; the left-wing press also used a number of incidents as a springboard for a campaign against the colour bar. The Home Office found it necessary to circularize chief constables of the desirability of maintaining complete equality in practice; and Brendan Bracken, as Minister of Information, published a strongly worded newspaper article on the subject. An incident in which a dance hall was closed to all coloured customers as a result of a ban imposed by local American officers gave rise to a widely reported case in 1943; the defendant, a West Indian, was prosecuted for failing to perform Home Guard duties as a protest after being excluded from the dance; the Recorder imposed a fine of one farthing on appeal and awarded costs to the defendant. He was one of a party of 345 West Indians recruited, as skilled craftsmen, to work during the War in factories on Merseyside. The success of this scheme, Overseas Volunteers, which was carefully planned and supervised by the Ministry of Labour, and for which Mr. (now Lord) Learie Constantine acted as Welfare Officer, had a good deal to do with subsequent development of immigration to Britain from the West Indies. Although initial difficulties were encountered in persuading employees to accept West Indian workers and in providing accommodation, both problems were eventually overcome. Most of the workers concerned went back to the West Indies when the scheme was wound up in 1947, but the unfavourable employment conditions they encountered there caused quite a number to consider returning to Britain again. The experience of the Royal Air Force contingent, who had mostly been returned to the West Indies on demobilization, was similar.

The 1946 Report on Jamaica gives a depressing account of the amount of unemployment immediately after the War.[1] It had been particularly difficult to take effective steps to find employment for returning ex-servicemen. With their comparatively favourable experience of British conditions, both the ex-servicemen and the volunteer workers seem to have had considerable influence on the build-up of migration. Previous migration between the West Indies and Britain had been almost entirely confined to the middle and upper classes. War service for the first time brought working-class and lower middle-class West Indians to Britain.

The first indication of the new migration movement came in June 1948, when the former German pleasure cruiser, the *Empire Windrush*, which had been chartered to take European migrants out to Latin America, called on return at Kingston. Enterprising advertising and the acute shortage of passenger transport to Great Britain ensured that the liner was booked to capacity. The arrival of a comparatively large number (492) of immigrants caused a sharp reaction in Parliament and the Press. Emergency welfare arrangements were made and the immigrants eventually found work without too much difficulty. The *Empire Windrush* was followed in due course by the *Orbita*, with 108 passengers, and the *Georgic*. However, total migration from the West Indies at this stage was very small and, until 1951, never realized a figure of 1,000 in any year.

In the decade 1911 to 1921 and again during the Second World War, the United States was the main receiver of Jamaican immigrants or migrant workers. During the War nearly 50,000 farm workers were recruited to work in agriculture, but after the War recruitment dropped sharply, and with the passing of the McCarran-Walter Act in 1952 migration to the United States from Jamaica was restricted to 100 a year. Britain then became possibly the only major industrial country open to large-scale migration from the West Indies. By 1954, immigration to Britain from the West Indies—and in particular, from Jamaica—began to assume numerically significant proportions, and increased rapidly until it reached its first plateau in 1956. From 1955 onwards the Home Office has maintained records of all arrivals and departures of Commonwealth travellers from which can be calculated the number of net arrivals in any one year. These figures relate to all persons travelling on a passport of Commonwealth countries. Not all these people will be permanent immigrants, students and long-term visitors are included in the tabulations, but for the Caribbean group it may be assumed that almost all immigrants would be seeking work and semi-permanent residence in this country.

The migration from the Caribbean was characterized from the start by a high proportion of women, by a low incidence of return migration, and by its responsiveness to the labour market in Britain. Labour shortages, in particular the acute shortage of unskilled labour, had not been met either by the European Volunteer Workers, or by the immigration of Southern Irish workers. The result was that in the period up to 1956 the West Indians who arrived were absorbed without great difficulty into the British labour force, although at the expense of some downgrading in status compared with their position in the West Indies. Just how powerful were the 'pull' factors in British industry in attracting migrants is discussed in Chapter 7.

No effort was made, with one exception, to match employment vacancies with the supply of migrant labour available before the process of migration got under way. This is the sharpest of the many contrasts between the Commonwealth immigrants and those who were recruited under the European Volunteer Worker scheme. The exception was that of the Barbadian migration. Direct arrangements were made by the Barbadian Immigrants Liaison Service with London Transport Executive (from 1956) and the

British Hotels and Restaurants Association for the recruitment of skilled labour in Barbados, and initial responsibility was undertaken by the employers for the accommodation and welfare of the recruits.

Towards the end of 1955 the British economy went into a period of recession and, following the fall in the demand for labour, migration from the Caribbean remained below the level of 1956 for three years. During 1960 it leapt to a new peak. There were by the end of 1959 approximately 126,000 West Indians living in Britain who had arrived since the end of the War. It was from their letters home that potential migrants heard about conditions in England. Jobs were once more available but pressure to impose controls was beginning to be seen as a serious threat, with the result that in 1961 and the first half of 1962 the rate of immigration was maintained at the high 1960 level and in these eighteen months net arrivals amounted to 98,000 persons (see Figure 6.1).

Although the vast majority of both men and women coming to Britain during the 'beat the ban' period were coming primarily for economic reasons, in order to work, a powerful secondary reason was the presence in Britain of family or of relatives. A sample study taken in 1962 of Jamaican emigrants, mainly destined for Britain, found that over 70% had relatives in their country of destination and about 50%, mainly women, had partners there.[2]

The threat of controls had an even more striking effect on immigration to Britain from India and Pakistan. From the time the Home Office began to maintain records in 1955 until the end of 1960 the number of net arrivals from these countries remained at a comparatively low level, but in the eighteen months prior to control the figures show a dramatic increase (see Figure 6.1).

The origins of large-scale migration to Britain from India and Pakistan are, as in the case of the West Indies, found during the Second World War. Before the War, Indian seamen formed part of the coloured communities in the ports. During the War, large numbers of Indian seamen jumped ship in Britain, and moved inland to work in factories. The Indian population in some British towns increased considerably—for example, in Birmingham it grew from an estimated 100 in 1939 to 1,000 in 1945, largely because of the movement of seamen into the city. After Partition, jumping ship into Britain continued to play a part in the migration from Pakistan.

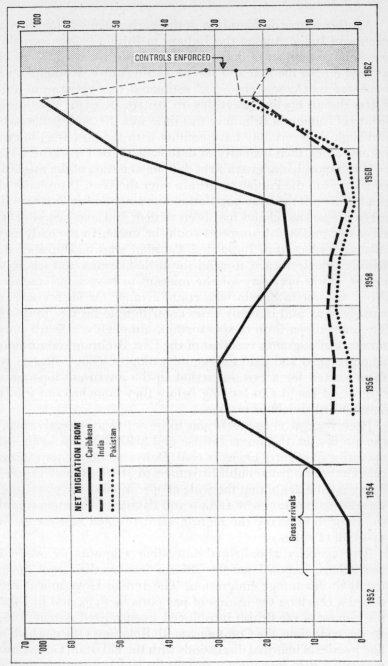

Figure 6.1. Estimates of immigration, 1952–30 June 1962

Sources: 1952-4, Home Office (House of Lords, Hansard, pp. 1038-9, 15 February 1956); 1955-June 1962, Home Office estimates of net arrivals.

Another source of migration at this early stage was middle-class groups in India. Among the Indians in Britain before 1951 there was a large number of doctors and students, many of whom had arrived during the War and stayed on afterwards. Kondapi, in his book *Indians Overseas 1938–49*,[3] estimated that there were about 1,000 Indian doctors practising in Britain in 1949. Yet another group of Indians in Britain at this time was the Sikh pedlars, but although they certainly have contact with the post-1945 migrant communities, their own origins date back to the First World War.

It is impossible to give a firm date for the start of the migration of Sikhs from the Punjab to Britain after the War. It probably did not begin until the large population movements after Partition had taken place, land claims had been settled, and some assessment of economic and social prospects could be made. In the early 1950s pioneer settlers from India and Pakistan who had prospered in British industry began to send for their kinsmen and fellow villagers. It was necessary for the migrant to have some contact or direct sponsor in Britain who could arrange for his housing and employment, and in many cases contribute to his fare to Britain. The most direct form of sponsorship, although it affected only a minority of migrants, was that of the East Pakistani restaurateurs, who arranged and paid for the migration of fellow villagers who then worked for a certain period in the restaurant for nominal wages and board and lodging before they launched out into the general British labour market.

However, travel agents began to be active at an early stage in the ports and the large towns, and within a few years were operating in country towns as well. Dahya mentions, for example, that Pakistani agents established offices in Mirpur town in 1956–7.[4] There is little doubt that the scale of operations of the travel agents was the main reason why Indian and Pakistani migration was able to attain so suddenly the high levels it reached in 1961 and the first half of 1962.

The agencies also helped intending migrants to evade the restrictions, imposed not by Britain but by their own governments to discourage emigration. The Indian Government introduced a check on the issuing of passports in 1955, and in 1958 at the request of the British introduced a centralized system of issue. At the same time, the Commonwealth Relations Office, which had had a series of informal discussions with the Pakistani Government, persuaded it to introduce a system by which intending migrants who wished to leave for England had to deposit a substantial sum of money—Rs. 2,500 (about £187 10s.) to cover the cost of their return air fare to Britain. All the various systems of control tended to work in an arbitrary and unsatisfactory way. The various illegal practices employed by the travel agents to get their clients to Britain developed essentially as a black market to get round restrictions imposed at first not by Britain but by their home governments. The practices continued in 1962 when the British controls took effect, but their heyday was over in 1964 when the issue of C vouchers for unskilled workers ended.

Sometimes ingenious methods were used by travel agents: legitimate passports would be obtained for travel from India to Mauritius or Singapore, and migrants would go by that route to Britain. In Pakistan, passports were obtained for journeys to visit Muslim holy places and migrants would go via the Middle East. Punjabi Sikhs were even disguised as Pakistani Muslims and smuggled through in the same way. Illiterate East Pakistani peasants sometimes arrived in Britain as 'students'—they travelled to Karachi, where an agent wrote on their behalf for a place in an educational institution in Britain. Upon acceptance, the necessary documents could be obtained. The most common of the illegal methods was, however, by means of forged passports endorsed for Britain. Passports were obtained from those already in Britain and a new photograph substituted. This practice reached such a pitch in the Indian community in Britain that the Indian Workers' Association conducted a campaign through a direct approach to Pandit Nehru, who was in England for a Commonwealth Prime Ministers' Conference, for the substitution of genuine for forged passports obtained in good faith. The campaign eventually succeeded.

In one outstanding case, restrictions on the issue of passports to Britain were reversed. In 1961, when control looked to be imminent, the Pakistani Government withdrew restrictions and promoted the migration of 5,000 people to Britain. This was intended to help some of the Mirpuri families due to be dispossessed by the construction of the Mangla Dam, but also included some people not affected by the dam project.

The proportion of women among the Indian and Pakistani migrants was much lower than that among the West Indians. A study in Southall in the late 1950s estimated that the proportion of women in the Sikh community there was as low as 4%.[5] The threat of control caused many more Sikhs to bring their wives to England after 1960,[6] but among the Pakistanis there were very few women indeed before 1962. In Bradford, one of the main areas of Pakistani settlement, the 1961 Census revealed 3,376 men and only eighty-one women. The Pakistanis who arrived between 1959 and 1962 and who constituted the majority of the immigrant population were mostly young and unmarried. Their predecessors who came in the middle fifties, sponsored by former seamen, were somewhat older and the majority were married. It is these men who have brought over their wives since 1962.[7]

To put this immigration into perspective we need to look at the evidence of the two censuses taken at the beginning and towards the end of the period. The 1951 Census showed up the numerical insignificance of all the coloured minority groups. If allowance is

Table 6.1. Estimated immigrant population in England and Wales, 1951 and 1961

Area of Origin	1951	1961
India	30,800	81,400
Pakistan	5,000	24,900
Ceylon	5,800	9,000
West Indies*	15,300	171,800
West Africa†	5,600	19,800
Far East‡	12,000	29,600
Total coloured population	74,500	336,600
Cyprus and Malta	24,700	66,600
Total Commonwealth	336,400	659,800
Irish Republic	472,100	644,400
Aliens	378,400	415,700
Total resident population	43,758,000	46,105,000
Coloured persons per 1,000	1·70	7·30

* Includes British Guiana and British Honduras.
† Includes Gambia, Ghana, Nigeria, Sierra Leone.
‡ Includes Hong Kong, Malaya, and Singapore.

Source:
Amended Census estimates. (For discussion of amendments see Chapter 10 and Appendix III.4.)

made for the fact that the birthplace criterion employed by the census classifies white-skinned British citizens as Indians, the remaining brown Indians are relatively few (for a full discussion see Chapter 10). At that date the coloured population born overseas was hardly more than 75,000, amounting to only 1·7 persons per 1,000 of the total population.

Table 6.1 shows how the position changed in the ten years between 1951 and 1961. The coloured population born overseas increased to a third of a million, and over half the increase came from the West Indies. In 1961 it amounted to 7·3 persons per 1,000 of the population. But the increase was not so great in absolute terms as the amount of public debate might have suggested. Citizens of the Irish Republic remained in 1961, as in 1951, the largest of the ethnic minorities in Britain. Within the inter-censal period the absolute increase among the Irish was still larger than the number of West Indians arriving in the same ten years. The number of aliens also was greater than the coloured population.

NOTES TO CHAPTER 6

1. *Annual Report on Jamaica for the Year 1946* (Colonial Office, H.M.S.O., 1949), quoted in G. W. Roberts and D. O. Mills, 'Study of External Migration affecting Jamaica 1953–55', *Social and Economic Studies* (Vol. VII, no. 2, 1958).

2. O. C. Francis, 'The Characteristics of Emigrants just prior to changes in British Commonwealth Immigration Policies', published in *The Caribbean in Transition* (Institute of Caribbean Studies, University of Puerto Rico, 1965).

3. C. Kondapi, *Indians Overseas 1938–49* (New Delhi, Oxford University Press, for Indian Council of World Affairs, 1951).

4. B. Dahya, 'Study of Pakistanis in Bradford' (for the Institute's 'Survey of Race Relations in Britain', 1968).

5. G. S. Aurora, *The New Frontiersmen* (Bombay, Popular Prakashan, 1967).

6. A. Patnaik, 'Study of Sikhs in Southall' (for the Institute's 'Survey of Race Relations in Britain', 1968).

7. B. Dahya, op. cit.

7 The Dynamics of the Migration

It is popularly believed that the prime reasons for the migration from the coloured Commonwealth are the poverty, deprivation, and over-population of the sending societies as opposed to the general wealth and, in particular, the generous social services of the United Kingdom. It is also believed that once such a migration is in motion it will continue as long as the sending societies are at a lower level of material wealth than the receiving society, and thus the spectre of a Britain with standing room only is raised. This explanation does not, however, account for the reasons why the migration from the Commonwealth countries started at one particular moment in time, why the numbers of migrants arriving in the U.K. rose and fell, and why the proportions of men and women kept changing within the migration.

A detailed study made by Ceri Peach[1] of West Indian migration to Britain shows the relative influence of changing conditions in the West Indies and Britain on the migration flow. Peach studied the migration rates between 1955–61 of the various West Indian islands and British Guiana and compared these to indices of population pressure, per capita income, unemployment, economic growth, and so on, of these islands. His finding was that adverse conditions in the West Indies should be considered as a permissive and not a dynamic factor in the migration, 'they [adverse conditions in the West Indies] allow migration to take place; they do not cause it'.[2] This conclusion was based on his finding no correlation between different rates of migration from each island and conditions in these islands when comparing each island against the next.

Peach did find, however, that the rates of migration from each island tended to follow the same pattern between 1956 and 1961: migration rose in all the islands in the same year despite the fact that their rates of economic growth did not rise and fall together. This led him to the conclusion 'that trends in migration are governed by factors external to the West Indies'.[3] The external factor that determined the rise and fall in migration was the demand for labour in the United Kingdom. Using as the index of labour demand the number of outstanding vacancies in each quarter kept by the Ministry of Labour, he found a correlation between rises in labour demand and rises in the rate of migration. This is illustrated in Figure 7.1 which is derived from quarterly figures of outstanding vacancies and West Indian arrivals. The downturn in the economy from the latter half of 1956 to the end of 1958 is reflected in the lower arrival figures. It will be noted that if a lag of three months for migration is allowed for, then the directions of change of labour index and of the level of migration are in agreement.

Peach further argues that if it is labour demand that determines trends in migration then this will have the greatest effect on male immigration and least on the migration of women and children

Figure 7.1. Quarterly figures of employment vacancies and West Indian arrivals, 1956–1960

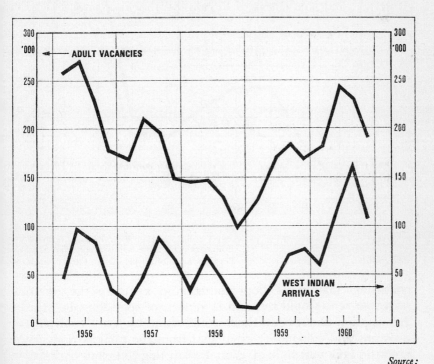

Source :
G. C. K. Peach, *West Indian Migration to Britain*, Table 18 ('Adult vacancies' figures from Ministry of Labour, 'West Indian arrivals' from Migrant Services Division).

who in many cases will be joining a relative who has already migrated. He shows convincingly that throughout the period of recession, as numbers fell, the proportion of men in the migration fell, and with recovery it rose as the overall figures rose. In 1960 arrivals were the highest yet recorded and the proportion of men was the highest since the boom year of 1955 (see Figure 7.2).

Peach suggests that there are two types of intending migrant, firstly the solid core who would come whatever the conditions,

Figure 7.2. Arrivals of West Indian men and women, 1952–30 June 1962

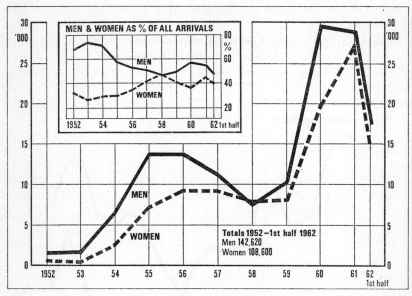

Sources:
For 1952–54 Home Office; 1955–61 Migrant Services Division; 1962 Home Office estimates.

consisting mainly of dependants, and secondly the 'floating migrants' who would respond to reports of conditions in Britain. Information about conditions would come by letter from earlier migrants and evidence is cited that from the early period of the migration the vast bulk of West Indian migrants had contacts in Britain.[4] He thus concludes 'conditions in Britain were the major determinants in the trends of that migration'.[5]

The migration of Indians and Pakistanis followed a very different pattern from that of the West Indians. As described earlier (and illustrated in Figure 6.1), the migration from India and Pakistan whilst of earlier origin did not develop into a substantial mass movement until 1961. The sudden change in migration movements in 1961, when net inflow increased nearly sixfold over the previous year, is explicable in terms of three factors affecting migration. First, there was the fear of control in Britain. This affected the organization of transport and the activities of travel agents in India and Pakistan who exploited and helped to create the demand. In turn, this led to the wide-scale avoidance and the removal of controls which had previously been imposed by the Indian and Pakistani Governments to restrict immigration to Britain. The effect of labour demand in Britain on migration before 1961 is more difficult to assess for Indians and Pakistanis, but if one allows for a greater time-lag than that shown by the West Indians then the very small net inflows in 1959 following two years of almost continuous fall in labour demand may be significant (Figure 6.1). But it was undoubtedly fear of control that completely changed the well-established pattern of migration.

Two main sets of conclusions are possible from this examination of migration from the Caribbean and Asia in the period up till the introduction of control in 1962. First, the major determinants of the migration were in Britain, but, as Peach has said, from 1961 'political forces overtook those of economics in the commanding position;'[6] secondly, the introduction of control and the political agitation that led to control distorted the pattern of migration and induced many people to migrate, at unpropitious times, who possibly would never have migrated. (Peach shows, for example, that the rise in the West Indian figures in 1961 and 1962 for the first time took place against the economic indicators.[7]) Thus one comes to the paradoxical conclusion that the most vigorous proponents of control created the very situation that they most feared by inducing a far higher rate of migration than had ever occurred before. The effect of the Commonwealth Immigrants Act was not only to increase the number of immigrants in this country, including their dependants who followed much later, but to increase the rate of arrivals to such an extent that in eighteen months the net inflow was almost as great as that of the previous five years. This massive increase was to compound the real problems which were in the United Kingdom and not at the gates.

THE IMMIGRANT AND LABOUR DEMAND

The movement of Commonwealth immigrants into Britain in the 1950s was not a unique phenomenon when viewed against general movements into Britain. In the years immediately after the War, labour shortages in Britain were so intense that, apart from schemes for former allies and displaced persons, active recruitment was carried out by the Ministry of Labour in various parts of Europe to attract foreign workers. Between 1945 and 1957 there was a net immigration of more than 350,000 European nationals into the United Kingdom.[8] Despite this large influx and continuing migration from Eire, one of the main problems that has affected the British economy throughout the fifties and sixties has been shortages of labour. Lack of spare capacity, both labour and capital, in the economy has been blamed for the recurrent cycles of 'stop-go' that have plagued the British economy. A situation of over-full employment has meant cost inflation and balance of payment problems that have led to deflationary measures by Government.

Studies of the employment of coloured immigrant workers found that many employers only started employing coloured labour in times of great labour shortage. The works superintendent of a Midlands foundry described the position as follows: 'The big influx of labour began in 1954. At this time you couldn't get an armless, legless man never mind an able-bodied one'.[9] As we have seen, a few employers, such as London Transport, the National Health Service, and the British Hotels and Restaurants Association, made direct arrangements with the Barbados Government for the recruitment of skilled labour. These employers took initial responsibility for the accommodation and welfare of the recruits, but they were the exception, and otherwise no effort was made to match employment vacancies with the supply of migrant labour before the process of migration got underway.

Most of the European countries with high growth rates have been the recipients of migrant flows, often larger than that of Britain. The extent of the differences in culture and economic development between the receiving European Economic Community countries and the sending countries has often been comparable to the differences between Britain and the Commonwealth countries. West Germany, France, Holland, and Belgium have imported much of their labour through official and semi-official recruitment schemes which paid for the passage and undertook responsibility for initial welfare and accommodation. In contrast, Britain took in labour from the Commonwealth for which it did not have to find accommodation nor pay the costs either of recruitment or transport.

In what types of jobs and in what industries did the coloured immigrant initially find work? Usually it was in an industry that was losing ground as far as pay and status were concerned (for example, public transport), or in those jobs that were considered unpleasant by the host community (for example, in foundries), or that entailed long and awkward hours. In general, the employment most easily available for the newly-arrived coloured immigrant was the sort of employment that the English worker did not want. In times of full employment with the demand for more and more skilled and/or highly-paid labour the local labour force became more upwardly mobile. This movement upwards left a vacuum into which replacement labour had to be attracted.

The economic costs and benefits of the immigration are discussed in Chapter 30. We are here concerned only with the question whether to import labour from Europe and the Commonwealth was the best method of meeting the labour demands of British industry. Since 1945 it has been often alleged that British industry has been wasteful and uneconomic in its employment of labour and that the responsibility for this lies both with management and unions. It can be argued that a migrant flow of labour has delayed the much needed structural changes necessary in industry by supplying a pool of cheap, available labour, and there is undoubtedly some truth in this argument, but it fails to take into account the very varied factors peculiar to each industry in which immigrants were employed. While structural reorganization may well be an ideal long-term solution of Britain's recurring labour shortages, most employers would certainly have and did use a series of short-term measures that seemed to offer a quicker and more certain solution. In some of the industries in which immigrants found work there was little room for major redeployment of labour, and in some instances the immigrant worker was more amenable to change than the local worker. It can also be argued that if unions and management in this country had been more willing to accept a drastic re-apportioning of labour together with concomitant redundancies, there might have been less demand for immigrant labour.

There does, however, remain a hard core of jobs filled by

coloured immigrants that because of their unpleasant nature, low pay, or socially arduous hours were almost impossible to fill, especially in those regions where there were many better jobs, in terms of pay, conditions, and status, and the demand for these better jobs was growing. It is unlikely, in the face of competition, at home and overseas, that wage rises sufficiently great to overcome English labour's reluctance to enter the less well-regarded jobs would have been possible in all cases.

It is possible that greater capital investment in industry might have reduced the demand for immigrant labour, but this too is open to doubt. In the one study[10] carried out in a section of the wool textile industry in Yorkshire, it was found that the employment of immigrant (Pakistani) labour had facilitated capital investment in the sample of companies studied. The reason for this was that the new machinery was so expensive that it was necessary to have some form of shift working which was in the main manned by Pakistani labour. Similar parallels probably exist in other industries where new machinery necessitates shift working and employers find it is only possible to operate this machinery by a heavy reliance on immigrant labour, due to English labour's reluctance to work at night or on changing shifts.

More efficient organization of the labour force or greater investment might have been the ideal answer to many of the problems of labour shortage. However, given the conditions existent in British industry in the 1950s or even in the present day, these methods of dealing with shortages of labour supply were never the most probable. If the coloured immigrant had not come to Britain the major employers would probably have attempted to widen their area of recruitment to other parts of the U.K., Eire, and Europe. It is possible that similar schemes to those run by the European Economic Community countries would have been set up. In some cases wage rises would have attracted more labour but the scope for these increases was limited and it should be noted that the greatest demands for the type of labour the immigrant supplied were in regions like the London and Birmingham areas where the highest average pay in this country is found.

The distribution of coloured immigrants in this country has been determined by the same factors as affected their migration. In those areas where low-paid workers are moving out the immigrant has moved in to take their places. Peach has summarized the position of West Indians saying, 'they have gone to the decreasing urban cores of expanding industrial regions'.[11] This conclusion is as applicable to Indians and Pakistanis as to West Indians. They have not settled in areas of low labour demand such as Wales, Scotland, or the North-East. The industries which have offered work to the coloured immigrant are in the main the service and older manufacturing industries at the centres of the great cities and rarely the new industries in the suburbs and beyond.

NOTES TO CHAPTER 7

1. G. C. K. Peach, *West Indian Migration to Britain* (London, Oxford University Press, for Institute of Race Relations, 1968); also Peach, 'West Indian Migration to Britain: the Economic Factors', *Race* (Vol. VII, no. 1, July 1965).
2. Peach, *West Indian Migration to Britain*, p. 92.
3. Peach, *West Indian Migration to Britain*, p. 36.
4. G. E. Cumper, 'Employment in Barbados' *Social and Economic Studies* (Vol. 8, no. 2, 1959), p. 129, and R. B. Davison, *West Indian Migrants* (London, Oxford University Press, for Institute of Race Relations, 1962), p. 23.
5. Peach, *West Indian Migration to Britain*, p. 49. See also Davison, *West Indian Migrants*, p. 23.
6. Peach, *West Indian Migration to Britain*, p. 49.
7. Peach, *West Indian Migration to Britain*, p. 46.
8. A. T. Bouscaron, *International Migrations since 1945* (New York, Praeger, 1963). Gross figures were considerably larger but a large number returned to Europe.
9. Quoted by Peter Wright, *The Coloured Worker in British Industry* (London, Oxford University Press, for Institute of Race Relations, 1968). See also Sheila Patterson, *Dark Strangers* (London, Tavistock Publications, 1963).
10. Brian Cohen and Peter Jenner, 'The Employment of Immigrants: A Case Study within the Wool Industry', *Race* (Vol. X, no. 1, July 1968).
11. Peach, 'Factors affecting the Distribution of West Indians in Britain', *Transactions and Papers 1966*, No. 38 (Institute of British Geographers). See also Peach's analysis of the West Indian's role as a replacement population in *West Indian Migration to Britain*.

8 After Control

We have shown in Chapter 7 how the flow of net arrivals experienced a violent upswing in 1961 and the first half of 1962 in response to the threat of control. The aim of this chapter is to describe what has happened to the flow of immigrants since then. Within the account of the total net addition which has taken place between July 1962, when control was introduced, and the end of 1967, we shall review the importance of the Indian, Pakistani, and West Indian sectors. From the much closer control which has been effected since 1962, valuable information is furnished about the relative importance of voucher holders and dependants, students, and others for settlement. Within this account we are also able to show how many men, women, and children have arrived among those immigrants who are most likely to become long-term settlers in Britain. We also have information about the professions of people admitted under the voucher scheme, which forms an integral part of the control system.

Control of Commonwealth immigration and the successive refinements introduced since July 1962 have had three broad effects. The balance of the immigration has been shifted from the Caribbean to India and Pakistan (see Table 8.1 and Figure 8.1), the balance within the labour force has been switched progressively from unskilled to skilled and professional workers (see Table 8.2), and the balance within the immigration has changed from a preponderance of wage earners to a preponderance of dependent wives and children (see Figure 8.2).

A brief résumé of information on net arrivals from the beginning of 1955 through to 1967 is set out in Table 8.1, below. The whole series may conveniently be broken into three time periods; the first comprises the calendar years 1955 to 1960 inclusive; the second covers the next year and a half up to July 1962 which provided such a high proportion of all immigrants; the third begins in July 1962 and covers the whole period since control up to the end of 1967. Roughly, each of these periods has provided one-third of all net immigration from the three areas taken as a whole, but the changing balance between Asians and West Indians is very striking.

Table 8.1. Net arrivals from India, Pakistan, and the West Indies, 1955–67

	India	Pakistan	Jamaica	Rest of Caribbean	Total
1955–60	33,070	17,120	96,180	65,270	219,540
1961–30 June 1962	42,000	50,170	62,450	35,640	203,470
1 July 1962– 1967	95,850	64,340	31,380	27,780	231,830
Total	171,720	131,630	190,010	128,690	654,860

Sources:
1955–30 June 1962 Home Office; 1 July 1962–7
Commonwealth Immigrants Act 1962 Statistics.

While more than half the total West Indian immigration took place before 1960, there has been a great falling off since the introduction of controls (see Figure 8.1). Exactly the reverse is true of immigration from India and Pakistan. The period since control has produced more than half of the Indian total and nearly half of all the Pakistanis.

In our analysis of arrivals before July 1962 we showed the regulating effect of employment vacancies in this country on the West Indian migration until the threat of control disturbed the pattern after 1960. With the passing of the 1962 Commonwealth Immigrants Act, the Ministry of Labour applied a selective system of regulation through the issue of employment vouchers, designed to meet the needs of the market. There were three categories of voucher: for those who had specific jobs to come to (A), for those who possessed special skills or qualification (B), and for unskilled workers without definite prospects of employment (C). Overall priority was given to the A and B categories, and within the C group applications, which at first were dealt with on a 'first come, first served' basis, special consideration was given to those who had served with the Armed Forces in the Second World War or later. Later, in July 1963, a modification was made to ensure that no Commonwealth country received more than one-quarter of all C vouchers in any one year. With the issue of the White Paper (Cmnd. 2739) in August 1965 it was announced that category C vouchers would be discontinued, but in fact the Ministry had ceased to issue them from the previous August.

Figure 8.1. The changing balance between Indians, Pakistanis, and West Indians, 1955–67

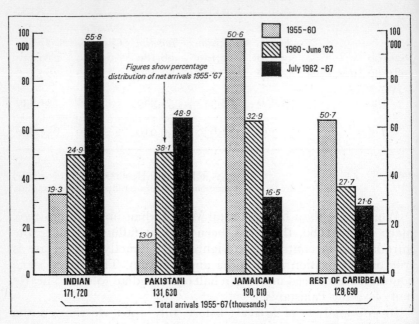

Sources:
1955–June 1962, Home Office; July 1962 onwards, Commonwealth Immigrants Act 1962, Statistics.

The very great number of applications for C vouchers undoubtedly led to this decision. In the first eighteen months after control there were over 300,000 applications in the pipe-line, mainly from India and Pakistan where the system was highly organized by the network of travel agents.

In this period just over 40,000 C vouchers were issued, of which nearly three-quarters went to Indians and Pakistanis and only 10% to West Indians (see Table 8.2). Thus the system was already discriminating very severely against West Indians who received no more than a further 240 vouchers in this category before they were discontinued. The West Indies fared even worse with B vouchers. Because there were not enough skilled and professional men and women wishing to emigrate, the West Indies received only 520 vouchers in the five and a half years up to the end of 1967, or less

Table 8.2. Vouchers issued, July 1962–67

Year	A Vouchers Job assured		B Vouchers Special skills		C Vouchers Unskilled		All Vouchers	
	To Indians and Pakistanis	To West Indians	To Indians and Pakistanis	To West Indians	To Indians and Pakistanis	To West Indians	To Indians and Pakistanis	To West Indians
1962	1,200	650	2,650	60	12,100	2,230	15,950	2,940
1963	2,990	820	7,540	160	17,220	1,960	27,750	2,940
1964	3,310	3,220	5,800	180	1,120	240	10,230	3,640
1965	2,650	3,080	5,760	90	—	—	8,410	3,170
1966	600	970	4,600	20	—	—	5,200	990
1967	700	900	4,700	10	—	—	5,400	910
Total	11,450	9,640	31,050	520	30,440	4,430	72,940	14,590
Percentage of all Commonwealth Vouchers issued:	32%	27%	74%	1%	72%	10%	61%	12%

Source:
Commonwealth Immigrants Act 1962, Statistics.

than an average of 100 a year in the whole period, whereas no less than 31,000 went to India and Pakistan.

The recruiting schemes operated by London Transport and the British Hotels and Restaurants Association enabled West Indians to avail themselves of A vouchers, but even this facility was severely curtailed by the White Paper which set a ceiling of 7,500 vouchers a year for the whole Commonwealth (with an additional 1,000 for Malta) and gave preference to B voucher holders. No country could receive more than 15% of the limited supply of A vouchers and this limitation in effect meant no more than 300 a year. The effects are clearly shown in Table 8.2.

To sum up, between the introduction of control and the end of 1967, India and Pakistan received 72,940 vouchers of all kinds while the whole of the West Indies and Guyana could do no better than 14,590. The issues to India, Pakistan, and the West Indies formed 73% of all vouchers issued in the Commonwealth.

But not all vouchers issued were in fact taken up, partly because there were long delays between application and receipt, partly because in 1962 and 1963 the recession in the U.K. was operating as a regulator, and partly because some who applied, mistakenly thought that a voucher was the equivalent of a free passage to the United Kingdom.

Table 8.3 shows the number of voucher holders who entered the

Table 8.3. Voucher holders arriving in the U.K., 1962–67

Country of origin	1962	1963	1964	1965	1966	1967	Total
India and Pakistan	1,040	21,890	7,120	6,310	3,150	2,930	42,440
West Indies	1,600	2,070	2,645	1,990	630	620	9,550
West Africa	640	1,390	820	280	60	30	3,220
Australia, Canada, and New Zealand	900	1,450	820	750	320	260	4,500
Malta and Cyprus	316	1,289	1,332	990	731	633	5,291
Rest of Commonwealth	624	2,041	1,968	2,560	569	507	8,269
Total Commonwealth	5,120	30,130	14,705	12,880	5,460	4,980	73,270

Source: Commonwealth Immigrants Act, 1962, Statistics

United Kingdom from all parts of the Commonwealth from after control was introduced until the end of 1967. In the whole period 120,000 vouchers were issued and 73,270 voucher holders entered the U.K. It will be seen that India and Pakistan took up 42,450 of the 72,940 that were issued; the Caribbean countries received far fewer (14,590), but were able to use a higher proportion (10,570).

From the beginning of August 1965 the White Paper selected for entry under the B voucher people with certain special qualifications or skills and particularly doctors, teachers, and graduates in science or technology who must have had at least two years' experience in employment since qualifying. Table 8.4 gives a breakdown by skills of vouchers issued in the years 1965, 1966, and 1967. The proportion of doctors, engineers, and scientists drawn from India and Pakistan is very striking.

Table 8.4. B vouchers issued, 1965–67

Country of Origin	Teachers	Doctors	Engineers and Scientists	Other Skills
India	2,942	3,986	4,439	1,113
Pakistan	577	1,264	632	107
Caribbean	47	19	9	53
Rest of Commonwealth	708	462	529	4,628
Total Commonwealth	4,274	5,731	5,609	5,901

Source:
Ministry of Labour.

While the Commonwealth Immigrants Act 1962 took away the right to enter the United Kingdom from all Commonwealth citizens except those issued with vouchers, wives, and children under 16, were free to accompany or to join husbands or parents already here. Other dependants admitted at the discretion of the authorities included elderly parents of Commonwealth citizens already settled in this country.

Table 8.5 shows the number of dependants arriving from the Commonwealth since control. Figure 8.2 relates the information in Tables 8.3 and 8.5 to show the changing ratio of voucher holders to dependants during the period, from India and Pakistan, from the

West Indies, and from the rest of the Commonwealth. It can be seen that the balance has shifted progressively from wage earners to dependants. In the first eighteen months the numbers of voucher holders and dependants were approximately equal for the Commonwealth as a whole but since 1964 the ratio has radically changed until now it is less than 1:10.

Table 8.5. Dependants arriving in the U.K., 1962–67

Country of origin	1962	1963	1964	1965	1966	1967	Total
India and Pakistan	1,560	6,620	8,770	12,800	13,340	15,820	58,910
	500	3,300	7,050	6,760	9,320	17,500	44,430
West Indies	3,730	7,890	11,460	11,150	9,870	11,210	55,310
West Africa	890	2,290	2,490	2,445	1,860	1,080	11,050
Australia, Canada, and New Zealand	610	1,770	1,720	1,990	2,900	2,730	11,720
Malta and Cyprus	625	1,487	2,240	1,629	889	787	7,657
Rest of Commonwealth	915	2,873	3,730	4,441	3,851	3,683	19,493
Total Commonwealth	8,830	26,230	37,460	41,210	42,030	52,810	208,570

Source:
Commonwealth Immigrants Act, 1962, Statistics.

Figure 8.3 shows the number of wives and children who have entered the country from India, Pakistan, and the West Indies. It will be seen that there are differences within the three groups in the proportion of women to children arriving. Until quite recently the number of Indian mothers was approximately 40% of the total, but in 1966–7 there has been a rise not only in the number but in the proportion of children arriving. The proportion of Pakistani children has always been higher and in 1967 amounted to 72%. The entry figures make no distinction between girls and boys but it has been usual for boys to join their fathers leaving sisters and mothers behind. (A survey conducted by International Social Service at London Airport in January and February 1967 revealed that out of 387 unaccompanied children under 16 arriving from Pakistan (80%) and India (20%) only four were girls.)[1] The West Indian pattern is different again. Children have outnumbered women by about 4:1 but between 1966–7 the ratio increased very

Figure 8.2. Voucher holders and dependants arriving July 1962–7

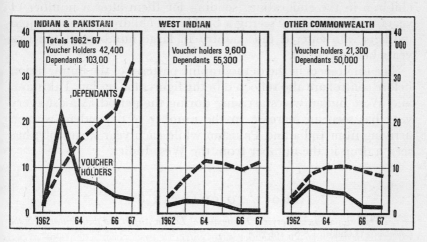

Source:
Commonwealth Immigrants Act, 1962, Statistics.

Figure 8.3. Dependent women and children arriving July 1962–7

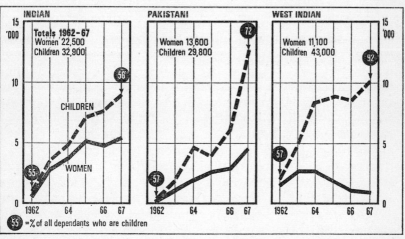

Source:
Commonwealth Immigrants Act, 1962, Statistics.

H

heavily. It has been customary for the mother to precede her children in the emigration, sending for them after a number of years, and we are now seeing a backlog of children coming to join mothers who entered the country in large numbers in the two years before control.

The differences in the demographic patterns of the immigration before control are also reflected in the figures for Indian, Pakistani, and West Indian wives arriving during the period. Almost every year has seen an increase in the number of dependent women arriving from India and Pakistan while each year since 1963 has seen a drop in the number from the West Indies.

NOTE TO CHAPTER 8

1. International Social Service, *Immigrants at London Airport and their Settlement in the Community* (London, I.S.S., 1967).

PART III THE EVIDENCE FROM THE TWO CENSUSES

9* Introduction

In Part III we shall be analysing the evidence of the 1966 10% Sample Census for what it can tell us about coloured immigrants. Our first task is to estimate the total coloured population and its distribution. The main body of Part III is devoted to an analysis of the coloured immigrants in the two main areas of settlement in Britain, the London and West Midlands conurbations. We shall describe their population structure and family composition; give a picture of how they are housed and how they are employed; and compare them with other immigrants and with the population as a whole. We shall also try to assess what changes took place in all these fields in the five years since the 1961 Census. Finally, we shall relate this evidence to other material in order to describe the economic circumstances of coloured immigrants.

The intelligent analysis of race relations in Britain is everywhere subject to difficulty and misconstruction because of the dearth of reliable information. One of the chief aims of this section of the Report is to set out clearly the available facts so that an informed general public may more accurately judge the issues before it. Since much of the information available is open to criticism from several quarters, we think it is necessary to devote a few paragraphs to the nature of our material and the problems associated with it.

Special tabulations of persons who in 1966 were resident in particular immigrant households were commissioned from the General Register Office. An initial search was necessary to locate immigrant heads of households and over the whole country this would have been an expensive procedure. We therefore decided to concentrate our attention on areas where the rate of return per 1,000 records searched would be highest. On the basis of the distribution of the coloured population in 1961, we chose only the London and West Midlands conurbations, and within these two areas only five groups: those born in India, Pakistan, Jamaica, elsewhere in the Caribbean, and British West Africa (Gambia, Ghana, Nigeria, and Sierra Leone). In order to obtain relevant comparable information we also selected the Cypriot population

* Chapters 9–12 have been contributed by Mrs. Valerie Jackson.

for similar treatment, and, in two special zones, English and Irish household heads. In addition we commissioned tabulations of everyone within these eight nationality groups. We should perhaps remind the reader that in 1966 this was in fact not a full count but a 10% sample. Issues of sampling variation and bias in selection are mentioned later.

In concentrating our attention on a special analysis of immigrant conditions in the London and West Midlands conurbations, we are consciously excluding 40% of the coloured immigrant population from our analysis; while this has been explained on the grounds of economy it is important to review the kinds of biases which are introduced; we shall also review the advantages. The major question we have to ask is this: does the sample for which we have special information differ significantly from that remaining elsewhere? One obvious feature comes to mind, relating to the regional distribution of Pakistanis; on this basis we do not have as full a cover of the Pakistani population as the others, because of the concentration of Pakistanis in the West Yorkshire conurbation. Outside this general criticism, we can argue that the London and Birmingham conurbations afford significant comparisons, representing as they do two rather different types of industrial complexes.

We have shown in Chapter 6 that migrants had been coming to the United Kingdom at a steady pace for many years; many of them in the early stages were professional people and they were chiefly concentrated in the London area. In 1951 the London conurbation contained 35% of the country's Indian population. As a result of this, in 1961 and even in 1966, the immigrant population of London contains a large element of the earlier type of professional migration as well as the younger, industrially attracted immigrants. In making a special analysis of the situation in Birmingham where there was little or none of this earlier professional migration, we think we are getting close to a purer representation of the recent immigrants. Since in 1961 the West Midlands contained 27% of all coloured immigrants resident outside the London conurbation, this was clearly the area to choose if we were not able for financial reasons to extend our analysis to the whole of the country.

Within the London and West Midlands conurbations we have selected two tracts for special study. In London the central study zone coincides exactly with that reviewed in detail in an earlier study by R. B. Davison,[1] and for which comparable information is available in 1961. Davison's study related to seven London boroughs, Battersea, Camberwell, Deptford, Hackney, Lambeth, Paddington, and Stoke Newington. They were chosen because they contained a high concentration of West Indians in 1961, and do not form a contiguous area (see map, Appendix III.1). Our information for 1966 relates to the exact area studied in 1961. The area contained about 900,000 persons in 1966 and 72,000 of them were coloured. The inner Midland area comprises a continuous area formed by the central wards of Birmingham, West Bromwich, Walsall, Wolverhampton, and the former borough of Smethwick. The exact wards, which were chosen on the basis of how many coloured persons were present in 1961, are listed in Appendix III.2. This area contained about 650,000 persons in 1966, with almost 60,000 coloured persons.

The selection of these two special study areas has permitted sensitive study of two or three select topics. We have been able to trace the degree of change in housing conditions over the five years 1961 to 1966. Comparable dynamic analyses of employment and demographic characteristics, though less dramatic, provide material which is central to our analysis of the changing conditions of immigrants. In designing the Census analysis, we had in mind that a comparison of the inner West Midlands tract with the remainder of the conurbation would afford a comparison of the older and more recent areas of immigrant settlement. In fact, our analysis has failed to reveal any significant differences between residents of the inner and outer tracts, other than those which stem from the nature of the housing stock. We find this negative evidence significant in itself.

In some places we have amalgamated tables for the inner and outer West Midlands areas, and the London material is also presented as a whole. In some of these cases we have found no significant differences between the separate immigrant groups, and in other groups the number of respondents in the smaller sections was not large enough to provide any useful information. We have not reviewed the matter of sampling variation explicitly. At these levels of aggregation, sample size is relatively large and the importance of statistical error thus reduced. Throughout, care has been taken not to push the validity of comparisons beyond what may be statistically justified.

But there are problems inherent in census material. The central problem is that the range of inquiry open to the nationally

sponsored and legally required census is far more restricted than
might have been logical for a survey concerned primarily with the
situation of coloured immigrants in British society in 1966. This
means that our analysis will ask questions which the census can
answer only obliquely. We would like to investigate how far
fertility levels have changed in the immigrant societies as a response to different mores and different housing conditions. In fact
the fertility measures which the census permit are very crude and
this important question cannot be fully answered satisfactorily.

The question of nationality, colour, and birthplace is a further
example of the limitations of our material. In general the census
classifies persons according to their place of birth. Some analysis of
nationality is available though not generally cross-tabulated
enough to identify separate national groups. This involves two
kinds of misfit groups which arrive by the same process of trying to
indicate colour by birthplace. There is a substantial number of
white persons born in India and Pakistan, children born to members of the Colonial Civil Service and of the Armed Forces, and to
others whose commercial interests led them to reside in these
countries. We have called these people 'white' Indians throughout
the whole of the analysis. Since they form a substantial part of the
total Indian population resident in the United Kingdom it is
important that we devote a little space to saying how we resolved
this problem.

From the 1961 Census of population it is possible to identify
roughly the number of white Indians. At that date there were
76,000 persons resident in England who were born in India but
with United Kingdom citizenship by birth or descent. The similar
figure for persons born in Pakistan amounted to almost 6,000. In
1961 the white Indians constituted 50% of the total enumerated
Indian population. It is clearly important that they are excluded
from our analysis, though this can be done only with limited
precision. The nature of the adjustments that we have made and
the assumptions on which they are based are set out in Appendix
III.3.

This unorthodox editing of census material may be defended
upon several counts. In the first place, a straight analysis of
Indians as recorded for census purposes provides an amalgam of
two vastly different populations. To the social scientist, the
average of these two is a completely useless concept. The authors
consider that however erroneous they have been in making these

adjustments, the adjusted material is vastly more useful than any such artificial admixture. In our major tabulations of special census material, much data for the Indian population is quoted in two forms, before and after adjustment. With this information, the sceptical reader will be able to satisfy himself on the nature of our assumptions, if he chooses.

The lack of congruence between nationality and skin colour also causes difficulties in the other direction, since in census terms all children born to foreign parents resident in the United Kingdom are naturally not recorded in the foreign birthplace tables. We have used a method, which is described in Appendix III.3, to arrive at an estimate of the total coloured population so that children born in this country are included.

Any discussion of the strength and weakness of census analysis must refer to the question of under-enumeration which occurs in every census. Where the sample is 10% there is more room for error and it is likely to be greatest among those whose housing conditions and working hours are unorthodox. Single persons, whether in shared dwellings or living alone, are apt to be missed and so the extent of under-enumeration among immigrants may be fairly high. This matter is discussed in Appendix III.3. In our analysis we shall try from time to time to indicate the likely effect of under-enumeration particularly relating to single males.

Whatever the weaknesses of the census, it does provide, within the limits of its range of inquiry, a comprehensive photograph of demographic, economic, and social conditions throughout the whole country. The censuses of 1961 and 1966, particularly the latter, are major sources of information for this study. For the social scientist the strength of the census lies in its comprehensive coverage of areas which, over a long period, have proved central to much social research. Here we are able to ask a series of questions of the whole population, or of parts of it. The census enables comparison of separate groups within the whole. In particular we are able to compare coloured immigrants with the white migrant groups, the Irish and Cypriots, as well as with the population born in the United Kingdom.

NOTE TO CHAPTER 9

1. R. B. Davison, *Black British* (London, Oxford University Press, for the Institute of Race Relations, 1966).

10 The Number and Distribution of Coloured Persons in England and Wales, 1966

1. NUMBERS

The question of how many coloured people are currently resident in Britain is difficult to answer. As we have indicated, there is reason to believe that the census counts which are basic to our reckoning were deficient, particularly among Pakistanis. In addition, the census does not identify non-whites directly, but tabulates all residents by birthplace. Thus children born in one country to natives of another will generally be classified incorrectly, if we argue directly from birthplace to colour of skin. In particular, this means we have to take care in estimating the number of coloured children born in England and Wales. The estimation of the total coloured population resident in England and Wales at census date 1966 thus involves two separate procedures, a sharpening of census estimates by reference to other sources, and an adjustment to accommodate children born in the host country.

Table 10.1 shows how the total Commonwealth population and its major component parts have increased from 1951 through 1961 to 1966. The data have been amended to remove the white Indian and Pakistani population.

In 1951, the total census-enumerated Commonwealth population, including Colonies and Protectorates, amounted to 336,000 persons. By 1961 the figure had almost doubled to 660,000, and a further 280,000 persons were added in the five years between 1961 and 1966. By the latter date there were 942,000 Commonwealth natives enumerated in England and Wales. These substantial increases are entirely consequent upon increases in the Commonwealth coloured groups, whose total population increased from 75,000 persons in 1951 to 336,600 in 1961, and 595,100 in 1966. The changes which have occurred reflect the net balance of arrivals and deaths, since births occurring to these populations within the United Kingdom escape our attention on the birthplace criterion. Because the coloured immigrants are young there would be very few deaths. Changes, therefore, stem almost entirely from new arrivals.

Continuing our consideration of the coloured population born

Table 10.1. Estimates of selected immigrant populations in England and Wales, 1951, 1961, and 1966

Area of origin	1951	1961	1966
India*	30,800	81,400	163,600
Pakistan*	5,000	24,900	67,700
Ceylon	5,800	9,000	12,900
West Indies†	15,300	171,800	267,900
West Africa‡	5,600	19,800	36,000
Far East§	12,000	29,600	47,000
Total coloured	74,500	336,500	595,100
Cyprus and Malta	24,700	66,600	90,800
Total Commonwealth	336,400	659,800	942,300
Irish Republic	472,100	644,400	674,600
Total population	43,758,000	46,105,000	47,135,500
Coloured persons per 1,000	1·70	7·30	12·6

* These are derived from census estimates as follows:

> 1951—110,767 Indians and 11,117 Pakistanis,
> 1961—151,435 Indians and 30,737 Pakistanis,
> 1966—232,210 Indians and 73,130 Pakistanis.

We have shown in Appendix III.3 that we think these included the following numbers of white Asians:

> 1951—80,000 Indians and 6,130 Pakistanis,
> 1961—76,000 Indians and 5,840 Pakistanis,
> 1966—68,600 Indians and 5,400 Pakistanis.

† Including British Guiana.
‡ Countries included are: Gambia, Ghana, Nigeria, and Sierra Leone.
§ Included are: Hong Kong, Malaya, and Singapore.

Source:
Amended Census Estimates, 1951, 1961, and 1966.

abroad, it is possible to make some adjustments for census under-enumeration, on the basis of Home Office records of arrivals since 1955. An example may be useful. In 1951, the Census recorded only 6,447 Jamaicans in the whole of England and Wales. Now from 1955 to the end of 1960, net listed arrivals, which themselves may not be a complete record, amounted to 96,180. If no other Jamaicans had arrived from census date 1951 to the end of 1954, and if none had died, we should expect the 1961 Census to enumerate 102,627 persons, plus the proportion of the 40,000 net arrivals in 1961 which came into the country before the Census date, late in April. In fact the Census enumerated only 100,051 persons, which is probably an under-estimate of 15,000 persons. This form of adjustment embraces errors from three sources. Since to our knowledge there has been a steady inflow of immigrants from the early fifties, this method underestimates the total population in 1961 by the amount of net immigration before complete records were initiated; it also fails to take account of under-enumeration in the 1951 Census. On the other hand, there will have been some deaths to Jamaicans resident in the host country, though these would not exceed about 1,000 during the whole inter-censal period. Our adjustments can therefore only be rough ones, but we think they are worth making; clearly this is a step in the right direction. We should point out that while the census data we are using relate only to England and Wales, net arrivals relate to the United Kingdom. But the censuses of 1961 and 1966 indicate almost no change in the component parts of Scotland's coloured population over this period. We are therefore safe in assuming that the under-enumeration indicated does not represent a diffusion over the border.

Making a systematic adjustment for each of the countries listed in Table 10.1, we estimate that the total of Commonwealth coloured residents at the 1966 Census who were born abroad was 711,000. This suggests that the census derived estimate of 595,100 was too small by 116,000, so that the census count enumerated only 84% of the total coloured Commonwealth native population. Under-enumeration was particularly severe among Pakistanis, of whom, on this estimate, only 62% were enumerated in 1966. Details are shown in Appendix III.4.

Next it is necessary to make some estimate of the number of children born in the United Kingdom to coloured parents. The population under 15 years enumerated in households where, for example, the head is Jamaican, is compared with the number of census enumerated Jamaicans under 15 years of age. Since this latter group comprises Jamaican natives, we assume that the excess indicates the number of children born into Jamaican households while in Britain. The evidence which enables us to estimate the number of children born here is derived from our special tabulations for the London and West Midlands conurbations. We find no reason to doubt that these areas adequately represent the country as a whole. Appendix III.4 presents detailed calculations and further comments on the validity of the procedure. Considering first only the census enumerated population, we calculate that in 1966, 595,100 census enumerated immigrants were in households, which contained a further 189,000 children. The number of children in West Indian households is particularly high and they amount to over 60% of the total.

But our final estimate of the number of children in immigrant households must take cognizance of census under-enumeration, and the method we have adopted is described in Appendix III.4.

Table 10.2 draws together our final conclusions on the size and composition of the coloured population in England and Wales at census date 1966. An estimated total coloured population of 924,300 persons comprises 710,900 Commonwealth immigrants

Table 10.2. Total estimated coloured population resident in England and Wales, 1966 Census, by country of origin

Area of origin	Born overseas	Born in the United Kingdom	Total
India*	180,400	43,200	223,600
Pakistan†	109,600	10,100	119,700
Ceylon	12,900	3,200	16,100
Jamaica	188,100	85,700	273,800
Other Caribbean	129,800	50,500	180,300
British West Africa	43,100	7,600	50,700
Far East	47,000	13,000	60,000
Total	710,900	213,300	924,200

* Excluding white Indians.
† Excluding white Pakistanis.

Source: 1966 Census of Population and our own calculations.

including children born abroad and 213,300 children born in this country. Within the total population, Jamaicans form the single largest group, about 30%; *in toto*, West Indians, 49%, are more important than the Indian and Pakistani group, 39%. It should be emphasized that the total of 924,200 persons represents close to a minimum at census date 1966. We shall discuss in Chapter 30 the importance of births and net arrivals since then; our conclusions there suggest that the total coloured population in England and Wales amounted to 1,113,000 by mid-year 1968.

2. DISTRIBUTION AND CONCENTRATION

The aim of this section is to attempt some comprehensive analysis of the settlement pattern of coloured persons in England and Wales. In this we are limited by the extent of census material, for which the smallest unit of enumeration is generally the local authority area.

The 1961 Census forms a useful benchmark, but while we can make some rough adjustment to exclude white Indians and Pakistanis, we cannot account accurately for the number of coloured children born in this country. The major part of this analysis deals, therefore, with changes in the number of adult immigrants, and no allowance has been made for possible differential under-enumeration.

Our analysis concentrates on the four major coloured groups, Indians, Pakistanis, Jamaicans, and other Caribbeans, and we shall compare the distribution and concentration of these groups at 1961 and 1966. Excluding white Indians we estimate that there were 277,000 persons within these four ethnic groups living in England and Wales in 1961. The distribution of these people within the conurbations and the rest of the country is set out in Table 10.3.

At that time, 71% of these coloured immigrants were in the six major conurbations, with Merseyside and Tyneside playing very minor roles in the total pattern. In contrast, London and the West Midlands conurbations contained 47% and 14%, respectively, of the country total. The regional pattern does not vary much from one ethnic group to another, but the proportion of Pakistanis in the Yorkshire conurbation is relatively high. In 1961, 41% of all Indians and Pakistanis were in towns outside the conurbations, while 80% of West Indians were within them.

We have next to consider what became of the new migrants arriving between 1961 and 1966. By this latter date there were an additional 213,000 coloured persons in the whole of England and Wales. The proportion of the total coloured population in these areas in 1966 had changed hardly at all; it was 72%. In fact, from region to region, the general pattern was that new immigrants tended to make their home on the basis of the regional distribution in 1961. This was remarkably true for the West Indians who have

Table 10.3. Census enumerated coloured population (000's), regional distribution, England and Wales, 1961

Area of origin	Greater London conurbation	West Midlands conurbation	South East Lancashire conurbation	Merseyside conurbation	Tyneside conurbation	West Yorkshire conurbation	All conurbations	Elsewhere	Total
India*	27·0	9·0	2·6	1·4	1·1	3·0	44·1	36·5	80·6
Pakistan†	5·4	6·0	1·0	·2	·4	4·8	17·8	7·1	24·9
Jamaica	53·3	20·1	3·9	·4	·1	2·5	80·3	19·8	100·1
Rest of Caribbean	45·3	4·7	1·7	·7	·2	2·7	55·3	16·5	71·8
Total	131·1	39·8	9·2	2·7	1·8	13·0	197·5	79·9	277·4

* Excluding white Indians.
† Excluding white Pakistanis.

Source:
1961 Census.

maintained a high degree of concentration in the conurbations
Indian and Pakistani migrants did not follow their earlier patterr
so closely. Almost twice as many Indians moved into the Wes
Midlands as would have been expected, and rather fewer Pakistanis. A relatively larger build-up of Indians also occurred in the
Yorkshire conurbation. In all, 12% of all new Indian or Pakistan
migrants made their way into this conurbation, the largest ne
addition to occur outside London and the West Midlands.

The overall significance of these four coloured groups within the
total population varies from place to place. It is probably correc
to say that the degree of concentration is generally much less thar
popular opinion believes. In England and Wales as a whole, the
1966 Census suggests that only 1·2% of the population belongs to
one of these four groups. In the whole country there were only six
local authorities with more than 5% of the population coloured
and all these were London boroughs. (They were Brent 7·4%
Hackney 7·1%, Lambeth 6·7%, Haringey 5·6%, Islington 5·4%
and Hammersmith 5·4%.) Even if 25% under-enumeration o
immigrants had occurred, the number of places in which the
proportion of coloured immigrants was greater than 5% woulc
still be under a score.

We have shown how the immigrants who arrived between 1961
and 1966 moved into regions which already contained sizeable
immigrant populations. If new immigrants were to move into
close proximity with their predecessors this would clearly increase
the degree of concentration. Table 10.4 shows to what extent thi
has happened. In 1961, there were almost exactly 100,000
Jamaicans in England and Wales, according to the Census. There
were thirteen local authority areas with a Jamaican population
exceeding 2,000 persons (and most of these were London boroughs). These thirteen places accounted for 56% of the tota
Jamaican population at that date. A further twelve local authority
areas, again mostly in London, had a Jamaican population o
between 1,000 and 2,000 persons, accounting for another 16% o
the Jamaicans. Thus, 72% of all Jamaicans were in places wher
1% or more than 1% of the total Jamaican population wa
concentrated.

Analysis of the change in concentration between 1961 and 196
has to take account of the total increase in the number of Jamai
cans in the country. By this latter date the Jamaican populatio
had increased to 152,000, so a place would need to contain a littl

over 3,000 Jamaicans to include 2% of the total Jamaican population. Table 10.4 below brings together material for our four
major immigrant groups according to this principle. Thus we are
able to compare levels of concentration and changes occurring
from 1961 and 1966.

Table 10.4. The changing concentration of coloured minorities, 1961
and 1966

(Figures represent the percent of each immigrant population which is
contained in local authority areas where there is a given percentage of
that group's total population.)

Degree of concentration	West Indian 1961 Jamaican	1961 Rest of Carib- bean	1966 All West Indians	Indian* 1961	1966	Pakistani 1961	1966
2% or more	55·7	41·3	57·8	11·3	24·7	33·5	28·8
1·5% to 2%	5·2	8·5	6·8	12·3	15·6	3·5	9·1
1% to 1·5%	11·2	12·8	6·5	22·2	23·3	6·5	17·6
Under 1%	27·9	37·4	28·9	54·2	36·4	56·5	44·5

* Excluding white Indians.   *Source:*
Calculations from Censuses, 1961 and 1966.

In 1961 concentration was particularly acute in the Jamaican
population with 56% of the total population in places at or above
the 2% level. At that date, 33·5% of the Pakistani population was
in the 2%+ category; in sharp contrast, the Indian population
was relatively dispersed with over 50% of the population living in
places with less than 1% of the total and with only 11% at the 2%
level. For these estimates the white Indians have been excluded on
the most conservative assumption, that they are widely dispersed
in the population. It is very clear therefore that, however we
measure it, the West Indian population was far more spatially
concentrated than the Indian and Pakistani in 1961.

By 1966, the degree of concentration in the West Indian and
Pakistani population had increased a little and in the Indian
group had increased considerably. By this time a pattern began to
emerge where the middle ranges of concentration, between 1%
and 2%, were becoming of increasing importance in the Asian
population, though at the 2% or more level West Indians were
still by far the most concentrated.

11 The Changing Demographic Scene, 1961 to 1966

Since the control of immigration, the number of women and children admitted to the United Kingdom has increased while the number of persons coming to work has been reduced to a trickle. Immigration control has thus had major demographic effects on the composition of the coloured population. This chapter aims to trace some of these changes. Again, much of the information we would like is only partially available, but we shall draw upon our special tabulations for the London and West Midlands conurbations to make inferences relating to the whole of the country.

1. MALE DOMINANCE AMONG IMMIGRANTS

We begin with a discussion of the balance between males and females within the immigrant populations. In the English population at large, the sex ratio, number of males per 1,000 females, has increased slightly, from 924 in 1951, to 937 in 1961 and 940 in 1966. In an ageing population like ours it is usual for this ratio to decrease over time because women's life expectancy has improved more than that of men. But over this period the sex ratio has changed in the other direction, a direct result of the high proportion of males among immigrants. Among the coloured population the sex ratio is estimated at 1,252 in 1951, 1,548 in 1961, and 1,384 in 1966. This means that 63% of the net increase in the coloured population from 1951 to 1961 was male, compared with only 56% from 1961 to 1966. At this point, it is perhaps wise to remember that census under-enumeration has probably excluded more males than females; it is thus likely that the true sex ratios are higher even than these figures.

The dominance of males in the immigrant population has thus declined a little since 1961. The left-hand side of Table 11.1 shows the sex ratio at 1961, at 1966, and among net arrivals between these two dates. It is of particular interest to note that net arrivals of West Indian women have exceeded those for men during this period. Among the Indian and Pakistani migrants, the percentage of males has been reduced but is still very high. Relating this change to the evidence on arrivals since 1962 in Chapter 8, which indicated a large swing towards female immigrants, we should remember that the first year after the 1961 Census was that which encountered the tremendous influx of immigrants 'beating the ban' and a high proportion of these were Indians and Pakistanis. In this respect, the inter-censal change represents the net effect of two conflicting trends.

Table 11.1. Male dominance among immigrants, male per 1,000 females, 1961 and 1966

| Area of origin | England and Wales | | | London conur-bation 1966 | West Midlands conur-bation 1966 | West Yorks conur-bation 1966 |
	At 1961	Arrivals 1961–66	At 1966			
India*	1,568	1,373	1,479	1,520	1,644	1,640
Pakistan†	5,380	3,541	4,231	2,890	9,451	5,394
Jamaica	1,258	773	1,066	989	1,181	1,356
Other Caribbean	1,264	809	1,026	1,048	1,152	1,145
British West Africa	1,949	1,452	1,614	1,572	—	—
All coloured	1,548	1,279	1,384	1,230	1,754	4,418
Cyprus	1,273	1,016	1,191	1,182	1,484	—
Ireland	925	234	912	870	1,122	1,045
Total population	937	—	940	916	979	949

* Excluding white Indians.
† Excluding white Pakistanis.

Source:
1961 Census, and 1966 Special Tabulations.

The right-hand side of Table 11.1 shows how the sex ratio of immigrants varies with the economic structure of various conurbations. The London conurbation attracts a high proportion of women among the English population and this pattern is repeated for all immigrant groups. In fact, there are more Jamaican women in London than men. The higher proportion of women immigrants in the London area probably reflects a concentration of higher status occupations, to which persons would be more likely to migrate with a spouse. We also have to consider the employment potential for higher status female migrants in executive and professional careers. In direct contrast, the Birmingham area has higher sex ratios than the country as a whole, an indicator of the role this area plays in the economic structure of the whole country. An economy based primarily on metal trades and heavy manufacturing offers opportunities for unskilled and semi-skilled males. Women may be employed in transport or in catering, but there is

I

little here to attract the higher status immigrant with a non-working wife.

2. MARITAL STATUS

The question of domestic arrangements among various minority groups raises issues of cultural values as well as the problems associated with the usual shortage of women among migrant populations. In this respect, the census is of limited value, since it merely asks for legal marital status, and does not inquire, nor should it be implied, that a married person is resident with his or her spouse at the time of enumeration. We should also add that the extent of common law unions, generally believed to be widespread among West Indians, cannot be satisfactorily assessed. Since the number of married men exceeds the number of married women in most immigrant groups, it is clear that the percentage of married males is not a useful concept for analysis.

Table 11.2. The married population, 1961 and 1966

	1961		1966	
Area of origin	Percent of females, 15+ married	Married women per 100 males 15+ years	Percent of females, 15+ married	Married women per 100 males 15+ years
India*	55·4	47·5	66·5	50·1
Pakistan†	62·1	11·3	79·7	14·5
Jamaica and			71·6	67·8
other Caribbean	58·8	45·6	65·7	60·8
British West Africa	54·7	26·0	83·6	51·9
Cyprus	71·2	52·4	59·0	59·6
Total population	63·7	70·4	63·6	70·0

* Excluding white Indians. Source:
† Excluding white Pakistanis.   1961 Census (six conurbations), and 1966 Special Tabulations.

If we relate the number of married women within each immigrant group to the related adult male population, we get some idea of how many men in that group could be living with a spouse in the country. This is, of course, a rough estimate since it assumes all women returned as married in the census are resident with a spouse from the same racial groups. It would be inaccurate because of marriages between different racial groups, but we think the measure still gives some general indication of how many men may be in a current marriage.

Material on this is presented in Table 11.2. Among all coloured immigrants the percentage of eligible women who are married has increased from 1961 to 1966. The rates of women married seem remarkably high, but on reflection various features contribute to this. Among Indians and Pakistanis, it is customary for marriages to take place at an earlier age than in western countries. In addition to this, the immigrant populations are particularly young, so few widows are included in these special groups.

If, however, we relate the married women to the male population of marriageable age, the imbalance of marital status among the immigrant groups is still very evident. In 1966 it was still true that only 15% of Pakistani males could possibly have a Pakistani wife in this country. But the effect of migration control is evident in the degree of change in this measure from 1961 to 1966. West Indians and Africans have achieved considerable success in improving their marital status position during this period.

On these measures it is difficult to make direct comparisons with the degree of marriage within each respective home country, precisely because the measures we have here are affected by rates of widowhood which in turn are responsive to age structure differences. Since our immigrant populations are young, we should take this feature into account. But a general review of age specific census data relating to these nationality groups within their own countries provides some interesting comparisons. Nuptiality is lower among Indians and Pakistanis and higher among West Indians than would be the case at home. In both these cases immigrants have tended to conform to the English pattern, which means more marriage for West Indians and less for Indians and Pakistanis. What the data cannot tell us is whether there is an immigrant response in the host country or a process of selection at source. Logically we must expect that arrivals from India and Pakistan have been selective of people with later marriage patterns, who might be relatively middle class, or who failed to marry young for economic reasons. But among West Indians it seems possible that greater economic prosperity, housing difficulties, the absence of close kin, and perhaps social pressure, have increased the degree of marriage thus reducing the number of common law unions. This would be quite in line with the standard interpretation of marriage within Jamaican society which is entered into only when the partners can afford the privilege and responsibility of matrimony.[1]

The figures presented in Table 11.2 relate to the London and West Midlands conurbations combined, and of them the London group forms by far the greater part. But it does seem that the degree of marriage among all immigrant groups is higher in Birmingham than in London, where there is a considerable student element—particularly in the Indian, Pakistani, and West African population. We shall, however, show in Chapter 12 that the degree of home ownership was remarkably high among all coloured immigrants in 1966. It would seem likely therefore that this may be an important influence on West Indian marriage patterns in Britain.

3. AGE STRUCTURE

A wide variety of migration studies have revealed a consistent tendency for immigrants to be drawn predominantly from the younger age groups, particularly the under 30 year olds. This would lead us to believe that a large proportion of all coloured persons resident in Britain in 1966 would be under 45 years of age. Now, in general, the age distribution of coloured immigrants is significantly different from the population at large, and one feature of this reflects the relative importance of children in the immigrant community. But to assess the age structure over the whole range, it is necessary to form a composite age structure from persons born abroad and their children, wherever they were born. This has been done for material at 1961 and 1966. With one or two exceptions, which are indicated below, there is a remarkable similarity in age distributions for males and females; the material also indicates no significant differences between the selected areas of London and Birmingham and the rest. We have, therefore, combined data for males and females, and present single estimates for each ethnic group at 1961 and 1966 (Figure 11.1).

The material reveals significant differences between age structures of various immigrant groups and these are in turn different from the structure in the whole community. In 1961, 17% of the total West Indian population in the six conurbations was under 5 years of age, compared with only 8% in the comparable total population.

We think it is wise to remember that the figure of 17% is almost certainly too high since under-enumeration would tend to exclude older rather than young West Indians, but we cannot at this stage reject this evidence completely. In 1961 the average length of stay for the bulk of West Indian and African immigrants would have been only a few years, and since migrants generally are without children at the time they migrate (or leave them behind in the first instance), there was a deficiency of children between 5 and 14 years of age at this time. Even so it seems likely that almost 30% of the coloured population in 1961 was under 15 years of age; this figure compares with only 23% in the total population.

A major second conclusion relates to the relative youth of the immigrant adult populations. Outside the Indian group there is probably not more than 10% of all coloured migrants over the age of 45 years. This compares with 38% in the total population of the six conurbations.

The similarity between the West Indian and African age structures has already been mentioned and that between the Cypriot and Indian population should also be pointed out. The relative maturity of these latter two groups in 1961 stems from their longer average period of residence in the host community. In 1961, the balance between recent and older migrants was such as to produce a more normal age structure than for the groups of more recent immigration.

Changes occurring between 1961 and 1966 will reflect a degree of ageing in the immigrants who were in England in 1961, but largely the arrival of newcomers. Coloured immigrant populations have become of slightly younger average age, although the percentage of persons 45 years and older has hardly changed. The chief factor of note is the remarkable increase in the West Indian child population. In 1966, we estimate that 38% of all West Indians were under 15 years of age, compared with only 23% in the total population. By this date wider differences between various coloured groups begin to emerge. Because the Pakistan population contains very few women, new additions of children are more usually achieved by children coming to join parents already in England. The system is not as fruitful of young children as among other groups where the proportion of new births within England and Wales is probably much higher.

With differences developing between various ethnic groups with respect to age structure, an average relating to all coloured persons

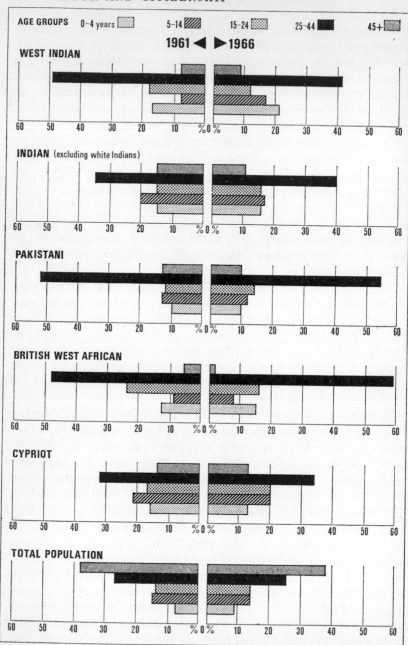

Figure 11.1. Percentage distribution of populations by age, coloured
immigrants and control groups, 1961 and 1966

Sources:
1961 Census (six conurbations), special calculation by Brian
Cohen;[2] 1966 Census, Special Tabulations.

as a whole is of limited validity, though it does provide a method of quick comparison. The age structure changes which have occurred and the manner in which they relate to the changes in the total population are summarized in Table 11.3. The swing towards young people in the coloured population is a very clear feature of the inter-censal period, but Figure 11.1 shows that this occurred almost wholly among West Indians.

Table 11.3. A comparison of percentage age structures, 1961 and 1966

| | 1961 | | 1966 | |
Age	All coloured groups	Total population	All coloured groups	Total population
Under				
15 years	29	23	34	23
15–24 years	16	14	13	14
25–44 years	45	26	42	25
45 + years	10	37	11	38

Sources:
As for Figure 11.1.

In order to give some broad indication of variations within the total immigrant population we have calculated median ages for adult males and females separately, for the London and Birmingham areas. Consistent with our hypothesis that migrants are selected from particular age brackets, irrespective of country of origin, these median ages display remarkably little variation from one group to another. But a slightly younger age distribution for females is revealed. In the London area, we estimate that 50% of all immigrant Indian men over 14 years (excluding white Indians) were under 31 years of age in 1966. The highest median age was for Jamaican males, at 32 years. All the coloured immigrant groups had median ages within the range, although for the Irish the median age of adults was 41·5 years and for the English, 44 years. In every case but one, the immigrant women were slightly younger, with a median age about one year below that for males. But in London the median age for immigrant women was significantly higher than for men, while in Birmingham immigrant women were a little younger than the men. This is probably related to the fact that there were more wives among female immigrants in Birmingham, and probably less independent female migrants.

4. FERTILITY

In view of their age structure it is not surprising that the rate of natural increase is high among immigrants, for the greater part of all immigrants are within the reproductive ages, and we have shown that the percentage of women that are married has been increasing. We now propose to investigate what the census can tell us about differential fertility. It will be necessary to review how far current trends reflect age structure features. We shall also review fertility as revealed in this country in the light of what we know about levels of fertility in the home countries.

Except in particular localities, we have no vital registration, so it is not possible directly to identify births to coloured persons; our analysis must rest on census material, and this creates methodological difficulties. We have records which indicate the number of children in households where the head of household belongs to separate ethnic groups. This allows an analysis of children born in this country in the London and Birmingham areas, but raises the question of mixed marriages. In 1961, about 80% of all West Indian households of two or more persons were ethnically homogeneous. Among Asians there were more mixed marriages, but again the white Indian element is difficult to extract. Thus, while West Indian paternity probably indicates that the mother is also West Indian, we cannot be certain that this is true for all groups. While we are able to make an analysis of births per mother, ethnicity must be defined in terms of the household head.

Without vital statistics, it is usual to estimate fertility from a census by relating the number of children within a given age bracket to the number of women in the fertile age groups. Thus we calculate child-woman ratios, relating the number of children who are under 5 years, under 10, or under 15, to the number of women who are from 15 to 44 years, and we may choose to consider only the married women. In some sense, therefore, we can calculate the average number of children per mother, but problems arise because the women may have different age structures within the 15 to 44 years group. In our case we have shown that immigrant women are significantly younger than English women; thus a high percentage of all immigrant women in the fertile age groups will be in the younger age brackets, significantly under 35 years of age. We may put the matter another way round. If we average the number of children under 5 years among all women from 15 to 44 years, the figure will be lower for English women than for immigrants because in the former group a significant proportion of women over, say, 35 years will no longer have children under 5 years of age, although they might have children under 15 years. On the other hand, if we carry out our analysis in terms of the children under 15, the measure is clearly biased in favour of the English women, since in general the immigrant women have not been married long enough to have children of this age. Taking this as the stronger argument, the analysis set out below is couched in terms of children under 5 years to women from 15 to 44 years. The matter of estimating fertility levels before family building is completed will be taken up again later in this section.

Taking the ratio of children under 5 years to married women from 15 to 44 years we find significant excess fertility in all immigrant groups including the Irish, but excluding the West Africans who we know have a predisposition to send their children back to the homeland.

Table 11.4. Children under 5 per 1,000 women aged 15–44 years, 1961 and 1966

Area of origin	1961	1966
India*	830	771
Pakistan	1,338	979
West Indies	576	821
British West Africa	572	510
Cyprus	740	604
Ireland	n.a.	768
Total population	396	434

* Excluding white Indians.   *Sources:*
1961 Census, amended from special calculation by Brian
Cohen; 1966 Census, Special Tabulations.

The degree of variation between 1961 and 1966 is partly a result of the effect of immigration control, since there were more Indian and Pakistani women by 1966. At both dates there is considerable excess fertility among the immigrant groups. The high figures among the Indian and particularly the Pakistani population to a large extent reflect the shortage of women in their populations; but the change occurring in the West Indian population is significant. We also think it is important to note that Irish and Cypriot fertility exceed that of the total population by 77% and 30% respectively in 1966. In fact, on this measure, West Indian fertility is only 7% higher than that revealed among Irish residents in the London and Birmingham conurbations.

It is a common practice for West Indians to send infant children home to their grandparents. The number of children recorded as returning to the West Indies between July 1962 and December 1965 was 8,200, not all of whom would have been born here or would have been under 5 years old. Adding all these children into our fertility analysis, that is, making a maximum assumption, would increase the child-woman ratio by about 10%.

We have investigated the differential in child-woman ratios between the London and Birmingham areas; the results are remarkable. Among the English, marital fertility is 25% higher in the West Midlands than in London. What is perhaps surprising is that the pattern of immigrant fertility shows the same differences in the two areas. Consistently, fertility is higher in Birmingham than in London but the pattern of differentials within each area, that Asians have about 40% more children within marriage than the English, and West Indians about 60% more, is remarkably constant.

It is important to view immigrant fertility in relation to what might be expected on the basis of birth-rates in the home countries. Applying what we know of fertility levels in the West Indies, we should expect about 80% more children than in the English control group; vital registration in India is highly undeveloped, but the best information available suggests that births would be higher than the English group by about 130%. In this light, the achieved fertility of immigrants in the host community is clearly lower than might have been expected. If we further look at the pattern of marriages, we find that rather less Indian women are married in Great Britain than in their home communities, though we have suggested a form of social selection. Probably immigration is selective of women with lower marriage rates and also with lower fertility within marriage. But a contrary situation arises when we review the position of West Indian women. In the West

Indies, only 45% of all women from 15 to 44 years of age were reported married in the 1960 Census. British returns indicate that about 70% of the London and Birmingham samples were married. We cannot be certain that common law unions have not passed for marriages in the 1966 English Census, but it is argued that such a high rate of permanent or semi-permanent sexual unions puts the female population under considerable risk of conception. In this light, the lower fertility achieved by West Indian women in the host community than in their home community is also the more remarkable. We wish we could say how far the adoption of contraception has been instrumental in this, or conversely how much of this is due to the absence of a maternal grandmother.

Recent evidence from Birmingham, where births to non-European parents are separately recorded, shows a progressive decline in the number of births to West Indians in each year since 1963.[3] The number of births in 1967 was 25% lower than the peak figure in 1963. If the adult West Indian population has increased by immigration over this period the crude birth-rate will have fallen considerably; if it has remained stationary the fall in the birth-rate has been 25%. The census shows an increase of 45% in the West Indian immigrant population from 1961 to 1966. Most of this increase would have taken place in the first two years of the period. In this time the number of births increased by less than 30% and then began to fall. We think this is very significant evidence of a fertility response to a new environment. As the median age of West Indian women in Birmingham was only 30 in 1966 the fall in the birth-rate cannot be accounted for solely by the reduction in fecundity which normally occurs in the late 30s.

At the beginning of this section, attention was drawn to the limited nature of the fertility measures which are available from census counts. It was indicated that the base population of immigrant women is likely to be concentrated in the younger age groups, while our comparisons have been drawn with English, Irish, or Cypriot populations where more older women, from 30 to 44 years, are present. Thus, while our measures indicate only an excess of 40 to 65% fertility, we still have to ask what is likely to develop at later stages. The point at issue may be put very simply. If contraception is more readily adopted in the English population than among immigrants, then the full effect of fertility differential will not be evident until the immigrant women have passed through the whole of their reproductive span. An earlier study carried out in Sparkbrook, Birmingham, encountered the same methodological problem.[4] Among a carefully selected sample the average number of live births per woman ever pregnant was 2·7 for English women and exactly the same for West Indian women, but the average age of English women was 41 years, in comparison with only 31 years for the West Indians. Furthermore, there were not enough older West Indian women living in Sparkbrook at that time to justify any age standardized comparison among the older groups. The Sparkbrook study revealed high Indian and Irish fertility, with a small excess in the West Indian community at age 30 years. At this age, English women had had about 2·1 pregnancies compared with about 2·7 for West Indians, 3·4 for Irish women, and almost 4·0 for Indians. But fertility control is most effective in reducing unwanted births above this age. Until we have the fertility experience of immigrant women through their whole reproductive life, the question of differential fertility cannot be properly answered.

5. FAMILY STRUCTURE

The fertility analysis so far presented has been related to the total population of females within each ethnic group. A more sensitive analysis of family structure is possible, which enables us to review the importance of children in households. Table 11.5 shows the percentage of households where there are no children present at all, the relative importance of families with three or more children, and the average number of children among all households which have children. (We have called a household with one or more children under 15 years of age, a family.) Again, ethnicity is defined in terms of birthplace of the household head. For 1961 we have information only for the six chosen nationality groups, but in 1966 we have some comparable information for households where the head was born in England or Ireland, but only drawn from the inner zones of London and Birmingham. In order first to assess the general level of family size among immigrants in relation to the general population, we shall start by reviewing data for 1966; we shall then return to earlier figures, to get some notion of how family size has changed in the five years.

Because the English residents in the inner London and Birmingham areas are considerably older than the immigrants, there are far more households without any children under 15 years among the English than among immigrants. It is generally known that family size is larger in the suburbs than in the central city because people with growing families move out to acquire more space, and we shall show later that average household size in the English population is smaller in the centre of the conurbations than outside.

We are thus comparing immigrant family size derived from the whole of the London and Birmingham conurbations with a selected English group.

Table 11.5. Family structure, 1961 and 1966

Area of origin	Percent of all households without children		Average number of children in families		Percent of all families with 3 + children	
	1961	1966	1961	1966	1961	1966
India*	51	50	2·02	2·35	26	36
Pakistan	55	62	2·28	2·30	32	34
West Indies	56	36	1·97	2·43	25	35
British West Africa	53	69	1·79	1·87	20	22
Cyprus	36	34	2·12	2·13	30	30
Ireland†	n.a.	46	n.a.	2·52	n.a.	42
England†	n.a.	69	n.a.	1·85	n.a.	20

* White Indians *not* excluded.
† Data refer to selected control zones only.

Source:
1961 Census, and 1966 Special Tabulations.

About 70% of English households have no children; among the Irish 46% have no children, but figures are much lower than this for West Indians, 36%, and Cypriots, 34%. A differential is also evident between the London and Birmingham areas, which applies to immigrants and English alike. In London, Indians, West Indians, and Cypriots have between 35% and 45% of all households without children; comparable figures in Birmingham run from 25% to 30%. Among West Africans and Pakistanis there are as many childless households as in the control population.

Not only is there a higher propensity for households to contain children, but the average number of children in families is also larger. Compared with 1·85 children under the age of 15 years in each English family, there are between 2·30 and 2·43 children in the major coloured immigrant groups. West Africans have only as many children as the control population, but we know that a significant proportion of West African children return to their parents' homelands for their early childhood. On average the three major immigrant groups have about 33% more children in families than the English families. We should also note that we have not been able to correct these data to exclude the white Indian population; it is likely that the true difference is even higher than that. Directly related to the greater average number of children per family, there are also more families with three or more children among the immigrant groups. About one-third of all immigrant households are as large as this, compared with only one-fifth in the English population. But a striking feature of the material is the large average family size among the Irish population. This comes as no surprise, but the degree of the excess, that Irish fertility on these measures exceeds every other immigrant group, is worthy of note in the current controversies.

Changes occurring between 1961 and 1966 reflect the large number of births occurring to immigrants in this country as well as the pattern of arrivals since control. It has been estimated that about 90% of all children under 5 years of age in 1966 had been born in the United Kingdom. The percentage of all West Indian households without children thus fell from 56% in 1961 to 36% in 1966; it has risen marginally among Pakistanis and West Africans. The average number of children in households was also smaller in 1961, but then almost certainly larger than the comparable English figure, which we can only estimate. Similarly, there were slightly fewer families with three or more children at the earlier date.

The above material is important for our analysis because it lends itself directly to analysis of family structure. To some extent we can remove the basic age structure bias which is present in all earlier tabulations by concentrating merely on families which have children under 15 years of age; broadly speaking, this restricts our attention to strata of the population which are comparable. On these data there seems to be good evidence that families are larger among the immigrant groups by about one third. But we must again remind the reader that the control data we are using relate to English and Irish households enumerated in the selected boroughs of the London and Birmingham conurbations, and not to the total conurbations. If tabulations covering the whole of the English population were available the differential would be reduced, but certainly not removed.

SUMMARY

We have traced various changes in the demographic structure of the immigrant populations between 1961 and 1966. These are indicative of the normal kinds of demographic changes which occur to a young population passing through the phases of migration, marriage, and family building.

Migrants are generally young, under 30 years of age when they move, and generally single. After settling into the new community, new alliances, usually within the supportive atmosphere of each ethnic minority, lead to marriage and the procreation of new off-spring. The initial imbalance between males and females in the immigrant population is redressed by marriage outside the group or by the later arrival of eligible mates. The delay in marriage which is consequent upon migration and the time it takes to settle into the new community usually lowers overall fertility compared with the level occurring in the home country, or at least delays it.

Much of this is evident in the material we have outlined above. West Indian migration has been peculiar in that the percentage of women migrants was remarkably high. The rate of entry of newcomers has fallen off very greatly since 1962 with the result that population has aged slightly. The number of marriages has increased and fertility has fallen, if we relate the levels in this country to what would have been likely in the West Indies. The declining West Indian births in Birmingham do suggest that the major period of family building has now passed for this group.

The situation with respect to Asian immigrants has been different. The balance of sexes was overwhelmingly in favour of the males, and the time sequence has also been different since they arrived later than the West Indians. By and large it has taken the Indian and Pakistani groups a longer time to draw their families to them or to enter marriages. The number of families being re-united is still high. For this group we are currently witnessing the family building stage, with consequent high birth-rates. Whether the recent reduction of births evident among West Indians will be repeated is a question which the next five years will answer.

NOTES TO CHAPTER II

1. Judith Blake, *Family Structure in Jamaica* (New York, Free Press of Glencoe, 1961).
2. Special calculations by B. Cohen and P. Jenner, for the Institute's 'Survey of Race Relations in Britain', derived from 1961 Census.
3. Statistics compiled by the Public Health Department, Birmingham.
4. J. A. H. Waterhouse and D. H. Brabban, 'Inquiry into Fertility of Immigrants: preliminary report', in *Eugenics Review*, Vol. 56, no. 1, April 1964.

12 Housing

1. HOUSING CONDITIONS OF IMMIGRANTS

The disadvantages of coloured immigrants in respect of their housing conditions are generally understood, although as yet no single comprehensive housing survey has been taken. The material presented derives from our special census tabulations and hence it relates only to the London and West Midlands conurbations. It has been argued elsewhere in this report that the immigrants who live in these two areas do not differ substantially from the immigrant population at large. In respect of housing, this is clearly not the case. Even for the population at large, housing conditions vary from one part of the country to another, with overcrowding and multiple occupancy particularly concentrated in the London area. It is obvious, therefore, that the housing conditions of the immigrant population in our two chosen areas will reflect conditions obtaining there. Thus we must state at the outset that our special material affords us a description of two particular areas rather than a complete analysis. Many of our results will stem in part from the type of housing stock which these two areas enjoy. That the areas are substantially different in their housing stock enables us to measure the nature of the immigrant response to different types of housing pressure.

We shall first describe conditions within these two major zones, the London and West Midlands conurbations. The reader will recognize immediately that such a large territorial expanse as either of these areas includes tremendous variation in housing stock and conditions; analysis in smaller territorial units would be preferable. The inner West Midlands tract serves as a valuable area in which to contrast housing conditions at closer quarters. In these wards the type of housing available to all comers is far more homogeneous than in the conurbation as a whole; thus we can argue that differences between immigrant and English housing conditions are more likely to indicate social processes than simply variations in the housing stock. Our London selected boroughs tend to offer the same kind of comparisons. Since this area was selected with other criteria in mind, we cannot here suggest that conditions in the seven selected boroughs indicate

London immigrant housing at its worst. But we can indicate that in some parts of the inner conurbation conditions are considerably more severe than in the London conurbation as a whole. Paddington may be used as an example; here housing density is particularly high among West Indians. Conditions may be as extreme as this in other boroughs for which we do not have this particular information. We can use material for these selected boroughs only to suggest the degree of variation and the extremes of hardship which may exist elsewhere.

Throughout this chapter we shall review various aspects of housing conditions within the five major coloured immigrant groups. Where possible, comparisons are made with two white immigrant groups, the Cypriots and Irish, and with a control group of English residents. Occasionally, only two figures will be compared, one relating to the aggregated five coloured immigrant groups, the other to the English group. The greater part of this analysis refers to conditions revealed by the 1966 Census. Finally, we shall make some brief comparisons of housing conditions in our seven selected London boroughs in 1961 and 1966. This enables us to show the changes that have occurred within a particular area which exhibited the extreme housing conditions revealed in Davison's study of Jamaicans.[1] (See map in Appendix III.1.)

(a) Housing Density

In an extensive analysis of housing conditions in the British conurbations in 1961,[2] firm proof was established of the overriding validity of persons per room as the most useful single diagnostic of housing conditions. Such a measure, therefore, will form a useful point of departure for this analysis. Table 12.1 shows persons per room in the London and West Midlands conurbations. The five major coloured immigrant groups are listed and may be compared with the Cypriot immigrant population and a residual category formed by excluding these six immigrant groups from the total population of each conurbation. A consistent wide differential is immediately evident. All immigrant groups are living at close to one person per room in comparison with only about 0·6 persons per room in the control population. There is little variation within the immigrant community and the situation is remarkably similar in London and in the West Midlands. In the selected London boroughs density is particularly high among the coloured immigrants; we think it significant that here, as in Birmingham, the

K

Table 12.1. Persons per room, London and West Midlands conurbations, 1966

Area of residence	India*	India†	Pakistan†	Jamaica	Rest of Caribbean	British West Africa	All coloured immigrants	Cyprus	Ireland	England
London conurbation	0·80	0·93	0·99	1·07	1·14	1·10	1·05	0·94	n.a.	0·57
West Midlands conurbation	1·06	1·13	1·09	1·09	1·08	1·00	1·10	1·01	n.a.	0·58
Selected London boroughs							1·19	0·49	0·93	0·62
Selected Midlands wards							1·14	1·04	0·92	0·56

* Not adjusted for white Indians.
† Adjusted for white Indians or Pakistanis.

Source:
1966 Census, Special Tabulations.

Irish enjoy lower housing density than the more recent immigrant groups. Because of the general level of housing conditions, density is higher within the selected London boroughs even for the control population, but whereas the English group housing density is only higher by 9%, among all coloured immigrants as a combined group, density is 13% higher than in the conurbation as a whole. A similar differential against immigrants in the inner area is revealed for the Birmingham study zone.

While the general level of housing density in persons per room is about 85% higher in the coloured immigrant groups than among the native English population, it is important to review how this comes to be so. Is it a question of larger households in the immigrant population or of smaller dwellings? The left-hand side of Table 12.2 shows that households of coloured immigrants are larger than English households in both areas. In the English population, West Midlands households are larger than London households because of the importance of single and young married persons in the capital city. This tendency is present in the immigrant population, to an even greater extent than among the English group, a feature which probably reflects the importance of the coloured student population in London.

The major reason why average household size is larger in the immigrant population than among the English is demographic. Some of this stems from higher fertility among the recent immigrants, for example there are more three-or-more child families among West Indians than among the English. But much of the cause may be traced to age structure differences. Since immigrants are predominantly young, as yet there are almost no two person households where the children have grown up and left home. The 'empty nest' stage, which accounts for a substantial part of all two person households in the English population, is many years away for the immigrant groups. In addition to these demographic features, economic pressures, particularly those arising from oppressive mortgage arrangements, may encourage immigrant households to take in lodgers. Elizabeth Burney has suggested that immigrant households are further enlarged, often beyond comfort, when members of the extended family network arrive from abroad expecting shelter and hospitality.[3] As a result of these various features, immigrant households in the London conurbation are 30% larger than those of the English population; in the West Midlands the differential is even greater at 57%.

Table 12.2. Household size, number of persons and rooms per household, London and West Midlands conurbations, 1966

Area of residence	Persons per household				Rooms per household			
	All coloured immigrants	Cypriots	Irish	English	All coloured immigrants	Cypriots	Irish	English
Selected London boroughs	3·47	3·38	3·17	2·66	2·93	3·58	2·72	4·29
Rest of London conurbation	3·61	3·93	n.a.	2·83	3·57	4·45	n.a.	4·86
Total London conurbation	3·57	3·89	n.a.	2·72	3·40	4·11	n.a.	4·79
Selected Midlands wards	4·78	5·09	4·14	2·89	4·20	—	4·52	5·20
Rest of West Midlands conurbation	4·69	—	n.a.	3·12	4·70	—	n.a.	5·29
Total West Midlands conurbation	4·76	5·04	n.a.	3·03	4·32	4·98	n.a.	5·25

Source:
1966 Census, Special Tabulations.

Differences between the inner and outer tracts of each conurbation are also instructive. In the population at large, it is usual for the average household to be lower in the central city because it contains a high proportion of young people with no families and of the elderly. In short, young couples without children choose to live centrally, and to move to the suburbs when children demand play space. We have to remember that our material reflects family size and the presence of lodgers or older generation in-laws. *None the less, the pattern of outwards diffusion of larger families is particularly clear among the Birmingham English population, a feature which has not been achieved by the Birmingham immigrants. It would seem that the normal pattern of suburbanization among households with young children is being frustrated.*

A second feature which enters into our calculation of persons per room is the number of rooms which each separate housing unit provides. An analysis of rooms per household shows that on average, an immigrant household contains about one less room than an English one in Birmingham and about 1·4 less in London. Within this pattern, West Africans are particularly at a disadvantage, but we have shown that they also have less persons per household, so housing density is not much affected. On average, immigrant households have 29% less space than the English in the London area and 18% less in the West Midlands. Thus we may conclude that high housing density among the immigrant population is caused by both these factors. In the West Midlands the number of persons in each household is the major contributory cause of high density. In London the blame must be equally shared between this feature and the number of rooms which each accommodation affords.

(b) Sharing Households

The question of the number of rooms which form the average housing unit is closely related to the degree of shared accommodation, for shared housing units are generally smaller than unshared ones. The census distinguishes between a dwelling—a structurally separate accommodation with independent access to a street or public hallway, and a household—a group of persons who live and eat together. Thus, where a dwelling has been divided but not structurally altered, it will contain sharing households. Much of this sharing is accompanied by shared use of various facilities; for example, a sharing household will probably only have shared use

Table 12.3. Percentage of all households which are sharing households, London and West Midlands conurbations, 1966

Area of residence	India*	India†	Pakistan	Jamaica	Rest of Caribbean	British West Africa	All coloured immigrants	Cyprus	Ireland	England
London conurbation	39·2	56·8	64·1	70·8	73·8	75·6	70·1	54·9	n.a.	31·2
West Midlands conurbation	29·2	34·1	41·3	43·1	43·3	70·3	40·9	21·4	n.a.	4·2
Selected London boroughs							83·9	62·0	60·3	39·2
Selected Midlands wards							44·0	30·3	25·9	6·6

* Not adjusted for white Indians.
† Adjusted for white Indians or Pakistanis.

Source: 1966 Census, Special Tabulations.

of a bath, although it may have exclusive use of its own water closet. But not all housing facilities are shared because property has been subdivided. Some older dwellings are structurally deficient, many have no bathroom, and some residents are still forced to share the use of an outside toilet with adjoining houses.

Table 12.3 shows that 70% of all immigrant households in the London conurbation are sharing accommodation. In this area, the level of sharing is high in the English population too, but it is twice as high for immigrants. In the West Midlands 40% of immigrants are sharing accommodation, and this is an area where the general level of sharing is below 5%. Within the immigrant population Indians have the smallest amount of sharing and West Africans the largest, a pattern which is consistent in both study areas. The much higher level of sharing which is evident in the London area reflects to some extent the nature of the housing stock. The large Victorian four-storey buildings form a considerable part of the housing stock of the inner middle ring boroughs. Such property is far less common in the West Midlands.[4]

We might ask whether the number of persons per room is high among sharing households only. Unfortunately we can show that this is not the case. Table 12.4 shows that immigrants in non-shared accommodation also live at higher densities than their

Table 12.4. Housing density, sharing and non-sharing households, London and West Midlands conurbations, 1966

Area of residence	Persons per room		Persons per household		Rooms per household	
	Immigrant	English	Immigrant	English	Immigrant	English
London conurbation						
Sharers	1·19	0·66	2·93	2·09	2·45	3·16
Non-sharers	0·90	0·55	5·08	2·91	5·62	5·26
West Midlands conurbation						
Sharers	1·39	0·77	3·32	2·18	2·39	2·83
Non-sharers	1·02	0·57	5·74	3·06	5·64	5·36

Source:
1966 Census, Special Tabulations.

English counterparts. For the sake of brevity, the material is presented only for the combined immigrants group, thus comparisons with the English groups are highlighted. In both areas there is a substantial difference between sharers and non-sharers. Non-sharers, by far the minority of immigrants in the London area, have larger units of accommodation, in fact larger on average than the English non-sharing group, but they also have almost twice as many people in each household. The total effect is that average housing density is still very high. In comparison with average household size, households among non-sharing immigrants are certainly very large. Such large households suggests the presence of lodgers and relations within an extended family system.

Table 12.5. Percentage of persons living at more than one, and more than one and a half persons per room, London and West Midlands conurbations, 1966

| | All coloured immigrants | | English | |
Area of residence	More than 1 p.p.r.	More than 1·5 p.p.r.	More than 1 p.p.r.	More than 1·5 p.p.r.
London conurbation	51·5	27·7	11·1	2·8
West Midlands conurbation	57·4	30·0	12·3	2·9
Selected London boroughs	63·2	36·9	13·1	3·3
Selected Midlands wards	59·3	31·4	14·3	4·4

Source:
1966 Census, Special Tabulations.

Such extremes of housing density mean that a high proportion of residents are living at more than one person per room. (For census purposes in 1966 the number of rooms includes all living rooms, bedrooms, and a kitchen, or scullery if used for cooking.) In both the London and the West Midlands conurbations, about 12% of all persons outside the immigrant groups live at this density. Between 50% and 60% of the coloured immigrants live at densities exceeding one person per room. The distribution within this high density category is also instructive. By far the larger part of English residents in this high density group are living at less than 1·5 persons per room. In the immigrant groups taken as one unit, almost half of all high density residents (and this means 30% of the total population) live at more than 1·5 persons per room.

(c) Household Facilities

In general, there is a far higher degree of sharing in the London area than elsewhere, a feature which stems from the nature of the housing stock. The large Victorian London terrace house lends itself fairly readily to subdivision, and varying degrees of structural alteration may be observed. In contrast, the terrace houses which are indigenous to the immigrant wards in Birmingham are far smaller and offer little opportunity for conversion. Thus, while the total amount of sharing is less in the Birmingham area, the hardship which sharing engenders may be greater; sharing a small terrace house results in higher overall densities and also in a high degree of sharing without duplication of essential facilities. To some extent, therefore, the nature of the housing stock has resulted in a more satisfactory form of conversion in the London area than elsewhere.

The census recognizes two types of sharing household, those with exclusive use of their own kitchen, defined in terms of a stove and sink, and those without such exclusive use. The difficulty of preparing meals using shared cooking facilities hardly needs to be elaborated, though it is possible that among immigrants, where we believe all male households to be more common, the hardship of sharing may be alleviated by pooling resources. Table 12.6 shows that in London, sharing with a kitchen is generally more usual than sharing without one, a pattern which is maintained for all ethnic groups, including the English. But the absolute level of sharing is much higher among the immigrant groups than among the English. Thus, about 25% of all immigrant households are sharing accommodation without their own cooking facilities, compared with only 10% of the English.

The situation in the West Midlands is rather different. In the population at large the degree of sharing is altogether lower. Sharing among immigrants is extremely high in relation to the English population and sharing without exclusive use of a kitchen three times more usual than sharing with one. In fact, the degree of sharing without a kitchen is higher than in the London area. In London two-thirds of all sharers have their own kitchen facilities; in the West Midlands only one-quarter do so. Among those sharing without kitchen facilities the West Africans are again in a particularly disadvantageous position. In both areas the Indian population fares best among the immigrant groups; this may possibly stem from the religious importance of dietary restrictions.

Table 12.6. Percentage of all households which are sharing households, with and without kitchen, London and West Midlands conurbations, 1966

Area of residence	India*	India†	Pakistan†	Jamaica	Rest of Caribbean	British West Africa	All coloured immigrants	Cyprus	Ireland	England
London conurbation										
With kitchen	30·3	43·9	36·0	44·5	48·3	47·5	45·4	49·8	n.a.	20·3
Without kitchen	8·9	12·9	28·1	26·3	25·5	38·1	24·7	5·1	n.a.	10·9
West Midlands conurbation										
With kitchen	9·6	11·2	13·6	7·3	11·9	34·0	10·3	15·6	n.a.	2·6
Without kitchen	19·6	22·9	27·7	35·8	31·4	36·3	30·6	5·6	n.a.	1·6
Selected London boroughs										
With kitchen							51·3	52·3	52·6	36·8
Without kitchen							32·6	9·7	7·7	2·4
Selected Midlands wards										
With kitchen							10·7	21·2	15·2	4·3
Without kitchen							33·3	9·1	10·7	2·3

* Not adjusted for white Indians.
† Adjusted for white Indians or Pakistanis.

Source: 1966 Census, Special Tabulations.

Our special tabulations also enable us to say how many households are sharing a bath and how many are without one completely. Since immigrants are generally found in areas of larger dwellings it is generally true that they are in accommodation affording shared use of a bath and water closet. In contrast, the small terrace house without a bathroom is more commonly the home of long settled English population than of immigrants. In London, where the total stock of larger houses is sufficient to meet a large proportion of immigrant housing demand, few immigrants are in these smaller houses. The position contrasts sharply with that in the West Midlands, where the total stock of larger housing is proportionately much smaller. Hence, many immigrants are living in the smaller houses, many of which are without bathrooms at all and have only shared toilet facilities.

Table 12.7. Households sharing facilities, London and West Midlands conurbations, 1966

Area of residence	Percent of households sharing bath		Percent of households without bath		Percent of households sharing W.C.	
	All coloured immigrants	English	All coloured immigrants	English	All coloured immigrants	English
London conurbation	50·9	11·8	14·1	14·8	53·2	15·1
West Midlands conurbation	26·0	3·1	31·4	14·1	39·4	5·6
Selected London boroughs	59·4	15·1	18·5	29·5	62·8	23·2
Selected Midlands wards	27·3	4·3	34·1	38·5	42·3	12·6

Source:
1966 Census, Special Tabulations.

Table 12.7 indicates the degree to which households are sharing a bathroom or water closet; the percentage of all households without a bath at all is also listed. For brevity all immigrants are tabulated as one group. As a general rule, the degree of variation from one immigrant group to another is very small; where Asians are living in households which share a bath and water closet, this also tends to be the case for West Indians. The only consistent variation is that West Africans suffer the highest degree of sharing.
In the London conurbation, about 15% of all households are

without a bath, English and coloured alike. Because they tend to
be concentrated into the larger houses, over 50% of all immigrant
households are sharing a bath compared with only 12% of the
English group. The different situation in the West Midlands
chiefly reflects differences in the housing stock there, but the
differences between immigrants and the English population are
more acute. It is again true that the percentage of households
sharing a bath is much higher for coloured households than for the
English, but households without a bath at all are also very common among immigrants.

In other words, there are more immigrants in small terrace
houses in the West Midlands area, chiefly because there is nowhere
else for them to go. This results in high housing densities and, if
these houses are shared, facilities are generally not duplicated,
for lack of space; as we indicated earlier, this also produces a
high proportion of sharing households without kitchen facilities.
But, generally, there is less sharing in the West Midlands than in
London, 40% compared with 70% (see Table 12.6). The material
suggests that the small Birmingham terrace house has provided
an acceptable housing niche for those immigrants who are fortunate enough to afford unshared accommodation.

(d) Housing Tenure

We are fortunate that the census allows an analysis of the tenure
under which households occupy their accommodation. Major
categories (which include about 95% of all tenancies) are as follows.
Occupancy as:

    (i) an owner-occupier,
    (ii) renting from a local authority,
    (iii) renting unfurnished from a private company or landlord,
    (iv) renting furnished from a private company or landlord.

Information on the types of tenancies taken up by the aggregated immigrant groups and the English population in both
complete conurbations is set out in Table 12.8.

As a general rule, newcomers within any society will experience
particular hardship in competing under unregulated conditions
for those social facilities which are in short supply. The housing
situation provides excellent evidence of this. In the situation of
excess demand which has existed in the London housing market
for so long, newcomers are at a severe disadvantage. The kind of

Table 12.8. Housing tenure, London and West Midlands conurbations, 1966

Area of residence	Owner-occupiers		Renting from a local authority		Renting unfurnished		Renting furnished	
	All coloured immigrants	English	All coloured immigrants	English	All coloured immigrants	English	All coloured immigrants	English
London conurbation	32·6	43·5	4·2	22·2	18·1	28·3	43·6	2·6
West Midlands conurbation	60·1	42·3	8·2	39·1	10·0	14·6	21·4	1·3
Selected London boroughs	22·2	14·0	5·2	33·3	23·5	44·1	48·2	6·2
Remainder	36·4	46·4	3·9	21·1	16·1	26·8	41·9	2·2
Selected Midlands wards	55·7	29·9	8·1	35·9	10·3	26·5	22·9	4·0
Remainder	73·9	45·4	6·2	40·0	6·8	11·5	16·7	0·6

Source:
1966 Census, Special Tabulations.

long-standing family influences which are necessary to obtain unfurnished rented accommodation cannot yet be theirs,[5] and to qualify for council housing generally requires five years' residence. As a result, we find a high proportion of all immigrant household squeezed out from the arena of preferred housing into the other alternatives, either to take rented furnished accommodation or to buy property. Thus, in the London conurbation 44% of all coloured immigrant households are renting furnished accommodation, in comparison with only 3% of the English group. In the West Midlands the comparable figures, 21% and 1%, respectively are as remarkable.

The high degree of owner occupancy is perhaps surprising particularly when we consider the areas in which immigrants are concentrated. Table 12.8 also indicates the relative importance of owner occupancy in the selected areas of London and Birmingham and in the remainder of each conurbation. The differential between the immigrants and the English is striking. *In the inner London boroughs, 22% of immigrant housing is in owner occupancy in the central Birmingham area 56% of immigrant household heads are owner-occupiers. In both areas this is nearly double the figure for the English.* In the outer Birmingham area, the degree of owner occupancy is particularly high, at almost 74%. The question of how the immigrant manages to pay for his house need not concern us here, but both Rex[6] and Burney[7] have shown how the financial strain of meeting mortgage repayments creates pressure to take in lodgers and paying guests. Our own evidence on the average household size in non-sharing households would certainly lend support to this theory. The evidence from the West Midlands outer tract clearly suggests that the social osmosis which produces a redistribution of immigrants away from their earlier sites of settlement will be achieved by the immigrants purchasing for themselves what is available to their own pockets and tastes. We do not suggest that there has been a move to suburbia. The number of immigrants in this outer area in households without baths suggests that the move has been to the smaller Victorian terrace houses in wards probably adjacent to the wards tabulated in the selected area.

Figures 12.1–3 indicate significant aspects of the immigrant housing situation. Figure 12.1 shows a high average density for persons per room among immigrants. This is a result of larger families and smaller housing units. Figure 12.2 presents informa

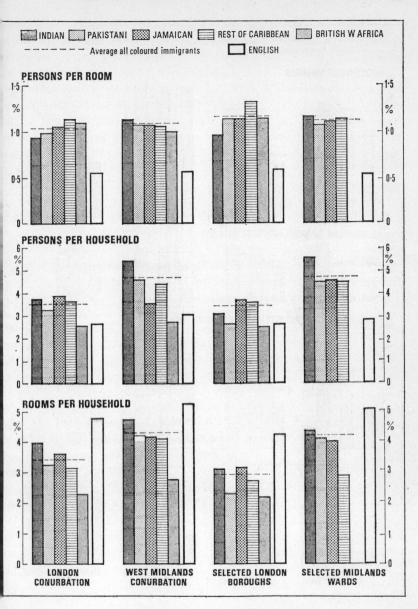

Figure 12.1. Housing density, 1966

Source:
1966 Census, Special Tabulations.

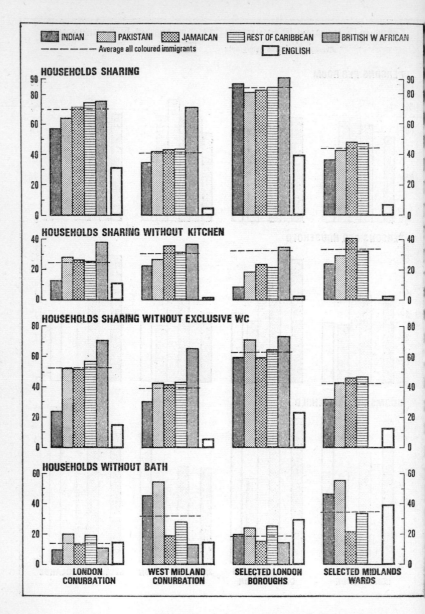

Figure 12.2. Housing, sharing and amenities, 1966

Source :
1966 Census, Special Tabulations

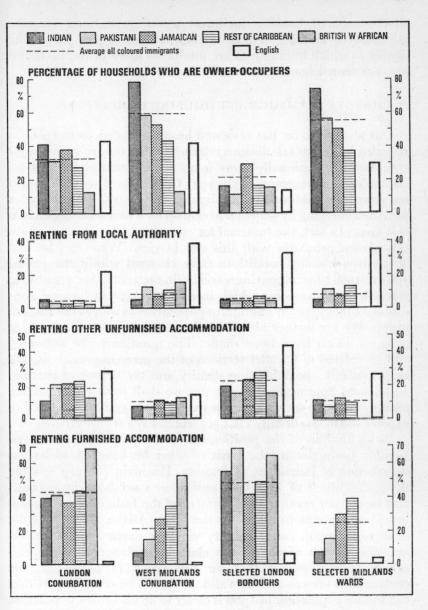

Figure 12.3. Housing tenure, 1966

Source:
1966 Census, Special Tabulations.

L

tion on shared housing facilities; again immigrants are disadvantaged. Housing tenure is indicated in Figure 12.3. The
degree to which immigrants are unable to share in the preferred
areas of rented housing is clearly displayed.

2. CHANGES IN IMMIGRANT HOUSING CONDITIONS,
   1961 TO 1966

Our analysis so far has reviewed housing conditions in 1966, as
revealed by census tabulations relating to the country's two major
conurbations. Nationally there is no housing material which relates solely to immigrants in the 1961 Census, but Davison's report
on Jamaican and other immigrants in central London does
provide something by way of a backdrop for a minor excursion into
this area.[8] In fact, the material for our selected London boroughs
was chosen primarily with this end in view. What can be said
about how housing conditions have changed within the period
1961 to 1966? By comparing various characteristics we are able to
trace the improvements which have been made in housing conditions of the coloured immigrant population as well as the English
group. We are further able to differentiate between the levels of
progress which have been made. The question to be answered
will be related to parallel sections of the preceding analysis. We
shall first talk about housing density and the degree of sharing,
and shared housing facilities. Later we shall review the housing
tenure profile, to see what major explanations can be suggested to
explain the major density changes which have occurred.

In his analysis of the position in 1961, Davison selected seven
London boroughs on the basis of what he believed to be the
distribution of Jamaicans in London. His main concern was the
living conditions of Jamaican and other Caribbean immigrants
and he did not make any adjustment of the Indian and Pakistani
immigrant groups to allow for the white Asians. In view of the
need to maintain comparability we have carried out a similar
analysis, though of course the changing balance of white and
brown Indians means that for this group in particular, the
comparisons are not strictly valid. It should be remembered that
the Indian population in 1966 is closer to an all-brown population
than it was in 1961; that since white Indians are likely to be of
higher social status than the brown, the changes between 1961 and
1966 would be to lower the social status of the total Indian population as the white Indians become a decreasing part of the total.

(a) Housing Density and Shared Accommodation

In 1961, housing density was extremely high in the seven London boroughs, with over 50% of all West Indians living at more than 1·5 persons per room. Table 12.9 shows how this

Table 12.9. Changes in housing density, seven London boroughs, 1961 to 1966.

Area	Percentage of population at more than one and a half persons per room		Percentage of households sharing accommodation		Percentage of persons living in households with less than four rooms	
	1961	1966	1961	1966	1961	1966
India	24	21	52	56	52	41
Pakistan	29	23	57	71	57	54
Jamaica	53	34	76	82	65	53
Other Caribbean	63	43	82	84	83	66
All coloured	52	36	74	79	69	56
Ireland	32	18	50	60	59	40
Cyprus	41	24	51	62	53	43
England	8	3	30	39	40	22

Sources:
1961: R. B. Davison, in *Black British*;
1966: Census, Special Tabulations.

compares with density among the Irish and Cypriot populations, as well as a major control group where the head of household was born in England. Taken on average (over the four coloured groups listed), 52% of coloured immigrants were living at this high density compared with only 8% of the English group. The Irish and Cypriot population take up an intermediate position. By 1966 the amount of this high density living declined, so that only 36% of the aggregated coloured immigrants were at this density, compared with a much reduced 3% in the English population. We have already shown how high housing density related to the number of households in shared accommodation. It is surprising to find that the level of really high density living was reduced to this extent during a period when the degree of sharing increased. In the coloured population 74% of all households were sharing accommodation in 1961, compared with 79% in 1966, an increase of 5%. Moving from a much lower starting level the comparable increase among English sharing households is almost one-third,

from 30% to 39%. We cannot show the total importance of sharing accommodation within this total spectrum of high density
living, but we do have information on the number of households
living in three rooms or less (and many of these would be sharing
accommodation). In 1961, Davison reports that 83% of West
Indians from outside Jamaica were living in three rooms or less;
on average the coloured immigrants had almost 70% of their
population in this type of accommodation, compared with only
40% for the English group. By 1966 these levels had been
reduced to 56% for immigrants and 22% for the English
group.

Without a similar analysis relating to other London boroughs
it is not possible to give any authoritative explanation of how the
degree of sharing accommodation has increased while the degree
of high density living and the number of households in three or
less rooms has declined. These seven boroughs, which by 1961
already had large immigrant populations, provided some of the
earliest areas of immigrant settlement. Between 1961 and 1966 we
suggest that the process of take-over by the immigrant groups was
accelerated during a period when general control of housing
density was tightened up in the hands of the local authorities.
Such a dual process seems to have produced a general lowering of
housing density at the same time as the degree of shared accommodation has increased.

It is perhaps important to point out that while we can review the
housing conditions of particular ethnic minorities in these seven
boroughs in 1961 and 1966, it is by no means certain that we are
talking about the same immigrants. The roles which the areas of
early immigrant settlement play in providing housing are
important, though their nature is complex and not yet well
documented. We have suggested that as immigrant areas become
saturated, other properties are subdivided and enter into the
immigrant housing market; thus the immigrants form a rising
percentage of the total population. Our special tabulations from
the 1966 Census relate to particular boroughs as they were in
1961. Although by 1966 they had been amalgamated with others
into a new configuration of boroughs, we do have some exactly
comparable information on the number of immigrants and
English in these areas at both dates. In 1961 the four immigrant
groups we have mentioned contained only 46,700 persons; by
1966 the comparable figure was 81,600.

Table 12.10. Selected ethnic groups, seven London boroughs, 1961 and 1966

Area of origin	1961	1966
West Indies	39,840	71,980
India and Pakistan	6,870	9,660
Cyprus	8,013	3,620
Ireland	44,270	47,020
England	657,150	608,900

Source:
Censuses, 1961 and 1966.

Among the groups which we can identify (which comprised 83% of the total population of these boroughs in 1961) there has been a population decline of 15,000 persons. This is chiefly made up of an increase of 35,000 coloured immigrants and an offsetting decline of 50,000 in the English population. This process of population replacement has been accompanied by an increase in the degree of sharing accommodation, although it would seem likely that the amount of high density occupation has been curbed by action of local authorities.

In view of the increase in the number of persons in shared households, we might ask what has happened to the level of amenities which these groups enjoy. Table 12.11 shows that the number of households with no bath has declined in both the immigrant and the English groups, immigrants from 25% to 18% of all households, English from 37% to 30% of all households. We have suggested elsewhere that the reason why immigrants are in households with a shared bath rather than without one relates to the type of property subdivision which has been undertaken in the London area. The number of houses with exclusive use of their own water closet has also improved among immigrants and English alike, from 70% to 77% for the English group, from 27% to 59% for immigrants.

When we look into the matter of housing tenure, the apparent inconsistency between increased sharing and a general improvement in the level of housing facilities is easily explained. Taken over the whole area, a significant amount of property has been taken into local authority ownership. The housing tenure of the English group is indicative of the overall picture. In 1961, 13% of

Table 12.11. Changes in housing amenities, seven London boroughs,
1961 to 1966

	Percentage of house-holds with no bath		Percentage of house-holds with exclusive use of water closet	
Area of origin	1961	1966	1961	1966
India	13	13	49	62
Pakistan	17	21	39	36
Jamaica	25	15	26	40
Other Caribbean	32	25	19	35
All Coloured	25	18	27	59
Ireland	37	30	48	58
Cyprus	36	19	48	54
England	37	30	70	77

Sources:
1961: R. B. Davison, in *Black British*; 1966: 1966 Census, Special Tabulations.

the English householders were owner-occupiers and 24% were
renting from the local authority; a further 55% were renting
unfurnished accommodation, while the remaining 7% were in
rented furnished accommodation. By 1966 the degree of owner
occupancy and renting furnished accommodation had not
changed, but about 10% of the whole group had transferred from
renting unfurnished accommodation into the local authority
group. Amalgamating these two groups to avoid the effect of this
transfer we may say that the general distribution between these
three major housing types has not changed for the English group,
remaining at 13%, 77%, and 7% through the spectrum. Among
immigrants, however, there has been a significant transfer out of
the renting furnished category, from 64% of households in 1961 to
only 44% in 1966; about one-quarter of those transferring out
have become owner-occupiers and one-quarter have acquired
council tenancies, while the rest have moved into rented unfurnished accommodation. (See Table 12.2.)

It has already been pointed out that length of stay in an area is
significant in getting a share of that accommodation which everyone wants, namely local authority and rented unfurnished
accommodation. It is interesting to note that immigrants in these

Table 12.12. Changes in housing tenure, seven London boroughs, 1961 to 1966

Percentage of all householders who are:

Area of origin	Owner-occupiers		Renting from local authority		Renting unfurnished		Renting furnished	
	1961	1966	1961	1966	1961	1966	1961	1966
India	16	21	7	10	26	38	48	38
Pakistan	18	12	5	4	16	15	58	69
Jamaica	25	29	1	4	12	24	61	42
Other Caribbean	9	16	1	7	14	28	75	48
All coloured	18	23	2	6	15	26	64	44
Ireland	8	7	15	28	40	38	34	24
Cyprus	34	29	6	12	30	22	28	31
England	13	14	24	33	55	44	7	7

Sources:
1961: R. B. Davison, in Black British;
1966: 1966 Census, Special Tabulations.

selected London boroughs have 32% of households in this sector of the housing supply schedule compared with only 22·3% in the London conurbation as a whole, and only 18% in the West Midlands conurbation. *The process of diffusion into the preferred sectors of the housing market has, however, taken place with little support from the local authority sector. By 1966, only 6% of all coloured immigrants had obtained council tenancies, compared with 28% of Irish immigrants and a third of the English-born population.*

(b) Who Benefits Most?

So far we have simply related changes occurring within the housing spectrum for both the English and the immigrant groups. We have indicated no glaring cases of the English improving their relative position more than the immigrants. Indeed, since the immigrants in 1961 are at a different level in the housing market, more sharing, more high density living, less facilities, and so on, it is difficult to decide how we should evaluate the degree of change which has been described. An example may be instructive. The percentage of population living at more than one person per room has declined from 23% to 13% in the English control group and from 71% to 61% in the aggregated immigrant group. Who shall say which improvement is the more significant? If we take the percentage improvement, the percentage of all people at this high density has declined by 43% for the English group but only by 15% for the combined immigrant population. But what exactly does that tell us?

When we come to compare the rate of improvement among various immigrant groups, we find it more open to reasonable analysis since, on the whole, we are operating at about the same level of amenities as at the starting point of our analysis. A method of calculating the percentage change in each variable from 1961 to 1966 and then ranking the degree of improvement allows some general analysis of which groups have fared well out of the changes and which not so well. On eight out of nine housing scores the Pakistani group is distinguished by a particularly poor record. Indeed, there are some cases where the trend for the Pakistani population has been contrary to the general one. For example, the degree of owner occupation has declined and the degree of renting furnished accommodation has increased from 58% to 69%. But we should point out that the sample of persons in these wards was very small. A total of only 250 households (a full count of those the census enumerated) is not a very firm basis for the generalization which the material suggests. The people who have distinguished themselves by a successful rate of improvements are the Caribbeans from outside Jamaica. The degree of very high density (over 1·5 persons per room) has declined markedly and in housing tenure there has been a movement from rented furnished accommodation into owner occupation and into local authority housing. By 1966 35% of all 'other Caribbeans' households were in local authority or rented unfurnished accommodation, which is high in relation to other recent immigrants in this area and to immigrants in the London and West Midlands conurbations generally (see Table 12.8).

But we should again remark that the group which has shown the highest degree of improvement from 1961 was at that date the most disadvantaged; at that date it had an average rank score on nine different measures of 6·7, where the rank of 7 indicates the lowest position. We should also note that the Pakistanis were not so heavily at a disadvantage in 1961 with an average rank score of 4·3. Thus the Pakistanis have moved downwards in the housing market from a less serious position in 1961. This is consistent with other information suggesting that the more recent immigrants are from East Pakistan where the general standard of living is lower than in West Pakistan.

Table 12.13 provides a summary of how the average standard of housing has changed from 1961 to 1966 and also indicates some measure of how the absolute levels stood at both dates. Rather than use an amalgam of absolute figures we have ranked the various ethnic groups on each of the variables and calculated an average rank score. It is very clear that West Indians have enjoyed the greatest improvement, while, as we have indicated above, the Pakistanis' relative position has deteriorated.

However, the rapid improvements which have taken place in living conditions of those West Indians from outside Jamaica has only been sufficient to reduce the degree of variation in housing conditions. That their level of housing amenities in 1966 was still the lowest except for the Pakistanis is substantially the result of a large increase in the number of their people who moved into these boroughs during the previous five years, an increase which was accompanied by a considerable increase in average household size.

In terms of the social costs of poor housing it is important to

Table 12.13. Average rankings* on housing characteristics and average household size, selected London boroughs, 1961 and 1966

Area of origin	Level of housing amenity 1961	Level of housing amenity 1966	Degree of improvement 1961–6	Average household size 1961	Average household size 1966
India	3·0	2·8	3·7	2·79	2·94
Pakistan	4·3	5·2	6·6	2·75	2·69
Jamaica	5·7	4·2	2·9	3·28	3·73
Other Caribbean	6·7	5·2	1·8	2·84	3·57
Ireland	3·7	2·6	3·8	3·18	3·17
Cyprus	3·1	3·4	5·1	4·23	3·38
England	1·4	1·4	4·6	2·74	2·66

* Highest ranking 1.

Sources
Calculation for 1961, R. B. Davison, in *Black* *British*; and 1966 Census, Special Tabulations

review average household size, both in cause and effect, in relation to restricted housing facilities. We suggest that the ravages of overcrowding and shared housing facilities are more serious among groups where the average household size is larger, just because this probably means there are more children in the households. Conversely, sharing may enforce less hardship among two-person families, particularly where both partners are out at work during the day. But it is precisely these smaller households which fit more easily into shared accommodation, and this is generally a concomitant of high density and poor housing facilities. The final two columns of Table 12.13 show average household size among all ethnic groups at both dates of our analysis. There has been a slight decline in average household size among the English control group, consistent with the slight increase in the amount of sharing. It is, therefore, significant that on balance this has occurred without any relative deterioration in the average housing level. Equally, that the Irish have improved their level of living with no increase in average household size suggests the relative competitive strength of the longer settled residents of the community.

In contrast, changes among the coloured immigrants tend to bear out the hypothesis suggested above, that improvements are partly a result of some of the larger households being forced out of the worst shared accommodation. Cypriots have a reduced level of

ousing amenity and smaller households, and Pakistanis, already
eparated out on account of their relatively poor performance,
ave a significant decline in level of housing conditions with only a
light fall in average household size. At the other end of the spec-
rum the improvements among West Indians are accompanied
by a substantial increase in the number of persons in each house-
old.

A comparison of the level of housing amenity in 1966 with
average household size at that date provides a useful summary to
his brief analysis of the dynamics of changing housing conditions
n this area. It is very clear that the West Indians have experienced
a considerable improvement in their level of housing conditions
over the period of analysis and it is comforting to think that the
action of the local authority in stepping up the degree of local
authority ownership has reduced the overall degree of variation
n housing standards from one ethnic group to another. But considering the level of housing standards in 1966 with average
household size at that date, it is amply clear that it is still the West
Indians who form the most disadvantaged group. The evidence is
that the changes introduced have not been more than a palliative
to poor housing conditions in these areas. In the face of the tremendous increase in the number of immigrant residents in these
boroughs from 1961 to 1966, much remains to be completed
before anything like an even distribution of housing resources will
be achieved.

NOTES TO CHAPTER 12

1. R. B. Davison, *Black British* (London, Oxford University Press, for the Institute of Race Relations, 1966).

2. Unpublished research papers of the British Universities Census Tracts Committee, E. Gittus, *et al.*

3. Elizabeth Burney, *Housing on Trial* (London, Oxford University Press, for Institute of Race Relations, 1967).

4. The special study area referred to in J. Rex and R. Moore, *Race, Community and Conflict* (London, Oxford University Press, for Institute of Race Relations, 1967) includes a high proportion of large Victorian houses. Sparkbrook cannot be taken as typical of the whole of the Birmingham or Wolverhampton inner wards.

5. P. Willmott and M. Young, *Family and Kinship in East London* (London, Routledg and Kegan Paul, 1957).
6. Rex, op. cit.
7. Burney, op. cit.
8. Davison, op. cit.

3 Employment

In order to assess the information available from the 1966 Census on the position of the Commonwealth immigrant in the field of employment, the analysis in this chapter will be sub-divided into seven sections. The first five sections will look at, in turn, economic activity rates, industrial status, and distribution by occupation, industry, and socio-economic group. A further section, utilizing both the Census and Ministry of Labour data, will examine unemployment. Each of the foregoing analyses will be looking at the same population from a different viewpoint, whilst in the last section an attempt will be made to present a more composite picture of the coloured immigrant in employment.

Unfortunately, it has not proved possible to present estimates of the Indian and Pakistani population excluding the white Indians,* as has been done in the previous chapters. This is due to the fact that it has been more difficult to estimate the activity rates and employment position of white Indians than their demographic structure, housing, and fertility. What can be stated is that their occupational distribution is more heavily concentrated at the upper end of the employment scale and that the distribution given for Indians in the tables that follow should probably be adjusted downwards for occupations of higher status. How far this correction should be made, however, is not readily apparent. The proportion of white Indians amongst the total Indian-born in the West Midlands is lower than in Greater London and, therefore, the West Midland figures probably give a truer picture of the position of Indian immigrants. It should also be remembered that there is a component of professional Indians (and Pakistanis) in the enumerated population. This is of greatest importance in the London area, so that, even after the exclusion of white Indians, we would expect the Greater London occupational distribution to be slanted towards higher status employment than that for the West Midlands.

Throughout the sections on employment that follow those

* In this context white Indians refers to those persons born in India or Pakistan of European (usually English) parentage.

immigrant groups that fell below a certain size are excluded. Thi means that, apart from economic activity rates, no information given on Pakistani females in either conurbation, or India females in the West Midlands. No information of any kind is give for persons born in British West Africa or Cyprus for the Wes Midlands conurbation. Information for persons born in the 'Re of the Caribbean' for the West Midlands is in certain instance merged with figures for 'All the Caribbean'.

1. ECONOMIC ACTIVITY

All the male immigrant groups in both conurbations, with on exception, have higher proportions of their population (15 yea and over) economically active* compared to the population as whole (see Table 13.1). The reason is mainly that the proportio of retired persons in the immigrant groups is far lower than for th total population. All groups have higher rates of economic activit in the West Midlands than in Greater London; this is mainly du to the presence of large student populations in London whic reduce the proportion of those economically active (see Appendi III.5 for figures of retired and students).

For women the position is more mixed (see Table 13.1), an in both London and the West Midlands, West Indian wome have substantially higher rates of economic activity compared t the total population. Whilst the Indian and Pakistani women hav economic activity rates fairly similar to those of the total popula tion in London, their rates in the West Midlands are very muc lower. The reason for this major difference is probably to be foun in the nature of the population enumerated as born in India whic was discussed earlier. In this context the economic activity rat for the West Midlands seem more significant than those fc London.

The position of African men, whose economic activity rates an at striking variance with all other groups, is explicable when on looks at the figures for students (see Appendix III.5). Nearly on third are students, and it is this factor which gives them their ver low economic activity rate. Among African women there is also very high proportion of students, but despite this they have a hig economic activity rate. It is worth noting that if one conside persons coming to this country to study as a separate, distinc

---

* Persons are defined as economically active if they are in employment or if they a seeking employment.

Table 13.1. Percentage of population (15 and over) economically active, for selected birthplace groups and the total population, Greater London conurbation and West Midlands conurbation, by sex, 1966

Birthplace	Males		Females		Females (adjusted for part-time work)†	
	Greater London conurbation	West Midlands conurbation	Greater London conurbation	West Midlands conurbation	Greater London conurbation	West Midlands conurbation
India	88·5	92·9	50·3	16·0	46·4	14·2
Pakistan	89·9	97·6	43·4	17·0	41·0	16·0
Jamaica	94·5	97·1	66·4	66·4	63·7	63·2
Rest of Caribbean	92·4	97·7	67·0	65·7	63·6	60·8
All of Caribbean	93·5	97·2	66·7	66·3	63·7	62·7
British West Africa	64·9	*	63·0	*	61·7	*
Cyprus	89·4	*	46·9	*	45·0	*
Total population	85·8	87·5	49·6	48·1	42·4	39·5

* The sample enumerated is too small and economic activity is not calculated.
† Female percentages have been adjusted on the basis that a person in part-time work is treated as 50% economically active, whilst a person in full-time work is fully economically active.

Sources:
1966 10% Sample Census, Special Tabulations; figures for total population from Table 13, *Economic Activity Tables*, Part I, H.M.S.O.

group from the resident immigrant population, then the economic activity rates of nearly all the immigrant groups would be even higher, especially for males in London.

Between 1961 and 1966 there was little change in the economic activity rates of Indians, Pakistanis, and Caribbeans in the Greater London conurbation. All the male groups showed marginal increases, whilst the females remained fairly steady. One would have expected that with the number of births and the increasing arrivals of dependent children between 1961 and 1966, the very high economic activity rates of West Indian women would have fallen, but this did not happen.

In general, therefore, it can be said that the immigrant groups have higher economic activity rates than those of the total population. This is less true of women, though West Indian women (the biggest numerical group) are much more likely to be working or looking for work than the total population. If one makes an adjustment to activity rates for part-time work (as is done in Table 13.1), then the differences between West Indian women and the total population are further accentuated, due to the much higher proportion of the total population who only work part time.

2. INDUSTRIAL STATUS

An analysis of industrial status identifies those groups within any population employed in an industrial society who are in a minority; for example, the self-employed and managers. The majority of the population, immigrant and total, is found in the residual category 'other employees'. In this analysis of industrial status, reference will often be made to this residual category, and in the data presented in Table 13.2 it is also more statistically significant than the other categories, in which numbers enumerated were often small. In effect, the 'other employees' category represents the rank and file of the employed population—that is, those not in authority (managers, etc.) or partly insulated from authority (professionals, etc.). Thus, one can say that the percentage of any population falling into the 'other employees' category gives an approximate indication of those who have failed to climb the ladder of our hierarchical society.

The data presented in Table 13.2 show the industrial status of men in both conurbations, and it can be seen that all the immigrant groups have higher proportions of their population in the 'other employees' category than the total population for either area. Cypriots, who are only marginally more represented in this category than the total population, have a very high proportion—nearly a fifth of their population—in the self-employed category. All the other immigrant groups are far less well represented in the ranks of the self-employed than the total population. Similarly, no immigrant group is as well represented as the total population in the managerial, foreman, and supervisors category. This is especially true of the West Indian group in London and all the immigrant groups in the West Midlands. In general, the status of all immigrant groups is less favourable in the West Midlands than in London, which is also illustrated by the relative size of the 'other employees' group in the two areas.

One way of expressing the data presented in Table 13.2 is to say that whilst three out of every ten of the total population have succeeded in climbing out of the 'other employees' category in Greater London, only one out of twenty Jamaicans has so succeeded. In the West Midlands, the comparative picture is one in four for the total population, but only one in ten for Indians and three out of a hundred for Jamaicans and Pakistanis.

For women the differences between the immigrant groups and the total population are less significant than for men. This is mainly because, even in the total population, only a very small proportion (about one-tenth) fall outside the 'other employees' category. All the immigrant groups are under-represented in the managerial category and generally over-represented in the trainee category. However, all the female immigrant groups have a larger proportion in the residual group than the total population.

In summarizing the information on industrial status it is worth repeating that all the immigrant groups of both sexes in both conurbations were markedly under-represented in the managerial group. This under-representation was least for the Indians in London, and this fact, together with the contrasting profiles of Indians in London and the West Midlands, serves to confirm our earlier remarks concerning the nature of the population enumerated as born in India in the Census.

An interesting sidelight is to compare the two West Indian groups with one another. Whilst West Indians are generally regarded as a homogeneous group by the English, it will be seen from Table 13.2 that the Rest of the Caribbean group has a

M

Table 13.2. Industrial status of those in employment for selected birthp[lace] groups, by percentage, by sex, 1966

(a) *Males—Greater London conurbation*

	India	Pakistan	Jamaica	Rest of Caribbean	All Caribbean	British West Africa	Cyprus	To[tal] popul[ation]
*Number in employment**	35,470	9,140	32,400	29,340	61,740	7,940	17,940	2,41[0]
Self-employed	3·7	6·0	1·5	1·2	1·4	0·9	19·6	7
Managers, foremen, and supervisors	8·3	4·4	1·1	2·7	1·9	2·9	5·9	15
Apprentices, articled clerks, and formal trainees	4·2	4·7	1·9	2·5	2·2	7·9	3·2	4
Professional employees	8·2	4·2	0·4	1·2	0·8	5·7	1·7	4
Other employees	75·6	80·7	95·1	92·4	93·8	92·6	69·7	69

(b) *Males—West Midlands conurbation*

	India	Pakistan	Jamaica	Rest of Caribbean	All Caribbean	To[tal] popul[ation]
*Number in employment**	12,450	11,170	13,050	3,290	16,340	763,
Self-employed	2·9	1·8	0·8	1·5	0·9	4
Managers, foremen, and supervisors	2·2	0·7	0·3	0·9	0·4	12
Apprentices, articled clerks, and formal trainees	2·9	0·3	1·8	3·3	2·1	4
Professional employees	2·6	0·3	0·2	0·3	0·2	3
Other employees	89·5	97·0	96·9	93·9	96·3	75

* Figures for the number in employment have been multiplied by ten, as the size of the sar[...] was 10% of the total population.

Sou[...]

1966 10% Sample Census, Special Tabulations; and figures for [...] population from Table 13, *Economic Activity Tables*, Part I, H.M.[...]

marginally higher industrial status than that of the Jamaican group. This difference also holds true for women in both conurbations.

The large proportion of Cypriots who are self-employed is almost certainly a reflection of their concentration in the catering and clothing industries. Similarly, the over-representations in some female immigrant groups of trainees is probably due to the presence of large numbers of student nurses. Taking these two points into consideration and allowing for the ambiguities in the Indian census sample, it seems fair to conclude that the industrial status of the selected immigrant groups under examination is considerably lower than that for the total population.

3. OCCUPATION

The occupational distribution of male immigrant groups in London shows a fairly wide spread over a number of occupations with considerable diversity between different groups. There are no overwhelming concentrations (except possibly for Cypriots) of any immigrant group in any occupation. Table 13.3, which shows those occupation orders* in which 7·5% or more of any immigrant group were enumerated by the Census, illustrates this point. Contrary to popular belief, the majority of West Indians are not transport workers. Although the category of Transport and Communication workers is one of the most important, it only contains just over 15% of economically active males.

In the West Midlands the pattern for male immigrants shows greater concentration and less difference between each immigrant group. Over one-fifth of the males of each immigrant group are labourers and this rises to over one-half for Pakistanis. A large percentage of these labourers work in engineering and allied trades. Contrasts which appear between London and the West Midlands are most apparent for the Indian and Pakistani-born populations. Whilst both groups in London are fairly well represented in clerical and professional jobs and have low percentages in labouring jobs, the reverse occurs in the West Midlands.

There is a certain similarity between male and female patterns. Indian-born women are very well represented in clerical and professional jobs in London; the most important occupations for West Indian women are service jobs (over one-quarter). Cypriot

---

* The Census divides the population into twenty-seven major divisions (occupation orders) and over 200 minor sub-divisions (unit groups).

Table 13.3. Distribution in major occupations* for selected birthplace gr{
by percentage, by sex, 1966

(a) *Males—Greater London conurbation*

	India	Pakistan	Jamaica	Rest of Caribbean	All Caribbean	British West Africa	Cyprus	T{ popu
Number economically active†	*36,530*	*9,440*	*33,710*	*30,240*	*63,950*	*8,480*	*18,700*	*2,46{*
Selected occupations								
VII. Engineering and allied trades workers n.e.c.‡	13·7	11·0	17·4	15·4	16·4	12·1	9·1	1{
VIII. Woodworkers	—	—	9·1	7·7	8·4	—	—	2{
XI. Clothing Workers	—	8·1	—	—	—	—	9·3	1
XVIII. Labourers n.e.c.	—	—	20·7	15·1	18·1	—	—	6
XIX. Transport and communications workers	7·6	—	12·4	18·3	15·2	10·7	—	10
XXI. Clerical workers	17·9	12·9	—	—	—	21·8	—	11
XXIII. Service, sport, and recreation workers	—	13·2	—	—	—	—	33·9	7
XXV. Professional, technical workers, artists	18·1	12·3	—	—	—	17·5	—	11

(b) *Males—West Midlands conurbation*

	India	Pakistan	Jamaica	All Caribbean	T{ popu{
Number economically active†	*12,630*	*11,470*	*13,530*	*16,910*	*777.*
Selected occupations					
V. Furnace, forge, foundry, rolling mill workers	15·9	—	8·6	7·8	4
VII. Engineering and allied trades workers n.e.c.	19·2	22·3	25·3	25·7	28
XVIII. Labourers n.e.c.	26·6	53·1	22·9	22·5	7
110. Labourers n.e.c. in engineering and allied trades§	*9·9*	*37·4*	*11·8*	*11·9*	*3*
XIX. Transport and communications	—	—	9·8	10·3	6

* Footnotes opposite, p. 157

le 13.3—*cont.*

(c) *Females—Greater London conurbation*

	India	Jamaica	Rest of Caribbean	All Caribbean	British West Africa	Cyprus	Total population
ber economically active†	*16,220*	*23,510*	*20,340*	*43,850*	*5,150*	*8,170*	*1,611,140*
ed Occupations							
Clothing workers	—	15·6	10·8	13·4	7·6	64·5	4·7
Warehousemen, store-epers, packers, bottlers	—	—	—	—	11·1	—	3·5
I. Clerical workers	45·5	7·5	13·4	10·2	21·4	8·1	35·7
9. Typists, shorthand riters, secretaries	*26·9*	*—*	*—*	*—*	*7·8*	*—*	*13·9*
o. Clerks, cashiers	*16·5*	*—*	*—*	*—*	*10·3*	*—*	*18·9*
II. Service, sport, and creation workers	9·9	27·9	22·2	25·3	17·5	13·6	21·4
V. Professional, technical orkers, artists	18·6	13·5	22·0	17·4	19·0	—	10·4
3. Nurses	*—*	*12·8*	*14·3*	*13·5*	*13·4*	*—*	*3·9*

(d) *Females—West Midlands conurbation*

	Jamaica	All Caribbean	Total population
Number economically active†	*7,720*	*9,670*	*447,110*
Selected occupations			
VII. Engineering and allied trades workers n.e.c.	39·5	37·8	15·0
XXIII. Service, sport, and recreation workers	14·2	14·5	20·4
XXV. Professional, technical workers, artists	15·9	16·4	7·4
183. Nurses	*15·8*	*16·3*	*2·7*

rcentages have been shown for immigrant groups only in those occupations where 7·5% or e of the economically active are enumerated. A dash (—) does not mean that no members of group were in that particular occupation but only that less than 7·5% were enumerated. gures for the number economically active have been multiplied by ten as the size of the ple was 10% of the total population.
.e.c.' after an occupational description means 'Not Elsewhere Classified'.
nit groups (identified by 3-digit code numbers) are sub-divisions of the occupation order ntified by Roman numerals) directly above them.

Sources:
1966 10% Sample Census, Special Tabulations; figures for total population from Table 13, *Economic Activity Tables*, Part I, H.M.S.O.

women are the great exception, where nearly two-thirds are clothing workers. In the West Midlands, engineering occupations are the most important for West Indian women (over one-third). Nursing, whilst it is an important occupation for West Indian women, is not the largest in either conurbation.

How does the occupational distribution of the immigrants compare with that of the population as a whole? In Table 13.4 some of the major differences are shown for men, and some indication is given of those occupations in which immigrants are either heavily under- or over-represented. In London, the greatest over-representation is for Cypriots in service occupations and, to a lesser extent, for West Indians as labourers. Africans and Indians are over-represented and West Indians under-represented in clerical and professional occupations. Other occupations in which immigrant groups were over-represented include West Indians as woodworkers and transport and communications workers, and Pakistanis and Cypriots as clothing workers. In the West Midlands, there was a very large over-representation of all male groups, especially of Pakistanis, as labourers. The other major over-representation was of Indians as furnace, forge, foundry, and rolling mill workers.

Table 13.4. Over- or under-representation* of different immigrant groups in different occupations, 1966

(a) *Males—Greater London conurbation*

Occupation	India	Pakistan	Jamaica	Rest of Caribbean	All Caribbean	British West Africa	Cyprus
VIII. Woodworkers			+	+	+		
XI. Clothing workers		+					+
XVIII. Labourers n.e.c.			+ +	+	+ +		
XIX. Transport and communications workers				+	+		−
XXI. Clerical workers	+		−	−	−	+ +	−
XXII. Sales workers			−	−	−	−	
XXIII. Service, sport, and recreation workers	+						+ + +
XXIV. Administrators and managers			−	−	−		
XXV. Professional, technical workers, artists	+		−	−	−	+	−

Table 13.4.—*cont.*

(b) *Males—West Midlands conurbation*

Occupation	India	Pakistan	Jamaica	All Caribbean
V. Furnace, forge, foundry, rolling mill workers	+ +			
VII. Engineering and allied trades workers n.e.c.	–	–		
XVIII. Labourers n.e.c.	+ +	+ + + +	+ +	+ +
110. Labourers n.e.c. in engineering and allied trades	+	+ + +	+	+
XIX. Transport and communications workers	–			
XXI. Clerical workers		–		
XXII. Sales workers	–		–	–
XXV. Professional, technical workers, artists	–		–	–

* Over- or under-representation has been calculated from the difference between the percentage of those in employment for the immigrant group in question in a particular occupation and the percentage of the total population in the same occupation. Only differences of 5% or more are shown and plus (+) denotes over-representation, minus (–) under-representation of the immigrant group in comparison to the total population.

+ or –	Difference between 5% and 9·9% inclusive
+ + or – –	Difference between 10% and 19·9% inclusive
+ + + or – – –	Difference between 20% and 34·9% inclusive
+ + + + or – – – –	Difference between 35% and 49·9% inclusive

Sources:
1966 10% Sample Census, Special Tabulations; Table 13, *Economic Activity Tables*, Part I, H.M.S.O.

For women (not shown in Table 13.4), in London the greatest over-concentration was as clothing workers for Cypriots and, to a much less degree, for West Indians. In the West Midlands, West Indian women were very heavily over-represented in engineering jobs. They were also over-represented in both conurbations as nurses.

One way of contrasting the occupational distribution of immigrant groups with that of the total population is to compare their numbers in the main 'white-collar' jobs—that is, clerical, sales, administrative, and professional jobs. The 'white-collar' analysis is shown in Table 13.5, and it will be seen that for males in London there were very considerable differences between the different groups. Both Indians and Africans were better represented than

Table 13.5. Distribution in main 'white-collar' occupations of selec
birthplace groups by percentage, by sex, 1966

(a) *Males—Greater London conurbation*

	India	Pakistan	Jamaica	Rest of Caribbean	All Caribbean	British West Africa	Cyprus	Tot popul
Number economically active*	36,530	9,440	33,710	30,240	63,950	8,480	18,700	2,468
Occupation								
XXI. Clerical workers	17·9	12·9	1·9	5·6	3·6	21·8	3·3	11
XXII. Sales workers	5·9	4·8	0·8	1·0	0·9	1·3	5·7	8
XXIV. Administrators and managers	3·4	2·0	0·2	0·5	0·3	1·3	1·4	5
XXV. Professional, technical workers, artists	18·1	12·3	1·6	4·7	3·0	17·5	3·6	11
Total % of E.A. in above occupations	45·3	32·0	4·5	11·8	7·8	41·9	14·0	36

(b) *Males—West Midlands conurbation*

	India	Pakistan	Jamaica	All Caribbean	Tot popul
Number economically active*	12,630	11,470	13,530	16,910	777,
Occupation					
XXI. Clerical workers	1·7	0·9	0·5	0·7	5
XXII. Sales workers	3·6	1·2	0·4	0·4	6
XXIV. Administrators and managers	0·9	0·1	—	0·1	4
XXV. Professional, technical workers, artists	5·9	1·0	0·8	1·4	8
Total % of E.A. in above occupations	12·1	3·2	1·7	2·6	24

* Footnotes on p. 162

le 13.5—*cont.*

(c) *Females—Greater London conurbation*

	India	Jamaica	Rest of Caribbean	All Caribbean	British West Africa	Cyprus	Total population
ber economically active* bation	*16,220*	*23,310*	*20,340*	*43,850*	*5,150*	*8,170*	*1,611,140*
. Clerical workers	45·5	7·5	13·4	10·2	21·4	8·1	35·7
I. Sales workers	5·7	1·3	1·5	1·4	1·4	3·3	10·0
V. Administrators and anagers	1·2	0·2	0·1	0·1	0·8	0·4	1·1
. Professional, etc.,	18·6	13·5	22·0	17·4	19·0	1·8	10·4
of whom 183 Nurses†	*1·0*	*12·8*	*14·3*	*13·5*	*13·4*	*0·5*	*3·9*
l % of E.A. in above cupations	71·0	22·5	37·0	29·1	42·6	13·6	57·2
l % of E.A. in above cupations (excluding nurses)	70·0	9·7	22·7	15·6	29·2	13·1	53·4

Table 13.5—*cont.*

(d) *Females—West Midlands conurbation*

	Jamaica	All Caribbean	Total population
Number economically active*	7,720	9,670	447,110
Occupation			
XXI. Clerical workers	2·3	2·5	26·3
XXII. Sales workers	0·9	1·2	11·1
XXIV. Administrators and managers	—	—	0·5
XXV. Professionals, etc.,	15·9	16·4	7·4
of whom 183 Nurses†	*15·8*	*16·3*	*2·7*
Total % of E.A. in above occupations	19·1	20·1	45·3
Total % of E.A. in above occupations (excluding nurses)	3·3	3·8	42·6

* Figures for the number economically active have been multiplied by ten as the size o
sample was 10% of the total population.
† Unit Group 183 nurses is a sub-division of occupation order XXV Professional, Tech
Workers, Artists.

Sou
1966 10% Sample Census, Special Tabulat
Table 13, *Economic Activity Tables*, Part I, H.M.

the total population, and Pakistanis were only slightly under-represented compared with the total population. The representation of the West Indian groups (especially Jamaicans) and Cypriots was markedly inferior to that of the total population in 'white-collar' occupations.

In the West Midlands, all the male immigrant groups were badly under-represented in 'white-collar' jobs and all were less successful in this respect in the West Midlands than in London, even allowing for the differences in occupational structure between the two areas. Indians were the best represented of all immigrant groups in these jobs, their percentage being about half the percentage of the total population, but Pakistanis and West Indians were hardly represented at all in these occupational categories.

For women, the 'white-collar' or 'white-blouse' analysis in Table 13.5 includes and excludes nurses; throughout the text nurses will be excluded when referring to 'white-blouse' occupations.* In London, Indian women were better represented in these jobs than the total population, whilst all the other immigrant groups were heavily under-represented. Women born in Africa and the Rest of the Caribbean fared about half as well as the total population, but Cypriots and Jamaicans only one-quarter as well. In the West Midlands, West Indian women did very much worse than the total population in 'white-blouse' jobs and were much worse represented than their sisters in London in these jobs.

Up to now we have only discussed occupational distribution at one moment in time (1966). To assess the nature of change over time we need to examine 1961 data as well, but unfortunately these are available for London only, therefore limiting this aspect of our study. Whilst the percentage of men in the total population in 'white-collar' jobs increased between 1961 and 1966, all the immigrant groups showed a drop in the proportion of males in these jobs (Table 13.6). This decrease was greatest for the Indians and least for the West Indians. For women, all groups, including the total population, showed increases in the percentage in 'white-blouse' occupations between 1961 and 1966. However, Jamaicans, who in 1961 were the least well-represented group, showed the smallest increase in the five-year period (Table 13.6).

* Nurses are excluded from the analysis of 'white-blouse' occupations in order to highlight a position which might otherwise be masked by their inclusion. This is especially so in view of the high concentrations of certain immigrant groups in this occupation.

Table 13.6. Comparison of percentage in 'white-collar' occupations in the Greater London conurbation, 1961 and 1966, for selected birthplace groups and the total population

| | Males | | Females* | |
	1961	1966	1961	1966
India	50·2	45·3	66·8	70·0
Pakistan	34·5	32·0	—	—
Jamaica	4·8	4·5	7·5	9·7
Rest of Caribbean	11·9	11·8	15·1	22·7
All Caribbean	8·0	7·8	10·6	15·6
Total population	35·8	36·9	51·1	53·4

* Female data exclude persons enumerated in sub-unit 183 nurses at both dates.

Sources:
1966 figures from Table 13.5; 1961 figures calculated from Table A.4 Census 1961, England and Wales, Commonwealth Immigrants in the Conurbations, H.M.S.O.

As far as other occupations are concerned West Indian men became slightly more concentrated and over-represented as wood-workers, transport workers, and engineering workers in London. These occupations were three of the four most important for West Indians, but in the fourth, labouring, there was a decline both in concentration and in over-representation. The concentration of West Indian women in nursing also declined between 1961 and 1966.

Before attempting to draw any conclusions from the analysis of occupation, certain points need to be made concerning the nature of the enumerated groups. The problem of interpreting census data concerning persons born in India has already been referred to. The evidence on occupational distribution, especially the comparison for men between London and the West Midlands, seems amply to confirm the suspicions that persons born in India enumerated in London are atypical. This is not only because of the large numbers of white Indians but also because there is a heavy concentration of middle-class and professional Indians in London. Thus, the data for the West Midlands give a much truer representation of the profile of the typical Indian immigrant. This conclusion applies—although to a more limited degree—to the Pakistani immigrant as well. Certain inferences can also be drawn regarding the African population which seem to differentiate that group from the typical immigrant situation. Approximately one-third of the male African population (15 and over) are students, and it would seem fair to hypothesize that a very large proportion of the African working population are ex-students whose educational attainments are very much higher on average than those of any other immigrant group or of the total population. The occupational distribution of Africans would tend to confirm this assessment of the nature of the African population. We propose, therefore, in what follows, to refer rather less to Indians, Pakistanis, and Africans in London and more to what are regarded as typical immigrant groups.

Certain general assessments of the position of coloured immigrants are possible. The occupational distribution of immigrant groups differs not only from the general population but also from each other. In general terms, immigrants are less well-represented than the total population in those occupations usually considered most desirable, and over-represented in those occupations considered most undesirable. In many respects the over-concentration of immigrants in labouring jobs is even more disturbing than their virtual absence in 'white-collar' jobs, especially in the West Midlands. Again, occupationally, coloured immigrants are not a homogeneous group; one must discuss the separate situations of Indians, Pakistanis, and West Indians. Even this is often a gross over-generalization, as can be seen for West Indians, where persons born in the Rest of the Caribbean consistently show higher percentages in 'white-collar' jobs and lower percentages in labouring jobs than Jamaicans, and this is so in both conurbations.

Within immigrant groups there are also differences in occupational structure between London and the West Midlands that are not wholly explicable by the overall differences of the occupational structure of the two areas. All immigrant groups show a less favourable occupational structure in the West Midlands, and whilst this may be due in part to a difference in the kind of persons enumerated and in the overall occupational structure in the two areas, it may also indicate the differing attitudes of the population in the two areas to the employment of coloured immigrants.

Implicit in this discussion is the assumption that before any immigrant group can be regarded as having achieved some sort of reasonable *modus vivendi* within the field of employment, its members must have a comparable opportunity to that of the general population. It must be equally possible for them to achieve a wide variety of occupations, especially those that are generally regarded as the elite occupations. We know that this stage has certainly not yet been reached, but there is no direct information from the Census as to the causes. In general, the unfavourable occupation distribution of the immigrant can be ascribed to two reasons. Firstly, inadequate skills, education, or, in general, factors personal to the immigrant, and secondly, the attitudes of the general population to the employment of the immigrant.

One can approach this question obliquely by examining the fact that West Indian women are heavily over-represented in nursing. It seems fair to state that the skill and educational levels of nurses are certainly not less than the majority of 'white-blouse' occupations examined in Table 13.5. It is therefore pertinent to note that in the West Midlands nurses were four times as numerous as 'white-blouse' workers for West Indians, but for the total population the situation was completely reversed and there were sixteen times as many 'white-blouse' workers as nurses. The reasons for these immense differences are complex, but it seems fair to suppose that the reasons why West Indian women are markedly under-represented in 'white-blouse' occupations cannot be solely their lack of suitable qualifications, but must also include in some measure the disinclination of the general population to see them in these occupations. It is also unlikely that the skill levels of West Indian men and women are so disparate that the under-representation of West Indian men in 'white-collar' jobs is not also due in part to the same reasons.

Finally, and most crucially, an examination of the data for London in 1961 and 1966 showed no sign of the occupational structure of immigrants coming any closer to the occupational structure of the total population. What changes there were, as far as West Indian men were concerned, showed very slight moves to greater concentration in certain occupations; there was no evidence that between 1961 and 1966 they were moving into those occupations in which they were markedly under-represented.

4. INDUSTRY

A further approach to the examination of the employment structure of immigrant groups is to look at their distribution by industry. This is a completely separate operation from the preceding section on occupation; it may be confusing to the reader a many of the names used for occupation and industry orders are similar. Specifically, this section refers to the industry in which a person works, whatever his job, whilst the previous section dealt with the job a person did, whatever the industry in which he worked. Thus, a transport and communication worker (occupation) can work in any industry, and workers in the transport and communications industry can have any occupation. In some instances, such as clothing workers in the clothing industry, the figures for occupation and industry closely reflect one another, but in many instances there is very little relation between the two different sets of figures. (An extreme example of this is that in 1961 only 10% of Commonwealth immigrants working in the construction industry were defined occupationally as construction workers.)

The major details of the distribution of the different immigrant groups in 1966 is shown in the Table In Appendix III.6. Only a few salient points will be discussed here. As with occupation, the industrial distributions of the immigrant groups differ one from another and show a greater diversity in London than in the West Midlands, but this is in part a reflection of the different industrial structures of the two areas. The largest concentrations of male immigrant workers in London are those of Cypriots, in miscellaneous services (mainly catering), and West Indians, especially those born in the Rest of Caribbean, in the transport and communications industry. Apart from these two industries, no other employs more than a fifth of any male immigrant group. In the West Midlands, however, there are very heavy concentrations of Indians and Pakistanis in the metal manufacture industry and of Pakistanis in the metal goods industry. These two industries, together, employ over half the Indians and Pakistanis employed in the West Midlands. West Indian males are also concentrated in these two industries, but to a much lower extent.

Over 60% of Cypriot women in London are employed in the clothing industry, and this is by far the largest concentration of any group in either area. West Indian women in both areas are to be found in fairly large numbers (approximately one-quarter) in medical and dental services. The metal goods industry in the West Midlands employs about a quarter of the West Indian female employed population.

The major differences in the industrial distribution of immigrant groups and that of the total population are illustrated for males in

Table 13.7. It should be noted that data for the immigrant population and the total population have been tabulated under different
criteria and are not strictly comparable. Data for immigrants have
been collected on the basis of where they live and data for the
total population on where they work. In Table 13.7, however,
the differences are great enough for this discrepancy to be
ignored.

The greatest degree of over-representation of immigrant groups
is generally in those industries, mentioned above, in which most
immigrants work. The most significant fact of under-representation is that, apart from Indian, Pakistani, and Cypriot men in
London, there is an under-representation of immigrants of both
sexes in both areas in the distributive trades.

Table 13.7. Over- or under-representation* of different immigrant
groups in different industries, 1966

(a) *Males—Greater London conurbation*

Industry	India	Pakistan	Jamaica	Rest of Caribbean	All Caribbean	British West Africa	Cypriot
VI. Engineering and electrical goods	+						
XII. Clothing and footwear		+					+ +
XVII. Construction	–	+					
XIX. Transport and communications			+	+ +	+	+	–
701. Railways			+	+	+		
702. Road passenger transport				+			
707. Postal services and telecommunication						+ +	
XX. Distributive trades			–	–	–	–	
XXII. Professional and scientific services			–			+	
XXIII. Miscellaneous services		+					+ +
884. Catering, hotels, etc.		+					+ +
XXIV. Public administration and defence							–

* Footnote opposite, p. 169

Table 13.7—*cont.*

(b) *Males—West Midlands conurbation*

Industry	India	Pakistan	Jamaica	All Caribbean
V. Metal manufacture	+ + +	+ +	+ +	+ +
VI. Engineering and electrical goods		−	−	−
VIII. Vehicles	−			
IX. Metal goods not elsewhere specified		+ +		
XVI. Other manufacturing industries			+	
XVII. Construction		−		
XIX. Transport and communications				+
XX. Distributive trades	−	−	−	−

* Over- or under-representation has been calculated from the difference between the percentage of those in employment for the immigrant group in question in a particular industry and the percentage of the total population in the same industry. Only differences of 5% or more are shown and plus (+) signs denote over-representation, minus (−) signs under-representation of the immigrant group in comparison to the total population.

+ or −	Difference between 5% and 9·9% inclusive.
+ + or − −	Difference between 10% and 19·9% inclusive.
+ + + or − − −	Difference between 20% and 34·9% inclusive.

Sources:
Derived from 1966 10% Sample Census, Special Tabulations; Table 16, *Economic Activity Tables*, Part I, H.M.S.O.

Another way of looking at the industrial distribution of immigrant groups is to examine it, as is done in Table 13.8, in terms of those working in manufacturing, services, construction, and transport and communications. This shows that all immigrants, except African males in London, have a higher proportion employed in manufacturing industries than the total population. Similarly, all immigrant groups, except African and Cypriot males in London, have a lower proportion than the total population working in service industries. These statements on distribution in manufacturing and service industries hold true for both sexes in both areas.

Turning to the question of any change that occurred between 1961 and 1966, it can be said that there was no sign whatever that the industrial distribution of male immigrant groups moved towards that of the total population. In fact, what indicators there were suggest that if there was movement, albeit very slight, it was in the opposite direction. Thus, between 1961 and 1966 persons born in the Rest of Caribbean were more greatly concentrated in the transport and communications industry. Also,

N

Table 13.8. Distribution of different immigrant groups in manufacturing and service industries, by percentage, by sex, 1966

(a) Males—Greater London conurbation

Industry	India	Pakistan	Jamaica	Rest of Caribbean	All Caribbean	British West Africa	Cyprus	Total popula
Number in employment*	35,470	9,140	32,400	29,340	61,740	7,940	17,940	2,684,
Manufacturing†	40·5	46·8	46·1	36·7	41·6	23·6	36·7	34·
Construction (XVII)	5·8	2·8	17·9	10·8	14·5	5·7	6·1	10·
Transport and communications (XIX)	14·9	9·0	18·2	26·2	22·0	22·0	4·4	12·
Services‡	38·4	39·7	15·8	25·2	20·4	47·6	50·9	42·
Industry inadequately described	0·6	1·6	2·0	1·1	1·6	1·0	2·0	0·

(b) Males—West Midlands conurbation

Industry	India	Pakistan	Jamaica	All Caribbean	Total popula
Number in employment*	12,450	11,170	13,050	16,340	807,
Manufacturing†	77·9	87·9	74·5	72·5	62·
Construction (XVII)	5·1	1·5	7·7	7·7	9·
Transport and communications (XIX)	6·0	1·9	10·3	11·8	5·
Services‡	8·9	6·8	5·8	6·7	22·
Industry inadequately described	2·0	2·0	1·7	1·4	0·

* Footnotes opposite, p. 171

ble 13.8—*cont.*

(c) *Females—Greater London conurbation*

Industry	India	Jamaica	Rest of Caribbean	All Caribbean	British West Africa	Cyprus	Total population
nber in employment*	15,520	21,940	19,180	41,120	4,760	7,900	1,641,440
nufacturing†	27·9	47·3	37·8	43·0	35·0	68·8	27·7
nstruction (XVII)	1·4	0·4	0·2	0·3	0·2	0·3	1·4
ansport and communications XIX)	5·8	5·4	5·6	5·5	5·3	0·8	4·6
vices‡	64·4	45·0	55·1	49·7	58·0	27·1	65·7
lustry inadequately described	0·5	1·5	1·4	1·5	1·5	2·9	0·6

(d) *Females—West Midlands conurbation*

Industry	Jamaica	All Caribbean	Total population
*Number in employment**	7,150	8,930	453,480
Manufacturing†	62·2	61·8	47·0
Construction (XVII)	0·1	0·2	1·2
Transport and communications (XIX)	3·6	3·6	2·4
Services‡	32·3	33·2	49·1
Industry inadequately described	1·5	1·6	0·3

igures for the number in employment are multiplied by ten as the size of the sample was 10% the total population.
Manufacturing industries include Industry Orders I–XVI and XVIII.
ervice industries include Industry Orders XX–XXIV.

Sources:
1966 10% Sample Census, Special Tabulations;
Table 19, *Economic Activity Tables*, Part I, H.M.S.O.

whilst the total population showed, between the two dates, increases in the proportion in service industries and decreases in manufacturing, all the immigrant population showed changes in the opposite direction. For females, however, there was a very slight tendency for their industrial distribution to move towards that of the total population.

To sum up, therefore, one can say that the industrial distribution of the immigrant groups examined differs one from the other and also from that of the total population. There are industries in which immigrants are scarcely represented (e.g., distributive trades) and others where they are heavily over-represented (e.g., metal manufacturing in the West Midlands). These differences are probably more accountable in terms of 'clean' and 'dirty' jobs, employers' preferences, and local labours' reluctance to meet the demands within certain industries rather than the particular skills possessed by the immigrant. Generally, the immigrant worker is more likely to be found in a manufacturing industry than the population as a whole and less likely to be in a service industry. Finally, between 1961 and 1966, there was little sign of the distribution by industry of immigrants coming any closer to that of the total population.

5. SOCIO-ECONOMIC STATUS

Finally, the position of the immigrant in the field of employment will be looked at from the point of view of his socio-economic status. Seventeen socio-economic groups are identified by the Census and people are allocated to these by reference to their occupation and employment status. Each of the socio-economic groups is drawn up by the Registrar-General so that it ideally contains people whose social, cultural, and recreational standards are similar. In turn, these groups are reducible to seven categories, the first six of which can be said to be in some sort of ranking with regard to the general standing of the occupations in each category in the eyes of the general community. Thus, in rank order, the first six categories are: (1) professionals, (2) employers and managers, (3) non-manual workers, (4) skilled manual workers, (5) semi-skilled manual workers, and (6) unskilled manual workers. The seventh category includes members of the Armed Forces and those with inadequately described occupations, and will be ignored in this analysis.

Due to a lack of comparative data for the total population in the

conurbations, the data presented in Table 13.9 refer to the selected
London wards and the selected Midlands wards referred to in
Appendix III.1 and 2. For both areas and for both sexes all the
coloured immigrant groups are under-represented in the top three
socio-economic groups compared with persons born in England
and Wales and in Ireland. For males in both areas all the immigrant groups (except Pakistanis in the West Midlands) have fairly
similar proportions to the English group in skilled manual work.
All the male immigrant groups are over-represented in semi-
skilled manual work and heavily over-represented in unskilled
manual work compared to persons born in England and Wales.
The distribution of West Indians in London and the West Midlands, and Indians in the West Midlands in skilled, semi-skilled,
and unskilled jobs is, interestingly, not very dissimilar to that of the
Irish. Pakistanis in the West Midlands come out as the group with
the lowest overall socio-economic status, with over 55% in the
unskilled manual worker category compared to less than 8% for
those born in England and Wales. In both areas, West Indian

Table 13.9. Percentage socio-economic distribution* for different
immigrant groups for selected areas, 1966

(a) *Males—selected London boroughs 1966†*

	Jamaica	Rest of Caribbean	All Caribbean	Ireland	England and Wales
Number economically active‡	12,070	8,430	20,500	14,400	206,750
1. Professional workers	0·4	0·4	0·4	1·0	3·1
2. Employers and managers	0·3	0·3	0·3	3·6	8·3
3. Non-manual	2·3	7·8	4·6	13·2	22·1
4. Skilled manual and foremen	42·8	37·2	40·5	36·5	39·6
5. Semi-skilled manual	24·1	30·5	26·7	19·7	15·7
6. Unskilled manual	27·0	22·4	25·1	24·8	9·9
7. Armed Forces and inadequately described	3·1	1·3	2·3	1·2	1·2

* Footnotes to Table 13.9 appear on p. 175.

Table 13.9—*cont.*

(b) *Males—selected Midlands wards*†

	India	Pakistan	Jamaica	All Caribbean	Ireland	England and Wales
Number economically active‡	8,260	8,860	10,190	12,840	13,190	138,740
1. Professional workers	1·4	—	0·3	0·4	1·5	3·0
2. Employers and managers	1·0	1·1	—	—	2·4	7·0
3. Non-manual	3·5	2·0	1·2	1·7	5·6	14·2
4. Skilled manual and foremen	41·5	15·5	46·3	46·1	40·2	47·0
5. Semi-skilled manual	20·4	24·4	27·3	26·2	26·0	19·9
6. Unskilled manual	30·1	55·1	21·7	22·2	23·3	7·7
7. Armed Forces and inadequately described	1·8	1·9	3·2	3·1	1·2	1·0

(c) *Females—selected London boroughs*†

	Jamaica	Rest of Caribbean	All Caribbean	Ireland	England and Wales
Number economically active‡	8,450	5,500	13,950	8,500	146,820
1. Professional workers	—	0·2	0·1	0·4	0·8
2. Employers and managers	0·1	—	0·1	2·3	3·7
3. Non-manual	19·4	23·6	21·1	36·8	50·6
4. Skilled manual	8·7	9·7	9·1	5·6	8·5
5. Semi-skilled manual	60·0	53·1	57·3	38·9	24·4
6. Unskilled manual	8·8	11·5	9·8	14·9	11·0
7. Armed Forces and inadequately described	3·0	2·0	2·6	1·3	1·0

Table 13.9—*cont.*

(d) *Females—selected Midlands wards†*

	Jamaica	All Caribbean	Ireland	England and Wales
Number economically active‡	5,920	7,470	5,450	91,110
1. Professional workers	—	—	0·7	0·4
2. Employers and managers	—	—	2·2	3·1
3. Non-manual	17·1	17·8	20·4	38·6
4. Skilled manual	14·2	14·6	8·7	12·1
5. Semi-skilled manual	55·5	55·1	53·4	35·1
6. Unskilled manual	8·3	8·0	11·7	10·1
7. Armed Forces and inadequately described	4·9	4·4	2·9	1·1

* Categories used in tables consist as follows:
   1. Professional workers, Registrar-General's S.E.G., 3, 4
   2. Employers and managers, Registrar-General's S.E.G., 1, 2, 13
   3. Non-manual, Registrar-General's S.E.G., 5, 6
   4. Skilled manual, Registrar-General's S.E.G., 8, 9, 12, 14
   5. Semi-skilled manual, Registrar-General's S.E.G., 7, 10, 15
   6. Unskilled manual, Registrar-General's S.E.G., 11
   7. Armed Forces and inadequately described, Registrar-General's S.E.G., 16, 17
† For areas covered by selected London and Midlands wards, see Appendix III.1 and 2.
‡ Figures for the number economically active have been multiplied by ten as the size of the sample was 10% of the total population.

Source:
1966 10% Sample Census, Special Tabulations.

women are heavily concentrated (over half) and heavily over-represented in semi-skilled work compared to English women.

Should one wish to examine the distribution of Commonwealth immigrants in terms of class, then it is a good approximation to say that the top three categories in Table 13.9 are non-manual workers and middle class and the bottom three are manual workers and working class. Table 13.10, therefore, shows for the two conurbation centre areas the percentage middle and working class for males. It will be seen that all the coloured immigrant groups are predominantly working class—that is, over 90%, whilst for persons born in England approximately 65% in London and approximately 75% in the West Midlands are working class. Conversely, there is a virtual absence of the middle class in immigrant groups. The position of the Irish is interesting in that they are in an intermediate position between the English and the coloured immigrants, and in the West Midlands they are much nearer the position of the other immigrant groups than that of the English.

An examination of change between 1961 and 1966 in the socio-economic status of the different coloured immigrant groups leads to the conclusion that there has been little or no change in the five-year period. One trend that may become significant is indicated by a small upgrading within manual occupations for West Indians in London with a decreased proportion of unskilled and an increase in skilled manual workers. The only changes across the manual–non-manual line have been a very slight decrease in the proportion in non-manual occupations.

Table 13.10. Percentage of middle class and working class* for different immigrant groups for selected areas, 1966

(a) *Males—selected London boroughs*

	Jamaica	Rest of Caribbean	All Caribbean	Ireland	England and Wales
Middle class	3·0	8·5	5·3	17·8	33·5
Working class	93·9	90·1	92·3	81·0	65·2
Other	3·1	1·3	2·3	1·2	1·2

(b) *Males—selected Midlands wards*

	India	Pakistan	Jamaica	All Caribbean	Ireland	England and Wales
Middle class	5·9	3·1	1·5	2·1	9·5	24·2
Working class	92·0	95·0	95·3	94·5	89·5	74·6
Other	1·8	1·9	3·2	3·1	1·2	1·0

* Middle class: categories 1, 2, and 3; working class: categories 4, 5, and 6; and other: category 7 (see Table 13.9). *Source:*
Derived from Table 13.9.

To summarize the information on socio-economic status, it can be said that all the coloured immigrant groups have a considerably lower status than that of those born in England and Wales. Their status is also lower than that of the Irish. The immigrant group with the lowest socio-economic status is undoubtedly the Pakistanis in the West Midlands. The middle-class element in the coloured immigrant populations is extremely small in the two areas examined, but it should be stressed that the socio-economic status of those living within the two conurbations but outside the 'centre' areas is slightly higher. Finally, one can conclude that between 1961 and 1966 the socio-economic status of the different immigrant groups did not rise and they continue to occupy a low position in our social hierarchy.

6. UNEMPLOYMENT

Having completed our picture of immigrants in employment, we can now examine certain aspects of immigrant unemployment. In this area, unlike the others we have examined, precise and regularly collected data are available from a source other than the Census. The Ministry of Labour collects data on a quarterly basis for persons, 18 and over, who are registered as wholly unemployed and for those who have temporarily stopped work in England, Wales, and Scotland. It is this data which will be used for the discussion.*

The current method of counting the number of Commonwealth immigrants unemployed started in 1963, and the period that we will review is from February 1963 to May 1968.† At the start of the period the number of unemployed immigrant males was nearly 27,000, and it had fallen to about 12,000 a year later. It reached a trough between 1964–6 when the number unemployed was between 4,000 and 5,000. From August 1966, when the male immigrant unemployed numbered nearly 5,000, it rose to nearly 13,000 by February 1967 and remained around that level until May 1968. For female immigrants a similar pattern can be observed, with a high initial level in February 1963, steadily falling

* We would like to thank the Department of Employment and Productivity (formerly the Ministry of Labour) for supplying this information; the responsibility for the interpretation of these figures is that of the authors.

† Throughout this section on unemployment, figures refer only to coloured Commonwealth countries and exclude Australia, Canada, New Zealand, Cyprus, Gibraltar, and Malta.

until August 1966, and then rising fairly sharply until February 1967, since when there has been a slow but steady fall.

Contrasting the figures of unemployed immigrants with the rise and fall of unemployment in the total population, it will be

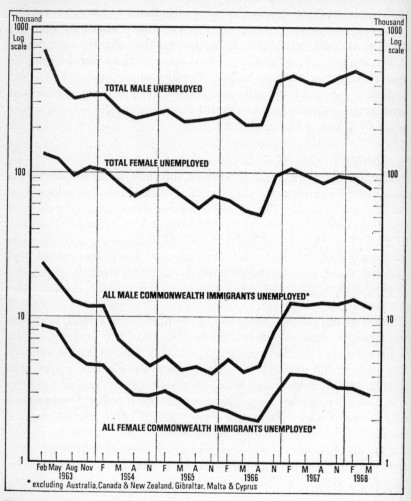

Figure 13.1. Persons 18 and over registered unemployed by sex and country of origin, between February 1963 and May 1968

Source :

Figures for Commonwealth immigrants from un-published data supplied by the Department of Employment and Productivity. Figures for total population from Ministry of Labour Gazette.

seen from Figure 13.1 that the immigrant unemployment follows that for the total unemployed population very closely, falling as total unemployment falls and rising as the total rises.

Another way of comparing the figures for the immigrant unemployed with that for the total population is to take these figures as a percentage of the figures for the whole population. It will be seen from Figure 13.2 that in 1963 about 4% of all male unemployed were Commonwealth immigrants, but during 1964 a steady fall occurred, so that by November 1964 less than 2% of all unemployed were Commonwealth immigrants. Throughout 1965 and 1966 this position was maintained, but in 1967 the proportion rose to between 2·5 and 3%. The levels for females were generally higher, but they tended to follow the same trend as for males. Thus, in February and May 1963, over 6% of all females unemployed were Commonwealth immigrants and at its lowest point in November 1966 the figure is just over 3%. This rose again to 4·5% in August 1967 and has since declined to about 3·5% in May 1968.

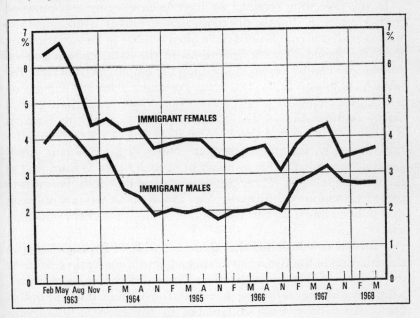

Figure 13.2. Immigrant unemployed as a percentage of total unemployed by sex, between February 1963 and May 1968

Source:
As for Figure 13.1.

It is unfortunately not possible to compare the rates of unemployment between immigrants and the whole population. The difficulties of making reasonable estimates of the immigrant working population would make the exercise hazardous.

However, the comparisons made above do yield some interesting points. Changes in the numbers of immigrant unemployed are in the same direction and the movement has the same timing as for the total population. What is noteworthy about these movements is that when the trend of unemployment rises, the proportion of immigrants amongst the total unemployed also rises. Thus, in times of rising unemployment Commonwealth immigrants tend to be harder hit than the general population. For the female Commonwealth immigrants the proportions were generally higher, as has been indicated, and this may be because proportionately more immigrant females seek employment as compared with the total female population.

7. CONCLUSIONS

In the preceding sections we have been viewing a population from a series of slightly different angles, and it is therefore not surprising if our conclusions have often tended to be variations on the same theme. Despite limitations in the data, certain general conclusions can be drawn concerning the employment of coloured immigrant groups in the two areas examined. The first conclusion is that the employment structure of coloured immigrant groups differs considerably and is generally less favourable (as far as it is possible to judge it in these terms) than that of the total population. Secondly, the employment structures of the different immigrant groups often differ as much from each other as from that of the total population. These differences show how fallacious it is to regard Commonwealth immigrants as a homogeneous group and that policies based on this assumption would probably be ineffective.

A further conclusion is that there are wide differences between the situation in the two areas examined, and these again underline the dangers of over-generalization. These differences suggest that, with the differences in the social and economic background of areas, there have been differences in the type of immigrant attracted into these areas and in the response of the local population to the newcomers. There are also indications that, for a complex of reasons, the general achievement of coloured immigrants is higher in London than in the West Midlands.

Finally, the concentration of coloured immigrants in certain sections of employment and their absence in others, coupled with the fact that there has been little or no change between 1961 and 1966, gives most cause for concern. If this pattern continues into the 1970s, then the assessment that the situation is still fluid and has not hardened into a rigid class-colour or caste-colour structure may well be over-optimistic. The basic problem should not, however, be seen in those sectors of employment that have over-concentrations of coloured immigrants, but in those that have few. It is in the occupations and industries where the coloured immigrant is rare or absent that the answers to concentration, lack of achievement, and frustration are to be found.

14 The Household Expenditure of Immigrants*

We still have no official information on the household income and expenditure of immigrants: the 1966 Census contained no questions on these subjects; in the Family Expenditure Survey there was no breakdown of the information by the birthplace of heads of households or some such criterion. In this chapter, a survey of the income and expenditure of immigrant households in Birmingham, carried out in 1966–7,[1] is compared with the Family Expenditure Survey for 1966.[2] All the figures and data given below can be assumed to come from these sources, except where it is explicitly stated otherwise.

Since the information about immigrants comes mainly from Birmingham, it is worth asking whether the conclusions are likely to be valid for the rest of the immigrant population. Most of the immigrants are concentrated either in the West Midlands or in Greater London. From Census data it appears that there are more clerical and professional workers among the immigrants, especially among Indians and Pakistanis, in London than in the West Midlands, and, of course, fewer manual workers.[3] One would expect the incomes of immigrants in London to be on average rather higher than in the West Midlands, not only because of the higher general level of incomes in London, but also because the average earnings of professional and clerical workers are significantly higher than those of manual workers. Of the latest arrivals among the immigrants in Birmingham, a much larger proportion were clerical workers, so the position may be changing.

The mean earnings of men in all occupations in the West Midlands are roughly the same as for the country as a whole, while the mean earnings of women are rather less. The distribution of household incomes, however, is roughly the same as that for the whole country. This means that if the immigrants in Birmingham were representative of the West Midlands population in general, their income pattern should be very similar to that of the United Kingdom as a whole. This turns out not to be the case, as might be expected.

* This chapter has been contributed by A. H. Vanags.

1. IMMIGRANT HOUSEHOLDS

In order to draw useful conclusions about the comparative economic circumstances of the immigrants, it is important to take into account employment status, family composition, and other sociological or demographic factors which influence the income and expenditure of households.

Table 14.1. Occupational status of heads of household

	Total population	West Indian	Indian	Pakistani
	%	%	%	%
Professional and technical	6·4 (8)*	6	6	6
Administrative and managerial	8·6 (11)	—	—†	0·5
Teachers	1·8 (2)	—†	4	—†
Clerical	6·6 (8)	3	4	5
Shop assistants	1·0 (1)	3	5	2
Manual	51·2 (67)	86	76	86
Retired and unoccupied	23·9	3	4	—
Armed Forces	0·5	—	—	—
Total	100	100	100	100

* The figures in brackets are the proportions in the various categories when the 'retired and unoccupied' group is taken out.

† The West Indies and Pakistan had some teachers, but less than 0·5%; similarly, India had some administrative and managerial, but less than 0·5%.

Table 14.1 compares the occupational status of heads of households for the U.K. as a whole with that of the three immigrant groups. Two things stand out. One is that the immigrants have no significant numbers of retired people (nearly all of those in the 'retired and unoccupied' group are unemployed); the other is that the immigrants are heavily concentrated in the manual category. These figures bear out the view that nearly all the claims by the immigrants on the social services are likely to be by the very young or the sick (or the unemployed). This view is further strengthened by the age structure of the immigrants. Among the heads of immigrant households interviewed in Birmingham only 16% or less were 45 or over, and most of them, some 70 to 80%, were in the

25 to 44 age group. The comparable U.K. proportions are 60% who are 45 or over and only 36% who are between 25 and 44.

It is commonly believed that immigrant families are much larger than those of the indigenous population. This is not borne out by the figures on the average size of households; indeed the average size of a Pakistani household is much less than that for the U.K. as a whole. These figures, however, mask the true

Table 14.2. Size of households

Number	Total population	West Indian	Indian	Pakistani
	%	%	%	%
1	14	35	41	64
2	30·8	12	10	12
3	21·1	11	8	11
4	18·7	11	9	6
5 +	15·4	30	33	8
Average size	3·33	3·23	3·31	1·91

position. It can be seen from Table 14.2 that the majority of immigrant households fall into one or other of the extreme categories: that is, either they have only one member or they have more than five members; remarkably, nearly two-thirds of all Pakistani families have only one member. The truth is that the figure for the average size of household is depressed by the fact that the dependants of the head of the household do not come here until some time has elapsed. For households where the head of the household arrived in this country before 1959, the average size in 1966–7 was for West Indians, Indians, and Pakistanis, 3·59, 5·43, and 2·67, respectively, while for those who arrived after 1962, the average size was 1·80, 2·20, and 1·30. This still leaves Pakistani households with a very small average size, which is accounted for by the fact that as many as 44% of the earliest arrivals were still single member households. Of the comparable West Indian and Indian groups, only 29% and 4% were still single member households.

2. IMMIGRANT INCOMES

Tables 14.3(*a*) and (*b*) show the distribution of net income, average income, and average household size for the immigrants and for certain selected U.K. groups. For the immigrants, net income is based upon the stated 'take home pay' of the respondents in the Birmingham survey, while for the U.K. groups the information is based on the Family Expenditure Survey. The distribution of income is given in much more detailed form in the Family Expenditure Survey than was available for the immigrants, so Table 14.3(b) is only an estimate to make the U.K. data comparable.

Table 14.3(a). Immigrant incomes

	Up to £17	£17–£23	£23 and more	Average income	Average household size
	%	%	%		
West Indian	34	32	34	£21 19s. 0d.	3·23
Indian	30	35	34	£23 2s. 0d.	3·31
Pakistani	51	36	13	£17 18s. 0d.	1·91

Table 14.3(b). Incomes of total population

	Up to £17	£17–£23	£23 and more	Average income	Average household size
	%	%	%		
U.K. as a whole	35	20	45	£23 10s. 0d.	3·03
U.K. manual workers	23	27	50	£24 3s. 0d.	3·43
West Midlands	33	20	47	—	—

There are two related but different questions on which the comparative income data may throw some light. One is the relative welfare or standard of living of the groups under consideration; and the other is whether or not immigrants earn less than white workers in similar jobs. The Birmingham data is more useful for the first question than for the second. Tables 14.3(a) and (b) suggest that the West Indians and Indians are rather worse off per head than the rest of the population, whereas the Pakistanis are better off. This type of crude comparison per head is, however, not really adequate, as the household composition of the immigrants is so different from that of the U.K. households. In addition, the

186 COLOUR AND CITIZENSHIP

Pakistanis form a special group, because most of them are single member households.

Table 14.4 gives the distribution of income, average income, and average household size for the earliest immigrants. This group gives a more satisfactory basis of comparison than taking all the immigrants together. Many more of the households of the earliest immigrants, except for the Pakistanis, have completed families and are therefore more like the average U.K. household. From Table 14.4 it can be seen that for all three groups of the earliest immi-

Table 14.4. Incomes of immigrants who arrived before 1959

	Up to £17	£17–£23	£23 and more	Average income	Average household size
	%	%	%		
West Indian	30	31	39	£24 2s. 0d.	3·59
Indian	13	29	58	£29 14s. 0d.	5·43
Pakistani	31	48	22	£21 1s. 0d.	2·67

grants, average income is higher than for the immigrants taken together, irrespective of their date of arrival, but the average size of household is also higher. Indeed, the increase in the size of household is proportionately larger than the increase in income, so that the position per head is worsened.

Tables 14.3(a) and (b), and 14.4 also give the distribution of income for the groups under consideration. For the U.K. as a whole, 45% of households and for U.K. manual workers, 50% of households have net incomes in excess of £23. For West Indians, Indians, and Pakistanis the proportions in 1966–7 were 34%, 34%, and 13%, respectively. If one takes only the earliest arrivals, the proportions of immigrants with incomes in excess of £23 improve to 39%, 58%, and 22%, respectively. Although for all groups the size of household goes up with income, this is more so in the case of the immigrants. This again means that immigrant households become worse off per head relative to U.K. households as household income rises.

The Birmingham survey does not provide direct evidence on the earnings of the immigrants. It is, however, possible to get a rough guide if one considers the average number of workers per household and compares this with the income data. For the earliest arrivals, the average number of workers per household in 1966–7, for West Indians, Indians, and Pakistanis was 1·69, 1·62, and 1·1, respectively. The comparable figures for U.K. manual workers and the U.K. as a whole were 1·75 and 1·36. These figures are rather surprising, particularly in the case of the Indians in view of the relatively large incomes they have. However, one must remember that the income figures used here are net figures, and the immigrants have much larger families and many of them would be claiming allowances for dependants abroad.

There is other evidence which suggests that coloured workers do earn less than their white counterparts, and that the difference may arise because coloured workers are less frequently offered overtime. This was the finding of a survey carried out in Nottingham.[4] A survey of white and coloured households living in Lambeth also found that there was a discrepancy in average earnings between white and coloured manual workers and that this difference was greatest for skilled manual workers.[5] On average, skilled coloured workers were found to earn £3 10s. 0d. per week less than white workers, and the average difference for the whole sample was £2 10s. 0d. It is of interest to see how the incomes of the immigrants vary with the length of time they have been here. Table 14.5 provides the relevant data. In all three groups household income increases with the length of residence in the U.K., but in the case of the West Indians the increase is not very large compared with the other groups and appears to be explained by the increase in the number of workers per household. In the case of the Indians and Pakistanis the change is significant and is not entirely explained by the increase in the number of workers.

3. IMMIGRANT HOUSING

Income is not the sole criterion by which the welfare of households may be assessed. Housing is the most important single item of expenditure in the budgets of households and its costs and availability must therefore be taken into account.

Table 14.6(a) provides a breakdown into two categories, rented and owner-occupied, of the type of accommodation for the immigrants and for the U.K. and U.K. manual workers. Table 14.6(b) provides the same breakdown for the earliest group of

Table 14.5. Change in incomes through time

Date of arrival in U.K. of head of household:	West Indian			Indian			Pakistani		
	-1959	1959-62	1962-	-1959	1959-62	1962-	-1959	1959-62	1962-
	%	%	%	%	%	%	%	%	%
Up to £17	30	38	33	13	25	43	30	54	72
£17-£23	31	32	40	29	39	37	48	34	24
£23 and more	39	31	27	58	36	21	23	12	4
Average income	£23 2s.	£20 7s.	£20 10s.	£29 14s.	£22 0s.	£20 12s.	£21 1s.	£17 12s.	£14 8s.
Average household size	3·59	3·21	1·80	5·43	3·23	2·20	2·67	1·78	1·30
Workers per household	1·69	1·39	1·1	1·62	1·2	1·18	1·1	1·03	1·0

Table 14.6(a). Type of accommodation

	Total population %	Total population: manual workers %	West Indian %	Indian %	Pakistani %
Rented	53·2	61	59	64	74
Owner occupied	43·5	35·5	40	36	26
Rent free	3·3	3·5	—	—	—

Table 14.6(b). Type of accommodation for the pre-1959 immigrants

	West Indian %	Indian %	Pakistani %
Rented	46	33	56
Owner occupied	54	67	44

immigrants, which is perhaps the most useful group for comparison because the more recent arrivals would not be expected to settle in for some time. Moreover, most of the more recent arrivals belong to single person or small households and would not be expected in any case to be owner-occupiers. This is reflected in Table 14.6(a), which shows that nearly 60% and more of all the immigrant groups live in rented accommodation, this being a much greater proportion than for the general population. The pattern is quite different if only the earliest group is considered. Of these only the Pakistanis have a higher proportion renting their accommodation than the general population, and even they are renting less than U.K. manual workers. Among the West Indians and Indians, the proportion who rent their homes is less than the proportion who do so both among the U.K. population in general and among U.K. manual workers. Conversely, of course, a larger proportion of them are owner-occupiers, which is a remarkable phenomenon. It is particularly remarkable in the case of the West Indians, since as many as 29% of the earliest arrivals still belong to single member households, and one can fairly safely assume that nearly all of these are renting their accommodation. This means that a very high proportion of West Indian families proper are owner-occupiers.

Table 14.7 shows how the type of accommodation varies with the income of households. At low incomes the proportion of owner-occupiers is larger among the general population than among the immigrants. For all four groups, the proportion of owner-occupiers naturally rises as income rises, but for the immigrants it rises much faster, so much faster that in all cases the proportion of owner-occupiers among those with incomes in excess of £23 is larger than for the general population. For West Indians, the rise in the proportion of owner-occupiers as income rises is particularly sharp, so that 70% of them are in this category as compared with only 53% for the general population. The key to the difference between the immigrants and the rest of the population may lie in the availability of local authority housing; 30% or more of the general population live in accommodation rented from local authorities, and in Birmingham the figure is about 36%, whereas for the immigrants in Birmingham it is only just over 8%.[6]

This discrepancy is, of course, partly a consequence of the fact that eligibility for council housing depends upon length of residence in the area. The Lambeth survey provides rather more information on this question. Households were divided into those who had been resident in Lambeth for more than five years and those who had been resident there for less than five years. The former category were considered as eligible for council houses. Among those who were eligible, 22% of the white households lived in council accommodation as compared with 10% of the eligible coloured households. On the other hand, 41% of the eligible coloured households were owner-occupiers, whereas only 26% of the comparable white group were owner-occupiers. These figures do not necessarily reflect the demand by the various groups for the different types of housing.

There is not much information available regarding the relative costs of buying accommodation for the immigrants and the rest of the population. A survey in Bristol did find that on average the repayment period for mortgages was shorter for the coloured immigrants than for the other groups considered.[7]

The costs of rented accommodation are, however, much better documented. Table 14.8 provides estimates of the average rents paid by the immigrants in the Birmingham survey and compares

Table 14.7. Type of accommodation by income

	Total population			West Indian			Indian			Pakistani		
	−£17	£17-£23	£23+	−£17	£17-£23	£23+	−£17	£17-£23	£23+	−£17	£17-£23	£23+
Rented	63	56	44	82	66	30	81	71	43	85	70	o4o
Owner-occupied	32	40	53	18	34	70	19	29	57	15	30	
Rent free	5	3	3									

Table 14.8. Average weekly rents

	West Indian	Pakistani	Indian	Total population		Total population: manual workers	
				Unfurnished	Furnished	Unfurnished	Furnished
All	£2 18s. 0d.	£2 5s. 0d.	£3 2s. 0d.	£2 0s. 10d.	£3 15s. 0d.	£2 1s. 6d.	£2 19s. 0d.
£17-£23 group	£2 18s. 0d.	£2 14s. 0d.	£3 0s. 0d.	£2 3s. 0d.	£3 10s. 0d.	£2 2s. 0d.	£3 4s. 0d.

them with the average rents paid for furnished and unfurnished accommodation in the U.K. as a whole and for U.K. manual workers. It also provides this information for the £17 to £23 income groups. From census figures we know that less than 15% of English households in Birmingham who rent their accommodation rent furnished accommodation,[8] while the Family Expenditure Survey shows that the proportion who rent furnished in the country as a whole is smaller still. This means that most households in the U.K. pay a rent which is much closer to the figure for unfurnished rents in Table 14.8 rather than the higher figure for furnished accommodation. The average rents given in Table 14.8 are unweighted averages, but, again from census data, we know that about two-thirds of the coloured immigrants in Birmingham who rent their accommodation, rent it furnished. It is this factor which seems to be responsible for the higher rents paid by the immigrants. They would, of course, generally be paying more even for unfurnished accommodation, because on average their tenancies would have been established more recently when rents have been rising. All the immigrants tend to pay more rent the longer they have been here. The average rent paid by the earliest arrivals is, for West Indians and Indians, £3 7s. 0d. and £4 10s. 0d., respectively, as compared with £2 11s. 0d. and £2 9s. 0d. for the latest arrivals. It seems that the demand for extra housing caused by the growth in the size of household offsets the other influences which in general might lead to less rent being paid with longer residence.

The Lambeth survey provides some more detail on how the immigrants fare in comparison with the white population. In order to eliminate the influence of long tenancies among the white population, those households who had been at their present address for five years or less were considered. Amongst this group it was found that the average rent paid by white households was £3 12s. 0d., while for coloured households it was £4 5s. 0d. The average for all households irrespective of how long they had been at their present address was £3 2s. 0d. Again, there is no breakdown by furnished and unfurnished, so it is not possible to say how this might have affected the figures. The average size of white households is 2·7, as compared with 3·6 for the coloured households, but the average size of those which had moved to their present address in the last five years is not known. Two other results of great interest were obtained: one was that at all levels of income, white families paid less rent than coloured families, and the other was that at all levels of rent paid, the quality of the housing (in terms of the availability of certain amenities) which the coloured families lived in was inferior to that of the white families. It was also found that of those who were owner-occupiers, white households had better quality housing.

4. SAVINGS AND REMITTANCES

The Birmingham survey also obtained information on the household expenditure, savings, and remittances of the immigrants. It is not possible to say how reliable the data are, since they are based on what they said they spent, saved, etc., rather than upon written records. The median levels of household expenditure for West Indians, Indians, and Pakistanis, respectively, were £9–£10, £11, and £7–£8, which is a pattern roughly in keeping with the relative sizes of the households of the three groups. Among the Pakistanis 77% of the households spent less than £10 per week, again reflecting the fact that most of them are single person households. In the case of the Indians and Pakistanis, household expenditure increased with the length of time they had been here, but for the West Indians this was not significant. Since expenditure tends to reflect income, this appears to be a corollary of the fact noted earlier, that their household incomes did not increase very significantly with time. On the other hand, the size of West Indian households did increase with time, just as it did for the others, which suggests that they became relatively worse off the longer they had been here. The Bristol survey also found that West Indians' housing standards, in terms of overcrowding and sharing basic amenities, deteriorated the longer they had been in the St. Paul's area.

The information on weekly savings and remittances suggests that the total proportion of income saved by the immigrants is relatively high. Remittances were claimed to be separate from savings so that the *total* weekly savings is the sum of the two items. This gives weekly savings for West Indians, Indians, and Pakistanis, respectively, of £4 1s. 0d., £4 9s. 0d., and £4 17s. 0d. On average, £1 7s. 0d., £1 7s. 0d., and £2 5s. 0d. was sent to their home country. The low level of remittances among the Indians reflects the fact that 53% of them send nothing at all. This finding, however, conflicts somewhat with the results of a survey of Indian households carried out in 1965 in Southall,[9] where it was found that the average weekly remittance was £2 12s. 0d., and that 15% sent nothing or sent something only 'now and then'. Of the West Indians and Pakistanis in the Birmingham sample, 28% and 23%, respectively, sent nothing back.

Table 14.9. Remittances by date of arrival

	pre-1959	*1959–62*	*post-1962*
West Indian	£1 6s.	£1 10s.	£1 1s.
Indian	£1 1s.	£1 6s.	£1 14s.
Pakistani	£2 5s.	£2 11s.	£1 12s.

Table 14.9 gives estimates of the average weekly remittances by the date of arrival for each group. For the Indians there is the expected falling off with time, but for the West Indians and Pakistanis less is remitted by the latest arrivals than by either of the earlier groups. Table 14.10 provides estimates of remittances,

Table 14.10. Remittances and savings for the £17–£23 group

	Savings	*Remittances*	*Total*	*Average income*	*% of income*
West Indian	£1 18s.	£1 6s.	£3 4s.	£19 11s.	16·5
Indian	£2 7s.	£1 5s.	£3 12s.	£19 15s.	18
Pakistani	£2 17s.	£2 7s.	£5 3s.	£19 9s.	26

savings, and the proportions of net income which these represent for the £17–£23 income group. This income group has been chosen because the estimates of average income are more reliable than for the two extreme categories. It can be seen that total savings, that is savings plus remittances, are a very high proportion of net income, varying from 16·5% for the West Indians to 26% for the Pakistanis. This compares with just over 5% of net income saved by the U.K. population, in general, and by U.K. manual workers. Even if remittances are excluded from savings, since these are often payments for the support of dependants abroad which the average resident of this country would be supporting at home, the proportion of income saved by the immigrants is still much higher than the average. It is nearly 10% for the West Indians, and considerably higher for the others, in particular the Pakistanis. These results are not really surprising: the immigrants are on average much younger than the population as a whole and almost none of them would have reached the stage in life when they would be dis-saving. As income rises the proportion of total savings which is sent home falls off quite sharply.

5. CONCLUSIONS

Putting together all this information about the circumstances of the immigrants, it is not easy to reach unequivocal conclusions. One thing, however, seems clear. The character of the Pakistani immigration is different from that of the others. Even after seven years or more, nearly half of them have no family over here, and the level of remittances remains high for the earliest arrivals. Savings are high, household expenditure is low, and the amount spent on rent, even by the earliest arrivals, is low. Many of the Pakistanis exhibit the characteristics of transients, which is quite unlike the others, in particular the Indians.

No really clear-cut conclusion about welfare, in terms of the household incomes of the immigrants relative to the general population, emerges from the Birmingham results. The distribution of household sizes is bi-modal for the West Indians and Indians, and heavily skewed for the Pakistanis. This contrasts with the much more regular size-distribution of U.K. households. As a consequence, the average figures for income for the immigrants, and in particular the Indians and West Indians, do not really reflect the incomes which *most* of the households have. At best, one can make the conjecture that the better-off the Indians and West Indians become, the worse-off they are in comparison with the equivalent U.K. income groups.

The average household size for the higher income households for the U.K. is certainly less than four, and although it is not possible to get exact figures for the household sizes of the higher income groups for the immigrants, it is well in excess of four for the Indians and West Indians.

One quite striking result which does emerge is the increase in household incomes through time of the Indians and the Pakistanis; this is especially marked in the case of the Pakistanis. For the Pakistanis, the incomes of the earliest arrivals are about 44% higher than those of the latest arrivals, while the increase in the number of workers per household is only 10%. For the Indians, these figures are 44% and 37%, respectively, which is still some improvement. The position of the West Indians, on the other hand, appears to deteriorate: the incomes of the earliest arrivals are about 18% higher than those of the latest arrivals, but the number of workers per household is greater by about 54%. This worsening in the position of the West Indians is confirmed by the fact that the household expenditure of the earliest arrivals is not significantly greater than for the latest arrivals, despite a doubling in the size of household.

It is in the cost and availability of accommodation where the immigrants appear to be at a disadvantage when compared with the rest of the population. Even the Pakistanis, with their small households, pay more rent than the rest of the population, and all the evidence suggests that this does not reflect higher quality but that the reverse is true, namely that the immigrants pay higher rents for worse quality accommodation. Since local authority housing is probably not available to many of the immigrants, they are forced to choose between renting furnished and buying their own homes. In view of the high rents and lack of security in furnished accommodation, it is not surprising that they appear to choose the latter as soon as they can afford it.

There are many things which it has not been possible to discuss because of the lack of adequate information. For instance, the diversity of the standards of educational qualifications in the countries of origin of the immigrants makes it difficult to make any investigation of the relationship between educational qualifications and income. In the Birmingham survey, a crude measure of educational attainment was used, namely the age at which the respondent ceased schooling, but no correlation was found between this and income. It would also be of interest to know the extent to which the immigrants are in occupations commensurate with their skills. The main problem, however, remains that of getting information on a comparable basis. Statistics by birthplace for the numbers unemployed are now available and one must hope that this will soon be the case for income and expenditure in the new Family Expenditure Survey.

NOTES TO CHAPTER 14

1. A survey of the income and expenditure of immigrant households was commissioned from Robert Radburn by the Institute's 'Survey of Race Relations in Britain'. It was conducted in Birmingham through West Indian, Indian, and Pakistani interviewers. The responses were derived from a quota sampling of areas identified as being

settled by immigrants. The sample contained 302 West Indian, 311 Indian, and 307 Pakistani households. Of these, the heads of household of 126 West Indian, 70 Indian, and 84 Pakistani households arrived in this country before 1 January 1959; 146, 115, and 149, respectively, arrived between that date and 31 December 1962, and of the remainder, 30 West Indians, 126 Indians, and 74 Pakistanis arrived after 1962. The proportions of the various nationalities in the last group appear to reflect the overall pattern of immigration since 1962. The West Indians and Indians were interviewed partly between December 1966 and February 1967 and partly between August and September 1967. This means that the figures which are in money terms, such as income, may be slightly inflated when compared with the Family Expenditure Survey for 1966. However, no significant difference was found in the results for the two dates, so the information has been compounded. The Pakistani households were all interviewed between October 1966 and February 1967.

2. *Family Expenditure Survey Report for 1966* (London, H.M.S.O., 1967).

3. 1966 Census, Special tabulations, prepared for the Institute's 'Survey of Race Relations in Britain' (see Chapter 13).

4. F. J. Bayliss and J. B. Coates, 'West Indians at work in Nottingham', *Race* (Vol. VII, no. 2, October 1965). Bayliss and Coates found that two-thirds of the English in their sample took home over £12 per week, whereas the proportion of West Indian men with similar earnings was 50%. Englishmen tended to work longer hours than the West Indians and this was presumably because they were offered more overtime.

5. This survey of housing occupancy was commissioned by Lambeth Borough Council from Research Services Limited in 1966, and quoted by Elizabeth Burney in *Housing on Trial* (London, Oxford University Press, for Institute of Race Relations, 1967).

6. 1966 Census, Special tabulations.

7. A. H. Richmond and M. Lyon, 'Race Relations in Bristol: a study of St. Paul's' (for the Institute's 'Survey of Race Relations in Britain',1968).

8. 1966 Census, Special tabulations.

9. Narindar Uberoi Kelly, 'The Singhs of Southall' (for the Institute's 'Survey of Race Relations in Britain', 1968).

PART IV POLICIES AND PRACTICES

15 The Genesis of Official Policy: On the Procrustean Bed

We shall be concerned in Part IV with the policies and practices devised within our own society and their effect on the processes of adjustment and inter-penetration which took place between the newcomers and their new surroundings. In Part III, we considered the situation of the migrants and its development over time: the policies and decisions taken during this period and the manner in which they were implemented were major factors in determining the evolution of that situation. The content of these decisions, their scope, and the manner in which they were taken depended to a substantial extent on factors external to the migration. The British system of government possesses well-marked characteristics: the dispersal of power (*de facto* rather than *de jure*); distinctive patterns of communication between institutions and individuals (horizontal rather than vertical, in Richard Rose's phrase); and haphazard provision for the dissemination of information within the system. These characteristics influence the way in which any new policy issue is defined and acted upon. Weaknesses in the system, although they vary in detail from one situation to another, are inherent and have a pervasive effect on the evolution of policy in all social problem areas.

However, despite these deficiencies in the system, new policy issues which call for remedial action usually pass through a series of processes: discussion, consultation, debate, legislation, leading finally to administrative action. These processes did not occur in this instance, for reasons which we will outline in Chapter 16. Ministers and civil servants had accepted a proposition which had been defined contemporaneously with the migration and whose significance had increased alongside the numerical growth in the migration. This was, that the right to self-determination on a basis of equality in the countries of the New Commonwealth, on the macro level, should be reflected on the micro level in the treatment of their citizens in the United Kingdom. In Part I, we described this period as that of 'status'—that is to say the one in which the sole aim of policy was to preserve the equality of status of the newcomer. The point of reference for this doctrine lay not in administrative practice but in the law. That is, the law conceived of as the quintessence of colour blindness: a Diceyan incarnation of ideal- ized opinion. Equality before the law served as a symbol of the community's intent; the words of Lord Justice Salmon, passing sentence on youths convicted of participation in the first serious challenge to the notion that these ends could be achieved by proclamation, achieved something of the status of a sacred text.[1] But the role of law in this situation was limited by the concept of the place of law in society, held both by the judiciary and the executive. To both, the notion that the law might guarantee not only civil rights but social rights through legislation against racial discrimination was quite unacceptable. The law's main function was its symbolic colour blindness. In fact, although we have no space to go into the arguments here, the view that English law (common law or statute law) has recognized no distinction by colour or race was certainly mistaken, as Hepple has shown.[2] But it was the perception of the law by the policy makers that was important.

The doctrine of equality by proclamation, confined in practice to the assurance of legal rights, had far-reaching consequences. It was, for ten years, the back-cloth against which all policy decisions were taken. And the responsibility for such co-ordination of policy that could be exercised (consistent with the view that no specific policies should exist) passed from the Colonial Office to the Home Office. The nature of the activities undertaken by that department—essentially regulatory functions related to the immigration process—was in itself a further restriction on the evolution of official action.

One further consequence of this basic policy decision was that, in the words of Lord Gardiner, reviewing the situation in 1965, 'the matter was just thrown onto the desks of local authorities and it was left entirely to them'.[3] And ministers who were reproached in Parliament or by local authorities for this act of de facto devo- lution replied that central government could accept no special responsibility for groups that had no special characteristic of any relevance: the existing system could make adequate provision for their needs. One response, that epitomizes them all, is that of the Home Secretary, Gwilym Lloyd-George, in 1956:

We look after them, as we look after every other citizen, to the best of our ability. I have no information that there is any particular problem as far as these people are concerned.[4]

Dignified, to paraphrase Bagehot, the superstructure of the policy may have been, but efficient it was not.

A major cause of the failure and missed opportunities in this field, which we shall be describing in Part IV, stems directly from allowing the existing local services to take the strain, for the link between centre and periphery is, in practice, one of the weakest points in our system of government. Local authorities have been entrusted with a vastly increased range of responsibilities in the social welfare legislation passed since the War. And although government departments determine the broad lines of policy, the methods of supervision employed leave a wide area of discretion to the local authority. Essentially, the method of central control is financial; the clumsy and undiscriminating machinery of the subsidy is the instrument by which social priorities, determined centrally, are put into operation. On detailed issues, arising from the execution of this policy, Whitehall must cajole rather than control.

Professor Griffith has enumerated some of the sources of potential weakness in the relationship between centre and periphery which may limit the capacity of local authorities to execute policy on any complex or controversial issue. These are: inadequate definition of the policy by the department concerned; failure of the department to gather adequate information on which to base policy; inadequate financial provision for the service concerned; and restricted resources on the part of the local authority.[5] On this issue, weakness under the first two heads was implicit in the limited scope of the policy adopted centrally. And since, as a result of this policy, no special financial provision could be made from the centre, the resources available were bound to be inadequate. The limits of action were defined by this limitation—with the additional complication that the whole question of immigration was beginning to acquire by the late 1950s an aura of potential controversy which constituted an additional inducement to refrain from too active an involvement. This was another reason why the needs of a dispersed and powerless minority for whom no spokesman existed were unlikely to be catered for, in a system where the distribution of resources is customarily determined in finance committees by 'the relative needs of the different services, by the view taken of their priorities and by the political or personal strengths or weaknesses of members and officers'.[6]

Such action as was taken during the 1950s was therefore severely

P

restricted; the form that it took tended to be determined by the capacity of local government officers—as defined by their training and attitudes—to handle the specific problems that arose. Here, the existing philosophy of certain branches of local government service were of considerable significance. Thus, the medical officer of health's regulatory function—the confining and eventual eradication of the environmental causes of ill-health—led public health officers to conduct a vigorous and at times punitive campaign against the improvised solutions reached by immigrants to their accommodation problems. In this activity, health departments frequently cut across the policy of housing departments, with whom their responsibilities interlock. Both the priorities determined at the centre for housing policy and the preferences of local authorities indicated a concentration on slum clearance programmes to the exclusion of the problems of the twilight zones of multi-occupied housing in which immigrants were chiefly to be found. The basic attitude to the latter was generally one of avoidance. Other local government departments contented themselves with the application of general policy. Children's departments and welfare departments applied standard case-work procedures, innocent of any recognition of the difficulties arising from cultural diversity. Local education authorities struggled on with the processes of teaching, solving as best they could the complex linguistic difficulties which frequently arose. Until, eventually, the scope of the problem forced a recognition that some form of special measure must be introduced, whatever the damage to the standing of the individual immigrants concerned.

This process of groping towards *ad hoc* solutions was as true of the local agencies of central government—offices of the national assistance board and employment exchanges—as of the departments of local government. In both instances, a process of feedback to the centre gradually began to take place. This proceeded rather faster in the case of departments where the style of administration involved a degree of contact with local government on the part of administrators or through an inspectorate. Moreover, although the official position remained unchanged until long after the sheer scope of the difficulties rendered its absurdity self-evident, the informal swapping of experiences between local authorities, discussions and professional conferences, and the demonstration function of certain activities had by the end of the 1950s eroded it in practice. As we indicated in Part I, the legitimacy of action directed specifically to needs deriving from the presence of coloured minorities in Britain gradually became accepted. The first attempt to give coherent expression to this new orthodoxy was the Prime Minister's White Paper of 1965, *Immigration from the Commonwealth.*[7] Our review of policy turns on the axis of this White Paper, which we define in Chapter 16 as introducing a period in which a 'Little England' policy was adopted. Unlike the labels which we have attached to earlier periods, which described states of affairs rather than consciously determined policies, this is a description of a serious attempt at a co-ordinated programme with clearly defined objectives. It is true that the period of *laissez-faire* had been ended three years earlier by a Conservative administration which almost outdid the Opposition with expressions of regret at the step that it was taking to control the entry of immigrants from the Commonwealth. But apart from the creation of an advisory body and the belated recognition in the Department of Education and Science that the local authorities could no longer be left to cope, that Administration took no specific policy initiatives in this field. Control, an expedient rather than a policy, dominated their thinking.

Against this background, the 1965 White Paper stands out as the first systematic review of policy and attempt to define remedies. Part II, drafted by the only department which really knew its own mind—the Home Office—deals with the restriction of immigration and the means by which it is to be controlled. As such, it is merely a further stage in a debate which had already been opened. The novelty lies in Part III of the White Paper, which deals with policies of integration. This section is Janus-faced. The sections on departmental action look into the past; Whitehall holds up a cracked mirror to itself, reflecting chiefly failures of comprehension and imagination. But the final sections on the evolution of policy and the devising of special means to deal with the problems that had arisen represent a new departure, stemming largely from the appointment of a co-ordinating minister. That these structures eventually proved inadequate is less important than the fact that they could at last be contemplated without self-conscious references to the dangers of unequal treatment. There are other valid criticisms of the White Paper to be made, notably that it lacks a point of reference in the reality of the situation, as a result of the failure to undertake effective gathering of information, symbolized in the universal reluctance to provide statistical information on this subject. Roy Jenkins was able to make this deficiency good during his term at the Home Office by setting in train the processes that led up to the P.E.P. investigation into the extent of discrimination.[8] His attempt at a concerted programme and the development of the special agencies which was involved, flawed though it was, is so important that we have considered it separately, as a case study (Part VI). What follows in this section is a review of the evolution of policy nationally—that is, in Whitehall and in Westminster—over the whole period of the migration leading up to Jenkins' assumption of the Home Secretaryship. It is followed in turn by an examination of practice in a number of particularly significant policy areas. One such area, where the evolution of policy from the application of universal values, to a pluralistic concept in which special measures are not merely justified but necessary, is education (Chapter 18). In this case, the comparatively early involvement of central government and the pressure of events made the transition a relatively painless one. In other fields, starved of direction and resources, improvised solutions have compounded difficulties (Chapter 20). The crucial area of housing stands mid-way between these two situations: the general trend towards more centralized planning and a recognition that there must be some form of planned allocation of resources has emerged only after a long struggle, the course of which has had concrete implications for race relations (Chapter 17).

Despite the discontinuities produced by the fact that local authorities possess different powers in different fields and by the variety, in practice, from one local situation to another, these case studies should be seen as running parallel and reflecting the general evolution of practice at local authority level, first in a state of nature and later against the background of the assumption of an increasing degree of responsibility by central government. At the end of the period we are considering, this recognition of responsibility on the part of central government extends to a degree of direct intervention and to a willingness to consider the problems of the areas of immigrant settlement as a whole.

In Part IV we also consider the role of one other agency of government—the police (see Chapter 20). Their position is of particular interest in that they have been assigned a double custodial role—both of the values embodied in law and in the more literal sense of the maintenance of public order. This function of social control came in due course to be in tension with a new task of community relations assigned to them when policy took its new direction under the Home Secretaryship of Roy Jenkins. The problems that arose as a result can, in some senses, be taken to epitomize the strains undergone by the system of government in its painful transition from an official policy of *laissez-faire* to one in which equality has to be not proclaimed but planned—the subject of specific and planned innovations. In addition, we shall look at the active involvement of voluntary organizations, religious and secular, both those with a general concern and those specifically evolved to meet the needs of this situation (see Chapter 21). As we have already suggested, the fluctuation in their significance has depended not so much on their own activities as on the importance attached to them centrally.

The influence of public opinion, both as projected through the mass media and as reflected in public opinion polls, grew throughout this period and its relevance was first recognized and eventually exaggerated. But, we will reserve our discussion of the content and changes in attitudes until a later section (Part VII). Instead, we will end Part IV with a brief review of the evidence obtained in the course of the P.E.P. inquiry into the extent of discrimination. The evidence from this inquiry stands both as the verdict on the efficacy of policy during this period and as a reminder that there has been a missing term in the whole discussion to date—the immigrant and his perception of the situation. The immigrant response and its effects on the evolution of the situation will be the subject of a separate section, later in this report (Part V).

NOTES TO CHAPTER 15

1. R. *v.* Hunt and others (*Times* law reports, 16 September 1958).
2. Bob Hepple, *Race, Jobs and the Law in Britain* (London, Allen Lane, The Penguin Press, 1968).
3. 264 H. L. Deb., Col. 166, 10 March 1965.
4. Quoted in Paul Foot, *Immigration and Race in British Politics* (Harmondsworth, Penguin Books, 1965).
5. J. A. G. Griffith, *Central Departments and Local Authorities* (London, Allen & Unwin, 1966), p. 562.
6. Griffith, op. cit., p. 505.
7. Cmnd. 2379, *Immigration from the Commonwealth* (London, H.M.S.O., 1965).
8. Published as W. W. Daniel, *Racial Discrimination in England* (Harmondsworth, Penguin Books, 1968).

16 The Decline and Fall of Laissez-Faire: Politics and Race Relations, 1955-65

One of the major obstacles confronting anyone proposing to discuss official policy on immigration and race relations in the period leading up to the Labour Government's White Paper of 1965 is the widespread belief that no such thing existed. This is a view common to all shades of opinion: it is one of the main themes of Paul Foot's devastating polemic;[1] Enoch Powell employs it as the cornerstone of his jeremiads on national negligence.[2] Politicians nearer the centre of the spectrum have repeated it; Henry Brooke, who as a senior minister in the fifties was as closely concerned as anyone with these questions, told the House of Lords in 1966 that:

> If only these problems had been thought out in advance, and if only action had been taken in the 1950s to keep the pace of immigration at a rate which the country could successfully absorb, without risk of over-heating the points of friction . . . we should have far more cause to be proud of the way this country grew to be a multi-racial society.[3]

Similarly, Lord Gardiner, Lord Chancellor in the incoming Wilson Administration, told the House in the previous year that in his view:

> The actions, or rather the inaction, of the last two Administrations means that neither our children nor their children will ever see the England which we have been used to seeing, because for good or ill England has become a multi-racial society.

And this was chiefly because:

> Just as until 1962 we had no real national plan about immigration, so we had no national plan as to how those who were here were to be integrated or assimilated into the population.[4]

The implication could hardly be clearer; no policy except control and that introduced belatedly. Control, moreover, as an expedient and not as part of a fully thought out programme. And the conclusion often drawn is that most of the difficulties that have subsequently arisen stem from this initial failure to plan.[5] Yet on close examination, it becomes clear that the view that the immigration was allowed to develop in a totally unplanned and higgledy-piggledly way cannot be entirely sustained; and the indictment of the Labour Government of 1945–51, and, in particular, the Conservative Administration that followed it, for failing to anticipate the difficulties that their successors would encounter, does not entirely fit the facts. But both the policies and the practices of the earlier period have been almost entirely covered by the detritus of succeeding epochs, and patient archaeological work is required to uncover the remnants of the structures constructed to deal with what was seen as an incipient problem of some importance. That these structures were in many ways inadequate to the problem cannot be disputed; nor is there space to do anything more here than indicate their existence. But they are of some importance because their existence reflects with clarity the initial assumptions with which the British Government approached the immigration of people who were then described as 'coloured colonials'. It was the modification of these assumptions, for reasons almost entirely extrinsic to the migration, which later brought about a sharp change of policy, and in turn produced the stereotype of complete inactivity which is now almost universally accepted.

We have already seen how wartime circumstances led to the importation of a number of skilled workers from the West Indies to work on Merseyside, and to the recruitment of men to the Armed Forces, particularly the R.A.F. The way in which the scheme for the employment of these workers was run under the joint supervision of the Ministry of Labour and the Colonial Office exemplifies the benevolent paternalism of this phase in the migration, and reflects general policy towards dependent colonial territories at this period. The manner in which the scheme was run down is also a reflection of a general belief about the undesirability of importing coloured labour on a permanent basis, on the grounds that it would not be in the best interests of the country or the migrants to do so. This belief was stated in perhaps its most extreme form by the Royal Commission on Population which was sitting at this period (although it did not report until 1949). A systematic policy of immigration, the Commission argued, 'could only be welcomed without reserve if the migrants were of good human stock and were not prevented by their religion or race from intermarrying with the host population and becoming merged in it'.[6] It is important to stress that these views, although their overtones at twenty years' range are distasteful, do not imply an explicitly racialist element in policy-making. Rather, they reflect a general view shared by all policy makers at this period and strongly influenced by the colonial experience. It is this view that led the Labour Government, when acute labour shortage forced it in 1947 to reconsider the restrictive immigration policy that all Administrations had followed since the First World War and embark on an extensive recruiting campaign, to turn to the Displaced Persons camps of Europe rather than to the colonies, despite the success of the Merseyside experiment. And it is against this background that the official reaction to the first substantial migration of coloured workers from the West Indies, in the liner *Empire Windrush* in June 1948, should be seen.

Concern, but concern coupled with acceptance of a degree of responsibility, was the keynote of the response of the Colonial Office (as the department chiefly concerned) to the arrival of the *Empire Windrush* and the persistent, though small scale, movement from the West Indies that followed. The Colonial Office was able to exercise a degree of supervision over colonial immigrants, and make some provision for their welfare, but in the matter of control over entry it was not able to satisfy its critics. This was largely as a result of the new initiatives in policy taken by its neighbours in Whitehall, the Commonwealth Relations Office. The decision of the Attlee Government to give independence to India and Pakistan and to accept Republican India's application to join the Commonwealth led to a far-reaching modification of the concept of Commonwealth. One of the tangible signs of this modification was the British Nationality Act of 1948, a codification of nationality law which allowed the newly independent countries of the Asian Commonwealth to fit their citizenship provisions into a new overall framework for British citizenship. This bipartisan measure had the then altogether marginal effect of removing any immediate prospect of Colonial Office control over the movement of citizens 'of the U.K. and colonies' to the United Kingdom.

When it became clear that the migration would not merely continue, but increase, both Government and Opposition took advice. The Labour party consulted an eminent academic student of the subject, Professor Kenneth Little, but no action was taken on his suggestion that legislation against discrimination should be introduced.[7] The Government had meanwhile turned to its interdepartmental working party for advice. This had been set up to supplement the Colonial Office Advisory Committee established in 1947, and was based (a factor of some importance) on the Home Office. The working party came to the conclusion that immigration from the West Indies would grow and that steps should be taken to deal with the situation that would arise as a result. Like the Royal Commission on Population, the working party was concerned with the possibility of an inassimilable minority being created by migration: granted the current philosophy, those steps could only be control, and the working party was reconvened in 1954 to consider ways in which this could be introduced.[8]

But although the working party seems to have been convinced of the necessity for a system of control equivalent to that operating in the case of aliens, the decision was evidently put off. And after the Election—at which the Conservatives obtained an increased majority—the conclusion reached was that there should be no control. That was the burden of the Prime Minister's somewhat oblique reply to Sir Cyril Osborne in the House of Commons on 10 November 1955.[9]

There are a number of possible explanations for this decision, which was to have a decisive effect on the development of race relations in Britain. The first can be found in the general evolution of policy on the colonies and the Commonwealth. By the mid-1950s it was becoming increasingly clear that several colonies were moving towards independence, and presumptively a place in the Commonwealth, at a faster rate than had previously been anticipated. The general acceptance of the changed nature of the Commonwealth, and the increasing stress on the importance of its multi-racial composition, made the approach of independence for the Gold Coast particularly significant and underlined the importance of making room for new members as equal partners. More specifically, the erratic progress of the West Indian colonies towards some sort of federal structure had gathered a certain amount of momentum. Under the circumstances, the Commonwealth Relations Office, perhaps more than the Colonial Office, had a vested interest in staving off any measure that might revive notions of the dependent or separate status of the African or West Indian colonies. Moreover, there was the possibility that the authorities in territories moving towards independence might themselves assume responsibility for their nationals in the U.K. The Senior-Manley mission, despatched to Britain by the Jamaican Government, recommended such an arrangement.[10]

At the same time, the bipartisanship, that had characterized policy towards the evolving Commonwealth, had received a severe check as a result of a basic disagreement between Government and Opposition about the proper course of development for the settler colonies of East Africa, and more particularly Central Africa, where the Labour party had withdrawn their initial support for the new Federation. In this atmosphere, any decision on the control of immigration from the colonies would certainly be controversial, as the Home Office explicitly recognized.[11]

On the other side, there was not much active pressure for control outside Parliament. In the absence of public controversy, the private pressure of the Commonwealth Relations Office and Colonial Office seems to have outweighed the arguments advanced by the Home Office and the joint working party. Sir Anthony Eden opted for inaction; and his decision opened a new phase in the development of policy on this issue.

If the animating principle of the first stage in the evolution of race relations was welfare, that of the second was status, and its motto 'Civis Britannicus Sum'. The prospect of control, contemplated with equanimity by ministers in 1955 and positively flaunted before the House of Commons, receded with astonishing rapidity; and an expedient ostensibly rejected only on grounds of administrative complexity was rapidly transformed into a breach of tradition to be avoided as a matter of principle. A similar process occurred on the other side of politics. The Labour Opposition's position had previously been equivocal; the London Members who had questioned ministers from the beginning of the 1950s were patently sympathetic to the notion of control. But their colleagues on the whole were not; and their acquiescence in Government policy helped to create the informal coalition which has since been made the scapegoat for any and all undesirable side-effects of the migration, under the label of 'high-minded Liberalism'—which, in the strict sense that laissez-faire was the basic philosophy involved, is for once accurate.

A few Members had evolved a position for themselves. Some, by relating the migration to their personal convictions on race relations—Cyril Osborne at one extreme, for example, and Fenner Brockway at the other; a second group, mostly Labour Members, by reference to conditions in their constituency; and a third, in relation to policy they had helped to formulate at an earlier stage—unreconstructed advocates of the paternalist wel-are approach, like Patrick Gordon Walker or Lord Home. But these were a small minority, and their concern with the subject was muted by the lack of occasion to express it and by the general debate on the future of the Commonwealth.

All this assumed greater significance than it might otherwise have done as a result of the shift in the balance of interests within Whitehall. The British Caribbean Welfare Service, set up as a result of the Senior-Manley Report, began in June 1956, housed in the Colonial Office student department, where it inherited the work and files of the welfare section of the Colonial Office, but subsequently moved out and started a separate existence. With this act of internal decolonization, the Colonial Office's direct concern with the subject was substantially reduced. The main responsibility subsequently rested with the Home Office, whose responsibility consisted chiefly of keeping a watch over the turnstile (in 1955 it turned this to some account by instituting a system of counting the clicks, although the information obtained was not made available until some time later). A debate in the Lords in November 1956 gave the Home Office an opportunity of putting the departmental case in public. The debate had been initiated by Lord Elton, who touched with greater reserve than he was subsequently to show on the possibility of control. In his reply, Lord Mancroft explained that control had been considered two years before but rejected because of administrative difficulties. After giving some remarkably accurate population forecasts (in a field where forecasts are notoriously fallible), he let the cat half out of the bag by adding: 'Her Majesty's Government are satisfied that, if the necessity arose, it would be possible to devise legislative and administrative measures which could be put into operation at short notice and would be reasonably effective.'[12] In other words, the administrative difficulties were not as significant as they might seem. But when the Home Office was next called upon to brief a minister for a debate in the House, the line adopted was rather different. Answering a debate in the Commons in February 1958, Patricia Hornsby-Smith told the House that the British Caribbean Welfare Service was doing excellent work; and that the Government was 'certainly not complacent about this problem'.[13] The tone of her speech suggested strongly, in its contrast with Mancroft's, that laissez-faire had also established itself at the Home Office.

However, there are signs that this process was contested. The inter-departmental working party had reconstituted itself in the winter of 1956–7, and repeated the inquiries carried out in 1953. The occasion for this renewed activity was the appearance of, for the first time in substantial numbers, immigrants from India and Pakistan. Entering the employment market at a time when it had itself not fully recovered from the deflationary effects of the Suez crisis, these new migrants caused considerable alarm in the West Riding and provoked the junior minister responsible (Miss Hornsby-Smith) into the comment that the newcomers were giving the Home Office 'a headache'—'they come in by air and at once begin to draw National Assistance'.[14] Consultations were begun with the governments concerned and in June 1958 the Secretary of State, Lord Home, was able to tell the Lords that the Indian and Pakistani Governments 'are now taking a variety of further measures designed to reduce the flow of migrants coming to this country'.[15] He hoped that 'the problem will sort itself out in the very near future'. In this deceptively favourable way the new doctrine of bilateral voluntary controls was launched as a quasi-solution, and had a brief vogue with each party in turn before being finally discredited in 1965. The major advantage of this approach, that it did not infringe the principle of Commonwealth status, arose from the fact that it was negotiated between equals. The disadvantage lay in its unenforceability, which in turn sprang from a fatal uncertainty about division of responsibility.

With these voluntary restrictions on migration from the Indian sub-continent (regarded in Whitehall as potentially exceptionally awkward) in operation, and with migration from the West Indies falling sharply in response to the decline in demand for labour, the Government looked for a brief moment as if it could have its cake and eat it. Effective results were being achieved by controls that were not controls, and by the operation of the economic regulator. But increasingly there were signs that difficulties that had arisen in certain local authority areas would not fade away with the passage of time, in the absence of Government intervention, and that the withdrawal of such services as had existed was difficult to justify, in practical terms.

In one or two cases Members were prepared to take up their local grievances, and in one instance this produced results. In an adjournment debate in November 1957 a series of London Labour Members harassed the Parliamentary Secretary to the Ministry of Housing (J. R. Bevins) about the inadequacies of the local authorities powers under the 1957 Housing Act to such good effect that he was constrained to initiate a series of discussions with local authorities. Although these had no immediate results their consequences were to be seen in part in the legislation of three years later (discussed in Chapter 17); more important, these discussions were an important inroad on the publicly expressed position that equal citizens could not be made the occasion for any special measures for relief of their difficulties. A social policy department had accepted some degree of responsibility for the situation that had arisen. But this was an exception.

The immediate effects of the disturbances which took place in Nottingham and Notting Dale in August and September 1958 was to blow away the complacency with which the subject was still clothed and leave the Government's lack of policy indecently exposed. Reactions within the Government were mixed. A small faction wished to introduce immediate control over immigration, using (as Lord Mancroft had predicted in 1956) the measure drafted in 1955. Lord Home, possibly somewhat isolated from departmental advice in Vancouver,[16] gave immediate public expression to this position. But the majority view was that bilateralism, which was apparently working adequately with the Indians and Pakistanis, should be extended to the West Indians. But neither Norman Manley nor the ministers of the embryonic West Indies Federal Government were prepared to accept any responsibility for such a solution. Faced with this refusal, the Colonial Office fell back on its old expedient and established a new committee to succeed that of 1947: this committee's specific objective was to associate the welfare operations of the British Caribbean Welfare Service with the machinery of Government in a form of loose co-ordination. On the general issue, a compromise decision was taken, which consisted of employing the machinery of bilateral consultation to introduce deportation provisions for Commonwealth or colonial citizens involved in serious crime. This line was duly adopted for the Home Secretary's speech to a concerned audience at the Conservative Party Conference, who passed by a substantial majority a motion calling for control; most Members thought that his speech meant legislation in the following session. As for the rest, Government spokesmen could refer critics to the sonorous words of Lord Justice Salmon, sentencing the nine youths convicted for assault during the disturbances:

You are a minute and insignificant section of the population who have brought shame on the district in which you lived and have filled the whole nation with horror, indignation and disgust. Everyone irrespective of the colour of their skin, is entitled to walk through our streets with their heads erect and free from fear. This is a right which these courts will always unfailingly uphold.[17]

Outside Whitehall the disturbances had a further important result, in that they pushed the Opposition into a position of outright resistance to the control of immigration. Both Hugh Gaitskel and Jo Grimond were initially inclined to favour the deportation of convicted criminals, but in the debates at the end of the year the spokesmen for the Labour party nailed their party's colours firmly to the mast by opposing control in any foreseeable circumstances.

A further result of some significance for the evolution of policy was the involvement of a whole range of new bodies, involving intellectuals and churchmen, predominantly but not exclusively middle-class Labour supporters, concerned to find non-racial solutions in the context of the new concept of the multi-racial Commonwealth. The newly formed British Caribbean Association epitomized this body of opinion in a Parliamentary context with its immediate lobby for an educational programme and official support for Fenner Brockway's anti-discrimination legislation.

Finally, for the first time, the significance of public opinion in this context was invoked. But, just as at an earlier stage the view of local authorities had seemed remote from the legitimate concerns on which policy making should be based, so at this point Lord Salisbury's rather incongruous attempts to demonstrate, with opinion poll evidence, that in writing to *The Times* and speaking against uncontrolled immigration of 'men and women of African race' he was speaking for the common man, made little impression on spokesmen of either party.

The period directly after the disturbances was the silver age of the status theory of Commonwealth immigration. A perceptive commentator writing in *The Economist*, after discussing departmental views with every appearance of inside knowledge, added that 'they [that is, officials] think that the liberal line—uncontrolled immigration—can be held for a few more years, but not indefinitely . . . this school in Whitehall and beyond feels that when the tide of colour rises to a ceiling as yet unspecified . . .

British voters will demand that some check is imposed'.[18] These forebodings notwithstanding, the Government persisted with the course of action determined upon. Consultations proceeded, but with agonizing slowness ('I am sorry that they are not quicker', the Home Secretary told the House rather pathetically). Attempts to spatchcock the deportation provisions into the Street Offences Act were beaten off.

Attention was to some extent diverted from what the Government was attempting to achieve by the extra-Parliamentary activities of Sir Oswald Mosley. His Union Movement had been as surprised as anyone by what had occurred in Notting Hill, but they were brisk enough in their efforts to exploit the situation. Early in 1959 Mosley announced his intention to contest the North Kensington seat at the forthcoming general election, his platform epitomized in the statement, 'we are going to treat these people fairly but we are going to send them home'. Evidence soon began to show that Mosley was gaining ground, and when a West Indian carpenter, Kelso Cochrane, was stabbed to death in the same area by an unknown assailant in May, the danger of further disturbances forced the Government to make another lengthy self-exculpatory statement. 'I am satisfied', the Home Secretary told the House of Commons in June, 'from consultations which I have had with my colleagues mainly concerned and from consultations which have taken place with local authorities, voluntary bodies, the official welfare organisations, and the police that everything possible is being done and that every effort will continue to be made in areas where there is a large coloured population to encourage their effective integration into the community.'[19] And further than that, with a general election imminent, the Government was not prepared to go.

As the Election approached the subject began to sink below the political horizon, and Mosley's failure at the polls, where he obtained less than 3,000 votes and lost his deposit for the first time in his career, added a sour smell of failure to the generally squalid impression made by the way in which he had presented his case.[20] This failure of explicit opposition to continued uncontrolled immigration, coupled with the handsome majority obtained by the Government at the Election, gave it the last of a series of breathing spaces. The fact that it failed to use it to any effect, either by taking the plunge and adopting control, or by devising positive policies with a degree of direct central intervention, is intimately bound up with the new departure on colonial policy adopted by the Macmillan Administration after October 1959.

Although Iain Macleod, who succeeded Lennox-Boyd as Colonial Secretary, has subsequently denied that the policies he adopted on coming into office represented any significant change from those of his predecessor, he is in a minority of one in doing so. The gradualist approach of the Lyttleton–Lennox-Boyd period, with the emphasis on economic viability, the creation of a sound administrative infrastructure, and above all the reluctance to interfere with the *status quo* in the settler colonies of East Africa, was replaced by a deliberate assault on the problems of these colonies and of the Central African Federation. The various stages in this initiative need not concern us here: what was important for present purposes was the impact of this policy at Westminster.

The pace of change proved too much for some Conservatives and eventually provoked Lord Salisbury's notorious attack on Macleod ('too clever by half'). But it also had the effect of stealing the clothes of the Opposition, who had no choice but to fall in behind the initiatives taken by the Colonial Secretary: accordingly, the centre of gravity of colonial policy moved sharply to the left. The keynote oration of this period was the Prime Minister's 'wind of change' speech in Capetown in February 1960 (perhaps more radical in style than content), and one of its major symbolic acts was the decision to allow South Africa to leave the Commonwealth in the following spring. Both reflect the diminishing significance attached in official policy to the position of the white man in Africa, and in this realignment, a minor though significant element was a countervailing belief in the importance of the black man in the new dispensation for the Commonwealth. As the Colonial Secretary saw it (the Press reported at the time), the introduction of control over West Indian immigration at a time when the Federation was at last getting on its feet and preparing for independence would be a substantial setback for this limb of his policy.

But while the tide was running powerfully in one direction in colonial policy, another current of opinion within the Conservative Party had begun to run with increasing strength. As a result of the general election, a group of Members from the Birmingham area, several of them newly-elected, had come together to launch a systematic campaign for the introduction of controls. These Members could claim direct constituency experience of the difficulties associated with immigration—a claim which, for reasons of electoral geography, was previously mainly confined to Labour Members. Of the problems themselves there could be no longer any serious argument, although the basic causes of the difficulties remained in dispute; the housing situation in particular now demanded some form of action and the Ministry of Housing was being strongly pressed by local authorities, particularly Birmingham. But perhaps most significant, these Members were claiming that the view they were putting forward was representative of public opinion at large. In this claim they were assisted by the setting up in the Birmingham area of a lobbying organization, the Birmingham Immigration Control Association. This Association brought together in the simulacrum of a mass organization a number of local figures who had been campaigning for some years, with the assistance of extensive publicity from the Press, for the control of immigration. This now became a demand for a complete stop for five years. Throughout the year leading up to the introduction of legislation an elaborate minuet was danced by the Birmingham Conservative Members and B.I.C.A.: a step or two closer when the Members' campaign at Westminster was making an impression on the Home Secretary, and a step back when B.I.C.A. contested the municipal elections of 1961 against a Conservative candidate. But the chief importance of the B.I.C.A. campaign in Birmingham and the West Midlands was that it provided the Birmingham Conservative Members with a means of demonstrating, in a way that polls could never do, that public opinion was aroused on the issue. And those local Members who disagreed with the campaign, particularly Sir Edward Boyle, were made to feel the weight of the people's displeasure.*

The confluence of these two tides began to produce rough water for ministers very early in the new Parliament. The Home Secretary was able to beat off Osborne with a repetition of the old story about consultation, but had to receive the deputations (in some instances, 'all-party') which Harold Gurden (Selly Oak, and secretary of the Birmingham Conservatives) organized and read the evidence that he provided. In July 1960, Butler had the

---

* Or were intended to. In fact, the avalanche of postcards intended to harass Sir Edward piled up harmlessly at Empire House (Birmingham Conservative headquarters).

Q

support of Gordon Walker, for the Opposition, in resisting a demand by Norman Pannell for control; but this support merely underlined the dilemma of the Home Secretary—the coalition between the two Front Benches on colonial issues was becoming an embarrassment on this sector of the front.

The difficulty was sharpened by the substantial rise in the migration from the West Indies in 1959 and 1960; and in August 1960 the Colonial Secretary made a further attempt to persuade the Jamaican Government to restrict the number of emigrants through passport limitations—the figure of 15,000 per annum was mentioned. Almost equally disturbing was the patent erosion of the bilateral agreements between the British Government and the Indian and Pakistani Governments, brought about by systematic forgery of passports and evasion of control by racketeers manipulating the migration for profit (see Chapter 6). As a result, the Home Secretary decided that the question of the mechanics of control should be thoroughly re-examined by the interdepartmental standing committee. Their report came down in favour of a system of control based on the availability of employment and incorporating checks on health and criminal record.

This move, which was accompanied by particularly detailed leaks to the Press (possibly by ministers anxious to test the temperature of the voter), caused a good deal of anxiety. It also provoked a strong reaction within Whitehall from the Commonwealth and Colonial Offices. The affront to the susceptibilities of territories shortly to become independent, it was argued, would be insupportable—a view reinforced by the Prime Minister-designate of the Federation, Sir Grantley Adams, on a visit to the United Kingdom early in 1961. The Treasury was known to be anxious about the prospect of losing a beneficial supply of extra labour for an economy in a state of expansion. The political arguments cut both ways: as *The Times* pointed out, was it seemly for a Home Secretary with a liberal reputation like Butler's to capitulate to pressure of this kind?

In the circumstances, it was decided to make one more attempt at a bilateral solution. The Prime Minister himself paid a visit to the West Indies as part of a trip which included Washington and Ottawa. The results were disappointing. The West Indian Governments remained unprepared to take any responsibility for a decision which would certainly be exceedingly unpopular with their electorates. An attempt to interest the United States and

Canadian Governments in increasing their quota and draining part of the surplus died stillborn. The Prime Minister left with President Kennedy (who as a young Congressman had spoken against the McCarran–Walter Act on the ground that it unfairly penalized the West Indies) a memorandum on the subject, but with no result.

Despite this disappointment, the Colonial Office was able to strike a bargain with its colleagues. In April 1961 Macleod, as Colonial Secretary, issued a statement which indicated that 'the Government... have at present no plans to introduce legislation directed to bringing immigration from any Commonwealth country to a halt'. The gloss that lobby correspondents were able to put on this statement was that there would be no control until the West Indian Federation had safely established itself; that was, until 1962 at the earliest. Further delegations and questioners on the subject of control were held at arms' length by ministers until the recess with a repetition of the familiar line about constant vigilance. The hopes of the control lobby were transferred to the Conservative Party Conference at Brighton in October, for which numerous resolutions on control had been submitted.*

In the event, these hopes were not disappointed. Not, as Cyril Osborne suggested, because a letter he wrote to the *Daily Telegraph* the day before, and distributed personally on the conference hall steps on the morning of the debate, was so eloquent as to finally tip the balance, but because of the events that took place in the interim. The first was the decision of the Jamaican electorate, on 21 September, at the urging of Sir Alexander Bustamante and his Jamaica Labour party, not to consent to their country's participation in the Federation. Secondly, the Prime Minister's decision to move Iain Macleod from the Colonial Office to the leadership of the House of Commons removed, as one paper put it, 'the main obstacle'. The plans proposed at the beginning of the year by the Home Office and the Ministry of Labour could be put into effect without further delay. R. A. Butler, in a speech of exquisite ambiguity, made the fact that control was impending clear to the Conference but the timing and processes opaque. And in the manner of his announcement, which was designed to avoid giving the misleading impression of yielding to right-wing pressure, he created a source of substantial extra difficulty for the Government.

* Eventually, forty.

The passage of the Commonwealth Immigrants Bill in 1961–2 has been as fertile of myths as any single event in the history of race relations in Britain. But matters of party mythology are not our concern here, except in so far as they affected subsequent formation of policy. More significant, perhaps, was the way in which control of immigration as the fundamental issue was pushed by virtue of the debate to the forefront and kept there for long enough to fix it permanently in the public mind as the crux of the entire question of race relations. In the early 1950s, control could be discussed across the floor of the House by Members of all shades of opinion as an element in a programme designed to promote the welfare of the newcomers. If, as ministers of both parties indicated, control could not be introduced, this was for reasons that were largely technical. After the Eden Government's decision not to introduce control, technicalities were erected into a principle, to which each party in turn adhered. This principle was increasingly held as prohibiting any measure of interference in the processes of migration, at any stage.

By 1961, pressures forced one party to relinquish its grip on the principle. In the process, the significance of control in terms of the standing of the Commonwealth had become such as to exclude any possibility of reversing the decision of the status period (1955–61) and introducing other measures for the newcomers' welfare or a broader programme directed to the problems of the areas in which they had settled. The passage of the Act introduced, one might say, a period of diminished responsibility. Control was achieved, and with it an end to the status debate. But the welfare issue remained virtually untouched, for reasons that had become obsolescent.

The conflict over the Commonwealth Immigrants Bill was to a very striking degree a symbolic one; the issue of control was debated by reference to its impact on the Commonwealth. It is true that Labour, in their reasoned amendment, stressed the irrelevance of the measure and immediate needs in areas of settlement, but this line of criticism was not developed at any length (except briefly, at a later stage, by Marcus Lipton): moral indignation about post-Imperial obligations was more effective in shaking the ranks of Tuscany.

The achievements of the Labour party, in modifying a bill whose provisions—based on a system of entry on employment vouchers—were by subsequent standards mild, were detailed at length by Eric Fletcher in his speech at Third Reading in March 1962. These were: early renewal (in 1963), easier entry for residents, a broader definition of students and dependants, the institution of entry certificates, and the publication of instructions to immigration officers. The degree to which these achievements did not represent a total success was reflected in the melancholy winding up speech by Denis Healey, who carefully reserved the Labour position on renewal of the legislation, and by the Oppositions' poor showing in the vote that followed. But at the time, the damage to the Conservative party looked quite extensive. Abstentions and outright opposition in several sections of the party had been frequent. Ministers, who had 'hated the necessity for the Bill', stressed that it represented 'control rather than a stop', and accepted the need for frequent review of the situation, were anxious to forget the episode. Control was duly introduced, with comparatively little difficulty, at the end of June, and a new advisory committee, the Commonwealth Immigrants Advisory Council—set up as a result of proposals made during the passage of the Bill—was left to review the situation in a nightwatchman role. Virtually unnoticed, the Migrant Services Division of the West Indian Federal High Commission, the chief prop of the welfare system, was broken up, and the Colonial Office Coordinating Committee slipped quietly into oblivion.

For a brief period it seemed as if the Labour party might be prepared to try to fill the policy vacuum. A sub-committee of the Home Policy Committee under the chairmanship of Harold Wilson began to consider positive measures for integration. In due course a drafting committee published recommendations in pamphlet form, *Integrating the Immigrant*. A liaison organization, the British Overseas Socialist Fellowship, was set up at Transport House to co-ordinate party activity on this front.

An encouraging scattering of coloured Labour candidates at the council elections suggested a response, and perhaps a mediating role for immigrants entering British politics on the lines of the Democratic party in the United States. But the energies of the radicals were diverted to a prolonged campaign to keep first Colin Jordan, then Oswald Mosley off the streets; 'punch up politics' and petitions campaigning for legislation against incitement to racial hatred (in which the major Jewish organizations made one of their rare interventions in this field) served as a surrogate for direct involvement in race relations. In Parliament, hostility was canalized into a campaign against the incoming Home Secretary, Henry Brooke, for a series of decisions on the deportation of Commonwealth citizens and aliens. The attention of the Labour movement itself was increasingly diverted by the approaching prospect of power and by the emergence of a new major issue. The party debate on the Common Market at Brighton marked, in Hugh Gaitskell's 'Vimy Ridge' speech, the apogee of the party's commitment to the Commonwealth; but neither of the main speakers made any reference whatever in the course of a lengthy debate to the relationship between Commonwealth membership and immigration control.*

In January 1963 Hugh Gaitskell died, universally regretted, and in his first major speech as leader Harold Wilson committed the party to the support of Fenner Brockway's Bill, now incorporating provision of racial incitement and without the clauses on employment (to which trade union members had objected). There was nothing in this to foreshadow the drastic modification to the party's line which took place during the year. Indeed, evidence during the spring and summer from by-elections suggested that the issue was no longer salient; substantial Labour victories in West Bromwich (where Maurice Foley for Labour came out for repeal of the Act) and Deptford against opponents basing their campaigns on the presumed local resentment on the issue indicated as much. The only shadow on proceedings was cast by a cloud no bigger than a man's hand at Smethwick, where the Conservative achievement in winning a seat against one of the strongest of all municipal election swings reflected the diversion of the energies, objectives, and personnel of the local immigration control association into the local Conservative party.

Nor was there any evidence of concern on the part of the Government. Control itself, in the Government view, required no further debate: action had been taken. The C.I.A.C. had already produced one report;[21] oversight of the situation was in reliable hands, and voluntary efforts were making headway in local situations. There were still more serious things to worry about: in the summer of 1963 the Profumo scandal broke and with it the festering scandal of Peter Rachman, the slum landlord.†

In this atmosphere, might not the Labour party have a

---

* Contrary to another myth, there was never any pledge to repeal the Act.
† The involvement of West Indians in both did not go unnoticed.

responsibility to avoid any controversial commitment that would jeopardize a long awaited election victory? Donald Chapman, a conspicuous opponent of the 1961 Bill, thought so; the campaign that might be provoked could be of 'Zinoviev letter' proportions. With this in mind and informal soundings by the Whips suggesting anxiety in the constituencies, the Shadow Cabinet met to consider their line in the debate on the renewal of the Act (for whose early arrival the Opposition was responsible). After acrimonious debate a solution was found: bilateral controls. This was duly put forward by Wilson in a debate that revealed considerable disarray in the Labour ranks. Henry Brooke had no difficulty in disposing of the argument for the further consultation with the Commonwealth which Wilson offered as a price for unopposed renewal; the Opposition were forced to divide the House.

Increasing evidence of local concern, open dispute at Southall, and a Conservative victory at Smethwick (where the Conservative leader, Alderman Griffiths, made the uncharacteristic mistake of telling *The Times* Midland correspondent what he felt on the issue) were a source of embarrassment for both Government and Opposition alike. But for the former there was a way out.

Control had, after all, been introduced by the Conservative Government as a deliberate act of policy. Beside this, the reports of the C.I.A.C. and their recommendations for action were of marginal significance. Henry Brooke had told the Commons in November 1963 that he would not want to suggest that all those 300,000 applicants awaiting vouchers would have necessarily entered the country if controls had not existed. By July 1964 he was implying the opposite in the House, and by September the claim that their entry had been averted was official party policy.

Certain Conservatives were prepared to push the matter further. In July, a meeting of the Birmingham group of Members, under the chairmanship of Geoffrey Lloyd, made the case for a full-blooded campaign based on stringent Conservative controls against Opposition laxity. However, the Birmingham initiative failed to carry the Conservative party. Other Birmingham Members organized a counter-statement and the general impression current when the campaign at last began was that the issue would not be debated between the parties. This was very much to the taste of the Labour party's N.E.C., whose efforts to obtain an

agreed line on immigration for the party manifesto led to prolonged bickering. Since the beginning of the year, Transport
House had answered the increasing number of inquiries about the
party's position on the issue by phlegmatically issuing a duplicated resumé of the key passages in Wilson's speech of November
1963. A party committee under Anthony Greenwood, established
with a publicity fanfare after that debate to work out new policies,
sat from January 1964 but never completed its deliberations. But
the election campaign clearly demanded something better; with
infinite pains a package was put together: bilateral controls, the
Brockway Bill, and aid to areas affected by immigration. With
the subject raised more and more frequently in Wilson's whistle-
stop tours, and the developing Conservative strategy of referring
to the numbers they had kept out (now putatively swollen to a
million, by the inclusion of dependants, in speeches made by the
Prime Minister in Birmingham and Bradford), a clear statement
became impossible to avoid. Wilson provided a substitute of a
kind, with some off-the-cuff remarks, at a mass meeting in the
Bull Ring at Birmingham, and a few copies were hastily run off
in Transport House; but these, and the confused variety of statements by individual candidates, did not correct the impression
of a party increasingly on the defensive on this issue.

It was in this posture that the new Labour Government was
disclosed on taking office, deprived by electors of the Parliamentary services of the Foreign Secretary, Patrick Gordon Walker,
defeated at Smethwick. This was generally seen at the time as a
clear expression of popular resentment, frustrated too long by
neglect, and acted as an immediate stimulus to action; the fact
that it was by and large working-class Labour supporters who
seemed to be involved intensified the pressures on the Government
to devise some form of policy which could be put into early effect.

The initial strategy adopted fell into three parts. First, the
Commonwealth Immigrants Act was renewed as an interim
measure. Secondly, a mission was to be sent to Commonwealth
capitals to try to negotiate bilateral agreements (eventually
headed by Lord Mountbatten).* Thirdly, the new Prime Minister
established his radical *bona fides* by a sharp attack on the new
Member for Smethwick, who would, he said, spend his short
Parliamentary career as 'a kind of Parliamentary leper'. These

* Except in Pakistan, where he was not permitted to participate in the mission's
activities.

initiatives taken, a search for positive policies was put in hand. In March 1965, the Prime Minister, after reviewing immigration policy and the need to 'stamp out evasion at source', announced the appointment of Maurice Foley, Member for West Bromwich, as the minister responsible (in a personal capacity) 'for the co-ordination of effective executive government action with, and through, local authorities and voluntary bodies to see that much speedier action is taken on integration, in the widest sense of the word, in terms of housing, health, education, and everything that needs to be done'.[22] The Prime Minister also announced the redemption of his party's pledge to introduce legislation 'to deal with racial discimination in public places and with the evil of incitement to racial hatred'.

In taking these steps, the Government's mind could not help but be wonderfully concentrated—first, by the failure of the Foreign Secretary to return to the Commons at Leyton (this Waterloo for the opinion polls was widely, but probably inaccur-ately, put down to the immigration issue and intensified the bogey effect now associated with it), and second, by the unmistakable signs that the Conservative party was considering a move to the right to accommodate the new currents of opinion out of doors. Sir Edward Boyle, Home's initial choice as spokesman on Home Affairs, was replaced in April by Peter Thorneycroft, who began taking a sterner line. A speech in February by the Leader of the Opposition demanded far stricter controls, and, after some elaborate backstage manœuvres, party opinion was induced by the Whips to coalesce round a motion, moved by Sir Cyril Osborne, for stricter control. This move, though partly frustrated by an inter-party group, which thereby won itself undying fame that long survived its own short existence, did demonstrate that most of the Conservative Front Bench now saw nothing odd in going through the lobbies in support of a man whose views had once been derided on both sides of the House. And it was clear that in devising its long-term policy the Government would have to have regard for the constant danger of being outflanked by its political opponents.

The second major initiative, foreshadowed in the Prime Minister's announcement of March, was the introduction of the new legislation on discrimination and incitement in April 1965. In drafting this legislation, the Home Secretary, Sir Frank Soskice, had the advantage of two previous detailed examinations of policy on this matter. One was his own, conducted in Opposition at the request of the N.E.C.; the second was by a committee of the Society of Labour Lawyers, who had been given the job of revising the Bill so often moved without success by Fenner Brockway, within the limits accepted by Brockway himself. Had he wished to do so, he could also have drawn on a third memorandum prepared by a splinter group from the Society of Labour Lawyers calling for extension of the Bill to housing and employment, enforcement by conciliation, and the setting up of an agency to oversee the process. But neither the Home Office nor the Lord Chancellor, to whom this memorandum was submitted, were prepared to act on it.[23] Those who drafted it responded by embarking on a systematic lobbying campaign, employing a series of different avenues. First, the newly formed Campaign Against Racial Discrimination (see Chapter 25) amended and then took over the responsibility for the proposals. Secondly, the lobby used their contacts with the Society of Labour Lawyers to persuade that body to issue an endorsement of their proposals. Thirdly, Maurice Foley, the minister responsible for co-ordination, was lobbied, and convinced. And finally, contact was made with the Opposition.

The new Conservative spokesman on Home Affairs, Peter Thorneycroft, saw the potential of the conciliation principle and persuaded the Shadow Cabinet and party Home Affairs Committee, whose initial instincts had been to oppose the Bill outright, to adopt the solutions of a reasoned amendment criticizing the drafting of the Bill and calling for the introduction of the device of conciliation. After narrowly obtaining a Second Reading for the Bill, the Home Secretary withdrew the contentious sections, substituting conciliation for criminal penalties and establishing a national agency, the Race Relations Board, to supervise the conciliation process through local committees. The scope of the Bill remained restricted to public places, and the incitement provisions were untouched; in this form, the Bill survived Committee stage—largely in consequence of a curious alliance between the Home Secretary and Conservative backbenchers— and passed into law. It seemed, as a student of the subject has commented, 'a haphazard, secret and inefficient process';[24] but at least it had provided the initial basis for future measures in this field by establishing an administrative agency, in the shape of the Race Relations Board.

Having evolved a solution of sorts to one policy problem, the Government now had to deal with the two main prongs of the March announcement—the integration programme and a new policy for immigration. By June, the failure of the Mountbatten mission had become evident. With the final collapse of bilateralism, any chance that the Government might have had of completing its *volte face* on the issue under cover of the symbols of Commonwealth (and, at one remove, monarchy) disappeared. Not only was consent not forthcoming, the Commonwealth as an institution in British politics could no longer bear the weight of controversy. A Labour Government had, like its predecessor, to evolve its own solution, in the knowledge that a Conservative party group, sitting under the chairmanship of Selwyn Lloyd, were likely to propose extremely drastic solutions—perhaps 'one in, one out', possibly a check on dependants. (In the event, its proposals, endorsed by the Home Affairs Committee in July, were milder and overtaken by the Government's own programme.) This situation gave rise to complaints that the parties were engaged in a species of Dutch auction. The Government's bid, put in 'by a committee presided over by Herbert Bowden, without waiting for [Maurice] Foley's report',[25] was contained in the White Paper on Immigration Policy,[26] which was published on 2 August from the Prime Minister's Office.

This White Paper, together with the Race Relations Bill that preceded it, represents the distillation of official thinking on race relations in the period immediately after Labour obtained office. It falls into two main parts: a section dealing with immigration policy, and a second with departmental proposals and the creation of a new agency to deal with problems of integration. The latter will be discussed subsequently: at the time, it attracted less controversy. It was the first which provoked immediate dispute. What was proposed was, first of all, a reduction to 8,500 in the rate of employment vouchers issued, including a special allowance of 1,000 vouchers for Malta; entry of unskilled workers was to be abolished; 'strict tests of eligibility' were to be applied to the entry of dependants; powers of medical examination extending to dependants were to be sought; and, finally, new powers were to be sought to combat evasion, including an extension of the Home Secretary's power to repatriate.

The proposals in Part II of the White Paper attracted widespread criticism on the well-justified grounds that there was an invasion of civil liberties involved in the provisions for deportation and some aspects of the proposals on dependants. Furthermore, despite the elaborate consultations that had taken place, the solutions reached, and in particular the selection of the number of employment vouchers to be issued, seemed arbitrary. But, perhaps the most potent case for the resistance of Labour supporters to the proposal had less to do with their content than with the manner in which they were presented and the psychological shock administered to their beliefs about the party. Here was clear evidence that the party of the Commonwealth, faced with an admittedly difficult situation, had taken the same line as its predecessor. In *The Economist*'s telling phrase, they had 'pinched the Tories' white trousers'.[27] The White Paper gave birth to another lobby (the Campaign for A Rational Immigration Policy); more effective in private than in public, the campaign obtained some useful concessions, notably the setting up of a formal inquiry (the Wilson Committee) into immigration control procedures. But despite these activities, the principles promulgated in the White Paper are still at the time of writing those on which policy on immigration (as distinct from integration) is based.

Looking back over the final stage in the passage of the immigration issue from the periphery of British politics to the centre, several features stand out. First is the role of public opinion. Just as local authorities and their anxieties, at first regarded as marginal, were gradually accepted as important, and even admitted as an element in decision taking by the end of the Macmillan Administration, so by the time of the Labour Government's White Paper, the role of public opinion had been accepted as a major factor in the situation, where four years before it had been rejected as an irrelevance, and before that assumed to be in line with the climate of opinion at Westminster. It is arguable that the neglect of public opinion wasted an important opportunity; certainly this was the argument repeatedly advanced by the British Caribbean Association. Although the opinion poll data (analysed in Chapter 28) is patchy, it does suggest that if during or immediately after the debate on control in 1961–2 positive proposals had been introduced, they might have commanded public support. But the emphasis on the need for control *pur sang* helped to create the anxieties it was intended to calm, with the curious result that public concern was eventually prayed in aid of policies that had helped to create it.

Secondly, 1965 was the end of ten years' battle by the Colonial and Commonwealth offices, dating from their victory of 1955, to keep Commonwealth interests in the range of those which would be considered when immigration policy was made. A major reason for this defeat was the decline of the importance of the Commonwealth in domestic politics. Even before his death the position of Nehru as the neutralist mediator of the Commonwealth had been seriously damaged by the Goa episode. The decline of Ghana into dictatorship and the instability revealed by the East African army mutinies helped to intensify the general mood of disillusionment with Africa, initially induced by the chaos in the Congo. By 1964, Enoch Powell was urging the Conservative party to cut its losses and forget the past commitment to the Commonwealth. If the Commonwealth survived into the period of Labour rule, it did so as an element of much-reduced significance in domestic politics. The concept of preferential treatment as of right for Commonwealth citizens was replaced by an increasingly insistent demand that the system of control be assimilated into that operated for aliens, and, as Labour modified its policy in the Common Market, a willingness to accept with equanimity the prospect of those provisions of the Treaty of Rome on the movement of labour which had been used to make Socialist flesh creep in 1962.

In essence, the immigration policy of 1965, as accepted in substance by both parties, was a 'Little England' policy, based unilaterally on the social and economic needs of this country as the Government defined them at that stage. This approach could reasonably be represented as selfish—for example, in its emphasis on the entry of skilled and professional migrants from under-developed countries, but its defenders represented the measures being taken as essential to the introduction of a systematic programme of integration. 'Without integration, limitation is inexcusable; without limitation, integration is impossible', ran the syllogism put forward by Roy Hattersley, who had been among the earliest to repudiate his past position on immigration control publicly (in March 1965) and was shortly to become a minister.

The abandonment of the metropolitan role for the United Kingdom was not quite final; efforts were made to preserve the fiction of non-discrimination in entry and some vestigial preference for Commonwealth citizens in certain sections still existed.

But, by this point, the Home Office had won the inter-depart
mental battle lost by the Commonwealth departments and it
victory was shortly to be symbolized in the transfer of the junio
minister responsible for integration to that department, there to
combine the roles of supervisor of immigration procedure with hi
previous responsibility. In this victory the changing official per
ception of what was at stake is neatly summarized. From being
an aspect of this country's relationship with the world outside
this matter had become a wholly internal problem, and one o
regulation: control at entry and control of the situation resulting
from entry, preservation of the Queen's Peace, prevention o
discrimination and incitement to racial hatred, and the averting
of inter-racial conflict.

This is, of course, not to imply that an effective Home Secretary, a co-operative Home Office, and efficient non-officia
agencies could not devise viable policies within this framework;
in Part VI the subsequent period of the Home Secretaryship o
Roy Jenkins is examined and assessed with these considerations
in mind.

NOTES TO CHAPTER 16

1. Paul Foot, *Immigration and Race in British Politics* (Harmondsworth, Penguin Books,
1965).
2. See, for example, his article in the *Daily Telegraph*, 16 February 1967, and, of
course, his speech of 20 April 1968 in Birmingham, reprinted in *Race* (Vol. X, no. 1,
July 1968), pp. 94–9.
3. 277 H.L. Deb., col. 695, 3 November 1966.
4. 264 H.L. Deb., col. 166, 10 March 1965.
5. Max Nicholson, *The System* (London, Hodder and Stoughton, 1967), p. 384.
6. Report of the Royal Commission on Population (Cmd. 7695) (London, H.M.S.O.
1949), para. 329.
7. Bob Hepple, *Race, Jobs and the Law in Britain* (London, Allen Lane, The Penguin
Press, 1968), p. 129.
8. William Deedes, in *Race without Rancour* (London, Conservative Political Centre,
1968), says that the matter was first considered by ministers in 1956–7. Since he was
himself a junior minister at the Home Office at that time his evidence is valuable; but
the chronology given here is accurate and has been checked.
9. This problem is dealt with at greater length in N. Deakin, 'The Politics of the
Commonwealth Immigrants Bill', *Political Quarterly* (Vol. 39, no. 1, January–March
1968), pp. 25–45.
10. C. Senior and D. Manley, *A Report on Jamaican Migration to Great Britain* (Kingston, Government Printer, 1955).
11. Deedes, op. cit., p. 9.
12. 200 H.L. Deb., col. 420, 20 November 1956.
13. 585 H.C. Deb., col. 1426, 3 April 1958.

14. *Daily Herald*, 8 May 1958.
15. 209 H.L. Deb., col. 617, 10 June 1958.
16. Foot, op. cit., p. 31.
17. *R. v. Hunt and others*, *The Times*, 16 September 1958.
18. *Economist*, 29 November 1958.
19. 606 H.C. Deb., col. 369, 4 June 1959.
20. See K. Kyle, in D. E. Butler and R. Rose, *The British General Election of 1959* (London, Macmillan, 1960).
21. C.I.A.C., *Report* (Cmnd 2119), (London, H.M.S.O., 1 July 1963).
22. 708 H.C. Deb., cols. 249–50, 9 March 1965.
23. The events leading up to the Race Relations Bill of 1965 are described in detail in K. Hindell, 'The Genesis of the Race Relations Bill', *Political Quarterly* (Vol. 36, no. 4, October–December 1965), pp. 390–406.
24. Ibid.
25. J. Rex, 'The Race Relations Catastrophe', in *Matters of Principle: Labour's Last Chance* (Harmondsworth, Penguin Books, 1968), p. 71.
26. Cmnd 2739 (London, H.M.S.O., 1965).
27. *Economist*, 7 August 1965.

17 Policies and Practices I: Housing

It was in the field of housing, by common consent the one which acts as the crucial determinant for the newcomer's future in this country, and that of his family, that the inadequacy of the White Paper of 1965 was most obvious. 'In housing above all', Elizabeth Burney has commented, 'immigrants expose the reluctance of Britain's social, political, and economic institutions to serve the demands of the weak, the unfortunate, and the unorthodox';¹ and this reluctance emerges with copybook clarity in the White Paper of 1965. 'The sole test for action in the housing field', it states, 'is the quality and nature of housing need without distinctions based on the origin of those in need.'² But no sooner is this statement made, which implicitly recognizes the possibility of variations in the extent of the need which is to be satisfied, than the draftsman shies away from its implications. 'The solution must lie in a determined attack on the housing shortage generally and particularly on the shortage of accommodation to rent on reasonable terms.' And on the crucial question of finance the White Paper adds: 'In the case of housing, subsidies and grants from the Exchequer are directly related to specific local authority projects so that increased capital expenditure by a local authority in this field will automatically attract increased Government assistance.' And finally, and most olympian of all: 'As time goes on, immigrants will qualify for rehousing by local authorities either by virtue of residential qualifications or through being displaced by slum clearance or other redevelopment. Thus it will become commonplace for Commonwealth immigrants to be rehoused by local authorities in pursuance of their normal statutory responsibilities. This in itself will tend to break up excessive and undesirable concentrations.'

In order to understand why a Labour Government should sidestep in this way the implications of its own expressed determination to assist both local authorities and immigrants, it is necessary to look beyond the banalities of the White Paper to the housing situation as a whole and its development over the period of the migration. In this way the 'strain' and 'tension', the 'acute hortage' and 'serious problems' with which the draftsmen of the White Paper sought to cover the nakedness of their proposals can be traced to their source.

'Commonwealth immigrants do not cause the housing shortage. It existed before they began to arrive in large numbers.'³ A statement of the obvious, but a welcome one. In fact, in 1951 (when the previous Labour Government left office) there would have been no need to labour the point, because a housing shortage was patently visible for all to see. Putting it at its simplest, the Census of 1951 showed that there were 13,117,868 private households in England and Wales but only 12,079,712 private dwellings. 'This disparity of 1,038,156', Alderson comments, 'was the measure of the overcrowding that everyone had either experienced or observed. There were families living in lodgings, with parents, or with friends, for want of the physical availability of separate houses.'⁴ This situation had been reached after six years of strenuous and not wholly unsuccessful effort by the Attlee Government to make up the deficiencies caused by the failings of the pre-War years and the very substantial damage caused by enemy action during the War. Through a willingness to intervene directly at all stages in the processes of providing houses, often in ways that were genuinely innovatory—the New Towns, new concepts of planning, even the much maligned prefabs—the Labour Government had, until the all-devouring demands of the export drive began increasingly to divert resources from domestic social expenditure, made some impact on the problem that faced it on assuming office. Above all, its policy was one based on the local authorities: a battery of controls and quotas ensured that their share of the new housing constructed exceeded by an overwhelming margin that put up by private builders.

Labour's Conservative successors were elected in 1951 having promised to build 300,000 houses a year, and kept that promise. The 1961 Census, taken after ten years of Conservative rule, shows that the disparity between the number of private households and the number of dwellings in England and Wales had shrunk to only just under 55,000. But this crude index of success is grossly misleading, because it conceals both the scope and the extent of a crisis which arose in the interim, during the years of migration from the New Commonwealth—a crisis which bore particularly hard on those newcomers entering the labour market in London and the West Midlands.

R

To some extent this crisis was a by-product of the solutions adopted by the Churchill Government in its successful drive to achieve the housing target it had set itself. To put it in over-simple terms, the emphasis was switched from the public to the private sector: controls were removed and development charges abandoned, and local authorities were encouraged first to lower the size and some of the standards of the new housing they were constructing and then to concentrate their energies on slum clearance and the rehousing of those displaced in the course of this operation. But within the private sector the erosion of the supply of private rented accommodation, which had begun as early as the First World War with rent control provisions, and was accelerated under the 1945 Labour Administration, with its emphasis on the expansion of the public sector, did not cease. Financial biases in the system in favour of the owner-occupier (through tax relief on the interest payment on mortgages and eventually his exemption from the payment of tax on his house as a capital asset under Schedule A) made the landlord role an even less attractive proposition. As the Milner Holland Report puts it, 'the very taxes which have made the life of the landlord so difficult have enhanced the benefits of being an owner-occupier'.[5]

This shrinkage in the private rented sector was accelerated both by the process of making new accommodation for sale available on a far greater scale than before, particularly in the suburban belts surrounding the major conurbations (thus diverting potential users from private renting), and through the further demolition of slum property. And, whatever its intentions, the Rent Act of 1957 further accelerated, rather than reversed, the shrinkage of private rented accommodation at moderate rents. Also, by limiting the local authorities capacity to produce new housing, both by cutting the Exchequer subsidy (from 1956) and by making them compete for funds in the open market at the prevailing interest rate rather than at preferential rates through the Public Works Loans Board, the Government effectively diverted the bulk of their energies to slum clearance which again bit into the cheap rented sector. A side effect of this process was to limit their ability to deal with the problems of those newcomers to the conurbations who are the natural clients for the lodging houses and boarding houses in the inner areas of large cities.

From the middle fifties onwards one particular problem began to emerge with increasing clarity and command public attention.

This was the question of the so-called multiple-occupied houses in the inner areas of large cities—the substantial Victorian housing abandoned by the middle-class owners to whom it had originally belonged. The shrinkage of the private sector had brought increasing pressure to bear on the supply of rented accommodation and driven prices upwards—especially in furnished accommodation and other lettings not subject to control as a result of the 'creeping decontrol' provisions of the Rent Act. By the late 1950s, the first of a succession of linked scandals about the homeless in London—usually working-class households with large families and low wages—began to break surface. In the grim paradox of misery and suffering for a minority in the middle of increased comfort for the majority there was ample material for impassioned exposés.

Although various explanations have been advanced for this acute shortage cheek by jowl with rising standards, they all boiled down basically to one word—'maldistribution'. As Donnison puts it:

> Increasing wealth is not spread evenly, like jam, across the country. It accumulates more rapidly in the economically growing centres through a concentration of relatively modest wage differentials and varying levels of employment, particularly among women. If left to accrue without any deliberate plan it can render housing scarcities in these regions worse.[6]

This is precisely what it did in London in the 1950s.

Moreover, like the Royal Commission on Population of 1949, the planners had totally failed to grasp the implications of the changes in family structure which had begun to become evident after the end of the War. Glass and Westergaard comment that between the two Censuses of 1951 and 1961:

> Substantial movements of internal migrants and immigrants have occurred at a time of significant general changes in the demographic and social structure of the population; migration has contributed to these changes, to the consequent shifts in housing demand, and to severe housing shortages, especially in the crucial zones of transition.[7]

The human consequences of this planning failure, and the inability of either central government or local authorities to deal with an unforeseen situation, can be seen in the phenomenon of multi-occupation. It is to the circumstances of squalor and stress produced by multi-occupation that newcomers of all colours drawn by the economic needs of the city, have had to adapt themselves. And it is these circumstances that provided the basic ingredients for Perec Rachman's operations, first on a small scale, and then, after the Rent Act of 1957, on an increasingly wide front until his activities were fortuitously revealed by an irrelevant scandal. Rachman seems to have developed to its highest pitch the art of forced 'gentification' (to use Ruth Glass's term): a process by which tenants paying a controlled rent are dislodged by unscrupulous manipulation of inter-racial tensions, to be replaced by profitable middle-class newcomers.[8]

The incapacity of local authorities in London to deal with this new situation is tellingly summed up in one phrase from the evidence given to the Milner Holland Committee: that the situation was such that any action by the local authority was 'creating a battlefield where the local authority cannot provide the ambulance service to take off the wounded'.[9]

This failure is particularly important since, despite the restrictions placed on their role by the Conservative Government, the local authorities still occupy a central position in the provision of housing. It is the crux of Rex's analysis of the situation of the newcomers in Birmingham that, as he puts it, 'the system of housing allocation is one of the two major determinants of the structure of race relations in Birmingham'[10] (the other is differential access to employment). The control of local authorities over the access of potential clients to adequate accommodation, which often appears to be exercised capriciously (indeed, in one area council housing *was* at one point allocated by ballot), gives them a central role in the problems of the inner city and its inhabitants. But this does not exhaust the list of the powers they can exercise on their own initiative. Apart from the selection of tenants, their allocation within local authority owned housing, the operation of differential rent schemes, and the general management of their property are all areas within which the Ministry's writ does not run. Outside their own estates, demolition or closing orders on individual unfit buildings, and enforcement of public health provisions are also subject to only the most general central supervision. Over and above these important aspects of housing policy, all of which are relevant for newcomers, the detailed decisions on the deployment of financial resources and the structures devised to implement the local housing authority's policy are fundamentally matters of local discretion. The Ministry's rule, at least until the mid-1960s, has been basically regulatory.

Alderson's cynical advice to the potential client, bent on securing accommodation from the local authority, is that 'the man who set about it efficiently would get an essential job, marry young, father a child a year, find himself a slum flat, share it with another family, and develop chronic ill-health. With all these qualifications he could even expect to get a home before he was 30.'[11] The extent to which this represents reality depends on a number of factors. First, the ideological bias of those responsible for determining policy locally. Within the broad lines laid down for them by central government (by legislation, White Paper, or exhortation through circular), most big city authorities have approached the problems thrown up by the growth of multi-occupation and immigration of all kinds on the basis that they are an irrelevance, and that those affected are 'transients' who would not—or should not—require council accommodation. In other words, the problems are a distraction from the task of providing adequate accommodation for those locally born or based members of the working class who have lived for too long in poor housing— back-to-backs or small by-law terraced housing (or, in the case of London, tenement blocks)—or with in-laws. This is a serious problem which has rightly preoccupied many authorities, but it is vital to distinguish it from the question of the 'twilight zone' of multi-occupied housing.*

Partly this reluctance to become involved in the problems of the twilight zone has been a function of the political pattern of the 1950s; most of the authorities affected were Labour controlled throughout this period, and, as Elizabeth Burney suggests, 'most Labour councils make a habit of resolutely ignoring immigration, to the extent of, wherever possible, ignoring the presence of immigrants'.[12] The existence of a twilight zone of rented accommodation in which (as we saw in Chapter 12) the immigrants were initially able to house themselves without too much difficulty, has made it possible to overlook their presence for some considerable

---

* In part, geography makes much of the distinction clear. Poor accommodation of the first kind is mainly to be found in Lancashire, South Wales, and the West Riding; sometimes it is owner-occupied and where it is rented (in single family occupation) the landlords who own it are often as poor as their tenants. (As in Lancaster, or in the Deeplish Survey in Rochdale.) The slum clearance drive of 1955 aimed at dealing with this problem; and the review of the situation conducted in 1966 (*Our Older Homes*—the Denington Report) indicated that substantial progress had been made.

time. (And it is possible for local authorities to argue that the newcomers should take their chance on the market—particularly if they are single men earning quite good money, as many new-comers are, and if rented accommodation is available, at whatever price.) And partly, official reluctance is a function of an exces-sively local approach to public housing. Successive reports and Ministry circulars since 1955 have urged on local authorities the importance of considering need before residence; but, although it is improbable that any local authority now gives more points for British nationality than damp, distinctions continue to be made, both in obtaining access to the waiting list and in progress on it. This in turn is related to the kind of local politician who serves on housing committees. Margaret Stacey has commented that:

local authorities in all except new and expanding towns tend to be overweighted by Councillors and Aldermen of long local residence, members of a strong in-group attached more to maintaining the *status quo* than to welcoming strangers. The result is something like the old Elizabethan poor law.[13]

Equally, the willingness of local authorities to tackle complex and delicate problems like those arising from multiple-occupation may be related to the internal structure of local government. Problems thrown up by such conditions may affect three or four departments, and new solutions may involve a degree of colla-boration which in some authorities (often for reasons of person-ality) is not feasible.

Alternatively, the capacity to undertake the kind of long-term planning which is often necessary may not be present. Eric Butterworth's conclusion on Bradford was that:

the bureaucratic machine is better at collecting material than it is at evaluating it or disseminating its results through the structure. In no department of the local authority does there appear to be a clearly worked out, long-term policy to meet any of the various contingencies which may arise.[14]

Finally, there may be a conventional wisdom, built up from experience of dealing with quite different kinds of minorities. 'Segregation' is a term that has a long history in the public housing field, and *de facto* separation by age or class is becoming increas-ingly a feature in housing of all kinds. If slum clearance or redevelopment does, for purely accidental reasons, involve an authority in rehousing coloured families, it often seems to draw on its previous experience with other low-status groups and acts accordingly. Thus, as Elizabeth Burney observes, 'any housing visitor can show you the "problem corner"—and there, like as not, will also be seen coloured faces'.[15] The American housing specialist Alvin Schorr comments:

one wonders whether residential segregation may serve as a substitute for other forms of discrimination. Will Great Britain face a similar development in housing when distinctions are not so readily made on the basis of accent and education?[16]

But over and above all these ideological and structural reasons which made local government unable to deal with the problems of the twilight zones and their inhabitants comes the sheer scope of the problem. And this in turn brings one back to London, where all the processes described above are to some extent relevant, though the dimensions of the difficulty are obviously crucial.

The Milner Holland Committee, after a careful review of the trends in the London situation, concluded that:

Young people seeking the cheaper and smaller units of accommodation have traditionally relied on privately rented housing, often furnished, often in multi-occupied property. Competing with them for this accommodation are low-income families with young children, elderly people, and others—for example, migrants from Ireland and further afield—who for various reasons have been unable to find homes better suited to their needs. As these pressures increase in Inner London, as conversion and improvements take place, attracting the better-off household capable of paying the higher rents which follow such modernisation, and as slum clearance proceeds, raising standards and reducing densities, there are signs that the sub-division and multiple occupation of housing tends to spread outwards.[17]

The Committee isolated eight boroughs in which housing conditions displayed signs of increasing stress—Willesden, Kensington, Stoke Newington, Hackney, Hornsey, Lambeth, Islington, and Hammersmith. Only Paddington among London boroughs had a higher proportion of coloured immigrants than these eight. Both because it attracted some of the more flagrant exploiters of tenants and because it has been the scene of a number of notable social studies, Kensington has rightly acquired most attention among the boroughs affected; but in some ways Lambeth presents a more interesting example of these trends at work. The nature of the area is different: most of Lambeth was middle class in living memory, whereas parts of Kensington went straight into multi-occupation. The Medical Officer comments that in Kensal New Town:

houses intended for the middle classes were colonised from the outset by what Charles Booth described in 1891 as 'riff-raff' driven from the slums of Tyburnia on the construction of the Great Western Railway and from the Lisson Grove area by the Great Central Railway. They are unique in that they have not descended into multiple occupation. They have been in this state from their beginnings about 100 years ago.[18]

Central Lambeth (or rather Brixton) served as a reception area for newcomers from the beginning of the migration. The first steps taken by the local authorities were in co-operation with the initial efforts of central government to arrange for their absorption: but the welfare phase gave place to the *laissez-faire* period, and Lambeth Borough Council were left to deal with its problem as best it could. Late in 1954, the Mayor and the local Member, Marcus Lipton, led a deputation to the Colonial Office. But Lord Lloyd, the Under-Secretary of State, told the deputation that central intervention was not justified; it would interfere with the Ministry of Labour's efforts to disperse the coloured population through allocation of employment vacancies. Although he sympathized with the local authority's dilemma and its contention that any action it took would be regarded by the public as giving unfair priority to 'coloured folk', it would have to rely on its own resource. Lipton's constant references to that rebuff in Parliament are a refrain that punctuates the periodic pleas of *non possumus* by Government spokesmen throughout the 1950s. The local authority, discouraged by its experience, tried one more gambit; it wrote to the L.C.C. and to government departments asking for assistance.

The Minister of Housing, Duncan Sandys (Member for next-door Streatham), replied in April 1955 that:

The Minister is of course aware that this migration is creating special difficulties for certain local authorities, of which your Council is one. He appreciates that the strict application of the provisions for dealing with overcrowding which are contained in the Housing Acts would be difficult in the present circumstances. But this duty to deal with the housing problems which have already resulted from the immigration remains with the housing authority.[19]

Armed with this helpful advice the Council relapsed into near-total inaction—a policy described by its advocates as 'we are all Lambethans now', and by its opponents as the 'Nelson's eye policy'. Although the only positive measure taken in the 1950s was the purchasing of two roads in the heart of the Brixton settlement area, Geneva and Somerleyton Roads, from the Beauchamp Estate, the fact that the leases were due to expire in 1966, and that with them the responsibility for the inhabitants (then thought to be overwhelmingly coloured) would fall to the Council acted as a time bomb, ticking through the years of *laissez faire*. In the event, the sleeper awoke a year early. A combination of events—trouble on one of the large new council estates in the area (an L.C.C. one) over the rehousing of a West Indian family, fears—quite unfounded —on the part of the Member for his seat, the reorganization and enlarging of the Borough under the provisions of the London Government Act, the advent of a new and energetic housing manager, and chief public health inspector—all contributed to the change of line. Policy proposals were drawn up (including the suggestion that not more than 5% tenancies on any one estate should be allocated to coloured tenants) and a full dress meeting was held with the ministers responsible for London housing (Robert Mellish) and immigration (Maurice Foley). Demands were presented and when they were not met a carefully calculated press leak displayed the Council like Pearl White tied to the tracks, helpless in the face of onrushing disaster while ministers skulked with complacent villainy in the undergrowth.

One of the demands that the Council had made was for a full-scale research project; and when the Government declined to support one the authority arranged it themselves through a third party.[20] The findings of the study are chiefly valuable for the light they cast on the solution devised by West Indians for their housing problems, in a situation of some difficulty in which the local authority had declined to intervene directly.

First, and predictably, the study showed few West Indians in local authority accommodation—5% in all, compared with 20% of the local white inhabitants. This was scarcely surprising in view of the pains taken by local politicians in the 1950s to avoid direct responsibility for rehousing immigrants and to emphasize the unlikeliness of their obtaining council accommodation except in the acquired property which forms a substantial proportion of publicly-owned housing. As the 1961 Census results (which found that 38% of Jamaicans in Lambeth were owner-occupiers, 49% renting furnished, and 11% renting unfurnished) would suggest, one solution that was being extensively adopted was house purchase. But the majority (two-thirds, in fact) were still renting accommodation. Here the coloured tenant was getting bad value for money. Most (three-quarters) of the coloured heads of household were earning under £22 per week; about half of them were paying over £4 per week in rent; whereas over three-quarters of the equivalent white sample were paying less than £4. A third of coloured tenants had no rent book. Although the average household size was 3·6 persons in coloured households and 2·7 in white, multi-occupancy was not a function of family size alone, independent of colour: of all households with children, only 17% of white families were in multi-occupation compared with 67% of coloured families. Nor were higher rents the consequence of late arrival in the district or the areas in which coloured newcomers settled. Although their socio-economic profile was very similar to the general population in the core area of settlement, the immigrants were worse off for amenities (sole use of toilet, cooking facilities, and water supply) than the bulk of the population in that part of the borough: 23% of the coloured families had none of them, compared with only 3% of whites.

But despite the fact that they were getting poor value for money, the West Indians struck roots in Lambeth. Thirty-nine per cent of the coloured sample had lived in the borough for over five years, and such movement as had taken place tended to be within the area. Only 20% of those who had considered moving intended to leave the borough. Most of the families had passed through the various stages of expansion through migration; only 14% now expected to be joined by further children from overseas. Indeed, nearly three-quarters of all coloured children aged 11 or under turned out to have been born in Britain—and over half in Lambeth (we are indeed 'all Lambethans now').

In sum, the Lambeth sample conformed very closely with the people of a migrant group in a big city, performing essential services but failing to obtain accommodation on an equitable basis or, until lately, any intervention on their behalf by the local authority. But despite the handicaps which the evidence clearly reveals the solutions reached have their own viability.

This same element of turning forced solutions to positive advantage is true of the substantial number of newcomers, from all ethnic groups, who have found the solution to their housing difficulties through house purchase. Elizabeth Burney comments that immigrant owner-occupation is 'a very positive source of physical and social improvement in many areas now written off as "decayed"'.[21] But like those who seek to become clients of the local authority, the intending house purchaser has to deal with a custodian acting on behalf of the established system—in this case, the estate agent. The estate agent is not subject to any form of statutory control (although a voluntary estate agents' council is now in existence). Both as a result of this lack of supervision and of the ambiguity in the nature of estate agency (is it a profession or a trade?), there have been too many instances of estate agents, operating in areas of immigrant settlement, committing malpractices. These range from straightforward misappropriation of deposits through manipulation of prices and 'blockbusting' (inducing panic flight by white residents), to suppression of relevant information, for example, about clearance schemes. Apart from outright abuses, agents have tended to interpret their role as involving authority to direct coloured newcomers into areas which they conceive to be suitable for them. This has in some instances had the effect of reinforcing patterns of concentration, although it is fair to add that in some cases they may have successfully interpreted their clients' wishes.

Agents may also play a substantial part in relation to the other main difficulty facing prospective buyers—the financial aspect. Raising sufficient funds to take the first step and put down a deposit is not as difficult for most immigrants as it would be for white house purchasers at an equivalent social and economic level. Co-operative financial arrangements among West Indians, known as 'pardner' or *sou sou* schemes, according to island of origin, can bridge the gap; for Asians, funds loaned by the community elders, raised between kin, or simply saved through substantial overtime working play an equivalent role. But the question of loan finance is more difficult. Many building societies are reluctant to help immigrant house purchasers, either through anxiety about their reliability, or because of the nature of the property which is available to them, or from a combination of the two. Occasionally, estate agents are able to act as go-betweens, either with the more respectable companies, or with the less scrupulous loan and investment companies which have flourished at the immigrants' expense. With or without the intervention of a third party, borrowing from these companies involves the house purchaser in a cycle of difficulties stemming from the necessity to keep up excessive payments which may well land him in serious difficulties with the local authority. In this situation the local authority itself can make a significant contribution by making funds available for borrowing by potential house purchasers and, with a few conspicuous exceptions, local authorities have in the past generally risen to the situation. In particular, since 1963 life has been made very much less difficult for all intending purchasers, who for reasons of income or pigment make unattractive clients for building societies, by the existence of the London County Council (and subsequently Greater London Council) 100% mortgage scheme. This scheme, which has been justly described by Elizabeth Burney as one of the most important of all policy innovations affecting newcomers, illustrates the advantages of having an authority with concurrent jurisdiction, operating at some distance from the restrictions imposed by local circumstances and local loyalties. If obtaining mortgages from this source turned out to have its special hazards— Lambeth in their active phase used the list of G.L.C. mortgagees as the basis for their drive against overcrowding—these were minor compared with the advantages for immigrants, who took to the scheme with enthusiasm. Moreover, surprisingly few abuses resulted.*

However, the heyday of council mortgage schemes now lies in the past—in fact it only lasted two years, 1963–5, by coincidence following close on the peak period of Commonwealth immigration. The decline began in 1965, when the Government restricted councils to the amounts they had lent in the previous year. In 1966, they were given a little more scope, but told to keep to various 'needy' categories—interpreted in various ways. Since 1966, the money has been cut back still further (with less emphasis on 'social' priorities, except in the narrow sense of people who will create a vacant council tenancy if they buy a house). In the summer of 1967, the G.L.C. scheme dried up entirely, and has now only reopened for very restricted categories of people— G.L.C. tenants, people displaced by G.L.C. redevelopment, people moving to New Towns. The Government seems to hope

* It should be pointed out that there is one factor which enables the G.L.C. to function more freely in this field—the fact that it is not a health authority and does not have the same anxieties about the implications of immigrant house-buying that obsess some local authorities.

that the option mortgage scheme will be of more use than 100% council mortgage—but it seems to be virtually alone in this.

In the solutions reached by the new Lambethans after ten years of nightwatchman rule by their Borough Council there were many substantial drawbacks: some of these are vividly illustrated in the flood of cases reaching South London rent tribunals throughout the 1950s and early 1960s. But there are also virtues—as Elizabeth Burney puts it:

> There is a good deal that is warm, sociable and attractive about central Brixton as its West Indian inhabitants have made it; a great potential for planners to build on if they only knew how.[22]

A verdict that many who know the area would gladly endorse. But the point is that the solutions are makeshift: the danger has been underscored by Ruth Glass, who refers to the 'quasi-solution' of allowing immigrants to remain in reception areas. It is easy to counterpose another quasi-solution—the adoption by the G.L.C. of a systematic policy of dispersal through its overspill estates and, to the extent that it is able to direct the process of recruitment, through New Towns. Although the vision of New Towns as 'anti-ghettoes' is an attractive one, this argument overlooks a series of practical difficulties which would prevent the G.L.C., even if it had been minded to do so, from embarking upon any policy initiative in this direction.

The attitudes and ambitions of the migrants themselves are one vital variable; that of the local population another. (Further data on this important aspect will be presented in Chapter 28.) Both these variables operated in a different manner from Lambeth in Ealing, where the Sikh immigrants' aspirations to home ownership and the defensive attitudes of respectable working-class inhabitants towards their property collided at an early stage. This is the kind of area in which the belief that immigrant entry lowers the value of property is universal; hardly won security and the status attached to possession of property have made it an article of faith which is in turn employed as a rationalization for hostility towards those who appear to pose the threat. Although clear-cut evidence has yet to be assembled, a general review of the situation by Professor John Denton uncovered no reliably substantiated incidents to justify the stereotype.[23] Although he found that estate agents often stated it as a general rule, they would then deny that it applied locally. A follow-up study in Southall itself, by Denton, reveals a property market still buoyant despite steady (and bitterly resisted) expansion of the Sikh settlement there. In Oxford, the dispersal of immigrant housing in small clusters and scattered units throughout most of the working-class neighbourhoods suggested that white property owners have not found in practice that the presence of coloured owners in their neighbourhoods harm property values. A study by Valerie Karn in a West Yorkshire town,[24] based on evidence made available by the local authority in connexion with its mortgage scheme, showed that immigrant house purchasers were paying 8·5% over the district valuer's valuation for houses they bought, compared with 2·7% for white purchasers, and that 6% of immigrant buyers were paying 30% or more over-valuation. This finding lends support to the mirror-image complaints by immigrants that they frequently pay far over the market price—and often for substandard property ('rubbish sold dear', in the Milner Holland Report's phrase).

It would be fair to add that Miss Karn's findings, which are supported by other investigators who have worked in areas of Indian settlement, relate to a town where competition for housing is at a low level. But conflict of a still sharper kind occurred in Birmingham, where some of the factors discussed above can be seen in operation in their starkest form.

The initial pattern of settlement in the West Midlands and in particular Birmingham followed broadly the same pattern as in London. Even by 1951, the immigrant population was not as concentrated as the popular image suggested, but the same marked tendency that was present in London, for the newcomers to cluster in an inner belt around the city centre partly composed of larger Victorian housing, was emerging with clarity. Behind this developing pattern lie a series of interlocking causes, which are summarized by Rex and Moore in *Race, Community and Conflict*, their study of Birmingham and one of its twilight areas, Sparkbrook.

Throughout most of the period between the initial settlement and the White Paper of 1965 Birmingham City Council was Labour-controlled; and for a large part of that period one or two powerful individuals dominated policy-making. Initially, anxious to devise acceptable means of cutting down the numbers of coloured newcomers to the city, these leaders had accepted with extreme reluctance the official Labour line on immigration, which they linked directly with the problems of the inner belt round the city's core, which was then undergoing a drastic facelift intended to drive home the image of a dynamic and successful commercial centre—and civic leaders. In 1955, a deputation from the local authority saw the Colonial Office, armed with a resolution calling for immediate controls on immigration, and only subsequently was the Council prepared to accept that such controls could not for the moment be introduced. In January 1956, the Corporation took what was then an unusual step by establishing a post of Coloured People's Liaison Officer, based on the local authority's own offices. The style in which the officer went about his work was subsequently a subject of some criticism, on the ground that the needs of immigrants were handled as individual exercises in case-work, rather than as a whole. But the existence of some form of provision enabled the local authority to view itself as making a significant effort in this direction.

By 1960 it had become clear that the solutions devised in the 1950s by Conservative ministers were not going to be adequate to the problems of the twilight zones. Ministers visited some of the areas affected; and what they saw there convinced them that the case for further action, which had been pressed on them with increasing force by local authority members and outside experts, had substance. One of the junior ministers at the Ministry of Housing summarized his experience when introducing, in 1961, the new legislation devised to meet this situation. He talked of:

basement areas used as common refuse dumps, roofs used for garbage disposal, entrance halls bearing the marks, if I may use the term, of a common pissoir, with contraceptives strewn on the rickety Dickensian staircases, often with the plaster peeled off and the bare lattice boards exposed; broken window panes, exposed and dangerous electrical fittings, and common lavatories and bathrooms of almost indescribable sordidness.[25]

To deal with this kind of situation, and others less dramatic but possibly still more productive of misery, local authorities were armed by the Housing Act of 1961 with a series of new powers. By Section 12, the authority is empowered to make orders applying management regulations to houses in multiple occupation in an unsatisfactory state; Sections 14 and 15 empower the authority to issue orders requiring certain work to be undertaken; Section 18 enables it to carry out the work in default and charge for it; and Section 19 empowers the authority to fix a limit on the number of individuals who should live in a house. Equipped with these new powers, Birmingham Corporation began an assault upon conditions in the twilight zone.

The effects of this assault fell almost exclusively upon immigrant landlords, for reasons which have been examined by Rex and Moore in their examination of Sparkbrook. Briefly, their view is that as a result of certain imperatives in the social organization of the city, a system of housing classes has been erected: a property-owning bourgeoisie which has tended to escape from the city to suburban security; the bulk of the working class, who have created 'a new public suburbia' in council estates; well-established tenants of self-contained housing; and lodging house landlords, and the tenants of furnished accommodation and lodging houses, who 'need no qualification at all apart from their willingness to pay a high rent in relation to housing space offered during an insecure tenancy'. For various reasons, the newcomer to the city is generally excluded from all but the last two categories; 'competition', Rex and Moore argue, 'leads to the formation of groups, very often on an ethnic basis, and one group will attempt to restrict the opportunities of another by using whatever sanctions it can'. Some migrants can overcome the consequences of this struggle, if they are adequately motivated, but the coloured newcomer suffers from particular handicaps in relation to his skin colour. He is not the author of the city's housing problem, but he is only too likely to be made the scapegoat for it.[26]

This process of scapegoating is particularly prone to occur in the case of the immigrant—usually, in Birmingham, an Indian or Pakistani—who adopts the solution of becoming a landlord. From the ideological position taken up by both major parties the immigrant by this act puts himself beyond the pale. To the Socialist, whose ideal concept is of housing as a social service and whose prejudices against the private landlord are sanctified by anecdotes from a generation of struggles, he becomes a 'coloured Rachman' —a convenient stereotype, in wide use among Labour councillors in the early 1960s. To the Conservative, who sees the basic answer, like ministers in the 1950s, in terms of a property-owning democracy of owner-occupiers, he is a caricature of the ideal. Samuel Smiles in black face who refuses to confine his enterprise within reasonable bounds. Quintin Hogg is said to have laid it down that 'a terrace of working-class houses is not a suitable field for Christian investment': a house built for the Victorian middle class, its

gentility defiled by the new uses to which it has been put, is not
to many Christians a suitable object for Muslim investment. To
neither, in the Birmingham situation, was the case for the landlord
a convincing one. The fact that he might have been driven to
adopt the role of landlord through necessity rather than desire,
and that the methods he employed to buy the house might mean
that he found himself painfully squeezed financially and that he
might have binding family obligations to discharge cut no ice.
The full weight of the Council's drive against overcrowding and
poor conditions fell squarely upon the Indian and Pakistani landlords.

Rex and Moore are not attempting to suggest that there was
anything improper in the actual prosecutions; although special
landlords' courts had to be set up to cope with the prosecutions of
landlords, they conclude that justice was done and go out of their
way to pay tribute to the part played by the public health inspectors. What they do suggest is that the local authority took an
excessively narrow and rigid view of its role in relation to the
problem of the twilight area and those in it.

Birmingham (who burnt their fingers when they tried to intervene directly, through compulsory purchase) mounted an energetic assault upon multi-occupation and its attendant problems,
with the express intention of containing the problem to the inner
city areas. When the powers conferred by the 1961 Act proved to
be inadequate for this purpose, even as amended in the Housing
Act of 1964, Birmingham Corporation promoted its own private
Bill in 1965, with all-party support, to provide for the registration
of housing in multiple occupation and the refusal of registration
in cases where either the applicant or the area is considered
unsuitable by the authority. A certain amount of opposition was
provoked by this action. Critics argued that the powers given to
the authority might be used to create and perpetuate 'coloured
ghettoes', and the local authority did not help its case by frankly
admitting that it was the Pakistani landlord it was trying to
contain. But, in practice, the objection to the Bill (which permitted
the applicant refused registration a right of appeal to the county
court) lay not so much in its possible use as an overt instrument of
discrimination—which would in any case never be permitted by
the Ministry, which has to approve the scheme made under the
Act—as in the general negative approach towards the problem
that it revealed, and its dubious effectiveness. Seen in this light,

s

it becomes yet another case for criticism of the White Paper, that virtually the only innovation that it commended in the housing field was the introduction of legislation along similar lines by other local authorities.*

Within the framework of this policy, it is fair to add, some changes have been taking place. In a long report issued in mid–1968 the Council, now under Conservative control, was able to point to an increased number of coloured people going into council accommodation—250 per year, with 16% of the waiting list composed of immigrants. The report adds, 'the Council has always insisted upon immigrant families being treated in precisely the same way as everyone else in terms of offers of accommodation',[27] although the Housing Department had earlier been quoted as saying that 'many Indians and Pakistanis refuse any but "patched" houses because these are the only council houses near to the main centres of their communities'.[28] Moreover, a quarter of the mortgages granted by the local authority were given to immigrants 'mainly on the older type of property'. But, for the Corporation, this policy had its dark side: 'inspectorial effort' had to be devoted to ensuring that conditions were observed—the authority was involved in a repetition and extension of its experience with lodging houses.

The general impression from this progress report is that the basic determinant of policy did not seem to have changed—'slum clearance', the report adds, 'will automatically engulf the poor properties unworthy of being improved, but there are relatively few immigrants in unfit houses'.[29] In other words, the increasing trend towards concentration is likely to persist, unbroken either by direct intervention by the local authority or voluntary dispersal. Only a determined application of improvement procedures in the inner ring is likely to bring about a long-term improvement in the situation.

Faced with a problem of a similar character (though smaller scale) to that of the London boroughs, it cannot be said of Birmingham Corporation either that it failed to formulate a policy or that it failed to act. In part, one could argue, as Rex and Moore have done, that political imperatives left the city Fathers with fewer options than their London opposite numbers. Certainly as

* At the time of writing four other local authorities have responded to this invitation, which is likely to be superseded by the introduction of legislation by the Government itself.

we have seen, political considerations were much more to the fore in the Midlands than in the London area. The protest movement, which appeared in its most striking form in the successive Immigration Control Associations, was not (as its organizers liked to maintain) a genuinely popular movement, but there is no doubt that it tapped real resentments. The rationale may not be very coherent—the chairman of one Midland Association told Elizabeth Burney that: 'You may say what's the difference except skin but I tell you they *are* different in ways we don't understand'—but the feeling is strong, and for this reason the 'suburban noose' is drawn tighter round the West Midland conurbation than it is anywhere else in England. The few attempts by ambitious Indians and West Indians to obtain housing in the privately developed estates of lower priced housing characteristic of the area have almost invariably provoked outbursts of intense hostility.

These outbursts have been particularly prone to occur on the fringe of the Black Country, in Wolverhampton—where, as Elizabeth Burney suggests, status differentials in housing being particularly difficult to maintain are particularly ferociously defended. The restriction of options open to immigrants, once again trapped between the slum-cleared centre and the 'suburban noose', is therefore even more marked than in Birmingham. The local authority has gone some way towards meeting the needs by making local authority housing available. Immigrants, once they have surmounted the difficulty of qualifying in a selection scheme which emphasizes a differential qualification period for the non-English born, are getting rehoused. But far more coloured people —proportionately nearly twice as many—find themselves on the pre-war estates, where known troublemakers are to be found and where disturbances involving coloured tenants took place in 1965. In part, this is a function of the selection scheme. Applicants for vacancies are graded from A1 to C3 and the preconceptions of the housing visitor are likely to ensure that the immigrant does not obtain the B2 or higher mark that is required to qualify him for post-war accommodation. If this does not take place, the dispersal policy of the local authority, which overrides the selection system, may bring about the same result.[30] Wolverhampton, a city which currently has far less difficulty than many London boroughs, has rather unfairly become the epitome of a local authority with 'immigrant problems'. To the extent that this is true, the cause is

not material difficulty but local attitudes. The inflexible paternalism of the local authority is effective, within its limits; but the
failure of imagination, symbolized in the reluctance to employ the
mortgage weapon to open an escape route for the immigrants who
wish to put into practice the process of dispersal to which the
Council itself is pledged, shows up these limits clearly.

These West Midland authorities, conscious of working within a
framework of restrictive opinion as well as restricting circumstances, have duly plumped—unlike their East Midland neighbours
—for containment. Their methods have already been discussed;
the manner is squarely in the sanitary tradition of British local
government. Schorr has suggested that housing policy in this
country 'is informed by the Victorian conviction that cleanliness
and sanitation will in themselves produce satisfaction, if not saint-
liness. . . . The poor, it goes without saying, are the natural
customers of a sanitary policy.'[31] And the disadvantaged immigrants are even more so. This is not to say that the problems of
single men in lodging houses do not have important public health
elements: merely that the emphasis is often maintained after the
original justification has ceased to be important. A typical statement of the sanitary position in relation to the immigrants has
come from a Northern medical officer of health:

bad housing conditions are not infrequently associated with unemployment, poverty, a low standard of personal cleanliness and hygiene,
defective maternal care and ignorance and fecklessness. Such conditions
are especially likely to flourish among an immigrant population,
irrespective of colour or creed, with defective standards of hygiene and
social conduct.[32]

Thus, to dragoon an immigrant household into compliance with
the provisions of the Housing Act is not only to protect them
against disease but to improve their social standards, employment
prospects, and even morality.

Other local authorities did not face the same imperatives as
Birmingham and the Black Country authorities: their minds were
not wonderfully concentrated. In some cases, a combination of the
local housing circumstances and the attitude of the newcomers
towards housing made a defensive posture tenable, in a style that
makes Lambeth's *laissez-faire* approach look like a dynamic
assault on the problem. Such an authority was Bradford.

Butterworth has described, with a tinge of irony, how each

successive cohort of ministerial visitors has complimented Bradford on the way in which it has approached the problems involved
in playing host to the largest concentration of Pakistani immigrants
in the country.[33] He suggests that a good deal of this apparent
success can be put down to local circumstances, and picks out the
housing field as one in which the city has been particularly
fortunate. Bradford, with a declining population linked to a
declining industry (wool textiles), has a large stock of mid-
nineteenth-century housing. The worst of this was the back-to-
back cottages—now partly eliminated by the slum clearance drive
of the mid-1950s. The growing residential segregation by class,
characteristic of other major cities, has meant that the larger
houses of the same vintage, built in inner wards have been
deserted by their original middle-class occupants. It is in these
inner wards that the Pakistani migrants, arriving to make good
the labour shortage in the textile industry, first settled: by 1966,
the two wards of Listerhills and Exchange had probably the
highest proportions of immigrants of any local electoral area in the
country, and 1,275 out of 1,417 lodging houses known to the
Council were owned and occupied by Indians and Pakistanis. But
the crucial difference lay in the fact that there was scope for
movement into adjoining areas: movement that became extremely
important as family reunions made conditions in the lodging
houses, acceptable to single men, undesirable for families with
women to protect (with all the cultural restrictions of purdah and
male jealousy). By July 1965, just before the White Paper, the
Health Department estimated that there were 1,400 families in
the city. Butterworth describes the developing trends:

> One is the movement outward from the centre, which is particularly
> characteristic of homes occupied by families but which also applies to
> some lodging houses. The second is the movement into streets of smaller
> houses by families with limited resources, working against the original
> tendency which has been noted for immigrants to be found on the
> margins of clearance areas rather than in the middle of them.

Nor did the local authority employ any of the other means of
intervention open to it. The slum clearance programme concentrated, with a considerable degree of success, on the back-to-
back cottage housing: 20,000 of the 30,000 remaining dwellings
of the worst vintage were cleared by 1962. But immigrants were
not affected by this programme, since they had not occupied this

housing in any numbers. Indeed, by the time the clearance programme neared its end many of the local white inhabitants were themselves not taking advantage of the opportunity to be rehoused by the authority. The low price of housing—both rented and for purchase—meant that the authority was competing directly with the private sector; anxiety that it would not be possible to let off the housing that the local authority operated had, by the mid-1960s, reduced the qualifying period on the waiting list to nil. But immigrants, with easy access to house purchase, were on the whole slow to take advantage of this opportunity—unlike Asian immigrants in some other West Riding towns—and the local authority has preferred not to encourage them. Possibly the authority's experience with a hostel it operated may have coloured the attitude towards immigrant tenants. This scheme failed, partly because the rents charged were a good deal higher than those that single men, intent on saving the maximum from their earnings, could expect to pay in ordinary lodging houses, but chiefly because the local authority was out of touch with the culturally-determined requirements of potential clientele. At any rate, by 1966 only forty-four council houses were occupied by immigrant families, and Butterworth comments that 'the majority of immigrants applying for local authority housing appear to be marginal to the immigrant community'.

Other means of positive intervention were also neglected: no mortgage scheme was thought necessary, and no steps were taken to ensure that improvement grants were used. With the pressure of multi-occupation at an acceptable level and a gradual process of dispersal taking place, the local authority could afford to let matters take their course; the absence of any substantial degree of organized pressure from public opinion or the press made the option all the easier to take.[34] But the spectacle of the levels of the housing market standing unused in favourable conditions presents an unhappy contrast with those areas where endless manipulation could achieve no result.

Other authorities stand midway between Bradford and London in the degree of freedom which they have had to deal with the particular difficulties of multi-occupation and the newcomers.

The St. Paul's area of Bristol is one in which the phenomenon of multi-occupation alongside substantial settlement of coloured immigrants has been studied.[35] The general profile of the area is not unlike that of Sparkbrook: a stable working-class community with a substantial degree of owner-occupation (61% of a sample of the white inhabitants were Bristol-born), broken up by patches of larger houses in multiple occupation in which the newcomers have tended to settle. Over a quarter of the West Indian households in the sample survey were overcrowded (using the measure of 1·5 persons per room) and 'one of the most significant findings was that there was virtually no social class gradient in the degree of overcrowding'. Similarly, the effects of the disadvantage of colour showed up in the poorer conditions, measured in terms of amenities, in which coloured families lived; and no less than 59% of West Indians felt that they had to make do with worse housing than in the West Indies (a drastic complaint, to anybody familiar with living conditions for unskilled manual workers in the Caribbean).

Relationships in St. Paul's between the various ethnic groups were characterized by cautious neutrality. Nearly a third of the white respondents spontaneously volunteered hostile comments about coloured newcomers, and, when pressed, two-thirds of whites were prepared to blame them for the continuing housing shortage, and a half to claim that they could recognize an immigrant-owned house from its exterior. But although these dissatisfactions had evidently led nearly two-thirds of the sample to consider moving (as had half the West Indians questioned), a substantial minority remained attached to the area, despite their anxiety about the low status increasingly attached to it. In fact, almost exactly one-third of those questioned declared themselves either satisfied or very satisfied with it. Workplace contact aside, the different groups were able to maintain a largely independent existence, and sources of competition and conflict were not such as to engender substantial (or 'realistic', as Richmond puts it) causes for hostility.

In this situation the role of the local authority is of considerable significance; and a special study was made of the rehousing of West Indians on the city's estates. A one year qualification period operated at the time of the study, and the average time taken by West Indians in the sample to obtain housing was two and three-quarter years. The main obstacle in the way of the West Indian applicant lay not so much in the process of selection—indeed the West Indians who had larger families and lived in poorer conditions were rehoused, on average, earlier than an equivalent white sample—as in finding out about the procedure. Given this fact, it is hardly surprising that over one-third of the successful applicants had English wives who could be presumed to know the ropes. Once arrived on the estate, the relative lack of competition for housing worked in the newcomers' favour; the processes by which they were selected were accepted as fair. And in many ways the West Indian sample approximated very closely to the normal pattern for successful applicants for council housing—in terms of skills, family size, and aspirations. But this does not necessarily imply an immediate 'fit': 'estate life', Lyon comments, 'is so finely organized around differences in status that whatever status attribute newcomers possess is likely to be critical for their prospects and their integration'—the danger in this instance being that the low esteem in which St. Paul's is held might be an alternative (and perhaps even stronger) reason for their rejection than skin colour. In practice, this process of rejection did not appear to be taking place. The West Indians, who 'wanted very much to be judged on their individual merits and not to be stereotyped as coloured people', appeared to be achieving their objective and adapting successfully to the rather tepid social life of the estate, with its emphasis on family and shrinking away from excessive contact with strangers. In many ways these particular newcomers were better equipped for success in this environment than less stable West Indian families would be; but even granted that they were to some extent a self-selected sample, the ease of their acceptance and adjustment is impressive, and suggests that the anxieties of some local authorities about accepting responsibility for rehousing coloured immigrants on ordinary estates are exaggerated.

The West Indians on the Bristol estates, however, remain a very small minority—although the P.E.P. investigation in 1967 suggested that more West Indians were prepared to consider the possibility of council accommodation (41%, in fact) than was commonly supposed.[36] A more frequent route to local authority housing lies through clearance schemes; and this leads more often to the patched or compulsorily purchased house in council hands, for reasons which are endemic in the selection process. Immigrants may, as we have seen, also be subjected to a process of 'scattering' in poorer class housing. The P.E.P. investigators' dry comment on one alibi for this process is, that while one of the 'justifications for this was that it made life easier for the immigrants by preventing unpleasantness, it was also true that it made life easier for the authority'.[37] But even these fortunates constituted a small minority (possibly even as little as 1%), as the P.E.P. investigation of the extent of discrimination was shortly to show. The majority were evolving their own solutions, as we have seen, and this solution almost invariably involved both multi-occupation and house purchase. Although these solutions carried with them a built-in source of friction, the reaction of the members of the host community remained throughout this period remarkably calm and balanced (see Chapter 28).

Some local authorities had the capacity to tackle the problems of multiple occupation constructively and were not deterred when this involved them in accepting responsibility for the coloured inhabitants of the area. Leeds was one, and Lambeth was eventually to become another. It is no reflection on their virtue to say that these were often also the authorities least under pressure. But the majority of those authorities were content to hold the line either noisily (like Birmingham) or silently (like Bradford), or else to shelter behind the convenient proposition advanced by successive governments, and reaching its apotheosis in the White Paper. This was that no special measures were necessary to deal with the problem of the twilight areas over and above those taken in 1961 and reinforced in 1964. Early in 1964, Sir Keith Joseph, the Conservative Minister of Housing, told the Commonwealth Immigrants Advisory Committee—who had produced a paper on immigrant housing with some useful (if peripheral) proposals[38]—that the solution of the immigrants' housing problems was well under way. His successor, Richard Crossman, sharply rebuked Sir George Sinclair, who tried to induce him to introduce a systematic rehousing programme. 'The local authorities with the worst problems to overcome in housing are by no means always those with a high proportion of immigrants',* he said in a written answer. 'Any special help should be given where the housing needs are greatest—on housing, not on racial grounds.'[39]

Some of those who criticized this approach were misunderstood (or misrepresented) as arguing for a specific programme for immigrant housing. Such a policy (perhaps loosely modelled on the Dutch programme for the resettlement of 'repatriates' from Indonesia, who were allocated 5% of new housing by central government) would certainly have been out of the question—as the C.I.A.C. had already indicated. Richard Crossman's repeatedly-taken high moral line with his critics appeared to be

* A point evidently not appreciated by the draftsmen of the White Paper (para. 34).

based on this view.[40] But this was not what critics, such as John Rex, were arguing. Their proposition was that there was a category of problem specifically affecting coloured newcomers which was being generally neglected, and they were putting forward a detailed case for remedial action based on a revised conception of the local authorities' role. Their view might be summarized as holding that the actual living conditions, rather than terms of tenure, or ethnic origin, or age, or location of the dwelling, should be the crucial factor in determining whether the authority should intervene; and that in a responsible system of local government this would be recognized and acted upon. In default of such action (either through parochialism, inertia, or lack of resources), there should be some form of intervention from central government.[41] In other words, responsibility for the situation must be accepted: the compromise between the market and the provision of housing as a social service had failed. Action should be linked with the provision of other services, and, with it, an attempt to relate the allocation of housing to the provision of new jobs. Discrimination against immigrants as such, represented a substantial additional handicap which might require additional corrective action, but this was the secondary, and not the primary justification for action.

The White Paper of 1965 represents the Government's rejection of this proposition, just as the narrowly-drawn Race Relations Bill of 1965 indicated the extreme reluctance and caution with which the Government had moved to take specific remedial action to deal with discrimination itself. And although the promised White Paper on the housing programme duly appeared in November 1965 as *The Housing Programme 1965–1970*,[42] the crucial uncertainty about the nature of the problem persisted and partly vitiated the analysis. 'First priority will be given', said this White Paper (paragraph 39), 'to relieving the acute shortage of houses to rent in the conurbations—especially in areas which attract newcomers including immigrants from the Commonwealth—and to clearing the great concentrations of slums' (a juxtaposition which perpetuates the confusion that has fogged the issue from the outset).

Earlier, the problem is brought into the sharper focus—'it would be criminal, at the present time, not to allow for an even faster rate of growth of building to let. Shortages fall heaviest on those least able to pay a high rent for their homes'—but the remedies are not —'the only remedy is an increase in public sector building'.

Generally, the White Paper contained some proposals that were new, and several more that were useful. But the rethinking of overall policy towards the inner cities was put off for another working party, another research project (the customary ritual reference to desirable new studies which characterizes all this Government's official documents), another White Paper.

But clearly the situation was not going to rest there. The stimulus of the Milner Holland Report was succeeded by that of the Denington Report on older housing.[43] Continued evidence of pressing need in the major conurbations accelerated a convergence of views on the proposal, originally advanced by the Milner Holland Committee, to designate inner areas as 'areas of special control'.

Some of these themes were gathered together and specifically related to the problems of coloured immigrants in two reports written by the National Committee for Commonwealth Immigrants' Housing Panel.[44] These reports were presented to successive Ministers of Housing and received with some sympathy—especially after James MacColl had taken over responsibility for the subject at junior minister level. But the only specific action that followed was the calling of a conference of local authorities, and this, through a process well described by John Rex,[45] became perverted into a forum for complaints by local authorities. Official policy continued to stress the importance of treating the subject within the overall context of housing policy and when pressed ministers fell back, as Lord Stonham did in November 1966, on platitudes. 'There is', he said, 'no immediate solution to this extremely difficult housing problem; only enough low rented houses will provide the cure.'[46]

The lever which made a breach in this wall was in fact not specifically devised to deal with housing difficulties—the Plowden recommendations for educational priority areas, with their emphasis on urban renewal through community renewal provided the necessary impetus for change. The Department of Education and Science acted rapidly to introduce positive discrimination in these areas, and the next White Paper from the Ministry of Housing, *Old Houses into New Homes*,[47] contained welcome recognition of the need to consider the problems of areas of multi-occupation as a whole—'the keynote of the proposals is that the local authorities are positively concerning themselves with the conditions of the unsatisfactory private housing in their terms', the

Report concluded. They should do this in terms of 'whole areas not just individual houses'. A range of new powers is proposed in order to enable this process to take place, but legislation has yet to be introduced and the situation is confused by a series of new proposals made in the immediate aftermath of the renewed debate about immigration in the spring of 1968. Faced with heavy pressure from local authorities, the Government fell precipitately into the opposite posture from their previous stand. An 'Urban Programme' was announced by the Prime Minister in a speech on May Day, which would have the effect of subsidizing local authorities in areas affected by immigration at the expense of those not so affected. The presence of immigrants had ceased to be an irrelevance or a misfortune to be accepted philosophically by the local authority: it had become a factor which justified direct intervention from the centre on a substantial scale. The implications of this startling change of policy, the details of which were softened by a later announcement, will be examined in Chapter 29.

Before this remarkable reversal, the Government did introduce one other measure relevant to our theme, in the Housing Subsidies Act of 1967. This involved a change in the situation of non-profit making housing associations in relation to subsidies which improved their viability. The role of housing associations in this field has yet to be discussed in this Report; the evidence is patchy, although a number of pioneer associations have been active in the field since the mid-1950s. At the height of the *laissez-faire* period, these associations, the Aggrey Association in Leeds and the Coloured People's Housing Association in Nottingham, made a useful contribution in meeting urgent need, but by the early 1960s these associations were no longer meeting the demands of immigrants, who could afford to pay more for housing and were increasingly inclined to turn to house ownership as the preferred solution. In London, the Metropolitan Coloured People's Housing Association performed the same role, but survived to change its name and identity when a new wave of associations arose in the 1960s. These were based partly on the public indignation aroused by exposures of the worst effects of abuses in the private rented system: 'Shelter', a fund raising and publicity organization, has helped to focus this indignation and harness it to providing resources for associations. In a recent report, *Notice to Quit*, Shelter has drawn attention to the continued deterioration in the situation of tenants in twilight areas and the relative ineffectiveness of the 1965 Rent Act, which was introduced in an attempt to stabilize the position by conferring security of tenure in the private sector. In these circumstances, associations working in collaboration with local authorities, as the Mulberry Housing Trust has done in North Paddington, can make an important contribution, as a safety net for cases which the local authority are unable for a variety of reasons to help. But, as those who work with them would recognize, their role is at present a palliative one and long-term solutions to major problems of immigrant housing are not likely to be found in this direction. On balance, Elizabeth Burney's rather harsh judgment seems justified; efficient associations have been few and their direct contribution slight, although they have provided a psychologically gratifying outlet for activity on the part of some local voluntary organizations—a point we shall return to in Chapter 21.

We have traced the evolution of policy on housing in some detail, because housing is in so many ways the crucial determining factor for the coloured newcomer. The familiar illustration is of the triangle of forces: housing for the adult, at the apex, determines education for the child, which determines employment for the adolescent. The failure in Government policy in this crucial field was initially, to a large extent, the result of a general misunderstanding of the processes at work in the housing situations in major conurbations. Not until the 1965 White Paper, when the causes of demographic change were better understood, the bulk of the Rowntree research projects had become available, and the Milner Holland Report published, was the evidence available on which to base a revised policy.

This is why the major sin of commission must be laid at the door of the Labour Government even if its predecessors' sins of omission are equally important. For the effects were the same in both cases: local authorities were left to struggle with the problem without adequate resources. Not every minister stated the position as brutally as Duncan Sandys did to Lambeth Borough Council in 1955, not every measure taken by central Government in this period was irrelevant to their needs—the 1961 Act gave positive assistance where it was properly used. But, in general, the critical policy decisions for the newcomer were taken in fragmentary fashion at the local level. And the consequences for them depended a great deal on three linked elements in the local situation. These were the age and composition of the local housing stock (a quirk of local history could decide this), the numbers and ethnic composition of the incoming groups, and the situation and response of the local population. The last could change without relation to the real structure of the situation: satisfaction or resentment, as Donnison has pointed out, are related to perceptions as much as to actual experience. The failures and successes of local government policy were also crucial in shaping the developing pattern of race relations, not only in other local authority services but also in other spheres of social contact where concentration and poor living conditions determine the reception that the newcomer receives.

NOTES TO CHAPTER 17

1. Elizabeth Burney, *Housing on Trial* (London, Oxford University Press, for the Institute of Race Relations, 1967), p. 2.

2. Cmnd. 2379, *Immigration from the Commonwealth* (London, H.M.S.O., 1965), para. 35 *et seq.*

3. Ibid.

4. S. Alderson, *Britain in the Sixties, Housing* (Harmondsworth, Penguin Books, 1962), p. 13.

5. *Report of the Committee on Housing in Greater London* (Cmnd. 2605, The Milner Holland Report), (London, H.M.S.O., 1965), p. 41.

6. D. V. Donnison, *The Government of Housing* (Harmondsworth, Penguin Books, 1967), p. 179.

7. R. Glass and J. Westergaard, *London's Housing Needs* (London, Centre for Urban Studies, 1965), p. 3.

8. There is a full account of this process in Appendix II of the Milner Holland Report, op. cit.

9. Milner Holland Report, op. cit., p. 96.

10. J. Rex and R. S. Moore, *Race, Community and Conflict* (London, Oxford University Press, for Institute of Race Relations, 1967), p. 35.

11. Alderson, op. cit., p. 94.

12. Burney, op. cit., p. 188.

13. M. Stacey, 'A Fair Deal for Migrant Housing', Institute of Race Relations *Newsletter* (June 1966), p. 15.

14. E. Butterworth, 'Immigrants in Bradford', for the Institute's 'Survey of Race Relations in Britain'.

15. Burney, op. cit., p. 76.

16. A. Schorr, *Slums and Social Insecurity* (London, Nelson, 1964).

17. Milner Holland Report, op. cit., p. 105.

18. Evidence submitted to the Milner Holland Committee.

19. Quoted in Burney, op. cit., p. 112.

20. Discussed in Burney, op. cit., Chapter V. The study was carried out by Research Services, Ltd.

21. Burney, op. cit., p. 56.

22. Burney, op. cit., p. 145.

23. John Denton, 'Immigrants and House Prices', *New Society* (No. 291, 25 April 1968), pp. 602–3.

24. Reported in a paper presented to the Third Annual Conference of the Institute of Race Relations, 19 September 196 .

25. Earl Jellicoe, Parliamentary Secretary, Ministry of Housing and Local Government, quoted in Peter Hall, *London 2000* (London, Faber, 1963), p. 25.

26. See the discussion in Rex and Moore, op. cit., Chapters 1 and 2.

27. Report of conference held by Birmingham Corporation to consider problems of immigration, 14 May 1968, p. 61.

28. Valerie Karn in *Race* (Vol. IX, no. 1, July 1967), p. 103.

29. Birmingham Corporation conference report, op. cit., p. 63.

30. For a full discussion, see Burney, op. cit., Chapters VII and VIII.

31. Schorr, op. cit., p. 135.

32. Quoted in Burney, op. cit., p. 167.

33. Butterworth, op. cit.

34. See, for example, for the role of the local press, Eric Butterworth, 'The 1962 Smallpox Outbreak and the British Press', *Race* (Vol. VII, no. 4, April 1966).

35. A. H. Richmond and M. Lyon, 'Immigrants in Bristol' (for the Institute's 'Survey of Race Relations in Britain').

36. W. W. Daniel, *Racial Discrimination in England* (Harmondsworth, Penguin Books, 1968), p. 195.

37. Ibid., p. 190.

38. Commonwealth Immigrants Advisory Council, *Report* (Cmnd. 2119), (London, H.M.S.O., 1963).

39. 710 H.C. Deb., col. 49–50, 6 April 1965.

40. As in a speech to the Institute of Housing Managers, reported in the *Guardian*, 17 September 1965.

41. For example in his article 'Houses and Colour', *Views* (no. 7, Spring 1965), pp. 61–4.

42. *The Housing Programme 1965–1970* (Cmnd. 2838), (London, H.M.S.O., 1965).

43. Central Housing Advisory Committee, *Our Older Homes: a call for action* ('The Denington Report'), (London, H.M.S.O., 1966).

44. *The Housing of Commonwealth Immigrants* (London, N.C.C.I., 1967), and *Areas of Special Housing Need* (London, N.C.C.I., 1967).

45. In *Matters of Principle: Labour's Last Chance* (Harmondsworth, Penguin Books, 1968), pp. 70–84.

46. 277 H.L. Deb., col. 733, 3 November 1966.

47. *Old Houses into New Homes* (Cmnd. 3602), (London, H.M.S.O., 1968).

18 Policies and Practices II: Education

1. BACKGROUND

The arrival and the education of the children of Commonwealth immigrants in British schools began to be seen as a problem in the early 1960s. During the 1950s, although there was a small but regular inflow of children from the West Indies coming to join parents in Britain, the vast majority were left behind in the first stage of the migration process. Nevertheless, the remarkably high proportion of women among the Caribbean migrants indicated that there was a strong possibility that once a home could be made and the fare money raised, the children would follow. As far back as 1958, one or two schools in a very few places began to notice an increase in the numbers of non-English speaking Indian pupils, but, as shown in Part II, migration from India and Pakistan only reached significant levels in 1961. Although some Indian wives and children did arrive during the 'beat the ban' rush, the family character of the Indian and Pakistani migration did not become clear until after the Commonwealth Immigrants Act statistics were published on the numbers of dependants entering the country.

Some schools already had a cosmopolitan range of nationalities among their pupils, having absorbed and educated children of the earlier post-war European immigrants. In the 1960s, however, rapid rates of increase in the number of children arriving, and their entry into schools at all ages and throughout the school year, many from non-English speaking homes, were problems for which the education system was quite unprepared. This chapter describes the policies which were developed in response to this situation.

The power to formulate policies and to put them into practice lay with a number of different institutions, national and local: the Department of Education and Science; the institutes and colleges of education, responsible for teacher training; local education authorities, in particular their directors of education and their own local inspectorate (if any); and the individual head-teachers and teachers in the schools. Thus, there was a highly dispersed pattern of power and responsibility. The linking institution was

H.M. Inspectorate. 'No other Department', wrote Professor Griffith, 'supervises and assists the work of the local authorities to the same extent as does the Department of Education and Science through the medium of the H.M.I.s.'[1] However, over the education of immigrants, although individual H.M.I.s gave help and tried to stimulate interest, it was eventually left to the Schools Council, set up in 1964, to draw the threads together by commissioning a national report on the developing problems and policies of local authorities and teachers.[2]

The difficulties which the schools experienced were to a great extent due to certain basic deficiencies and inequalities in the education system, which were documented in a series of massive and detailed reports which appeared between 1959 and 1967 (1960, Crowther; 1963, Newsom and Robbins; 1967, Plowden).[3] These deficiencies hindered the schools in meeting the educational needs of the children from overseas, and affected the way in which the children were initially received. The inequalities narrowed the opportunities of children of immigrants just as they narrowed those of children of English parents. The local chief education officers, and the head teachers in the schools, on whose shoulders fell most of the responsibility for dealing with the arrival of immigrant children, had to accept most of these things as part of the facts of educational life.

2. THE DISPERSAL POLICY

Departmental thinking can be traced through four documents: *English for Immigrants*, a pamphlet published in 1963 mainly concerned, as the title suggests, with methods of teaching English,[4] the Second Report of the Commonwealth Immigrants Advisory Council in 1964,[5] Circular 7/65 issued in June 1965,[6] and finally, the White Paper of August 1965 which, with slight changes, incorporated the Circular.[7]

The most important of these documents in the development of policy making in relation to education was the Second Report of the C.I.A.C., completed in December 1963 and published early in 1964. The C.I.A.C. had been set up by the Conservative Government to advise the Home Secretary on matters relating to the welfare and integration of immigrants. While the Second Report, dealing with immigrant pupils, referred to certain general problems in the education system—such as the shortage and maldistribution of teachers (which affected the reception of

T

immigrant children in the schools)—it did not deal directly with them, and indeed found itself not competent to do so.[8] Its main concern was with the role which the schools might play in achieving integration through the cultural assimilation of children of immigrants.

A national system of education must aim at producing citizens who can take their place in society properly equipped to exercise rights and perform duties the same as those of other citizens. If their parents were brought up in another culture and another tradition, children should be encouraged to respect it, but a national system cannot be expected to perpetuate the different values of immigrant groups.[9]

Although this formulation was later modified by the Schools Council[10] and rejected by the N.U.T.,[11] the emphasis on the school's role in the cultural assimilation of immigrants has not disappeared. Yet the attention paid to the subject was far more a reflection of certain general views and anxieties about the presence of immigrants than of the actual problems of cultural conflict with which immigrant children and their teachers had to cope.

There is no analysis in the reports of the C.I.A.C., the Schools Council, or the N.U.T. of what British values are. Jennifer Williams, in her description of schools in Sparkbrook, gives her views of how the teachers interpreted them:

The teachers see their role as putting over a certain set of values (Christian), a code of behaviour (middle-class), and a set of academic and job aspirations in which white collar jobs have higher prestige than manual, clean jobs than dirty . . . and interesting responsible jobs are higher than just 'good money' jobs.[12]

No item here was likely to excite the active opposition of immigrant parents. Caribbean immigrants were Christian, and both Muslim and Sikh religious groups were tolerant about Christian teaching in the schools. Immigrants were no different from British parents in having 'middle-class' aspirations for their children.

Integration was perceived by the C.I.A.C. very much in terms of social contact within the school between immigrant and native children. To achieve this, and to prevent any interference with the 'normal' routine of a class, the C.I.A.C. assumed that it was essential for the proportion of immigrants in a school or class to be small. Paragraphs 25 and 26 of the Report express better than anything else the beliefs and hopes which under-pinned official policy making until well after 1965:

The presence of a high proportion of immigrant children in one class slows down the general routine of working and hampers the progress of the whole class, especially where the immigrants do not speak or write English fluently. This is clearly in itself undesirable and unfair to all the children in the class. There is a further danger that educational backwardness which, in fact, is due to environment, language or a different culture may increasingly be supposed to arise from some inherent or genetic inferiority.

But something more than academic progress is involved. Schools want to give their immigrant pupils as good an introduction to life in Britain as possible. The evidence we have received strongly suggests that if a school has more than a certain percentage of immigrant children among its pupils the whole character and ethos of the school is altered. Immigrant pupils in such a school will not get as good an introduction to British life as they would get in a normal school, and we think that their education in the widest sense must suffer as a result . . . we were concerned by the evidence we received that there were schools in certain parts of the country containing an extremely high proportion of immigrant children. Moreover, the evidence from one or two areas showed something a good deal more disturbing than a rise in the proportion of immigrant children in certain schools; it showed a tendency towards the creation of predominantly immigrant schools, partly because of the increase in the number of immigrant children in certain neighbourhoods, but also partly because some parents tend to take native-born children away from schools when the proportion of immigrant pupils exceeds a level which suggest to them that the school is becoming an immigrant school.

The Report concluded that the location and catchment areas of schools should be planned so that they remained mixed, and that dispersal of children would be preferable, as a last resort, to *de facto* segregation.

The drafting of the C.I.A.C. Report coincided with the first political crisis about immigrant children in the schools. This was a protest organized by white parents of children attending two primary schools in Southall, against the presence of immigrant children (mainly Indian). About 60% of the children in one of the schools were children of immigrants. Southall was, in fact, one of the two areas referred to in the C.I.A.C. Report where the build-up of immigrant children had so disturbed the Committee.

Sir Edward Boyle, then Minister of Education, attended a meeting of the parents at the school. He refused to countenance any suggestions that the immigrant children be educated separately, or that children then attending the school should be moved. However, it was subsequently agreed that Southall would in the case of future admissions of immigrant children into schools 'disperse' them and try to maintain a limit of about 30% in any one school. Sir Edward explained to the House of Commons in November that year: 'If possible, it is desirable on education grounds that no one school should have more than about 30 per cent of immigrants.' It was, he said, 'both politically and legally more or less impossible to compel native parents to send their children to school in an immigrant area if there are places for them in other schools. . . .' Sir Edward went on: 'I must regretfully tell the House that one school must be regarded now as irretrievably an immigrant school. The important thing to do is to prevent this happening elsewhere.'[13]

This was the origin of the official dispersal policy, which subsequently became the main plank in the programmes which the Government recommended to local education authorities. As suggested in the middle of the Southall crisis in 1963, the dispersal idea may be interpreted first of all as a rejection of any policy of separate education for immigrants, i.e. of a 'separate but equal' philosophy. But it also implied a belief by the Department of Education and Science (D.E.S.) that the schools could correct, through their placement policies, the effects of residential concentration and of the transfer of white children to other schools by their parents. This transfer process was given great importance.

The only italicized paragraph in Circular 7/65 occurred in the section headed, 'Spreading the Children':

It will be helpful if the parents of non-immigrant children can see that practical measures have been taken to deal with the problems in the schools, and that the progress of their own children is not being restricted by the undue preoccupation of the teaching staff with the linguistic and other difficulties of immigrant children.[14]

By the time the official dispersal policy came to be set out in the White Paper in August 1965, it was presented not only as an aid to integrating immigrant children, and a way to prevent any fall in the standards of the schools, but also as a help to the organization of special English classes for immigrant children. There is almost an implication that the policy should apply only to non-English speaking children:

In order to maintain the standards of education in schools attended by large numbers of immigrant children with language difficulties, special arrangements must be made to teach them English. . . . This will often mean special classes . . . for at least part of the day, although from the beginning they should join as far as possible in the normal social life of the school. . . . Such arrangements can more easily be made, and the integration of the immigrants more easily achieved, if the proportion of the immigrant children in a school is not allowed to rise too high. The Circular 7/65 suggests that about one-third of immigrant children is the maximum that is normally acceptable in a school if social strains are to be avoided and educational standards maintained. Local Education Authorities are advised to arrange for the dispersal of immigrant children over a greater number of schools in order to avoid undue concentration in any particular school.[15]

It is interesting to note that if the teaching of English to non-English speaking children was the goal, then having too few of them in a school could be to their disadvantage. The D.E.S.'s own pamphlet *English for Immigrants* had in 1963 suggested that in such cases, non-English speaking pupils should be brought together for classes in one school.[16]

This multi-purpose policy had, in 1965, no statistical basis. How many children of immigrants were there in the schools, how many of them had inadequate English, how many schools contained more than 30%; these questions could not be answered. (The D.E.S. began to collect statistics in 1966.) No definition of the term 'immigrant pupil' had been given. The definition of 'immigrant pupil' eventually adopted for statistical purposes included, first, children of immigrant parents born overseas, who had come to Britain, and secondly, children born in Britain to immigrant parents who had arrived within the previous ten years (the date being moved up each year).

Problems were related solely to the overall numbers of 'immigrant pupils' in a school, and no distinctions about the various age-groups were made. The problem of language was in one sense exaggerated; when the statistics were collected it was found that half the total number of immigrant pupils had no language problem. On the basis of the D.E.S.'s own criteria for judging language ability, only a quarter of the immigrant pupils were found to require special teaching.[17]

In another sense the language problem was under-estimated, for the White Paper was complacent about the need for more specialized materials, and for more in-service training courses, in English as a Second Language (E2L). 'Increasing interest is being taken,' says the White Paper (para. 47), and 'many people feel the need for further research and for the development of new materials and teaching aids.' The problems of each school depended a good deal on the previous experience of the teachers. Sometimes a school with a high proportion of immigrant pupils experienced less 'strain' than one with fewer, because the former was used to dealing with children with linguistic and cultural difficulties. The problems of linguistic differences were not new. The Schools Council in Working Paper, No. 13 (para. 10) reproduces the following fascinating quotations from the Newbolt Report of 1921: Newbolt was looking for 'a source of unity to be found in the teaching of children' in all kinds of schools. He was looking for a 'possible basis for national education' something that would 'obliterate or soften the line of separation between the young of different classes to bridge the social chasms which divide us'. In the end he concluded that: 'English in the highest sense was "*the* channel for formative culture for all English people".'

There is little doubt that the official dispersal proposals, in Circular 7/65 and in the White Paper, tended to reinforce popular views about the danger of English children being held back. It was believed by a number of teachers that the standards of their non-immigrant pupils were falling. This was put in perspective two years later when the I.L.E.A. published the report of a study of fifty-two primary schools, where immigrant pupils formed more than one-third of the pupils. Two-thirds of the head teachers questioned felt that there had been some fall in the intelligence of their non-immigrant pupils, i.e. these children were less able than the ones of previous years. This change was due to the fact that the ablest families had been moving out of the area.* About one-third felt that there had also been some under-achievement by non-immigrant pupils, i.e. that they were not doing as well as they could. This might in theory, said the Report, be due to the existence of increased class rolls, to higher pupil-teacher ratios, to a concentration of the teachers' attention on the immigrant pupils, or to a lack of mutual stimulus from other non-immigrant pupils.

---

* This movement out of certain areas of the large towns was not new. Its cause was the increased housing opportunities for people after the War, to which public housing contributed as much as private. Slum clearance schemes also altered the balance of the population in the inner city area.

But the Report found that in fact the average class rolls, and the average pupil-teacher ratio in these schools, although high, were slightly lower than the average for the whole I.L.E.A. The non-immigrant pupils in the schools, who were transferring to secondary schools in September 1966, achieved scores in English, Verbal Reasoning, and Mathematics which were the same as the average for all transfer pupils in all the Authority's primary schools.[18]

The D.E.S.'s stress on dispersal meant that a chance was lost to inform the public and the people working in education about the work being done in some schools with large immigrant intakes. Spring Grove, in Huddersfield, is perhaps the best known example. Its experiment in language teaching was already receiving attention.[19]

At the beginning of the decade, Spring Grove was an ordinary primary school, with a growing proportion of immigrant and non-English speaking pupils. Under the guidance and initiative of the Headmaster, Trevor Burgin (now advisor to the Huddersfield L.E.A.), and with the co-operation of the local authority, it gradually developed a 'school within a school' for non-English speaking pupils. This had the double effect of providing the non-English speakers with the grounding in English which they desperately needed, and of preventing the ordinary class teachers from being overwhelmed with problems they could not adequately cope with. The proportion of immigrant children in the school rose to about two-thirds, and of coloured children to over half. The proportion of all children gaining grammar school places was maintained, and so was the loyalty of many native parents, some of whom continued to send their children to Spring Grove even when the family moved away from the area. Huddersfield subsequently adopted a dispersal scheme, but without abandoning the principle of specialized and intensive teaching of non-English speaking children. The moral of the Spring Grove experiment was that in discussing how to avoid teacher strain, maintain standards, and satisfy the education needs of different groups of immigrant children, the number of immigrant children in the school was not the only nor even the most important factor: the organization and the quality of the teaching were at least equally vital. Spring Grove did experience a huge change in the kind of pupils it taught, and it changed its organizational character to meet this. Nevertheless, it remained both a good school by conventional standards and a multi-racial one.

Reactions to the Dispersal Policy

The official dispersal scheme had a cool reception. Ealing and Bradford L.E.A.s had already adopted their own dispersal schemes West Bromwich, Halifax, Huddersfield, and Hounslow L.E.A.s were to follow, although each scheme differed from the others in important ways. The I.L.E.A., Birmingham L.E.A., and a number of other authorities rejected the proposal. Some authorities rejected dispersal because it violated the principle of the neighbourhood school, and because of the belief among teachers that the contact with immigrant parents, which was possible only if the school was close to the children's home, was of real benefit in any attempt at integration. There were particularly strong objections against the movement of infants (5–7 year-olds) long distances from home. Another reason for rejecting the policy, in some authorities, was that it was seen by immigrant parents to be discriminatory—it removed the right of parents to choose their children's school and its manner of presentation tended to confirm popular prejudice that immigrant children held back native ones.

The selection of children for dispersal on grounds of origin, rather than on an educational criterion, worried many commentators on Government policy. The Plowden Report recommended: 'Dispersal may be necessary but language and other difficulties should be the criteria employed.'[20] In the only detailed study of a dispersal policy in action, the education committee of Ealing International Friendship Council also recommended in 1968 that any future dispersal should be based upon language difficulty, not origin.[21] In both cases, the recommendations were based on the desire to get away from racial distinctions, but did not go to the root of the problem of how best to organize language-teaching.

But apart from these disagreements of principle, there was perhaps a more decisive reason for rejection and that was the practical difficulty of moving only immigrant children, and the political difficulty of moving both native and immigrant children, or 'swapping'. The official dispersal policy excluded the dispersal of English children. The administrator, therefore, had to find receiving schools with spare places to which the immigrant children could be taken. The lower the quota, the more schools he would have to find, and the larger the number of children who would be likely to have to be 'bussed'. Meanwhile, because immigrants frequently lived in areas of falling population, especially of the young, the schools in those areas would be likely to have empty places. The Ealing dispersal scheme has, in fact, run into quite serious difficulties of this kind. The original quota of 30% has been raised to 40%; and although immigrant children form only about 16% of the total Ealing school population and about 30% of the Southall school population, the authority requested neighbouring boroughs to receive some of the children being dispersed because they could not be accommodated in Ealing's own schools—a request which was turned down.

A fourth reason for rejecting the official dispersal policy may have been the reluctance of some L.E.A.s to tackle possible receiving schools which did not want to accept an intake of immigrants. It is hard to assess the strength of this. Certainly, in Ealing the anti-immigrant Residents' Association has opposed the dispersal policy.

3. LOCAL EDUCATION AUTHORITIES

While the D.E.S. might recommend, it fell to the L.E.A.s to take what action they thought necessary. Some rejected the idea of any special measures at all. For most of those who felt that they had to take some action, the problem was regarded primarily as one of resources. The main task which these L.E.A.s shouldered was the organization of special language classes for non-English speaking immigrant pupils. *English for Immigrants*, published by the D.E.S. (then the Ministry of Education) in 1963, contained an excellent early statement of the necessity for *teaching* English to pupils whose command of the language was inadequate, and suggestions about how this could be administered. The writer stressed the need for 'a carefully planned, intensive course making full use of modern methods of language-teaching.' This applied to both junior and secondary school children. 'Such special classes', the writer went on, 'should be staffed by teachers with some knowledge of modern methods of teaching English as a Second Language.'[22] At this time, however, there were almost no such teachers in Britain, there were no in-service courses for teachers, graduates of university courses in E2L were going abroad to teach, and little or no thought was being given to attracting them back to teach non-English speaking immigrant children, or to helping those who came back seeking work of this kind. There were no books or classroom materials designed for teaching English to children of immigrants in Britain.

Many L.E.A.s found it hard to find and hold their ordinary teachers, quite apart from getting teachers specialized in E2L. This situation led some authorities to employ immigrant teachers specifically to teach immigrant children, not always to the benefit of the children or the longer term professional prospects of the teachers themselves. For example, when Southall's dispersal scheme started in 1964, only five out of twenty teachers of immigrant reception classes were English, five were Anglo-Indian, and the rest Indian or Pakistani.[23] Not all the Indian and Pakistani teachers spoke Punjabi, the language of most of the immigrant children, although the idea that they did seems to have been the reason for at least some of the appointments.* The teacher shortage in some areas with many non-English speaking pupils was nominally improved by more generous allocations under the D.E.S.s teacher-quota system. But this could not increase the supply of teachers or of specialized E2L teachers, and in some areas additional posts in the quota were not fully taken up. Institutes of education were slow to respond to the need for teachers prepared for work with immigrant children, including E2L work (see below).

Financial contribution from the centre came in 1967, when the Home Office began to provide a 50% rate support grant, under section 11 of the 1966 Local Government Act, towards staffing services affected by the presence of immigrants in a local authority area. Of a total estimated expenditure by local authorities in 1967–8 of just over £3,100,000, nearly £1,900,000 was claimed for education staff (which might include teachers, non-teaching aides, and welfare workers). Thus, the Government contributed just under £1m. to local authorities in 1967–8 to spend on schools with immigrant children.[24]

In general, however, the context of nearly all local authority policy-making has been one of serious shortage of staff and expertise, and it must be assessed against this background.

The different administrative arrangements made by L.E.A.s to provide special language-teaching have been examined in detail

* The White Paper treated the training of teachers of immigrant pupils, and the training of immigrant teachers, in the same sentence: 'Arrangements have been made or are under discussion for the provision of special courses of training, both for English teachers of immigrant children and for teachers and potential teachers among the immigrants themselves. . . .' (Para. 45.)

by Nicholas Hawkes,[25] and reviewed in less detail in the Schools Council Working Paper No. 13[26] and in June Derrick's book, *Teaching English to Immigrants*.[27] Although these accounts date from 1965–6, they cover the main forms of organization adopted, which are summarized below.

The first of these, and the method which separated non-English speaking (N.E.S.) children least from the normal activities of the class and school, was that of normal placement plus some special tuition in 'Withdrawal' groups or classes. This is the most common form of provision in Birmingham and some other Midland L.E.A.s and is also used by many schools in Inner and Outer London. There is a good deal of variation in the quality of language-teaching in 'Withdrawal' classes, in the size of groups taught, and in the amount of special tuition per week. An extension of the 'Withdrawal' class idea is the part-time centre, to which N.E.S. children are brought from a number of schools for half the day, after which they return to their normal school. Part-time centres have been used in Leeds and Batley in the West Riding, and also exist in Islington and a few other areas in London. Some authorities found that the transportation of the children used up valuable time which could have been spent on teaching. The main difficulty which administrators and teachers have both expressed is how to combine sufficient teaching of English to non-English speakers with the maximum participation in the life of the school. There is little doubt that the most satisfactory way to combine these goals in schools with high proportions of N.E.S. children is to have a specialized language-teaching department within an ordinary school, and this has been achieved in a handful of schools throughout the country (of which the best known are probably Spring Grove in Huddersfield, and Gillespie School, Islington (I.L.E.A.)), but it requires teachers specialized in E2L and plenty of classroom space.

A far more common arrangement adopted by the schools with large intakes of non-English speaking children is the reception class. This was advocated in *English for Immigrants* and in Circular 7/65, and had, in theory, the same virtues as the special English department, in permitting intensive teaching without separation from the school. In some schools, reception classes have grown into special English departments, as numbers increase and the experience of the teachers grows. The advantage of this specialization is often lost, however, when the children are spread in many reception classes, either through normal placement, or through dispersal schemes. An extreme case is Ealing, where there are over sixty reception classes. In Bradford, where there is also a thorough-going dispersal scheme covering children of all ages, the L.E.A. made no special language provision for either infant or junior school children, but the receiving schools often set up reception classes staffed by ordinary teachers. These arrangements should be contrasted with Huddersfield's policy of trying to concentrate non-English speaking children in a number of full-time language centres attached to schools where they are taught English before being dispersed into other schools.

Full-time language centres, separate from ordinary schools, began to be set up as a response to the influx of Indian and Pakistani children aged 13 + in 1965. The influx was an unforeseen result of changes in immigration policy in the White Paper. Families wishing to be re-united in Britain had to bring their children in before they reached the age limit of 16, and those whose motive in coming was not family feeling but economic ambition also had to come as young teenagers. In response to the arrival of Asian teenagers with inadequate English, Bradford and Birmingham set up full-time reception centres for children of this age group, and some other L.E.A.s have followed suit. One L.E.A., Batley in the West Riding, with a higher intake of young non-English speaking children than of older groups, set up a full-time centre for primary school children, while the older ones attended only part-time classes.

In judging these various arrangements the vital factor to look for is the quality of the language-teaching: a similar administrative arrangement could produce both good and bad. It is now generally agreed by experts in the field that children whose English is inadequate, even the youngest age groups, benefit from special teaching of English. If they are left to 'pick up' the language, they may be able to manage socially in day-to-day contact, but they will not be equipped educationally and when they leave school will not be able to compete equally for any jobs needing even minimum qualifications. The type of arrangement necessary will obviously depend on the number of such children in an L.E.A. and the way they are distributed in the schools. In some ways, so far as language learning is concerned, concentration is an advantage, because special arrangements must then be made, if only to enable normal classes to proceed. June Derrick, in her book *Teaching English to Immigrants*, clearly favours full-time tuition because of the close personal attention it permits: 'There is no doubt that intensive language-teaching is the most effective, and that the biggest gains are made when the teacher sees his pupils often.'[28] But this judgment presupposes that there will be an expert teacher. The touchstone for deciding for or against particular methods is whether they allow or provide low pupil-teacher ratios, and teaching adapted to the age and ability of the pupil.

In achieving these goals, the solution adapted by Birmingham L.E.A. is interesting. A department for the teaching of English as a Second Language was set up under R. D. Chapman as early as 1960. The Authority is one of those which had and have great difficulty in getting and holding teachers. The Burnham Reports following the 1944 Education Act ended the practice of paying teachers in certain areas more than those in other areas (with the exception of London), so that financial incentives were not available, except for head teachers and deputy heads, in the light of the special circumstances of their particular schools. In addition, Birmingham had to face the general lack of teachers qualified in E2L. It therefore built up a team of peripatetic teachers specifically for language-teaching in schools where the number of non-English speaking children was too small to justify a full-time class. As they were not attached to any single school, they could be paid above the national basic scale by being remunerated as holders of additional graded posts. By spring 1968, there were fifty-two full-time and some part-time peripatetic teachers, dealing with some 2,000 children, in specialized 'Withdrawal' classes, with another 250 children attending full-time language centres. (The number of specialized teachers since then has increased.) Beginners were getting seven or eight lessons a week, each lasting forty to forty-five minutes. 4,600 children were at that time assessed as in need of special English tuition. An important aspect of the Birmingham scheme was that it provided its own built-in training element, including evening classes and workshop sessions. These extended, in 1968, not only to the new recruits to the specialist team, but to the city's ordinary class teachers. The Language Centre provides a headquarters, and is also a meeting place for teachers of *foreign* languages who have found E2L methods helpful. This is one example of the way in which the development of techniques of teaching E2L has had 'fall out' benefits of wide application, not only in the teaching of foreign languages, but also in the teaching of English to English children.[29]

One of the achievements of Birmingham's Department for the Teaching of English as a Second Language has been the establishment in 1968 of a C.S.E. examination, which has now been taken over by the West Midlands Examination Board. This, together with the teaching materials produced by the Leeds Project, should provide some objective basis for assessing the adequacy of the administrative arrangements for teaching English. Although in many parts of the Midlands and the North of England, and in some London boroughs, language-teaching provision has increased, by no means all the children classified as being in need of intensive help are yet receiving it. Moreover, the D.E.S.'s method of collecting statistics on language ability almost certainly underestimates this need.[30]

In infant schools in particular, where the foundation of all subsequent ability to learn is laid, almost nothing has been done. There is still a tendency for infant teachers to reject the need for special language teaching for this age group, particularly in schools where the proportion of non-English or poor English speaking children is low.

4. A.T.E.P.O.s, THE N.C.C.I., AND THE LEEDS PROJECT

One of the great difficulties facing teachers of immigrant children, whether in ordinary classes or special language classes, was the absence of suitable written and other teaching material, and of information on the background of the children which could help them to understand the children's difficulties. The initiative in providing such material was to come not from the top but from the base.

The first voluntary Association of Teachers of English to Pupils from Overseas was established in the West Midlands as early as 1962. It had from the start close links with the Birmingham L.E.A. R. D. Chapman, its founder, headed Birmingham's special language department. Covering a very wide area, it had a circulation list of about 100 and an active membership of thirty or forty, including both teachers in primary schools, and university lecturers. In March 1965, the London A.T.E.P.O. was formed. During the following three years, branches were formed in the West Riding, Coventry, Bedford, Slough, and Derby, and the A.T.E.P.O.s have now been federated. Their main function has been to provide 'emergency do-it-yourself' work to help teachers deal with everyday teaching. This has meant organizing

conferences and work-shop sessions, circulating duplicated biblio-
graphies and teaching notes, and setting up study groups on
special subjects. The A.T.E.P.O.s have also functioned as ginger
groups to obtain more resources and help from L.E.A.s through
developing fruitful links with local H.M.I.s and administrators.
Getting more adequate training facilities has been one of the main
objectives, and the A.T.E.P.O.s have also tried to build up contacts with colleges of education.

Another voluntary organization, whose impact upon the situation was less immediate but covered more ground, was the
Education Panel of the National Committee for Commonwealth
Immigrants. The Panel brought together for monthly meetings a
number of educationalists of high calibre, and operated as a
stimulant to action on the part of established bodies, in particular
the institutes and colleges of education. In 1967, the teacher training sub-committee held two major conferences on the subject,
organized with the co-operation of H.M. Inspectorate. Two
pamphlets, one on the educational background of West Indian
children, the other giving practical advice to teachers of E2L,
were published.

It was largely as a result of A.T.E.P.O. and N.C.C.I. pressure
that some progress was made in teacher training. In September
1965, Ann Blatch, formerly a teacher in Huddersfield, started the
first one-term in-service training course in E2L at London
Institute of Education, attended by fifteen teachers. In 1967, her
course was taken over by the I.L.E.A. In July 1968, the N.C.C.I.
was able to list only two colleges of education which provided
similar in-service training.[31]

A small number of colleges of education were in 1968 providing
optional courses in the teaching of immigrant children, as part of,
or as a supplement to, their basic training courses. These have not
yet had time to make an impact in the classroom. Edge Hill
College of Education at Ormskirk, a pioneer in the field, now offers
a course in the education of children of immigrants as part of a
more general three-year course combining teaching with social
work methods.

Thus, most of the burden of teacher training has been placed on
the L.E.A.s and the teachers' own voluntary groups. Some
L.E.A.s have provided a range of in-service training. (The
I.L.E.A. holds, in addition to its one-term course, one-week full-
time courses for its new recruits from training colleges, part of an

existing training provision for teachers going to schools with special difficulties.) But not all L.E.A.s were interested, and it was not impossible in 1967 for a probationary teacher to find herself, without warning or preparation, placed in charge of a reception class for forty infant children of immigrants.

The hesitant development of in-service training seems to indicate the absence of a concerted drive by the D.E.S. to get courses set up and attended. There would have to have been two aspects to this: first of all, a serious attempt to persuade the institutes of education, and, through them, the colleges, to set up courses; secondly, some effort to impress upon local education authorities that they should release teachers to attend courses. One of three one-term courses in English as a Second Language for immigrant children had to close because local authorities were reluctant to release teachers. Yet for many other one-term courses, this reluctance was not apparent.

Meanwhile, the most important attempt to meet the needs of teachers on a sufficiently large scale arose from the initiative, late in 1964, of June Derrick, then lecturing in the Department of English, University of Leeds. She drew up a proposal for the establishment of a national centre to provide practical help to schools admitting large numbers of immigrant pupils. The proposal was submitted to the newly established Schools Council, whose reaction was to sponsor a feasibility study, undertaken by June Derrick, to find out the extent to which local education authorities were aware of the factors involved, the size of the immigrant in-take into local authority schools, and the nature of the pedagogical problem. The results, which have never been published in full, formed the first comprehensive study of local authority practice, and, in fact, of teaching practice in the individual schools. It seemed likely to the Council that the survey would show the need for development work in the preparation of new materials suitable to the classroom situation and the real life experience of the immigrant children. On the basis of June Derrick's report, a three-year development project ('the Leeds Project') was set up at the Institute of Education of the University of Leeds in September 1966, with an initial budget of £50,000 later raised to £77,000.

The objectives of the Leeds Project were to provide teaching materials for pupils with inadequate English, of Asian and Southern European parentage. Its first aim was the production of an introductory two-term course for children aged from 8 to 13. Approximately 150 teachers in thirty-eight L.E.A.s were involved in trying out the new materials during the Project, so that, in effect, it also functioned as a training for teachers. The introductory course was published in January 1969. But in addition, it was planned to produce a more advanced course for the same age group, a course for the newly-arrived teenagers, and to conduct research into the situation of 5–7-year-olds. The Leeds Project was therefore oriented in an extremely practical way, and began to affect the school situation from the start, through the teachers involved in the trial of the new materials and by becoming, inevitably, an information source for many others. In the autumn term of 1968 the small project staff were committed to running two complete short courses in different colleges of education. The Leeds Project may be said to represent the first attempt by any of the central institutions of the educational system to tackle the problem of resources. June Derrick's feasibility study, together with the report on infant schools subsequently conducted for the Leeds Project by Diana Stoker, remain the only comprehensive and detailed studies of what is actually taking place in schools where there are immigrant pupils with inadequate English.

5. WEST INDIAN CHILDREN

All these activities were devised to meet the needs of the non-English-speaking child, and in the provision of special classes, the production of materials, and the analysis of the classroom situation, attention has in practice been focused on children of Asian or Southern European parents. Only in a few exceptional schools and authorities is there evidence of a serious attempt to meet the education needs of children of parents from the Caribbean countries, or to help class teachers to overcome the difficulties which they feel in tackling the problems.

Children of West Indian parents, the largest of all the immigrant groups, have been a source of bafflement, embarrassment, and despair in the education system. They have complicated the attempts to define the term 'immigrant pupil' and to assess the linguistic needs of immigrant pupils; in class, they have often presented problems which the average teacher is not equipped to understand, let alone overcome. Those teachers who are interested—perhaps members of A.T.E.P.O.—have been groping towards understanding and practical solutions. But there has so

u

far been no study completed, comparable to June Derrick's survey for the Schools Council, to provide an overall picture of what is happening to these children in the schools, and an idea of the numbers of children who have special difficulties and of those who do not.

Both June Derrick and others were aware of the need for analysis and for the production of materials to help teachers of West Indian children, and in 1967, a project with aims similar to those of the Leeds Project began at Birmingham University, under Professors Sinclair and Taylor. The Schools Council contributed the budget of £20,000. The lack of an objective study has meant not only that teacher training and teacher-aid programmes have been held back, but also that almost all comment tends to be about 'problem' children. Moreover, the problems are often defined exclusively from the point of view of the teacher, who may not be free from bias. These, for example, were some of the comments of one teacher in a secondary modern school in Handsworth:

The expansion of the number of coloured children from immigrant sources has considerably added to the difficulties of teaching and maintaining discipline. . . . [A] certain amount of colour consciousness seems to exist, further problems and difficulties are caused by poor speech, bad housing conditions, and also the inability of some immigrants' parents to appreciate the conditions and conduct considered to be acceptable by the host community. Most of these difficulties lie with the Caribbean immigrant group.

. . . colour consciousness seems to manifest itself in unacceptable reactions to criticism and from marked scowling to outright muttering, flouncing and outbursts of uncontrolled temper and . . . resentment of individual remedial treatment. . . .

When Caribbean children come here the freedom of English schools goes to their heads . . . unfortunately, these children are not used to moving in a controlled manner, their free movement reaches unacceptable levels; it is reproved and this is seen as an example of prejudice. 'The White children do it, why can't we?' Some feelings of prejudice may be an echoing of parents' attitudes who see prejudice in the refusal of Unions and employers to accept lower standards of trade skills.

. . . our older pupils blithely state that they are going to stay for a fifth year to take a fifth year G.C.E. course and become electrical engineers, without any conception of what is truly involved in achieving such a laudable ambition. . . . When boys . . . find their schemes are not capable of fruition, they are inclined to blame colour prejudice rather than their own lack of suitable qualifications.[32]

A counter example, to illustrate that some teachers did see problems from the child's point of view is provided by Audrey Allison, a teacher in an E.S.N. special class in a Bristol secondary school. This was part of her description of her most difficult West Indian pupil who arrived in her class from Jamaica in September 1963, aged 11 years 10 months.

[He] could neither understand nor be understood for about three months, after which he built up a resistance against all the new conditions around him and retired into a refusal to make any approaches to them. . . . [He] said that the people in the next room hated him. I presumed that his parents tried to keep him quiet and well-behaved at home as the neighbours were in such proximity . . . this seemed to frustrate him greatly . . . and he was very noisy, excitable and aggressive in class, could not sit still for long, nor walk around the school in a controlled way. . . . He refused to speak to me, turning away from me, with a sulky expression and eyes downcast, often shut. . . .
He is an intelligent boy and his lack of education was obvious to him; this hurt his pride. He refused to tackle seriously any new piece of work. He shut his mind against Reading, but found he could easily understand Arithmetic, so began to work at this quite well. However, if he made even the smallest mistake, when I pointed it out, he would turn away, refuse to listen . . . and usually would tear up his book, or scribble over every page. . . . I am sure that his hurt pride made him unable to accept the fact that everyone makes mistakes. In the last two months this attitude seems to have disappeared.
. . . his father, who visited the school after his first report, advised us to beat him every morning until he cried. . . . Eventually, in about March, I discerned signs of his being able to trust me and to understand the nature of the relationship I offered. Things have gradually improved since then. He began to read in June and is now working well, as his ability is slowly fulfilling the needs of his intelligence.

She adds that this was the most difficult pupil of all the West Indians she had taught, but that the same attitudes and reactions existed to a lesser degree or with shorter duration, in nearly every West Indian pupil who had arrived from overseas, and had been placed in her (special) class. Most of the other West Indian pupils in the school had been placed in lower streams of normal classes, with the exception of a minority who had done very well, some of whom had been transferred to a grammar school.[33]
The problems faced by very many pupils who have come from the Caribbean, or whose parents did, seem to spring from several different sources. There is, first of all, for a minority of these

children an unexpected linguistic barrier when they first enter school; they cannot follow the teacher, nor make themselves understood. Unlike children from non-English speaking homes, they are unlikely to have been warned about this. A rather larger proportion may be able to follow and make themselves understood, yet their command of English may be inadequate for educational purposes. In a return which Birmingham L.E.A. made to June Derrick's Schools Council inquiry in 1965, of 8,242 immigrant pupils so designated, over half were children of West Indian parents. Nineteen per cent of the West Indian pupils in the I.L.E.A. sample were said to need further intensive language-teaching. The D.E.S.'s criteria for assessing language ability are likely, as John Power has argued, to conceal rather than to illuminate the linguistic needs of West Indian children.[34]

Secondly, many of the problems the children have derive from economic circumstances. Children of West Indian parents born in Britain are likely to have lived a very confined pre-school life, without toys, and, since both parents probably work, without having spent much time playing with the parents. Those who arrive from the Caribbean may have had more freedom to develop in their earliest years, but have probably received an inadequate, and 'formal and arid' primary schooling, which Elsa Walters has described in vivid and in many ways devastating terms.[35]

Thirdly, the children's parents may place a greater burden upon them than would the average British parent. They are likely to have great expectations both of the children's progress at school, and of their contribution to domestic and family chores at home. They will probably share with many English parents a lack of understanding of modern teaching methods. The parents' expectations of academic work may well have a stimulating effect for the children who have had an opportunity to develop and who are bright; but they are likely to depress the confidence of the children who have lacked such opportunity.

Finally, there are the problems which West Indian pupils have which derive directly from their teachers and the school system in Britain. There is the problem of prejudice, and of the effect of teachers' expectations upon the children's progress, regardless of their intelligence, the importance of which has been demonstrated.[36] The problems of discrimination and expressions of racial prejudice in the wider society must inevitably affect the relationships which can be formed in the classroom, between pupils of different racial origin, and between teacher and pupil. There have been complaints by teachers in secondary schools that West Indian pupils gang up together.

Another problem which adversely affects West Indian children is the high degree of teacher mobility in some areas, which, together with the fact that the children may also often be moving home, hinders the development of a stable relationship, which might otherwise be possible, between pupil and teacher. This hurts all children, of course, but the stability is likely to be particularly important for West Indians, because many have been separated from their mother through migration, and may be having to form new relationships at home just at the time when they have also to form them in school.[37]

The quality which emerges most strongly from any account of the difficulties of Caribbean pupils is that of frustration; it is clear that many children have had their natural ability and energy thwarted from a young age. Those arriving from the Caribbean will have lacked the sort of primary schooling which has allowed an increasing number of English children since the War to acquire a good mastery of basic learning skills. The children are in danger of losing confidence in themselves, and feeling that they have failed their parents; or they may want to demonstrate their worth, but be unable to do so in terms which either their parents or their teachers understand and approve of. To complicate matters, their teachers and their parents are likely to ask different things of them.

The vast majority of these children have simply entered ordinary classes in their local schools, and have been dependent upon the interest and energy of the class teachers. Some of them have received special teaching in remedial classes. Indeed, at first it was not uncommon for head teachers to turn to their remedial teacher to deal with all immigrant pupils, including non-English speaking ones. Few West Indian children have been included in the more specialized language classes developed by some authorities. The justification for placing children in remedial classes, full-time or part-time, is that in a good class there will be small-group work, and plenty of individual attention. This can also be said of some special schools for E.S.N. children, in which a disproportionate number of West Indian children are placed. A teacher may be able to adapt her methods to the needs of West Indian pupils. On the other hand, placement in a remedial class or E.S.N. schools may reflect poor assessment of a child's potential. The lack of a culture free, or culture fair, test of ability, which would enable an objective assessment to be made, has been one problem. The I.L.E.A. Report commented:

One of the Authority's medical officers with long experience in the examination of educationally sub-normal children feels that some of the migrant children, especially West Indians, admitted to E.S.N. schools, may well have intellectual potential above the level of their assessed I.Q., their level of achievement having been depressed by inadequate or narrow previous education.[38]

6. ACHIEVEMENT

The problems of Caribbean children in schools overlap with those of Asian and South European and other non-English speaking groups, and also with those of some English children. What prospects have all the immigrant pupils of achieving educational equality with English children of English parents, i.e. of achieving a similar spread of attainment? Two studies suggest that those who have had all their schooling in the U.K. are doing at least as well as their English peers, but the number of such children surveyed is only just over 100, and there is some evidence to suggest that within this group, children of parents of some nationalities may do worse than others.[39] It would be rash to generalize about the achievements of the 'second generation' on the basis of research so far conducted. Reports from teachers of immigrant children in infant schools give ground for concern that a lack of knowledge of English, or lack of mastery of other basic skills, may hamper immigrant pupils at each subsequent stage in their school career. There are, of course, counter-examples, children who start in a backward primary group, and finish in a grammar school sixth form. But enough is known generally about the cumulative effect of 'failure' in the early stages of learning, for this to be regarded as a major handicap for immigrant pupils. Apart from the Leeds Project, and the subsequent Birmingham one, the greatest single contribution of policy-makers at the centre would be the implementation of the Plowden 'Education Priority Areas' strategy, and the opening of nursery schools promised under the 'Urban Programme'.

As for the children who are themselves immigrants, it is fairly certain that *as a group* they will find themselves in the 'below average' categories of attainment, and that their academic attainment will be less than their spread of intelligence would have permitted. Some of the greatest educational problems are arising in the 13 + age group. This has implications for the provision of further education and industrial training which have so far not received very much consideration. There is a danger that because of the demand for formal qualifications and age restrictions on the entry of trainees and apprenticeships, some of the younger generation are likely to find themselves in a lower occupational class than their parents.[40]

7. CONCLUSIONS

There is no doubt that the most important single decision during the entire evolution of policy was that taken by the Schools Council in 1965 to commission June Derrick's study of L.E.A. and classroom practices. It led, of course, to the productive and immediately useful work of the Leeds Project. More significant, however, was the perspective of the Project, which provided a more realistic and a more reputable basis for the development of policies in the future. This perspective was radically different from that of the Commonwealth Immigrants Advisory Council in its Second Report, of the Department of Education and Science in its Circular 7/65, and of the Government in the White Paper.

The main policy issue defined in the earlier period, 1963-5, was the problem created by the numbers of immigrants entering the schools. The policy-makers' main concern was to minimize disturbance to the normal (i.e. the previous) routine of the class or school. They expressed fear lest the class teachers would devote too much time to immigrant at the expense of non-immigrant pupils. The school's role in the process of integration was seen as a social one: it would train immigrants to be British, and provide a location where they could mix with English children.

The Leeds Project was set up to equip teachers for a specific education job—the teaching of English as a Second Language. It was concerned to do this whether the teacher had 2% or 100% of immigrant pupils in his class. The proportion of children with inadequate English would affect the organization of language classes, but teachers with low proportions needed help as much as those with high proportions. The evidence from June Derrick's and Diana Stoker's reports suggested that some of the most effective teaching of non-English speaking children was taking place in schools which had had high intakes of immigrant pupils over a number of years. The greatest danger, stressed in both reports, was not that immigrant pupils received too much attention, but that the attention they received was too limited and too inexpert and that they became mere passengers, instead of participants, in the educational process. This danger was greater where they formed very low proportions in class. The reports found that the simple presence of immigrant and native-born pupils in a class, still less in a school, did not amount to integration in any real sense. Without more attention to their particular educational needs, the children were unlikely to be able either to join in the life of the school, or to compete on equal terms after leaving school.

The main instrument of official policy, devised on the basis of the pre–1965 perspective, was dispersal: L.E.A.s were advised by the D.E.S. to intervene to prevent the proportion of immigrant pupils rising above a third in any school. But the main policy imperatives revealed by June Derrick's and Diana Stoker's reports were the need to provide materials, books, and in-service training for serving teachers; to alter initial training courses so that language-teaching for immigrants was included; and to provide nursery schools in areas of immigrant settlement. Neither June Derrick nor the other Leeds Project staff came to any firm conclusion about the dispersal schemes which were operating. But the reports suggested that placement schemes such as the dispersal schemes should be judged on their contribution to the educational needs of the immigrant pupils.

The whole question of the educational effect of dispersal schemes was given only cursory attention when the policy was first proposed. For some, the point of the policy was to make life easier for teachers in schools which would normally have large intakes of children of immigrants. For others, the policy was a way of preventing the development of 'all immigrant' schools, which were per se undesirable. For still others, dispersal was an essential basis for cultural assimilation, including the learning of English. We have seen how in the White Paper all these notions were contained in the official justification of the dispersal proposal. Little or no thought had been devoted to a clear analysis of the nature and the extent of the educational needs of the immigrants. It was wrongly assumed that an influx of immigrant pupils into a school automatically hampered the chances of native English children in the school and that the children were competitors for the teacher's attention under all circumstances. (The development of techniques of teaching English as a Second Language, in which the Leeds work has made its contribution, has shown that in this field, at any rate, the 'fall-out' benefits in teaching English to English children, and in teaching foreign languages, are considerable.)

Official policy gave the accurate impression of having been devised under the pressure of circumstances and based on received ideas. Central to both was the concept that, as a result of the coming of immigrant pupils, the schools were changing for the worse. Many of the schools attended by immigrant children were in *areas* which had been changing—the 'twilight areas', described by Ruth Glass and by Rex and Moore, from which younger families had been moving since the end of the War because of the improvement in housing and in employment opportunities. These general changes were largely ignored by the policy makers in education until the publication of the Plowden Report at the beginning of 1967. The kind of children attending these schools was changing, the 'character' of the schools was changing, and the arrival of immigrants, with particular problems, was only part of this process. The official dispersal policy, with its emphasis on preserving the normal routine of a school, was in a sense a Canute-like attempt to prevent change. It is significant that the actual quota figure chosen—30%—was not related to the residential distribution of immigrants within a local authority area. It was based on an idea of how many immigrants a school could 'absorb' without changing its 'character'.

The dispersal proposals were not linked with any real attempt by the D.E.S. to tackle the lack of resources, particularly the shortage of appropriately trained teachers, and of equipment to help them. As a result, they appear as an attempt to dodge the issue of resources, by making the problem 'disappear' by sleight of hand. When there were only a few children of immigrants in a class, they often hardly impinged at all on the teacher's consciousness. The dispersal policy also fitted some teachers' definition of their problem in terms of discipline: they wanted to reduce the numbers of immigrants in order to reduce their disruptive potential.

Some, but not all. As we have seen, there was a powerful feeling among many teachers, especially those in primary schools, that the schools should serve the neighbourhoods in which they were sited.

These teachers were prepared to adapt their techniques, and to give their time. They received no leadership from the D.E.S., practical or political, in a situation in which there was a need for in-service training, for liaison between teachers, and for teachers' centres. Above all, there was a need for an interpretation of events which would attract teachers into schools with immigrant pupils, rather than repel them from the situation. This was not provided.

Why was it that the central response to the presence of immigrant pupils was so negative and so slow? It is impossible on the basis only of published material to give a full answer. One can only suggest the reasons. The D.E.S., the most 'interventionist' in style of all the social service departments, was at its weakest when it came to planning for new developments in the system.

Theoretically, H.M.I.s could have foreseen the increases in the number of children of immigrants, and could have made plans to provide the necessary information and to examine in advance the various arrangements which would be necessary to receive and to teach the children. This was not done. Some of the reasons are suggested in the Report of a House of Commons select committee on the H.M.I.s published in September 1968.[41] It is clear from the evidence to the committee that the individual H.M.I.s in the field are hard pressed and do not have sufficient specialist skills. One witness, who had himself been an H.M.I., told the committee that the H.M.I.s 'had allowed themselves to be divorced from the general sociological field', and one of the recommendations was that 'attention should be paid to . . . the need to have within the Inspectorate some Inspectors with special knowledge of social developments affecting education'. The other significant point brought out by the committee was that communications between the Inspectorate and the D.E.S. left much to be desired. One witness to the committee described the methods of diffusing information as 'a bit primitive'. Thus, the conditions of work of the H.M.I.s and their relationship with the D.E.S. were not likely to produce the kind of planning which would have been necessary if the D.E.S. itself were to adopt a very positive role. Moreover, as John Power has pointed out:

The structure and traditions of the Department would . . . have tended to inhibit its Inspectors from doing more than arranging (or stimulating others to arrange) various conferences and courses, while hoping that interested groups and individuals among teachers and others might emerge to take more positive and independent action. . . .[42]

One result of the 30% quota set by the official dispersal policy was to make the preservation of inter-racial schools appear to be more difficult than was in fact the case. The figures obtained by the D.E.S. from their Form 7i returns from schools show how many 'immigrant pupils' there are in every school in January each year. The degree of concentration of the 'immigrant pupils' has not been published.[43] However, figures for the I.L.E.A. were as follows in January 1968: half the 'immigrant pupils' in primary schools attended schools in which they formed less than 30% of the pupils; a further 28% attended schools where they formed between 30 and 50%; only 6·5% or about 2,700 children were in schools, sixteen in all, where they formed more than 60%. In secondary schools, 78% of 'immigrant pupils' attended schools where they formed less than 30% of the pupils, and 0·8% or 174 pupils went to one school, where they formed more than 60%.[44] The figures include, of course, Cypriot and Italian pupils. They exclude children born in Britain of immigrant parents who arrived more than ten years previously, i.e. before January 1958. These children are not defined as immigrants, and are therefore not counted. The figures are not therefore a precise reflection of the racial composition of the schools, but they give a general indication of it. On the basis of the I.L.E.A.'s experience, if inter-racial or, at any rate, international schools are the goal, then Britain has already achieved this as far as the overwhelming majority of the children of immigrants are concerned.

Nevertheless, so long as present housing policies are pursued there will be some predominantly 'immigrant' schools and some predominantly 'black' schools. What kind of attitude should be taken towards them? Should chief education officers try to break up concentrations by dispersal or other means?

The terms, of course, cover a number of different kinds of schools: the large mixed international school; the school with a high proportion of Indian or Pakistani children, first or second generation, who share with each other a common language and cultural background; the school whose pupils are children born in Britain to parents who emigrated from the West Indies. It is necessary to recognize that some of these schools may be as good or better than predominantly English, or predominantly 'white' schools. The I.L.E.A. report, which dealt mainly with educational problems, noted that:

> In some underprivileged areas many immigrant children are providing a reservoir of ability which is very welcome in the secondary schools. In many primary schools also, children of immigrant families especially if they have had a full primary school education in this country, are contributing both to the intellectual and social quality of the school. [45]

This is not surprising, at least as long as housing discrimination restricts immigrant families with supportive 'middle-class' attitudes to education in 'immigrant' school catchment areas. At present, neither the proportion of immigrants in a school, nor the proportion of black or brown children, indicates a degree of 'badness' of the school.

At the same time, in some L.E.A.s, officials refer to the 'ghetto areas' as though the degree of segregation and inferior education which exists in the northern U.S.A. existed in Britain too. Yet those predominantly 'immigrant' schools which are deprived in terms of educational resources, or which serve deprived areas, join other 'white' schools which have similar problems. Plowden showed this, so did Newsom and, more recently, Sir Alec Clegg's report to the West Riding Education Committee. [46]

It is difficult to be precise about the extent to which the predominantly 'immigrant' schools are different from any other schools, whether they tend to lose teachers more than other schools, whether staff-pupil relationships take a different form, whether the pupils attain less than they might have done in more racially mixed schools. We know very little about what the children's parents want, or the pressures on a parent who chooses an interracial or predominantly 'white' school in preference to his near neighbourhood 'immigrant' one. The orthodoxy, most clearly expressed by the C.I.A.C., was that the danger of predominantly 'immigrant' schools lay in depriving immigrant children of the benefits of a 'normal' school, and the company of English children. This was a judgement which fitted the prevailing view that the tensions between 'host' and 'immigrant' were not problems of race relations.

It is a judgement which can still be made by those who would deplore the isolation of any ethnic group that would deprive the children in their formative stages of all contact with their English peers. They would judge that these children might not be adequately prepared for the predominantly white society in which they will be living. They would also wish to avoid a 'colonial' situation with schools which are predominantly 'black' and staffed by white teachers. On the other hand there is also the judgement that for a young child and its immigrant parents there is no substitute for the neighbourhood and the neighbourhood school.

So long as present housing policies are continued some neighbourhoods will increasingly become coloured quarters and there will be a growing number of predominantly immigrant schools. In fact, if we look ahead, the danger which may face the predominantly immigrant schools is not that they will be different but that the differences will be misinterpreted. It is that those in authority—local administrators, head teachers—will perceive an identity between colour and inferiority, and as a result the schools, and the children in them, will receive inferior treatment. The best argument for dispersal policies is that this perception—the identification of colour and inferiority—will inevitably influence the allocation of resources and the attitude of teachers. But this may not be inevitable, particularly if the Plowden policies are fully implemented and the multi-racial schools, whatever their 'racial balance', share in general improvement based on compensatory education. If the multi-racial schools are as good as any others and, equally important, are perceived to be so, then the self-fulfilling prophecy linking colour and inferiority will be invalidated. This in itself will have significant consequences for race relations in Britain. But if this advance is to be made, radical changes in the whole basis of teacher training and the allocation of resources must take place. And this will require an unequivocal political commitment.

NOTES TO CHAPTER 18

1. J. A. G. Griffith, *Central Departments and Local Authorities* (London, Allen & Unwin, 1966), p. 523.

2. For a description of the report, carried out by June Derrick, see *English for the Children of Immigrants*, Schools Council, Working Paper No. 13 (London, H.M.S.O., 1967).

3. *15 to 18* (The Crowther Report) (London, H.M.S.O., 1960). Terms of reference: to consider in relation to the changing social and industrial needs of our society, and the needs of its individual citizens, the education of boys and girls between 15 and 18, and in particular to consider the balance at various levels of general and specialized studies and to examine the inter-relationship of the various stages of education. *Half our Future* (The Newsom Report) (London, H.M.S.O., 1963). Terms of reference: to

consider the education between the ages of 13 and 16 of pupils of average or less than average ability who are, or will be, attending full-time courses either at school or in establishments of further education. *Higher Education* (The Robbins Report) (London H.M.S.O., 1963). Terms of reference: to review the pattern of full-time higher education in Great Britain, and in the light of national resources to advise H.M. Government on what principles its long-term development should be based. In particular, to advise whether there should be any changes in that pattern, whether any new types of institution are desirable, and whether any modifications should be made in the present arrangements for planning and co-ordinating the various types of institution. *Children and Their Primary Schools* (The Plowden Report) (London, H.M.S.O., 1967). Terms of reference: to consider primary education in all its aspects and the transition to secondary education.

An excellent summary of all these reports and the Albemarle Report on the Youth Service has been written by Anne Corbett, for the Council for Educational Advance 'Much to do about Education—a critical survey of the fate of the major educational reports'.

4. *English for Immigrants*, Ministry of Education pamphlet No. 43 (London, H.M.S.O., 1963).

5. Second Report by the Commonwealth Immigrants Advisory Council (Cmnd. 2266) (London, H.M.S.O., February 1964).

6. *The Education of Immigrants*, Department of Education and Science Circular 7/65 (June 1965) to local education authorities and certain other bodies.

7. *Immigration from the Commonwealth* (Cmnd. 2739) (London, H.M.S.O., August 1965).

8. C.I.A.C. Report, op. cit., para 14.

9. Ibid., para 10.

10. Schools Council, Working Paper No. 13, op. cit., paras. 22–3, 26–7.

11. National Union of Teachers, *The N.U.T. View on the Education of Immigrants* (London, N.U.T., 1967).

12. J. Rex and R. Moore, *Race, Community and Conflict* (London, Oxford University Press, for Institute of Race Relations, 1967), Chapter 10, by Mrs. Jennifer Williams.

13. Hansard, Vol. 685, cols. 433–44, 27 November 1963.

14. Circular 7/65, op. cit., para 8.

15. *Immigration from the Commonwealth*, op. cit., paras. 41–2.

16. *English for Immigrants*, op. cit., p. 15. The pamphlet contains a lengthy discussion of a number of ways of organizing the teaching of English within a school.

17. D.E.S., *Statistics of Education*, Vol. 1 (London, H.M.S.O., 1966). There were 131,043 'immigrant pupils', making 1·8% of all pupils: 44% came from the West Indies, 19% from India, 10% from Cyprus, and 6% from Pakistan. Forty-nine per cent had no problem with English; 26% had reasonably good spoken English but weak written English; 19% had some English but needed further intensive training; 6% had no English. The quarter needing further intensive language teaching made up 0·45% of the total school population. For a critical analysis of the Department's criteria of assessing language ability, see John Power, *Immigrants in School: a survey of administrative policies* (London, Councils and Education Press, 1967). *Statistics of Education* (1967) gives the total of immigrant pupils as 183, 776 (unlike the 1966 figures, this includes schools which had less than ten 'immigrant pupils').

18. Inner London Education Authority, *The Education of Immigrant Pupils in Primary Schools: report of a working party of the inspectorate and the school psychological service* (London, I.L.E.A., 1967), para. 44, and Appendix 3, Table F.

19. T. Burgin and P. Edson, *Spring Grove: the education of immigrant children* (London, Oxford University Press, for Institute of Race Relations, 1967).

20. Plowden Report, op. cit., Chapter 6, para. 119, Recommendations.

21. Ealing International Friendship Council, Education Committee, *The Education of the Immigrant Child in the London Borough of Ealing* (London, E.I.F.C., 1968).

22. *English for Immigrants*, op. cit., p. 15.

23. Notes on visits to Southall by the Institute's 'Survey of Race Relations in Britain', in 1964.

24. Estimates submitted to the Home Office by local authorities under Section 11, Local Government Act, 1966.

25. N. Hawkes, *Immigrant Children in British Schools* (London, Pall Mall Press, for Institute of Race Relations, 1966).

26. Schools Council, Working Paper No. 13, op. cit.

27. June Derrick, *Teaching English to Immigrants* (London, Longmans, 1966).

28. June Derrick, op. cit., p. 17.

29. The benefits also derived from the re-organization of a school to create smaller classes; see, for example, H. Bulla, 'Immigration—past, present and future: attitudes and official policies of local officials in West Bromwich . . . to . . . coloured Commonwealth immigrants' (Dissertation for B.A. degree, University of Bradford, 1966). See also, the case of the class with only one English girl, *Daily Telegraph*, 7 November 1968.

30. See, for example, John Power, op. cit.

31. N.C.C.I., *Practical Suggestions for Teachers of Immigrant Children* (London, N.C.C.I., 1967).

32. Association of Teachers of English to Pupils from Overseas, Midlands Branch, Work Group on West Indian Pupils, *Report and Supplement*, A. Crump (ed.), February–May 1966.

33. Audrey Allison, 'Some case histories of West Indian children illustrating a few educational problems' (private communication to the Institute's 'Survey of Race Relations in Britain', 1965).

34. J. Power, op. cit.

35. Elsa Waters, 'Some factors in the background and experience of West Indian children which may affect their progress and behaviour in English schools' (paper offered for discussion by members of a child guidance clinic and possibly to be presented to the British Psychological Society, unpublished).

36. See, for example, C. Bagley, 'The Educational Performance of Immigrant Children', commenting on the I.L.E.A. Report, in *Race* (Vol. X, no. 1, July 1968).

37. See, Sylvane Wiles, 'Children from Overseas' (2), Institute of Race Relations *Newsletter* (June 1968), para. 4, Separation of the Child from Parents.

38. I.L.E.A. Report, op. cit., Appendix II.

39. Ibid., Appendix III, Tables A–E. Also, Alan Little *et al.*, 'The Education of Immigrant Pupils in Inner London Primary Schools', *Race* (Vol. IX, no. 4, April 1968); and Sylvane Wiles, 'Children from Overseas', (1) and (2), Institute of Race Relations *Newsletter* (February and June 1968).

40. See, for example, Peter Townsend's prediction in *Policies for Racial Equality*, A. Lester and N. Deakin (eds.), (London, Fabian Society, 1967).

41. House of Commons Papers, 400, part 1 and 2, Select Committee on Education and Science (H.M. Inspectorate).

42. John Power's book review in *Education* (Vol. 131, no. 23, June 1968), p. 766.

43. Figures published since this was written give the number of schools in England and Wales with proportions of immigrant pupils of 2–20% and over, 20–33⅓%, and over 33⅓%, at January 1967. See, Statistic of Education 1967, tables 23 and 24 (1968, London, H.M.S.O.).

44. Unpublished figures supplied by the I.L.E.A. research department.

45. I.L.E.A. Report, op. cit.

46. Sir Alex Clegg, 'The Wastage of Human Potential in Education' (West Riding Education Committee). See also, A. Clegg and B. Megson, *Children in Distress* (Harmondsworth, Penguin, 1968).

INTRODUCTION

In Chapter 7 we discussed the dynamics of the migration to this country from the Commonwealth and concluded that the prime moving force was that of economic opportunity. From our discussion of 1966 Census data, it became clear that, as yet, the coloured immigrant communities have not achieved anything like a comparable position to that of the indigenous population. And the census data suggests that in part this was due to the reluctance of employers to employ immigrant labour for reasons above and beyond those of skill. In this chapter, we wish to pursue this topic further and examine it in the whole context of industrial relations and labour management. While attention will be paid to the skills of the coloured worker, our primary focus will be on the host society's reaction to the presence of the coloured worker in the labour force. Specifically, this means the examination of the attitudes and behaviour of employers and employees, the policy and the practice of management and unions, and the intervention or non-intervention of the Government and other public bodies.

Before proceeding, it is necessary to reiterate the crucial importance of equality of opportunity in the field of employment and its relation to housing and education.

The inter-relationship between housing, education, and employment has already been stressed; and it is worth stressing again in this context. Low income coupled with financial instability are direct corollaries of poor or restricted employment opportunities, and these in turn close many of the avenues of escape from the initial areas of reception for the immigrant with their inadequate housing. These areas are also often those with the poorest educational facilities. Thus, the children of the original immigrants may receive an education which is less than adequate and leaves them ill-fitted for the labour market. If the children of immigrants also find their employment opportunities restricted for reasons not directly related to their education, then the whole vicious circle is repeated and reinforced. But although a great deal of discussion in political circles and the press has been devoted to the problems of concentration of coloured communities and incipient ghettoes, and those of schools with high proportions of coloured school-children, far less has been said about the restrictions on employment opportunities for coloured workers, which has been one of the main factors responsible for the concentrations in housing and education. It is one of the contentions of this chapter that problems in the field of employment are inextricably bound up with those of education and housing, and that problems in these two fields, which have received the lion's share of the attention of politicians, administrators, commentators, and the general public, are insoluble without due attention and energy being devoted to the equally important field of employment.

1. THE PATTERN OF DISCRIMINATION

The assumption has been made in this chapter that restrictions on the opportunity in employment of the coloured worker exist at present in the British labour market and that this is not solely due to the skills or lack of skills that the coloured worker possesses. As our starting point, we will examine the direct evidence for this assumption, before placing the discussion in the context of labour relations generally. The most important evidence is contained in the P.E.P. Report,[1] which was based on research carried out in six selected areas in 1967. Using a threefold approach—interviewing immigrants, interviewing persons in a position to discriminate, that is, employers, and situation testing—the investigators concluded that there was substantial discrimination, largely based on colour, against coloured applicants applying for jobs. In interviews with representatives of Ministry of Labour employment exchanges and private employment bureaux, it was reported to the P.E.P. investigators that a large percentage of the users of these facilities discriminated against coloured labour. On another level, a recently published study by Bob Hepple cites seventy-five selected examples of discrimination, reported in the press, covering engagement procedures, training, promotion, terms and conditions of work, dismissal procedures, and trade union practices.[2] In studies, such as those by Sheila Patterson in South London[3] and Peter Wright in the Midlands and the North,[4] evidence of discrimination against coloured workers is presented. The Race Relations Board Annual Report shows that by far the largest single category of complaints that it had received was in the field of employment, even though the Board's powers at that time did not cover complaints of this kind.[5] This material and a mass of

w

supporting evidence suggests that discrimination against coloured workers has been widespread and pervasive.

The pattern of discrimination against coloured workers in British industry disclosed in these investigations appears to be so all-embracing and operates at so many levels that an innocent stranger (or a frustrated coloured job applicant) could well believe that it is the result of a centralized directive, enthusiastically implemented, that the employment of coloured labour be restricted to those jobs that white men do not wish to have. This would be a mistake: none of the central triumvirate of the Government, the C.B.I. (for employers), or the T.U.C. (for workers) has ever laid down a deliberate policy which would have the effect of discriminating against the coloured worker. Such statements as there have been since the 1950s from these bodies have almost always stressed a belief in the importance of equal opportunity irrespective of race, and expressed confidence in the inherent sense of fair play of the British public—and in particular, of employers, workers, and customers—to see that discrimination on the grounds of race does not occur. But despite these pronouncements, the P.E.P. Report showed that nearly a quarter of firms in areas where there were fairly large numbers of coloured workers did not have any coloured employees and that most of the remainder placed severe limitations on the types of jobs that coloured workers could do. The Keighley Junior Chamber of Commerce reported in 1966 that they could not find a single white-collar job for coloured school leavers in the town and had found amongst employers in the town every attitude from 'wooden indifference to frank hypocrisy'.[6] It is this discrepancy between public pronouncement and general practice which we will examine first, before looking at the whole pattern of industrial relations in Great Britain as it affects the coloured worker.

A feature of industrial relations in Great Britain is the pre-eminence of voluntary procedures—as opposed to legally-enforced rules—devised to regulate work conditions and behaviour. These voluntary procedures have been under attack from various directions in the past few years, but industry has attempted, usually successfully, to keep the settlement of disputes within industry despite increasing Government pressure, especially over wage-bargaining. The recent report of the Royal Commission on Trade Unions and Employers' Associations (the Donovan Report) again emphasized the role of voluntary bargaining between employer and employee and suggested that the law had little role to play in industrial relations.[7] Furthermore, many of these voluntary agreements are the product of informal decisions taken at plant or shop-floor level. Coupled with this method of decision-making, there is a strong streak of conservatism that runs throughout British industry. The resistance to change is tenacious, on the part of both management and workers.

Thus, the coloured worker in Britain, since the 1950s, has been attempting to enter an industrial system resistant to change, in which decisions are often taken not at national or even regional level but at plant level. In this situation, the employer faced with a coloured job applicant was far more likely to be influenced by local and personal factors than the remote declarations of racial equality by the Government, the T.U.C., and the C.B.I.* In some cases, probably a small minority, the employer would refuse to consider employing a coloured man because of his strong prejudicial feelings on the grounds of race. More frequently, especially in the earlier days of coloured immigration, the coloured man was an unknown quantity, and the employer's attitude to his employment potential may well have been influenced by uninformed views derived from the British colonial experience. These responses often lumped together the vast diversity in origin and experience of West Indians, Africans, Pakistanis, Indians, and others into one omnibus category of 'blacks' or 'natives' who were thought to be incapable of all but the simplest and most repetitive tasks.

Employers were not only doubtful of the possible contributions that a coloured man could make or was capable of making, but fearful of the effect on the other workers or customers of using this unknown and visibly different source of labour. The benefits to be obtained by employing coloured labour usually seemed too small, when balanced against the apparent dangers of upsetting other workers and customers, for many employers to risk the experiment. For their part, workers were suspicious of coloured labour and of the use that employers might make of it. It was feared that coloured workers might be used as strike-breakers and that unscrupulous employers would pay coloured workers lower than standard wages. Workers were often as ignorant and suspicious of standards prevailing in the countries from which the immigrants

---

* The C.B.I. made no specific statements on racial equality prior to 1967. See below, Employers' Associations, in this chapter.

had come as their employers and were unwilling to believe that the West Indian or the African could be a skilled man.

Most employers therefore approached the question of whether to employ coloured immigrants with some trepidation. Often the easiest answer was to let someone else sail the uncharted seas. In a conservative milieu where anything new and strange could disturb the delicate equilibrium of industrial relations, the best policy seemed to be to stay with the known, tested labour supply. A few employers and workers were willing to give the newcomers a fair chance to prove themselves. But the foundations of a pattern of discrimination against the coloured worker was laid down by the mass of employers, unwilling to look at this new source of labour unless they had no other choice.

However, due to continuous labour shortages, some employers found themselves during the 1950s and early 1960s in a situation which seemed to them to offer no other choice than the employment of coloured labour. Peter Wright, in his study carried out in the Midlands and North of England between 1961 and 1964, found that fifty out of sixty-eight companies employing coloured workers cited the lack of an alternative source of labour as one of the reasons for their initial employment.[8] Similarly, other studies in other parts of the country have found that employers have only started to recruit coloured labour in times of grave labour shortage. But, as Wright points out, 'the distribution of jobs available to coloured people did not occur evenly throughout status levels. Generally speaking, the coloured worker tended to obtain the jobs which the white workers valued least.'[9]

In a situation in which only certain employers were willing to employ coloured workers, and then only for limited types of jobs, a system of quotas grew up. Investigators have found in many firms informal quotas—agreed between management and workers—limiting the number of coloured employees to 5%, 10%, 20%, or 30% of the workforce in the company or in a department. Employers expressed the fear that if they employed too many coloured workers they would become known as a coloured factory and local white labour would no longer wish to work for them. Certain jobs and departments within firms became known as 'coloured', and, in turn, the pressure on those who were willing to recruit coloured labour became more intense. Once it was known by labour exchanges and the coloured community that a particular firm would employ them, the number of applicants they received increased and demands for quota restrictions would also increase. Some employers, less scrupulous than others, took advantage of the employment difficulties of coloured workers and confirmed the worst fears of English workers by using coloured labour as cheap labour, often to work in intolerable conditions. These were exceptions, but rare though they may have been, they exacerbated suspicions between white and coloured labour.

Bars on the promotion of coloured labour, either to better jobs in terms of pay and conditions or to supervisory positions, became fairly general throughout industry. Of these two positive kinds of promotion, instances of upgrading to supervisory positions with some authority over white workers have been almost non-existent. The P.E.P. Report stated from their interviews with employers that only the first type was at all common: as they put it, 'at manual worker level coloured people had positions of authority only over other coloured people'.[10] In his study, Wright reported that it was rare for coloured workers to obtain jobs in supervisory positions, and similar reports have been made by Patterson in South London and McPherson in Tower Hamlets.[11] The reason for this bar on promotion has generally been a fear of the resistance of white workers to taking orders from coloured workers. This bar on promotion has also had an effect on recruitment in jobs where a worker might reach a supervisory position over a number of years.

In this way, despite repeated Government statements and exhortations and T.U.C. resolutions on equality of opportunity, a pattern of discrimination has been established in employment. This discrimination has manifested itself in recruitment, the type of job available, quotas, ethnic work units, and opportunity for promotion. It was caused by the mass of employers and workers acting in what they perceived to be their own best interests. Employers, unwilling to experiment and fearful of disturbing the industrial peace, and workers, suspicious of both the coloured man and their employers, combined to exclude the stranger.

2. OFFICIAL POLICY

(a) Government

Throughout the 1950s and the early 1960s, the official policy of the Government was occasional exhortation, not usually backed up by any action. In Whitehall, the attitude was determined, up to 1961, by the Treasury's belief that immigration from the Commonwealth was a bonus to the economy; this view reinforced the general opposition to the idea of control. Tentative moves were made by the Government at times when the possibility of friction arose. In periods of recession and at the time of Notting Hill, Government exhortations became frequent. Fears of unmanageable entry of unskilled Asian workers led to agreements with the Indian and Pakistani Governments to limit migration by powers of passport control. But apart from this, the general policy was one of *laissez-faire*: it was assumed that such problems as arose in the field of employment would work themselves out over time. By 1961, the only action of any kind that the Ministry of Labour had taken was in the previous year, when it started taking unofficial counts of coloured unemployed. After the Commonwealth Immigrants Act of 1962 this was changed to counts of Commonwealth immigrant unemployed.

None the less, the mechanism of control employed in the Commonwealth Immigrants Act of 1962, and reinforced by the White Paper of 1965, was economic—the availability of employment or the work skills of the immigrant—although the reasons adduced for control were the strains imposed by migration on social services and amenities. There was, and is, no necessity for the social and economic imperatives to run parallel; often, they are in direct conflict. Indeed, those areas where economic considerations would be most favourable to the entry of immigrant labour are usually those where social strains are likely to be greatest. The use of the employment machinery as the means of control can only have been chosen on the basis that it is a convenient administrative device (already tested through years of use for aliens), and has nothing whatever to do with the employment situation in Britain.

The Government was involved from the very start of the migration, however, with the coloured worker's search for work. Sheila Patterson reports the manager of a South London employment exchange as saying: 'Even without reading the papers I can always tell when a new shipload's arrived. Next morning there'll be seventy or more round at the exchange bright and early. You can't say they're not keen to work.'[12] Both Banton[13] and Patterson found, in London in the early 1950s, that in certain exchanges arrangements had been made for all coloured immigrants to be interviewed by one of a particular group of clerks. The explanation was that more attention by sympathetic clerks could be given to the particular difficulties of coloured immigrants. This practice was discontinued after charges of segregation were made. In general, however, employment exchanges were run on the general *credo* of public service with no discrimination on grounds of race.

The non-discriminatory stance of the employment exchanges came into direct collision with employers' preferences. Until 1954, any vacancy notified which put 'unreasonable restrictions' on the kind of worker wanted was to be refused. From 1954 until 1964, exchanges were to attempt to persuade an employer to change his mind, but if this was not possible they were to accept 'no coloured' or 'whites only' requests. This policy left the employment exchanges in a peculiarly ambiguous position, in which they could be accused of pandering to an employer's prejudice. Their answer to this charge was that they were protecting a coloured job applicant from the humiliation of unnecessary rejection on grounds of race. It is possible that one reason why the Ministry of Labour did not take a harder line with employers was that from 1956 onwards employers no longer had to notify vacancies to employment exchanges but could rely solely on private bureaux and other means. A fear that the number of vacancies notified would fall too drastically may have influenced ministerial policy.

In July 1964, the Minister of Labour told the House of Commons that exchanges had to note restrictions laid down by employers, otherwise they would send men for jobs they had no chance of obtaining and would be unable to continue the process of persuasion to have these restrictions withdrawn. Later in his speech, after critical questions, the Minister said, 'to the extent that where it is shown that continued resistance is due to prejudice, eventually and after due consideration we are prepared to withdraw the facilities of the employment exchanges'.[14] The final sanction of withdrawing facilities has almost never been used and the procedure by which this is done is extremely cumbersome.[15] The policy was further strengthened towards the end of 1966, but the Ministry will still accept quotas where a 'reasonable proportion' of coloured workers are employed. The new Race Relations Act 1968 also legitimizes quotas in its racial balance clause. It has been suggested by David Beetham that the cumbersome nature of the method of withdrawing facilities is an indication of the great reluctance to endanger the voluntary and co-operative relationship between officials and employers.[16] This is probably not only an accurate assessment of policy with regard to employment exchanges, but also an explanation of the Government's reluctance to take any active steps in the whole field of employment over the period up to 1968.

The Youth Employment Service has faced the same problems as the labour exchanges; they have become increasingly involved in the question of discrimination as the numbers of young coloured school leavers increase. A report covering the three-year period up to March 1968 suggests that immigrant school leavers present two different sorts of problems for the Y.E.S.[17] First, some have not reached adequate educational standards and are not fluent in English, and secondly, that 'some of the less able school leavers (and their parents) tend to be over-ambitious'. A greater difficulty faced by the Y.E.S. has been the reluctance of employers to employ coloured school leavers, although it is suggested that the Y.E.S. has had some success in persuading employers to change their practice. Generally, little difficulty was reported in obtaining industrial apprenticeships, but reluctance to employ immigrants in the service industries was most apparent. Although discrimination was gradually diminishing, the Report concludes, 'complete equality of opportunity is still to be achieved'. Beetham, who examined the work of the Y.E.S. in Birmingham, found that immigrant school leavers were more difficult to place than native-born school leavers and involved more work for the Y.E.S. Beetham also reported that the Y.E.S. was successful in persuading employers in some cases to drop discriminating practices.*

Attempts to introduce legislation against racial discrimination in employment in the period before 1965 came to nothing. Fenner (now Lord) Brockway introduced a private member's bill in 1956, which included clauses that specifically attempted to deal with discrimination in employment. But in Brockway's bill of 1960, and subsequent bills, provisions covering employment discrimination were dropped, partly as a result of pressure from the trade union group of Labour M.P.s. Proposals to amend the 1965 Race Relations Bill to cover employment among other things also failed. Suggestions that the Government should amend the Fair Wages Resolution, which all government contractors have to agree to comply with, to include a non-discriminatory clause have not been implemented.† However, a few local councils, starting

---

* For a further discussion of the Youth Employment Service see Chapter 24.

† Roy Jenkins, as Home Secretary, undertook in 1966 to inaugurate early consultations on this issue, but at the time of writing (late 1968) no action has been taken.

with the London Borough of Camden in 1966, have incorporated a non-discrimination clause for all contractors to sign.

A further indication of the Government's attitude was the unwillingness until very recently to collect statistics by colour or origin. It was felt that the keeping of such statistics was in itself discrimination and would create racial problems where none or very minor ones existed. This attitude permeated not only central government departments and the nationalized industries but also local government and private industry. Thus, the usual response to an inquiry about how many coloured workers a company employed was the ritual statement that because the firm did not discriminate it did not keep such records. This attitude to keeping such statistics has been gradually eroded since 1967. There is general agreement that accurate information is necessary if realistic policy decisions are to be made, and with the keeping of such records it is more difficult to keep discrimination hidden. [18]

An excellent example of keeping statistics relating to colour which concerns the Government's role as an employer is shown by the differing situations in the Army and the Royal Air Force. Both services state, quite unequivocally, that coloured Commonwealth servicemen are dealt with in exactly the same way as other servicemen. In response to inquiries in mid-1968, the Army was able to supply an analysis of coloured male soldiers by rank, length of service, and so on, while the R.A.F. stated that it had no records as to whether a man was coloured or not.* In the event of charges of racial discrimination being made against either service, the Army is in a better position to refute them. [19]

The information supplied by the Army is of great interest and is summarized in Table 19.1. The progress made by coloured soldiers (no information was available concerning officers) is described by the Army authorities as encouraging, and the figures would seem to confirm the statement that 'the coloured soldier has every prospect of getting a really square deal in the Army' (letter, 11 September 1968). In view of the very marked reluctance of private industry to promote coloured workers to positions of authority over white workers, the fact that over 40% of coloured soldiers are N.C.O.'s is quite striking. Some 60% of

---

* Information supplied by letter from the Ministry of Defence (Army), 11 September 1968, and from the Ministry of Defence (Air), 13 August 1968, to the Survey of Race Relations. The interpretation of information supplied in these letters is that of the authors and not that of the Ministry of Defence.

all coloured soldiers are tradesmen, which is another interesting comment on private industry's assessment of the coloured worker's skills. As far as distribution is concerned, every single major arm or corps of the Army has coloured N.C.O.s of the rank of Sergeant or above. The lower percentages of coloured soldiers in the higher non-commissioned officer ranks seems to be almost entirely due to shorter length of service. This is borne out by an examination of the figures for coloured soldiers with nine or more years' service, of whom over half hold the rank of Sergeant or above.

Table 19.1. Rank distribution of coloured male soldiers

Rank	Less than 3 years	Length of Service completed 3 years and under 6 years	6 years and under 9 years	9 years and more	All	Percentage distribution
Warrant Officer I	—	—	—	5	5	0·2
Warrant Officer II	—	—	—	15	15	0·7
Staff Sergeant	—	—	—	23	23	1·1
Sergeant	1	3	34	50	88	4·2
Corporal	9	61	226	57	352	16·8
Lance-Corporal	37	119	205	16	376	18·0
Private	552	397	261	16	1,228	58·8

Source:
Unpublished data supplied by Ministry of Defence (Army) in letter of 11 September 1968.

The role of the Government as an employer is of great importance and it has been suggested by some critics that its record does not always reach the exemplary standards to which it should aspire. Hepple, in his recent book, suggests that the provisions of the Nationality Rule in the Civil Service often are too stringent and lead to curious exclusions, unjustifiable by any rational approach to the question.[20] The impact of these rules often falls hardest on the children of European refugees. One of the strangest anomalies recorded is the requirement that Bank of England employees be British by both birth and parentage. It is not known whether this requirement remains in force now that the Race Relations Act 1968 has become law.

The most recent information available on the employment of coloured personnel in the Civil Service was given by Mr. John Diamond in a parliamentary reply to a question on the subject, on 23 July 1968:

On an estimate made last September at least 16,400 in the Home Civil Service: of these over 50 were in Administrative and equivalent grades; some 8,000 in the clerical, sub-clerical and equivalent grades; and about 8,000 in industrial grades. The Government do not recognise any distinction of this sort.

Again, these figures (which exclude the National Health Service) are illuminating when compared to private industry's fears regarding coloured workers in higher status jobs, but unfortunately the figures supplied by Mr. Diamond in his answer are not detailed enough to permit any systematic analysis. The best one can say is that there are significant numbers of coloured employees in the higher ranks of the Civil Service.

Through the medium of the National Health Service, the Government does employ a very large number of coloured workers ranging from highly qualified medical staff to ward orderlies and catering staff. As was seen in Chapter 13, medical and dental services account for extremely large percentages of certain immigrant groups. The Minister of Health, in reply to a question on 7 May 1968, gave some information on this matter which is summarized in Table 19.2. As can be seen, whilst approximately half the junior doctors working in N.H.S. hospitals were born outside the U.K. and Eire, only about one-sixth of those in the grade of Senior Registrar were born outside the U.K. and Eire. The number of coloured nurses, especially West Indians, is very substantial, but there is evidence that there is discrimination against them in teaching hospitals, where the national figure is said to be only 1 to 2%.[21]

The largest number of jobs within the public sector are those in nationalized industries, local government, and municipal undertakings, and it will be convenient to consider here their policies and practices. In theory, most of the nationalized industries have operated a policy of non-discrimination on the grounds of race. However, as in most of these industries recruiting is at local level and as those responsible for recruiting are to be found at many levels in the hierarchy, practice has varied widely. Practices in different nationalized industries and different sections of these

Table 19.2. Number of medical staff* in the grades of Senior Registrar and below working in N.H.S. hospitals in England and Wales, 30 September 1967

	(1) Total staff	(2) Born outside U.K. and Republic of Eire	(3) (2) as a % of (1)
Senior Registrar and below	12,182	5,668	46·5
Senior Registrar	1,369	228	16·7
Grades below Senior Registrar†	10,813	5,440	50·3

Notes: * Locum staff and General Practitioners holding hospital appointments excluded.

† Grades below Senior Registrar are those of Registrar, Junior Hospital Medical Officer, Senior House Officer, and House Officer.

Source:
Written answer, Mr. K. Robinson, Minister of Health, Hansard, Col. 57–8, 7 May 1968.

industries have covered nearly as wide a spectrum as those in the general field of employment.

Probably the most important employers of coloured labour in this category have been British Rail and London Transport. Both have recruited labour directly outside the U.K., in Barbados, and both have employed coloured workers from the very earliest period of coloured migration. It is easier to describe London Transport's policy and practice than that of British Rail, as the former has a very highly centralized recruitment and promotion system, while that of the latter is far more diverse. Recruitment by London Transport for bus and train staff has operated on a basis that would seem to be free of discrimination. Promotion up to certain levels would also seem to be in general non-discriminatory, but there has been a reluctance on the part of the L.T.B. to promote coloured workers to supervisory positions, expecially where they would be in the public view. The absence of coloured bus inspectors has been a matter of considerable comment in this context,[22] but in the latter half of 1968, the first coloured L.T. bus inspector was appointed. There are no coloured station-masters on London Transport although there are a few station inspectors. As promotion on the railway side is to a very great extent a question of seniority, the absence of coloured staff at station-master level does not necessarily indicate any discriminatory practices. London Transport also employs on the permanent way some coloured gangers (equivalent to charge-hands).

In general, the L.T.B. has followed a policy of dispersing coloured workers, where possible, without restricting itself to any quotas. This has helped the absorption of coloured workers and has given the L.T.B. more flexibility in its recruitment policies. It is possible that the greater difficulties experienced by the L.T.B. on promotion on the buses is due to the peculiarly exposed position of a bus inspector compared with most supervisory jobs, including those on the railways.[23] But until London Transport grasps the promotion nettle more firmly, especially on the buses, some doubts will remain about its policy.

The picture of British Rail is far more confused, but if it is fair to infer from the evidence that there are obstacles to promotion in London Transport, then it is also fair to infer that obstacles exist on British Rail and that the ceiling at which non-discrimination stops is lower. In certain areas, no coloured staff have been recruited, while in others, there have been bars on coloured workers except in the lowest grades. Often, wide variations in recruiting policy have been seen in adjacent areas falling under different jurisdictions. Thus, in 1961 there were no coloured staff at Paddington, although other railway terminuses near by employed large numbers. In 1966, a West Indian working as a guard at Marylebone applied for a transfer to Euston and was officially informed that it was a policy at Euston not to employ coloured guards. Following disclosures in the press, the policy at Euston—stated to have been agreed between management and men—was rescinded and the transfer effected.

Many municipal bus companies and also bus companies which are subsidiaries of the Transport Holding Company (a public corporation) have operated, and some still continue to operate, bars on the recruitment of coloured staff. Directors of transport companies have stated that coloured conductors and drivers are unable to do the work or are unacceptable to the general public—despite the contrary experiences of those bus companies who do employ coloured labour. One explanation for the absence of coloured staff has been that white labour is available—an ingenuous explanation that implies coloured labour will only be

considered if white labour do not want these particular occupations. On certain occasions, publicity about colour bars has forced
bus companies to change their policies. An illustration of this was
the storm over the Bristol Omnibus Company's operation of a
colour bar in 1963. After much national and local press publicity,
the chairman of the Transport Holding Company, who held a
controlling interest in the Omnibus Company, intervened, and
made it clear that a colour bar could not be tolerated. It was
stated that the Holding Company had earlier issued a general
directive forbidding discrimination, but that this had been ignored
locally.[24]

In the nationalized industries, while the policy is one of non-
discrimination, the different levels at which decisions affecting
employment are taken make for variations in practice. In local
government, diversity of policy as well as practice is to be found.
Different departments of local authorities are often almost
separate enterprises, and it is not unknown for one department of
an authority to recruit coloured labour and another department
of the same authority to operate a colour bar. Most of the major
local authorities do employ coloured staff in both white-collar and
manual jobs, and some local authorities have been among the best
in offering full opportunities for coloured staff. In some cases, the
opposite is true, especially in transport departments (see above).

Local authorities are large employers of professional staff and
some have shown a reluctance to employ coloured staff for these
positions. This applies especially to doctors, who apart from their
medical duties also have considerable administrative responsibility. Similar reluctance has been shown over the employment of
accountants and social workers (except where they would work
with the coloured community). In two instances, however,
coloured staff have reached the very highest levels in local government.

Discrimination undoubtedly exists in many forms in employment in the public sector, but certain aspects differentiate it
sharply from that in the private sector. Due to its nature, public
employment recognizes standards of pay, unions, and so on, and
the extreme exploitation of coloured workers, such as occurs—if
only occasionally—in private employment, is rare or non-existent.
The use of ethnic work units, which is fairly common in some
sectors of private industry and which produces a situation of
go-betweens, straw-bosses, and is an open invitation to corruption

and bribery, is also rare or unknown in public employment. Finally, discrimination in much of the public sector is restrained by the *credo* of non-discrimination. In the final resort, discriminatory practices in central government employment and the nationalized industries are the responsibility of a minister of the Crown who is forced to act if the discrimination is too blatant and the publicity too great. Throughout the field of public employment those who make policy at all levels and those who implement policy are publicly accountable. While this public accountability is not of such a searching quality as to eradicate discrimination, it is usually sufficient to limit its scope and to inhibit to a degree those who would practice a policy of discrimination. Hence, while discrimination exists in the field of public employment, the coloured worker is likely to find that his employment chances are a great deal better than normally obtain in private employment.

(b) Trade Unions

Trade unions play an extremely important role in the system of industrial relations in this country. Over eight million workers (approximately two-fifths of the labour force) belong to the 160 unions affiliated to the Trades Union Congress. At its annual conference in 1955, the policy of the T.U.C. was stated clearly and explicitly:

This Congress condemns all manifestations of racial discrimination or colour prejudice whether by Governments, employers or workers. It urges the General Council to lose no opportunity to make trade union attitude on this issue perfectly clear.

Since then, a series of resolutions have been passed at annual conferences of the T.U.C. declaring the trade union movement's opposition to all forms of racial discrimination. This policy of non-discrimination is also officially followed by every individual trade union, although only one union has a rule that expressly prohibits racial discrimination.[25] The trade union movement as a whole, therefore, stands firmly on a policy of equality and non-discrimination. But a closer examination of the situation shows that policy and practice are not always in step.

At the centre, the policy is clear, but as one moves nearer the shop-floor, the picture becomes more blurred. Few instructions and little advice seem to have filtered from national offices of unions to regional, district, and branch officials. Beryl Radin, writing in 1966, revealed that the T.U.C. had not communicated with local trades councils on the subject of co-operation with the local voluntary liaison committees set up to promote integration.[26] Furthermore, trade union policy has been plagued by a confusion very similar to that of the Government. This derives from the view that to make any special provision for the particular needs of coloured workers would be to act in a discriminatory manner which would only create or accentuate problems. Thus, few unions provided any literature of even the most basic type in languages other than English, little attempt was made to explain the role of unions to coloured workers—many of whom were strangers to British industrial procedures—and sometimes no active attempt was made to recruit them.

Some union officials have gone to some lengths to recruit coloured workers, but these seem to have been a minority. Indians and Pakistanis, especially, have been seen as more difficult to deal with than other coloured immigrants. One union official described what he thought was particularly needed when working with immigrants (mostly Indians and Pakistanis): 'You have got to spend more time with them than English people. You must remember that you are talking with people who by and large have never heard of a trade union before. . . . You must use language which is simple . . . to avoid misunderstanding.'[27] A more common attitude has, however, been that there is no need to take any special measures at all.

One major source of friction has been the control exercised by unions, mainly craft unions, on the entry of new workers into their trades. Historically, these unions have always demanded that before anyone can become a member of the union they must serve an approved apprenticeship, and in certain trades employment without the union card is almost impossible. Many of these unions refuse to accept that any immigrant worker has had the training and the experience to reach the skill standards required by the union. The requirements of these unions are not only an obstacle to the employment of coloured immigrant workers but also to other immigrants, and even products of Government retraining schemes. The Donovan Commission reports that about two out of every five trade unionists (about three and three-quarter million) worked in a closed shop. Of these, about three-quarters of a million worked in a 'pre-entry' closed shop, i.e., where a worker had to be a member of a trade union before he could obtain the job.[28] Related to this is the control exercised by some unions on entry into approved apprenticeship schemes. In certain industries, local branches of unions have the right to determine the number of apprentices who can be trained and also either to approve or to nominate who these apprentices should be. Preference is given to those apprentices who have some connexion, usually family ties, to present and past members of the union. These conditions militate against any outsider, and especially the young coloured worker, obtaining an apprenticeship.

Most of the evidence available on trade union membership suggests that West Indians are as willing to join as English labour when approached. A study carried out in Nottingham found that rates of union membership of West Indians and English were very similar.[29] Radin reported that almost all unions stated that coloured workers were as receptive to join the union as were English workers, if not more so. In some instances, unions have been introduced into factories that were previously non-union by immigrant workers.[30] Despite this, there has been a widely reported feeling among trade union officials that immigrant members do not pull their weight in union activities, although there has never been any suggestion that at times when industrial action has been taken by unions immigrant members have been anything other than wholehearted in their support.

The most detailed study of the interaction of unions and coloured workers is one currently being carried out in Bradford by a team under the direction of Mrs. Sheila Allen, and some of their preliminary findings are worthy of note.[31] The most frequent response of trade union officials to questions on recruitment was that no special difficulties were encountered in the recruitment of immigrants. Where difficulties were cited they included language problems, and disillusionment with and lack of trust of unions. One respondent commented: 'We do not seem able to get the trust and understanding of these people. . . .' However, nearly all the trade union officials thought that the unions were doing everything possible to involve immigrants in union affairs. Despite this, the Bradford study showed that immigrants were unionized to a much lesser degree than indigenous labour and that this was due only in part to the type of industries in which they worked. One explanation offered was that in the trades in which immigrants were most concentrated, unions were often weak and did not pursue active membership policies. It was suggested that any ignorance and suspicion which the immigrants may have shown was equalled by that of many of the officials themselves.

On the other side of the picture, immigrant workers' views of trade unions were also studied.* Just over half the Pakistanis interviewed thought that trade unions could be of help to immigrants, but many of these replies were qualified and conditional on trade unions changing certain of their practices with immigrant workers. Often Pakistani respondents felt that unions had not helped them in the various problems on the shop-floor, had not responded to their industrial needs, and were only helpful for English workers. Immigrant views could be summed up as a series of demands for direct representation in the union structure, especially where a majority of workers were immigrants.

The Bradford study concluded that while immigrants may be accused of only 'taking' from the unions, this criticism also applied to the vast majority of union members. No evidence was found of blacklegging by immigrants, but unions had failed to take action, 'not only on the level of disputes and compensation—but also on the general level of discrimination'. It is suggested that the problems raised by immigrants are only part and parcel of the problems faced by unions and that better communications within unions are by no means the whole answer.

The policy of many immigrant organizations is to encourage their members to join trade unions and actively participate in their affairs. Beryl Radin found that a number of unions had coloured shop stewards and also a few coloured branch chairmen, treasurers, and other officials, sometimes in predominantly white branches.[32] Other studies have also indicated the presence of coloured shop stewards. Participation of coloured members in education courses and week-end schools run by unions has also been noted. But the extent of these activities is limited: it would appear that few, if any, coloured trade union members have reached the higher decision-making positions in trade unions or are paid full-time officials of unions.

Fear of immigrant labour under-cutting and depressing wages has been expressed by unionists. Frank Cousins, General Secretary of the Transport and General Workers Union, has discussed this:

some employers have used the situation in order to maintain low levels of wages. This in itself has been a criticism against our coloured

---

* Only Pakistani responses have as yet been analysed.

colleagues. I know of many passenger organisations that have recruited workers in the West Indies and the reaction of my own British trade union colleagues has been 'they wouldn't have had to do that if they had paid the right rates of pay'.[33]

This feeling coupled with past memories have made many unionists suspicious of the coloured immigrant workers. In the immediate post-war years some unions negotiated agreements with employers regulating conditions for the recruitment and employment of foreign labour, mainly directed against European labour. Although no written agreements at industry-level relate to colour or to Commonwealth citizens (except in shipping), it would be strange if the feeling that produced anti-European agreements had no carry-over to the later arrivals on the industrial scene.

Two of the worst cases of a breakdown of confidence between coloured workers and unions have occurred in strikes at factories in Preston and Southall. In the strike at Preston, there was what seemed to be a lack of consultation and effective communication between union officials and the coloured workers (whose representatives they were supposed to be) in new agreements with the management. The workers, mainly Indian, did not accept the agreement which raised their work load for a small wage rise and went on strike. Their fellow white workers did not support them and the union stigmatized the strike as 'racial' and gave it no support. After a bitter three-week strike, the strikers returned to work.[34] Interestingly, Radin reported that at a course arranged by the unions this strike was discussed and the white shop steward stated that they had miscalculated the situation.[35] By accepting dual standards, first the coloured workers and subsequently the white workers were compelled to accept the conditions originally given only to the coloured workers.

In the Southall strike, district officials of the union gave support —to the extent that they were able to do so—to the strikers (mainly Indian). The union had been introduced into the firm (which was extremely anti-union) by Indian workers with the aid of the I.W.A. (Indian Workers' Association). After a long history of disputes, the sacking of an Indian led to a full-scale strike. While officials of the union on the industrial side supported the strikers, the administrative wing of the union refused to make the essential declaration that the strike was official. After a six-week strike the workers returned to work beaten and disorganized. Peter Marsh, in his study of the strike,[36] showed that the indecisive attitude of the union was the result of structural factors: the union officials responsible for sanctioning strike benefit and declaring a strike official are separated from those officials responsible for organizing workers and negotiating on their behalf. Added to this there were complications in communication and inflexibility of interpretation by certain union officials, all of which led to the Indians involved believing that the union had totally failed them.

More recently, in the summer of 1968, the outcome of a strike in Queensbury, Middlesex, in a not dissimilar situation, was markedly different. Coloured workers, mainly Pakistanis, who had introduced the union to another firm that had resisted unionization, went on strike over bad working conditions and low wages. The firm involved attempted to hire temporary workers through an agency and advertised for students in order to break the strike. The union, however, came to the support of the strikers and forced the agency to withdraw and paid strike benefits. Various trade union groups in the area supported the strikers and the firm finally negotiated a satisfactory settlement with the union.[37]

Any assessment of union practice is undoubtedly complicated by two interrelated factors; first, the autonomy of many branches and, secondly, the difficulty of carrying white workers in support of union policy. Thus, the actions of many local branches—openly expressed opposition to the employment of coloured workers or hostility towards the wearing of turbans and beards by Sikhs—are in part due to local officials giving expression to the feelings of their white members. Similarly, the refusal of local officials to support coloured workers' complaints can be due to a fear that they would not be able to carry their members with them. These incidents are in themselves a reflection on the inability of the unions to educate their members in the basic principles of trade unionism—unity and brotherhood.

The inability of unions to educate their members is not so surprising when the attitudes of some leading trade unionists are examined. The belief that coloured workers contribute little and take greatly is not entirely absent among the upper echelon of trade unions. The *Guardian* reported Sir William Carron (shortly to become Lord Carron) as telling his union's conference that it would be interesting to have detailed figures of the grand total consumed in educational grants, Health Service expenses and subsistence payments to 'the ever-growing number of individuals

who are not born in this country and who have in no way contributed towards the setting up of the fund into which they so
willingly dip their fingers. As they so succinctly put it—in such a
surprisingly short time after their arrival—"they know their
rights".[38]

The existence of stereotypes sometimes seems to be as marked at
leadership level as among the rank and file.

To sum up, the reactions of the trade unions to the coloured
worker have been varied. Their general policy has been welcoming, but in practice they have often acted in ways which have
alienated the coloured worker. In general, however, the sins of the
unions have been the same as those of the Government—those of
omission rather than those of commission. They have failed, with a
few notable exceptions, to organize and involve the coloured
worker, or to make allowances for the differing cultural and
industrial backgrounds from which coloured workers have come.
Moreover, they have displayed a rigidity and lack of understanding in their dealings with coloured workers which could still have
grave repercussions. Finally, and most crucially, the unions, again
with a few notable exceptions, have failed to educate their
members to face the challenge presented by the presence of the
coloured worker in British industry.

(c) Employers' Associations

The role of employers' associations in the field of industrial
relations is, in general, far more limited than that of unions. Their
role in bargaining is usually confined to industry-wide agreements
on wages and hours of work. As the Donovan Report points out,
negotiations on bonus rates, piece rates, and conditions of work
are a product of bargaining between shop stewards, or less
frequently local union officials, and local management.[39] The
questions that would affect the coloured worker, such as quotas
and promotion, would not usually involve an employers' association. It is only in the event of disputes arising that an employers'
association might be involved. Despite this, employers' associations
can be influential in advising their members on the adoption of
policies and of representing their members' views to the Government and the general public.

The Confederation of British Industry, which is analagous to the
T.U.C., made no statements and gave no hint of its policy on the
question of race prior to 1967. Since that date, increasing interest

has been shown in this question, presumably as a result of the fact that proposals on the extension of the Race Relations Act to employment were being considered. As discussions on legislation have progressed, so different strands of the C.B.I. position have emerged.

The first response of employers has been that the problem is minimal. At a conference on racial equality in February 1967, a spokesman of the C.B.I. stated: 'our [C.B.I.] experience is that up to now no serious problems have arisen'.[40] In a similar vein, the Director of the Engineering Employers' Federation (the largest industry association in the country) stated: 'We have in our industry to our knowledge little evidence of a serious state of discrimination.'[41] Since the publication of the P.E.P. Report in April 1967, the playing down of discrimination as an important factor has been more muted.

A second response has been that discrimination is more a question of employee and customer resistance rather than the prejudice of the employer. Thus: 'The employer is not . . . an entirely free agent. He has to take into account the attitudes of his other personnel and . . . of his customers. In neither case is he in a position to dictate. . . .'[42]

The third and most important response has been that the established voluntary machinery in use in industry was more suitable for dealing with complaints of racial discrimination than was intervention by an outside body. A statement, prepared in January 1967 by representatives of the C.B.I. and the T.U.C., opposed legislation and expressed confidence in the well-tested voluntary procedures which had proved successful in the past for the variegated problems of industrial relations, which they felt could be adapted to deal with this problem.[43]

The C.B.I. recommended that employers' associations should begin discussions with the appropriate unions. As a result of this, the Engineering Employers' Federation and the Confederation of Shipbuilding and Engineering Unions drafted a memorandum of agreement on racial discrimination. This declared that 'allegations of discriminatory practice . . . can more suitably be considered and dealt with through voluntarily-established machinery than through statutory resources'.[44] Voluntary machinery was to be set up utilizing existing machinery and procedures for certain types of complaints and special arrangements for the others. The Engineering Employers' Federation have followed up the draft memorandum by publishing and distributing a pamphlet on the subject.[45]

The strength of C.B.I. and T.U.C. opposition to the 1968 Race Relations Act is discussed elsewhere, but essentially it should be seen as part of industry's traditional dislike of government intervention in its affairs.[46] The particular shape of the enforcement procedures of the 1968 Race Relations Act for employment cases is a prime example of the tenacity of voluntary procedures in industry and of the shaping of new administrative instruments to the old existent pattern.

The policy of the C.B.I. and of other employers' organizations over the presence of the coloured worker in British industry is basically similar to that followed by the Government and unions. Until 1967, no indication was given of the presence of coloured workers, and one can only assume that they did not consider the question worthy of attention or hoped that if nothing was done it would disappear unnoticed. Since then, stimulated by the threat of legislation and intervention in their preserve, the C.B.I. has shown greater activity and has helped to set up machinery that seems to have two distinct purposes: first, the reduction of discrimination by enunciating a general policy of non-discrimination and attempting to contain it by the creation of *ad hoc* machinery, and secondly, the avoidance of outside intervention. It is difficult not to feel that it is the second of the two purposes that has been the prime mover in the activity of the C.B.I.

3. THE COLOURED WORKER

Employers often cite the lack of adequate skills as the reason why they do not employ coloured workers either throughout their organization or in particular posts within the organization. Complaints are made of coloured workers' qualifications and abilities, their slowness, the quality of their workmanship, their inability to communicate in English, their attitude towards work and supervision, their frequent job changing, and the length of time it takes to train them. These and other similar complaints by employers and also at times from fellow-workers and union officials have been put to nearly every investigator of the situation of the coloured worker in industry.

Various estimates of the skill levels of coloured workers prior to migrating to this country have been made, but the translating of skill levels between countries makes an assessment in British terms difficult. Peter Wright has suggested that an estimate of West

Indian skills carried out by the Ministry of Labour Staff Association in 1955 is the most realistic.[47] According to this estimate, 13% were skilled, 22% semi-skilled, and 65% unskilled. Wright is also of the opinion that Indian and Pakistani immigrants are on the whole less skilled than West Indian immigrants. In his study, Wright found that the majority of employers thought that the skill levels of coloured workers were lower than those of British workers. Opinions were more mixed as to whether coloured workers were as hard working as British workers. A small minority believed them to be more hard working, a larger minority less hard working, and the majority assessed them as about as hard working as British workers. Just over half Wright's respondents said that coloured workers were less flexible and needed more supervision than British workers. Finally, the majority of firms said that the labour turn-over of coloured workers was lower than for British workers.

One of the most interesting facets of Wright's study was his description of the different way in which different employers assessed the situation. Not only did different employers assess coloured workers differently, but often they contradicted each other's assessments. Furthermore, while some employers thought that West Indians were good workers and other groups bad, other employers gave reverse assessments. In one firm it was claimed that Pakistanis were more educated than Indians, and in an adjacent firm that Indians were more educated than Pakistanis. Both firms preferred to employ the group believed to be less educated.

In a study in the wool textile industry in the West Riding in 1967, twelve out of fourteen employers found Pakistani workers generally comparable in all respects to local labour.[48] Some employers thought that Pakistani labour was superior to other labour that could be recruited for these particular jobs. However, two employers thought that Pakistani labour was inferior with regard to both the quality and quantity of work. Possibly, the most significant point made by many of the respondents satisfied with the standard of Pakistani labour was the need for careful selection. A similar emphasis on careful selection, this time of West Indian workers, was made by employers to Sheila Patterson in her studies in the late 1950s in South London. Quite a few employers indicated that there had been initial problems with standards of work until they learnt to select good West Indian workers.

A study of employment opportunities in office jobs, undertaken by Julia Gaitskell in 1966–7, showed that the belief that coloured workers were not suitably qualified for white-collar work was widely held and self-reinforcing.[49] While the average standard of coloured applicants was probably lower than that of white applicants, many of those with suitable qualifications were rejected. Sometimes the justifications produced to prove that the coloured applicant was not suitable in terms of skill were highly improbable. The manager of one company explained why he had rejected an applicant for a secretarial post—'Asian . . . a charming woman, 40-ish, capable, been here a long time. Her English was good although not her first language. But we both felt [he and the personnel officer] that if she got excited her English would fall down.' Later in the interview he expressed the opinion 'they [coloured people] do get wildly excited'. An even more interesting comment from another company was: 'He [Lieutenant-Colonel of Engineers, a graduate of Rangoon University] had Sapper experience in the post-war Indian Army. Hard to judge whether he was any good . . . it was not the British Army, after all.' Private employment exchanges reported that, even with British qualifications, it was extremely difficult to place coloured applicants in office jobs.

In the very different environment of the East End of London, McPherson found that opinions as to the skills of coloured workers varied as much as elsewhere.[50] In some cases, coloured workers were considered the most valued workers in firms whilst in others, they were thought to be lazy and poor workmen. In one case, a clothing manufacturer stated that he would not employ immigrants as they could never become tailors or cutters—they were not born to it. This was a surprising statement as the clothing industry had the highest percentage of immigrant workers of any industry in the area and immigrant workers were generally reported to be highly valued by their employers.

Lack of facility in English is often cited as a bar to the employment of coloured workers, especially Indians and Pakistanis. The general impression is that nearly all can speak no English. Yet in the Bradford study, out of 187 Pakistanis interviewed, only thirty could speak no English at all and fifty-seven were classed as fluent speakers of English.[51] Further support as evidence can be deduced from the fact that the third largest employer of Pakistani labour in the West Riding wool textile study operates a policy of employing only workers who could speak some English.[52] It therefore seems likely that the inability of Pakistanis to speak English has in the past been greatly over-estimated. This would mean that a far wider range of unskilled and semi-skilled jobs should be open to a larger number of Pakistani workers.

Another widespread belief about coloured workers is that they frequently change jobs, especially if they think they can earn more money. A study carried out in Nottingham in 1963 found that 63% of West Indian workers had been three years or more in their longest job.[53] The P.E.P. inquiry found that nearly half of all immigrants had been in their present job for three years or more.[54] There is also evidence that the Barbadians, directly recruited by London Transport, have a much lower wastage rate than all other London Transport staff.[55]

Many employers state that coloured workers make extravagant claims about their skills and past experience. Most investigators would agree that some coloured workers, especially those unfamiliar with British working conditions, do overstate their abilities. However, the blanket disbelief that some employers and trade union officials have shown over claims to skills, whether acquired in Britain or abroad, is undoubtedly unjustified. Radin found that trade union officials who gave coloured workers trade tests to prove their abilities were satisfied that many reached the required skill levels. Private employment bureaux reported that well over a third of coloured applicants for clerical work did reach an adequate standard.[56]

When one examines the evidence about coloured workers' abilities, the most striking thing is the apparent conflict of evidence. Sometimes a person will contradict himself, as did one union official when he said that immigrants were 'pretty good workmen' and 'take pains', later said that the 'danger' was that they are 'not concerned with quality', and finally, that their attitude parallelled any newcomer to the mill.[57] However, one major difference does emerge and that is that most employers who report favourably on coloured workers either mention the importance of good selection or differentiate between good and bad coloured workers whom they have employed.

The success and undoubted capacity of coloured workers in a whole variety of occupations, ranging from doctors to textile workers, from administrative class civil servants to London Transport staff, shows that within the coloured population all grades of skill and industry are present. Whether the distribution of these skills is present in the same proportions as for the local population is doubtful, but it does mean that individual coloured workers stand to suffer from the generally held stereotype of the unskilled. It seems possible that the assessments of coloured workers' abilities given by some employers and trade union officials owe as much to their own personal attitudes and stereotypes as they do to the real qualities of the workers concerned. Similarly, beliefs about the capacity of Pakistanis to communicate in English could well owe much to the stereotypes held by the British. The irony is that the employer with 'bad' immigrant employees will probably fulfill his own worst fears and confirm his own stereotypes.

4. THE INDUSTRIAL RELATIONS SYSTEM

A useful analytical framework has been suggested by Hepple for discussing the position of the coloured worker in the British industrial relations system.[58] Hepple discusses the different factors which make up and which influence the rules of the industrial relations system. In this context, 'rules' is used as a generic term to describe all the means by which jobs are regulated—for example, custom or collective agreement. Two different kinds of rules are identified—internal and external rules. Internal rules are those that are settled autonomously within a particular enterprise and external rules depend on the participation and consent of persons outside the enterprise. Examples of internal rules which affect the coloured worker would include shop-floor 'understandings' about numbers to be employed, barriers against promotion, allocation of overtime, ethnic work units, and separate facilities. External rules would include D.E.P. labour exchange policy on job referrals, the intervention of union officials either for or against job discrimination, legal rules, and the activities of bodies outside industry such as community relations groups.

Another factor discussed by Hepple is the effect on these rules, especially the internal ones, of the context of the industrial relations system and changes in this context. Thus, change due to technological or market factors can have the effect of changing the rules governing the employment of coloured workers. In the West Riding study of the wool industry quoted earlier, the installation of new machinery changed the rules of the job so that male night labour replaced female day labour.[59] This change in the rules allowed Pakistani labour to be employed. However, technological change and new investment will not always work in favour of the coloured worker. The availability of certain jobs may be reduced by technological change and the jobs most threatened will usually be the least skilled jobs in which, as we saw in Chapter 13, there are disproportionate numbers of coloured workers.

Hepple states that the internal rules which are generally discriminatory in nature are strongly entrenched and highly resistant to change. As the practice of workshop bargaining grows (and the Donovan Report recommends a strengthening of this process and its official recognition), so the pattern of inequality will continue. The changing focus of power in industry is of vital importance to the position of the coloured worker, for it is the internal rules decided at shop floor level that place the greatest obstacles in the way of the coloured workers. The external rules are moving in the opposite direction, becoming increasingly anti-discriminatory (especially with the new Race Relations Act 1968), but it would seem to be a classic case of needing to run fast just to stay in the same position.

CONCLUSIONS

For any new and easily identifiable minority group entering a society, one of the main, if not the main, determinants of achievement in the field of employment is the reaction of the host society. This was and is especially the case with the inflow of coloured workers to the British industrial system. For workers with little or no capital, the possibility of establishing themselves outside the existing framework is severely limited, and they must therefore enter the tightly organized industrial system controlled by British employers and workers and not by members of their own minority groups.

Our analysis of the British reaction to the presence of coloured workers has of necessity been general in nature. In part, this is due to the extreme diversity of the employment scene where employers range in size from the Government and nationalized industries, employing hundreds of thousands, to small private employers. But among private employers the range also varies from the industrial giants with a hundred thousand or more employees throughout the country, with thousands of employees in a single plant, to the small shop, workshop, or garage employing one or two employees. The diversity of employers is mirrored by that of the degree of organization of workers, which varies within industries and between industries, and is often dependent on the nature of the work and the size of the firm. The inter-dependence of the job for which a coloured worker is being recruited and the jobs of other workers varies from one place of work to another and again makes it more difficult to generalize. The picture is therefore one painted with a heavy brush; but, despite the very real and important differences between employers, industries, regions, unions, and each particular and peculiar local situation, certain general patterns have been the rule. Employers willing to accept coloured workers for reasons other than labour shortages, workers willing to accept coloured workers as fully equal, especially in regard to promotion, have been exceptions and not the rule.

The one fact that stands out above all others is that throughout the field of employment, discrimination is widespread and pervasive. It manifests itself in recruitment, training, promotion, and a host of other ways. This discrimination is not a result of any centrally inspired policy of government, unions, or employers' organizations, but is determined by decisions at local level. As long as the criteria by which management are expected to make their decisions are short-term and limited, then the situation of the coloured worker can be expected—without active intervention from outside—to remain on the margins of the industrial relations system. The role in which British industry has cast the coloured worker is that of spare man or reserve—to be used only when necessary.

The immediate costs of such policies are not borne by the discriminators but by the wider society. The decisions, freely taken at the periphery, become a practice with long-term implications so damaging that a decision must finally be taken at the centre to intervene, however reluctantly. The alternatives are, to allow the situation to deteriorate, or to break the tradition of non-interference in industrial relations. In fact, the problem of the coloured worker is only one of many examples which have arisen through the individual decisions of a host of employers. A classic problem of this type is the education and training of workers, where the decisions of employers, based on their own short-term and limited criteria, have continually failed throughout the nineteenth and twentieth centuries to produce sufficient adequately-trained manpower. It has been the role of the State to provide this through its ever-expanding education system and by training schemes, culminating in the Industrial Training Act 1964, which statutorily imposes 'non-profitable' duties on employers.

In effect, the question of the coloured worker raises the whole question of whether private industry has a social role as well as a business role. Decisions taken by private industry can, and often do, have vast social consequences, and whilst, as far as the business efficiency of any single firm is concerned, these may seem irrelevant, the State sometimes places obligations upon each individual firm that seem generally to be justifiable. Prime examples of this are recent acts such as the Contracts of Employment Act 1963, laying down minimum periods of notice, and the Redundancy Payments Act 1965, giving an employee an entitlement to redundancy pay from the employer. Some private companies, usually the very largest, consider that their social role is important and contribute money, materials, and manpower to local educational and community facilities. The degree to which this is part and parcel of public relations is debatable, but undoubtedly many companies go much further in these and other activities than would be justified by balance-sheet consideration.[60]

The conflict between the short-term, limited considerations of employers and the wider, long-term needs of society has meant that the Government has a crucial role to play in the satisfactory absorption of the coloured worker in industry. In such a situation, a hands-off non-interfering policy of doing nothing for fear of discriminating in favour of the coloured worker is a policy of acquiescing in widespread discrimination. With the growth of the coloured population and discriminatory practice, a whole host of new fears and practices grew up. Much of the responsibility for this has lain with the Government—first, for allowing the situation to deteriorate, and then, when finally it was decided to take action (in 1968), for permitting the action to be half-hearted and lacking in conviction.

Part of the paradox of the British resistance to the entry of the coloured worker is that often this resistance has gone much of the way to reinforcing the worst fears of the resistors. Each particular group of British workers, each individual employer, and each union branch, acting on what it perceived as its self-interest and excluding coloured workers, has created situations which seem to confirm their worst fears. Unions, inactive in recruiting, have seen the exploitation of coloured workers with its inevitable side-effects on their own members. Factories or departments, protecting themselves against coloured workers, have seen factories or departments near by with majorities of coloured workers.

As in so many other spheres, the coloured worker in the British industrial relations system is less of a problem and a challenge in himself than an indicator of much that is inefficient, poorly organized, and socially unacceptable in the whole system. The coloured worker is also a prime example of the inability of the system to adapt to the pace of change which is the single most important factor in our social and economic life. As the Donovan Commission indicated, informal structures have grown up alongside formal ones, and the attempt to fit the informal structure to the formal has inevitably led to severe frictions. But the Donovan Commission, which was attempting to catch up with changes that have been taking place over the last fifty years, failed totally to look at a more recent development—the coloured worker and discrimination. The most careful search of Donovan will reveal only passing comment on race or colour.

Will it need more dockers marching—and another Royal Commission—to convince those who are called on to implement the Donovan reforms that 'racial disputes' are not on the periphery of our industrial situation, but symptomatic of its most central conflicts?[61]

NOTES TO CHAPTER 19

1. Political and Economic Planning Report, *Racial Discrimination in Britain* (London, P.E.P., 1967), and W. W. Daniel, *Racial Discrimination in England* (Harmondsworth, Penguin Books, 1968).
2. Bob Hepple, *Race, Jobs and the Law in Britain* (London, Allen Lane, The Penguin Press, 1968), Appendix 1.
3. Sheila Patterson, *Dark Strangers* (London, Tavistock Publications, 1963 and Penguin Books, 1965). Also *Immigrants in Industry* (London, Oxford University Press, for Institute of Race Relations, 1968).
4. P. Wright, *The Coloured Worker in British Industry* (London, Oxford University Press, for the Institute of Race Relations, 1968).
5. *Race Relations Board Report 1967–8* (London, H.M.S.O., 1968).
6. Keighley Junior Chamber of Commerce, Immigrant Project, published 1967.
7. Royal Commission on Trade Unions and Employers' Associations, 1965–8 (The Donovan Report) (London, H.M.S.O., Cmnd. 3623, 1968).
8. Wright, op. cit., pp. 44–6.
9. Ibid., p. 46.
10. Daniel, op. cit., p. 108.
11. 'A Study of Immigrants in East London Industries' sponsored by the Councils of Citizens of East London and Tower Hamlets, conducted by K. McPherson 1966–8. (To be published in *Immigrants and Employment in Tower Hamlets and in Croydon: two case studies*, Institute of Race Relations Special Series, 1969).
12. Patterson, *Dark Strangers* (Penguin), op. cit., p. 126.
13. M. Banton, *The Coloured Quarter* (London, Cape, 1955), p. 134.
14. H.C. Vol. 699, col. 16, 20 July 1964.

328 COLOUR AND CITIZENSHIP

15. Hepple (op. cit., p. 71) states that up to November 1967 the sanction of withdrawing employment exchange facilities has occurred only once.

16. D. Beetham, *Immigrant School Leavers and the Youth Employment Service in Birmingham* (London, Institute of Race Relations Special Series, 1968), p. 39.

17. *The Work of the Youth Employment Service 1965–8*, a report by the National Youth Employment Council (London, H.M.S.O., 1968), pp. 4–6.

18. A complaint by an M.P. (*The Times*, 7 September 1968) that the keeping of statistics on colour by the London Transport Board was discriminatory was almost certainly mistaken. The P.E.P. Report and other investigations have shown that the keeping of records which are available for investigation is usually a sign of a non-discriminatory or less-discriminatory policy being followed.

19. Since this chapter was written, it was disclosed in the press (*Daily Express*, 6 December 1968) that the Army had set a quota of 3% for coloured recruits. Questioned on this, the Secretary of State for Defence stated that no coloured man had ever been turned away as a result of this quota. In view of the changed circumstances he had decided that there was no longer any need for this type of limitation (*The Times*, 12 December 1968).

20. Hepple, op. cit.

21. Hepple, op. cit., p. 181. An article published since this chapter was written by Oscar Gish, 'The training and advancement of non-British nurses', Institute of Race Relations *Newsletter* (November–December 1968), would seem to confirm the existence of discrimination in training and in promotion to senior nursing posts.

22. See *The Unsquare Deal* (London, West Indian Standing Conference, July 1967), and also *Guardian* 3, 5, and 11 April 1968.

23. We wish to acknowledge the help given by Mr. Dennis Brooks. He has been carrying out a study of coloured immigrants in London Transport, commissioned by the Institute's 'Survey of Race Relations in Britain'. All interpretation of the information supplied by Mr. Brooks is that of the authors of this Report.

24. For a fuller discussion of the Bristol dispute, see Institute of Race Relations *Newsletter* (June 1963), pp. 4–7.

25. Hepple, op. cit., p. 83. An attempt was made at the 1967 T.U.C. Congress to move a resolution that all unions should have a rule prohibiting racial discrimination.

26. Beryl Radin, 'Coloured Workers and British Trade Unions', *Race* (Vol. VIII, no. 2, October 1966), pp. 157–73.

27. P. Marsh, *The Anatomy of a Strike: Unions, Employers, and Punjabi Workers in a Southall Factory* (London, Institute of Race Relations Special Series, 1967), p. 118.

28. Donovan Report, op. cit., Chapter XI. Information used is derived from W. E. J. McCarthy, *The Closed Shop in Britain* (Oxford, Blackwell, 1964).

29. F. J. Bayliss and J. B. Coates, 'West Indians at work in Nottingham', *Race* (Vol. VII, no. 2, October 1965).

30. See, for example, Marsh, op. cit. The I.W.A. has been especially active in the introduction of unions.

31. Unpublished research conducted by Mrs. Sheila Allen on the work situation of Pakistanis in Bradford, supported by the Institute's 'Survey of Race Relations in Britain'.

32. Radin, op. cit.

33. N.C.C.I., *Racial Equality in Employment* (Report of Conference held in London, February 1967), pp. 98–9.

34. P. Foot, 'The strike at Courtaulds, Preston', Institute of Race Relations *Newsletter* (July 1965, Supplement).

35. Radin, op. cit.

36. Marsh, op. cit.

37. Information from local newspapers, especially *Wembley News*, and strike leaflets (July 1968).

38. *Guardian*, 25 April 1967.

39. Donovan Report, op. cit.

40. N.C.C.I., *Racial Equality in Employment,* op. cit.

41. Ibid., p. 88.

42. Ibid., p. 2.

43. *Sunday Times,* 29 January 1967.

44. Hepple, op. cit. The full memorandum is printed in Appendix III.

45. Ivan Hattingh, *Race Relations and the Engineering Industry* (published by the Engineering Employers' Federation, December 1967).

46. An excellent illustration of industry's attitude towards legislation is given by Les Cannon of the E.T.U. in *Electron* (Journal of the Electrical Trades Union, Vol. 56, no. 5, May 1967). Cannon argues that in the cases of housing and insurance it is not difficult to identify discrimination and legislation should be strengthened, but that industry was too complex to be dealt with in the same way.

47. Wright, op. cit.

48. B. Cohen and P. Jenner, 'The Employment of Immigrants: a case study within the wool industry', *Race* (Vol. IX, no. 1, July 1968).

49. Research conducted by Julia Gaitskell into attitudes and policies of large office employers in Croydon, 1966–7 (to be published in *Immigrants and Employment in Tower Hamlets and in Croydon: two case studies,* Institute of Race Relations Special Series, 1969).

50. McPherson, op. cit.

51. Allen, op. cit.

52. Cohen and Jenner, op. cit.

53. Bayliss and Coates, op. cit.

54. P.E.P. Report, op. cit.

55. Brooks, op. cit.

56. Gaitskell, op. cit., and P.E.P. Report, op. cit.

57. Allen, op. cit.

58. Hepple, op. cit., and more especially paper by Bob Hepple, 'Employment', for the UNITAR-IRR 'Comparative Study of the Effectiveness of Policies and Measures Against Racial Discrimination'.

59. Cohen and Jenner, op. cit.

60. The social role of private industry is a topic being increasingly discussed in the U.S.A. See *Report of the National Advisory Commission on Civil Disorders* (Kerner Report) (New York, Bantam Books, March 1968), especially Appendix H.

61. Bob Hepple, 'The Donovan Report and Race Relations', Institute of Race Relations *Newsletter* (October 1968).

1. THE HEALTH AND WELFARE SERVICES

The health and welfare of the immigrants have become problems for British society in very much the same ways as did other aspects of their lives. They became symbols—and symbols charged with emotion. The extreme stereotype of the coloured immigrant, which was circulated widely, was of someone who brought disease into the country, and who, once here, created a risk of epidemics because of his origin and living conditions. On the welfare side, the immigrant was seen as a sponger, living on benefits, or as part of a group which, collectively, caused shortages of essential services: housing, educational facilities, maternity beds in hospitals. The arrival of immigrant families in the main towns and cities has put additional pressure on certain services, and has given rise to the need for certain changes in those services and in the training of the staff who man them. But taking the social services as a whole, as Mrs. K. Jones has shown, the immigrants are an asset, not a burden:

The adult working population supports the old in the community. An inflow of young adult immigrants therefore—so far as current expenditure on the social services is concerned—provides a once and for all gain for thirty years in which they add to contributors but not to dependants. This more than outweighs the additional social service costs which may be incurred because of the immigrants' special health or educational requirements.[1]

The high rate of economic activity of the immigrants and their age structure has given them an overall 'positive balance'. At the same time it has meant that the immigrants are brought into contact with a range of services dealing normally with the health and welfare of families; and that the people operating those services face problems of language, cultural conflict, and cross-cultural communication. Poor housing conditions mean that certain services are likely to be under extra pressure; and in general the economic situation of the immigrants and their various cultures are likely to involve some deployment of extra resources, or new approaches in some existing services. Evidence submitted jointly by the National Committee for Commonwealth

Immigrants and the Institute of Race Relations to the Seebohm Committee, in September 1967, rejected the concept of special services designed specifically for immigrants. But it added: 'At the same time, we accept that within the services special provision must be made for those needs of the immigrant communities which are specific to those communities.'[2] As in the field of education, the Government, therefore, has been faced with two problems: prejudice, and the need to devise acceptable means for making positive provision for specific needs. At least until 1965, positive policy-making and its finance was left to the local authorities and local services. After 1965, the establishment of the National Committee for Commonwealth Immigrants and the passage of the 1966 Local Government Act meant there was some overall administrative perspective and some Government help. But until 1968 the Government's attention was largely focused upon the point of entry.

(a) Health Controls

The legal position on control based on public health considerations at the ports of entry evolved in the following way. In 1936, the Public Health Act gave the Minister of Health power to make regulations to prevent the risk of the importation of quarantinable diseases. Under the Public Health Ships and Aircraft Regulations 1966, any person thought to be suffering from one of these diseases (plague, typhus, cholera, smallpox, yellow fever, and relapsing fever) could be placed in quarantine. These powers applied to any person arriving at a port of entry. Under the consideration of provisions relating to aliens in the Aliens Order 1953, immigration officers could refer any alien for medical examination, and refuse permission to land either for reasons of public health, or if he were likely to be a burden on the health services. But until 1962, Commonwealth citizens could not be refused permission to land, and could only be examined if they presented an immediate danger to public health under the regulations governing quarantinable diseases. Under the 1962 Commonwealth Immigrants Act, all Commonwealth citizens, except dependants entitled to enter and returning residents, became subject to medical examination at the ports of entry. With the same exceptions, they could be refused permission to land on grounds of health: either if they were a danger to public health, or if they were suffering from an illness which meant they would not be able to support themselves and their families. The Instructions to Immigration Officers issued in 1966 stated that, with the exception of entitled dependants and returning residents, 'where a Medical Inspector certifies that it is undesirable for a person to be admitted for medical reasons or that he is suffering from mental disorder the Immigration Officer should refuse admission unless there appears to be strong compassionate reasons for not doing so'.[3] Finally, under the Commonwealth Immigrants Act 1968, all Commonwealth citizens entering Britain, including entitled dependants and returning residents, became subject to medical examination at the ports of entry. No powers were taken to refuse permission to land to dependants and returning residents, but they, like other Commonwealth immigrants, could be admitted subject to the condition that they reported to a medical officer of health in the area where they were going to live. To fail to comply with this condition was an offence punishable by a term of imprisonment, and the possibility of a recommendation for deportation. The 1968 Act put into law policy recommendations made in the 1965 White Paper.

The British Medical Association was the most active lobby pressing for more stringent health controls at the point of entry. Between 1956 and 1964, the Representative Body of the Association passed eighteen resolutions urging some form of medical examination prior to entry. Early in 1965, the B.M.A. set up a small working party 'to investigate the health problems of immigrants to this country and the possible risk of their bringing in, undetected, diseases which are potentially dangerous to the rest of the community'.[4] The Committee recommended that all immigrants should be medically examined before entry to Britain and that those found to be suffering from certain diseases, which were listed (twenty—including epilepsy, drug addiction, and alcoholism), should be excluded. The B.M.A., the Government in the 1965 White Paper, and, later, the National Committee for Commonwealth Immigrants all endorsed the view that medical examination should preferably take place in the country of origin, before departure. This was in accordance with the practice of most other countries, and it would be, if a practical system could be evolved, obviously more efficient and humane. But in a letter to general practitioners sent out on 4 January 1965, the Ministry of Health stated: 'the proposal to secure a chest X-ray in all cases before departure from the country of origin has been very fully explored and not found to be practicable.' And it is notable, moreover, that the B.M.A. recommended that any system 'should utilise the services of Government Medical Officers from this country and, through them, of local doctors approved for the purpose by the Government of the U.K.'[5]

Given the general suspicion with which immigration officers regard all documentary evidence of the would-be immigrant's right to enter Britain, in any case of dispute, it is doubtful if any system of medical certification conducted in the country of origin would be practical. The B.M.A. recommendation that any immigrant suffering from certain diseases should be excluded has not been implemented in the case of entitled dependants and returning residents. There has, however, been a gradual extension since 1965 of measures to ensure that immigrants register with a doctor in Britain, are examined, and receive any necessary treatment. Throughout, the numbers of those refused entry on health grounds has remained small. In 1964, of 16,929 Commonwealth immigrants examined, eight were refused entry.[6] In 1967, of over 20,000 examined, fifty-eight were refused entry.[7]

The Ministry of Health's view of priorities was set out in its letter of 4 January 1965 to G.P.s. The main task was 'to ensure that at an early date [immigrants] learn how to use the Health Service, and in particular, for us to secure by voluntary action that those from countries with a high incidence of tuberculosis—particularly from Asia—have a chest X-ray as soon as possible after their arrival in this country'. The follow-up arrangements outlined in the letter were: first, that immigrants referred for examination at ports of entry were to be given printed leaflets in various languages encouraging them to register with a G.P., so that an X-ray could be arranged if necessary (X-ray apparatus was installed at London Airport at the beginning of 1965); secondly, the British addresses of these immigrants were to be sent to their local medical officers of health for further follow-up. (These measures covered only those referred for examination at ports of entry.) Thirdly, the Ministry went on to say that it was hoped to arrange that *all* dependants arriving with entry certificates issued in their country of origin would have a tear-out slip in their passport with their British address on it. This would be torn out by the immigration officer at the port of entry and sent on to their local medical officer of health. Despite certain obvious limitations (printed leaflets would have to be read to illiterate persons; those coming with entry certificates are only a proportion of the total dependants arriving), these measures appear to have made an impact. In 1965, Islington's Medical Officer of Health was able to trace two-thirds of those referred to him from the airports, and in Bristol the proportion was three-quarters.

Three months later, a second letter from the Ministry to medical officers of health encouraged them to extend local preventive tuberculosis services, including X-ray facilities and B.G.C. vaccination for children, and for adults where necessary: the Ministry would supply the vaccine.

(b) Tuberculosis and Venereal Diseases

Of all the specific diseases to which immigrants were thought to be susceptible, tuberculosis attracted the greatest attention. Rates of T.B. infection among certain immigrant groups were found to be substantially higher than the average. In Bradford, in 1961, the incidence of tuberculosis was 23·94 per thousand in Asians, compared with 0·64 per thousand in the whole population.[8] In the early 1960s, although the Pakistanis in Bradford formed only about 2% of the total immigrant population in Britain, they contributed nearly 10% of all tuberculosis notifications. The 1965 B.M.A. Report estimated that about half the cases of tuberculosis in Pakistanis, identified in the first year after arrival, would have been identified by an X-ray at the port of entry or in the country of origin. Eric Butterworth discusses the effect of the Bradford environment on the incidence of the disease: the effect of often overcrowded lodgings, and of employment in the wool industry, where occupations involving the carding and combing of wool have always been associated with a high incidence of tuberculosis.[9]

Bradford has recorded the incidence of tuberculosis among Asians since 1952. The peak year in the 1950s was 1954, when there were 667 new notifications, of which 340 were in Asians. Since then the number of cases in non-Asians has fallen. The Asian rate also began to fall, but rose again in 1961, 1962, and 1963, that is, during and just after the period of a very high rate of entry prior to the Commonwealth Immigrants Act. Since 1964, new notifications have again started to fall and there was a 24% fall in cases of pulmonary tuberculosis in 1965 compared with 1964. This was certainly in great part due to the vigorous preventive action taken by the local health authority.

An extensive programme of prevention was begun in the city

in 1956. Mobile radiography units operated at the places of employment of Pakistani workers, and during the high unemployment period 1962–3, at the employment exchange. A three-phase programme, started in 1965, covers all immigrant school children, pre-school children, new arrivals to the city, and those already settled and registered with a G.P. Most of the immigrant population of the city has now been covered.

Tuberculosis rates for other immigrant groups are far lower. The B.M.A. Report quoted the following figures collected in Birmingham in the two years, 1960–2: notification rates for men were 0·67 per thousand for the English, 2·1 for the Irish, 1·3 for the Caribbeans, 4·5 for the Indian, and 94·7 for the Pakistani (which also included those from Ceylon).

The pattern of tuberculosis among immigrants is that perhaps half the cases are imported and then spread to compatriots. The pattern of venereal diseases, which has also received considerable attention and is well categorized as part of the British response to the immigrants, is rather different. The B.M.A. Report found that 'it is the experience of venereologists in charge of clinics that gonorrhoea and syphilis amongst male immigrants are most frequently contracted after arrival and often through the agency of white prostitutes'. Hinds gives a brief but vivid account of the way in which a white prostitute may exploit the colour factor,[10] and Dahya describes a similar process of systematic exploitation of immigrants by pimps using white prostitutes.[11] In contrast to tuberculosis, the overall number of reported cases of venereal disease in the total population has been rising since 1957, and by 1965 had reached about 80% of the previous peak, just after the Second World War.[12]

This rise has been a world-wide phenomenon and is not confined to countries with significant immigration. In terms of the numbers of those to be treated, the B.M.A. Report found that syphilis was not a problem, but that gonorrhoea was. Caribbean patients formed 28% of male patients in 1962. Since then the number of Caribbean patients and their proportion in the total has fallen, and in 1966 they formed 18% of the total. In 1965, 83% of the female patients were U.K.-born, 8% Caribbean-born, and 9% were born elsewhere. (The proportion of Caribbean female patients had fallen since 1963.) The comparatively high rates—in proportion to the numbers at risk—came, therefore, just after the high immigration rates before the Commonwealth Immigrants

Act. The steady fall in the number of cases of venereal disease in immigrants since then can be taken to be the result of the formation of families or stable unions. As the B.M.A. Report pointed out: 'we do not consider that medical examination of immigrants to exclude cases of disease is as important as measures to improve contact tracing and to provide better social circumstances and readily available facilities for diagnosis and treatment.' No policy measures designed for particular national groups have been taken.

(c) Demands on Hospital Services

Pressure on local health and welfare services has, in a few cases, been a problem of numbers, the most notorious example of this is the problem of pressure on maternity beds. The areas in which many immigrant families have settled are those from which native-born families have been moving for some years in search of improved housing opportunities. The result of this movement, out and in, is that in some areas of poor housing a very high proportion of the young families are immigrant families. Richmond's Bristol survey demonstrated this clearly: he found that the Caribbean-born population of St. Paul's contained a higher proportion of 'normal' households than the other national groups.[13] But the restricted supply of suitable housing means that homes are too crowded to permit home confinements. At the same time, the number of live births per thousand of the population is higher for most immigrant groups—partly because, as groups, they have a higher proportion of women of child-bearing age and a very low proportion of old people.[14]

It is against this background that figures like those for West Bromwich in 1964 should be seen: 688 'white' mothers had their babies at home, and 953 in hospital; twelve 'immigrant' mothers had their babies at home, and 217 in hospital. The percentage of hospital births was approximately 58% for 'white' mothers, and approximately 94% for 'immigrant' mothers. The total population of West Bromwich was an estimated 97,000, and the immigrant population an estimated 8,000.[15] Dr. Galloway, the Medical Officer of Health for Wolverhampton, has said that 'social grounds were responsible for two-thirds of the admissions of immigrant mothers in Wolverhampton, and for only a fifth of the other mothers who had their babies in hospital.[16]

The assessments of need are made by a domiciliary midwife.

Dr. Galloway's account of the policy measures taken in response to the need for beds was as follows: 'Due to limitation of beds (which is remediable) and to limitation of staff (which is less remediable) the institutions can meet the demands made upon them only by resorting to the early discharge of patients for nursing at home by domiciliary midwives.' Thirty-five per cent of Wolverhampton births in 1966 were home confinements, 63% were hospital confinements, but the mothers were discharged early, and only 2% of mothers had their full stay in hospital after having their babies. Dr. Galloway did not assess the medical effects of this, and it would presumably depend on a number of factors such as the percentage of first babies in each group, the quality of home nursing which could be provided, and the home conditions. Wolverhampton midwives have, as Dr. Galloway added, been equipped with V.H.F. radio equipment to speed communication. It should also be added that the shortage of staff—medical, nursing, and midwifery—has been met to a very great extent by immigrants from the Commonwealth and other overseas countries.

Apart from the problem of maternity beds, immigrant groups make less demand upon hospital services than the native born. The total number of hospital beds available (December 1966) was divided as follows: geriatric, 31,482; mental illness, 138,734; chronic sick, 26,612; subnormality, 61,698; and paediatrics, 6,469.[17] Given the age-structure of the immigrant population, we can say that they provide few geriatric patients. The same is true of demand for places in local authority homes for the aged. Immigrants are unlikely to contribute to residents, because of the small proportion of over-65s in the immigrant groups, and the strong cultural traditions in which grandparents remain within the family and are cared for by their grown-up children.

In the mental health services there are no overall figures showing the proportion of Commonwealth-born patients. Christopher Bagley[18] and Dr. Farrukh Hashmi[19] have drawn attention to stress factors in Britain which may cause mental illness among some immigrant groups. Local studies which have been carried out do not enable any overall conclusions to be drawn. Indeed, it has been suggested that the relative incidences of mental illness are a function of the diagnostic process and have little objective value. A study of patients attending psychiatric clinics in four areas of Birmingham with high proportions of immigrant residents disclosed that on average 9·31 immigrants per thousand suffered some form of mental illness, compared with 6·14 per thousand British inhabitants.[20] In an earlier study in three London mental hospitals, only eighteen out of some 18,000 patients were West Indian, which seemed to indicate that the rates for severe psychiatric illness was not high in this group. The results of a six-month study of a group general practice in the same area as the three hospitals suggested that there was a high rate of less severe psychiatric illness among West Indians. Ari Kiev concluded, on the basis of these and some other local surveys, that 'it appears likely that the incidence and prevalence of severe psychiatric illness necessitating hospitalisation is low, while the prevalence of minor psychiatric disorders is much higher than might be expected'. He found that there was no evidence of 'broad differences' in the susceptibility to illness of West Indians and English born.[21]

Broadly, the position within the hospital service is that while immigrants from many Commonwealth countries contribute heavily to the staff, they are apparently under-represented among the patients. The exception is in maternity and child welfare services. This is an area where, as in services for the old, the links between local health authorities and the hospital services are closest. The midwifery service is provided by the local authority, so that the early return of mothers from hospital after having their babies falls directly upon a local authority service. (No extra grant for midwifery is payable under Section 11 of the 1966 Local Government Act.)

But the absence of a general quantitative burden upon the health services does not mean that there are not conditions or problems of health, and even survival, which be may said to be related to belonging to an immigrant group. Higher tuberculosis rates among Pakistani workers have already been referred to. This is a fairly simple matter: the causes are understood, the people exposed to the condition are not hard to trace, and techniques for prevention and treatment are already available. There are, however, a series of health and welfare problems which have been found to arise particularly among immigrant mothers and babies whose prevention and solution are not so easily arranged. Some children of immigrant parents have been found to present symptoms which were common to poor working-class children before the War—deficiencies in diet have resulted in anaemia and in the appearance of rickets in some children.[22] A study of 100 immigrant mothers found that many were suffering from severe depression.[23] A study of young children found a withdrawal, non-communication syndrome occurring specifically in children of West Indian parents—this had sometimes been misdiagnosed as deafness.[24] The case histories of the children in this last study frequently shared the following characteristics: maternal depression, economic pressures on the parents, mothers too exhausted to give time to or enjoy their children, inadequate housing, inadequate care of children, and multiple fostering (i.e., child minding). There have been deaths from fire, often caused by oil-heaters which may be the only available form of heating in some buildings.[25]

There are lessons here about problems of diagnosis, about health education, about the provision and supervision of day nurseries and nursery schools, and about housing policies. It provides an extreme example of the way in which the particular health or welfare problems of immigrants are frequently associated with quite clearly defined economic or social pressures, while at the same time policies to deal with the problems are complicated by cultural and sometimes linguistic differences.

(d) The Failure to provide for Cultural Diversity

Apart from illnesses requiring hospital treatment, the normal health and welfare of immigrants and their families, as for everyone else, are the responsibility of local authority health and welfare services and the general practitioners. Local authorities are required by law to provide a number of services, including health centres, maternity care, midwives, health visitors, home nursing, and vaccination and immunization. Schemes are submitted to and approved by the Ministry of Health and the responsibility for putting them into practice lies with the local authority departments. The only form of control exercised by the Ministry from the centre is the withholding of recommendations for loan sanctions, which does not affect projects financed through current expenditure, and, in general, the Ministry's approach has been to leave as much responsibility as possible with the local departments. Local authority child care services come under the Children's Department of the Home Office which has its own inspectorate; the Advisory Council on Child Care advises the Home Secretary on any matter required and can initiate topics; and the Central Training Council is responsible for training in the service. A local authority may employ a family case-worker and may subsidize an intensive case-work agency such as a family service unit, and an advisory service such as a citizens advice bureau. If we include the housing visitor, the T.B. visitor, and the public health inspector, there is a considerable array of doctors, social workers, and officials who are meeting the immigrant as patients, 'clients', 'cases', 'problems', or offenders. Not under the local authority, but still having an important role in the welfare of the immigrant population, are the local officials of the Ministry of Social Security and the staff of local employment exchanges, both of them responsible for paying or withholding benefits.

The relationships between the individual and any of these representatives of authority is quite different from the relationship between workmates or neighbours. Here, the point of the contact may be to elicit or impart information, to assess what action a department must take, or to persuade an individual himself to take action. Cultural misunderstanding and conflict, and racial prejudice and discrimination, are likely to appear. These are major issues which the presence of immigrants raises for the health and welfare services. Another is the question of whether the diffuse structure can provide the required action.

Bessie Kent has shown the inadequacy of some basic principles of social work when the case-worker is dealing with someone from a different cultural background: the need to be treated as an individual; the need to express feeling; the need to get a sympathetic response to problems; the need to be recognized as a person of worth; the need not to be judged; the need to make his own choices and decisions; the need to keep secrets about himself. All these 'needs', listed in a social work manual, she shows to be inappropriate and misleading for various groups. Cultural differences of this kind are a source of irritation or worse for the case-worker:

British social work is based on the belief that man can alter his own destiny; confronted with a client whose culture has taught him that man is a pawn of destiny and can do nothing except to meet with dignity whatever fate has in store for him, the British social worker will not only have an opposing perception as to the fundamental purpose of existence, but may well be infuriated by the client's 'refusal' to do anything about his problems.

Or again:

conditioned as she has been to the idea that man is basically evil and that only through self-discipline and training can be he saved from the folly of self-indulgence ('spoiling'), particularly as regards sexual behaviour, she will be frightened by clients who are at ease with their bodies and unafraid of their emotions.[26]

These are some of the difficulties which affect the social worker engaged in trying to help a client. Other social workers—health visitors, midwives, T.B. visitors, housing visitors—are not concerned with the social inadequacy of an individual so much as with his social circumstances. This applies particularly to housing visitors whose scanty training is scarcely adequate equipment for the complex process of assessing the needs of individuals from differing cultural backgrounds. Elizabeth Burney has shown the danger of bias in any system which accords them too great a degree of discretion.[27] In the case of the health visitor or the general practitioner, the straightforward problem of language may be the main difficulty. Dr. Simpson, a Bristol G.P., has given some vivid examples of language difficulties, and various solutions adopted to overcome them.[28] For example, he made some use of language cards for hospital patients, giving various medical phrases in different languages with the English translation. He also made a note of the medical terms used by his Jamaican patients, which often differed considerably from the normal English ones.

Some of these difficulties have important implications for social work training. Here again, change may be inhibited by a very diffuse structure with many kinds of training institutions, covering many disciplines. There is no doubt, however, that the experience of social workers coming into contact with immigrant families is one factor contributing to a general re-thinking of methods. The National Committee for Commonwealth Immigrants has been working with the Association of Social Work Teachers (which spans disciplines and different institutions) to produce a pamphlet suggesting possible changes in the syllabus. Through the London Boroughs Training Committee it has organized four two-day courses for senior social workers, and a pilot project of a series of weekly seminars for residential staff. These courses or seminars cannot, of course, amount to training in themselves. The purpose has been to provide some orientation for professional groups who are bound in the course of their work to come into contact with immigrant 'clients'. They are seen as a stimulant to more widespread and systematic changes in training within the professions and groups affected.

In some cases, failure by immigrants to make use of a specially provided service has been attributed to lack of attention by the local authorities to cultural difference. Bradford failed to recognize the household structure of the Pakistani male immigrants in the city: the physical arrangements, with communal kitchen and sitting-room, separate from the bedrooms; the fact that many households were composed of close-knit kinship groups. When it provided a hostel without communal rooms, and with the cooking stove in the self-contained bedrooms, it failed through lack of tenants. In addition, the rent of the hostel rooms was too high to attract the immigrants.[29] In other cases, cultural misunderstanding has been suggested as a reason for excessive use of a service by an immigrant group. In a controversial paper, Katrin Fitzherbert argues that the numbers of West Indian children received into care (short or long term) 'give an exaggerated picture of the size of the problem of deprivation among West Indian children, and reflect the reluctance of the Children's Department to treat West Indians as a separate cultural group, with distinct family patterns and attitudes to child-rearing'. She argues that social workers tend to assume that West Indian parents are less capable than they in fact are; and adds that so far from being unable to make effective use of services many West Indian parents see the child care service as a convenient, rather than a last resort, service.[30] In reply, Mary Dines argues that, on the contrary, pressure of circumstances—in particular the need for both parents to work, and the lack of day nursery care—create realistic grounds for families to require help from local authorities, especially if the mother has to go into hospital or becomes otherwise unable to look after her children.[31] The crux of the problem is the difficulty of distinguishing preferences and choices which may be culturally based from those which are imposed by circumstances. 'It is important', Mrs. Dines adds, 'not to confuse situations that arise through force of circumstances with any natural inclination to lead a particular way of life.' The controversy serves to illustrate the recurring problem: to what extent can separate criteria be applied in the case of minority groups and what are the consequences of applying them? Respect for the other cultures can produce a pluralist solution based on parity of esteem; or it can tip over into 'separate but equal'.

In this debate the generally welcomed recognition of cultural diversity between ethnic groups has sometimes led to an unjustified assumption of socio-economic homogeneity within them. Eric

Butterworth quotes statistics showing infant mortality rates among immigrants and children of unskilled and semi-skilled workers which are increasingly relevant in this context. In 1965, the average rate of infant mortality in Bradford was about 25 per thousand, but this dropped to 10 per thousand in professional class homes, and rose to 30 per thousand in homes of unskilled and semi-skilled workers. Among immigrants, the rate was 50 per thousand in 1965 but this dropped to 35 per thousand by the end of 1966. In his summing up on health and the Bradford local authority, he writes: 'the pattern of health is more likely in future to approximate to social class rather than ethnic characteristics'.[32] The same analysis could well be applied to welfare services, with the proviso that the future significance of colour is still unknown. Emphasis on the possession of differential characteristics by one minority or another may also lead to the assumption that this characteristic is unique to an immigrant group. On investigation this may be found to occur in native-born people as well. Dr. Simpson writes: 'Having decided to keep a record of patients that are co-habiting because it is part of the Caribbean way of life, I find that it is not uncommon among the English' among all age groups.[33]

One service which has encountered particular difficulties arising from culturally-based variation in outlook is the youth service—to which immigrant parents' attitudes have tended to be suspicious or uncomprehending. Yet the available evidence suggests that the rate of delinquency among coloured adolescents is well below average. These low delinquency rates are particularly marked in view of the failure in the past of the youth services to make provision for immigrants. This was sharply criticized by the Hunt Report, *Immigrants and the Youth Service*.[34] The youth service is there described as already understaffed and reluctant to take on an additional burden. But the socially cohesive potential of the youth service cannot be over-estimated. The work done for immigrants in this as in all fields varies greatly from area to area. In Birmingham, an assistant for youth work has been appointed at the Institute of Further Education at Sparkhill. In Bristol, a youth field worker, financed by the Rowntree Trust, instigated the establishment of a multi-racial youth centre with a youth leader. Here, strong emphasis was placed on securing parental understanding and co-operation in the early stages, as there has usually been no parallel with the youth club organization in the culture of origin.

There has been some demand from national groups for separate youth clubs of their own. But the Hunt Report felt that although such organizations might be useful as interim measures, 'integration is better served by multi-racial contacts within the existing Youth Service than by separate provision'.

Youth clubs could provide a continuation of the multi-racial contacts which occur in schools but which tend to diminish after school leaving age. But the numbers involved are still only small. Only 10% of young immigrants in Bradford belong to youth organizations, and the highest proportion, in Birmingham, is only one-third. Without specific funds and training programmes for leaders the hopes for expansion are not high.

In general, the inadequacies of the local authority health and welfare services stem from structural weaknesses which have been analysed in the Seebohm Report. Within the existing framework, the basic philosophy concerning immigrants has in the past been that they should be taught how to use the existing social services. The voluntary liaison committees set up after 1965 under the National Committee for Commonwealth Immigrants were not intended to provide a separate service for immigrants, but to channel immigrants to available agencies which existed for the benefit of all.

But the success of any health and welfare measures has, as the Seebohm Report notes, to be judged within an existing framework of housing circumstances and income which may be the source of their problems. In the case of immigrants one has to add the consistent extra factor of discrimination. We shall be discussing this in detail when we deal with the P.E.P. Report. The late Dr. Yudkin put the case strikingly:

some of the problems are accentuated by the fact that many of the immigrants and their children are coloured. Extra poverty because some parents have to do work less skilled than they are capable of; extra overcrowding because of discrimination in housing; besides these, the prejudices of the white population make it difficult to find foster homes or adoptive parents for those children that need more permanent care.[35]

(e) Specific Requirements

Granted the problem of defining need, which we have discussed, there were from the outset certain obvious and specific requirements. One was for a programme of health education, and perhaps welfare education, explaining the working of the National Health Service and the social services. Considerable stress was laid on this important question of communication, both by the Commonwealth Immigrants Advisory Council and by the Government itself in the White Paper of August 1965. Part of the effort could be made through written information in various appropriate languages. A study of the literature which had been prepared— either by local authorities, or by private agencies or firms—was carried out by Tower Hamlets Liaison Committee in 1967.[36] What it found was a certain amount of literature in various languages, normally concerned with very basic public health matters—immunization and vaccination, chest X-rays, and treatment of venereal diseases. Some authorities had prepared leaflets about maternity and child welfare, including dietary matters, and a few authorities employed special interpreters attached part-time to their health departments. The overall impression was, however, patchy, and the report of the study made a plea for information produced centrally. The uneven response of local authorities on this matter reflected, of course, the general unevenness of provision of services and, in particular, health education. In 1964, a Joint Committee of Central and Scottish Health Councils on Health Education recommended more and stronger central organization.

Apart from health education, another obvious need was for healthy and safe day-care for pre-school-age children whose mothers were at work. There is no need to labour the point which has been most recently and forcefully made in the Plowden Report and the Seebohm Report and echoed by all organizations concerned with children's welfare. Nursery places would benefit all families where the mothers work, and among immigrants this means particularly the West Indian families. The evidence from the Midlands suggests that Indian and Pakistani women go out to work less, but, even then, mixed nursery schools would enable non-English speaking children to learn some English before going to school. What seems to have happened in nursery schools and day nurseries is that the responsibility has slipped between two departments—health and education—and passed to the private sector.[37] Since 1949, the number of day nursery places provided by local authorities has steadily declined, in accordance with the Ministry's policy that places be provided only for those in special need. Even since the arrival of immigrant families in the cities, the number of

z

nurseries has continued to fall. In December 1956 there were 547 local authority day nurseries, in December 1964, 455. Meanwhile, the number of registered private child-minders rose from 881 to 2,994,[38] and that of the unofficial child-minders, catering for a public largely composed of immigrant parents (as far as can be seen), even more rapidly. Associated with this growth was an increase in health hazards which caused anxiety to local authorities and voluntary organizations. It was expected that nursery education would be provided to an increasing extent in schools by the local education authorities. But this did not happen. 'It is amusing to consider', writes Mark Blaug, 'that the neglect of nursery schools in this country survived 20 years of overfull employment.'[39] Most parents were not amused. The result is that both local voluntary liaison committees and other voluntary agencies are struggling to provide 'pre-school play groups' and to put pressure upon local authorities to provide them. Provision either of day nurseries for babies, or of play groups for older children has not been made on the required scale. There is increasing pressure on local authorities to supervise child-minders more closely, but as yet no attempt appears to have been made to instruct them about the advantages of play, the provision of toys, and generally to take steps to bring the private sector up to the standard expected in the public one. This was one of the suggestions made in the London Council of Social Service's comment on the Plowden Report.[40]

(f) The Evolution of Policy

Until 1966, local authorities were presumed to be able to handle any special provision for immigrants with their own resources. The 1965 White Paper, in attempting to draw together the scattered wisps of official thinking and experience of practice, declared that the immigrants' needs were 'different in degree rather than kind', and the general objective must be 'to treat them in the same way as other citizens' (para 53). The Local Government Act of 1966, in Section 11, provided for a 50% rate support grant in respect of special staff, or extra effort by normal staff, due to the presence of Commonwealth immigrants having a different language or culture from the rest of the community. Total grants in the first year amounted to about £1½ million from the Government. In this, it marked a step forward from the position taken in the White Paper. However, it was left to each local authority to make expenditure claims according to its own priorities and policies, and there was consequently considerable variation between different authorities as to what they spent Section 11 funds on. In the first year of operation, 1967–8, the largest estimates in all major authorities, except Manchester, were for education. Manchester's largest estimate was for public health inspectors (£44,016), with education next (£36,260). Estimated expenditure on day nurseries varied considerably: Birmingham, £16,219; Wolverhampton, £1,173; Bristol, £11,600; Brent, £21,680; Ealing, £3,515; and Haringey, £1,540. (This should be distinguished from pre-school play groups, which would be paid for by local education authorities, who might have claimed part of the cost of teacher-attendants under Section 11 under 'Education'.) Estimates of expenditure on health visitors also varied. For example, Ealing's estimate was £18,253 (its second largest claim after education); Haringey's, which like Ealing has a large non-English speaking population, only £2,820.[41]

These variations do not only reflect the varying populations and proportions of immigrants in the local authorities, but also differences in policies towards immigrants, and, in particular, differences in health and welfare policies between authorities, which characterizes the administration of social welfare in Britain generally. What they illustrate in the present context is that although the Government, in its advance first from the *laissez-faire* position and then past the weak universalism of the 1965 White Paper, decided to make a substantial contribution to the costs of certain services through Section 11 of the 1966 Local Government Act, no overall guidance accompanied this provision. By 1968, however, there was a definite change in the approach of the central government. The Plowden Report established the principle of compensatory provision for deprived areas,[42] and a parallel concept of housing priority areas evolved from a variety of sources (as we have seen in Chapter 17). This process culminated in the announcement of the Urban Programme, which will be discussed in some detail in Part VIII. But we should note here that in the first year it is expected that the projects 'will be mainly in the field of nursery education, education and child-care and will cover the provision of buildings, staff, equipment and other items of expenditure'.[43]

The parallel to the field of education is in some ways a close one. The consequences of immigration for the health and welfare services were regarded as something which local authorities could handle without guidance, and, initially, without central funds. It was supposed that the particular problems of health and welfare experienced by immigrants would be dealt with in the normal way by the National Health Service and other social services, without specific reference to their special needs. The one subject on which special policies were thought necessary was the risk of the importation of infectious diseases and control at the ports of entry was gradually tightened, until in 1968 all immigrants became subject to examination, and to admittance on condition of reporting to a medical officer of health. All those except entitled dependants and returning residents could be refused permission to land on grounds of health. Only belatedly did any official recognition emerge that the process of migration and the functioning of control machinery might themselves generate welfare needs. The dispute over the new proposals for control in the White Paper of 1965 led to the setting up of the Wilson Committee on appeals procedure, and the Committee, basing itself in part on evidence gathered during a six months' study carried out at London Airport by International Social Service,[44] recommended the creation of an independent body to provide an advisory and welfare service.[45] An independent, unofficial body, backed by over 100 immigrant organizations, had already been set up—the Joint Council for the Welfare of Immigrants. And in July 1968, an *ad hoc* working party set up by the Home Office submitted proposals for the establishment of an independent Port Advisory and Welfare Service. Action on their recommendations awaits the overdue introduction* of legislation on the broader question of appeals.[46]

In general, the placing of problems of immigrant areas within an overall problem of urban deprivation is a hopeful step. Whether compensatory provision will be made on a large enough scale to make a significant difference is another question. There are indications that projects under the Urban Programme will not be left entirely to the local authorities, but will be planned in accordance with some overall perception of priorities. The assumption of a degree of central direction after a decade of drift comes opportunely: the recommendation by the Seebohm Report

* The Immigration Appeals Bill, introduced in November 1968 (after this section was written), provides under Clause 14 that: 'the Secretary of State may with the consent of the Treasury make grants to any voluntary organization which provides advice or assistance for, or other services for the welfare of, persons who have rights of appeal. . . .'

of a single local authority social work department should also encourage a planned distribution of resources by providing an instrument by which efficient allocation can be undertaken. But whether these developments in themselves are sufficient to justify optimism is another matter.

2. THE POLICE AND LAW ENFORCEMENT

Introduction

The survey among police officers, carried out for the Royal Commission on the Police (1962), revealed that many police said 'that coloured people had grown more resentful of them recently'.[47] In 1967, the late Sir Joseph Simpson (then Commissioner of Police for the Metropolis) wrote:

Complaints of police 'brutality', of West Indians afraid to complain at police stations for fear of being 'beaten-up', and protest marches and deputations in support of these allegations, have all been part of the deteriorating background to the pattern of police and immigrant relations during the last six months.[48]

The West Indian Standing Conference, in a study entitled *Nigger Hunting in London?*, claimed that 'threads of objectionable prejudice seem to be inter-woven into the fabric of police and immigrant relationship. It must be maintained that many instances have proven that the police are malicious and sometimes exceptionally hostile.'[49]

But although the claim that relationships between police and immigrants have been deteriorating is one that has frequently been made, culminating in a full-scale confrontation in the B.B.C. television production *Cause for Concern* in August 1968, objective evidence on the state of the relationship is not easy to come by. This is not because there is a shortage of assertions—all organizations connected with civil liberties or race relations have files full of complaints about police practice. The absence of validated material is an artefact of the machinery which exists to examine these complaints; and the way in which this machinery functions is at least partly responsible for the penumbra of suspicion cast on this topic. What does seem indisputable is that, at least in certain areas, an attitude of suspicion and mistrust has grown up between the police and the immigrant community—this, ironically, at a time when the police are trying to bring about a better understanding between themselves and immigrant groups, and when more police officers are devoting their attention to the problem than ever before. How then has this situation come about and how is it likely to develop? In order to begin to answer these questions, we will need to consider the place of the police in the structure of society, the function of social control which they perform and the specific tasks which they are called upon to undertake in order to discharge this function, and the effects on all these of changes in society as a whole.

(a) *The Life and Labour of the Police*[50]

The general objective of the police force laid down by the first Metropolitan Commissioner of Police still stands. This makes 'the principal object to be attained . . . [the] prevention of crime. . . . Security of the person, the preservation of public tranquillity and all other objects of a police establishment, will thus be better effected, than by the detection and punishment of the offender, after he has succeeded in committing the crime.' To this end a great deal of importance is attached to relations between police and public. Hence the sentiment expressed in the Report of the Chief Inspector of Constabulary in 1965, that the 'police service as a whole is deeply conscious of the need to have the goodwill and support of the public at all times',[51] is echoed in most official police reports and by most Home Secretaries, and is emphasized in police training.

This sentiment glosses over a fundamental conflict which derives from the nature of police operations. 'A police officer who by profession must be inquisitive and interfering',[52] must, at the same time, if he is to perform his function efficiently, try to maintain good relations with the community in which he operates. Thus a conflict arises for the policeman between carrying out the social role which the prevention of crime requires and performing the 'thief-catching' role, where he is exercising delegated authority. The police want to be respected and not questioned in the execution of their duty, but at the same time to have understanding and help from the public. This conflict is inadvertently expressed in a police report of 1958, where it is asserted that 'a selfish insistence on the right of the individual citizen, conveniently disregarding the rights of his fellow, has made it difficult to nip incipient trouble . . . in the bud'.[53]

The conflict is reinforced by the way in which policemen are constrained to work and live. Policemen are an identifiable minority and are to some extent shunned by the non-police public. This is particularly true where police houses are grouped together, and certainly for single policemen living in Section Houses. Thus, the Willink Commission survey found that 67% of policemen questioned said that the job adversely affected their outside friendships, though another survey, in urban areas alone, found that only 44% of policemen thought this.[54] The police are also expected to set an example in their private life for the rest of the community and the police disciplinary code reinforces this in encompassing their off-duty behaviour. And so the policeman is set apart from the rest of the community, yet is expected to be well integrated with that community to carry out a major part of his role.

In the decaying areas of cities where crime rates are often greatest there now tends to be separation of home area and work area. This can lead to a lack of identification with the area of work and a patronizing attitude towards the people who live there. The policeman takes on the attitude of those in his own area of residence, and non-identification, not isolation, then becomes a problem. Social isolation is reinforced by the irregular hours of work and by the liability to transfer, although this is now less frequent.

The hierarchical structure of police organization (based on a quasi-military model) may represent a potential source of tension. The values stemming from a structure of this nature may well come to be in opposition to the values associated with good community relations. This is another aspect of the policeman's dilemma, which is intensified by his social isolation.

This dilemma is not lessened by the discretion policemen can exercise in the course of their duties. It is central to their role as crime prevention agents. Discretion is essential 'on the beat' as it is the individual policeman who must determine the most appropriate action in dealing with specific situations which are or may lead to 'breaches of the peace'. Delegation of authority through chief constables down to station level is also essential where resources have to be disposed in the most efficient manner for prevention and detection of crime. Although it is a crucial element in police procedures, discretion can lead to abuses. This is witnessed by the number of complaints against individual policemen, which, even if not substantiated, may frequently turn on a disputed use of discretion. Discretionary powers inevitably lead to a style of policing which is discriminatory and involves risks; it can give rise to the feeling of being singled out for special attention. At the level of chief constable discretion can also give rise to conflicts and inconsistencies. For example, prosecutions for male importuning in Manchester increased dramatically with the change of the chief constable in 1959.[55]

In this situation the police's perception of the extent to which they have achieved their goal of good police–public relations is important. In 1966, the Metropolitan Police Commissioner thought that 'there had been a marked improvement in the attitude of the public towards helping the police'.[56] This is in contrast with the earlier findings of the Willink Commission Survey, which showed 'that police felt that a change for the worse had occurred in relations between themselves and the public',[57] despite the finding that the public's view of the police was an extremely favourable one. The difference in the police and the public's view of their relations is not so surprising as it might at first sight appear. A favourable view might have been predicted among the public at large. If the police have felt that public relations have deteriorated—and immigrant hostility is only part of that hostility—their perception is probably limited to those who have had 'contact' with the police. These pockets of poor opinion need to be located, in any assessment of how far minority views affect policing overall.

Two developments have militated against an improvement in police relations with the public. First, an overriding concern with the 'crime wave' has resulted in a concentration on the thief-catching role to the detriment of the social role. Furthermore, new legislation has increased police duties and increased the number of people who come into contact with the police for infringements of the law. This is particularly so in relation to motoring offences, which constitute a high proportion of all offences.

Public attitudes to the police are likely to vary from area to area and to depend to some extent on social class, but one obvious index of public regard for the police is the rate of complaints about police misbehaviour. Though changes in the procedure for recording complaints in 1964 may have caused administrative increases, two interesting examples indicate how complaints are a barometer of the public's attitude, though perhaps not so accurate as a measure of police misbehaviour. After the shooting of three policemen at Shepherds Bush in 1966, there was a 'distinct drop' in the rate of complaint.[58] The adverse publicity of the Sheffield inquiry contributed to the increase in the number of complaints in 1965. Table 20.1 indicates the rising trend of complaints over the last few years. But the proportion of substantiated complaints has not risen, notably in the Metropolitan area.

Table 20.1. Complaints and substantiated complaints against the police, 1964-7[59]

| | Metropolitan area | | All other areas | |
	Complaints received	Complaints substantiated	Complaints received	Complaints substantiated
1964	1,870	197	3,363	408
1965	2,460	237	6,736	756
1966	2,412	235	5,771	699
1967	2,639	220	5,885	756

The system of investigating complaints against the police through an internal quasi-judicial procedure has been the subject of much criticism, notably in Ben Whitaker's study of the police. Although the procedure has been revised since he analysed the drawbacks of the system, many of the criticisms he makes retain their validity. They have been cogently restated by Louis Kushnick, who comments on the machinery of investigation:

In the event of a conflict of interpretation or of opinion the natural tendency of the police, whether of the same force or from a different force, would be to define the problem in a similar way, because of their training, experience and concept of role. It seems necessary not only to ensure that justice be done, but that it be seen to be done, and therefore that there be some participation by an outside body which would not have the same biases. This, in all probability, would not affect the findings in the majority or perhaps even in the vast majority of cases. But it would be beneficial to the police in that these findings would be more likely to be accepted as being fair and objective, rather than being seen as the results of the police acting as judges in their own court.[60]

Another advantage of an independent system of inquiry would be that the rumours, that proliferate as a result of the way in which investigations and hearings are conducted at present, would have less uncertainty to feed upon.

On the other side, there are important practical objections to be raised against a system of independent review. Large numbers of complaints, many of them trivial, might choke any independent system. In many cases court proceedings will be pending; either the complaint must be investigated and hearings held while the case is still *sub judice* (which is unsatisfactory) or else complaint proceedings must take place against a background of a conviction or acquittal by a court. In the latter instance, there is an obvious danger that the results of court proceedings will determine the outcome of the complaint. In addition, there are arguments both from the standpoint of police practice and from what could be called police ideology. In the United States, systematic campaigns have been conducted by police associations who argue that independent review tribunals 'undermine police morale, impair their efficiency, and would paralyse them in dealing with violations of the law'.[61] This case has been put in a milder form in a recent report of the Chief Inspector of Constabulary: 'the principles to be considered in any system for dealing with complaints against the police from members of the public are that justice must be seen to be done . . . and that police morale should not be undermined in order to secure this objective', and, he adds, 'the present procedure seems to justify these principles'.[62] However, there is some doubt about whether the serving policeman accepts that the present system is satisfactory. Whitaker found that the majority of the policemen interviewed thought that serious complaints should be independently investigated,[63] but in the five years that have intervened since his inquiry, police opinion may have hardened against any system of external review.

As we have pointed out, the role of the police inevitably involves conflict and as an identifiable group, to some extent isolated from the community, they are a target for prejudice and resentment. The grievances and the resentment of the public are expressed through the complaints machinery which is not seen to be impartial and may thus tend to reinforce resentment and prejudice. This is as true whether the complaints are substantiated or not. Complaints adjudged frivolous, trivial, or deriving from a misunderstanding may be just as damaging to public confidence as a massive scandal. Many unsubstantiated complaints indicate a decline in police-public relations and, particularly where racial or class attitudes are involved, the need in a complaint procedure should be less to prove or justify behaviour as to reassure an offended person. The procedure is thus vital to the background against which police-immigrant relations need to be considered.

(b) Police–Immigrant Relations

Initially, the police were regarded by the authorities in Whitehall simply as the means of ensuring that law and order in areas of immigrant settlement was efficiently preserved. In other words, they should simply continue to execute the traditional function of keeping the peace. Thus, the Home Secretary was able in 1958 to pay tribute to the way in which the Metropolitan Police had prevented the disturbances in Notting Hill from getting out of control, and it was generally agreed that the disturbances in Dudley two years later had been handled with considerable skill by the local police. In addition to this function of preventing the emergence of open conflict between immigrant minorities and the white majority, the police were employed in an intelligence role— they were the medium through which most of the scanty information about the minorities reached Whitehall. At this stage, the idea that the police might perform a mediating role between the coloured and white communities had not yet been put forward: as we have seen, the general objective of official policy towards minorities in the late 1950s and early 1960s precluded any direct involvement of this kind. This confining of the police to a purely regulatory role may well have had something to do with the deterioration of relationships, which began to be noticeable in the early 1960s and which found expression in the increasing number of protests raised by organizations like C.A.R.D. and the West Indian Standing Conference. These complaints stemmed almost exclusively from the experience of West Indians. By the mid-1960s the rate of complaints by coloured immigrants in the Metropolitan Police area exceeded those made by the white majority by three to two. C.I.D. and senior police officers were virtually unanimous in the view that the relationship between the police and the coloured minorities had never been worse.

In this atmosphere, complaints about police misbehaviour have received a good deal of publicity. But as we have suggested, what has not been established is how much this reflects on actual police performance. To extend an earlier quotation: 'it is understandable that a police officer by profession must be inquisitive and interfering, will at times himself become the object of suspicion, particularly by those who themselves feel insecure or perhaps harassed'.[64]

Though senior police officers are often liberal in their views towards coloured immigrants and have become more understanding in their dealings with immigrant groups, it is not established whether their attitudes have influenced the police on the beat. Complaints (which do not of course customarily involve senior officers) are certainly becoming more frequent; but the fact that the rate of substantiated complaints is lower for coloured immigrants, at least in the Metropolitan area, than it is for white complainants (2·5% as opposed to 8·8%)[65] has been put forward as evidence that immigrants are particularly prone to make frivolous complaints arising out of their own insecurity (the 'chip on their shoulder'). However, it is of the essence of complaints that arise from insensitive or prejudiced remarks or behaviour by the police that they are difficult to substantiate and usually depend on the unsupported assertions of the complainant. The relative importance of these factors is difficult to establish, but there is no doubt that on a subjective level all those involved believe that there has been a sharp deterioration in the atmosphere.

Additional complaints may be generated by changes in the role of the police. Alternatively, the police may become 'objects of suspicion' for groups who themselves feel insecure. Moreover, where there are immigrant organizations which are capable of gathering and transmitting complaints effectively, it is possible that the rate will increase. Finally, changes in the situation of the immigrants and increased expectations may well create increased sensitivity and produce more complaints.

In short, the extent of actual discrimination practised by the police is not established. It is readily conceded by senior police officers and Federation officials that the police share the prejudices of the indigenous population.[66] Some add, however, that these do not influence police behaviour in carrying out their duties. But, granted the degree of flexibility deriving from the discretion exercised at all levels, it is difficult to be entirely confident on this score. Michael Banton's remark that 'to explain what a policeman actually does it is necessary to see his activities as being governed more by popular morality than by the letter of the law',[67] can readily be extended to behaviour of officers towards immigrants.

Many coloured immigrants, of course, live in the decaying areas near the centre of cities. As these areas often coincide with areas of a high incidence of crime, it will often happen that the inhabitants will have their reputation determined by the association with the area. For coloured immigrants, this reputation will be reinforced by their visibility. This must inevitably affect police attitudes, for it is in just these areas where police work is greatest that detection and apprehension take precedence over prevention. The policemen in these areas, who themselves will be visible, are thus more likely to be seen as a threat rather than a helpful ally.

If there were in fact a high recorded incidence of crime among immigrants in these central areas, there might be a realistic basis for differential treatment of immigrants on the part of the police. But this does not seem to be the case. The two main sources of information are an article by Bottoms,[68] and Lambert's unpublished work. Bottoms found, on the little evidence available, that crime among immigrants tended to be low except for violent crimes, where domestic disputes predominated. The rate of violent crime needs to be treated carefully as it probably involves people at greater risk by age and environmental factors than for the population at large. Coloured immigrants have also been over-represented in drugs charges, mainly possession of cannabis, as compared with the white population. It should be noted that 'the use of the drug is more natural, as the drug itself is more natural, than it is among the English'.[69] Lambert confirms these findings: 'fewer than 5% of arrests made in the significantly coloured neighbourhood are in fact coloured people. . . . Only in offences related to drug trafficking are coloured immigrants over-represented.'[70] These figures, apart from contradicting a widely-held stereotype (to which even the judiciary have been known to subscribe), also suggest that prosecution is not used by police as an instrument of discrimination—although it must be borne in mind that prosecution is the ultimate police sanction and there are lesser sanctions at their disposal.

There are certain bright spots around the country which should be noted. In Warley and Birmingham, when immigrant school children were asked about policemen they spoke in terms of the help, advice, and friendliness they received. This can be contrasted with the experience of a London police officer talking to a class of mainly West Indian girls, who met with the unanimous assumption that everybody who went inside a police station was beaten up.[71] For adult immigrants in West Bromwich, Detective Sergeant Till had 'helped them to organise peace and contentment' for which they presented him with a silver plate.[72]

(c) The Police and Integration

As the pendulum has swung away from the concept that the police role should be confined to the prevention of disturbances or open conflict and as the provision of special facilities designed to promote integration has become acceptable in terms of general policy aims, the Home Office have begun to consider measures for the promotion of better relations between police and immigrants. When he first came to the Home Office, Roy Jenkins made this one of the areas on which he placed particular emphasis. As the Chief Inspector of Constabulary put it in his first report to the new Home Secretary:

in 1966, you became responsible for co-ordination of measures to promote integration of coloured immigrants into the community and caused inquiries to be made about action that was already being taken by Chief Officers in areas in which it was known that large communities of coloured immigrants were resident. As the year advanced . . . the Police Service took a more intense interest in the problem.[73]

Two areas in which this intense interest was shown were in the field of liaison between police and immigrants through the appointment of liaison officers and in the recruitment of coloured policemen. In particular, the Metropolitan Police were concerned with the deterioration of the atmosphere and made increasing efforts to devise a structure which would enable this trend to be reversed.

Though police liaison officers existed before Roy Jenkins issued a circular on the subject of police authority in July 1967, this central initiative gave added impetus to the idea. What has not yet been properly established is the exact functions of the persons appointed as liaison officers. In the Metropolitan Police and elsewhere they are virtually self-appointed, in that officers with special interest in the field of race relations are asked to put themselves forward. This may, of course, lead to some very good work, but in general the lack of specific duties may result in little being done. In addition, as the appointment is not generally full-time there will be a tendency for police duties to override liaison duties, whatever they might be seen to be.

Little training is given to liaison officers; a two-day course of lectures at Scotland Yard was all the London ones had, and more training may well be necessary if they are to operate effectively. As the Metropolitan liaison officers are mainly those with an interest in the field anyway, the suggestion that there is a resistance to further training may not find support in reality.

So far the Metropolitan Police have about 100 liaison officers, twenty-five of whom sit on the voluntary liaison committees established under the auspices of the National Committee for Commonwealth Immigrants. Altogether, according to an analysis of the results of a questionnaire issued by the National Committee, thirty-seven local liaison committees have at least one police representative, generally of inspector rank or above; and ten have more than one. In nine cases, the representative is also the designate police liaison officer. The role of the local committees is characterized by a degree of ambiguity. The basic rationale for the participation of police officers in their activities has been presented by a serving police officer, in a paper prepared for the National Committee's Training Panel, as the promotion of improved communication and understanding and 'to lend stress to the principle that the administration of criminal justice in all its ramifications is totally a community responsibility'.[74] Some local committees, however, who see their role principally as acting on behalf of local immigrants, have concentrated on investigating instances of alleged 'police brutality' and attempting to press home such instances as occur with the police. Other committees, in contrast, try to build up a relationship with the local police force, based on exchange of information, lectures, and informal meetings—extending on occasion to cricket matches and socials. On balance, the majority of committees have concentrated on the latter style of activity and it is within this general framework of educational and social action that the work of police liaison officers has so far been. Great scope has been given to individual police officers of the uniformed branch in creating their own variations on the theme of liaising throughout London with the various committees set up under the auspices of the National Committee for Commonwealth Immigrants. One divisional liaison officer will make a personal liaison with one or more committees, sometimes as a mere observer, and at other times will fully participate in the work of the committee and its subsidiaries. Together with this activity, some officers have devised their own approach to the community at large by, for example, publicizing their availability at specified times at their police stations.

As a result of this facility of inter-communication making individual police officers aware of the need in the area for an increase of knowledge of the purpose and methods of the police by immigrants on the one hand and for dissemination of information within the force regarding the customs and origins of immigrants on the other, many lectures to mixed groups of officers and to groups of immigrants have been delivered by police or chosen authorities from among the immigrant organisations.[75]

A Department (A5) at Scotland Yard has been set up to co-ordinate the activities of the liaison officers, to carry on a dialogue with the leaders of the immigrant community, and to carry out a general education function.[76] This Department organized a two-day conference for liaison officers in the Metropolitan area which has been mentioned previously. It has also organized lectures for police officers on race relations and is now producing a leaflet explaining the police role to newcomers. It is intended to expand the activities of the Department in the future, when it will be divided into two parts—one concerned with race relations in general, high level liaison and initial training, and the other concerned with community liaison locally.

In the rest of the country, the liaison officer system is growing, with some variations on the Metropolitan system. Bradford, for example, has appointed a Pakistani and an Indian civilian liaison officer as well as a uniformed liaison officer. In all, over thirty police forces outside the Metropolitan area have appointed liaison officers, numbering about 100.

In provincial forces, the role of the liaison officer is also often not defined. Inspector J. P. Steer, the liaison officer for Warwickshire, when asked about his work, replied that: 'We are not setting out to be social workers. We have no terms of reference at all. . . . What we are trying to do is find out what they expect from the police and tell them where they stand and what exactly we can do to help them.'[77]

The immigrant community is to some extent suspicious of the liaison officers scheme. The West Indian Standing Conference (London Branch) is reported to have 'believed that police did not intend to treat black people fairly and impartially and that liaison on the part of the police was "simply to whitewash and hoodwink the community and especially the black community into believing that the police are the fairest in the world" '.[78] However, these public denunciations are not necessarily paralleled in private practice. Since 1964, the Standing Conference has maintained contact with the special officers appointed at Scotland Yard and although public criticism is frequently voiced, these contacts have been maintained. In the event of further revision of procedures by the police, it is quite possible that the Standing Conference's present critical line would be speedily amended.

It is too soon to say whether the liaison system will produce results. We have argued that some degree of conflict between the police and the immigrant community is inevitable—though by conflict we do not necessarily mean to imply violent conflict. The liaison system will not eliminate this but can bring about a better understanding of the particular causes of conflict. To tackle the problem successfully, the liaison officers should be full-time appointments and they should be full participating members of local committees. This will present the police with a difficult manning problem and, in a situation where there is a great man-power shortage, may not be possible. However, if the scheme operates successfully and some dialogue is established between the police and the community, this may compensate for the loss of a man on the beat. The liaison officer, in any case, need not be strictly off the beat but a free-ranging agent acquiring an intimate knowledge, if he does not already have this, of the problems within his particular division. In the future there should be scope for this officer to develop into a community liaison officer without particular reference to immigrants.

In order to produce effective liaison officers, there will have to be some definition of their function and, after this has been done, training appropriate to this function. This will at least guarantee a minimum service which will be known to be available. This again will cause staffing difficulties, but it may be a necessary short-term sacrifice if any headway is to be made.

It is essential that liaison officers are not seen in the context of a public relations exercise, an activity of which many police forces are becoming increasingly enamoured. This would be a negation of the concept of liaison between two equally concerned parties.

The second prong of the police effort to salvage the deteriorating situation is in the recruitment of coloured policemen. Unfortunately, the police have dragged their feet over this issue. There is little doubt that some chief constables, who were in principle favourably disposed towards recruiting of coloured policemen, allowed themselves to be dissuaded by fears of the reaction of serving policemen. There was widespread anxiety in the police about the capacity of coloured officers to exact from the public the degree of respect and compliance which the police would ideally like to receive; this found expression in an anxious correspondence in the *Guardian*.[79] Other critics, from a more positive position, were concerned that coloured police might be recruited merely in order to police areas of immigrant settlement. Until Roy Jenkins became Home Secretary, no real attempts were made to recruit coloured policemen, but, as a result of the stimulus administered by Jenkins, the policy of most forces changed from defensive assertions that no sufficiently qualified applicants had presented themselves to a positive attempt at recruitment. The Association of Chief Police Officers stated through their Secretary in October 1966 that they 'would welcome more coloured applicants'.[80] Yet a survey amongst policemen in the Metropolitan area revealed that 62% of those questioned 'did not want coloured policemen recruited in areas where there were large numbers of coloured immigrants'.[81] There are now seven coloured policemen in the country. In the Metropolitan area there are two coloured policewomen and one man, with another undergoing training.

One should add that there have been practical difficulties over the recruitment of coloured policemen. Part of the general shortage is due to the high standard, especially of physique, required and the conditions of work. Language is frequently cited as a barrier. The Metropolitan Police, for example, considered only one applicant in thirty suitable before 1964.[82] Though the total number of coloured applicants to date is not known, seven does seem a disproportionately small number in relation to the immigrant population.

The impact that the recruitment of coloured policemen could have had has to a great extent been lost. Belated attempts to improve the situation only serve to underline the previous reluctance of chief constables and the Metropolitan Commissioner. It cannot be that only since 1966 have there been suitable applicants. An appointment of a coloured policeman much earlier would have had a much greater impact on public and immigrant attitudes than it does now.

Finally, there are the police efforts to improve the training of new recruits and to educate serving policemen in social problems with particular reference to the immigrant community.

Police training for recruits consists of a twelve-week full-time course at a Police District Training Centre, followed by a two-year probationary period on the beat, during which time the constable attends classes and lectures under the guidance of a force training officer. In a document for the N.C.C.I., the Metropolitan Police state that the initial training:

concentrates mainly on criminal law and procedure with a distinct emphasis placed upon the public with a duty to treat all law-abiding citizens irrespective of their race, colour, creed and social position with unfailing patience and courtesy. The purpose is to train an officer to be a policeman first, and although consideration has been given to guiding the trainee towards an appreciation of what is required in community relations, race relations is only a small part of the formal training.[83]

Ninety-six lectures will have been delivered at the various recruit training establishments during the course of 1968. To quote further: 'The widely held opinion amongst senior officers that practical experience of the policeman has more importance in this field has a great deal to commend it.'[84]

Training thus lays stress on the legal aspects of policing with a smattering of information on community relations. It is presumed that knowledge about the community will be achieved through practical experience. Apart from the fact that policemen apparently think that 80% of the information they gain during their training course is of no use to them afterwards,[85] the attitudes they gain during their two years' practical experience are to a great extent derived from older policemen. In addition, prejudices are likely to be reinforced if the only practical experience of immigrants is gained on the beat, in areas where the general population is most hostile to the police, and where the older officers have little time for further training. The new recruit will neither be exposed to informed or balanced attitudes, nor will he have time to relate his experience to what he has previously learned about community relations.

Apart from this initial training course, there are special courses for particular types of police work—for example, the C.I.D.—which need not be discussed here. In addition, there is a special course for constables at the Police College at Bramshill House intended for those who show promise, and serving as an avenue for accelerated promotion. It is broader in content than most other police training, and includes economics, politics, and social studies. A shortened course on these lines during initial training would certainly provide a better background for policemen serving urban communities.

For higher ranks, the official further training courses for those singled out for eventual promotion to the highest levels are mainly (though not exclusively) concerned with police administration. No doubt this should be the main emphasis. But it can be argued that as policemen rise through the hierarchy they should gain a greater understanding of the complexity of life in an urban society and not just of one institution in that society. The popularity of university extension courses in criminology and special courses in social studies designed for police officers is evidence that the individual policeman is quite prepared to devote time and energy on his own initiative to equipping himself with information of this kind.

However, the most important part of all police training is that given to police constables, because, as one policeman has put it, 'it is not the Chief Inspector the immigrant is worried about—it is the policeman walking down the Harrow Road, now'.[86] It is, in fact, unlikely that one part of the training can be changed without some reshaping of the training at all levels. The course for probationary policemen has changed little over the last twelve years and, apart from the new situation presented by immigration, it is time that courses took account of the new environment and the changing expectations both of the police and the community. The legal aspects of policing should be less emphasized and less reliance should be put on the part played by experience on the beat in the local setting and the influence of older colleagues. A greater importance could be attached to social studies in the form of elementary psychology and sociology. In this way, the road to improved police community relations may be made a little easier.

Conclusions

The response of the police to the decline in their relations with the immigrant community has in some ways been encouraging, but it still leaves much to be desired. It would be unrealistic to hope for too dramatic a change, but already existing machinery can be adapted without too great a strain on police goodwill. The first way would be to create full-time liaison officers who would be community oriented, make the least possible use of uniform, and are trained at least to an elementary level in a social science. Their duties should have three main components. First, they should establish contacts in the community in order both to obtain a sounding board, and to function as a spokesman for the police. They should not perform general policing duties except in emergencies. Secondly, their duty should be to act on behalf of the community as a whole and to carry out an educative role in whatever way may be appropriate, either by talking to individuals or by discussing changes in certain police routines for dealing with specific incidents. Thirdly, and perhaps most important, they should help the police to understand the needs of immigrant communities and of particular areas.

Another change which should be urgently considered is in relation to the complaints procedure, into which an element of independence should be introduced. We have dealt earlier with some of the practical objections to such a change: although these should be taken seriously, they are not insurmountable. One way of resolving them might be to establish a small committee, with representatives from all interests involved, to make recommendations to the Home Secretary on the form that a new system might take. It may well be that such revised machinery would not make a great deal of difference to the outcome of most complaints, but it should have an effect on public confidence (which would in itself make the amendment worth while) and it would represent an important concession for the immigrant community. Equally, there is scope for changes in police training along the lines already discussed.

Generally, there is no doubt that the organization of the police is such that discrimination against any group in the community can be dealt with effectively. The way the police work is supervised and organized can drastically curtail the opportunities for discrimination. But against this must be set the question of police discretion which militates against the detailed supervision of the police task. However, the curtailment of discrimination does not so much require direct interference in detail as the adoption of disapproving attitudes and the disciplining of actions which are suspected as being discriminatory. This is why the Home Secretary's failure to persist in his earlier decision to introduce an amendment to the police disciplinary code, making it an offence to display prejudice or act in a discriminatory fashion, is regrettable. Although it has been strongly challenged by the Police Federation, it would stand as an official recognition that certain standards must be observed.

Finally, it is clear, that, as Michael Banton indicates in his study of the police, change in our society will modify both the role of the police and the expectations and attitudes of the general public. These changes will place a considerable strain on the police and test their adaptability to the limit. As so often, one of the functions performed by the immigrants has been to display in its sharpest form a dilemma already arising as a result of processes at work in our society as a whole.

NOTES TO CHAPTER 20

1. K. Jones, 'Immigrants and the Social Services', *National Institute Economic Review* (No. 41, August 1967), pp. 28–40.

2. Evidence (unpublished) submitted jointly by the Institute of Race Relations and the National Committee for Commonwealth Immigrants to the Committee on Local Authority and Allied Personal Social Services (The Seebohm Committee).

3. Commonwealth Immigrants Act, 1962: instructions to immigration officers (Cmnd. 3064), (London, H.M.S.O., August 1966). Supersedes instructions issued May 1962.

4. British Medical Association, *Medical Examination of Immigrants: report of the working party* (London, B.M.A., 1965).

5. Ibid.

6. *Annual Report of the Ministry of Health for 1964* (Cmnd. 2688), (London, H.M.S.O., 1965).

7. Cited by the Prime Minister, Rt. Hon. Harold Wilson, in a speech in Birmingham on 5 May 1968.

8. Eric Butterworth, 'Policies for Integration: a study of Bradford' (for the Institute's 'Survey of Race Relations in Britain').

9. Ibid.

10. D. Hinds, *Journey to an Illusion: The West Indian in Britain* (London, Heinemann, 1966).

11. B. Dahya, 'Pakistanis in Birmingham and Bradford' (for the Institute's 'Survey of Race Relations in Britain').

12. Statistics on the incidence of venereal disease are from the studies of the British Co-operative Clinical Group, 'The Gonorrhoea Study, 1965', *British Journal of Venereal Diseases* (Vol. 43, no. 1, 1967); R. R. Willcox, 'Immigration and Venereal Disease in Great Britain', *British Journal of Venereal Diseases* (Vol. 42, no. 4, December 1966), pp. 225–37; B.M.A. Report, op. cit.

13. A. Richmond and M. Lyon, 'Race Relations in Bristol' (for the Institute's 'Survey of Race Relations in Britain').

14. K. Jones, op. cit.

15. H. M. Bulla, 'Immigration—past, present and future: attitudes and official policies of local officials in West Bromwich to coloured Commonwealth immigrants', (Dissertation for B.A. degree, University of Bradford, 1966).

16. J. Galloway, 'Some Aspects of Immigration', *The Medical Officer* (Vol. 118, no. 5, 4 August 1967), pp. 69–70.

17. *Report of the Committee on Local Authority and Allied Personal Social Services* (Cmnd. 3703), (London, H.M.S.O., July 1968). (The Seebohm Committee.)

18. C. Bagley, paper presented to the Anglo-French Conference, Brighton, 9–13 September 1968.

19. F. Hashmi, paper presented to the Anglo-French Conference, Brighton, 9–13 September 1968.

20. Ibid.

21. A. Kiev, 'Psychiatric Illness among West Indians in London', *Race* (Vol. 5, no. 3, January 1964), pp. 48–54.

22. B. Gans, 'Health Problems and the Immigrant Child', in Ciba Foundation, *Immigration, Medical and Social Aspects* (London, Churchill, 1966).

23. C. Eric Stroud and V. Moody, 'One Hundred Mothers: a survey of West Indians in Britain', *Maternal and Child Care* (Vol. 111, no. 26, June 1967).

24. B. Gans, op. cit., and see also W. H. Israel, *Colour and Community: a study of coloured immigrants and race relations in an industrial town* (Slough, Council of Social Service, 1964).

25. G. Stewart Prince, 'Mental health problems in pre-school West Indian children', *Maternal and Child Care* (Vol. 111, no. 26, June 1967).

26. B. Kent, 'The social worker's cultural pattern as it affects casework with immigrants', *Social Work* (October 1965), pp. 14–22, and in Institute of Race Relations *Newsletter* (January and July 1968).

27. Elizabeth Burney, *Housing on Trial* (London, Oxford University Press, for Institute of Race Relations, 1967).

28. R. E. D. Simpson, 'Morbidity survey of a general practice with a large proportion of immigrants' (for the Institute's 'Survey of Race Relations in Britain').

29. Eric Butterworth, op. cit.

30. K. Fitzherbert, *West Indian Children in London* (London, G. Bell, 1967), sponsored by the L.C.C., Lewisham Children's Department and the London Boroughs Social Work Training Organization.

31. Mary Dines (London Council of Social Service) 'The West Indian Family', *Race* (Vol. IX, no. 4, April 1968).

32. Eric Butterworth, op. cit.

33. R. E. D. Simpson, op. cit.

34. *Immigrants and the Youth Service* (London, Department of Education and Science, July 1967). Chairman: Lord Hunt.

35. S. Yudkin, *The Health and Welfare of the Immigrant Child* (London, National Committee for Commonwealth Immigrants, 1965).

36. J. Ford and others (compilers), *A Survey of information provided for non-English speaking immigrants in their own languages by local authorities* (London, Council of Citizens of East London and Council of Citizens of Tower Hamlets, February 1967).

37. See, for example, National Labour Women's Advisory Committee, *Labour women's national survey into care of children: final report* (London, N.L.W.A.C., 1967), Part 4: The education of immigrant children.

38. The Seebohm Report, op. cit.

39. M. Blaug, 'Selectivity in Education', *Social Services for All?* Part Two (London, Fabian Society Fabian Tract 383, June 1968), p. 32.

40. Recommendations of the Immigrants Advisory Committee, Greater London Area, of the London Council of Social Service on *Children and their Primary Schools* (Plowden Report) (September 1967)

41. Estimates submitted to the Home Office under Section 11, Local Government Act 1966. H. of C. Written Answers, col. 98–9, 8 May 1968.

42. *Children and their Primary Schools: A Report of the Central Advisory Council for Education* (London, H.M.S.O., 1967), Chapter 5. Chairman: Lady Plowden.

43. Statement (press release) on the Urban Programme by the Home Secretary, the Rt. Hon. James Callaghan, 22 July 1968.

44. *Immigrants at London Airport and their Settlement in the Community* (London, International Social Service, June 1967).

45. *Report of the Committee on Immigration Appeals* (Cmnd. 3387), (London, H.M.S.O., August 1967). Chairman: Sir Roy Wilson.

46. See Joint Council for the Welfare of Immigrants, *Annual Report 1967–8* (43, Lady Margaret Road, Southall).

47. Ben Whitaker, *The Police* (Harmondsworth, Penguin Books, 1964), p. 14.

48. *The Job* (the newspaper for men and women of the Metropolitan Police), in the editorial 'Man to Man' (8 December 1967).

49. Joseph A. Hunte, *Nigger Hunting in England?* (London, West Indian Standing Conference, London Branch, 1966).

50. Much of the information for the section is drawn from *Police: a social study* (London, Church Information Office for Church Assembly Board for Social Responsibility, 1967); and Ben Whitaker, op. cit. The principal source, however, was from research commissioned by the Institute's 'Survey of Race Relations in Britain', as yet unpublished, by John Lambert, who has examined police operations in Birmingham.

51. *Report of Her Majesty's Chief Inspector of Constabulary for the year 1965* (H.C. 251), p. 72.

52. *Report of the Commissioner of Police of the Metropolis 1967* (Cmnd. 3659), p. 16.

53. *Report of the Commissioner of Police of the Metropolis 1958* (Cmnd. 8000), p. 20.

54. Royal Commission on the Police: minutes of evidence 1960–2 (Chairman: Sir Henry Willink) (London, H.M.S.O., 1963).

55. Ben Whitaker, op. cit., p. 30. Other examples of this sort of activity are to be found in M. Banton, *The Police and the Community* (London, Tavistock Publications, 1964), Ch. 5.

56. *Report of the Commissioner of Police of the Metropolis 1966* (Cmnd. 3315), p. 7.

57. Ben Whitaker, op. cit., p. 15.

58. Cmnd. 3315, op. cit., p. 30.

59. Compiled from the Reports of the Commissioner of Police for the Metropolis and the Reports of Her Majesty's Chief Inspector of Constabulary for 1965, 1966, and 1967.

60. Louis Kushnick, 'The Police, Minority Groups, and Independent Enquiry', *Race* (Vol. X, no. 1, July 1968), p. 90.

61. Ibid., p. 90.

62. *Report of Her Majesty's Chief Inspector of Constabulary for the year 1967* (H.C. 272), p. 85.

63. Ben Whitaker, op. cit.

64. Cmnd. 3659, op. cit., p. 16.

65. This analysis was obtained from New Scotland Yard A Department.

66. 'I wouldn't think of suggesting to you that the police force does not share proportionately the prejudice of the society from which its members are drawn, and to which they belong.' (Robert Mark, Deputy Commissioner of the Metropolitan Police Force, transcript of *Cause for Concern*, B.B.C. August 1968.)

67. Michael Banton, op. cit., p. 146.

68. A. E. Bottoms, 'Delinquency among Migrants', *Race* (Vol. VIII, no. 4, April 1967).

69. Letter from Rev. K. Leech in Institute of Race Relations *Newsletter* (October–November, 1967).

70. *Sunday Times*, 30 July 1967.

71. From John Lambert's material. But a small-scale study, conducted by the Metropolitan Police in North London, showed that police stations were frequently entered by local West Indians for a wide variety of purposes.

72. *Birmingham Post*, 25 April 1967.

73. *Report of Her Majesty's Chief Inspector of Constabulary 1966* (H.C. 544), p. 9.

74. N.C.C.I. Police Training Procedure and N.C.C.I. Role. Chief Inspector K. L. Lee (Metropolitan Police), NC/TRG/68/5, Appendix 2, p. 5.

75. Ibid., p. 3.

76. See *The Job*, 19 and 21 July 1968.

77. *Coventry Evening Telegraph*, 18 August 1967.

78. *Guardian*, 31 July 1968.

79. Letters to the *Guardian*, 19 and 30 November 1964.

80. *Evening Standard*, 12 October 1966.

81. *Bolton Evening News*, 8 November 1966.

82. Ben Whitaker, op. cit., p. 95. In the past, the failure to recruit coloured police has sometimes been put down to the low quality of applicants. In one year, for which information is available (1966), thirty-six coloured men applied to join the Metropolitan Police—five were asked to attend an interview, but four failed to turn up. The fifth was rejected as being below standard. Of the rest, over half were recent immigrants and the others were rejected for lack of education or on medical grounds. The Home Secretary regarded these results as disappointing. (740, H.C. Deb., Written Answers 278–9 (7 February 1967).)

83. Chief Inspector K. L. Lee, op. cit., p. 1.

84. Ibid., p. 2.

85. Ben Whitaker, op. cit., p. 109.

86. Transcript of *Cause for Concern* B.B.C. August 1968.

21 The Volunteer in the Vacuum

1. THE CHURCHES AND THE NEWCOMERS

A recent *Times* leader stated that:

Whatever else may be said of the record of the Church of England in the past ten years it cannot be denied that the Church as a whole and Churchmen as individuals have given witness to the need for racial tolerance.[1]

Do the records of not just the Church of England but of the Churches in England uphold this statement? Although in general terms they do, the activities of the Churches in dealing with specific problems leaves much to be desired.

Few people would deny that the Churches in Britain accept racial prejudice as being anti-Christian. This can be seen not only in the public pronouncements of leading Churchmen, but also in the various pamphlets published by church institutions and Churchmen. Set against this record are the activities of certain individuals who, at the time of the 1964 general election, made what can only be called racialist pronouncements, usually through their parish magazines.[2] Their statements were condemned by their fellow Churchmen, but no formal action was taken.

Though there is no lack of public statements and publications from the Churches bearing witness to the need for racial tolerance, few Churchmen would regard these as sufficient in themselves to demonstrate a Christian attitude towards coloured immigrants.

The relationship of the Churches to the community varies very much from denomination to denomination. The Catholic Church and, to a lesser extent, the Free Churches have strong working-class congregations. They are particularly strong in the central areas of cities. By contrast, the Church of England has suffered a great decline in these central areas, where the flight of the middle-class population has resulted in nearly empty churches.

The rapidly changing character of urban life has created a whole series of community problems for which the Churches have been unprepared. It is unfortunate that, until now, pastoral care has been concerned with individual church members in distress, and so has tended to ignore the condition of the wider community.

This blinkered view of the community is one important factor which prevents the Churches, especially those in the central, working-class areas, where the problems are most acute, from making a more effective contribution to community life. For the Catholic Church, this failure must be seen against a tradition of avoiding involvement in 'political' issues which are not seen to affect religious *practice*. The Free Churches' tradition of political involvement is rendered less effective by their small following. For the Church of England, local political action is not a feature of its activity.

This is all particularly relevant to the Churches' action in relation to immigrants, who, in the main, occupy the decaying central areas of cities. Thus, some Churchmen see the presence of immigrants, and coloured immigrants in particular, as just one aspect of the general problem of Christian action in a rapidly changing environment. Some take a narrower view and see the arrival of immigrants, especially the West Indians, as an opportunity for a Christian revival, for this group have strong church-going traditions. A similar attitude interprets the arrival of Asians as an opportunity for missionary work in the church backyard.

Whichever of these opinions is held, all Churchmen agree that the Churches have a vital role to play in achieving acceptance of the coloured immigrant. In fact, some think that they are uniquely placed amongst the institutions of this country to make the cause of racial harmony and integration their own.[3]

This unity, however, masks a difference in purpose, for integration has many interpretations. Various shades of opinion can be picked out. To some Churchmen, integration means 'they' adapt to 'our ways'.[4] This attitude seems implicit in the hostility of some Churchmen to the Pentecostal Sects and in the missionary attitude towards Asian immigrants.[5] The Church of England holds no one opinion on what is desirable. Integration can mean any group developing 'its own way of life in a measure of separation', 'changing both their culture and ours . . . into a new unity which is neither' or some mixture.[6] A more radical view would seek to 'create a new situation in which the indigenous population and the overseas people are woven together so as to become a new society'.[7] In this latter case, the problem of converting the indigenous population is seen as the hardest task facing the Churches. The migrants are seen to have indicated their adaptability by migrating.

Given that these differences exist, the overriding view is that the

Churches have an important role to play in achieving greater racial harmony. What then have they achieved?

The activities of the Churches can be divided into four broad categories. These are: pronouncements made at the national level by Churchmen and representative organizations, the dissemination of information and educational work, the activities of various institutions within the Churches, and activity by individual ministers and priests at local level. All are interconnected, but each can be examined separately.

The most critical aspect of the Churches' work in relation to immigrants is local action. 'The time has long passed for merely talking about multi-racialism and integration—though not all Church people even do so. Now—at once—we are called upon to put our preaching into practice.'[8] But a recent ecumenical symposium concluded that the Churches had 'failed to seize the initiative in extending friendship to the coloured immigrant',[9] and the William Temple Association said that 'the Churches have not been conspicuous in the work of social integration'.[10] Finally, the British Council of Churches' Standing Committee on Migration, after a full review of the situation undertaken in 1965, commented that 'the total effort is impressive but in relation to the size of the problem is quite insufficient'.[11]

Failure is often defined in terms of church attendance. This index is presumably based on the hypothesis that people attend church as a result of a conviction that Christianity is meaningful to them, in the community, in dealing with problems which confront them. If this index is accepted as valid, then the failure of the Churches, not only with immigrants, but also with the indigenous population, is abysmal.[12] From the patchy statistical evidence available, it seems likely that the congregation of all denominations in the large conurbations will be at most between 7 and 12% of the population aged 15 and over.

The West Indian migrants in London attend church rarely except for special services. In 1963, about 4% of the West Indians in London attended church regularly.[13] This may not give a representative picture for the whole country. R. B. Davison's sample contained a much higher percentage of regular attenders, with 44% of the male and 57% of the female immigrants attending regularly.[14] In Bradford, also, the rate of attendance seems much higher.[15] However, though the evidence is not completely consistent, the general opinion seems to be that there is a sharp fall-off in church attendance habits among West Indian and West African immigrants, although it would seem that the decline of church attendance habits has been overestimated.

There are of course many reasons why this has happened that have little to do with the attitude and actions of the Churches. The work habits and mobility of the immigrant population, combined with the English climate, all disrupt church-going habits, The Irish immigrants, coming from a similar climate to that of England, with strong inbred church-going habits, seem to have gone through a similar process. It is estimated, for example, that 30 to 50% of Irish Catholic migrants cease to attend Church soon after arrival in this country.[16] If this can happen where a church has such a strong influence on its members, which has many special institutions set up to help its migrant members, and is in many ways an Irish Church, it does not seem so surprising that immigrant groups from other denominations should fall by the wayside. Behaviour which is meaningful in Dublin or Kingston may not be so in London.

Against this must be set the feeling of many West Indian and West African Christian migrants towards their church. There is often a great disappointment at the sparse attendance and at the cool reception they feel they receive,[17] although some churches attract a large number of black immigrants who do feel 'at home'. It will often be the case that one or two churches in an area will account for all the church-going immigrants. The success is generally due to the efforts of the local minister, who often has a special interest in immigrants. The Seventh Day Adventists, for example, have been very successful in attracting West Indian migrants.

For the English Churches, success in attracting the coloured Christian immigrant is usually due to the activities of the local Churchmen. Where the churches have large West Indian congregations they will often also run advisory centres, community centres, and playgroups. Clifford Hill has described in detail the range of activities which conscientious local Churchmen will find themselves engaged in.

The Churchmen will also often be active in local statutory and voluntary organizations which are concerned with immigrants. There is little room for a comprehensive list of individual Churchmen's activities, but various examples spring to mind. The Methodist Mission in Notting Hill, which is run as a group

Ministry, has a strong community base, and one of its ministers is Chairman of the local Social Council. In Sparkbrook, the Reverend Jack Reed was the first Chairman of the Sparkbrook Association, which is very much a community association, and his church is very active in the immigrant community.

Finally, individual Churchmen have a most important part to play as mediators—sponsors, in Collins's terms—for immigrant members of their congregations. This may well extend beyond the simpler task of bringing the individual newcomer as a fellow member into the congregation, although even this task may not be straightforward. Robert Moore has shown how in Sparkbrook a combination of apathy and hostility in some congregations acted as an effective deterrent to immigrants seeking church membership.[18] Research, both here and in the United States, has shown that regular churchgoers are no less inclined than the population at large to display rejecting attitudes towards coloured people. In this situation the priest often has a difficult task to perform: he must reconcile the interests of the newcomer, while retaining the confidence of the existing congregation. Too often the tensions are resolved in favour of the latter, through either lack of conviction or a failure of comprehension.

However, the community based activities of some churches do indicate the great weakness of church attendance figures as an index of the success of the Churches. The contact of the local church with the immigrant community will be very much greater than church attendance figures indicate.[19]

Some mention needs to be made of the growth of Pentecostal Sects among the West Indian immigrants, which some Churchmen see as another indication of the failure of the English Churches. They are seen as undesirable *per se* as their congregations are almost entirely West Indian, and thus form the embryo of a segregated Church. It is thought by some Churchmen that these sects are attracting migrants who were members of the main English Churches in the West Indies. This hypothesis is not supported by much evidence and the main information seems to indicate that the growth is merely due to past practice. These sects are predominantly Jamaican in membership and in 1962 their membership was thought to be between 5 and 10% of the West Indian migrants.[20] Noting that two-thirds of West Indian immigrants came from Jamaica up to mid-1962, this figure should be compared with about 13% of the Jamaican population, who in

1960 gave their denomination as Church of God or Pentecostal.[21]

Whether the growth of these sects in this country is undesirable is a matter of opinion. The social functions they perform in giving comfort and practical help to their members should not be under-estimated. Their growth may be partly due to the hostile environment the coloured immigrant meets in England. Thus, rejected by the local working-class population and having no common feeling with the typical Church community, they may turn to these sects for comfort.[22] When the European Catholic migrants came to England before and after the War, their own priests came with them, conducting services for them and acting as a link with their native culture. It was not seen as sinister nor was it discouraged, and these priests still minister to the spiritual need of these European migrants.

We must conclude that even though there is not complete consistency in the evidence relating to the immigrants' participation in the churches locally, many Churchmen and immigrants feel that the Churches have failed locally to help them in a way that they could and should. It is not that individual Churchmen are not doing a great deal—some examples have already been given and more could be added: it is that there seems to be no drive for action on a broader front. The activities of the individual Churchmen are negligible when viewed against the overall task. As one said recently: 'You work away in your own little plot, with your nose to the grindstone, and when you have time to look up, the whole race situation seems to have become worse.'

There are signs, however, that this inertia is being overcome. Bishops are appointing chaplains with special responsibility for immigrants. Both the Roman Catholic Bishop of Birmingham and the Church of England Bishop of Coventry have full-time chaplains for immigrant affairs. The Group Ministry at Notting Hill was set up through action initiated at the Methodist Church Conference and the Methodists have national and local committees concerned with immigrant affairs. Of the denominations with large numbers of potential members from the Commonwealth in this country, the Roman Catholics, perhaps surprisingly in view of their experiences with previous migrations, have been slowest to devise new institutions for dealing with the problems of coloured immigrants. The emphasis in their effort has tended to rest on providing for students, particularly those from Africa.

There are other denominations whose interest is less direct, in that they have few members among the migrants, but who have none the less been exceedingly active. This is particularly notable in the case of the Quakers. The Race Relations Committee of the Society of Friends is a lineal descendant of the organizations set up during the Quakers' long campaign against slavery. The Committee has pursued an active role from the beginning of the migration and individual Quakers have been prominent in voluntary organizations working in this field. Under this heading we can also consider the Jewish community. American students of race relations frequently express surprise that there has not been in this country any commitment on the part of the Jewish community equivalent to that in the United States, where the work of the Anti-Defamation League has been very influential and the Civil Rights Movement has depended to a large degree on funds contributed by Jewish organizations and individuals. In practice, neither the example set in the United States, nor the analogy with the situation of the East European Jews entering Britain fifty years ago has generated sufficient interest in race relations to produce a significant institutional involvement. There have been exceptions in the case of both individuals and certain Synagogues, and the Council of Christians and Jews has been actively considering problems associated with the growth of prejudice for some years. But, generally, only the brief recrudescence of fascism on the pre-war model has been sufficiently powerful a stimulus to involve the Board of Deputies in this field; and, at least at the time of writing, interest has died down with the decline of such activities and failed to revive.[23]

So far, little has been said of the attitude of the Churches to Asian migrants. These include Muslims, Hindus, and Sikhs, whose religion has a strong influence on their social life and organization. This, together with language difficulties, has presented them with different problems of adjustment compared to the West Indian migrants. Not only have they to contend with racial intolerance, but also with religious intolerance.[24]

However, as there is no recent proselytizing tradition in all but a few Churches in England, it seems unlikely that the missionary activity will blossom. There is ignorance of the Asian religions and customs among Churchmen and this has generally resulted in misunderstanding. Add to this the language difficulties, and inaction is understandable. Individual Churchmen in particular areas have been very successful in giving pastoral help to migrants. The particular problems they have helped to deal with include the isolation of the Muslim women, difficulties in finding jobs, and in finding or establishing places of worship. A number of Churchmen have been involved in this field; viewed against the general potential of the Churches and the total task facing the community, their examples mark the inactivity of the Churches as a whole.

Since 1956, the Churches have been publishing various tracts on race relations. The British Council of Churches, to which all the main English Churches, except the Catholics, belong, has kept a watching brief on the migration from the outset, and published, in 1956, *Your Neighbour from the West Indies*, and, more recently, *Immigrants in Britain*. It acts as a mouthpiece for the Churches on immigrant matters. In 1958, after the race riots, it published a strongly worded resolution, and it has also commented on the discriminatory aspects of the various Commonwealth Immigrants Acts. In addition, the Church of England, through the Board of Social Responsibility, publishes information on its attitude to immigrants and produces information for its spokesmen. Various individual Churchmen, especially in the Nonconformist Churches, have published books and pamphlets on the Christian attitude to immigrants. The Catholic Church, through the Catholic Institute for International Relations (formerly The Sword of the Spirit) has also produced a series of pamphlets, as has the Race Relations Committee of the Society of Friends, which also issues a Newsletter. These all express liberal views and provide information intended to lay the various myths which have grown up about coloured immigrants. Together with this general educational material, the Churches have also published school and educational material on immigrants. The Christian Education movement and the C.I.I.R. have published teaching kits and the Student Christian Movement have produced a guide for teachers.

From the Churches' newspapers there has been a flow of information about immigrants and favourable comment on the activities of ministers working with immigrants.

In the speeches of the leaders of the Churches and in their communications to their 'flock', there has been a similar flow of liberal pronouncements on racial issues. Examples of this sort of activity are the speeches of the Archbishop of Canterbury, Lord Soper, and other Church representatives in the Lords on the various Commonwealth Immigrants Acts and Race Relations Bills. In 1968, the whole Bench of Bishops and the Nonconformist representatives voted against the Government on the question of admission of British citizens of Asian origin from Kenya. On a similar level are the speeches in the Convocations of York and Canterbury in 1959 and the motion recently passed by the Church Assembly which states 'that this Assembly welcomes the declared intention of the Government to extend the scope of the Race Relations Act 1965, and endorses the recommendations of the Street Report that the Act should be extended to include housing, employment, shops, and the provision of services (including insurance and credit facilities)'. This resolution was based on recommendations from the Standing Committee on Migration of the British Council of Churches. Also in 1968, Cardinal Heenan issued a pastoral letter, read in every church in his diocese of Westminster, on the treatment of immigrants. It cannot be doubted, after reading what Churchmen have written and said on racial prejudice and discrimination, where they stand. The main fault is the lack of a co-ordinated national campaign to attack discrimination. Communication of information and opinion on a broader front would add considerably to the effectiveness of a campaign for tolerance and charity towards coloured immigrants.

It is interesting to note that two of the three coloured immigrants writing in a recent Christian symposium on race thought that the Church leaders 'have been far too content to follow public opinion rather than trying to change it'.[25] In respect to racial issues this does not seem to be borne out, but it may well be the impression many people receive because of the lack of adequate communication between the leaders of the Churches and the congregations.

The Churches in England, and the Church of England in particular, own some very valuable assets, many of which are not utilized fully, even for ritual and congregational activities. The assets of the Churches which are of particular interest from the local communities' point of view are the churches and church halls. Control of these buildings is often split between the Diocesan Commissioners and the parochial councils. If there is agreement between these two bodies on the use of their buildings for social purposes, there is a great gain by the local community. If, however, as often happens, there is disagreement, or, more likely, a lack of local or Diocesan initiative, then valuable buildings remain under-used or unused. In addition, changes in use or redevelopment of church premises for housing or community centres are often prevented by the legal aspects of church ownership.

This problem can be overcome and there are various Christian Housing Associations who have built on church land. But this activity, however, is only touching the fringe of the problem—'the number of Churches considering using land for housing is very few indeed, despite the present need'.[26] (Direct help for the immigrant community through housing associations has also been undertaken; this will be discussed elsewhere.)

Connected with this problem of mobilizing church buildings for community activities is that of the duplication of buildings between denominations. This emphasizes the need for a national policy on the part of the Churches if any real progress is to be achieved. It impinges on the whole question of the role of the Churches in the urban areas with long standing social problems related to housing, health, and welfare. It will be mainly in these areas that immigrants will live for some time to come. The local Churchmen individually cannot be expected to deal with these problems unsupported, and the use of church buildings is one very vital aspect of the problem.

There is another group of assets over which the Churches, particularly the Church of England and the Catholic Church, exercise control, that of schools. In 1963, places in denominational schools both primary and secondary accounted for 21% of the total places available.[27] In primary schools alone the Churches have a much greater share of total places. They can thus have a strong influence on the educational policy on racial issues throughout the country, and some steps have been taken in this direction, as was mentioned earlier.

It has been suggested that the denominational character of the school may inadvertently exclude immigrant children.[28] For the Church of England primary schools this suggestion is not supported by the evidence available from the Department of Education and Science, as Table 21.1 shows. Roman Catholic schools, however, have a consistently lower than average percentage of immigrant pupils, especially in Birmingham, where they have 16,000 out of 110,000 primary school places and where there are numbers of West Indian Roman Catholics. It is interesting to note in this context that earlier this year Bishop Leary, Catholic Bishop of Birmingham, asked his school managers to take Asian children as pupils, wherever possible, to ease the burden on other schools in the area.

Table 21.1. Maintained primary schools, January 1968[29]

Number of immigrant pupils as a % of the number of school roll by denomination

	Church of England	Roman Catholic	County primary	All
Birmingham	13	1	11·1	9·7
Walsall	5·0	5·8	6·3	6·2
Warley	9·8	2·9	5·4	5·6
West Bromwich	27·4	8·4	11·1	13·2
Wolverhampton	12·1	6·9	9·8	9·7

The welfare services run by the Churches do not directly impinge on the problems that have been discussed. They reflect, however, aspects of Christian concern for the deprived members of the community, and the traditions of Christian action for the community. Consideration of these services draws attention to the Salvation Army and the Quakers who have made large contributions in the field compared with their following in the community. It also draws our attention to the sort of effort the Churches can make in areas where they feel Christian action is needed. If similar efforts could be made by all the Churches in tackling the problems in the decaying areas of cities, it would go some way to bringing some measure of social justice to those who live there.

2. VOLUNTEERS FOR INTEGRATION

It is impossible in a section of this length to cover all the varieties of voluntary organization which were set up to help solve 'race' or 'community' problems, or which, set up for other purposes, tried to influence the situation, to make their particular contribution. Attention here is mainly focused on local, borough, or neighbourhood-based committees set up to promote 'good relations' between immigrants and the native population. This is not to say that some national voluntary organizations were not particularly active: the Society of Friends Race Relations Committee, for example, and Community Service Volunteers. The former is a good example of an organization spanning the religious and secular spheres of activity, whose style was closely related to other organizations functioning at a local level. As we saw in the previous section, the leadership provided by most religious organizations is limited to the national level; it has been epitomized in the symbolic role of the Archbishop of Canterbury, the first Chairman of the National Committee for Commonwealth Immigrants. One curiosity has been that radical lobbying organizations have not participated in this field to anything like the extent that might have been predicted. One hybrid, Racial Unity, did combine the style of these radical organizations with the welfare approach of a religious body; but after an active existence during the earlier stages of the migration, it faded into inactivity. But the explicitly political organizations of the left, for example, the Movement for Colonial Freedom, have displayed only spasmodic interest in this field; the National Council for Civil Liberties' involvement is also of relatively recent date—basically, from the period of the Mosley punch-ups, in 1962. Despite the increased concern of the National Council and other radical bodies, their impact has in general not been great and it is at the local level that the main contribution of voluntary organizations has been made. The Community Service Volunteers is one of the few organizations that has applied in local situations a broad approach deriving from its general concerns.

From the beginning, as the preceding chapters have indicated, integration was regarded by Whitehall as essentially a matter for local institutions: local government, and local offices of central departments, assisted by the specialized services of the British Caribbean Welfare Service (later Migrant Services Division of the West Indian Federal High Commission). In addition, much was expected from voluntary organizations, for the inevitable complement of *laissez-faire* at the centre was reliance on volunteers. The move towards co-ordination, begun by the Commonwealth Immigrants Advisory Council in 1964, was eventually legitimized in the setting up of the National Committee for Commonwealth Immigrants, which sanctioned the concept of Government involvement, through the direction and financing of voluntary effort. But, even after the establishment of a fully-staffed central secretariat, co-ordination tended to be at best a loosely conceived operation. The central body dealt, one might say, with the N.C.C.I.'s output, with conferences, pamphlets, relations with local committees: the input—analyses, ideas, policy recommendations, written work—rested almost exclusively upon volunteer effort. For the specialist Panels of the N.C.C.I., which drew on the contributions of experts in the fields concerned, were also, in effect, voluntary bodies. (We have dealt with their contribution in discussion of the various subject areas with which they were concerned.)

In August 1965, when the White Paper was published, there were in existence three main kinds of local organizations: immigrant organizations, including some formed and run by West Indians but with an inter-racial membership; local 'campaign' committees, established to oppose racial discrimination; and local voluntary liaison committees, established with the broader aim of promoting harmonious integration of immigrant groups. The role of liaison committee was defined (in para. 66 of the White Paper) in terms of involving people of influence in the community as well as immigrants in the work of the committee. The majority of the English-formed local voluntary committees, in fact, adopted this strategy and it was these which were singled out for official recognition, and official support, in the White Paper and subsequently by the N.C.C.I. A major part of the N.C.C.I.'s work has been the promotion of such committees, and it contributes a matching grant towards the salary of liaison officers to serve with existing committees.* When a new committee is set up, local authority support is first sought—a procedure which can give rise to difficulties. However, the first two years of the N.C.C.I.'s operations saw a great increase in the number of committees and the appointment of thirty-two liaison officers.

Before the N.C.C.I. was established, the voluntary liaison committees† had a variety of sponsors: some were set up on the initiative of councils of social service, others were established by the local trades council, and some by the local authorities themselves. The degree to which immigrants joined in the formation of committees also varied.

Some committees dated from the early 1950s and had been intended to deal with problems created by the new arrival of immigrants: 'liaison' could mean co-operation between different social welfare and other agencies. Others had been formed after the 1958 Notting Hill and Nottingham 'riots' with the purpose of

* This section was written during the lifetime of the N.C.C.I. At the end of November 1968, the N.C.C.I. was replaced by the statutory Community Relations Commission which was set up under the 1968 Race Relations Act.

† The title of voluntary liaison committee was conferred on these organizations when the N.C.C.I. was set up in 1965. We use the term to describe them even before this date.

promoting racial harmony. But between the mid-1950s, when the liaison committees in their present form first began to appear, and their enshrinement in an official structure in 1965, the dimensions of 'race relations' in Britain were totally changed by a number of events and decisions of profound importance. Part of the difficulties that have subsequently arisen can be put down to these changes and the lack of flexibility in the structure devised for a different set of circumstances.

Mary Grigg has described the difficulties of the voluntary liaison committees in trying to adapt to a changing situation:

> The function of a liaison committee, which originally was to express the goodwill of the community, has now become a matter of grappling with the ill-will of the community. . . . [A] committee set up to cope with a limited local problem, can scarcely adjust itself overnight to understanding and tackling the local symptoms of a national disease.[30]

The perspective of the early voluntary organizations can be partly defined in negative terms: they did not see the problems as racial ones. As R. A. Burt put it: 'The dominant response of the formal social organisations dealing with the West Indian immigrant population has been a refusal to view the social problems within racial categorisations.'[31] Mary Grigg has characterized the voluntary liaison committees as 'the voice of conscience of the local establishment. They were built up on a belief that a few newcomers needed some help and friendly guidance and that there was nothing fundamentally wrong with the local community.'[32]

Some committees seem to have been overtly paternalistic: for example, the title of one formed in Bristol, Committee for the Welfare of Colonial Workers, which included representatives from the Co-operative Society, the Council of Social Service, the Council of Churches, the Chamber of Commerce, the Immigration Department of the Home Office, Her Majesty's Prisons, the National Assistance Board, and the Society of Friends.[33] This committee did not in fact survive the long winter of *laissez-faire* in the 1950s. More typical of the later pattern was the Nottingham Commonwealth Citizens Consultative Committee, formed in 1954 and sponsored by the Council of Social Service, the Council of Churches, and a number of local Commonwealth immigrant representatives. The committee had been formed partly at the instigation of Ivo de Souza, then Welfare Liaison Officer for West Indians at the Colonial Office and subsequently with the British

Caribbean Welfare service. Neither the local authority nor the statutory authorities initially played a prominent role. A three-year grant from the Pilgrim Trust in 1956 enabled the Committee to appoint a full-time secretary (Miss Dorothy Wood), and it was only in 1960 that the local authority became the main source of funds. The main purpose of the Nottingham Committee was quite simply to provide practical help for immigrants, and was in effect a broadening out of activities which had been started by the Council of Social Service as far back as 1951: personal counselling and an employment advisory service were two of the early services organized by the Committee, both in time handed over respectively to the Council of Social Service and the Ministry of Labour. In 1956, a Coloured People's Housing Association was set up, which over the following ten years bought about thirty houses. In 1959, Eric Irons, a leading West Indian member of the Association, was appointed by the local authority as an educational organizer with special reference to the needs of coloured people. Later he became a J.P.

The Notting Hill and Nottingham 'race riots' of 1958 did not fundamentally alter the perspective of these organizations. The most significant change seems to have been a shift away from the idea of 'welfare for immigrants' and towards an idea of 'education for the host community'. For example, one of the first actions of the newly formed Willesden Friendship Council was to commission research into the attitudes of local residents towards racial issues, to assess the amount of prejudice. On the basis of the findings, the author, Joan Maizels, urged that a major education programme be undertaken by the Council in co-operation with schools, trade unions, and so on.[34] Paradoxically, one of the effects of the Notting Hill episode may have been to disguise problems of discrimination. It is true that racial violence took place: but on the other hand, British society, in the person of Mr. Justice Salmon, condemned it, and some at least of the culprits were severely punished. There was a mushrooming of new voluntary organizations, most of which were concerned to preserve racial harmony. This change of definition produced a change of emphasis in the work undertaken. 'Bad' race relations were equated with mass violence; 'good' race relations merely with the absence of violence. This was particularly true of many local authorities. The attitude of many of the London boroughs in 1959 was, 'we have no problem' or 'we are watching the situation and it is fully under control'.[35] In other words, they viewed race relations as a problem of public order, rather than any other kind of problem. There was also a reluctance to become involved at all. In October 1958, the London Council of Social Service called a meeting to discuss the situation preparatory to establishing an immigrants advisory committee. Seventeen London boroughs sent representatives: Kensington was not one of them. The attitude of the local authorities was important not only because they had decision-making power but also because the voluntary committees were often dependent on them for funds, and any success they could achieve was to depend almost entirely on their relationship with their local authority. This failure in response on the part of the local authorities was significant not only in itself but because it closed the door to the possibility that other authorities would follow the example of Birmingham and of the consortium of Black Country authorities who had formed the Commonwealth Welfare Council for the West Midlands. The activities undertaken by the full-time officers working for these authorities consisted in part of welfare work (on the basis of individual cases) and also of referrals to local government agencies. This work, which, though limited in scope, was in its own terms effective, depended on a definition of the immigrants' position which was no longer acceptable.

The reluctance of the local authorities to commit themselves was also reflected in the avoidance of the issue by elected representatives. The possibility that they might intervene, in a mediating capacity or even as spokesmen for the minority, which was already for other reasons remote, receded even further. Only a few individuals conceived their role as including activity on behalf of immigrant constituents.

The various local 'liaison' committees set out to promote their goal of peaceful integration by undertaking a variety of activities on a rather limited scale. Mixed social gatherings, 'international' exhibitions, or events, functioned as symbolic offers of welcome to immigrants, and could provide mild propaganda for the host population if they were attended by local dignitaries. No commitment to a policy more specific than harmony and friendship was required. The function of the social occasions whether arranged by a club or a voluntary liaison committee could vary. If organized for no particular purpose than to 'mix' people, they could become a matter of non-representative English meeting non-representative immigrants, a dilemma familiar to many middle-class voluntary workers in other fields. Collins described such an organizatory meeting in a school 'on kiddies' chairs', in which the 'middle-class elite, M.P.s, reverends and idealists . . . unblinkingly faced the robustness of the migrants, and with their beautiful English manners politely observed the invisible gulf which existed between themselves and their dark brothers; that bridge which could be crossed only by the new West Indian quasi-elite, who inserted himself in the middle, in a kind of social no-man's-land.'[36] But where these meetings took place, to celebrate, for example, the opening of a new community centre for an immigrant group, they could be a kind of social sealing-wax, a friendship ritual closing a period of conflict about the establishment of the centre. Where they were for purposes of entertainment or enjoyment, they could simply provide just that.*

One of the main functions of some of the committees was a kind of U.N.-trouble shooter role: harmony in action. This involved the provision of 'conciliation' officers, to go and talk to the parties when cases of personal racial friction occurred. The best example is that of Willesden Friendship Council's work, in resolving or quieting disputes between landlord and tenant, in many cases immigrant landlords and native tenants, by sending a multiracial team to discuss the grievances. The technique was extended by some committees to cases of racial discrimination, prior to the 1968 Race Relations Act. In Nottingham, lawyers attached to the Housing Association formed by the Committee, also attempted to conciliate in cases of housing discrimination. Their experience indicated that without legal sanctions, such 'persuasive' work was doomed to failure. Effective action on this front had to await the passage of legislation against discrimination.

Despite its limited practical application, conciliation to clear up misunderstandings has on the whole been the accepted role of the committees. Protest, in the form of marches or demonstrations, tended to be discouraged. Most of the committees were inhibited from taking a more active part in opposing discrimination by their overall perspective: the need to preserve racial harmony and to bring people together. Exposing discrimination and fighting it was seen as likely, respectively, to make the coloured minorities feel

* One of the more elaborate attempts to arrange inter-racial activity was Willesden Friendship Council's jazz-ballet group, also described by Collins. He found that the Council 'presented a unique achievement in London between the migrant and the English where they managed to get the full support of the borough officials and the community as a whole'.

separate from the British, and to alienate the British from the voluntary liaison committees.

The voluntary liaison committees, both before and after the introduction of co-ordination, rejected confrontation, even as a last resort. This was due partly to a conviction that getting on with the powers that be was likely to produce better results than protest, partly to scepticism about claims of discrimination, and partly to the general view that sources of conflict between groups should not be stressed. The ambivalent approach to racial discrimination meant that few of the voluntary liaison committees in the post-1965 period played any part in the prolonged campaign to extend the Race Relations Act 1965. It led to radical criticism of their position, expressed by Dipak Nandy:

Voluntary liaison committees have always had a choice, one which has been masked by the imprecision of the concept of 'liaison' (for it suggests a symmetrical two-way relationship which does not obtain in real life). The choice is between interpreting the demands for equal opportunities of the minority to the dominant white society and, on the other hand, acting as spokesman of that society to the minority group. In effect, the voluntary liaison committees have uniformly chosen the second alternative.[37]

Most of the voluntary liaison committees, and many other voluntary organizations, attempted some form of work which can be classified as 'welfare' work: advising individuals, helping to fight court cases, setting up housing associations or children's play-groups, and so on. Inevitably, only a handful of people could possibly benefit from these efforts. Burt, for example, found that there was great praise, officially, for a housing association in Paddington, which after two years' existence had bought one house and re-housed five families. The local borough council had refused to grant funds to it.[38] As we have suggested earlier, housing associations have tended to be of restricted value to immigrants; but it was natural that voluntary liaison committees should wish to be involved in projects which appeared to have a practical application. Nevertheless, it is possible to name some groups (liaison committees and others) where 'welfare' work has either made an impression upon the existing social work agencies, or has had a political function in illuminating the need for national policy or municipal policy changes.

Since the end of the 1950s, and especially in the post-1965

period, voluntary liaison committees have been discouraged from undertaking welfare services specifically for immigrants, and from doing individual casework. They have come to see their role as one of encouraging the adaptation of existing statutory agencies to meet the needs of a society with immigrant populations: basically an advisory and information-giving role. If a local committee can muster sufficient expertise, then it is possible to see how this function can be useful to the various professional workers coming into contact with immigrant groups. Nottingham Voluntary Liaison Committee's work, in getting the Technical College and employers to establish training courses, is an example. The same committee raised with the city architect whether some houses could be built of a size to suit Indian extended families. Sometimes a committee may also be used by a local authority department to advise on or endorse a political decision. For example, Brent Voluntary Liaison Committee was asked by the local authority education department to comment upon the 7/65 Education Circular dealing with the 30% quota. But how much influence the voluntary liaison committee has depends to a great extent on the professional workers', or the local officials' own attitudes. The education department of an authority may have a closer relationship with a voluntary liaison committee than the housing department. This in turn may depend upon the fact that an education sub-committee of a voluntary liaison committee may be composed of teachers, whose conclusions will fall very much within an acceptable and known framework of reference. In the case of housing, the required policy will probably involve a radical departure from hitherto accepted principles. In acting as advisers, the voluntary liaison committees have to depend on their own expertise and upon diplomacy to make headway.* They are not expected to engage in political combat with local agencies or local authorities, and many would certainly be reluctant to do so: how could they win?

* Some of the limitations under which the voluntary liaison committees operate were inadvertently illustrated by Elizabeth Burney's findings on Nottingham's housing policies. Nottingham V.L.C. had been in existence for more than ten years, as one of the more active and committed of the local committees. Yet almost no coloured families had been housed on the council estates. Elizabeth Burney suggested that one reason for this was the 'extraordinary ignorance' among immigrants of Nottingham's council house system. This does suggest that the V.L.C. had, at least until recently (when an advisory service was established), failed to get through to its immigrant constituents. But of course there were other reasons why so few immigrant families were housed on council estates; as Burney says, there was 'a deliberate policy of re-housing them in old terraced houses acquired for the purpose'.[39]

However, since so much of the 'welfare' of immigrants, and the future of race relations, is dependent upon local political decisions, it must be expected that the more vigorous voluntary liaison committees will increasingly cross the line from adviser to protagonist. For example, Ealing International Friendship Committee has produced a detailed criticism of the local education authority's 'dispersal scheme' and called for basic changes in the way it is organized. [40]

The concept of 'community work' now adopted by the National Committee for Commonwealth Immigrants and the voluntary liaison committees has been best demonstrated in action by other kinds of organizations. The Sparkbrook Association, [41] working in an area with only 15,000 residents, has shown what can be done to improve the amenities and morale of a neighbourhood on a non-political basis. The incidental success of the Association has been to prevent problems of 'urban decay' turning into race relations' problems. Many of those who participated in the Association's work could have turned instead to anti-immigrant work. The Association had no views on some of the most important issues of race relations: such as immigration control; and locally, the implications for race relations of the Birmingham Corporation Act, which increased the local authority's power to limit multi-occupation. It was not intended to deal with racial injustice. Its function was to channel grievances into practical work to improve the area.

A broadly similar range of activities was undertaken by the Notting Hill Social Council in North Kensington. A deluge of voluntary organizations of all description had burst upon the area after the disturbances of 1958, but in most areas the sheer scale of the problem had been too much for their limited resources. As Burt commented in 1960, 'the necessarily limited scope of any individual welfare project in North Kensington can only be overwhelmed by the uncontrollable magnitude of the problem confronted in the area'. [42] The Social Council, based on a Methodist group ministry, survived, where other voluntary bodies were engulfed, to undertake a series of practical projects directed towards community organization to tackle grievances held in common: it was still functioning effectively when the flamboyant descent of a new wave of volunteers on the area in 1967 began the cycle of activity and frustration over again.

In a different style altogether were groups like the Islington branch of the Campaign Against Racial Discrimination. Local C.A.R.D. groups began to be formed in 1966, at first largely as a result of individual action rather than any central planning. Most of the groups followed patterns of action established by the earlier 'campaign' committees, such as the Campaign for Racial Equality groups in Leicester and Bradford: individual casework, collection of evidence of discrimination, 'counter propaganda', and protest action. One of the main activities of Islington C.A.R.D. was to organize tenants to protect or gain their rights under the various Rent Acts. This was a highly political group, formed to deal with racial injustice. Its activities were intensive and involved aggressive protests against some local landlords and sometimes the local housing authority. Its ideology was popular participation, not the provision of services. But, as in Sparkbrook, the effect was the joint organization of efforts to combat problems common to immigrants and non-immigrants.[43]

The voluntary liaison committees, working in areas with populations ranging from 100,000 to over 1,000,000, were not designed to do this kind of intensive local work. How they interpret the concept of 'community relations' remains to be seen.

One committee, the Camden Committee for Community Relations, has pushed the orthodox concept to the furthest point so far achieved. It is in Camden that the most ambitious campaign of public education has been undertaken and where the attempt to reach various key groups with influence over vital aspects of the lives of immigrants, like estate agents, has been tackled most systematically. Both in the provision of play groups and the sponsoring of housing associations, Camden's contribution has been better co-ordinated than that of other comparable committees. But even Camden was paralysed by the difficulties that arose in 1968, when the Government's casual treatment of the N.C.C.I. over the issue of the Kenya Asians split the whole voluntary liaison movement, and the wide range of activities undertaken, though impressive on paper, have had only a marginal effect on the lives of newcomers.

We have already referred to the Society of Friends Race Relations Committee. This committee, like the voluntary liaison committees, sets out to stimulate others to take action (in this case local action by Friends) and to educate the public. But it also has as one of its aims to influence national policy, which means that it is obliged to take up a position on national policy issues. The Committee has established a community centre in Islington; it has worked as a national lobby against the prevailing immigration policy and for the extension of the Race Relations Act 1965; and it has worked with the Immigrants Advisory Committee of the London Council of Social Service, and the N.C.C.I., in mounting conferences for professional groups who come into contact with immigrants. It affiliated with C.A.R.D.

One local organization has succeeded in combining the role of 'campaign' committee with the advisory and educative functions of the V.L.C.: the Oxford Committee for Racial Integration. This committee, using the threat of publicity as a sanction, has had some success in ending discrimination by local employers. It was unique in its acknowledgement of the extent of racial discrimination and the lengths to which its members and officers went in order to end it. O.C.R.I.'s negotiations were conducted not so much to deal with cases of friction but in order to end a discriminatory practice. O.C.R.I. members were willing, not to disturb public order, but to run the risk of being accused of doing so, in order to publicize and end discrimination. Their picket of Annette's Hairdressing Salon, after months of negotiation, was, however, very much out of line with the attitudes of most of the liaison committees. Both in Manchester and Brent, the local branches of C.A.R.D. complained that the voluntary liaison committees had tried to prevent protest action against alleged police misconduct in the area.

Looking back upon the whole period from 1955 to the present day, it is clear that it was too much to expect that 'integration' could be decisively promoted or affected by the local voluntary committees unless they had had more political backing. Race relations in Britain were formed by forces beyond their control and their own attitudes were influenced by the same forces. There was bound to be an element of 'tokenism' in the voluntary efforts to provide services which would be of real use to immigrants. Nevertheless, on a limited scale, the provision of a special training course, of a day-nursery, of a legal advice service, which would not otherwise have existed was not futile activity, especially in the smaller boroughs. Where the voluntary committees could have contributed more, but chose on the whole not to do so, was in anti-discrimination work. Here, many of the members shared the prevailing general view that the 'problems' derived from the strangeness of immigrants, rather than from racialism in the 'host' community or its institutions. After the P.E.P. Report (of which the N.C.C.I. was part sponsor) and the change in public attitudes towards discrimination, many of the voluntary liaison committees have devoted more attention to it—one or two have even been prepared to tackle complex and controversial issues like relationships with the police. But in general, the role which most of the officially recognized voluntary local organizations have adopted has been a confused combination of the advisory and the educational. The execution of this role is hampered by lack of access to sources of power and funds, and the voluntary liaison committees which have been 'pro-integration' have inevitably been attacked from both sides, an uncomfortable process for the liaison officers.

Community relations work, to be successful, requires special qualities in the liaison officer. First of these is a degree of professionalism which many of them have lacked, as a result of inadequate training. The officer should be able to originate and organize projects, and for this work he requires initiative but he must also be able to carry his committee with him. In some cases there has been conflict between the officer and his committee because each has had a different conception of his role: some committees and their executive have relied heavily on the liaison officer; some have required him to be a paid secretary and little else; and in others he has been controlled by the town clerk or some other official in the town hall. In matters of subordination he is in an ambiguous position; in the terms of the White Paper he is the direct servant of the committee, but his salary is provided by the N.C.C.I., which has to be satisfied about his competence before he is appointed. He depends on the N.C.C.I. in other ways: for training courses, for advice on his work, which is given through the development officers, and he may look to the N.C.C.I. for help in resolving conflicts that may arise between him and his committee officers. To these ambiguities in his operational subordination should be added the pressures from different elements in his 'constituency', who may interpret the purposes of the voluntary liaison committee in very different ways. As he is required to involve the whole community in this community relations work, he needs diplomatic skills of a high order.

The position of the N.C.C.I. itself has also suffered from similar ambiguities. It is the grant giving body and, in the words of the White Paper, it was expected 'to build up a comprehensive body of doctrine which can be flexibly applied to a variety of local situations'.[45] In fact, once a voluntary liaison committee has appointed an officer, the N.C.C.I. loses all direct power of control; it can only offer advice, which may be refused. As a result, no comprehensive body of doctrine has been built up and the flexibility has had to be very considerable.

Although the voluntary liaison committees have not been, nor attempted to be, 'mass' organizations in any sense, they have been in many areas, as Michael Dummett pointed out, 'the principal close contact that members of immigrant organizations had with the white community, and [have] determined the picture which they formed of what their supposed allies in that community were like'.[46] On the other side, for many of the English participants in the committees, contact with immigrant representatives was their introduction to the problems of racial discrimination. Ideally, this interaction between 'people of influence'—both from the 'host' and immigrant communities—would give the immigrants a share in the decision-making process, and increase the understanding of the English. But this ideal rested on an assumption about the goodwill of the host community—particularly the decision-makers—which has been steadily eroded in the past ten years. This does not mean that the strategy of seeking to involve people of influence has become invalid, although its validity may well vary from borough to borough. It does mean, however, that the methods used to achieve this, and even more important, the actual content of the involvement, need to be re-examined. In many areas, the committees may choose to function as propaganda groups and as local pressure groups, without engaging in protest action. But both roles depend upon the members of the committee having clear views on the general issues of immigration and race relations in Britain, and upon public policies, as implemented or devised at the local level. The danger facing the voluntary liaison committees is that they may become remote, both from the ordinary citizen, and from the springs of power within their area, and become window-dressing for local authorities indifferent and even hostile to equal rights for minorities.

3. THE ANTI-IMMIGRATION LOBBY

The task of the anti-integration groups was in many ways easier than that of the pro-integration ones. Their basic function was to be a political lobby for goals of extreme simplicity: 'a halt to immigration, and subsequently repatriation' of immigrants. That is to say, the basic concepts on which their policies were founded were simple, although their practical consequences would be complex and difficult (if not impossible) to implement. Both advocates and opponents accepted it as a basic proposition that there were problems. For the proponents, these were problems revealed by immigrants but not necessarily—or only to a limited extent— created by their presence. In consequence, they sought solutions, economic, political, psychological, which involved changing attitudes and reforming institutions in society as a whole. Their opponents, on the other hand, had no need to seek such elaborate and complex solutions, for, to them, all these problems would be solved by the single act of ending immigration or by getting rid of immigrants already here through 'repatriation'. For these groups the 'solution' had come first, an expression of their own hostility; and the problems were adduced as reinforcing evidence for their campaign. The initial impetus was given to this campaign by the Conservative Government's failure to defend an over-extended position credibly; and their task was made easier as the politicians, constantly conceding ground by urging or defending stricter control, identified the presence of immigrants with the existence of problems. But while the all-party formula evolved after 1964 was 'stricter control of entry, but equality in Britain', this proposition was not acceptable to the anti-integration groups.

In one sense this is understandable, since the opponents of integration were starting from a position of failure. As the Government's White Paper pointed out, by 1965, Britain was already a 'multi-racial' society. Not even the total ban on immigration sought by all the immigration control associations could alter that. And the Race Relations Acts of 1965 and 1968 together constitute a formidable obstacle to the removal of civil rights in Britain. But the constant attention focused upon immigration control has helped to affect the position of those already here as citizens. A few more turns can still be given to the screw of control, but the main interest of the anti-integration groups in the future is likely to turn increasingly to the situation in Britain. Not only because of the stricter controls at the gate, but also because of the kinds of organization which have increasingly become prominent.

Although a variety of right-wing racialist or 'nationalist' political parties have grown up in this country since the end of the Second World War, their importance should not be got out of proportion. Mosley's Union Movement; the League of Empire

Loyalists; Colin Jordan's National Socialist Movement; the British National Party: these organizations have obtained little significant support. They have been dependent upon the provocation of violent clashes and upon court cases for attention. Publicity is their life blood: only a temporary, and largely fortuitous conjunction of events in 1962–4, conferred any significance on them and that conjunction soon passed. More recently, the League of Empire Loyalists and the British National Party have united, together with some members of the newer Racial Preservation Society, to form the National Front. This, in turn, at the time of writing, seems to be splitting—a characteristic process in the sub-world of small extremist groups.

Most of the ground that has been made by extremist organizations has been gained by newer groups which are not political parties but are formed on an explicitly anti-immigrant platform. A series of such organizations appeared at the beginning of the 1960s: the Birmingham Immigration Control Association, formed in 1960, and the schismatical British Immigration Control Association, set up by Donald Finney in Smethwick in 1961. Their role in the debates on immigration control in 1960–2 and later in the electoral campaign in Smethwick has been examined by Paul Foot, who shows how they provided an essential ingredient in Peter Griffiths' success in 1964.[47]

These organizations evaporated after the Act of 1962, but some continuity can be traced through the Argus Briton's Rights Association, whose programme was as follows: to combat the establishment of a multi-racial society; to resist by all constitutional means enforced integration; to preserve and protect the English way of life and culture; and to combat the erosion of the individual Briton's rights. An American influence is apparent in the stress on the theme of individual rights, which derives partly from the provisions on racial incitement in Clause 6 of the Race Relations Act of 1965. It almost distinguishes these groups from the authoritarian 'nationalism' of the earlier political parties. The A.B.R.A. developed into another organization, the Racial Preservation Society, which added another theme: racial harmony. One of the beliefs of the Society is that the 'racial problems of the world cannot be solved by means of persecution, extremism, or by any form of violence but only by peaceful separation'.

The main tactic of the immigration control associations has been political lobbying through organized letter-writing to the local and national press, to M.P.s, and to other public figures. The following procedure has been recommended: 'first of all take leaflets [centrally supplied (ed.)] round to the houses next door. Next night call and ask if they are interested . . . but first of all write a number of letters to your local papers . . . sign them "English Rights Association" '. The R.P.S.'s main activity has been the printing and distribution of the *Sussex News* and the *Midland News*, its journals. Mass distribution of these papers has been made in the Midlands and the south of England and they have certainly reached a far larger audience than the shoestring magazines of the political parties of the far right. The contents of the papers have consisted of, for example, lists of scientists who believe that racial differences are more than a matter of physical characteristics; letters from apparently eminent supporters, or sometimes from the occasional educated coloured man who purports to utter threats based on the numerical strength of the immigrants; photographs, uncaptioned, of dark-skinned men with pale-skinned girls; various statistics of birth-rates, and disease and crime rates on an ethnic basis from the United States or Britain; and a wholly tendentious 'opinion poll'.[48] Members of the R.P.S. were eventually prosecuted under the Race Relations Act of 1965, but without success—largely, in the view of a well-informed observer, because the prosecution had not prepared its case with any understanding of the issues likely to be raised.[49]

Tenants' and residents' associations provide the other main institutional basis for organized opposition to integration. It would not be accurate to say that more than a handful of such organizations have been directly concerned with 'the race problem': none the less, attempts to prevent property sales or the letting of local authority accommodation to coloured people either through existing organizations or the establishment of *ad hoc* bodies has been quite common. Elizabeth Burney quotes one example of the way in which the issue is viewed. A Mr. Rhodes of the Clairegate and Blakely District R.A. told her:

The aim is to keep up the amenities—that means stopping the neighbourhood going downhill. It *will* go down, of course, but we may delay it. Oh, it means agreeing to maintain our gardens, and lobbying the Council to mend the pavement. Keeping out coloureds? No, we couldn't do it. They are bound to come. Other Associations have tried, but they've failed because people turn round and say 'You give me so much, or I'll sell to coloureds.' I've got strong personal views you know, but they are my own views. . . . you can't live in the same street as them.[50]

These anxieties over declining amenities are genuine: the perception of the coloured intruder as the cause of decline or the instrument of its acceleration is mistaken, but is commonly held and strongly entrenched, as data presented in Chapter 28 shows.

But other organizations are horses of a different colour. Some bodies describing themselves as residents' or tenants' associations, in fact appear to devote all their time to opposing immigration, sometimes in open or tacit alliances with other bodies, such as the National Front or the R.P.S., or with immigration control associations—for example, an organization with Mrs. Joy Page as secretary, calling itself the London and Counties Tenants' Federation. Mrs. Page has been a constant contributor to the local and national press with her letters calling for an immediate end to immigration. One characteristic example appeared in the Southall edition of the *Middlesex County Times*, in which she argues:

The country's doors are to be left wide open to the surplus populations of four of the quickest breeding peoples in the world; housing is to be made exclusively available for them in the Midlands—according to the Home Secretary; in spite of the country's economic cutbacks, even more of the taxpayer's money—£30,000 of it—is to be made available to the Archbishop of Canterbury's Immigration Committee. . . . And in a few days time we are about to be asked to accept an extension to the Race Relations Act which will enable immigrants to take over houses wholesale.[51]

Mrs. Page, to whom the *Daily Telegraph* has thought it right to open its correspondence columns on many occasions, also quotes a range of familiar, and often dated, statistics to support her case. When the 'national' Immigration Control Association was formed in June 1968, its fourteen committee members were said to include representatives from tenants' and residents' associations in Southall, Slough, Millwall, and South London. Its Chairman was a Conservative Councillor from Lambeth; its Secretary none other than Mrs. Page.

To an extent, the anti-integration campaigners are a stage army: the same names occur constantly; the letters they send to the Press are often virtually identical. A Black Country editor has commented:

With notable exceptions racialists seem even more illiterate than the people about whom they complain. Moreover they are surprisingly limited in their ideas and accusations. They persistently ring the changes on the same few allegations which we have long ago on careful investigation found to be untrue. They still send me the same old anti-immigrant poems, always with a naïve sense of discovery as if they had found a new Poet Laureate. The more serious social problems and their possible solution are never touched on by these people whose views are invariably negative and destructive and never constructive.[52]

But one or two organizations have gradually acquired a substantial membership, notably the Southall and District Residents' Association. This Association, which has been affiliated to the English Rights Association, began the election address, issued on its behalf for candidates in the 1968 local elections, under the heading 'Immigration':[53]

It is four years since the formation of the new London Borough of Ealing. How has Southall fared during this time? Firstly, what steps have been taken to control the flood of immigrants to Southall despite the shortage of housing accommodation, jobs and schools; what have the Council done in respect of petitioning the Minister of Housing and the Minister Education on these grave problems? Very little; and what about the Councillors you elected to represent Southall—'Complete silence' with the exception of two, Tom Steele and Bill Lamb who were expelled from the Labour Party in representing your views that our own people should be considered first in rehousing, and the residents' qualification should be extended to fifteen years for immigrants as against five years for our own people who have been on the housing list for years.

The address goes on to imply that immigrants throw rubbish in the street, and turn 'residential properties' into brothels. It opposes the education department's dispersal scheme for immigrant children: 'This cost the rate payers £22,500 in one year and it will become worse with the increasing birthrate of immigrant children.' The S.D.R.A. won two seats in these elections; it did not contest those seats where there was a National Front candidate.

The arguments of the more recent anti-integration groups are generally backed up by a recitation of problems which are said or implied to have been caused by immigrants. The difference between the supposed immigrant way of life and the supposed English one invariably involves a threat to the English. The evidence adduced is part medical, part anecdotal. One famous specimen, which has been circulating freely in several towns for some time, was included in Enoch Powell's Birmingham speech[54] —the little old lady and the grinning piccaninnies. Mr. Powell says that he had it from a correspondent in Northumberland. A variant of this theme, reported four years ago by Paul Foot, who had encountered it in five different cities, was the little old lady to whom indecent advances had been made by Indians.[55] Others ring the change on the theme of defilement—sexual and excremental. This aspect of anti-immigrant propaganda can really only be studied in psycho-analytical terms; those from whom these anecdotes originate are likely to be among the 10% of pathologically prejudiced identified in the attitude survey reported in Chapter 28. But by no means all of those who help to give circulation to these anecdotes fall into such a category.

The importance of the extremist groups has related largely to the changing political environment in which they have worked. Until recently, they have been far less numerous than the pro-integration groups, and still have fewer organized local activities. None of the 'nationalist' political parties have made any significant headway. Nor is it likely that they now will: the line taken by the major parties is such as to take the wind almost entirely out of their sails. But the impact of the newer groups has been greater than their numerical strength. Their main importance has been to act as a conduit for potentially non-racial discontents, convincing the anxious moderates that immigrants are to blame for the processes of social change and their side effects, in a way which the anti-immigrant politicians, with their aura of disreputability deriving from the pre-war activities of the British Union of Fascists, can never do. Over the long term, they have also been able to bring openly racialist arguments back into circulation, in the guise of a defence of English culture. It *is* a guise, or otherwise the same people might be working on the right wing of the pro-integration groups. Occasionally individuals have in fact moved between the two: and an important part of the achievement of bodies like the Sparkbrook Association is that they have been able to divert anxieties about changing environment into constructive channels.

The other achievement of the anti-integration groups has been to help persuade people in positions of authority—editors, M.P.s, local party organizers, trades unionists—who do not share their views, that public opinion is moving in the direction of greater hostility towards immigrants. Some need little convincing: such a view chimes in with their preconceptions. Not many have the confidence to consign their letters to the wastepaper basket.

Ultimately, the extent to which these bodies have been able to make an impact on the situation is a reflection of the extent to which the overall climate of opinion has deteriorated. Their room for manœuvre, and the way in which they have exercised it is a function of the performance of local and central government and, in particular, the politicians over the whole period of the migration.

NOTES TO CHAPTER 21

1. *The Times*, 6 July 1968, in a leader entitled 'The Tories and Race'.
2. The Rev. R. S. Pulford, who is a member of the Racial Preservation Society, is one notorious example.
3. C. S. Hill, *West Indian Migrants and the London Churches* (London, Oxford University Press, for Institute of Race Relations, 1963), p. 76; W. Wood and J. Downing, *Vicious Circle* (London, S.P.C.K., 1968), p. 66.
4. See M. Nesbitt in *Church Times*, 28 August 1964.
5. Both these attitudes are expressed in an article by Rev. C. S. Hill, 'Colour in Britain: A Christian Viewpoint', in *Congregational Monthly* (September 1965), p. 17. It is unfortunate, as it belies the good work the author has done amongst migrants.
6. Edwin Barker, *Commonwealth Immigrants: the Work and Attitude of the Church of England* (London, Board for Social Responsibility, 1963).
7. 'The Churches amid Growing Racial Tension in Britain', *Race Relations in Ecumenical Perspective* (Issue of November 1962, no. 4), pp. 9–10.
8. Wood and Downing, op. cit., p. 66.
9. C. S. Hill and D. Matthew (eds.), *Race: A Christian Symposium* (London, Gollancz, 1968), p. 175. See also, *Immigrants in Britain* (London, British Council of Churches Standing Committee on Migration, 1965), and Wood and Downing, op. cit.
10. Report of the William Temple Association, London Branch, August 1966.
11. Report of the Standing Committee on Migration of the British Council of Churches, 27 April 1965.
12. For the indigenous population, the Catholic Church is the exception. See, for example, 'Youth and Religion', *New Life* (Vol. 14, nos. 1 and 2), p. 358; and J. Rex and R. Moore, *Race, Community and Conflict* (London, Oxford University Press, for Institute of Race Relations, 1967), p. 79.
13. Rev. C. S. Hill, 'Colour in Britain: A Christian Viewpoint', op. cit., p. 16.
14. R. B. Davison, *Black British* (London, Oxford University Press, for Institute of Race Relations, 1966), p. 129.
15. See Eric Butterworth, *A Muslim Community in Great Britain* (London, Church Information Office for the Church Assembly Board for Social Responsibility, 1967), pp. 33–4.
16. John Archer Jackson, *The Irish in Britain* (London, Routledge & Kegan Paul, 1964), p. 148.
17. See, for example, E. James, *The Reverend Gentleman: West Indians and the Church in Britain* (Southend-on-Sea, Citizen Press, 1962). The same opinion is expressed in relation to West Africa in Anna Craven's *West Africans in London* (London, I.R.R. Special Series, 1969).

18. In J. Rex and R. Moore, op. cit.

19. See, Rev. C. S. Hill, *West Indian Migrants and the London Churches*, Chapter III; and the Methodist Church Manchester and Stockport District Christian Citizenship Committee: Social Responsibility Project, Group 6 Race Relations Report, August 1966, these give some figures for other forms of contact.

20. M. C. Calley, *God's People* (London, Oxford University Press, for Institute of Race Relations, 1965), p. 96 and pp. 122–3.

21. O. G. Francis, *People of Modern Jamaica* (Department of Statistics, Jamaica, 1962), pp. 9–10.

22. 'The Churches amid Growing Racial Tension in Britain', op. cit., pp. 9–10.

23. Since this was written the Board of Deputies has set up a Working Party on Race Relations to consider the most effective contribution which the Jewish Community should make to improve race relations in Britain.

24. Hassam Karmi, *Problems of Adjustment* (—, the author, January 1965), available at the Institute of Race Relations Library.

25. *Race: A Christian Symposium*, op. cit., pp. 195 and 197.

26. Memorandum from Rev. W. J. Milligan to the British Churches Housing Trust, January 1968.

27. *Facts and Figures about the Church of England—No. 3* (Central Board of Finance of the Church of England, 1965), Table 83.

28. See *Economist*, 2 April 1966. Denominational schools in Birmingham account for about 25% of all primary school places. The article contends that few of them are taken by coloured immigrant children.

29. Table 21.1 was obtained from the Department of Education and Science as a correction to the Written Answer, from Miss Bacon to Mr. C. Price in *Hansard*, 4 July 1968, which was incorrectly headed.

30. Mary Grigg, *The White Question* (London, Secker & Warburg, 1967), pp. 135–6.

31. Robert A. Burt, *Colour Prejudice in Great Britain* (Princeton, New Jersey, The Author, April 1960), p. 80.

32. Grigg, op. cit., p. 137.

33. Burt, op. cit., p. 104.

34. Joan Maizels, *The West Indian Comes to Willesden* (London, Willesden Borough Council, 1960).

35. Burt, op. cit., p. 116, interview with Nadine Peppard.

36. W. Collins, *Jamaican Migrant* (London, Routledge & Kegan Paul, 1965).

37. Dipak Nandy, 'An Illusion of Competence', in *Policies for Racial Equality*, A. Lester and N. Deakin (eds.) (London, Fabian Society, 1967).

38. Burt, op. cit., p. 109.

39. Elizabeth Burney, *Housing on Trial* (London, Oxford University Press, for Institute of Race Relations, 1967).

40. *The Education of the Immigrant Child in the London Borough of Ealing*, a report of the Education Committee of the Ealing International Friendship Council (April 1968).

41. For a full account of the work of the Sparkbrook Association, see J. Rex and R. Moore, op. cit., Chapter IX.

42. Burt, op. cit., p. 116.

43. See Nigel Baseley's (unsigned) article in *Campaign*, No. 1., Newsletter of the Campaign Against Racial Discrimination.

44. For a step-by-step account of the protest up to the trial, see Michael Dummett's article in *Campaign*, No. 2, Newsletter of the Campaign Against Racial Discrimination.

45. *Immigration from the Commonwealth* (Cmnd. 2739), (London, H.M.S.O., 1965), para. 73.

46. Michael Dummett, in a paper on immigrant organizations given at the Third Annual Race Relations Conference, September 1968.

47. Paul Foot, *Immigration and Race in British Politics* (Harmondsworth, Penguin Books, 1965).

48. See Manchester University Liberal Society, Study Group, *Anti-immigrant Organizations* (London, Union of Liberal Students, 1966).

49. Report (unpublished) for the Institute's 'Survey of Race Relations in Britain', by Professor Richard P. Longaker, Department of Political Science, University of California.

50. Burney, op. cit., pp. 212–13.

51. *Middlesex County Times*, 5 April 1968.

52. Talk by Mr. Clement Jones, Editor of *Express & Star*, Wolverhampton, at the Harrogate Conference of the Guild of British Newspaper Editions, 21 September 1968.

53. For a report on the election, see Graham Thomas 'The Council Election in Southall, May 1968', in Institute of Race Relations *Newsletter* (July 1968).

54. Reproduced in *Race* (Vol. X, no. 1, July 1968), pp. 94–9.

55. Foot, op. cit.

22 Some Conclusions: The Lessons of the P.E.P. Report

In Part IV we have considered the response of a number of different institutions, official and voluntary, local and national, to the new situation revealed by coloured immigration. These institutions were not in themselves in a static condition during this period. Indeed, the decade of the migration was one of persistent and accelerating social change in a number of different ways quite unconnected with immigration. In some cases, the response to the newcomers was a function of these processes and not the direct result of their arrival—for example, in the field of education, where (as we tried to show in Chapter 18) social change in the inner city had changed the composition of the schools before the immigrants came on the scene.

But despite the multiplicity of factors at work, it does seem possible to trace in the bewildering variety of processes taking place in the different fields we have described a coherent response to immigration, taking in all the various institutions in the host society and passing in succession through a series of metamorphoses. In a familiar metaphor, the newcomers acted as a catalyst, first illuminating the weakness of existing structures and then precipitating change. In its initial form, this response was determined by the values already implicit in the various institutions and their patterns of behaviour. To be specific, in the political system (after some initial uncertainty), the doctrine of the equal status of Commonwealth citizens and the undesirability of any actions that trenched upon this equality determined the shape of policy for the first years of the migration. In the educational system, the universalist view of the school as an instrument for producing cultural homogeneity and pursuing middle-class values determined the reception the first black (or brown) pupils received. In housing, the main policy aim was the provision of accommodation within the public sector on the footing of local preference, based on residence in 'classical' slum conditions. In the welfare services, the guiding principle was equal access for all clients to statutorily provided services, which seemed in the 1950s to be putting an end to poverty in the traditional sense of the term.

In the background, the police functioned as the guardians of public order, smoothing over such rough passages as took place with impartial zeal, and in the foreground, the voluntary organizations took on the responsibility for providing such welfare services as might be justified in the case of new immigrants, which were not available on a universal basis. This residual role of dispensing charity seemed particularly appropriate in the case of the Churches. In sum, the response in this period could be described as one of 'weak universalism'.

Then, partly as a direct result of the deficiencies of policy in the first stage, distinctive policy initiatives began to be taken in each of the fields we have discussed. The redefinition of the immigrants as a separate, problem-generating group began to take hold and provided the stimulus for the campaign to control their entry into the United Kingdom, which eventually became the dominating element in the political debate. In the field of housing, the initial willingness to accept a degree of concentration in inner city areas was replaced, once the sacrosanct status of the newcomers was terminated by the political debate, by an increasing tendency on the part of public health departments to enforce strict standards in the areas of settlement in order to control the multi-occupation which stemmed, at least in part, from the failure to take effective steps to deal with discrimination. In education, a special need—that of the non-English speaking child—was belatedly identified, but the remedial measure adopted was dispersal, extended to those children who differed from the majority only by virtue of skin colour, and designed to restore a degree of 'normality' to those schools that were in danger of becoming abnormal. The increasing threat to public order, perceived after the issue had become politically salient, was dealt with by increasing the sanctions against racial incitement—and thereby inflicting a permanent handicap upon race relations legislation. In employment, the multiplicity of local practice defied generalization, but permitted discrimination to take hold and grow deep roots, fertilized by the misleading and hostile folklore about the quality of immigrant labour and never effectively pruned by the Ministry of Labour. In this developing situation, the voluntary organizations could no longer act as effective front-runners: but the necessity for whole-hearted commitment on the part of the Government was shuffled off by the singling out of one kind of voluntary organization—the voluntary liaison committees, which were gathered together in 1965 under the wing of an official agency (the National Committee for Commonwealth Immigrants) and supplied with full-time staff and funds. As might have been expected, the scope of the task proved too great for the resources which could be deployed in this way and the National Committee ended its three-year career to the accompaniment of bitter—and unfair—accusations of having been the figleaf for the Government's otherwise naked racialism.

This second series of responses on the part of Government and official institutions at various levels, which flowed direct from the first, might be described as being based on a definition of 'weak selectivity'. In so far as these responses were the product of conscious decisions and were not merely spontaneous reflexes, the theme common to them is one of social control.[1] Policy was directed towards redeploying resources in order to maintain or restore the *status quo* that existed before the organism had received the stimulus of the newcomers' arrival. The important distinction was that a problem had been defined: the sense of shame about identifying differences was lost when the Serpent entered Eden in 1958, with the Notting Dale and Nottingham disturbances. But this identification was a negative one, in direct reaction from the initial failure to make one at all: there was still a reluctance to engage in selectivity in the positive sense.

As we have tried to show, the White Paper of 1965 epitomized the failure of this second response in its double inadequacy. First, the diagnosis was inadequate: the implication was allowed to appear that the newcomers were in some sense responsible for placing intolerable strain on the institutions and social services which had, in fact, failed to cope adequately with their needs. This formulation of the problem as an 'immigrant problem'—not the immigrants' problem—was at the root of the inadequacies of policy in this second stage. And second, the resources deployed to make good this deficiency were quite inadequate. An under-financed and ill-equipped organization produced by the recasting of voluntary effort was left to deal with the whole vast task of integration: the function of the local authorities and Government departments defined simply in terms of the intensification of their existing policy commitments—sometimes not even that. Even in its own terms—those of eliminating the main difficulties by the controlled induction of the first generation into British patterns of behaviour and the anglicizing of the second generation—the aims of policy were inadequately provided for. Only in the legislation against discrimination were the handicaps of the individual coloured citizen the focus of action: and in the Act of 1965 the areas tackled covered too small a part of the individual's experience to have much direct effect.

The failure of weak selectivity, delayed by the Herculean efforts of some of those involved in the voluntary and statutory agencies, eventually became clear; its failure began the process of producing the synthesis, which one could call 'strong universalism'. This consisted of an approach based on the concept of two categories of disadvantage affecting the vast majority of coloured people in Britain, who live in the inner city areas. There are those disabilities arising from the circumstances in which they live—which, since there are as yet no coloured ghettoes, as such, affect equal or larger numbers of white people: and there are those disabilities that affect coloured people by virtue of their colour. The latter are in practice largely the result of the discrimination which has been pervasive in the fields of housing and employment. The effect of these two sets of disabilities has been cumulative: and the consequences are best dealt with as a whole. But it was the revelation of the extent of the specific disabilities arising from discrimination which provided the main stimulus for a change of policy. The evidence which underlined the failure of the previous policy was contained chiefly in the P.E.P. Report on the extent of discrimination. We have described the political genesis of this report elsewhere (Part VI); what is important here is the situation it revealed. For the evidence of the P.E.P. Report showed that even had official policies been pursued more vigorously within their own terms of reference, they would not have achieved integration. Three major points emerged: first of all, the Report showed that most acts of discrimination in employment occurred without any assessment of the merit of the candidate, his qualifications, or suitability. In a large number of cases, rejection was stated to be because of his race or colour. Secondly, the Report did not support the view that with anglicization discrimination would cease; on the contrary, the findings suggested that the more English and the more skilled a person was, the more he was likely to experience discrimination. Thirdly, the Report drove home the lesson that one of the single most important causes of the relatively poorer housing conditions of immigrant families was racial discrimination. Quite simply, most of the private housing market, particularly in rented accommodation, was closed to the coloured man or woman.

THE EVIDENCE OF THE P.E.P. REPORT

The P.E.P. Report was commissioned in the autumn of 1966 by the Race Relations Board and the National Committee for Commonwealth Immigrants, to investigate the extent of racial discrimination in areas not covered by the 1965 Race Relations Act: employment, housing, and services such as insurance and car hire. We consider here its findings under the first two heads.[2]

The investigation was in three parts. Nine hundred and seventy-four interviews were conducted with immigrants from the four main Commonwealth migrant groups: West Indian, Pakistani, Indian, and Cypriot. Five hundred interviews were conducted with people in a position to discriminate. These included 175 national and local employers; 154 national and local trade union officials; staff in thirty-six employment bureaux, and in the Ministry of Labour employment exchanges in the six areas of the study. Two of the areas were in London, one in the South of England, one in the Midlands, and two in the North. The third part of the investigation consisted of 400 'situation tests', each with three applicants (English, Hungarian, and West Indian). The 'situation tests' were set up originally to provide an objective measurement of discrimination, and to check on what were assumed to be tendencies by immigrants to exaggerate the extent of discrimination, and by employers and others to minimize its extent. In fact, the evidence from either of the three types of inquiry would in itself have provided objective evidence of considerable discrimination.

Contrary to the expectations of those designing the inquiry, the survey of immigrants' own views revealed that beliefs about the existence of racial discrimination were not exaggerated, but closely related either to personal experience, or to knowledge of the experience of others. Indeed, when all three parts of the inquiry had been analysed, the Report concluded that immigrants tended to under-estimate the amount of discrimination which in fact took place.

(a) *Employment*

Seventy-two per cent of the immigrants interviewed believed that employers did discriminate, and in half these cases the belief was based on personal experience. Forty-five per cent of the West Indians interviewed, 35% of Indians, 34% of Pakistanis, and only 6% of Cypriots said they had personal experience of such discrimination. Half of those who believed in discrimination based their belief on knowledge of the experience of others. They were then asked to explain how they had managed to avoid it. In many cases, the answer was that they had applied only for one or very few positions since coming to Britain. Some put it down to luck, others to the possession of some special personal or occupational skill. The only other significant reason given was that offered by 41% of the Cypriots, who believed that they were members of a racial group which was not discriminated against. The experience of the Hungarian tester, in the 'situation tests', suggested that this belief was in fact a mistaken one, and that European immigrant groups did experience some discrimination, although not as much as the non-European groups.

The type of discrimination referred to in the claims was the refusal of a job. In half the cases, the person was applying at the time for an unskilled position, in 28% of the cases, for a semi-skilled or skilled manual position, and in 8% of the cases, for a clerical, administrative, or professional position.

In 14% of the cases, the person rejected was seen by the foreman or works representative, in a further 8% of the cases, by the manager, and in over half the cases, the rejecting was done lower down the hierarchy, by the man at the gate, someone in the personnel office, or the receptionist or inquiries clerk. This in itself was not a particularly startling finding, until the very frank 'reasons for rejection' are considered: a quarter of all those claiming personal experience of racial discrimination were told 'no coloured', others were told 'no foreigners' or 'English only', and a further small proportion informed that the 'coloured quota was full'. A few were offered a job on the telephone, but rejected on their arrival when they were seen to be coloured, and 8% were told they were 'unsuitable' without being asked for any details of skills, qualifications, or experience. Altogether, 42% were rejected either explicitly on grounds of colour or foreignness, or without any reason being given or inquiry made about their suitability for the position. A further 41% were told there were 'no vacancies' when in fact these did exist, since vacancies continued to be advertised or other (white) applicants were known to have got jobs at the time or subsequently. Thus, even on the basis of the subjective claims by immigrants that there was racial discrimination, the evidence was either conclusive or strong. A sample of forty of the firms against whom the claims were made was then tested, and in nine out of ten cases the claims were found to be justified.

In these follow-up tests, all the circumstances of the original claim of discrimination were simulated: the applications were for the same type of job, and were made in the same way and to the same type of person as in the real life incident. The testers were, however, exactly matched in their qualifications and in their work history. Objectively, they were all equally suited for the particular position. The coloured tester applied first, then the Hungarian, then the English. The results were as follows: in fifteen out of the forty applications, the English tester was offered a job, or advised to apply; in fifteen applications, he was asked to call back, told there would shortly be a vacancy, or details were taken for future reference; in ten applications, he was told there was no vacancy. The experience of the Hungarian was not the same: in ten cases, he was offered a job or advised to apply; in seven cases, he was encouraged to apply for a future vacancy; and in twenty-three cases, he was told there was no vacancy. The experience of the coloured tester was again different: in only one case was he offered a job or advised to apply; in two cases, he was encouraged to apply for a future vacancy; and in thirty-seven cases, he was told there was no vacancy.

Fifteen employment bureaux were also tested. This time, the testers were applying for vacancies in accountancy jobs. Two of them, one English (A) and one West Indian (B), were exactly matched in qualifications and work experience. A third tester, a West Indian (C), had better qualifications and more experience than either of the other two. They were looking for roughly similar kinds of jobs, and approached the bureaux in the order B-C-A. The English applicant was told of a possible twenty-three vacancies; the applicant B, with exactly the same qualifications, was told of five possible vacancies; and applicant C, the most highly qualified of the three testers, was told of eighteen possible vacancies.

The evidence from the survey of immigrants and the situation tests disposed of one of the major justifications which was put forward by employers to explain unequal treatment: namely, that coloured applicants were inferior and foreign, and rejecting them was merely a rational sorting out of the least suitable applicants. The Report revealed that colour was a major factor in recruitment decisions.

There was no evidence that knowledge of the English language, possession of English qualifications, or training, protected a man from discrimination. On the contrary, there was some indication that it was precisely the most 'integrated' members of the immigrant groups who tended to meet rejection; those who made little attempt to join English society were protected from rebuffs. The large majority of the sample of immigrants who had no formal qualifications made the lowest claims of discrimination: only 34%. Of the twenty-two people interviewed with English trade qualifications, fifteen claimed personal experience of discrimination; of the twenty-seven people interviewed with English school leaving qualifications, twelve claimed experience of discrimination; and four out of the five people interviewed with English professional qualifications claimed to have experienced discrimination. The Report gave some examples:

1. A West Indian, aged 34, came to Britain in 1956; building trade certificate obtained by part-time study at Polytechnic. Sent by union for a job as a cabinet maker: 'Saw the manager and he told me, "the men in this shop do not work with coloureds" ', and was shown the way out.
2. A Pakistani, aged 29, came to Britain in 1957; served apprenticeship in gas fitting; applied for a job as a gas fitter: 'I was told that I couldn't have the job as I was a Pakistani and coloured people couldn't go to work in white British homes.'
3. A West Indian, aged 29, came to Britain in 1961; City and Guilds Diploma in electronics, member of the Institute of Radio Engineers; applied to a national radio and television manufacturer; saw the Area Manager: 'He stated quite positively that it was not the company's policy to employ coloured people.' He applied to another employer: 'The receptionist said that all jobs are classified and must be filled by British nationals. When I pointed out that I was British, she said, "You must be English".' The informant was subsequently employed in the type of job for which he was applying. When a follow-up test was conducted, the West Indian tester was told that no personnel was employed in the type of work he was seeking; the English and the Hungarian testers, inquiring about the same type of work, were told that jobs were available if they wished to apply.

Claims of discrimination were also high among those with trade or academic qualifications achieved in their country of origin. This was perhaps understandable, because of the lack of comparability in qualifications (see Chapter 19). However, many of these informants had not been applying for jobs requiring their qualifications, but for unskilled or semi-skilled jobs. Daniel gives this summary of conclusions:[3]

In terms of formal qualifications, experience of discrimination was highest among people with the highest qualifications, including those with English trade, professional and school leaving qualifications.

In terms of English speaking ability, experience of discrimination was highest among people who had spoken only English as a child and lowest among those who had spoken no English.

In terms of job done before coming to Britain, experience of discrimination was highest among those who had been in full employment and lowest among people who had been unemployed.

In terms of length of time in Britain, the longer people had been here the more discrimination they had faced.

In terms of union membership, which provided some idea of the extent to which they wanted or were prepared to join English organisations, the proportion of union members experiencing discrimination was higher than the proportion of non-members.

Just under half the immigrants had been in their present job for over three years, and more than a quarter had held their present job for between one and three years, at the time they were interviewed. There was no evidence of the 'lack of staying power' of which some employers complained, and attributed generally to all coloured immigrants.

(b) *Housing*

The significance of the P.E.P. findings on housing lay in the light they shed on the private housing market, on which the overwhelming majority of immigrants are dependent.

Just over two-thirds of the total sample of immigrants in the survey believed that landlords did discriminate. The belief was greatest among the West Indians, and least among Pakistanis. Eighty-eight per cent of West Indians, 55% of Indians, and 44% of Pakistanis believed that landlords did discriminate. Personal experience of this was, however, much less than in the case of employment. Just under 40% of the West Indians, just under 20% of the Indians, and 15% of the Pakistanis claimed to have personal experience of discrimination by landlords. In half these cases the reasons given for the belief was that they were told 'no coloured' or had the door slammed in their face. The majority of those who thought that landlords did discriminate, believed this because of the experience of others. When asked how they themselves had come to avoid it, most of the Indian and Pakistani informants (over 80%), and over two-thirds of the West Indians, said that they had only applied for accommodation where they knew that they would be accepted. Very few Cypriots had experience of discrimination, which they rated as a less significant handicap than the British climate. Most of them either gave no reason for their escape, or attributed it to the fact that their group was not subjected to discrimination. The importance of the factor of colour was once again clearly demonstrated by these findings. In the total sample, 48% of the immigrants were in the process of buying their home, jointly or singly. The remainder were in some form of rented accommodation, virtually all in the private sector.

'Test' applications were made to 180 landlords (sixty in person, 120 by telephone), to eighteen accommodation bureaux, and to thirty estate agents. They were spread over all six of the areas in the survey.

In the case of the applications for private rented accommodation, the opposite procedure was adopted from that of the employment tests. These had mostly been follow-up tests, to check allegations of discrimination. In other words, there was already some evidence suggesting that discrimination was practised. In the housing tests, only those vacancies were selected which did not indicate any restrictions in their advertisements. The Milner Holland Report on London's housing had, in 1965, estimated that only 11% of all private rented accommodation vacancies advertized did *not* exclude coloured tenants. It was in this group that all the P.E.P. tests for rented accommodation were made. Each of the three testers—English, West Indian, and Hungarian—made half his applications in a 'middle-class' role and half in a 'working-class' role. The West Indian's two roles were a hospital registrar and a bus conductor; the Hungarian's an accountant and a van driver; the Englishman's a school teacher and a builder's labourer. Applications were made at short intervals in the order: West Indian, Hungarian, Englishman. The results were as follows: of sixty personal applications, the three testers were given the same answer on fifteen occasions. On thirty-eight occasions, the West

Indian was told the accommodation had been taken and both the others were told it was vacant; on four occasions, the West Indian was asked for a higher rent than the others; on two occasions, the West Indian and the Hungarian were told the accommodation had been taken, and the Englishman told it was vacant; on one occasion, the West Indian and the Hungarian were asked for a higher rent than the Englishman.

In the 120 telephoned applications, the three testers were given the same answer on forty-six occasions.

In the test applications to eighteen accommodation bureaux, the three testers were given the same treatment on four occasions. On ten occasions, the West Indian was refused or offered nothing, while the others were offered addresses or put on a mailing list. On one occasion, the bureau stipulated 'We do not let to non-English'; on three occasions, the West Indian was offered fewer addresses than the others.

Of the thirty applications to estate agents for accommodation to let, the three testers were given the same treatment on ten occasions. On sixteen occasions, the West Indian was either refused or offered nothing, while the others were given addresses, put on the mailing list, or asked to call back. On one occasion, the agent stated 'We do not let to coloureds', and on three occasions, the West Indian was offered fewer addresses than the others.

The interviews conducted with the staff of the bureaux and agencies indicated that the market was even more restricted for coloured applicants than was suggested by the results of the tests. The greatest difficulty was in unfurnished flats or statutory tenancies. The consensus of opinion was that only very infrequently was there an unfurnished flat on the books which could be offered to a coloured person. Unlike the findings of the employment tests, the Hungarian experienced almost no discrimination in housing. As in the case of employment, however, the class of the coloured applicant made little difference: there was no less discrimination against the West Indian tester in his role as a hospital registrar than when he was applying as a bus conductor. In fact, he tended to meet rather more hostility in his middle-class role.

In the 'situation tests' for house purchase, seven estate agents were approached in each of the six survey areas, and again the testers adopted middle-class or working-class roles. Of the forty-two applications, the three were given the same information fifteen times. On twenty occasions, the West Indian was treated differently from one or both the others: he was denied access to certain of the properties for sale, he was told that no mortgage would be available to him, or he was quoted less favourable terms for a mortgage.

The P.E.P. Report did not provide new information. The existence of discrimination on grounds of colour had been known to many groups of people: to some of the coloured applicants for jobs or housing; to staff in industry who made the decisions about hiring and to trade union officials concerned with hiring; to all those who read advertisements for housing and to all staff involved in the renting or sale of property; to readers of the Milner Holland Report. From time to time, feature articles had appeared in the press about discrimination, and situation tests had been carried out occasionally by journalists. The Campaign Against Racial Discrimination had, in the summer of 1966, set up 'situation tests' to reveal the extent of discrimination against second-generation coloured school leavers, and the results received coverage in the press. These fuelled the public discussion about whether 'the problem' was due to the foreignness of the immigrants or was due to racial hostility against non-Europeans. But the P.E.P. Report was the first systematic attempt to assess the extent of racial discrimination and its finding, that it varied in extent 'from the massive to the substantial', would have been anticipated only by very few people. The findings showed that the groups who were most physically distinct in colour and racial features from the English experienced the greatest discrimination, and that the group who were culturally most like the English, and who sought integration, were the most likely to experience rejection. In employment, the coloured applicant was twice as likely to be discriminated against as a white immigrant. In housing, the white immigrant experienced virtually no discrimination. The Report illustrated how the process of racial discrimination tended to push or keep immigrants in poorer housing and lower status jobs, reinforcing the stereotype and preventing integration.

In this way, the conditions under which the coloured minorities were struggling to establish themselves were brought home to the policy-makers and the public at large. The first half of the lesson, for future policy, which was implicit in the P.E.P. findings—that specific action was required to deal with the specific disabilities of coloured citizens—was applied by Roy Jenkins in the programme for action devised during his period as Home Secretary, which is described in Part VI. But the second half—that these remedies depended for their successful application on the reallocation of resources on a far greater scale within society as a whole in favour of the under-privileged areas and on a basis of need alone—is only now being learnt. The flawed initiative of the Urban Programme, discussed in Part VI, illustrates how much further there is to travel before those responsible for formulating policy and applying it in practice learn from the experiences we have tried to describe in this analysis.

NOTES ON CHAPTER 22

1. Dipak Nandy has described the various justifications for this objective in his essay 'An Illusion of Competence' in *Policies for Racial Equality*, Anthony Lester and N. Deakin (eds.), (Fabian Research Series 262, July 1967), p. 35.

2. *Racial Discrimination in Britain*. A report issued by Political and Economic Planning, London, 1967, based on research conducted by Research Services Ltd. A fuller version of the findings was written by W. W. Daniel of Research Services, *Racial Discrimination in England* (Harmondsworth, Penguin Books, 1968).

3. Daniel, op. cit., p. 81.

PART V THE IMMIGRANT RESPONSE

23 Adaptation or Withdrawal

INTRODUCTION

In Part V we shall look at the response of the immigrant communities to their new environment. We shall try to discern how far this response has been determined by their own cultural heritage and how far by their treatment in this country; the pattern of their settlements, for example, may be shaped by their cultural needs, by official housing policies and the forces of the market, simply by avoidance of discrimination, or by a desire for security. In Part II we described the forces which brought these migrants to Britain; we shall now examine the intentions with which they came and the way in which these intentions have been modified by events. If it is true that many who did not intend to stay permanently have now changed their minds, does this mean that their expectations have been fulfilled, or have they decided to stay in spite of disappointment, or even because of it? Or have they been forced to stay by immigration policy? Whichever of these possibilities is true, what will be the effect on their behaviour as a group in this country? This question will involve us in a discussion of the nature of their initial approach to British society, of the minimum demands that they made upon it, and of the concessions they were prepared to make in order to build a life here. In our discussion, we shall distinguish between the first generation, the true immigrants, and their children—whether they were immigrants, like their parents, or were born and brought up here. The concept of an immigrant-host relationship is already beginning to lose its relevance to a situation in which newcomers, however diverse their origins, are lumped together as coloured immigrants and are rejected because of their colour. As time passes and children who have been born here to immigrant parents begin to grow up, the concept will apply with even less force: there may well be a conflict of values within the home as the parents fear the effect upon their children of an alien culture, but whether or not this culture seems alien to their children will tell us much about the way these groups are adapting themselves and how far the children, who are British born, are allowed to feel that they are accepted by the wider society.

418 COLOUR AND CITIZENSHIP

We shall also examine the different kinds of leadership that have been thrown up within the communities; the role that the leaders play and the nature of their following. The quality and character of the 'leaders' and the extent of their influence can tell us a good deal about the nature of the immigrant communities, and the different ways in which they have reacted to changes in the political and social climate.

In Part IV we analysed the nature of the British response to the presence of coloured immigrants: in Part V we shall look at a response to a response. The variety of the response within the different communities arises from the great diversity within the immigration and displays almost the whole range of the modes of adaptation which were described in Part I of this Report. Although Part V is principally concerned with the response of minorities, it must be remembered that there is a constant inter-action between the minority groups and the majority and that this two-way relationship involves a measure of adaptation and acceptance on both sides. The process of mutual adjustment proceeds at a different pace for different groups and for different members within a group. Moreover, the process, once begun, is not in any sense irreversible. It is affected by many factors. There can be set-backs and regressions caused by frustration of hopes, by the behaviour of either side, by the influence of personalities, and by the effect of events in the sending countries or in other parts of the world, such as the persecution of a kindred minority. Reinforcements of a minority group by arrivals from the home country can also slow up the process, just as tolerant attitudes and behaviour on the part of the majority can accelerate it. In examining the response of the various communities, we must also remember that we are watching a process that is still in its early stages. The earliest of these migrations is barely twenty years old and the great majority of the immigrants from India and Pakistan have been in this country for less than ten years.

One further caveat. While culture of origin, motives, and expectations all affect the mode of adaptation, it must be remembered that there are considerable variations within each immigrant group which also enter into the equation. There are, for example, the differences between peasant and land-owner, between villager and townsman, between skilled and unskilled, English speaking and non-English speaking, literate and illiterate; there are differences of class and of caste, and between the religious and the secular. The list could be multiplied indefinitely, but these examples are given to remind the reader that, as the composition of the migrations was not homogeneous, the response within each immigrant group cannot be expected to be uniform.

1. WEST INDIANS

The West Indian migration to Britain was at no time highly organized. It is true that once it acquired a momentum, shipping lines responded to meet the demand; but from the almost casual beginnings (described in Chapter 6), there developed a flow from all the islands which was the result of a number of individual initiatives. At a later stage, the settlements were to be reinforced as relatives came to join relatives, and in this sense there was a measure of selection, but the migration remained a movement of individuals who financed their own passages and were not dependent on the sponsorship of influential fellow countrymen already in England, nor were they heavily indebted to travel agents.

The individualism of the immigrants and their heterogeneity has been one of the chief characteristics of this migration and has influenced the patterns of settlements. One instance of this has been the large number of women who came over alone in the early years, leaving their children and, in many instances, their partners behind. The basic social unit in most West Indian islands is either the nuclear family of husband, wife, and children, or more usually the grandmother family (see Chapter 5). The migrant's obligations were thus limited to the immediate family and there was no elaborate kin or village network such as that which was to have so much influence on development of the emigration from India and Pakistan.

Although there were no such networks extending to this country, there was a tendency, which remains, for people from one island to congregate together and for Jamaicans to settle according to their parishes of origin. But, apart from the pull of these local patriotisms and the tendency of all newcomers to keep together for mutual reinforcement and support, there was nothing in the culture or social organization of West Indians which would have kept this immigration concentrated in large separate settlements. They were, in fact, predisposed by their upbringing and by their familiarity with British customs and culture to adopt British ways and to adapt themselves to a British society which they were well fitted to enter through the mechanism of a highly stratified class system. Indeed, they were the most assimilationist of all the coloured immigrants in the sense that they regarded England as their mother country and, unlike other immigrants, they did not feel that they had to come to terms with an alien culture which might threaten their own. On the contrary, they expected to be welcomed by the Churches and were prepared to play an active part in parish life. It is true that many of them were countrymen, but while they may not have been prepared for the changes in style of life demanded by living in a city in a cold climate, these were impersonal forces with which they had to come to terms. What they were not prepared to meet was hostility.

(a) Expectations and Illusions

The West Indians were, in fact, the least prepared of all the immigrant groups for their reception in this country and the least equipped to meet antagonism. Their expectations were so high; the reality so different. In the West Indies, when they had encountered white people (and some from the country districts had hardly seen a white man), it was in positions of authority, as officials, employers, patrons, or as spiritual and intellectual mentors. On arrival, they were surprised to find white men performing menial tasks; they had not expected to be competing with them for jobs and housing. 'Now I was seeing my colonial society in a terrible light, I had never hoped to challenge the whites in Jamaica for a job. I realized in the confusion of the crowded station that I was starting on a desperate phase of life. If the white man was sweeping the streets, then any job I asked for would mean a challenge to him. I was not one of the "mother country's" children. I was one of her black children.' So Donald Hinds described reflections on the train from Dover to Victoria.[1]

The West Indian who comes to England faces a complex of problems which spring not only from his illusions about the nature of a white society but from his heritage and his colour consciousness. He has grown up in a colonial society in which the dominant culture has been overlaid on his African origins and in which the class structure is stratified by colour; where the poor are black and where social and economic advancement proceeds along an ascending order of ever lighter skin shade. It is not only that the poor are black but that what is black is rejected. Fernando Henriques has shown how in Jamaica the white bias affects not only social relationships but even affections within the home; the fairest child in the family will be the favourite, and thus colour frustration occurs from an early age.[2] Until quite recently this has been reinforced in the schools. The textbooks and readers show only white children, and white adults are seen to play all the dominant and attractive roles. Dr. Elsa Walters has pointed to the psychological damage which the child suffers. 'The acceptance of white skin as associated with all that is important enough to be in books, pictures and "school learning" tends to an unconscious rejection of a child's own colour.'[3] When he leaves school he will find colour discrimination in employment; in many stores, for example, the counter staff will be fair and the outside staff much darker. A constant association therefore exists between blackness and inferiority, producing an ambivalent attitude in West Indians towards their African origins.

Many came to England to escape from this system because they felt that there would be more opportunities for a black man than at home. It is not surprising that when they meet rejection in England they are left disoriented. As Mervyn Norris, a Jamaican student, wrote in his prize-winning essay in *Disappointed Guests*: 'Most West Indians I have met in Britain suffer from neuroses about colour. Partly they brought them to Britain, partly they found them there.'[4] They are not supported by the same strong sense of national identity as is the case with Indians and Pakistanis. If the Federation of the West Indies had not broken up, it might perhaps have conferred on West Indians in Britain some sense of a shared identity. Unlike other immigrants, West Indians are dependent for their cultural and religious life to a large extent on the institutions of the receiving society, and if the Churches should be thought to be failing them—and, as we have seen, their experience has been mixed but on the whole a source of disappointment—they are likely to be thrown all the more in on themselves.

On the evidence presented in Part III the West Indians still appear to be concentrated in the large conurbations and in the areas of original settlements in other cities. As they gather their children to them and build new families in this country, they have not been able to move out into the suburbs. They are still living in very overcrowded conditions with fewer amenities than English people living in the same neighbourhoods, and they are paying more for less. They are still concentrated in the same manual occupations and they appear to be earning less than Englishmen in similar jobs. In fact, as time goes by and their families grow, their standard of living appears to be falling, while their children, handicapped by long separation and by changing to another educational system, are emerging from school with fewer attainments than the average English child.

The variety between the West Indian islands and within their populations makes it dangerous to generalize about West Indians in this country. It would be wrong to think of these immigrants as a homogeneous group, or to expect the same response to British society from men and women drawn from different classes, from town and country, and from French- and English-speaking islands. Some West Indians have prospered here and are leading middle-class lives; others are to be found in the professions. But on the whole, the general impression is one of a gradual deterioration in their relative position over time.

This deterioration is the more disturbing because an emigration draws on some of the most enterprising elements in a population and we have seen that the West Indian migration in the mid-1950s contained a large proportion of skilled workers. This picture of insulation and comparative failure might perhaps be expected of an immigrant group separated from the receiving society by language and by the barriers of another culture, and which is unwilling to adapt itself to the new environment. But West Indians share a common language and a common faith with their hosts and the Caribbean culture is everywhere derived from that of the metropolitan countries.

(b) The Two Cultures

How great are the social and cultural differences? An extreme view is stated by Sheila Patterson in her study of Brixton. 'The West Indian newcomers differ from the British receiving society in social and cultural background at least as much as do such immigrant groups as the Italians, Latvians and Cypriots. These social and cultural differences . . . are often obscured, not only by the more immediate and obvious difference of pigmentation but by the facts of a common citizenship, a common language and a common adherence to Christian doctrine.'[5]

Mrs. Patterson was comparing and contrasting the typical West Indian whom she characterized as coming from a semi-rural colonial proletariat with the contemporary lower and lower-middle classes in Britain. Elsewhere in her book, she described Brixtonian *mores*, which are 'on the whole those of the respectable upper-working class or of the even more status conscious lower-middle or white-collar class' who expect from their neighbours certain standards of order, cleanliness, quietness, privacy, and propriety, with houses well kept and neighbours keeping themselves to themselves.[6] This is a class in which marriage is the norm and the unmarried expectant mother brings shame on her family. Mrs. Patterson maintained that no immigrant groups had so signally failed to conform with these standards as the West Indians.

Is this really so? There seems little doubt that many English people would agree. They see the relations between West Indians and the British as a meeting between two cultures. Thus Richmond found in the St. Paul's area of Bristol, where one-fifth of the population is Jamaican, that the vast majority of the English agreed that 'the immigrants' background and ways of life make them altogether different from English people around here'.[7] But there was little agreement on the specific ways in which the immigrants were different. Rex and Moore, on the other hand, found that the West Indians in Sparkbrook, although they came from a number of islands, had a 'largely English culture pattern', with their community and social activities centred around sports clubs; some of the West Indian families reminded them of the Victorian middle class; and they speak of the 'petit-bourgeois respectability which pervades so much of West Indian life'.[8] It is true that they found many unstable relationships, and mothers of children living without partners, but some at least of the disorganization of West Indian family life is the consequence of emigration, and of being forced to live in decaying areas of cities.

Which of these very different views is near the truth? In order to consider this adequately we must again look at the typical West Indian social structure. From the end of the eighteenth century, when the agitation against the slave trade began, the small white ruling group, which had always kept socially aloof, began increasingly to treat the coloured middle class as allies and to abandon or reduce the social barriers between them. When the slaves were freed, the result in many islands was to collapse a three-class system into two basic classes, distinguishing the ex-slaves, who in West Indian terminology were black, from the upper group, who were coloured or white. Colour in the sense of appearance as a key to descent has been of such importance in this society that colour terms are often used to indicate class and a man is spoken of as 'white' because he is rich or successful. But this class division along colour lines has also been reflected in a cultural division.

This was in a sense the most colonial of all societies, in that almost everyone from top to bottom accepted the ideas of the ruling group as to their own superiority. But it was only those who aspired to be 'white' in the special West Indian sense who adopted European values and followed European culture patterns; the rest of the population remained within an Afro-West Indian culture. The evidence suggests that the emigrants to Britain, particularly in the early 1950s, were socially ambitious to climb out of what Lowenthal calls, 'the black masses'[9]—Patterson's 'rural colonial proletariat'[10]—and eager to adopt the ways of the coloured group with its careful social gradings. As the emigration grew, it began to draw, particularly in Jamaica, on the rural unskilled Afro-West Indians, so that both elements are to be found in England.

(c) The Realities—Housing

From the earliest stages West Indians have had the greatest difficulty in finding houses.

I walk this town one night from the time I finish work till it was time to start work the following morning. In those days police didn't even bother to pick up a black man, because the jail would be a night shelter out of the rain and the cold. That day when I finish work I was feeling so rusty and tired that I drag myself to Charing Cross an' pay a penny an' got into the toilet determined to have a roof over my head that night. I remember that it was a small island man cleaning up the lavatory, I think he was a Bajan. I didn' pay him no mind, I decided that I would curl up on the toilet seat and go off to sleep. I was just dropping off into a sweet sleep when I hear the door breaking down, bam! bam! When I look up the black man climb over the top and see me sleeping. . . . Man that Bajan man carry on, you hear. 'Get outa there man! Is guys like you come to the white people their country and spoil it up. You should be ashamed of you'self man. You lettin' the race down, man.' So I come out and just look him over from head to toe and back again and said to him 'Is not me carrying down the race, boy. You see me coming to England going round cleaning up people's shit'.[11]

This was the experience of a Jamaican migrant in London in 1950. For those who arrived in the early 1950s the problem of finding somewhere to live was desperate. They came at a time of acute housing shortage, made worse for a coloured man or woman by racial discrimination by landlords.

The housing shortage and colour discrimination persisted throughout the 1950s. Broad demographic trends, planning and housing policies, and the operation of the private housing market all helped to determine what kind of areas and what kind of houses were available to the working-class newcomer to the large cities, whether he was white or coloured. He was forced to find shelter in the decaying areas of cities, which had been losing population, in the dilapidated homes of people who had moved away to the suburbs.

The neighbourhoods described by Rex and Moore[12] and the type of housing available to newcomers were equally typical of the London boroughs. Similar conditions awaited the West Indians in other parts of the country. Their choice was almost everywhere restricted. In Bristol, nearly half the West Indian population was concentrated in the St. Paul's Montpelier district at the time of the 1961 Census.[13] By 1965, when Richmond and Lyon conducted their survey, their number had increased by over 40%. The area was one of depressed and dilapidated working-class housing on the edge of the central business district. As Rex and Moore found in Sparkbrook, the area contained a large number of Irish and also immigrants who had arrived in the previous ten years from Europe and from other parts of England and Wales. On the other hand, house buying by West Indian and Indian migrants seems gradually to have enabled reasonably friendly households to have been created by groups of friends and relatives. Valiant efforts were made to turn a room into a home.

Mrs. Rocco lived in a small room just large enough to hold a bed, dressing table and wardrobe, everything as bright and gaily painted as possible in the dirty smoke-laden air which thickened the texture of the curtains, obliterating any colour or pattern. . . .[14]

Apart from problems of actually obtaining a roof over their heads, West Indians faced the difficulty of communicating with their English neighbours in those first areas of settlement. Even if there had been no cultural differences, the disparity between the ages and family structure of the two communities would have been a barrier. Young adults predominate in a migration but the English who choose to stay or are unable to move from areas like Sparkbrook and St. Paul's tend to be much older, with children who have grown up and left home. As there is so little communication between the generations, the English make no distinctions within colour and see every West Indian as a threat to the status of the area. Richmond found that the majority of the English were skilled artisans or clerical workers, and that many identified themselves with the middle class and voted Conservative.[15] Rex and Moore observed that nostalgia for the past glories of the neighbourhood added to the resentment of the older people in Sparkbrook. 'There is an element of fantasy for most of the older English who constantly refer to the "good old days" when all the big houses were nicely kept, the area inhabited by respectable people and the streets safe at night.'[16] It is true that such areas are generally regarded as of low status throughout the city, as well as by the residents, whether native or immigrant; but Lyon found that this feeling of loss of status produced a greater antipathy towards West Indians among their neighbours than among English residents elsewhere in the city.

It is this antipathy and aloofness which so largely determines race relationships. Far more than differences in culture, it affects the response of West Indians in their areas of first settlement. They see their relations with the English as relations between two groups in which the scope of integration is limited by the way they are perceived and treated by the dominant group. The crude characterization of the West Indians as an undifferentiated racial group and the hostility associated with it reinforces the solidarity of the immigrants with each other and forces them to cling together, forming a sub-group or ethnic colony which they hesitate to leave for fear of the insecurity of an unknown world that lies outside.

Dispersal at Bristol

Let us look by contrast at a very different picture which emerges in one city where West Indian families have succeeded in obtaining reasonably modern houses on council estates.

Rex and Moore have described the immigrant 'not as simply moving from one culture to another but as being cut off from his native culture and social signposts in a colony structure which belongs neither to his homeland nor to the society of his hosts'.[17] The danger for the West Indians is that they will be forced back into the colony when, if they could escape from it, many of them would find the social signposts in this country very familiar to them.

There is evidence that once they can move out, many of the barriers to social integration are removed. A study of forty-five

West Indian families who have been rehoused on council estates in Bristol affords a most encouraging picture of successful integration.[18] They were found to have a similar outlook to English families on the estates and they faced the same problems of making a start in finding friends. In many ways the West Indians were making a more positive contribution.

The overall picture is of a much richer social life than the sample of neighbouring English families (who were also interviewed). Many immigrants in the strange country value friendship highly and are determined to seek out friends and to retain them. Also, as many West Indians suggest, the ideals of privacy and restraint between neighbours is not a cultural norm in the West Indies, the different values and expectations of the immigrants being reflected in their patterns of social life in England and in the higher level of gregariousness.

The West Indian families form a tiny minority on the estates: there was never more than one family in any street. It might be thought that their successful integration was purely a result of dispersal, but dispersal was only one factor. The context of the changed environment was also highly relevant. The three council estates differ from one another; they include one of the newest in Bristol, expanding, well laid-out, and with the residents all relative newcomers, with young families predominating. It was on this estate that the majority of the West Indian families were living; but others were on one of the oldest pre-war estates, with a large number of poor, unskilled, slum clearance tenants paying low rents. This estate has a low reputation in Bristol. The other families were found on a third estate which lies somewhere between the other two, with a mixture of pre-war and post-war housing and a mixed population. It, too, is regarded by Bristolians as a rough area.

It is significant that the West Indian families seemed to be equally well accepted on all three estates and nowhere were they thought to be lowering the status of their neighbourhood. This is the more remarkable in view of the concern for respectability prevalent among the residents.

There is a widespread popular picture of West Indians noisily clustering together for solidarity in large colonies. If this were true of these families, they would be totally unsuited to estate life and would interpret the restraint and isolation of the small home-centred family life as another form of rejection. Some of them, it is true, were suspicious because they had not appreciated that this was the norm, but they were the exception. Most of the West Indians had settled in well although very few had been there longer than two years. Several who had come from an area of Bristol with a large Jamaican settlement felt that they had a much better chance on the estates of getting to know English people. They found them good and helpful neighbours and the estates friendlier places. They had been made welcome. Gardening was a useful common bond: one family who started laying out a lawn found one neighbour who came over to help and another who lent his lawnmower. The most successful relationships seemed to be established where there were families with children, although on the whole the West Indian children were younger than the English. Difficulties occurred with elderly, reserved neighbours, repeating the pattern of the gap between generations in the twilight areas.

The majority of the West Indians had formed good friendships among the neighbours. Most of these relationships involved mutual help, running errands and minding the children. There was nothing like the social isolation which was characteristic of so many of the English families who were interviewed. It was also very striking that there was little tendency for the West Indian families on the estates to draw together, although some of them made frequent visits back to St. Paul's to see friends or to shop for West Indian food. Equally striking was the low degree of prejudice among their English neighbours on the estates, few of whom were prepared to hold stereotyped views about colour but saw the West Indian families as individuals whom they welcomed or not, on their merits. The attitude of the majority was one of tolerance or casual acceptance.

In some ways, however, the West Indian families on the estates were not typical. Just over one in three had English wives; and this had undoubtedly helped them to find their way to a council house. In other ways, too, there was probably some self-selection; those who saw the council house system as a way to integration were those who felt prepared for it. They were certainly found to exhibit characteristics which helped them to fit into their neighbourhood, and which might not have been so common in St. Paul's. They were not prepared to join West Indian groups or associations, as they felt that if they were identified with any exclusively West Indian association this might prevent their being accepted on the estates. In this they preferred to behave as individuals, exhibiting the traits in the West Indian make-up which prompted the emigration and which, given favourable circumstances, should equip the West Indian for individual adaptation to an English environment.

(d) Adapting to Change

The West Indians who have come to Britain are a self-selected group. They have chosen to uproot themselves and better their prospects by seeking work here. From such people, with the preconceptions about England we have sketched, we should expect a readiness to conform to English cultural patterns, given encouragement to do so. And in fact this is happening. Most of the coloured Jamaicans interviewed by Richmond in Bristol supported the view that immigrants should adopt English customs and rejected the idea that immigrants cling together and do not want to be friendly with the English. It is ironical that the English in St. Paul's were quite unaware of this wish to conform and to be friendly and were convinced that the opposite was true. But this is hardly surprising in view of the prejudice among them and the almost total absence of communication. It was Robert Park who said: 'It is the essence of race relations that they are the relations of strangers.'[19]

Some English customs, however, are rejected. There is a strong element of Puritanism in many West Indians—part of the middle-class Victorian system of values to which they aspire. This makes them uneasy in the face of the relaxed standards of sexual behaviour of young adolescents in England: they are not willing for their own daughters to adopt the standards of their English peers, and, in an effort to protect them, they will often not let them join youth clubs or take part in out-of-school activities. The strong discipline which they enforce at home creates difficulties. After a long period of separation—frequently as much as eight years—it is often hard to establish a relationship with their children. Having left them in the charge of a grandmother, who may not have been able to manage them when they reached adolescence, the parents then try to re-assert their authority and this produces tensions. In their anxiety that their children should not let them down in a society where they themselves feel insecure, they are inclined to discipline them with some harshness which sometimes leads to a collision with the authorities, sometimes even to prosecution for treating their children cruelly by English standards. This experience leaves the parents bewildered and resentful, and the children disturbed by the strain of adjusting to the different standards required of them at home and at school.

But though they may wish to guard their children, they are not rejecting adult British society. They are often the main support of the Churches in working-class areas. That West Indians will usually participate in British institutions is shown by their readiness to join trade unions, in which many of them play an active part. Beryl Radin heard of many coloured shop stewards elected by predominantly white workers, and found a West Indian who was chairman of a branch with nearly all white members. She quotes a union official in London who reported that on two building sites where West Indians had been elected as shop stewards and where there were a number of Irish and other 'foreigners', the West Indians were the most 'English' of all the men there.[20]

If council housing were equally available to them, they would be following the normal British working-class housing pattern, but, until now, this avenue has been largely closed to them, and they have been forced to buy their houses. It is true that many prefer to own rather than rent; Lyon, for example, found that some of the estate tenants still hoped to buy their house even though it was a council house. In this respect, their aspirations are more like those of the skilled workers or of the middle class. On the other hand, the P.E.P. Report showed an increasing demand for council housing and this demand will certainly grow as coloured citizens become more aware of their rights.[21]

One of the indications that West Indians not merely observe English norms but have the qualities needed to resist the cultural influences of their neighbourhoods is their record in crime. They tend to live in areas of cities with the highest crime rates and the highest criminal residences; they also belong very largely to the age group (15 to 44) which is the most prone to crime; and yet the incidence of crime among this first generation appears to be far lower than for the population at large. John Lambert's study of the police division in Birmingham with the highest crime rate showed that West Indians (who, at the 1966 Census, though only 6.4% of the division's population, were concentrated in the criminal areas where they comprised 17% of the population) accounted for 3% of all indictable offenders.[22] As Lambert says: 'They seek success within the general framework of their own values and rise above the delinquent and criminal standards prevalent in the areas in which they live.'

At first sight this may seem surprising, because various observers have noted in the West Indies an attitude to authority in general which is usually thought to have developed from experience under slavery. 'The masses', writes Lowenthal, 'see formal law as a class weapon and policemen as their natural enemies.'[23] This hostility is partly due to the fact that much police activity is directed to practices which the middle and ruling classes regard as criminal but which are considered customary by the masses. Between the islands there are great differences—to someone who has lived in the slums of West Kingston, the police will look rather different than to a villager from Barbados: but so they will to the inhabitants of North and South Kensington. In some islands, the police are considered corrupt and biased against the working class, in others, they are still regarded with suspicion attaching to their long association with the colonial power. A distinction, therefore, may sometimes have to be drawn between attitudes to authority and attitudes to the police. West Indians observe administrative regulations; there is no Black Market in currency; West Indian children arrive in this country with entry certificates; and no attempts to evade passport control have been reported. We must also recall the points already made about the Caribbean social structure. There are two sets of values corresponding to the two basic classes. Among the immigrants to Britain there are very many who are moving away from the 'masses' into the section which is oriented to middle-class forms of behaviour, indeed, to Victorian respectability.

There are many other indications that a process of adaptation is taking place. There is the demographic evidence that West Indian women are marrying earlier and limiting their families. The evidence of the falling West Indian birth-rate in Birmingham (reviewed in Chapter 11) is supported from the records of general practitioners. In one Bristol practice with a large number of Jamaican patients, there is conclusive evidence of a sharp decline in the birth-rate over a period of five years.[24] In a study of 200 West Indian mothers in Reading, Professor Bell found that 90% were married, and that three-quarters of those who were unmarried when they came to England had got married within two years of their arrival.[25] For most of them illegitimacy carried no stigma at home, yet in England they felt it was important to legitimize their child. Bell also found that husbands were actively helping to rear the children, a very different pattern from that prevailing in some West Indian islands. With job security, men are more and more assuming the normal British role and responsibilities of the father of a family. But here again, it would be rash to generalize. Although many West Indian families appear to be conforming to the patterns of the English lower middle class, there are also many which preserve the matriarchal form. In these families, the stable unit is the mother and the children whom she has borne to several partners, and the partner in residence has little authority in the home. As we have seen from census evidence, a large number of West Indian women are at work. The life of many of these working mothers is especially difficult. They may be the main support of their families here, and they may be sending money home for children left behind. Their own mothers are not present to help them. They leave their infant children with child minders; their older children are often neglected. Because of their poverty and ignorance of the system, they often live in the most overcrowded conditions. It would be fanciful to speak of a process of adjustment in these immigrant families which are barely able to keep afloat.

Many West Indians do not regard themselves as immigrants. 'We are not immigrants in the true technical sense; after all, we are members of the Realm. We are British.' This remark, by a leading West Indian in Derby,[26] points to the dilemma of many West Indians in Britain and helps to show the difference between the way they and Indians or Pakistanis see themselves in their new country. It is false to think of them as a community apart. They came to England as individuals, as kinds of Englishmen, and not as nationals of a State: they remain as individuals, unorganized in any associations, their development shaped by their environment. Just because they lack a sense of national identity, they do not combine easily except in small scale co-operative savings schemes (the 'pardners') and they are suspicious of those who take initiatives and set themselves up as leaders. *Teamwork*, the now defunct magazine published by the West Indian Standing Conference, spoke bitterly of the complete anarchy which forms the patterns of West Indian society. But in the British context this reflects the view of a leadership whose flock will not follow. (This subject is considered in detail in Chapter 25.) It is significant that many West Indian publications have been started in this country and they have all failed, whereas the two Urdu papers, *Mashriq* and *Asia Weekly*, which serve the Pakistani community and bring them news of home, are flourishing. The failure of the West Indian papers cannot be explained simply in terms of organization, although a large part of the Jamaican market may be pre-empted by the *Weekly Gleaner* which is published in England and merely reprints items from the Jamaican *Daily Gleaner*. It is more likely that there is not a sufficiently strong sense of community among West Indians in England to support a publication. West Indians read English newspapers.

Their ties with home are with the family and very local. Those who regularly send money home are supporting children or parents; they are not as a rule transferring savings for investment in land or houses or for the support of a business, for they are not entrepreneurs at a distance, their life is lived here until success may enable them to return. Many of them think that they will return, but the longer they stay here and the more roots they put down, the more they are likely to change their minds.[27]

The West Indian emigration is now very nearly complete. Only a trickle of wage-earners and wives now enter the country and the numbers of dependent children will progressively decline as the backlog is made up (see Chapter 8). Professor Bell found that 77% of the West Indian mothers in Reading had all their children living with them,[28] and this was increasingly becoming the pattern. The Lambeth Housing survey found that in 1967 only 14% of the West Indian families had children likely to join them in the next two years.[29] So there will be very little reinforcement from home—the reverse if anything seems to have been taking place. The Home Office records for 1967 show fairly substantial numbers of Jamaicans leaving the country, with a net loss of Jamaican men; the trend is continuing in 1968. There has been a small but steady flow of West Indians returning home.[30] But it is not possible to be precise, as the records make no distinction between those who have been here on a visit or those who have been here for some time. It is generally the successful who return, intending to put their savings into a house and land, but they have found it difficult to earn a living and some reluctantly return to England within the two years allowed them.[31] Most of those who emigrate for economic reasons dream of returning home one day, and Donald Hinds claims that the dreams of the older generation are reproduced in the imaginations of their sons and daughters. However, unless the state of race relations deteriorates very much in this country, it is far more likely that the great majority of West Indians will stay for good.

(e) Disillusion

They will stay, but the danger is growing that they will with-draw into themselves and give up their attempts to approach the English and adjust to their ways. It is becoming clear to them that adjustment has to be all one-way. Experience of discrimination and rejection are causing West Indians to question the assump-tions which made them the most assimilating of the coloured immigrants. They are being forced to recognize that it is healthier for them to stay with their own kind. The experience of Wallace Collins is typical of many. A skilled carpenter, he was able to practice his craft and was at first well treated by his fellow-workers, but as he got better paid work he encountered massive hostility and was forced out of employment by the prejudice of fellow trade unionists. The final blow to his hopes and illusions occurred when he was sent by the employment exchange to a job and was told by the Irish foreman to fill a hole with a pick and shovel. He had admired the British way of life, and had mixed easily with the British at work and at play, but he finally decided that he had been wrong to try to escape from his Jamaican heritage.

Just to see Jamaicans let themselves go in England exhilarated and gratified me and I was awakened after five years in London to the significance of fellow West Indians there. . . . I wanted to be myself. I was ready to accept myself and not give a damn to what society says I should be. . . .

The antagonism which he experienced in his first five years in London had a cumulative effect.

I decided to quit the disenchantment, the uncompassionate yet polite monstrosity of the white man's society, where I quested for his daughter's hand in marriage, vied for promotion in his factory, con-fronted and fought for liberties daily; and at the same time tried to convince him that I was a genuine human being as he was, whereupon I wound up embracing his ideals and aspirations. This metamorphosis took place in me without my knowing it, until I began to intermingle with my own people. . . . I felt wanted and desired by my own people. I warmed to them and in my mind and heart I hugged them close to me. I belonged.[32]

Collins finally decided to leave Britain for Canada, but this is an escape not open to many. The disillusion and disenchantment is greater among West Indians than among any other immigrant group because they expected so much. The survey of immigrants conducted by P.E.P., as part of the inquiry into racial discrimination, found that over half the West Indians had found life in Britain worse than they had expected, while only 12% said that it was better. Their greatest source of disappointment was the racial and colour prejudice they had experienced, and unfriendliness to foreigners. Others mentioned difficulties in getting housing and jobs—difficulties sometimes caused by prejudice. The consensus of West Indian opinion revealed by the P.E.P. Report reflected two aspects of life in Britain for the black man or woman: the problem of survival and the problem of respect.

Yet what did they expect, what did they hope for? Knowledge of England varied; the degree of attachment to England varied; the degree of ambition varied. The element of risk had to be accepted as part of the decision to migrate.

Everybody is in flight and no one knows what he is fleeing to. A better break. A better break. That's what we say. And suppose this break doesn't come. Whatever it is let's suppose it doesn't turn up. What next? Tornado hates what he's going to, and yet he goes. The Governor doesn't care. He hates nothing and it seems he loves nothing. He simply lives. The others, all of us, simply go to this place which, for all we know, might be hell itself. Now it seems that if we got all the evidence in the world that it is hell, no one would want to turn back. . . . But if that break doesn't turn up? My God, what a flight. . . .[33]

So said Collis, a character in George Lamming's novel, *The Emigrants*, published in 1954.

The 'breaks' which the emigrants were seeking, those who had definite plans, were modest: the acquisition of a skill, by attending a full-time course or by studying at night; relatively secure employment; education for their children. 'To make a man o'yuhself, be somebody in the place you livin', keep yuh family clean, an' lead a decent clean life til the Almighty ready to give you leave.'[34]

The most difficult practical problem, as we have seen, was to get adequate housing, and many still find that they are worse off after several years in this country than they had been in the West Indies. They are also disappointed that they cannot get work appropriate to their skills.[35]

The economic struggle severely limited the lives they could lead. 'We stay at home, don't jump around much, we don't even have the money at the weekend to start anything. Just once a while we go to church, nothing, no show, nowhere. Can't afford to lose a shilling. . . .' That was the life which one of the couples interviewed by Betty Davison found themselves leading. They hoped to bring some of their children to join them in England. A taped message was recorded to send to them in Jamaica: 'Well, children, I long to see you, we have it very hard in England but by the mercy of God, one day, all of us will meet again.'[36] There was a striking contrast between the adventurous spirit in which the migrants set out, and the confined life which imposed itself upon them in Britain. Bound in space by housing, and in time by shift-work and overtime, the shape of life was laconically summed up in Rex and Moore's study of Sparkbrook by a 10-year-old West Indian girl: 'My mother has three children. We live in one room. My mum works on nights and my dad works days.'[37]

Richmond provides evidence of a fall in the social and occupational status of immigrants after arrival in Britain, but, as he points out, this tends to be a characteristic of all migrations. Immigrants generally have to accept a drop in status. But there were some aspects of disillusion which have affected those who have achieved success as well as those still struggling. West Indians had many illusions about the British and British society which were to be shattered, and in the process they began to lose their own sense of identification with Britain.

Does Mr. Clay know why West Indians come and will come to England? The British people whom I and the rest of us met were to us paragons of everything manly, courageous, wonderful. . . . How can I or any other West Indian live down this great lie? Is this the homeland of the great John Wesley, the birthplace of Nurse Cavell. . . ? It is not the material England alone that draws immigrants. England to the outside world stands for much more than Mr. Clay knows.[38]

The writer of this letter, to a provincial paper in 1958, expressed in passionate terms what has been repeated again and again by every West Indian writing or speaking about the 'integration' of his countrymen into British society. 'I remember Jamaicans crying when the *Hood* was sunk during the Second World War. We used to sing "Rule Britannia" as children. Whole classes would walk through the streets of Kingston singing it. . . .'[39]

If admiring Britain was admiring a certain way of life, and going to Britain a search to achieve it, it was only to be expected that the visible, tangible, social Britain on arrival would be different. But the worst was not that the real Britain failed to embody the idealized British way of life, but that the West Indians who considered themselves to be British, were treated as foreigners; and this, because of their race. 'Like every West Indian, I am part Englishman. I mean this, of course, in the sense that, having acquired the English language, the traditions and institutions of this country, it is natural for me to want to be here. The West Indian is essentially what British culture and influences have made him.' So wrote Albert Maria Gomes, former Minister of Labour and Commerce in Trinidad. He added, 'my admiration of the Englishman's country and way of life was as intense as my resentment of his overlordship'.[40]

The coloured man was assumed by the English to be lower class, and many stratagems were adopted to keep him there. Those West Indians for whom the migration to Britain had been a step towards middle-class status were doubly frustrated. Those who were fair skinned and already part of the middle class, found themselves sharply demoted. This became very clear to Gomes when he settled in Britain after previous visits as a V.I.P.: 'There are certain unusual features of my experience', he writes. 'I was accepted as a white person in Trinidad. For all practical purposes, I am "coloured" in England.' The educated middle class particularly resent that the British make no distinction between coloured people. The effect on a student was described by Kenneth Ramchand in his essay in *Disappointed Guests*:

Leaving the West Indies and coming to Britain is like entering a land where the natives suffer from a curious kind of colour blindness, in the contemplation of human groups. This special form of blindness manifests itself in an insensitivity to racial discrimination and variant shades within the category 'black'. It registers two crude categories, black and white.[41]

The denial of the Englishness of the West Indians was both a conscious and an unconscious action. It manifested itself in different ways: in the ignorance of British people generally about the Caribbean—their surprise that West Indians could speak English; in the emotionally charged terminology in which the word 'immigrant' was used constantly to mean 'coloured'; in the actual changes in the immigration laws made in 1962 and 1968. Wallace Collins described how odd he felt during the first debates about immigration control in 1961. He had then lived and worked in

Britain for about seven years, mainly as a cabinet maker and joiner: 'I felt like an overgrown child left on a doorstep who overhears the argument among unseeing neighbours among whom were some who meant well, and some who argued for the sake of arguing, whether or not they should take in the poor, unwanted black "chile".'[42]

The debates on immigration control in 1961 showed a troubled conscience, and control itself was introduced apologetically. By 1965, this was no longer the case, and by 1968, Enoch Powell's speech in April was followed by a razor slashing incident by youths at an 'inter-racial' christening in Wolverhampton. By 1968, most of the West Indian population in Britain had already been settled for some years, and had had sufficient opportunity to re-assess the situation, on the basis of their continuous daily experiences. All the same, Powell's speech came as a shock to many, and the High Commissioner for Jamaica issued a calming statement to Jamaicans in this country in an attempt to reassure them. He recognized that most of them would be bewildered and greatly disturbed and it was impossible not to be discouraged; while he would not expect his fellow Jamaicans to take insults lightly, he wanted to assure them that there were many people who were working together to improve race relations.[43] All the public debates about race relations, whether they concerned immigration control or the need for equal opportunities in Britain through the Race Relations Acts, tended to emphasize the differences between native English and Commonwealth immigrants.

Behind the public debates and the mass media coverage of race relations lay the individual encounters and the personal experience of discrimination. Could the Englishman any longer be trusted? Beryl Radin in her study of coloured immigrants in the trade unions quotes a West Indian who had been elected chairman of a branch with nearly all white members. 'I'd never put myself in a position where I'd have to depend on the loyalty of my fellow workers', he told her. 'I just don't feel I could depend on them if I needed help.'[44]

Many coloured immigrants are protected by their culture and the barrier of language from the full emotional impact of exclusion or rejection and many avoid situations where they might be rejected. But to the men and women who see themselves, not only not culturally different, but as inheritors of the same culture, the effect of discrimination is far worse. It is possible that now, after many years in Britain, many West Indians may resort to the same defensive avoidance as the Pakistani or Indian who has newly arrived and knows nothing of this country. But, unlike the others, West Indians have no cultural citadel, no communal institutions to which they can withdraw, unless it be to the refuge of the Pentecostal Church. It is true that the number of Pentecostals is growing in this country, but Malcolm Calley found no evidence to support his thesis that adherence to Pentecostalism would follow from a sense of alienation from British society.[45] There are West Indian leaders who assert that there is a distinctive West Indian culture and who see in a pluralist solution the only hope for the West Indian communities in Britain. Neville Maxwell, a former Chairman of the West Indian Standing Conference, is an articulate spokesman of this view:

For West Indians in Britain, the choice is clear although the means to the end, as is invariably the case, will not be achieved without great effort and self-understanding. That choice does not lie between swallowing everything English in order to become black Englishmen and women—if this metamorphosis is at all possible, not to mention allowable—and rejecting entirely things English.

That part of our culture which is English oriented—as history would have it—cannot be wished away. It is there and we must recognize it for what it is. Rather, the middle course lies in developing and consciously fostering what is best in our own sub-culture since our original African culture was ruthlessly suppressed and subordinated to the naked acquisitiveness of the Metropolitan country. West Indians in Britain should by now have discovered what customs, habits, modes of thinking and doing things are in their best interest. This process must have happened in view of the fact that contact with another culture or between a sub-culture and a dominant culture in its natural setting, must inevitably bring out in a pronounced way what was latent in the other. Re-appraisal and renewal thus leads to self assurance and unshakeable conviction.[46]

This conviction is to be found within the concept of Negritude, which, in the words of Leopold Senghor, quoted by Maxwell, involves 'the awareness, defence, and development of African cultural values'. Integration, in the sense of pluralism, should be the goal for West Indians and other minorities in Britain. 'Assimilation must be rejected for the misguided hoax that it is.'

But Maxwell is aware that the average West Indian immigrant is deaf to this kind of appeal. He is too preoccupied with the business of establishing himself and his family. In spite of the disillusion and the emotional withdrawal, the material ties with England have grown.

If the romance has gone, for the time being a more prosaic economic marriage remains. Those who have achieved some material success may take a realistic and detached view:

I was willing to put up with certain things because England had given me a job and a home, but I wouldn't consider bringing my parents to a country where an Enoch Powell or Duncan Sandys might cause them to be thought of as less than they are. As for my children, well, if this country can't take advantage of their education, then they can go to Canada or America like my brothers and sisters.[47]

The speaker, Sam King, ex-R.A.F., returned to Britain on the *Empire Windrush* in 1948. Unless another country appears to offer the 'break' that England has not, remigration is unlikely.

Christopher Bagley suggests that the West Indians' position in this country lies midway between that of the Negro in America and in Brazil.[48] In America, rising expectations are not matched by any improvement in status, while in Brazil the Negro is relatively satisfied with far poorer conditions. As West Indians begin to expect more but find that, despite their education and their skills, opportunities are denied them and there is a relative decline in their status, we shall grow nearer to the American situation.

I think the only difference between the people on the *Windrush* and our children is this: we came asking for our rights, they are going to demand them.

2. PAKISTANIS[49]

Of all the migrations from the Commonwealth, the Pakistani presents the greatest contrast to the West Indian. If to many West Indians Britain was the mother country, to Pakistanis it was a foreign land whose language, customs, religion, and way of life were totally alien to them. Their loyalties were to their own new nation, to their region, to their village, and above all to their kin. They came to England asking nothing of their hosts except to settle for a while, work, and earn for their families at home, to whom they meant to return.

What distinguishes this migration from all the others, and not simply from the West Indian, is its demographic imbalance. For

cultural as well as economic reasons it has remained predominantly male, selecting male children to join male relatives in this
country. The imbalance between the sexes is far greater among
East Pakistanis than among West Pakistanis, who have recently
begun to bring their wives over[50]—even then, those who do so are
generally men who came during the 1950s, and the number of
families in which a mother is present is still fairly small.

The all-male character of the migration is partly the consequence of the strict seclusion of Muslim women. It is far preferable to leave them under the protection of the joint family than to
expose them to an alien environment. But although this cultural
inhibition may have an important bearing on the way the Pakistani settlements develop in the future, it is only a partial explanation of what has been happening. The Pakistani emigration, unlike
the West Indian, became highly organized and depended on a
system of sponsorship and patronage which made it selective and
confined it to a comparatively few villages within a few areas. We
have seen that the economic success of the pioneer Pakistani
migrants, frequently merchant navy deserters, induced their kinsmen to jump ship and join them. These settlers later sponsored
other kinsmen by arranging for their recruitment as seamen, for
recruiting from Pakistani ports was largely controlled by the crews.
In this way, the flow was confined to the original emigrant areas
of Sylhet, Mirpur, and Campbellpur. When the recruits exceeded
the demand and the Pakistani Government began to restrict the
issues of passports, travel agents emerged to fulfil the new and
profitable role of supplying forged documents and of sending
'religious' travellers to Britain via the Middle East. The organization of this traffic depended to a large extent on there being sponsors in England who could provide shelter and an introduction to
a job, and in many cases, the money for the fare. The effect of the
1962 Commonwealth Immigrants Act was to perpetuate the selective process of migration, as kinsmen and fellow-villagers stood an
even better chance of being sponsored under the voucher system
than those who had no kinship links with Britain.

A very close reciprocal relationship is set up between sponsor
and client. Some form of sponsorship by friends and relations in
Britain on the basis of village-kin ties is a necessary insurance for
the immigrant against possible hardship during his early days in
Britain. This, as much as a desire to be with kinsmen and friends,
explains the emergence of village-kin groups in Britain, which has

become the pattern of settlement, not only among Pakistanis but among the Gujaratis as well.[51] The sponsor has an equal interest in the relationship. He looks first for kin to help him achieve his economic goals, whether in running a business or in managing houses. If close kinsmen do not exist, he sponsors distant kinsmen, friends, and fellow-villagers. It is not necessary for a prospective migrant to know his sponsor personally, provided there is a mutual friend known to both parties.

A Pakistani sponsor in Britain becomes a patron to all those whom he has sponsored, no matter how widely dispersed they might be in Britain. Each of them is linked to the other through ties of mutual aid and other reciprocal obligations. They forgather during holidays, visit one another in illness, entertain new arrivals and departing relatives, and sustain each other in times of crisis. In short, reciprocal obligations, consensus in decision making, and cohesion when threatened from outside characterize their social and economic relations in Britain as they do in Pakistan. This, however, takes place within a clearly defined patrilineage group known as a *baradari* or brotherhood, which comprises a number of extended families within a clan.

In Pakistan, men and adolescent boys spend their leisure hours in the company of male members of the *baradari* at the *baithak* (a kind of club or resting place). Here, a family's male guests will often sleep with their host or with another male member of the family. Among Pakistani immigrants in Britain, the sponsor and his 'family', or the house-group, are the substitutes for the traditional functions of social control exercised at home by the *baithak* and the *baradari*. Within the all-male dormitory houses, the Pakistani is reminded of his primary obligation which is to discharge his debt to his sponsor or to his family, who have probably mortgaged their land to pay for his passport and passage, and then to remit sufficient funds to Pakistan to sponsor other kin and to improve his family's fortunes.

The Pakistani sacrifices material comforts to pursue his economic objectives, and the dormitory house, with its low rent of 15s. a week, is an important means to this end. Food is bought on a co-operative basis at bulk rates and he can live on as little as £2 10s. 0d. a week, other expenses consisting of 2s. for flour, 7s. for milk, 16s. for groceries, and 10s. for bus fares. In his first few years every penny is saved to discharge obligations: many Pakistanis remit as much as half their earnings. It was estimated that in 1963 remittances amounted to as much as £26 million, or more than the inland revenue of East Pakistan.[52] The dormitory house also serves as a kind of insurance policy or provident society, for rent is excused to a kinsman who falls out of employment. It is, therefore, not surprising that a plan by the Bradford City Council to provide hostels for single Pakistanis, with separate cooking facilities in each room, at a rental of 30s. a week failed to evoke any response. Their goals are more likely to be reached through mutual support and austere living than through dispersal into the wider community.

Joint living in these dormitory houses with their group activities and total lack of privacy ensures that the immigrant conforms to the norms of his community in respect of diet, thrift, recreation, language, avoidance of contacts outside the sub-group, and modest hospitality to visiting kinsmen. Apart from visiting friends, leisure hours are spent in the house or in watching Indian and Pakistani films. This self-sealing process is carried over into working hours, especially if the immigrant is recruited into an ethnic gang, sometimes on the night shift, where contact with his employers is maintained through an English-speaking foreman.

These closely knit and self-segregated communities are served by their own shops and other services provided by fellow-countrymen: the growth of these services and the emergence of the Pakistani entrepreneur in the last few years is a measure of the growth of separate communities. In Bradford in 1967, there were fifty-one Pakistani grocers and butchers, compared with only two in 1959. By this date there were also fifty Pakistani schools of motoring. The number of cafés increased from three to sixteen, of barbers sixfold. The city now has five Pakistani banks. In 1967, an article in *Asia Weekly* compared Bradford's Lumb Lane to a bazaar in some prosperous city of Pakistan. The same kind of development has taken place around other Pakistani communities. For example, in Balsall Heath, whereas ten years earlier there were five Pakistani shops or cafés, in 1967 there were sixty. Glasgow's population of 7,000 Pakistanis is served by one hundred retail grocers and twenty-five wholesale stores.[53]

This picture of a community organized along village-kin groupings has emerged only in the last few years and is the result of massive reinforcement from Pakistan since 1961. In the earlier years, Pakistanis settled together irrespective of origin, but as the rate of immigration accelerated, sub-groups, based at first on regional identity, soon fragmented into village and kinship units.

The community was further divided by religious sects, namely, the Sunnis, Shias, and Ahmeddiyas. Within a sub-group based on a common area of origin, the immigrants confined their personal relations to their fellow-adherents. Since marriage does not take place across the Sunni-Shia and other sectarian boundaries, there are no kinship ties to bridge the gap. Thus, the growth of the Pakistanis in Britain has developed from a fusion of the migrant community to fission and segmentation. Personal relationships between immigrants from outside their area of origin are kept to a minimum. East Pakistanis live exclusively apart from West Pakistanis, even in London where the acute housing shortage might have brought them together. In Bradford, there is no sharing between West Pakistanis from different regions—Pathan tribesmen live on their own, Campbellpuris and Mirpuris avoid one another, and there is a similar division between Punjabis and non-Punjabis. Houses are apt to be grouped according to area of origin.[54]

This effect of fission through reinforcement is familiar from the pattern of settlement of immigrants in other countries,[55] but whether it will persist among the Pakistanis depends on the rate at which families are reunited in this country. If a wife comes to join a husband, the family moves to a house away from the areas of dormitory settlement. At first, such families were few and isolated, on the margin of the settlement, but already there is a perceptible clustering of family houses in certain streets cutting across regional and kin boundaries. We may postulate a sequence which begins with fusion and leads on to fission and segmentation. In its third stage families are thrown out to the margin, leading in the next stage to a clustering of family houses with a return to fusion, and finally to the stage where the dormitory house may itself become marginal. There are still Pakistani settlements which have been formed fairly recently, in places like Luton, Bedford, and Watford, which have not got much beyond the stage of fusion; earlier settlements in Bradford and Birmingham exhibit the second stage fully and the beginnings of the fourth stage of family clusters.

Before the 1965 White Paper virtually closed the door to adult male immigrants, it was possible for brother to replace brother in the emigration, and when Rex and Moore were working in Sparkbrook, in 1964, they found that many Pakistanis expected to follow this pattern. The effect of the White Paper was to substitute adolescent schoolboys for their uncles in the emigration; after a short period in English schools, they too would become worker-bees sending honey back to the hive. Thus, the Government restrictions did not change the pattern of the settlements except to lower the age of entry. But they did force the immigrant to face the fact that he would probably not return to his country, except on a visit. This may have led a certain number to decide to bring over their wives who would not have otherwise done so; subsequent restrictions imposed by the British Government accelerated the process. The effect of the 1968 Commonwealth Immigrants Act, which closed the door to dependent children unless both father and mother were in Britain, remains to be seen. It may result in many more wives coming over to join husbands, but cultural inhibitions may still prove too strong.

Meanwhile a distinction must be drawn between the majority who are still in all-male settlements and the growing minority of reunited families. The male settlers exhibit many of the character-istics of the transient. As we have seen in Chapter 14, their savings are very high and their standard of living remains low, although their earnings have risen significantly over time. They ask little of this country except to be allowed to earn and prosper materially. If this is conceded, they are not very much concerned with their social or political rights. 'The Pakistanis demand little of their hosts and are prepared to accept the Britons' definition of the relationship.' Michael Banton's observation, made in 1956, still holds true today.[56] The Race Relations Board has received very few complaints from Pakistanis. The P.E.P. Report showed that they are not particularly aware or resentful of discrimination because they avoid situations which would bring them into con-flict with outsiders, with whom they seek only a *modus vivendi*.[57] An analysis of the correspondence columns of the two weekly papers serving the community, *Mashriq* and *Asia Weekly* (with a circula-tion of 24,000 and 14,000, respectively, in mid-1967), revealed not one letter of complaint about racial discrimination. Almost every issue, however, contained protests against Pakistani authori-ties in Britain and in Pakistan alleging bribery and corruption.

The press in Pakistan is also full of complaints against a corrupt bureaucracy. Corruption operates at many levels: nothing very much is obtained for nothing. A great gulf divides officialdom from the illiterate masses. At all stages of emigration, money and *sifārish* (influence, connexions) are needed. Passports can be very expensive. Even the application forms for work vouchers were sold to the ignorant for 25 or 50 rupees. A racket is still being run by the peons in the British High Commission who make applicants pay for an entry permit. Remittances in many villages are paid to the recipient by the headmaster, who acts as local postman and deducts a percentage which he fixes himself.

As long as Pakistanis in England continue to think of themselves as an extension of their home society, they are likely to carry over attitudes learned at home towards authority. This explains the evasion of regulations, whether they emanate from the Pakistani authorities or the British. The Black Market continues to flourish, even though the Pakistan Government introduced a bonus voucher rate for immigrants in this country which gave them 75% above the normal exchange rate; income tax is evaded by claiming allowance for fictitious children in Pakistan;[58] and loopholes are found in the immigration laws by such devices as falsifying the ages of children, adopting the sons of fellow-villagers,[59] or by entering as tourists and marrying one of many 'professional brides' made available by agents.

Their attachment to their home society and to the joint family will remain very strong so long as Pakistanis remain 'bachelors' in this country. The head of the family has a hold over the married man in so far as he keeps his wife within the family home and arranges the betrothal of his daughters; if an unmarried Pakistani wishes to marry he depends on the head of the family for the choice of his bride.

Once a Pakistani decides to bring his wife and children to this country he is breaking out of the web of connexions that has tied him so closely to home, kept him sheltered from the outside world, and prevented him from psychologically putting down roots in Britain. Bringing over a wife and children is in many ways a most decisive step. It involves uprooting them from his family and removing them from the authority of the head of his family. He himself will move out of the dormitory settlement, away from the colony of single men, to his own house in another neighbourhood; he will have a stake, which is wider than his economic interest, in his adopted country; and will become more aware of the values of British society. All this does not mean that there will be any loosening of the bonds of his own culture: in fact, they may well become stronger.

The young male immigrant is as secular as his contemporary in British society. Dahya found very little religious observance among male Pakistanis; few said their prayers; few houses contained a copy of the Koran. Attendance at the mosque was very rare—at the festival of Id, the congregation had to be coached in the ritual. In Birmingham, Pakistani cafés remain open during the feast of Ramadhan and are much frequented. But the arrival of wives and mothers will serve to strengthen religious observance, for women say their prayers regularly and are regarded as the keepers of a man's conscience: it is they who transmit religious beliefs and values to the children.

When the children go to school, and particularly when daughters reach the age of puberty, a conflict of values arises which heightens the Pakistanis' consciousness of their culture. Faced with what they must regard as a challenge to the traditional upbringing of their daughters, Pakistani parents frequently insist on their wearing traditional dress which prevents their taking part in physical education. In doing so they are combining to make their first demands on the new society. Even if the mother raises no objection at this stage to her daughter's conforming with English custom, she may reassert herself at the time of leaving school and try to reimpose Pakistani standards of dress and behaviour. The permissive atmosphere of English co-educational schools is seen as a threat to morals and to parental authority as well as to Muslim culture. To meet this threat many communities are now providing facilities for the formal religious instruction of their children. In Bradford, for example, the majority of Pakistani children attend one of the two mosques, where, it is reported, they spend an average of fifteen to twenty hours a week, either before and after school on weekdays, or on Saturday and Sunday mornings.[60]

The arrival of wives in Britain serves to reinforce Muslim culture in other ways. They are kept in strict purdah and are effectively isolated from the world around them. A Muslim woman who visited several Pakistani families in Bradford reported on the extreme loneliness of the wives and their dependence on their husbands.[61] Removed from the companionship of other women in the joint family, they cannot leave their house without their husbands, who still spend their leisure with other men outside the home. The traditions and taboos of the joint family are carried over even into the small nuclear household: husband, wife, and children eat their meals separately and the wife must eat unseen by her husband. Even if there were not the barrier of purdah, they would be isolated by their total lack of English. As more families are reunited, this social isolation will no doubt be broken down, but it seems certain that the first generation will be zealous guardians of their culture and will see that it is transmitted to their children.

Pakistanis in Britain regard themselves as a people apart. They classify themselves as *Kālé* (black or coloured), and Europeans as *Gŏré lok* (literally 'white people'). Negroes are referred to as *Sidis*, irrespective of their origin, and are not part of the *Kālé* category. The distinction between *Kālé* and *Gŏré*, the insiders and the rest, is primarily a social distinction based on culture and religion, and the connotation of colour is often forgotten. The worlds of *Gŏré* and *Sidis* cannot be reconciled with the *Kālé*, whose legacy is regarded as a sacred trust from God. The terms are continually used by the Pakistani immigrants, whether they are peasants or members of the educated professional elite, and they serve to heighten the consciousness of racial, social, and cultural differences. This classification of the world into 'we' and 'they' has a close parallel to the practice of Jews, who refer to non-Jews as *Goyyim*, and it may tell us a good deal about the way this community will seek to maintain a separate cultural existence in Britain. This exclusiveness is also maintained in their attitude towards the Sikhs. Although the term *Kālā* can also be applied to Indian complexions and, broadly, to people of Indo-Pakistani origin, and although West Pakistanis, being Punjabis, share many cultural traits with Sikhs, for example language, folk music, and some of their diet, they maintain a distance from them and avoid personal relationships. They also stereotype the Sikhs, who are said to practise fraternal polyandry in this country and to eat tinned cat food and bully beef.

There is no sanction in Islam against inter-marriage with people of another faith, and Pakistani seamen who arrived in the early 1950s frequently married English wives.[62] But in spite of the very great preponderance of single men in the emigration, there appears to have been comparatively little inter-marriage with the *Gŏré lok*, although correspondence in the two Urdu papers shows that 'marriage out' is sufficiently widespread to be regarded as a deviant pattern of behaviour and a threat to the culture of the community. *Asia Weekly* recently sought the views of its readers on the subject: 'Can a white woman be a good wife?' In the correspondence, which ran for several weeks, readers wrote unfavourably about the white wives of their acquaintances, whom they found slovenly, domineering, and apt to be unfaithful. The letters were printed alongside photographs of girls in mini-skirts, girls smoking, and film stars with low necklines—the intention clearly being to show white women in an unfavourable light. There was an even more vehement correspondence in *Mashriq* on the subject of *Gŏrĕ* boyfriends, which began when a girl wrote that she felt there was no harm in having white boyfriends and that she was going to marry one with her parents' consent. Of all the letters received by the newspaper, not one was in favour of inter-marriage. Another heated correspondence was started when a schoolgirl wrote complaining that she had to wear traditional dress at school; not a single letter supported her; a letter from a woman university student maintained that traditional dress for Muslims is a religious injunction and when a people chooses to abandon it they do so at their peril; this was why the Arabs had lost the war against Israel.

These debates become a form of ritualized drama in which highly emotional and exaggerated views are expressed, to remind the readers of their basic values, their motives for emigrating, and their cultural ties.

Meanwhile, the majority of Pakistanis in this country remain single, and they appear to be achieving their economic objectives. The great mass of workers are still engaged in labouring jobs in textiles, heavy engineering, and in transport. It may be deplorable that they tend to be concentrated in industries which are declining and, for the long run, there is a danger that Pakistanis will be associated with this kind of occupation, unless a much wider variety of jobs and job opportunities is made available to them. But at this stage of the immigration there is, as we have seen, little feeling of discrimination, and, in many cases, there may be none because they are not looking for other types of work which might pay less: those who take white-collar work sacrifice material prosperity for status. Among Gujaratis, according to Desai, occupations which entail wearing a uniform are not highly regarded, as they lower the prestige of immigrants belonging to high castes.[63] This is not the case with Pakistanis, with whom to be a bus conductor or driver has a high status, because it requires a good knowledge of English and the uniform bestows authority on the wearer. However, from both Glasgow and Bradford, it is reported that Pakistanis are unwilling to accept promotion to Inspector as they would earn less and they are afraid of incurring resentment if they had to criticize and check white employees.[64] This is consistent with their general avoidance of situations which might bring them into conflict or competition with British workers.

Alongside the mass of manual workers, there is a class of entrepreneur who is prospering through providing services to his fellow-countrymen and has a vested interest in the immigrant community remaining separate. There are other successful Pakistanis whose savings go into investment in the home country. Dahya cites the case of a Mirpuri who came to this country in 1952. Between 1956 and 1962, he sponsored ten people, all of whom were married. Seven of them have now brought their wives and children over. Members of this group have between them five establishments in Bradford. During 1967, four of them invested 800,000 rupees in a modern block in a town in Jhelum district which consists of a cinema, a petrol station, and flats. The whole project will cost 1,400,000 rupees over the next four years. The original sponsor, who is completely illiterate, and his wife are responsible for managing the new property. (Rex and Moore also found that some of the most successful Pakistani shopkeepers in Sparkbrook were illiterate.)

A distinction must be made between the entrepreneurs, who live in or near the immigrant colonies, and the educated elite of Pakistani professionals resident in Britain, who are doctors, teachers, lawyers, journalists, and officials of the High Commission. The hierarchical nature of Pakistani society is carried over into the emigration, not in the settlement areas, but in the attitudes of the High Commission and of many of the elite who find the immigrants' way of life in Britain an embarrassment. The mass of the immigrants, in turn, feels that the High Commission is out of touch and does not look to it for leadership. There are members of the elite who have assumed the role of leaders and they are discussed in Chapter 25.

In spite of cleavages, particularly between East and West Pakistanis, and regional differences in village and kin loyalties, community feeling is strong among Pakistanis in Britain. It is founded mainly on pride in Pakistan and on a sense of belonging to a new nation. This patriotism operates in times of crisis, like the 1965 war with India, when large sums of money were raised for defence, and it expresses itself not only in loyalty to the home country but in the value attached to maintaining the culture and traditions and transmitting them to the children. The immigration is far too recent for there to be many signs of a process of adaptation to the norms of British culture; but it remains to be seen what effect the British educational system is having on the children. Even among the first generation of adults, there are already some indications of change. It may be a small thing, but the Asian film club in Bradford now finds that American and British films are more popular than Indian or Pakistani productions. This would have been unthinkable ten years or even five years ago. The secretary of the club, which shows films in three cinemas, was reported as saying that his clients are no longer so nostalgic for their home country.[65] Many Pakistanis offered their support to the shortlived 'I'm Backing Britain' campaign by offering one day's wages. *Asia Weekly* lent its support and ran a competition for letters on the subject and also an open meeting in Birmingham where donations were received.

We have seen that there has been a certain amount of intermarriage, and loneliness may lead to more as Pakistanis seek companionship among white girls. So long as the ratio between the sexes remains so unbalanced, there is bound to be a conflict between the claims of their culture and their human needs. But the Government's action in withdrawing their passport rights from Kenya Asians and speeches by Enoch Powell have thrown the Pakistanis back in on themselves. Some who had taken out British citizenship re-applied for Pakistani citizenship after the passing of the 1968 Commonwealth Immigrants Act. An editorial in *Asia Weekly*, however, which appeared in the week following Enoch Powell's Birmingham speech, advised its readers that the way to keep their self-respect was through political organizations. The paper was against any exclusively immigrant organization: Pakistanis should join one of the main parties in Britain and use their vote. They should make use of the democratic process to demand their full rights in this their second home. This sane response was a tacit acknowledgment of the real position.

Although it may still be psychologically important to the single male Pakistanis to think of themselves as 'birds of passage' and though they may express their intention to return to Pakistan, they know that they are unlikely to do so. Compared with what they can earn in Pakistan, where the average income is £30 a year, Britain is indeed an El Dorado, and their brick built houses, even though they have poor amenities, are *pukka*. So much is expected from them at home that even if there were no other motive for staying, they are more or less compelled to remain as worker bees outside the hive. Very few will return. For many the migration offers an escape from the hereditary bonds of caste, as caste distinctions can no longer be maintained in an urban society. Some men who have prospered have even been able to arrange marriages with women of a higher caste belonging to locally influential families, thus acquiring a new status—these marriages would never have been possible in Pakistan. There is an obvious contrast with the West Indian who finds his hopes of escape from the handicap of colour frustrated in the emigration.

3. INDIANS
(a) Sikhs

Of the three main constituents of the coloured immigration from the Commonwealth, the Sikhs are the most homogeneous, the most cohesive, and the best organized. As we saw in Chapter 5, they are drawn mainly from the Jullundur and Hoshiarpur districts, which are contiguous areas in the Punjab; they come mainly from large villages which have each contributed hundreds of members who settle together in the same cities in England.

The cohesion of the Sikhs is not solely an affair of group settlements of fellow villagers, but springs from their common religious faith and from their sense of belonging to a brotherhood which was forged in persecution. It is the cohesion of a people who have throughout their existence been a minority fighting—very successfully—for survival. Although their culture is as alien as the Pakistanis from the British, they have traditional ties with Britain which make England less of a foreign land. Their loyalty to the British in the Indian Mutiny and their martial qualities, which made them the backbone of the Indian Army and the favourites of the Raj, forged a long association with the British. The long tradition of migration—there is hardly a family in the Doaba that has not got some relative living abroad or in another part of India—prepared them for life in Britain and helped them to organize welfare services on a community basis which went farther than the mutual aid among village kin which we have seen among the Pakistanis. This vicarious experience of migration limited their objectives so that their expectations were not pitched too high, and, like the Pakistanis, they at first demanded little of this country except to be allowed to earn a living and remit their savings to their families. As with the Pakistanis, the emigration was initially confined to men, but, unlike the Pakistanis, the Sikhs brought over their families when the immigration control seemed to be imminent. This process continued and the balance between the sexes approaches the West Indian pattern, with the difference that, whereas there are still many West Indian women living alone in Britain, all Sikh women are living with their husbands. When a family is re-united, all the children come with their mother, instead of arriving one by one.[66]

It is villagers who have formed the bulk of the Sikh migration, the majority having been small farmers, belonging to the Jat caste. There were also a number of landless peasants of lower caste, including untouchables. Alongside these peasant migrants, there was a movement of educated urban Sikhs, engaged in the professions and in white-collar jobs in the Punjab, who abandoned their qualifications to accept labouring jobs in Britain in which they could earn more than as teachers, clerks, or non-commissioned officers in the Indian Army or the police in India. These migrants from the towns, whom Aurora calls middle class,[67] settled and worked alongside the peasants, and this again distinguished the Sikh from the Pakistani settlements, for among the Pakistanis there has been very little mixing of the landless peasant and the educated elite. This is, perhaps, one of the reasons why the Sikh communities have thrown up so many leaders and have been able to organize community services on such a scale. There is certainly a greater sense of identity between the illiterate and the educated among the Sikhs than either among Pakistanis or West Indians in this country.

The pattern of settlement and of employment depended very much on whether the immigrant knew English. The majority did not and many were illiterate. A knowledge of the language enabled a man to take employment working alongside an Englishman, for example in transport, with strong union organization. Again, he could find his own housing. But the majority had to rely on English-speaking compatriots who acted as go-betweens with employers who were willing to hire Indian labour in gangs for work in factories. In these factories, they were isolated by language and by their numbers from the English workers and, in many cases, by working on night-shift. The earliest Sikh settlers in Southall came along a chain which led from the Punjab to Woolf's rubber factory, whose personnel officer had met members of a Sikh regiment in the Middle East during the War and was prepared to take Sikh labour. Woolf's example was followed by a few other employers, and the concentration became so great that, by 1959, 70% of the Indian workers in Southall were employed in four or five firms.[68] As none of these factories were unionized, they were still further isolated, for membership of a trade union could have provided an entry into the wider community.

It was often necessary to bribe a foreman to get employment and, later, to be given overtime; to a Punjabi peasant, with no knowledge of England, this appeared to be a British norm of behaviour and affected his outlook on the new society. The lack of a union for the immigrant workers made them much easier victims; but many Sikhs disapproved of bribery and at a later stage they began to organize their fellows into unions in order to protect them from the arbitrary power of the corrupt foreman. However, the process of concentration and virtual segregation in all-immigrant shops continued, so that by 1965, 90% of the un-skilled labour at Woolf's consisted of Sikhs.[69]

The concentration in employment was repeated in housing. Few English people were prepared to take in Punjabis, and the early immigrants had great difficulty in finding lodgings; they were often exploited by their fellow-countrymen who bought houses and let off rooms or beds at high rates in very bad con-ditions.

You cannot imagine how barbarously we lived in those days. The front room had three beds, two of them double. The back room had a similar number of beds. The large front on the same floor had four beds. The two other bedrooms on the same floor had five beds. The number of people living there fluctuated between twenty and twenty-five. Some of the beds were used during the day by the night-shift workers and at night by the day workers.

The lavatory was blocked half the time so much so that people some times p—— in the bathroom sink. The bath, therefore, smelled terribly, besides being always dirty. God knows how things have changed.[70]

This overcrowding was forced on the immigrants, and although it enabled them to live cheaply and save to meet their obligations, it also brought the community into a disrepute from which it still suffers. At a later stage, Sikhs began to buy their own houses, two or three friends joining together to pay the deposit. When families were re-united a different type of overcrowding occurred, as heads of families felt obliged to house their kin in the small, single family, terraced housing which they were able to buy. But the arrival of women brought great changes. There was then someone at home to keep the house clean and attitudes to property began to change. In the period of the rush to 'beat the ban', every room in Indian-owned houses was used for sleeping, but three years later in many family houses the front rooms were reserved as sitting-rooms and furnished with three-piece suites. This improvement in the general standard of housing and the move towards a 'Western' style of living became accepted signs of economic success. They also led to a reduction in overcrowding, especially as younger kinsmen left to form their own households. But the concentration of Sikhs increased in certain areas as numbers grew, partly because estate agents confined the newcomers to certain areas that already contained numbers of immigrant houses. The rate of reinforcement from India is shown by the increase in the number of Indian-owned houses in Southall. In 1959, it was estimated that 163 houses were owned by immigrants; four years later the number had risen to 634.[71]

'We had started feeling British but then there were so few Indians but now there are so many of us that we have started feeling Indian again.'[72] This remark, by a Sikh who came to England in the early 1950s, illustrates the effect of reinforcement from home, but it does not tell the whole story of the consolidation within Sikh communities. A number of influences have operated to enhance their sense of identity and their cultural distinctiveness. Some of these influences come from within the community, others from their reception by the British. Most of the younger Sikhs cut their long hair, shaved off their beards, and discarded the turban even before they left the Punjab;[73] they were prepared to abandon these outward marks of their religious allegiance as they might be a handicap in getting employment in England. Once settled in England, others of the five distinguishing marks were also discarded—in particular, the bangle, which is dangerous and may even be lethal in industry. This, as Aurora points out, is evidence of pragmatism; since these outward signs have little utility in contemporary English life and since the identity of the group does not depend on them, their hold is loosened in a new social environment. But he also says that the older Sikhs feel ashamed if they cut their hair. It is generally the older village men and the younger urban Sikhs who are engaged in white-collar and other smart clean jobs who wear turbans in this country. Shaving may, however, follow a loss of faith and be a sign of lapsing; there was the case of the London Transport guard who returned to the faith, let his hair and beard grow, and was suspended for forty days for wearing a turban.[74] During this time prayers were said for him in the *gurdwaras* and when London Transport re-instated him there were three days of rejoicing. A visitor to any *gurdwara* finds many of the congregation clean shaven; and it is evident that religious observance is not necessarily affected. But the turban has become a symbol of their identity for Sikhs in this country which has increased in importance because employers, particularly in municipal transport, victimized members of the community for wearing them. This form of discrimination is perceived as hostility, and has produced the threat of industrial action and protest demonstrations which have rallied Sikhs from all over the country. This solidarity in defence of their social rights marks off the Sikhs from the other immigrant communities.

The Sikhs have shown that they are capable of collective action in other contexts. The workers at Woolf's, after four years of abortive attempts, eventually managed to organize a union. This was in the face of hostility from the company, while the organizers ran the risk of betrayal by fellow-workers who were the agents of corrupt foremen. Once the union was recognized, they came out on strike over the suspension of a worker and remained solid for six weeks, although the Transport and General Workers' Union refused to give official backing on the grounds that most of the workers had lost their membership in the union by not paying their dues. On these grounds the T. & G.W.U. refused to grant any strike benefits even to workers who were fully paid up. The Sikh community gave some financial support, but the strikers could not continue without union backing and were taken back on the company's terms; their local union was broken.

The history of this strike showed the weakness of the Indian workers faced with an industrial procedure which they did not fully understand. They had been wrongly led by trade union officials to suppose that they would have the official backing of the union; and they chose the worst moment to strike, during the Christmas slack period when the company could maintain production levels by hiring strike breakers. In spite of these overwhelming handicaps, and although the man suspended was unpopular with the workers, they were prepared to endure great hardship out of loyalty to the principle of collective action.

The solidarity which they showed in face of their employers masked internal divisions which have been endemic in Punjabi communities in this country. The non-collection of dues by shop stewards was the result of factionalism within the community, because shop stewards were elected on the basis of personal loyalties and were not considered representative of the workers as a whole. This state of affairs is a microcosm of the pattern of leadership in the Indian Workers' Associations (see Chapter 25). But we need to say something here of the limited part that the I.W.A. leadership has played in helping the immigrants adapt themselves to the new society.[75]

On arrival, the immigrants sought the help and protection of relatives and men from their own and neighbouring villages, who had already gained prestige through the money they had sent home to support their families. Some had bought houses in England and placed their clients under an obligation by providing tenancies. They knew the ropes and were able to do favours to their friends by getting them jobs and overtime and by acting as their intermediaries with officials, with building societies, and with other agencies in the new country. By creating these mutual obligations, they established their own personal followings, which they mobilized in their bid for leadership in the local I.W.A. elections, which convulse the Punjabi communities every two years.

The original objects of the Indian Workers' Associations that were formed in the early 1950s were to provide welfare services and recreation for the immigrants. They helped the new arrivals to help themselves in meeting the demands of life in an urban community, in finding jobs, and in dealing with British officials. They also provided club rooms where immigrants could meet one another and read Punjabi newspapers, and they organized Indian film shows, which were to become a lucrative source of revenue and power. In the early days of the immigration, they reinforced community solidarity—potentially very strong—and thus created a feeling of security, which probably helped the new communities to make an initial positive approach to their new environment. By inviting prominent Englishmen to sit on the platform at celebrations of Indian national days, they showed that they could establish friendly relations with the British and that the community was accepted as an important part of British society. In this way they were able to introduce their members to British institutions and they occasionally urged them to join trade unions.

The Punjabis readily accept this kind of lead: they felt that they should support the organizations which their British neighbours and workmates supported, otherwise they might gain the reputation of not being interested in the welfare of the community as a whole. The I.W.A.s were therefore reinforcing a positive disposition towards British institutions. But, as DeWitt John shows, they did not go much further than this. The energy of the leaders soon became taken up by the internal affairs of the I.W.A.s, and particularly by competition for office; few have been active in British organizations. They were more concerned with winning prestige within their own communities than with establishing links to the outside world. They were not in any real sense representing their communities to the British, nor were they interpreting British values to their followers by explaining to them how they were expected to behave in this new society. In fact, they were reproducing in a foreign context the atmosphere of Indian village politics.

Even if there were not these constant reminders of the flavour of home politics and the obligations to village kin, there were the ordinary ties with home through letters and new arrivals. Many immigrants return to their villages to visit their parents or their wives, to attend marriages, or to be married themselves. On these visits, they take and receive messages for their village kin in England whom they visit on their return. All this is characteristic of the early stages of any economic migration. The Boeing 707, which made the initial journey possible for so many in the 1960s, provides an easy link with home. The link is renewed and strengthened through the marriages arranged in the homeland.

We have seen in Chapter 5 that although Sikhism set its face against caste, it does survive in the Punjab as an occupational hierarchy based on birth within which caste endogamy is still generally observed. A great majority of the immigrants have their marriages arranged in the Punjab, and even when a marriage occurs in England, it is often arranged through the home villages; the link between Coventry and Newcastle is in Jullundur. However, Indian-born wives are preferred, as they are trained to accept the traditional position of Sikh women and the marriage is therefore thought to have a greater chance of success. There is also a doubt about Indian girls who have grown up in this country and have been exposed to English *moeurs*: it is safer to get a girl from the Punjab and in fact it is just as easy to arrange a marriage in India as in England. In his study of Sikhs in Vancouver, Mayer also found that 80% of the post-war marriages had been arranged in India and that even the second generation, born in Canada, accepted this practice.[76]

Apart from their importance in marriage, caste distinctions hardly survive the process of emigration. For men, leaving the village meant leaving caste. The first weakening of the system occurred on the long sea journey where the travellers were mixed up together and ate food prepared by cooks of another caste and in a common kitchen. Different arrangements were made for the women, who never accompanied their husbands but followed years later, invariably escorted by a close relative; by this time, travel was almost entirely by air and they were met on arrival by their caste-fellows. Housing conditions in England in the early days of the settlement made it impossible to keep up caste exclusiveness, and later, when families were re-united, the neighbours of a Jat family might be anyone from an untouchable to a non-Sikh. Friendships formed in the emigration cut across caste and created bonds of fictional kinship based neither on caste nor village membership. Thus, the men who worked to make the Shri Guru Singh Sabha *gurdwara* in Southall called themselves *Gurdwara Bhai* or Temple brothers. Aurora gives a ranking order of nine qualities thought desirable in the emigration; at the head of the list is a good knowledge of English, followed by influence with employers, leadership of the I.W.A., and so on, down to, unskilled worker earning and saving good money, in the eighth place, followed by membership of a high caste. Thus, the traditional criteria of social status are almost turned on their head in the diaspora. However, in some settlements, for example, in Coventry and Southall, there are two *gurdwaras*, distinguished by caste, the Jat which is the larger and more prosperous, and the Ramgarhia whose members are drawn from the carpenter and blacksmith castes and are regarded as belonging to a somewhat lower class.

The *gurdwara* plays a very important part in maintaining the internal cohesion of Sikh communities. It is at once a religious and a social centre where any Sikh may be sure of a welcome, and of receiving hospitality and, in theory, a lodging. The arrival of wives greatly strengthened the *gurdwaras*, for, like Muslim wives, the women are more inclined than their husbands to observe the prescribed rules of their religion. They tend to keep all the religious fasts and they maintain religious observance in the home. Moreover, no institutionalized form of social seclusion prevents Sikh women from attending any kind of public gathering.

The members of the *gurdwara* committee are leaders in the community. In some settlements, for example in Gravesend, they regard themselves as representing the whole Sikh community to the host society, in others, they are more concerned to preserve the faith and the unity of their co-religionists. Sectarian divisions and divisions between orthodox and more liberal *gurdwaras* are reflected in attitudes to relationships with the British: the orthodox fight for the preservation of Sikhism, for example, in agitating against any restriction on wearing turbans; the liberals are proponents of integration and, are more likely to be represented on multi-racial associations.

Some of the leaders of the religious communities maintain active connexions with India, making frequent visits to Amritsar. A significant development in the last few years has been the growth of missionary activity from the Punjab among communities in Britain. A number of Sants have recently arrived from the Punjab and demands are being raised by the recently formed *Shiromani Khalsa Dal* (a political grouping within the Sikhs in Britain) for Punjabi to be taught in the schools and for religious instruction to be provided by the local education authorities.[77] Most of the children who have been born in England can speak Punjabi, but cannot read or write it and do not know the *Gurmukhi* script in which the holy scriptures are written; and, although some *gurdwaras* run classes at the weekend, the London *gurdwara* at Shepherd's Bush started a monthly service in English some years ago 'because the number of young Sikhs was growing who were less conversant with Punjabi than with English'.[78]

The missionaries are not the only visitors from Amritsar. Sikh political leaders have shown an interest in tapping the growing wealth of the communities in Britain and in enlisting their support in the political struggles of the Sikhs in India. When Sant Fateh Singh, the President of the Akali Dal, visited England in 1966, his followers collected thousands of pounds in his honour. One month earlier, Harcharan Singh Hudiara, General Secretary of the Akali Dal, in a speech to the Sikh Cultural Society in Southall, 'thanked them for their help in forcing the Indian Government to accept the just demands of the Sikhs'[79] for a Punjabi speaking state (Punjabi Suba), which came into being in November 1966. The demand for Punjabi Suba was granted by the Indian Government under pressure in the middle of the Indo-Pakistani war in 1965, but the Sikhs are not satisfied with the boundaries under the award and are demanding that the capital, Chandigarh, and the great Bakhra dam shall be given to them (at present they are Union territory). These political issues are very much alive in the minds of many Sikhs in this country and are more vital to them than central British politics.

These were the forces that played upon the Sikh community to remind them of their cultural distinctness and their ties with India. Meanwhile, the arrival of their wives and children in the early 1960s changed the character of the settlements. Social life now revolves around the families and their home, and the I.W.A.s with their rivalries and their meetings have begun to lose their importance as a focus for the community. The decision to bring their families to Britain meant for many Sikhs that they were turning their backs on their old world and putting down permanent roots in the new.[80] They now began to emulate the standards of the respectable English working class and, as we have seen, they soon began to adopt English standards of housing and furnishing. The more educated among them left the original settlement area for better neighbourhoods within easy distance of the *gurdwara*.

But the majority, who brought over their wives because of the fear of coming immigration control, remain clustered in a few neighbourhoods and, as the English move out, there are fewer opportunities for mixing. In any case the wives are unable to communicate as they know no English. They were quite unprepared for emigration, and the transfer from rural life is a far more radical change for them than for their husbands. The wives have many problems of adjustment. They had been separated from their husbands for many years; and then they had to leave the shelter of the joint family and the company of other women. The self-sufficiency of an English house with its toilet and bathroom is no substitute for the social life which women enjoy in bathing together near the village well. Isolated by the barrier of language, they have felt the loneliness of their position intensely and at first were afraid to leave their houses. Many still remain cut-off from contact with the English world around them, shopping exclusively at Indian stores.

But, after a time, many Sikh wives began to go out to work. In the Punjab it is quite common for women to work in groups in the fields or, if from the lower castes, in domestic service, but for Jat women to work for hire would mean a loss of prestige, and yet the majority of the women whom Patnaik found working in Southall were Jats; there was no concealment, though most of them had hidden the fact that they were working from their relatives in the Punjab. Thus the Sikhs, confronted with a conflict between traditional values and the economic demands and opportunities of the emigration, have adopted two standards of social behaviour, one for their kin in India and another for their life in Britain. Yet going to work does not necessarily bring Sikh women into contact with English women; because they know no English, they tend to work in all-immigrant groups, with an interpreter who communicates with the foreman. Nor does it necessarily demand many cultural concessions. Traditional dress is such an important part of Indian culture that many women do not take a job if they are required to wear Western dress.[81] Most women who work in factories or bakeries continue to wear their traditional dress under overalls and they have a choice of food at the canteen.

These working wives are making considerable sacrifices for the sake of the family and its future. Being housewives as well as wage earners, they have little time to spare to attend language classes— nor do they have the desire. Most working mothers seldom go to the *gurdwara*. Patnaik found one mother who had cut her daughter's hair—something unheard of among Sikhs—as she had no time to plait it before sending her to school. So, in some ways, the working wives are lapsing members of the community, but they are often strict with their adolescent children; as they themselves are more exposed to an alien culture, they wish their children to be sheltered from it.

Although mature wives may work, it is considered wrong for a daughter-in-law to do so, who has to be sheltered even within the house. Recently arrived brides have few contacts with the English-speaking world and it appears that this next intermediate generation of mothers may be even more isolated than the women who preceded them from the Punjab. It is quite different with the daughters who go to school in this country. Many are allowed to work on leaving school—a radical break with the tradition in the Punjab that daughters, until they are married, may do nothing but help in the house. This has probably been the single greatest effect of English education, and inspires many conflicting emotions in Sikh parents. The compulsory school-leaving age has also had a significant influence in that it has prolonged the formal period of childhood, especially in girls, who in India are regarded as adults at puberty. For this reason, the disappearance of the single sex school is a cause of concern to many parents. Girls and boys may play together in the primary school, but after puberty girls are expected to return home immediately after school and change into traditional dress. However, there is not the same opposition to wearing school uniform as there is with Pakistanis and in this respect Sikh girls have greater freedom and can participate fully in school activities.

Education is valued for itself and as an avenue to a career, but the parents' lack of English often prevents them from visiting the school, or from understanding the permissiveness of English educational methods; they sometimes feel that their children are not learning enough and it is fairly common for them to engage a tutor. In some cases, children have been sent back to the Punjab to complete their education. But on the whole, they welcome the opportunities that are open to their children and are anxious for them to succeed, to qualify for a profession or for white-collar jobs, and to escape from the low status which is associated with manual work. Many young Sikhs now attend evening classes, but this was exceptional in the early 1960s. Aspirations are changing. All the same, parents are aware that their children are acquiring a different set of values at their school and from the friendships formed at school and they feel powerless to counteract them. Many children, conscious of the tensions which are set up in the home, do not discuss with their parents what they learn at school and they may grow away from them. This is a painful dilemma which faces all immigrant parents who entrust their children to an alien culture; but the process of alienation from the Sikh culture has not yet gone very far. Few of the young Sikhs who have now left school have had all their education in this country, and once they leave school there is very little mixing with their English peers except at work. (This is not true of the good games players who often join a team in a local league, but they are the exception; most of the Indian teen-agers are 'sports crazy' but generally play for all-Indian sides which compete with other teams within the league.) Indian boys spend their evenings doing their homework or visiting friends; they are not on the whole used to the idea of youth clubs and very few youth clubs welcome them. And if there is little mixing with English boys, there is practically none with West Indians or Pakistanis.

Many young Indians are attracted, as they grow up, to an English culture which offers them an avenue to a career and considerable freedom. But how much they will adopt any part of this culture depends in the short run on the attitudes of the British and the response of their own parents.

In certain communities the Sikhs have attracted hostility. The main reason was the sharp increase in numbers which built up in a short period before the Commonwealth Immigrants Act and which led to the overcrowding of houses. The pressure on local authority services found many councils totally unprepared, and the resentment came from local residents who feared for the value of their property and expressed their hostility through associations formed ostensibly to protect the amenities of the neighbourhood. The Sikhs have also had to face the open hostility of local councillors who wished to change the rules against them in the allocation of council housing; they have seen candidates in local and parliamentary elections standing on an anti-immigrant platform, and advocating segregated schools and restrictions on the sale of private property. Week after week they have been subjected to attack and abuse in the correspondence columns of the local press. This hostility to the Sikhs arose not only from the overcrowding of houses and the way their houses seemed to be neglected; there was also resentment at success. The Sikhs appeared to be entering the property market in a fairly large way when they bought two cinemas in Southall and a number of shops in the main shopping centre. There were complaints about the building of *gurdwaras* and of the sounds of the ceremonies that issued from them. There was agitation about the large numbers of Indian children in certain schools, although it may well be that anxiety about educational standards was rather a rationalization than the cause of resentment.

In face of this hostility the Sikhs have combined in their own interest. We have seen that they are capable of solidarity in organizing nation-wide protests against the Manchester and Wolverhampton transport organizations on the issue of the wearing of turbans. In certain areas, they have decided to use their political leverage by working through one of the main political parties. In Southall, for example, the I.W.A. delivered the Indian vote to the

Labour party in the Greater London Council Elections in the spring of 1964, and in the general election in October 'because it [Labour] is the party of the working class, because it stands for the Commonwealth rather than the Common Market, and because of its general policies—particularly housing'.[82] The I.W.A. Southall, has continued to support the Labour party, but in the local elections in 1968, two Sikh candidates entered the field for the first time, one in the Labour and the other in the Conservative interest.[83]

While hostility may cause the Sikhs to combine, it is also likely to reinforce their attachment to their own culture. The *Khalsa*, a militant sect or brotherhood formed by the last Guru in a time of religious persecution (see Chapter 5), has a large membership in this country—embracing the majority of Sikhs. At the time when the Manchester Sikhs were fighting the Transport Committee for the right to wear turbans, the Singh Sabha (orthodox) *gurdwara* in Southall reported that 135 Sikhs were baptised as *Khalsa*, of whom twenty were women. The two-edged sword had been specially brought over from Amritsar for the ceremony. To choose baptism would involve a decision to wear the five distinguishing marks of a Sikh (long hair, comb, short drawers, iron bangle, and sword). Growth in membership of the *Khalsa* may thus indicate a response to what is seen as hostility on the part of the British. To quote the 1931 Census of India: 'Whenever the martial spirit revives Sikhism also revives, and in times of peace there is a tendency for Sikhism to decline.'[84]

But hostility may lead to an increasing isolation of the Indian communities. The channels of communication between the Indians and British were always fairly narrow; the language barrier has prevented each side from learning about the culture and norms of behaviour of the other. The ignorance is profound. A comment by a Sikh anthropologist who worked for the Survey in Southall sums up the position in many communities:

There was not only a lack of understanding of the breadth of the cultural gap between the immigrants and the English and of the effort needed on both sides to bridge it, but there was no recognition of the fact that the immigrants were trying to tackle the problems as best they could. The general attitude can be summed up: 'Why don't the Sikhs assimilate?', 'Why don't they at least learn English ways if they are going to live in Southall?' And, the final condemnation: 'The Sikhs don't want to integrate.' The standards set for the immigrants, specially when seen from the Sikh point of view, were impossible. They were expected to unlearn a lifetime's experience in as little as six to ten years; adults were expected to adopt a new way of life, without even being told what the new life is. . . . The immigrants were left to manage as best they could and from the beginning the stage was set for later tensions. . . . The Sikhs needed to know of English ways in order to learn them; but the English needed to know of Sikh ways in order to teach them.

The character of Indian leadership may be changing as the composition of the immigration has been changed by Government policies. Since the 1965 White Paper, the majority of Indians entering the country have been graduates and they have little time for the parochial politics of the Indian Workers' Association; they are also much more conscious of the effects of discrimination than the peasants who preceded them, because they came hoping for professional positions and because, especially if they are teachers, they have been disappointed. Together with some of the old established leaders who may detach themselves from the I.W.A., they may move into British and inter-racial organizations and play their part in improving race relations in Britain. This would mean an opening up of the communities to the British scene even if the impulse behind it was defensive.

Meanwhile, Sikh communities are likely to remain fairly closely concentrated, mutually supportive and supplying more and more of their own services. There will be a certain amount of dispersal from the centres as aspirations rise and as the housing market permits, but the families who move out will want to remain within reach of the *gurdwara*, the cultural centre. The process of dispersal would accelerate if families could feel the same confidence of getting jobs and houses in the unknown areas as in the settlements where they can rely on community support.

At present we have a picture of Sikh communities which are not segregating themselves in the same way as some Pakistani settlements but at the same time are becoming self-sufficient and inward-looking. They keep to themselves, retaining their own values and norms of conduct, mixing very little socially with the English, and making little use of English institutions apart from their active membership in trade unions. They often settle their own disputes without recourse to the courts, and they regulate their social obligations by the traditional codes obtaining in the Punjab. Their ties to India in this first generation are still very strong.

This is to be expected with recent immigrants, but it is not only the barriers of language and culture that are keeping them separate; they are being virtually insulated in the poorer quarters of the towns where they have settled.

There are few examples of Sikh settlements in the Anglo-Saxon world which might give us some indication of how this community will develop in England. The Sikhs have generally settled in British colonial territories where they regarded the indigenous population as more backward than themselves and where they formed an artisan class, mid-way between the natives and the representatives of the colonial power. One of the few places where a comparison might be made is Vancouver, where the first Sikh settlement dates from the beginning of this century and was reinforced after the Second World War. Mayer found little basic social changes there; he writes of the uneducated Sikhs: 'It is as if they continued to act in the way they would have in the Punjab had they had the opportunities, but with a different social backdrop.' This was not true of the educated, many of whom had adopted the attitudes of white Canadian society. Mayer distinguishes between the educated India-born, who have adopted many Canadian ways but do not for example play Canadian games, and the Canada-born whose outlook is different from their parents', with whom tension is greater than is usual between generations: their contact with white society is of a different nature from the India-born; they are not yet real Canadians, but being between two worlds some of them join multi-racial gangs whereas the India-born act as a separate group. 'The former have a closer contact with white society even though it is the "problem" section.'[85]

At the time of his study, there had been very little inter-marriage although there were few Indian women in the settlement. In the few cases where it had occurred, the spouse was Canada-born. Opinion was strongly against such marriages as it was feared that the individual would be lost to the community. Inter-marriage was regarded as a severance from the community rather than as a link with the wider society. Religion had begun to lose its hold on the Canada-born, who could not understand the readings from the Holy Book. Mayer felt that there was a danger of the emergence of a 'cultureless' category of young people who would owe allegiance neither to Indian nor to Canadian society.

If the picture of this society has any relevance for this country, it will not be sufficient to rely on the English educational system to help the next generation to evolve towards some form of Anglo-Sikh culture. Western influences are at work on this new generation through the schools, newspapers, and the cinema, through employment and in the shops. There will be little fresh immigration of male workers and reinforcement from home will continue only through marriage. As families become more Westernized, they move outwards from the Sikh settlement areas leaving the strong village kin ties and following the pattern of living of the small 'Western' nuclear family. The traditional position of women has already begun to change. We have seen that caste distinction has virtually ceased except in marriage. The traditional relationship of parents to children will be altered as the children earning their own incomes will insist on greater independence. The level of aspiration has risen considerably. Unlike their fathers, few sons will be content with manual jobs. Moreover, their parents expect them to become British citizens, yet will be disappointed if they abandon Sikh customs. The children may grow up within an Anglo-Sikh culture, which may be neither Sikh nor English but the distinctive creation of the Sikhs in England. At present the communities retain the main content of Indo-Sikh culture. With so many forces playing on traditional Sikhism, the way in which these communities will develop is still very open: the direction they will take will depend to a large extent on the attitudes and policies of the British. Positive efforts by the Government and by local authorities will be needed to help adolescents to remain within their own culture while feeling at home in the culture of their adopted country.

(b) Hindus

We have been discussing the response of the Sikh communities, which form the bulk of the immigration from India, but there is also a substantial number of Hindus in this country. They have come mainly from Gujarat and have established themselves in tightly-knit Gujarati settlements, maintaining an existence quite separate from the Sikhs, from whom they are divided by language and religion. We are told by Desai that there are no Hindu temples in this country because the elaborate rituals which are required are forbidden by custom on a foreign soil.[86] But in any case, temple observance is on the decline among the relatively Westernized Hindus of Gujarat and the Punjab. Hinduism does not need to find expression in temple worship: it is a religion which is practised in the home. The Gujarati immigrants usually delegate their ritual duties, including even marriage and funeral rites, to members of their families who are in India, performing no more than a token ceremony in this country.

This is only one of the ties which bind Gujaratis to India. Because there are no cultural institutions or religious centres like the *gurdwara*, which might become a focus for the community, the joint family and the village-kin group assume even greater importance, and so does caste-affiliation. It is true that, as we have seen among the Sikhs, some of the most important caste distinctions do not survive in the emigration. Thus, in England, there is no prohibition against members of different castes or even untouchables eating together; and it is also impossible to maintain a hierarchical system which is based on a simple division of labour, with members of different castes dependent on one another for services and support, as in an Indian village. But this structure is very much weaker in cities than in villages even in India; Gujaratis are used to the idea of earning their money away from home and to the weakening of the caste system that results. They are accustomed at home to varying their attitude to caste as between home and place of work. None the less, the break is sharper in England; here, they are all economically dependent on the host society. However, the first generation of immigrants see their life in England in many ways as an extension of life in India, and in terms of the village society in India, caste retains its importance. The kin groupings in England often centre on one leader, who has influence because he helped the later immigrants to get to England and provided employment. The relationships of this sponsor and his clients are then governed largely by regard for the prestige that will accrue to both within the village in India. The relationship is similar to the hereditary relationship of patron and client in India, by which a landowner receives the services of a Brahman priest, of craftsmen, such as potters, and of labourers, in return for food, small payments of cash, and protection. In England, it is enforced by the fact that both parties are members of joint families in the traditional system at home and that their reputation there is of importance. It is through continued membership of the joint family that the immigrants retain their membership of the wider caste society in India.

It is not only mutual obligations that are regulated in terms of Indian society: the kin or village group and the immigrant household exercise supervision and strong social control over the behaviour of their members. Most disputes are settled by arbitration without recourse to the courts. Contractual arrangements made, for example, in the joint purchase of a house are not put in writing, as there are sufficient social sanctions operating here and in India to prevent default. There is pressure on members of the group to remit money for the support of their families in India, and a dutiful son gains prestige within the community. The controls are effective because the newcomer is dependent on the group for finding employment, for loans if he wishes to buy a house, and for most of his leisure hours, which are spent within the house or in visiting. Control of the group operates particularly strongly to prevent marriage with an outsider, which is prohibited to a Hindu. This prohibition applies not only to Sikh, Christian, Muslim, or Jew, but to persons of another caste, and though the effect of caste is in many respects so much weaker in England than in India, it is still strictly observed as to marriage. The group is able to bring powerful sanctions to bear on anyone who deviates: in the last resort he may be made an outcast and this means that he will be cut off from his parents or relatives, since, if he eats with them, they will also be outcast. Thus, marriage with a white woman means rejection and a complete break with the immigrant group. The breach is not only social: the person rejected is cut off from an elaborate network of help of many kinds. His partners in business or in the purchase of a house may lose confidence and demand separation; his creditors may want an immediate return of their loans. There is no one to turn to if he is out of work.

Most of the needs of these Gujarati communities are supplied by travelling grocers and hawkers whose customers are tied to them socially through village, kin, or caste membership, or through friendship. The service that is offered by the grocers has a twofold significance in keeping the community intact. Selling and delivering the groceries is a social activity, like visiting, and the grocer is a link in the social network. He also supplies all the family's dietary wants. Gujaratis are traditionally vegetarians and their cooking, which is elaborate, requires a great variety of spices not easily obtainable in England. By supplying this Indian diet, the grocers are providing a symbolic link with Gujarat. They are served by a number of Indian wholesalers: whether retailers or wholesalers, all their employees are Indian and this close commercial relationship keeps money within the group.

The emigration has followed much the same pattern as with the Sikhs. The men first established themselves and then called for their wives, who had been left in the protection of the head of the joint family. When a wife arrives in England, she is sheltered from the surrounding society, and very few go out to work as this would involve wearing English clothes and would mean an important cultural change. Although most of the women in Desai's group were literate, very few could speak English. Their children who have been brought up here act as interpreters for them. Because of the service provided by grocers and hawkers, the Gujarati wives have to make only minimal contact with the outside world.

Nearly all the Gujarati men in England are literate and a higher proportion than among the Sikhs have university degrees or some similar qualification. These men usually find they cannot get jobs appropriate to their qualifications, but many deliberately choose labouring jobs which, with overtime, give them a greater economic reward, or else work in transport, even though to wear uniform means a loss of prestige. It is more often men of the higher castes who are inclined to sacrifice pay to status by taking white-collar employment. In either case, there is inevitably a feeling of bitterness which does not arise with those former peasants now earning good money in factories.

The structure of the Hindu joint family and the caste system, with its strict rules as to marriage within the group, operate to shut the Gujaratis into their own society more closely than the Sikhs. Many factors combine to strengthen this encapsulation. The difficulties encountered over housing force them to combine with kinsmen to buy houses; for employment, they rely on sponsors from the village-kin group. If a leader emerges, he is bound to press for their needs as Gujaratis and to emphasize what distinguishes them from the native British. They were from the start less inclined than the Sikhs to accommodate themselves to British ways except at work, and British rejection has emphasized the tendency. As Desai has said:

Total participation would require from the immigrants varied and extensive cultural change. In fact, most of them accept only those cultural changes which are the minimum condition for making money. . . . In many factories, they behave as immigrant groups rather than as individual employees. Consequently, to some extent, they force their English co-workers to act in the same way. But from their side, because of cultural preferences (which include ideas about colour), English workers generally refuse to treat immigrants as individuals and limit or prohibit their participation. Where there is a wall, both sides have built it.[87]

NOTES TO CHAPTER 23

1. Donald Hinds, *Journey to an Illusion* (London, Heinemann, 1966), p. 51.

2. Fernando Henriques, *Family and Colour in Jamaica* (London, Eyre & Spottiswoode, 1953).

3. Dr. Elsa H. Walters, 'Some factors in the background and experience of West Indian children which may affect their progress and behaviour in English schools' (unpublished, 1966).

4. In *Disappointed Guests*, H. Tajfel and J. L. Dawson (eds.) (London, Oxford University Press, for Institute of Race Relations, 1965).

5. Sheila Patterson, *Dark Strangers* (London, Tavistock Publications, 1963), p. 7.

6. Patterson, op. cit., p. 198.

7. A. Richmond and M. Lyon, 'Study of the St. Paul's area and of three housing estates in Bristol', research commissioned by the Institute's 'Survey of Race Relations in Britain'.

8. J. Rex and R. Moore, *Race, Community and Conflict* (London, Oxford University Press, for Institute of Race Relations, 1966).

9. David Lowenthal, 'Race and Colour in the West Indies', in *Daedalus* (Spring, 1967), p. 595.

10. Patterson, op. cit.

11. Hinds, op. cit.

12. Rex and Moore, op. cit.

13. Richmond and Lyon, op. cit.

14. R. B. Davison, *Black British* (London, Oxford University Press, for Institute of Race Relations, 1966), Chapter IX contributed by Mrs. Betty Davison, p. 142.

15. Richmond and Lyon, op. cit.

16. Rex and Moore, op. cit.

17. Rex and Moore, op. cit.

18. Richmond and Lyon, op. cit.

19. Robert E. Park, 'The Nature of Race Relations', in *Race Relations and the Race Problem*, Edgar T. Thomson (ed.) (Durham (North Carolina), Duke University Press, 1939).

20. Beryl Radin, 'Coloured Workers and British Trade Unions', *Race* (Vol. VIII, no. 2, October 1966). See also, F. J. Bayliss and J. B. Coates, 'West Indians at work in Nottingham', *Race* (Vol. VII, no. 2, October 1965); Bayliss and Coates found that 66% of West Indian men were in trade unions, compared with 78% of white Englishmen in their sample.

21. Political and Economic Planning and Research Services Ltd., *Racial Discrimination* (London, P.E.P., April 1967).

22. John Lambert, 'Study of immigrant crime and the relations of the police and immigrants in a division of Birmingham', research carried out for the Institute's 'Survey of Race Relations in Britain'.

23. Lowenthal, op. cit.

24. Dr. R. E. D. Simpson, 'Study of a General Practice with a large proportion of immigrants', research commissioned by the Institute's 'Survey of Race Relations in Britain'.

25. Professor Robert R. Bell, of Temple University, Pennsylvania, 'The Lower Class Negro Family in the United States and Great Britain', unpublished paper presented

to University of Reading. Professor Bell's sample was 40% Barbadian; the rest came mainly from Jamaica.

26. In an interview conducted as part of a survey for United Nations Institute for Training and Research by the Institute of Race Relations (unpublished).

27. Richmond found that 55% of his West Indian sample in Bristol were definitely intending to stay in Britain, 40% were intending to return, 24% were not sure. This compares with an original intention to stay of only 17% and to return of 66%.

28. Bell, op. cit.

29. This survey of housing occupancy was commissioned by Lambeth Borough Council from Research Services Ltd. in 1966, and quoted by Elizabeth Burney in *Housing on Trial* (London, Oxford University Press, for Institute of Race Relations, 1967).

30. Registrar-General's Quarterly Return No. 477: 1st Quarter 1968 (London, H.M.S.O.), Appendix D., p. 34. The figures are derived from the International Passenger Survey and include any passenger who declares his intention to leave the country for at least a year.

31. See Betty Davison, 'No Place Back Home: A study of Jamaicans returning to Kingston, Jamaica', *Race* (Vol. IX, no. 14, April 1968). See also, the experience of a Jamaican, quoted by Donald Hinds, who returned to Jamaica after ten years in England and could not get a job ('Jamaica is not a poor man's country.'), Hinds, op. cit.

32. Wallace Collins, *Jamaican Migrant* (London, Routledge & Kegan Paul, 1965).

33. George Lamming, *The Emigrants* (London, Michael Joseph, 1954).

34. Lamming, op. cit.

35. Richmond found that 60% of the West Indians in St. Paul's felt they were worse housed than they were in the West Indies. Forty-two per cent of his sample who had been in Britain between six and ten years felt that they were worse off in 1966 than they had been ten years before.

36. Mrs. Betty Davison, op. cit.

37. Rex and Moore, op. cit.

38. Letter to the *Oldham Evening Chronicle*, 14 October 1958, in C. E. Fiscian, 'Minority Group Prejudice: a study of some sociological and psychological correlates of anti-English prejudice among West Indian immigrants to London' (Ph.D. thesis, 1960).

39. Quoted in 'Voyage to the Promised Land', Dick Adler, *Sunday Times* Colour Supplement (30 June 1968).

40. Albert Maria Gomes, 'I am an Immigrant', *Listener* (Vol. 80, no. 2062, 3 October 1968) (Third Programme Talk).

41. In *Disappointed Guests*, op. cit.

42. Collins, op. cit.

43. Summarized extract from a statement issued by the High Commissioner for Jamaica, 29 April 1968.

44. Beryl Radin, op. cit.

45. Malcolm Calley, *God's People: West Indian Pentecostal Sects in England* (London, Oxford University Press, for Institute of Race Relations, 1965).

46. Neville Maxwell, *The Power of Negro Action* (London, The Author, 1966).

47. *Sunday Times*, 30 June 1968, op. cit.

48. Christopher Bagley, 'Relative Deprivation and the Working Class Racialist', in Institute of Race Relations *Newsletter* (June 1968).

49. For this section we have drawn heavily on unpublished research conducted by B. Dahya in Birmingham and Bradford for the Institute's 'Survey of Race Relations in Britain', and also on unpublished research in Bradford commissioned by the Survey from Eric Butterworth.

50. Dahya reports that there were approximately ten East Pakistani wives in the whole of Bradford by 1967 and 142 East Pakistani dormitory houses. Similarly, in Balsall Heath there were ninety-two East Pakistani dormitory houses and only four family houses. The figures for West Pakistanis in Balsall Heath were 229 dormitories and seventy-nine family houses.

51. See R. Desai, *Indian Immigrants in Britain* (London, Oxford University Press, for the Institute of Race Relations, 1963).

52. *Why a Federation?* (Organising Committee, National Federation of Pakistani Associations, London, 1964); and a report in *Oldham Evening Chronicle & Standard*, 18 January 1964.

53. Karam Elahi, 'Some Aspects of Social Adaptation of Pakistani Immigrants in Glasgow' (M.A. thesis, Edinburgh University, 1967).

54. Dahya lists 983 Pakistani houses in Bradford in 1964, broken down as follows: 142 East Pakistani, 190 Chacci (Campbellpuri), 24 Pathan, 3 Gujarati Muslim, 135 Punjabi, 489 Mirpuri.

55. Price shows that the Greeks of Central Sydney, who had come from a number of islands and the mainland, were fusing together as a national group and assimilating themselves to Australian society; but thirty years later, after the Second World War, there was so much reinforcement from different islands that the Greek community broke up into a federation of Greek district groups and the process of assimilation was much retarded. In one case, the Kytheran Greeks, inter-marriage came down from 42% to 10%. C. A. Price, *The Cultural Integration of Immigrants*, W. D. Borrie (ed.) (Paris, U.N.E.S.C.O., 1959), p. 281. Also C. A. Price, *Southern Europeans in Australia* (Melbourne, Oxford University Press, 1963), p. 260.

56. Michael Banton, *White and Coloured* (London, Jonathan Cape, 1959), p. 123.

57. Over 70% of Indians and Pakistanis had never applied to a white landlord for lodgings. W. W. Daniel, *Racial Discrimination in England*, Penguin Special based on a P.E.P. Report (Harmondsworth, Penguin Books, 1968), p. 41.

58. The Inland Revenue, on the basis of a pilot study of 1,000 cases where 55% of claims for income tax relief for dependants were found to be fraudulent, estimated that the annual loss might be as high as £7 million, making a total loss up to 1967 of £28 million.

59. Children are legally adopted by *affidavit* and are either declared orphans or the progeny of the sponsor. This procedure, however, is not permanently binding in Pakistan where, under *Shariat* law, an adopted child has the status only of a 'ward' in relation to its guardian. Thus, many immigrants, in conformity with British law, have 'adopted' their nephews and cousins not only as an economic investment but also to qualify for income tax relief.

60. John Goodall, 'The Pakistani Background', in *New Backgrounds*, Robin Oakley (ed.) (London, Oxford University Press, for the Institute of Race Relations, 1968), p. 90.

61. Z. Dahya, 'Pakistani Wives in Britain', *Race* (Vol. VI, no. 3, January 1965), pp. 311–21.

62. Sidney Collins, *Coloured Minorities in Britain* (London, Lutterworth Press, 1957), pp. 160–73.

63. R. Desai, op. cit., p. 70.

64. Karam Elahi, op. cit.

65. *Bradford Telegraph & Argus*, 1 August 1968.

66. For this section we have drawn on unpublished research commissioned by the Institute's 'Survey of Race Relations in Britain' and conducted by Narindar Uberoi and Anjali Patnaik (both in Southall), by Ian Thomson in Gravesend. We have also drawn on DeWitt John, *Indian Workers' Associations in Britain* (O.U.P., for I.R.R., 1969).

67. G. S. Aurora, *The Frontiersmen* (Bombay, Popular Prakashan, 1967), pp. 18 and 30.

68. Ibid., p. 77.

69. Peter Marsh, *The Anatomy of a Strike* (London, Institute of Race Relations Special Series, 1967), p. 16.

70. Aurora, op. cit., p. 37.

71. *The Immigrant Community in Southall* (London, Economist Intelligence Unit, 1965), p. 6.

72. Patnaik, op. cit.

73. Aurora, op. cit., p. 94. Narindar Uberoi found that 75% of the Sikhs in Southall in 1965 were clean shaven.

74. *Guardian*, 31 August 1964.

75. John, op. cit.

76. Adrian C. Meyer, *A Report on the East Indian Community in Vancouver* (Working Paper, Institute of Social and Economic Research, University of British Columbia, December 1959), p. 18.

77. *Middlesex County Times*, 26 August 1966.

78. Preetam Singh, a London Barrister, introduced the service on 29 September 1963.

79. *Middlesex County Times*, 26 August 1966.

80. Aurora, op. cit., p. 117.

81. Narindar Uberoi, 'Sikh Women in Southall', *Race* (Vol. VI, no. 1, July 1964), p. 34.

82. *Middlesex County Times*, 11 April 1964.

83. For an account of this election see Institute of Race Relations *Newsletter* (July 1968), p. 281. Both Sikhs stood in a ward with a high Indian concentration. S. S. Gill (Labour) topped the poll, running over one hundred votes ahead of the second nearest Labour candidate. S. Mangat (Conservative) was narrowly beaten into fourth place and ran hundreds of votes ahead of his other Conservative colleagues. The Indian voting was clearly for personalities as much as parties. Labour won two out of three seats. The third went to a candidate from the anti-immigrant Residents' Association.

84. *Census of India*, 1931 (vol. 3), p. 305.

85. Mayer, op. cit., p. 27.

86. Rashmi Desai, op. cit., p. 93. Dr. Desai's is the only substantial piece of research which has been conducted among Hindus in England and for this section we have drawn on his findings.

87. Desai, op. cit., p. 87.

24 The Second Generation

What has surprised me is the fear some of these girls seem to have for the future. No matter how we try to advise and help them they are aware of a colour problem once they have to go out into the world and earn a living.

(Chief Inspector Ivy Kilvington of the Bradford Police, *Telegraph & Argus*, 4 April 1968).

Well let me put it this way. They think we are sub-human. They don't think us equal to them. So we have no right to own a house, have chairs, eat with a knife and fork, or drink from a glass, or dance to music, or us young girls wear mini-skirts. They don't think we are equal to that.

(16-year-old West African sixth form girl in a B.B.C. discussion programme, 9 September 1968.)

In this chapter, we will examine what is happening to the children of immigrant parents, how they appear to be equipped to enter British society, and how that society is receiving them.

A second generation is by strict definition those children who have been born to immigrant parents in this country, but for this chapter the definition has been extended to cover those who have had a substantial part of their education here. Their formative years will have been spent in England and within English schools before they enter the labour market. By this definition, there are still very few of the second generation in employment or even in our secondary schools. The great majority, especially of the Indian and Pakistani teen-agers, are in fact immigrants like their parents.

There were comparatively few Indian and even fewer Pakistani children in England before 1961 and those who have been born here have for the most part not yet left junior school. When, in August 1965, the Government lowered the age of entry of dependent children to 16, it forced many parents to interrupt their children's education and bring them over in their early teens, thereby creating problems for English schools and introducing children to the labour market a few years earlier than if the upper age limit had remained at 18. Despite a couple of years at school, these children are none the less first-generation immigrants, and may speak English hardly any better than their fathers. The large-scale West Indian migrations began at least six years before those of India and Pakistan and so we might expect the West Indian second generation to have progressed much further through the educational system, but even so few have as yet reached the labour market.

This position will change very radically in the next few years. In January 1967, there were about 115,000 children whose parents came from Africa, Asia, or the West Indies in primary and secondary schools in England, Wales, and Scotland (71,000 in primary schools, and 44,000 in secondary schools).[1] How radical the change will be is shown by the proportion of U.K.-born children in the schools of one local education authority. In Nottingham, in January 1967, only 7% of the coloured children in secondary schools were born in this country, whereas in the primary schools no less than 61% were born in the United Kingdom.[2] Thus, the number of children of immigrant parents leaving school who have spent a large part of their time in the British educational system will change dramatically during the next ten years.

The little research that has been conducted among teen-agers has not generally distinguished between recent arrivals and the established children. The evidence is mainly concerned with school leavers who are first generation. It can tell us something of what may await the second, but their future will be determined by the policies that are developed in housing, education, and employment, and by the state of race relations, not only in this country but elsewhere, particularly in the United States. The experience of the first generation of school leavers and the attainments of their parents may also affect their chances, for there is a danger of an increasing association in the minds of employers between colour and lack of skill. This kind of stereotyping, as Sheila Patterson has pointed out,[3] can be reinforced by the entry into the labour market of young immigrants who have had only a few years in school and have very imperfect English. It may make it difficult for the second generation to convince employers that they are up to local standards for skilled and white-collar jobs. And yet, being products of our educational system, they will be as well equipped as their white contemporaries. Whether they will have the same expectations as their white contemporaries (which may not be very high) or whether they will be less or more ambitious depends on a number of factors which will be different for each of the main ethnic groups. (David Beetham remarks, rather depressingly, that the 'socializing' process which makes for low aspiration on the part of the secondary school English child is not yet effective for the West Indian.)[4] To assume that the second generation will be less tolerant of discrimination than the first generation is to assume that they will have a different perception of their rights and that this different perception will automatically derive from being born and brought up in this country.

These children will still have certain handicaps and be subject to conflicts that are either not experienced at all or not as intensely by their English peers. Nearly all the Asian children and many of the West Indians will, at least intially, suffer from a lack of English or a lack of adequate English in the home. These are handicaps which belong to the early stages of an immigration. They are likely to be offset in very many cases by the support which the children receive from parents who are anxious that they should succeed at school and who value education for its own sake.

But there is a special hazard which awaits many West Indian and West African children whose mothers go out to work and have to leave them with child-minders. Many registered child-minders are conscientious and affectionate towards their charges: others regard them purely as a useful source of income. The horrors of child-minding have been often recorded. It is quite common for children to be left all day locked up in a room, never spoken to, except when food is brought to them, and given no toys to play with. Deprived of stimulation and play in their pre-school years, they may well become retarded and handicapped throughout their school career.[5]

Most of the abuses occur with unregistered child-minders, but registration does not necessarily protect the child. A recent inquiry found a registered child-minder operating in a house in Birmingham deemed an unfit dwelling by the Corporation.[6] It had no bath, no hot water, and the toilet was out of order. A senior official said: 'the Corporation has a duty to make the houses wind and waterproof until they are demolished but will not go beyond that state of repairs.' Aside from the condition of the house, the children had to be kept quiet because the child-minder's husband worked at night and needed to rest in the day. Public health officials are well aware of the abuses—in the words of the Medical

Officer of Health for the London Borough of Camden: 'Unsatisfactory child-minding has reached alarming proportions. And failure to meet the basic needs for physical, emotional, and mental development impairs the integration of the young child's personality.'[7]

Because so many West Indian and West African mothers go to work, the shortage of day nurseries and of licensed facilities of any kind may have grave consequences for this generation of coloured children.

In the previous chapter, we looked at the dilemma of parents who are torn between ambition for their children's future and anxiety that they may lose them to an alien culture; and we have seen how these anxieties can produce tensions within the home. For the teen-ager particularly, the conflict between the values of parents, school, and peer groups is likely to be felt more acutely than it will be by the average white teen-ager. The reaction of the coloured youngster in this situation is difficult to predict, but if white society continues to be rejecting there may be no socially acceptable way for them to express themselves, and this could in some instances lead to delinquent behaviour.

This brief introduction of the general situation of the coloured teen-ager presents rather a gloomy picture and what evidence there is, which we will now examine, gives grounds for qualified pessimism.

1. EDUCATION

There is no evidence on the distribution of coloured children between different types of secondary school for the country as a whole. The Department of Education and Science annual census does not publish this information which might serve as a rough index of educational attainment. The records of some local education authorities with substantial numbers of 'immigrant' children do, however, show that they are very under-represented in the selective schools. A Midlands city with a large coloured immigrant population may be typical of the general position at the beginning of 1968. In this city, more than 50% of the places in secondary schools are in grammar or comprehensive schools, but only 15% of all immigrant children (whatever their colour) were in these schools. It is true that many of these children are fairly recent arrivals, and what little evidence we have shows the importance of the length of time spent in primary education in this country.

Thus, Sylvaine Wiles' limited study of a boys' comprehensive school in South London found that, of the coloured immigrant children who had full education in the United Kingdom, a somewhat higher proportion were in the top stream than was the case with the native children, but that those who had less than full education here were overwhelmingly in the bottom two streams.[8]

In primary schools, similar factors seem to affect performance. In the I.L.E.A. study of immigrant pupils' performance at 10 +, based on teacher assessment and written tests, the two critical factors were competence in English and length of stay in this country.[9] This study (already discussed in Chapter 18), which was made in 1966 on 1,051 immigrant children (including 124 Cypriots), concluded that, 'although differences can be seen between immigrants who have received all or most of their primary schooling in this country and all Authority pupils, these differences are smaller than many people feared'. Performance improved continuously with increased length of stay and was 'most apparent in those . . . who had . . . a complete or almost complete primary education in the United Kingdom'. As a result, for those who had all their primary education here, 'significant differences [in performance] are no longer detectable by strict statistical test'. It should be noted, however, that this last conclusion was drawn from a cohort of only fifty-two pupils. 'Less precise indications suggest that those who come early also tend to be better adjusted, partly, perhaps, because they have less often been separated from their families.' This may in part explain why West Indian children did not perform as well as other nationality groups. For example, in the mathematics tests, 85% of the West Indian children were rated below the median, compared with 68% of the Indian and Pakistani children. However, these differences diminished with increasing length of stay.

It therefore seems that, apart from the handicaps mentioned earlier, those children who have had nearly all their primary education here will be on almost equal terms with their white contemporaries, at the start of secondary education. This still leaves a great many at a disadvantage—those who either come part of the way through primary education, or who have been separated from their families for extended periods.

It is important, in the future, that the coloured child is not judged as having a low educational potential. The I.L.E.A. Report, as we have seen, cites the opinion of one of its school medical officers, that some of the immigrant children, especially West Indians admitted to E.S.N. (educationally sub-normal) schools, may well have intellectual potential above the level of their assessed I.Q. A recent article in *Race* noted that 'low social class depresses a child's performance *independently* of his actual intelligence', and, possibly connected with this, that 'the teacher's perception of the child in his care is of fundamental importance for the child's intellectual status'.[10] In other words, teachers' attitudes and preconceptions can be decisive in determining a child's performance. Because many immigrant children now at secondary school have a poor record of attainment, there is a danger that teachers may perceive all immigrant children as being alike.

For these children to have an equal opportunity when they reach secondary school age some remedial measures need to be taken. The recommendation of the I.L.E.A. Report (drawing on the Plowden Report),[11] that 'compensatory education, supported by measures of positive discrimination, is urgently desirable not only for immigrant children but for all deprived groups', would if acted upon give some hope for the future. However, in the present economic environment, whatever the desires of the local education authorities, it is unlikely that sufficient resources will be available to deal with this critical phase in the education of the first generation.

2. EMPLOYMENT

For those leaving school, the opportunities for employment are critical for their future adjustment to society. 'No matter how we try to advise and help them they are aware of a colour problem once they have to go out into the world and earn a living.' It is not possible to say how generally this remark (which we quoted earlier) applies to coloured school leavers, for there is little evidence on the attitudes of the youngsters. Until now the Youth Employment Service has managed to place the great majority of those who sought their help. The report of the Y.E.S. points out, however, that in some areas immigrant school leavers are 'at a definite disadvantage' compared with local young people of the same standard.[12]

Many of the school leavers have used the service of the Y.E.S. In Birmingham, for example, Beetham found that 61% of the Asian and 79% of the West Indian school leavers in his sample found the Youth Employment Officer one of the most useful sources of information on jobs.[13] If they have recourse to the Y.E.O., they will in all probability be shielded from direct experience of job discrimination for the officer will not send them to employers who are known to discriminate.

In the opinion of the Y.E.O.s, school leavers have usually obtained jobs commensurate with their abilities. Beetham also thought that those in his sample did as well as white school leavers. There is little evidence about apprenticeships, but the attitude of the craft unions has been discussed in Chapter 19. In the Westhill survey in Birmingham, more than 20% (8) of the West Indians and 14% (5) of the Asian teen-agers in the sample had got apprenticeships compared with 23% of the white teen-agers.[14] In a limited study of West Indian school leavers in North London, four out of twenty-one had apprenticeships, compared with eight out of twenty-one of the matched English leavers; but taking together those who had either apprenticeships or 'on the job' training, the numbers of West Indians and English were equal.[15] From this limited evidence, it might appear that these teen-agers are not falling too far behind their white contemporaries.

There are, however, various qualifications to be made. The amount of time a Y.E.O. has to spend in placing a coloured youth is much greater than for a white youth, partly because a large proportion of the school leavers, until now, have had an imperfect command of English and partly because of discrimination. Sometimes whole sectors which supply typical school leaving employment, such as the retail trade, discriminate against coloured workers. The Y.E.S. reports that employers are reluctant to take coloured school leavers in hairdressing, catering, and office work.[16] Thus, language plus discrimination cut down severely on job opportunities.

The Y.E.S., as we noted in Chapter 19, also reports that over-ambition of some children in the lower ability ranges has created difficulties in placing them. Those who ask for jobs beyond their capabilities cannot easily be persuaded to take jobs that are appropriate to their ability. The Y.E.S. summer report for 1965 mentioned that an 'over large number' were seeking one of three specific careers: motor mechanic, television service mechanic, or electrical engineering, and were often refusing to consider good craft apprenticeships in other fields.[17] This could be due to inexperience, on the part of both the immigrant parents and their children, of what is required for certain sorts of jobs, but it also shows greater ambition than among corresponding English families. The socializing process mentioned by Beetham has not yet begun to work! It must be remembered, however, that much of this is the opinion of the Y.E.O.s. It could be argued that their expectations of the immigrant school leavers may have led them to label those who have not been satisfied as over-ambitious. The evidence to the Hunt Committee from some 17 to 20-year-old coloured youngsters indicated that those who complained about the Y.E.S. thought that the Y.E.O. had attempted to divert them from their desired course (which they had subsequently achieved).[18] These were all in white-collar jobs. Butterworth found that in Bradford about 60% of the coloured school leavers, at Easter 1966, thought they were in jobs below their ability, though the Y.E.O.s considered that this was true of only 10%.[19] Beetham, on the other hand, thought that the jobs desired by immigrant children in his sample were in much shorter supply than those desired by white school leavers and often required special qualifications which the children had not got; this, in his opinion, showed a lack of realism.[20]

Once these school children have found work, there is consistent evidence that the West Indians are less satisfied with their jobs than white or Asian teen-agers. The two surveys in Birmingham found that West Indian youths were less satisfied with their work than white youths and that the Asians were the least dissatisfied.[21] Figueroa, in his study of West Indian and English school leavers in North London, also found the West Indians less satisfied. There is no obvious explanation of why this should be so. It may be that they are more ambitious, or that they expect more, or that in fact they are doing less well. Figueroa found that during the first year of employment the West Indian boys had an average increase in wages of £1, compared with an average of £2 10s. for the English boys (the averages for the girls were £1 10s. and £2, respectively). 'We are aware that there is a growing bitterness and this could erupt in Britain.' This is the observation of the Secretary of the Methodist Church Committee on Migration in Manchester, reporting in 1968 on discrimination against coloured teen-agers.[22]

The Y.E.S. has been able to perform its useful service to coloured school leavers partly through its strong links with the schools. Any plans to weaken this link and transfer the service to the employment exchanges (which Birmingham has suggested) would, it is feared, lead to a deterioration of the service, especially through loss of experienced staff, and coloured school leavers would suffer.

The higher qualifications of the second generation will not necessarily lessen the discrimination. The findings of the P.E.P. Report are not reassuring. Although employers felt that the better educated immigrant would find employment more easily than the illiterate, P.E.P. found that the more qualified the immigrant, the more likely he was to experience discrimination.[23] There is already a feeling that the dice are loaded. In the words of a West Indian youth leader in Britain: 'There is a lot of fear and a lot of frustration among our young people.'[24] Unless the Race Relations Act 1968 changes this situation, it seems likely that coloured school leavers, who in the future will swamp the Y.E.S., as it is staffed at present, may not have a fair deal.

3. SOCIAL CONTACT

Friendships formed between white and coloured children are seldom continued beyond school, and even at school there is some awareness of colour prejudice, as children reflect the attitudes of their parents. It has been observed, both in primary and secondary schools with children of different nationalities, that the children are apt to choose their friends from within their own group and reject members of other groups, and that they show this in-group preference whether they are English or immigrant children.[25] However, it is on leaving school that teen-agers are made acutely aware of the distance that separates coloured children from their white contemporaries. 'Through the hostile [twilight] areas coloured youngsters walk in groups and avoid trouble. Our cities are full of young coloured citizens of Britain trying to tiptoe through society.'[26] This and the quotations with which we began this chapter are witness to the anxiety and frustration which is felt by many coloured teen-agers in the first generation. It is not possible to say how widely these feelings are shared or how intense they are, but their origin seems to lie far more in a sense of social rejection than from experience of discrimination at work. From the evidence in the previous chapter, we may say that the sense of rejection is likely to be most keenly felt by West Indian youth; youth clubs and other forms of youth organization are familiar in many West Indian islands, and West Indian boys would like to join in the activities of their white contemporaries if they were welcomed. In Pakistan, as we have seen, the adolescent boy spends his leisure time with older men, and girls are secluded at puberty. Organized youth activity, aside from sport, is unknown in rural India. Thus, it is not surprising that the Westhill survey found 'the West Indian youngster more successful in assimilating to the British way of life' and the Asian youngsters 'less advanced in social integration'. The survey found, for example, that West Indians were more likely to attend evening classes than the Asians, they enjoyed sport and music more, they were more likely to be members of a youth club, and especially to belong to a multi-racial youth organization.[27]

The Report of the Youth Service Development Council is less optimistic, finding 'the general picture far from encouraging'.[28] There are three main reasons for this conclusion. First, the immigrant children share the general deprivation of the area in which they live and so are socially disadvantaged. Secondly, the Report found little contact between coloured and white pupils after school. Finally, it found that the efforts of the youth clubs as a focus for social contact were good only by exception. Taken together, these indicators are important, because the Council found that the youth service attracted immigrants according to the degree of acceptance in the local community and according to the range of services available to young people locally.

If the West Indian child is more likely to suffer from a sense of rejection, his need for organized social activity is also likely to be greater than that of the Indian child. The latter returns from school to the warmth of his family and to a mother who is keeping the home, whereas many West Indian children come back to a house that is empty because their mothers are at work. There is also very little room for them in overcrowded lodgings and they have to seek their recreation outside the home.

West Indian girls may not be allowed the same freedom as their brothers for, as we have seen, there is a strong element of puritanism in many West Indian parents. Besides, they will often be expected, from an early age, to look after the younger members of the family and to do the housework. Thus, they may be discouraged from attending mixed youth clubs or from taking part in any social activity organized by the school.

Indian girls are sheltered in adolescence and are expected to stay at home after school and to change into traditional dress, but as they increasingly enter the labour market, it is probable, as we have shown in the previous chapter, that their economic independence will lead to some degree of social freedom. Even so, it is unlikely that there will be very much mixing with English boys and the sanctions against inter-marriage are likely to remain strong. If the Indian pattern of early marriage is continued in this country, many girls will be betrothed before they leave school and may be married by the time they are 18.[29]

Indian girls may gain a certain measure of freedom, but this is unlikely to be true for Pakistanis. With compulsory schooling until 15, Muslim girls can no longer be secluded at the onset of puberty, but out of school they will be kept virtually isolated for some time to come. The parents' insistence on traditional dress, even at school, cuts these girls off from their peers in recreation, and their isolation will tend to perpetuate their dependence on their own community. Their economic dependence on the male members of the home will continue because it is unlikely that many of these girls will be allowed to work on leaving school.

It would be misleading to assume that the social problems of these children relate only to immigrant youth; they are in fact a variant of the problems of all the young, especially in the deprived areas of large cities. The children of immigrants, may need some form of social activity even more than their white contemporaries, but their need is only greater in degree. Some communities will take to British institutions more than others, who may provide their own recreation in much the same way as the needs of Jewish youth were provided by Jewish settlements and Jewish youth clubs, supported by Jewish philanthropists. In any case, we must remember that youth organizations can only cater for a minority. It is desirable that the youth service should be opened as widely as possible to immigrant youth: its significance will be symbolic for it will be building bridges and keeping them open until they are no longer needed. However, the majority of the second and third generation will have to get across without them.

4. DELINQUENCY

On American experience, one might be led to suppose that the behaviour of the second generation would be more deviant than that of their parents or the indigenous population. What evidence there is indicates that the opposite may be true: but apart from the findings in Cardiff, which are discussed below, we must remember that we are still dealing with what is, in effect, a first generation. Lambert's study in Birmingham throws some light on the question.[30] He used various indicators of delinquent and potential delinquent behaviour and found that Asian children were markedly less delinquent in terms of approved school attendance than a comparable English age group: West Indian boys, though more prone to approved school admissions than Asian boys, were under-represented compared with white children. He also found that coloured children formed less than 10% of all young probationers, which was an under-representation and that more than half of these children were from mixed marriages. For children in care and in contact with the children's department, West Indians were slightly over-represented, and children of mixed marriages were grossly over-represented. Asian children were very much under-represented.

The evidence on children in care is confirmed by Butterworth for Bradford, and also by Katrin Fitzherbert's information on West Indian children in London.[31] She noted that children beyond parental control were often those who had been separated from their parents by migration. These late arrivals who come straight into secondary school have formidable problems of adjustment and are a 'transitional' generation. If this group is counted separately, as a temporary problem, then the West Indian children in care are under-represented.

5. OLDER SETTLEMENTS

Because the post-war immigrations are too recent to have thrown up a second generation, we have so far been discussing the evidence on what is predominantly a first generation of immigrant teen-agers; but there are some coloured settlements in England and Wales which have been established long enough for a second and even a third generation to have grown up in a British environment. These were the port settlements in Liverpool, Cardiff, East London, and in the North East, described by Richmond, Little, Banton, and Collins, who focused their research mainly on the first generation.[32] To fill part of the gap in our knowledge, Leonard Bloom has recently been studying the psychological consequences of belonging to a minority group in the Bute Town area of Cardiff, where Little carried out his pioneering research in the 1940s. Bloom's study, which is not yet complete, is particularly interesting because it includes three generations of coloureds and some post-war coloured immigrants, and compares and contrasts them with a sample of Italian and Greek immigrants of the first and second generations. The author has so far only conveyed his main impressions of his findings to us.[33]

The coloured people who settled in Bute Town after the First World War differed in many respects, and their experience was different from the post-war immigrants who were attracted to the centres of industrial production. These early settlers were African, Asian, and West Indian seamen who had been signed on in their home ports and who settled in Cardiff with the intention of continuing in the merchant service. They experienced great hardship. There were race riots in 1919, in which at least one coloured man was killed, and throughout the inter-war years their position remained very precarious. The depressed state of the shipping industry, colour discrimination, and the hostility of the National Union of Seamen resulted in chronic unemployment. Their numbers were comparatively low and because of the Depression they were not reinforced from home and few wives came to join them. Many of them married local white women and many of the second generation are the products of these mixed marriages.

Bute Town itself is not exactly typical of the areas to which the majority of post-war immigrants have gone. It is the dockland area of Cardiff, a peninsula shut off from the rest of the city, bounded by a railway and a disused canal. But what is significant is how few of the coloured people, whatever their generation, have left Bute Town and how few wish to. They lead an encapsulated life within what is virtually an enclave. Even after the coloured quarter was re-developed in 1965, the population stayed where they were, exchanging their old terraced houses for high rise apartment buildings. There are few jobs for them in the rest of Cardiff: not a single coloured inhabitant of Bute Town has reached the university.

On the other hand, the Greek and Italian immigrants who first settled in Bute Town are now scattered throughout the city, where they easily find employment. They have little doubt that sooner or later they will belong in Cardiff and that it is only a matter of time before they are fully accepted. But the coloured people have to face so complicated a pattern of rejection and acceptance that they have little basis upon which to make a rational prediction about their future. Bloom quotes one post-war Italian immigrant who spoke of his own difficulties but said they were small compared with what the coloured population has to face. Italians have come to Cardiff to work and to prosper; while they retain their sense of being Italian they seem to have achieved a remarkable degree of harmony between their Italianness and their Welshness. But the second generation of coloureds have not been able to find the psychological means to fight from within a society of whose response they are so uncertain. Their attitude towards this society is far more ambivalent than that of the older men whose experience of hardship and discrimination brought home to them the overriding importance of colour. These older men, like the post-war arrivals, are more aware of the differences between coloured and white than their children and grandchildren, who, while less prepared to admit to any difference between the races, are almost equally unready to move away from the security of Bute Town. They have to a large extent absorbed the values of the 'host' society but they live neither in an alien nor a local culture.

These are the adolescents grown to manhood whom Little observed in the 1940s. He found that caught in a conflict of loyalties between a dark-skinned father and a white mother they tended to withdraw and avoid identification with either parent.[34] This resulted in a generalized habit of detachment and the avoidance of emotional and intellectual problems. Little suggested that this psychological attitude contributed to a lack of educational incentive, which was intensified by the narrow range of employment open to coloured juveniles.

However, this second generation has had a much easier time than their parents, who have bitter memories of the struggles of the 1920s; their economic and, in some cases, their social position has certainly improved, and with greater familiarity they are able to face the discrimination that certainly exists. There is no longer the searing unemployment of the 1930s and the city's slum clearance has given some plausibility to the view that things are better, particularly as people want to believe that this is true. Like Little, Bloom found that the area is peaceful and juvenile crime lower than in adjoining neighbourhoods. But the general picture that Bloom draws is not very encouraging. We see a second and third generation which lives in a quasi-ghetto, is denied the opportunities available to white English-speaking immigrants, is less ambitious, and achieves less than they do. They are not without white friends outside the area and they have a fair amount of social contact with whites, but they fear that they will meet colour prejudice outside Bute Town. They choose to stay in the coloured quarter because it is safer to trust to their own kind. Yet no one relishes the prospect of being cut off from the main stream of Cardiff city life: it is accepted as a regrettable and unhappy consequence of the insecurity of being coloured in a white city.

A report of a Working Party of the Liverpool Youth Organisations Committee, published in October 1968,[35] found the position of the second and third generation of coloured youth in Liverpool as dismal as we have described it in Cardiff. They suffer the same psychological handicaps, they meet discrimination in employment, and when they move outside the coloured quarter they feel very insecure. The inquiry left the Working Party with 'a deep sense of unease'. They write of 'the long-standing myth in Liverpool of non-discrimination between people of different racial characteristics', which is a cloak for indifference and lack of understanding. They found evidence of hostility to colour in white down-town areas in a city which has had a coloured population for at least forty years.

They also feared that there is a danger of conflict unless an active policy of integration is urgently adopted. On the evidence of what has happened in Liverpool and Cardiff there is obviously no room for complacency about the future of the second generation of post-war coloured immigrants.

NOTES TO CHAPTER 24

1. Department of Education and Science, Statistics of Education 1967 (London, H.M.S.O., 1967).

2. Nottingham Education Authority Return for January 1968.

3. Sheila Patterson, 'A Hardening Colour Bar? 2. The Jobs', New Society (16 March 1967).

4. David Beetham, Immigrant School Leavers and the Youth Employment Service in Birmingham (London, Institute of Race Relations Special Series, 1967), p. 22.

5. See Dr. G. Stewart Prince, 'Mental Health Problems in pre-School West Indian Children', and Dr. C. Eric Stroud, 'One Hundred Mothers', in Maternal and Child Care (Vol. III, no. 26, June 1967).

6. The People, 17 November 1968.

7. Dr. Wilfrid Harding, Medical Officer of Health, Borough of Camden, quoted in the People, 17 November 1968.

8. Sylvaine Wiles, 'Children from Overseas (2)', Institute of Race Relations Newsletter (June 1968), p. 245.

9. Inner London Education Authority, The Education of Immigrant Pupils in Primary Schools, Report of the Working Party of Members of the Inspectorate and Schools Psychological Service (London, I.L.E.A., November 1967).

10. Christopher Bagley, 'The Educational Performance of Immigrant Children', Ra e (Vol. X, no. 1, July 1968).

11. *Children and their Primary Schools* (London, H.M.S.O., 1967) (The Plowden Report).

12. Department of Employment and Productivity, Central Youth Employment Executive, 'Work of the Youth Employment Service, 1965-8' (London, H.M.S.O., 1968).

13. Beetham, op. cit., p. 25.

14. F. Milson, *Operation Integration Two: The Coloured Teenager in Birmingham* (Birmingham, Westhill College of Education, September 1966).

15. Peter Figueroa, 'Study of West Indian School Leavers in North London', research carried out for the Institute's 'Survey of Race Relations in Britain'.

16. 'Work of the Youth Employment Service 1965–8', op. cit., p. 5.

17. See Beetham, op. cit., p. 20.

18. Unpublished evidence to a committee of the Youth Service Development Council (the Hunt Committee) 1967.

19. Eric Butterworth, 'Policies for Integration: a study of Bradford', research carried out for the Institute's 'Survey of Race Relations in Britain'.

20. Beetham, op. cit., pp. 17–18.

21. Westhill, op. cit., p. 6; Beetham, op. cit., p. 34.

22. Rev. Roy Allison, Secretary of the Methodist Church Committee in Migration, Manchester, *Guardian*, 26 February 1968.

23. *Racial Discrimination* (London, Political and Economic Planning, 1967).

24. *Daily Telegraph*, 10 April 1968.

25. Taysir Kawwa, 'Three Sociometric Studies of Ethnic Relations in London Schools', *Race* (Vol. X, no. 2, October 1968).

26. Stuart Hall, *The Young Englanders* (London, National Committee for Commonwealth Immigrants, 1967).

27. Westhill, op. cit., p. 10.

28. *Immigrants and the Youth Service*, Report of a Committee of the Youth Service Development Council (London, H.M.S.O., 1967), p. 3.

29. From research in Southall by Narindar Uberoi, carried out for the Institute's 'Survey of Race Relations in Britain'.

30. John Lambert, 'Study of Immigrant Crime and the Relations of the Police and Immigrants in a Division of Birmingham', carried out for the Institute's 'Survey of Race Relations in Britain'.

31. Katrin Fitzherbert, *West Indian Children in London* (London, G. Bell, 1967).

32. A. H. Richmond, *Colour Prejudice in Britain: a Study of West Indian Workers in Liverpool, 1942–51* (London, Routledge, 1954); K. L. Little, *Negroes in Britain: a Study of Racial Relations in English Society* (London, Kegan Paul, 1947); Michael Banton, *The Coloured Quarter* (London, Cape, 1955); and S. Collins, *Coloured Minorities in Britain: Studies in British Race Relations based on African, West Indian and Asiatic Immigrants* (London, Lutterworth, 1957).

33. Leonard Bloom, 'Study of Bute Town, Cardiff', research carried out for the Institute's 'Survey of Race Relations in Britain'.

34. Little, op. cit., Chapter 6.

35. Liverpool Youth Organisations Committee, *Special But Not Separate: a Report on the Situation of Young Coloured People in Liverpool* (Liverpool, Liverpool Youth Organisations Committee, 1968).

25 Leadership

In this chapter we shall consider the functions of leadership in the various immigrant communities. The leader has a double image: that which he presents to the host community, and its *doppelgänger*, which is displayed to his own. In the new social situation in which the immigrants find themselves, he acts as an interpreter of the values and practices of the host society for the newcomers. In some cases, this function is interpreted positively: the leader acts as a form of human bridge between the two parties. In other instances, it is defensive: the leader gauges the hostile reaction of the host community and provides evidence of that hostility and proposals for modifying it, avoiding its effects, or actively combating it. In each instance the *raison d'être* of the leader is interpretation; but many may not accept the necessity for such an interpreter or the legitimacy of those who appoint and recognize him. Thus, the dialogue that takes place between the immigrant leader and the potential sponsor in the host community may be a dialogue of the deaf in which each party mistakes or misrepresents the role of the other, and in which remarks may be addressed not to their ostensible audience but to a wider public.

The uncertainty that often surrounds the function of leadership is increased with the divisions between the various immigrant groups in Britain. The image is not merely doubled: it is kaleidoscopic, broken into a variety of small fragments. In this situation the self-appointed leader flourishes: the extent to which he is able to function will often depend more on the way in which the host community perceives him than on the degree of acceptance he has achieved among fellow-migrants. This abuse of leadership function, which may be revealed in circumstances humiliating to the immigrant community, may lead both to a repudiation of the necessity of leadership and to pressure to create organizations that transcend the divisions based on the circumstances and values of the sending society and the feuds and schisms that these generate.

The obvious basis of such an organization is the common and visible difference of skin colour that separates off the immigrant from the host community. This can take the form of common opposition to the political expression of the white man's dominant situation (in shorthand terms, imperialism); a common interest in the independence of countries affected by imperialism, especially in Africa; a concern for the condition of the Negro in the United States and a desire to emulate the Negro struggle for justice; or, more simply, a recognition of a common interest in the hostility of the host community to coloured immigrants in this country, and its expression in discrimination.

But so far, these common grounds of united action, although they have exerted a strong influence, have not yet produced a lasting and effective common organization to articulate them. The factors of disassociation (in Sheila Patterson's phrase)[1]—cultural traits (including language), class and national orientations, and incompatibility of material interest—have proved stronger than the grounds for association. This has not always been the case, and may not always be so, but, over the main span of the period under discussion, leadership in the various migrant groups has been fragmented, weak, and often unrepresentative, even of the limited interests of which it purports to speak.

The rapid growth and death of organizations and their adaptation to changing situations makes any clear-cut classification difficult. Organizations evolve, and split, changing title, rationale, and style of approach as they do so. Some exist without clearly defined leaders—some of the *ad hoc* economic self-help bodies ('Pardner' schemes) are a case in point. More common are the leaders without organizations. They may be a product of the definition employed: a leader is a man (or woman) whose name is well-known within a particular immigrant group and to whom the host community looks for a lead at moments of crisis—the so-called 'prestige leader'. The fact that such leaders rarely make any attempt to exercise the authority with which they are presumptively endowed, and which the host community assumes them to possess, is often irksome to other claimants to the leadership role, who base their claims on the importance of the organization that they lead. But these, too, often turn out on closer examination to be fictitious entities, mere paper panthers (as Dipak Nandy once described the United Coloured People's Association),[2] existing only in a filing cabinet, among friends and kin of the 'leader', or in his imagination. The significance attached to leadership among immigrants and hosts alike, and the style in which leadership functions are discharged have fluctuated widely over the period we are discussing. Indifference has existed on one side, and on the other, and for a period on both. The consequences of this fluctuation have been both to magnify and minimize the importance of individuals, frustrating able men at one time and exalting the insignificant and the frauds at others. The diversity of attitudes among migrant groups (see Chapter 23) and the varying reaction of the hosts in different situations also makes it difficult to construct watertight generalizations. But certain broad trends do emerge.

During the period before the Second World War a significant coloured leadership group could certainly be said to exist in this country. It was concerned largely with the wider issues of the future of the Empire and British colonies; the relevance of this concern to the British situation was the status of the coloured man, as an equal citizen. This ideological emphasis was intensified by the high proportion of students among the coloured community of the period: the style in which the campaign was conducted was chiefly through an alliance of sympathetic politicans in the host community (radical critics of the colonial system) and committed Christians (like the Quakers). Some headway was made by one organization, the League of Coloured Peoples, led by the West Indian, Dr. Harold Moody. In some ways this could still be described as the most successful attempt to create a unified organization based on the common factor of colour. But in the changed situation after the Second World War the League's methods were less relevant, and it gradually faded into inactivity. Moreover, the 'new migration' (as it was initially described) from the West Indies had new needs and invoked new responses in the host community. As we saw in Chapter 16 the approach of the United Kingdom authorities was initially pragmatic and welfare based, though limited in application. While the Colonial Office was content to take care of the basic problems on arrival, the need for the kind of self-help organizations that often characterized the early stages of migrations did not exist. On the other hand, the reluctance (at least after 1951) to go further and make provision for jobs and housing left the immigrant with a series of longer term practical problems whose solutions occupied all his energies. Sheila Patterson's study of the best known of the initial reception areas, Brixton, shows this process at work in great detail.[3] Once a series of solutions had been evolved to these difficulties, a number of small-scale organizations began to appear: they were largely based on the type of body familiar in the culture from which the immigrants had come.

The most important of these associations, in the earlier period of the West Indian settlement, were the self-help economic organizations, the 'pardner' schemes—formal only to the extent that they had a specific membership, and a 'banker' or secretary.

There were also the small Pentecostal sects catering for the religious needs of those immigrants who found English styles of worship or English attitudes towards religion disturbingly un-committed. 'The need for non-economic associational outlets is minimal', Patterson found:[4] or, as A. G. Bennett put it, through one of his characters in his novel of the early days of the migration, *Because They Know Not*: 'you read a lot of bunk about those things. The only society I join is Barclays Bank and some of the best people in the land are members like myself. I don't want to join anything else.'[5]

The resulting absence of any effective organization and leader-ship until the late 1950s can be explained, as we have suggested earlier, in two ways: first, in relation to the immigrants, and secondly—and equally—by reference to the hosts. It seems clear that the heterogeneity of the West Indian immigrants in par-ticular, in terms of origins, social class, and political orientation, was a powerful force hindering the growth of associations. But in this context one aspect of the division within the migration (perhaps particularly in the case of Jamaicans) seems especially important. This is the colour-class categorization which lies at the root of the organization of West Indian society and which has been described in earlier chapters. The failure of the British to make those fine distinctions based on shades of colour, when these categories are the basis of social differentiation in the sending culture, accentuates the need for the elite and 'white biased' middle and upper-lower class to keep their distance from the ordinary immigrant: it also means that, in Patterson's phrase, there is 'room at the top for those migrants who achieve moderate prosperity'.[6] By the mid-1950s, the first few Jamaican landlords and small businessmen had reached this position, and a crude economic hierarchy was beginning to emerge. But in approaching the host community these emergent leaders had two major difficulties to contend with. First, the reluctance of fellow West Indians to accept their claims to leadership—which were not an inherited claim derived from wealth or skin colour—and secondly, the ambivalence of their own attitude towards the host society. Was it a better measure of success to appear and to be accepted in the part of West Indian leader or simply to be accepted, without distinction of colour or origin, as a successful businessman? If the latter—and most of the cultural biases at this stage were in the direction of making the attempt to be recognized as British (or, at worst, black British), then there would be a risk of appearing needlessly conspicuous in an unrewarding capacity. Especially since, in order to be at all effective, leadership functions would have to be carried out flamboyantly to over-ride the suspicions of fellow West Indians.

In fact, the attitude adopted by potential leaders made little difference, because the prevailing values adopted by opinion formers in the host community after the mid–1950s were that any distinctions of colour were totally irrelevant or over-ridden by the possession of a common citizenship. Local authorities, unable to square this new attitude with their experience generally, relapsed into inertia; in such a situation there was no need for them to identify or make use of coloured leaders. In certain instances (see Chapter 21) local voluntary efforts filled the gap—a process which required identification of leaders, but only in certain limited and exceptional circumstances. Rex and Moore have described how in Birmingham, the Corporation's liaison officer, appointed in 1956, declined to recognize the existence of organizations or leaders, and dealt directly with individual immigrants.[7]

The disturbances of 1958 in Nottingham and Notting Hill at first seemed likely to precipitate a radical change in the situation. After all, after systematic hunting of black men, identified as such, had taken place, there was no point in pretending that the fair-minded British recognized no distinctions of colour. Two immediate possibilities existed: the fissures dividing the West Indians in England by class and island loyalty might close, and there might also be some attempt at a junction between the different ethnic groups. The riots also had the effect of mobilizing the previously rather passive and complacent body of opinion in British society which felt a general concern for race relations and there might have been a basis in the chastened and more realistic post-riot atmosphere for effective inter-racial organization. In the event, some attempt was made to organize in all three directions: all three failed.

Within the West Indian community the immediate reaction of many of the intellectuals who had been drawn to Britain by the better prospects here were certainly towards solidarity. But even in the first moment of rage and revulsion there was an ambiguity: on what terms was the process to be made—as an intellectual or as a West Indian? Thus the multiplicity of West Indian organizations which sprang up in late 1958, compared by Donald Hinds to the swelling of streams after summer rain,[8] remained rivulets and eventually dried up without being able to tap leadership skills and experience. Only one or two individual initiatives led to any results. The most significant was that of Claudia Jones, a Trinidadian and former member of the Communist Party of the U.S.A., who had been deported from the United States to Britain in 1957 after her conviction and imprisonment under the Smith Act. The *West Indian Gazette*, which she had started in the same year, rapidly gained circulation and became for a while an effective platform for the views of West Indians on major policy issues.

The attempts to put together a federal protest organization were also ineffective. One such body was formed, with active help from African student organizations (one of which, the West African Students Union, had a long history of active involvement in migrant politics in Britain) and a deputation went to the Home Office. But no progress was made in making contact with the organizations in the newest of the 'new migrant' groups—the Pakistanis and Indians.

In the case of the Indians, effective organization involving a substantial proportion of the migrants existed both on a local and a national level. Indian organizations in Britain go back to before the Second World War when they were concerned exclusively with the struggle for Indian independence. Although the main body of Indians in England were students or professional men, such as doctors, dentists, or occasionally lawyers, there was a small minority of working-class migrants who organized an Indian Workers' Association alongside the middle-class India League. When the migration from the Punjab began in the mid-1950s, the immigrants revived the Indian Workers' Association (which had meanwhile become dormant), beginning in 1953 with the Coventry Association.[9]

Although membership of the Indian Workers' Association is open to all Indians, it was in practice confined to Punjabis and involved, at this early stage, nearly all the immigrants from this group. There are a number of explanations for this phenomenon, which contrasts so sharply with the situation among West Indians. First, there is a general view among Punjabis in Great Britain that it is desirable that the community should present a united front to the outside world, in the interests of achieving integration—*Mel Jol*. Since the migration was homogeneous in its origins, this led to a high degree of conformity with values held in common. The internal organization of the community, with its originally strong emphasis on kinship ties and networks of mutual obligation, helped to draw individuals into participation in I.W.A. activities.

Almost equally important was the strength of the Communist Party of India among the migrants. It is necessary to stress that, in the Indian context, membership of the Communist Party conferred a good deal of prestige on the individual, and gave him a recognized position among those concerned with politics (effectively all male Punjabis). There is a strong tradition of Communist activity in the Punjab: until the Second World War, Communists formed a part of the Indian National Congress in the area. In post-independence politics, the Communist Party has functioned as an independent entity, but often in alliance with a range of other parties. As DeWitt John puts it: 'Punjabis have grown up in a political atmosphere where non-Communist and even conservative religious leaders co-operate with the Communist Party.'[10] However, it is expected of a member of the Party that he will be politically more zealous and less prone to corrupt practice than non-Communists. The prestige that has gone with observation of this practice permits the Communist to function in I.W.A. politics without the apparatus of contacts and kinship employed by the non-Communist politician. It also permits him to mobilize migrants for participation in I.W.A. activities—though not necessarily in action specifically directed to Party ends. John quotes one Indian Communist as saying:

I am ashamed of the Party branch. The Comrades are interested in the I.W.A. and nothing else. When we have a meeting to discuss the I.W.A., then all of the comrades come. But when we are going to discuss national or international issues only one or two come. It is a very bad record.[11]

Thus, the Communists within the I.W.A. acted as a ginger group on specifically I.W.A. issues, ensured a high level of interest in those issues and participation in action arising from them, and provided their leaders with a basis on which to run for office.

Included in the activities of the I.W.A., as we have seen, were a number of 'social work' functions, involving favours done and difficulties resolved for individual members of the community. By far the most pressing of these arose in connexion with the issue of passports, a long-standing grievance among Indians in England, who had often obtained entry by evasion of the control operated by the Indian Government over the distribution of passports, by forgery, or by substitution. Repeated attempts were made to interest the Indian High Commission and the Indian ministers visiting the United Kingdom in the situation of those migrants who were stranded in Britain with forged passports. Eventually, Pandit Nehru suggested (when approached in 1957) that representations would be more effective if a combined body was set up to speak on behalf of all the organizations. As a result, in 1958, the Indian Workers' Association of Great Britain was created.

The I.W.A.–G.B. had a wide range of aims written into its constitution. The safeguarding of the conditions of work of Indians in Britain through collaboration with British organizations, liaison with the Indian High Commission, educational work on the image of India, and social welfare work. In practice, the passport grievance became the main focus of its activities, and this campaign was conducted in opposition to rather than in collaboration with the High Commission. The passport racketeers, who were ultimately responsible for the situation that had arisen, had connexions with certain officials in England and the Punjab and proved difficult to dislodge; but by 1960 their resistance had worn down and the High Commission agreed to issue valid passports to all Indian citizens in England.

This important victory, in which the Communists in the I.W.A. played a major part, marks a high water mark in the effectiveness of a national organization. Shortly afterwards, it became the victim of one of the periodic schisms which are the occupational hazard of all Punjabi organizations. Ironically, it was not until its plans had been eroded by schisms that other migrant organizations at last began to make contact with their Indian opposite number.

The appearance of large numbers of West Indian organizations after Notting Hill proved to be a transitory phenomenon; but the reaction of the governments of Jamaica and the embryonic West Indian Federation to the riots had longer lasting consequences. The British Caribbean Welfare Service, set up after the Senior-Manley mission to Britain in 1955, was strengthened by the addition of new personnel and re-christened the Migrant Services Division of the West Indian Federal High Commission. Among the personnel drafted in were two trained community development officers, and these set about trying to organize a body which could act as a forum for discussions between representative West Indians in the London area. The organization that was created in this way was known at first as the Standing Conference of Leaders of West Indian Organizations in London, and met at the M.S.D. offices. Initially, Standing Conference was a discussion group, attended both by West Indians and white sympathizers. Among the organizations affiliated were not only sports clubs and social welfare bodies (generally the only bodies to survive for any length of time), but inter-racial organizations, including those set up on the initiative of members of the host community, such as the Parliamentary lobby, the British Caribbean Association. Members of the M.S.D. who were guiding the conference's activities encouraged this trend: they recommended West Indians setting up new organizations 'to keep such terms as "coloured" or "West Indian" from their titles and rather substitute such names as "inter-racial" or "commonwealth" '.[12]

Thus, the initial trend of Standing Conference's activities was towards providing a forum for discussion on the most satisfactory means of achieving integration, at which a number of sympathetic whites assisted. The rationale in this approach was that, as a result of the events of 1958, a difficulty had been created and a response was called for, but that the goodwill of the host community would re-assert itself, perhaps by a form of permeation through inter-racial organizations. Occasionally, Standing Conference heard reports of events in Notting Hill which suggested an opposite conclusion. These came chiefly from the Coloured Peoples Progressive Association, one of the few political organizations to survive the year after the riots, despite a destructive intervention in its affairs by Michael de Freitas (Rachman's chief collector and local frontman). But the scope of Standing Conference activities and the style in which they were conducted ('under', as the then Chairman put it, 'the protective wing of Federal Government')[13] allowed them to do no more than note what was happening.

Gradually, however, the atmosphere changed. By 1961, eighteen organizations was affiliated to Conference, and friction was growing between Conference and the M.S.D. A memorandum from the latter in September reminded Conference of its obligations to the High Commission, which had provided it with somewhere to meet. 'This postulates', the memorandum stated, 'that on its part the Conference should pursue no policy which might be embarrassing to the Commission.' 'That is not to say', it added, 'that the Commission wishes in any way to unduly control the scope of activities of Conference.'[14]

Two major events in 1961 precipitated a change of policy on the part of Conference. The first was the break-up of Federation, as a result of Jamaica's rejection of the concept at the referendum of September (see Chapter 16). There is no doubt that this came as a shock to West Indian leaders in England, much more accustomed than their fellow countrymen at home to contact with migrants from other islands,* and conscious of the increased prestige that an independent Federation would confer on them in Britain. All the leaders in Standing Conference appeared to have supported the concept of the Federation, regardless of their island of origin, and to have regretted its collapse. With the Federal Government went the Federal High Commission in the U.K. and its Migrant Services Division.

This material and psychological blow fell exactly at the moment when the British Government finally decided, after agonies of indecision, to control immigration from the Commonwealth (indeed, as we have seen in Chapter 16, the two events were interconnected). Thus, the presumption of British fair play, which was nurtured by the High Commission and to some extent justified by British reactions to Notting Hill, was finally exposed as unreliable and the strategy based upon it discredited.

For a while, it was possible to construct an alternative theory of benevolence in the host community, based on the Labour Party's resistance to the Commonwealth Immigrants Bill. At one stage it seemed feasible that Labour might be prepared to take on the role of a positive integrative agency for the new minorities, on the lines of the Democratic Party in the United States. Individual West Indians joined the Party, and made rapid progress.

Most of the activity which took place only touched the fringe of consciousness of individual West Indians; often it looked suspiciously like a cynical manœuvre designed to ensure that Labour pocketed a few extra votes. But it helped to prolong the view that a solution could be found within the existing system.

Nevertheless, Standing Conference began to move slowly away

* One of the main (ostensible) reasons for the breakdown of Federation was a dispute about freedom of movement between the various West Indian islands.

from the original concept of a discussion group on integration and to develop a policy based on the proposition that a separate solution not dependent on acceptance by hosts or support by the High Commission would have to be devised. The tangible sign of this change of policy was the campaign for a West Indian Social Centre. The intangible evidence of alienation was a willingness to shrug off the support of those whites who had been involved in the early activities of Conference, and a hardening resistance towards those investigators who wished to study the situation of the West Indian.

Generally, a strong sense of isolation permeated leadership during this period. Looking back on the riots of 1958 and its consequences, Team Work inquired, in 1963:

We look back on the result of all this activity, and what do we find? We find that the spell of conscientious activity lasted for a while, and then began to taper off, until today we are left with only a handful of West Indians who are still troubled with the knowledge that the survival of one depends upon the survival of all. For those who assumed the role of leadership during the riots and then lost interest when it no longer provided the opportunity for self-aggrandisement . . . we must apply different standards of judgement in order to measure the extent of their disgrace to themselves and to the rest of the West Indian community.[15]

As long as no urgent threat existed the Conference activists could denounce their supine fellow countrymen indefinitely—most of them would remain blissfully unaware of the denunciations. In a culture in which verbal communication is so much more important than the written word, only pressure from the outside could do the job for them: until then, Conference remained (as the Migrant Services Division before them had admitted to being) out of contact.

The Indian community was also under pressure, and the capacity of the I.W.A. to resist it had been diminished. The position of the High Commission had always been neutral, at best; it had 'discouraged political association among the immigrants, fearing it would make the immigrants more visible to the host society thereby increasing the latter's hostility to Indians'.[16] As long as the individual I.W.A.s functioned effectively as social work agencies on behalf of members, and some sort of effective federal body existed, this lack of support from the High Commission was of no great significance. Once the migrants could find their own way to the appropriate institutions and needed no intervention, the potential leader, in order to secure a clientele, needed to secure a firm footing in the esteem of the host community. This could only be done by securing recognized authority: hence the competition for office became greater and rivalries constantly fiercer. It was at this stage (in 1962) that the Chinese invasion of India occurred, with the immediate result that the prestige of the Communists in the Indian Workers' Association was severely damaged, and the Communist Party itself split between two factions ('left', or 'Maoist', and 'right', or 'revisionist'). The disintegration of what had previously been the main integrative elements in the I.W.A.s led to the final collapse of the Federal organization; the Birmingham I.W.A., mainly dominated by Maoists, quarrelled irreparably with the largest of the associations, Southall, which left the I.W.A. of Great Britain. Thereafter, the I.W.A.–G.B. functioned as an appendage of the I.W.A.-Birmingham. On a local level a series of splits occurred in almost all major associations, leading to loss of prestige and alienation of the graduates who formed the majority of the male migrants after the Act of 1962.

The schism in the C.P.-I. had the incidental effect of terminating an odd arrangement by which the C.P.-G.B. kept in touch with the Indian comrades. Rather than accept the Indians, with their overriding concern with communal affairs, as ordinary members of the Party, the C.P.-G.B. preferred to organize them in separate branches, with an English comrade as liaison officer. This arrangement suited the majority of Indians, who in any case despised what they perceived as the slack discipline and low standards required of new entrants to the C.P.-G.B.: the minority concerned with international issues were allowed to maintain direct contact with Party headquarters and on occasion write in the *Daily Worker*. After the schism those comrades who supported the 'left' C.P.-I. (who included most of the politically sophisticated) were summarily expelled by the C.P.-G.B. and set themselves up as an independent Association of Indian Communists. The remainder, who supported the revisionist 'right' C.P.-I., were absorbed into the main body of the C.P.-G.B., and their segregation thus terminated.

But in practice the link with the C.P.-G.B. had never been of real significance; the communism of the migrants was of purely Indian relevance. When, after 1962, the Punjabi communities in the West Midlands and Southall began to feel themselves under political pressure, they turned for support to the local Labour parties. Negotiations were conducted with the local parties by the serving officials, on the basis that the communities vote could be delivered to Labour in return for measures that would lift the pressure—for example, in relation to overcrowding. In the negotiations both parties were to some extent overbidding their hand; the Indian leaders, because they could only deliver a proportion of the vote at best, as a built-in consequence of factional schism, and because they were playing their hands for personal benefit, and the Labour leaders because they had no real intention of returning the favour paid, except by insignificant rewards (in the small change of local political patronage) to individuals. But in at least two cases pacts were in fact made, and Labour can be shown to have benefited at the General Election of 1964 in consequence. One form of defensive action, communal intervention in host community politics, had been devised to cope with the increasing hostility felt by all migrant groups.

Perhaps the least affected were the Pakistanis. Strong tendencies towards self-segregation had existed among the migrants from the beginning. Such organizations as did evolve—burial societies, mosque committees, and, occasionally, informal welfare organizations—were concerned 'with Pakistanis as a national group and not as immigrants in a foreign country'.[17] These were subject to further fissures in consequence of the linguistic and cultural divisions between different groups within the migration (broadly, between East and West Pakistanis), so that effective organization was very slow in emerging. The High Commission had made a number of gestures, in an attempt to cope; England was divided, in a kind of Cromwellian system, into a number of areas for which officers (in most instances Majors) on the High Commission staff were to be responsible. But Rex and Moore comment that the staff 'knew little of, and sympathised less with the interests of the ordinary migrant. It is an organisation of diplomats in a situation where sensitive community leadership and the skills of social work are needed.'[18]

A misleading appearance of involvement in host community activities was given by the candidature of individual Pakistanis in local elections in 1963 and in one case in the General Election of the following year. These were prestige candidatures: the audience was the immigrant community and the electoral processes were being manipulated to demonstrate the numerical support possessed by these individuals.

It is against this background that the attempt to form a National Federation of Pakistani Associations, in 1963, must be seen. If the Federation has never been very effective, this is largely because of its strong bias towards East Pakistan. But any organization, whatever its regional basis, would have to contend with the preoccupation of individual Pakistanis with their economic problems which has exceeded even that of the West Indians, and the fact that the individuals who have assumed the leadership role are even more isolated and atypical. Five years after its founding the National Federation was savagely attacked in an editorial in *Asia Weekly* which called for unity and deplored factionalism among Pakistanis and the failure of the so-called leaders to tackle the problems of the immigrants. 'We openly declare that the National Federation is a useless and meaningless organisation which is tantamount to saying that its title is a misnomer.'[19] The paper stated flatly that there is no association in any British city which could be said to be a representative organization of Pakistani immigrants. Factionalism was damaging the reputation of their country and the British complain that they do not know whom to recognize as leaders among all the pretenders. In the same week, *Mashriq* was advising Pakistani graduates 'to pack up their bags and go back home'; they were said to have become a nuisance to the true interests of the immigrants.[20]

The capacity to organize commercial operations, so clearly in evidence in the lodging houses of Sparkbrook, does not extend to the creation of effective defensive organizations. This can be partly attributed to the comparatively low level of hostility in the major area of Pakistani settlement, Bradford; but even where the pressure was strong, in Birmingham (where, as we have seen, Asian landlords formed a scapegoat group and were a subject of repeated prosecution for the local authority), the corresponding reaction was weak and ill-organized. An *ad hoc* body, the Commonwealth Property Owners' Association, was set up to deal with the situation, but soon flickered into inactivity.

So it was on divided and disorganized coloured communities that the results of the 1964 election and a consequent shock wave of alarm and confusion about immigration broke. For West Indian leaders, the lesson was clear enough. An expectation of fair play on which the original Standing Conference approach was based had changed first to apprehension and then to a certainty of foul deal-ling. But what morals should be drawn from this process for the approach to the host community? Or was any such approach now out of the question? If so, what was the alternative? Heineman points to one insidious solution to the individual activist's dilemma.

The fear of failing to gain recognition and independence may take the form among Conference activists not of identifying with the British in the hope of gaining status and acceptance that way, but rather in a desire to seem to be outspoken and angry about society, so that the isolation and powerlessness which are a part of daily existence can be viewed by leaders as being self-willed and not as a rejection by a society which he distrusts but into which at the same time he would like to gain entrance and acceptance.[21]

If this is right, it explains a great deal about the style of much of the protest adopted. Yet there were limits to this outspokenness; the anxiety of respectable men with their first foothold on the upward ladder not to jeopardize that respectability excluded drastic solutions like going to prison.

But it would be quite unfair to give the impression that no conscious attempt was made to think out an alternative pro-gramme. In Neville Maxwell's *The Power of Negro Action*, Standing Conference produced in 1965 a reasoned statement of policy. Starting from the rejection of the concept of assimilation as a goal for West Indians in British society, Maxwell concedes that 'by and large the West Indian until recently has been concerned less with the self-identification, West Indianism, negritude or call-it-what-you-will, than with the unconscious drive to establish a minimal level of communication with the native community'.[22] But now he has no alternative; white leadership and white perceptions of the Negro's place in British society are equally damaging to his future prospects in Britain.

The solution lies in capitalizing on weakness; the geographical concentration in the incipient ghetto and the preoccupation with 'bread and butter issues'. The concentration provides a framework within which to work, and the material obsessions become a conscious policy of economic development (the parallel made is again with the Jews), which means an emphasis 'not on trying to climb someone else's political ladder but on getting their fingers around the throat as it were of the economy'. In proper Smilesian style, what is required is an 'Operation Boot Strap'.[23]

In the meantime, anything which helps to provide a degree of unity and stimulate interest, even cricket, must be encouraged, and class divisions based on middle-class values minimized.

If the remedies proposed are Utopian, the analysis is convincing and provides an alternative to the increasing preoccupation with the Third World. Neither, however, are related in any effective way to the situation of the individual West Indian. In the provinces, the situation seems to have been broadly similar. A nominal Standing Conference existed in Birmingham at the time of Rex and Moore's study, but in practice it was the creation of an individual and did not survive his withdrawal from the scene.

From this powerlessness, and the cul-de-sac into which Indian and Pakistani organizations had run, the shifting in the host community attitudes towards immigrants in the period immediately after the 1964 general election offered two immediate prospects of escape. As we have seen in Chapter 16, the incoming Labour Government entered upon an anxious search for positive policy proposals. In March 1965, the appointment of Maurice Foley as Minister responsible for integration led to a period of ministerial visits during which he made a systematic attempt to canvas immigrant opinion. Although this consultation was not on the immigrant leaders' own terms, it represented a significant gain on the random discussions that had been the only previous form of contacts. Ultimately, these forays convinced Foley that the system of voluntary liaison committees that had been instituted and developed by Nadine Peppard should form the major part of the Government's effort on the integration front (see Chapter 26). This implied a systematic attempt, conducted with official funds, to draw immigrant leaders into participation as partners in the framework of policy-making nationally within the new National Committee for Commonwealth Immigrants. It was arguable (and indeed argued) that this policy represented a change of heart and deserved support. And the prospect of legitimization of status, with all the benefits of prestige that it would confer, was a powerful incentive to collaboration for many immigrant leaders.

One of the organizations that had meetings with Foley immediately after his appointment was the Campaign Against Racial Discrimination (C.A.R.D.). C.A.R.D. had been set up in December 1964. The initial impetus had come from the anxieties generated by the Smethwick episode among a number of white radicals associated with the Committee of 100 and a West Indian

Quaker, Marian Glean; the catalyst was provided by the visit of Martin Luther King to London *en route* to receiving a Nobel Prize. After a number of co-options, partly of community leaders unable to attend the initial meetings and also of sympathetic whites (who formed a minority of four on the provisional executive of thirteen members), C.A.R.D. began the painful process of defining its objectives.

The first Chairman of C.A.R.D. was Dr. David Pitt. One of the many areas of misunderstanding that arose subsequently lay in the simple identification of Pitt with the Labour Party—his position was in fact far more complex. Although he had indeed stood as a Labour parliamentary candidate and was a sitting G.L.C. Councillor, he was also heir to the earlier radical anti-colonialist tradition and at one time had been active in nationalist politics in Trinidad. He had served for some time on the executive committee of the League of Coloured Peoples. In his message in the Claudia Jones memorial edition of the *West Indian Gazette*, he indicated that he saw C.A.R.D. in the direct line of descent from earlier attempts to unite coloured people on an anti-colonialist footing. At the same time, he was not a West Indian 'leader' in any orthodox sense. Heineman comments that:

... to members of Standing Conference he can be seen both as a front and a challenge; he was someone who had achieved a certain level of success partly because he was a West Indian, and yet he did not seem to be as concerned with the West Indian community, in the way he should be (i.e. in the way they expected).[24]

By coming forward at this stage to lead them, he was signalling the possibility that the class differences, like cultural ones, might at last be overriden under the pressures of the situation. But there remained the latent threat of alienation from those who regarded themselves as qualified for leadership by their efforts, under difficult circumstances, to organize the community. Nevertheless, in February 1965 Standing Conference decided after some hesitation to affiliate to C.A.R.D.: in this they were followed by the Indian Workers' Association of Southall and the National Federation of Pakistani Associations.

It was part of the basic strategy of C.A.R.D. that the immigrant organizations were the key to the situation. Existing organizations were assumed to understand the situation at local level and to participate in it. Their claims to representativeness were taken (especially in the case of Asian organizations) at face value. And, despite anxious discussion of the need for C.A.R.D. activity at grass roots level, it was assumed that such activity would alienate existing organizations and could therefore only be conducted with their help and participation. As a result, C.A.R.D. emerged from its chrysalis stage at the founding convention of July 1965 as a federal organization, based on the assumption that a genuinely representative nature could be achieved by building coalitions.

C.A.R.D.'s early months had also been taken up with a long drawn out dispute about styles of protest and objectives. Should the main target be better legislation against discrimination or the repeal of the Commonwealth Immigrants Act 1962? As Heineman suggests, this debate ultimately proved to be of secondary importance to the structural decisions taken. The format of an organization of organizations had its credibility tested severely during the next stage in the evolution of race relations: but for the next year, at least, the federal structure remained largely intact. In practice (as Heineman argues) this amounted to little more than multiplying powerlessnesses, like zeros. But it was sufficient to preserve C.A.R.D.'s claim to be a representative organization.

After the White Paper, C.A.R.D. increasingly saw its position to be on the left flank of a radical coalition, its claim to representation based mainly on the participation of the largest of the Indian organizations, I.W.A. Southall. Standing Conference withdrew from C.A.R.D. after two members of the Executive Committee accepted invitations to serve on the new National Committee for Commonwealth Immigrants and it subsequently maintained a hostile neutrality. Its comments on the 1965 White Paper had denounced the 'voluntary liaison committees [and] numerous immigrant advisory councils which while providing harmless outlets for well-meaning people and "jobs for the boys" merely scratched the surface'. A 'more serious attempt should be made by those concerned to contact organisations which truly represent immigrants. In the past such contacts have been studiously avoided by all such goody goodies.'25 I.W.A. Birmingham ploughed its own Marxist furrow, concentrating increasingly on problems of the Third World. Other critics of the Government, mostly inside the Labour Party, had had their row at the party conference and obtained their concession (the Wilson Committee on Immigration Procedure): honour was satisfied. In the circumstances, a coalition of forces between Government and elements sufficiently representative of the immigrants (to outward appearances, at least) appeared possible. Provided, that is, that the official programme could be seen to diverge sufficiently from the lines laid down by the White Paper to command confidence, and that a personality not tainted by association with it was in overall charge. The appointment of Roy Jenkins as Home Secretary in December 1965 appeared to provide such an opportunity.

NOTES TO CHAPTER 25

1. Sheila Patterson, *Dark Strangers* (London, Tavistock Publications, 1963), p. 372.

2. Dipak Nandy, 'Fallacies of Parity', lecture given to Institute of Race Relations, 8 December 1967 (unpublished).

3. Patterson, op. cit., especially Chapter 17.

4. Patterson, op. cit., p. 363.

5. A. G. Bennett, *Because They Knew Not* (London, Phoenix Press, n.d.).

6. Patterson, op. cit., p. 377.

7. John Rex and Robert Moore, *Race, Community and Conflict* (London, Oxford University Press, for Institute of Race Relations, 1967), p. 160.

8. Donald Hinds, *Journey to an Illusion* (London, Heinemann, 1966), p. 136.

9. The passage that follows is based on DeWitt John's study of the Indian Workers' Association, *Indian Workers' Associations in Britain* (London, Oxford University Press, for Institute of Race Relations, 1969).

10. John, op. cit.

11. Ibid.

12. R. A. Burt, 'Colour Prejudice in Great Britain' (B.A. thesis, Princeton, 1966), p. 90.

13. Quoted in B. W. Heineman, Jr., 'The Politics of Race: a Study of the Campaign Against Racial Discrimination' (unpublished B.Litt. thesis, Oxford, 1967), p. 103.

14. Ibid., p. 106.

15. *Teamwork*, May 1963.

16. R. H. Desai, *Indian Immigrants in Britain* (London, Oxford University Press, for Institute of Race Relations, 1963), p. 103.

17. Rex and Moore, op. cit., p. 171.

18. Ibid., p. 171.

19. *Asia Weekly*, 10 February 1968.

20. *Mashriq*, 10 February 1968.

21. Heineman, op. cit., p. 137.

22. Neville A. Maxwell, *The Power of Negro Action* (London, The Author, 1965), p. 22.

23. Ibid. The implied reference is to the programme of economic development in Puerto Rico.

24. Heineman, op. cit., p. 148.

25. West Indian Standing Conference: statement on the White Paper of 1965.

PART VI ROY JENKINS AND LEGISLATION AGAINST DISCRIMINATION: A CASE STUDY

26 Clearing the Way

To argue (as we have done in Part IV) that the Government's White Paper in August 1965 was an almost wholly negative response, at a time when the situation demanded a rigorous analysis and proposals for administrative action, is not necessarily to suggest that none of the policy initiatives taken by the Labour Government in their first year of office had any constructive content. The appointment of Maurice Foley to the post of Co-ordinator of Policy on Integration in March 1965, at first on a part-time basis, was one such positive step; but its effects were largely vitiated by a combination of factors.

In the first place, Foley's initial departmental base in the Department of Economic Affairs, was not an ideal locale from which to direct policy on an issue on which effective determination depends chiefly on the attitudes in powerful departments in the main stream of Whitehall—the Ministries of Housing and Labour, the Department of Education and Science, and indeed the Home Office. Nor did the revised Committee of Junior Ministers constitute an adequate counter-vailing instrument of co-ordination. Foley's own style, a free-wheeling approach based on personal contact and face-to-face bargaining, and small staff, also largely excluded the prospect of the kind of patient negotiation based on extensive paperwork that would enable him to carry unpopular policy decisions against entrenched senior ministers in departments other than his own.

The first six months of the new Minister's activities were therefore mainly taken up with the task of public education; the co-ordination of the work of different departments took second place, with the result that the integration policy section in the White Paper (Part III) presented an unconvincingly negative and uncoordinated appearance.

And so, against a background of the deteriorating situation (described in Chapter 11) Foley found himself defending a White Paper, Section 2 of which (the new immigration proposals) he personally found distasteful and whose positive elements had clearly gone seriously awry. 'I grant you that none of the proposals to this end are very dramatic,' he said in a speech delivered immediately after the White Paper was issued, 'but . . . we cannot expect to solve the various difficulties which have arisen overnight by some master stroke of administrative action.'[1] This hardly argues great enthusiasm for a document for which he was on paper largely responsible; that he was able to defend it at all with a degree of success, both in public and in private, is an impressive tribute to the extent to which he had succeeded in his other capacity, as a personality capable of inspiring confidence. He had defined the strategy as one of achieving 'a mutual understanding— and I stress the word mutual'; a condition which 'will only be achieved when the collective social conscience demands that it should happen'. The social conscience 'will need to be stimulated in the right direction if it is to make the right demands'.[2] To some degree, this objective was achieved during the eighteen months of 'Foley's forays'. As Eric Silver put it when summing up his achievement at the end of this period in office: 'If we are less complacent now, Mr. Foley more than most is responsible for inducing a more sophisticated appreciation of what is involved. . . . As a one-man pressure group, inside and outside the Government', he continually put the case that 'race relations was not simply the dark side of other problems, that it had to be seen as a whole'.[3]

But it was precisely because a one-man pressure group was not in itself sufficient to provide the solid foundations for policy-making that the situation, immediately after the White Paper was issued, was so disturbing. A disconcerting impression of drift (reinforced by the eccentricity of the Government's performance on the Race Relations Bill in the spring of 1965) was undermining confidence in the Government's capacity.

The temporary suspension of discussion of the immigration policy set out in the White Paper brought about by the concession of a committee of inquiry (the Wilson Committee) into immigration procedures, seemed to leave the Government even more uncertain of its course. The Expiring Laws Continuance Debate in November 1965 illustrates this uncertainty with painful clarity. Winding up for the Government, Ray Gunter informed the House: 'I defend my stand on the White Paper on the very standpoint of the Christian Gospel'; and that his officials marked the cards of coloured workers as such, 'from a sense of Christian charity because they know that if they send a man to work he will be humiliated, often not because the management wants to humiliate him but because the man on the workshop floor will not accept him.' On the selection of a number for the allocation of work vouchers, he could only say that this was 'an exercise of judgment'.[4]

With such uncertainty prevalent, not only on the manner of execution of official policy but on the aims of that policy, it was clear that not even Foley's capacity for soothing the troubled breasts of members of local authorities could avert trouble, especially if the general election, which seemed increasingly likely to take place early in 1966, produced the same kind of exploitation of anxieties over immigration as had its predecessor. This, in broad outline, was the position when Sir Frank Soskice's increasing ill-health drove him into retirement and the Prime Minister appointed Roy Jenkins, at the end of December 1965, to be his successor.

In discussing the period that followed, it is impossible to avoid discussion of the personality of the new Home Secretary. The public persona, Welsh miner's son turned Whig, has fascinated journalists without stimulating any profound analysis; the oblique style seems to baffle, the highly polished surface to reflect the light without revealing the depths. Perhaps more relevant for the present discussion was the new Home Secretary's past political position, as a technocrat Socialist, seeking cures for economic malaise by efficient achievement of planned growth and, specifically, through early entry into Europe, balanced by an abiding concern for civil liberties. Also his political loyalties should be remembered—the admiration for Clem Attlee (whose biography he has written) and subsequently the close association with Hugh Gaitskell (in whom the balance between intellect and emotion had never appeared to better advantage than in the debates on Commonwealth immigration, but with whom he disagreed fundamentally in the linked debate on Europe)—and his publications— not only the scholarly biographies of Sir Charles Dilke, or Asquith, but that *locus classicus* of commentators on his Home Secretaryship, *The Labour Case*.[5] In this work, published for the 1959 General Election, Jenkins set out his criteria for a civilized bourgeois socialism. It was on Home Office issues, and perhaps in particular those (like the admission of aliens to Britain) which involved questions of individual liberty that Jenkins discerned the sharpest divide between the parties. He characterized his Conservative predecessors' policy on the admission of foreigners as 'more suitable to a police state, terrified of intellectual infection from the outside world, than to a Britain which is the traditional refuge of the oppressed'.[6] Heineman* has suggested that, in addition, the style and objectives of the Kennedy-Johnson administration (with which Jenkins was personally familiar) had made a strong impression on him.[7]

In short, the preoccupation with efficient management, balanced by a concern for the individual and his position *vis-à-vis* the bureaucracy, were together crucial in forming the assumptions with which the new Home Secretary turned to considering a problem which he identified from the outside as one which would define the style of his Home Secretaryship.

An immediate problem which arose as Jenkins began his term of office was the appointment of the first Chairman of the Race Relations Board. He brushed aside the considerations of his predecessor and the claims of other candidates, and appointed Mark Bonham Carter, the publisher and former Liberal Member for Torrington, a chairman capable of sophisticated analysis of the problem and with an equally acute sensitivity to the political overtones in the situation. The aimlessness and negative atmosphere of the debate (or rather the succession of statements on the on the subject of immigration) on the Expiring Laws Continuance Bill in November 1965 had provided convincing evidence that the task of defining the ultimate goals of policy was not an intellectual exercise but an immediate, practical imperative. The need was satisfied with characteristic neatness and precision in the first major speech on race relations, in the course of which Jenkins defined integration 'not as a flattening process of assimilation but equal opportunity, accompanied by cultural diversity, in an atmosphere of mutual tolerance'.[8]

These preoccupations with efficiency and intellectual precision also emerged in the identification of the first (and as it turned out chief) major policy initiative in this field—the extension of the legislation against racial discrimination to cover the fields of housing and employment. Initially, the emphasis was very much on the side of employment: this reflected the Home Secretary's own predisposition to view this field as the most important, and, to

---

* We shall be quoting frequently from Heineman during the course of this analysis. The fact that we do not always find his interpretation convincing should not prevent us from indicating how very much (and on occasion very obviously) indebted we are to him for his pioneer work.

some extent, the influence of his closest advisers. The full significance of housing, as the root cause of the cycle of discrimination,
was grasped less rapidly but eventually as surely as the super-
ficially more dramatic issue of job discrimination. There was no
question that the principle of extension was uppermost in the new
Home Secretary's mind from the beginning; it satisfied all the
criteria for a policy initiative. The rationale was capable of crisp
exposition, its importance was beyond question; the detailed case
was technical to some degree but also basic to a problem in human
rights and the argument would have to be balanced between the
two. It is true that powerful vested interests were involved in any
such extensions—both employers and trade unions could be
expected, for rather different reasons, to oppose a further Race
Relations Act. Also, that his predecessor, in persuading the House
to accept the much mutilated Race Relations Act of 1965, had
commented that 'it would be an ugly day in this country if we
had to come back to Parliament to extend the scope of this
legislation'.[9] But this could hardly be read as a binding commitment and the job of persuading the interest groups presented a
technical problem in political manœuvre which was not a deterrent to Jenkins and his chosen allies.

Moreover, the selection of the extension of legislation as the key
issue offered an escape from the blind alley of immigration policy
which the new Home Secretary clearly found extremely distasteful. It was implicit in any decision to advance on the legislative
front that the immigration flank would need to be stabilized. Now
that the Government's liberal critics had been bought off with
the Wilson Committee investigation, the main hazard was from
the right; and an almost uninterrupted series of concessions on the
numbers and composition of the immigration made the stabilization a difficult operation. Here, too, the new Home Secretary
attempted a formula, but although it had the lucidity of the
definition of integration—the flow 'should not be so high as to
create a widespread resistance to obstruct the integration process
[nor] so unreasonably low as to create an embittered sense of
apartness in the immigrant community itself'[10]—it neither
carried the same conviction nor achieved the same success.
Clearly, it was a relief when the *détente* of 1966 made it no longer
necessary to make up the case for continued immigration *de novo*.
Instead, it was possible to re-vitalize the stale vocabulary of the
debate and re-define its terms by placing the emphasis on a

comparatively new factor in the situation—the 'second generation' of coloured children, British-born or educated, shortly to leave school and compete for jobs and housing.

By filtering out the immigration elements of the situation and re-presenting the case as one of justice denied by the simple factor of skin pigmentation, this approach revived the moral issue in a sharpened form and provided the best justification for legislation against such capricious discrimination.

The selection of legislation as a leading issue necessarily implied the relegation of other and more complex issues to a lower priority. In January 1966, Maurice Foley joined Jenkins at the Home Office; this measure of consolidation of functions relating to immigration carried with it substantial drawbacks in terms of the association of the Home Office's necessarily negative responsi-bilities for immigration control with a positive integration function. This could be justified as appropriate while the senior Minister was prepared to tip the scales by placing strong emphasis on positive elements in official policy. Yet such an emphasis para-doxically left less rather than more scope for Foley's talents. In the immensely difficult task of restoring confidence in the period after the 1964 election and maintaining it in the teeth of the Government's ineptitude, his achievment was, as we have seen, considerable. But in the equally difficult job of outflanking entrenched opposition elsewhere in Whitehall and averting such potential disasters as the Ministry of Housing's ill thought out support for Birmingham Corporation's restrictionist housing Bill, Foley was no more effective operating from the Home Office than he had been in the D.E.A., and his small staff, imported unchanged from that department, had even less scope for operation inside the Home Office well. Certain policy initiatives on matters directly within the sphere of the Home Office were taken, for example, in relation to police practice; but even within the department Foley found the new scope of his responsibilities unsympathetic. And so, the clearly formulated aim of extending legislation against discrimination was not balanced by practical proposals for official action in other directions to promote integration. The Home Secretary talked bravely about the responsibility for providing an example but policy outside his department presented the same negative appearance as it had done in the White Paper.

A final characteristic of the style of Jenkins' tenure of office at the Home Office which is relevant to this field was his sensitivity to what was politically possible in terms of timing. Two things were clear, in this context, by the end of 1965: first, that the general election then pending would be of crucial importance in clearing or clouding the atmosphere—and that if the storm were safely weathered, controversial legislation would have to come early in the lifetime of the parliament. The first of the major speeches on race relations that Jenkins 'placed' at various stages of his Home Office career, like so many stepping stones across a potentially treacherous marsh, was therefore not made until after the Election.

In fact, uncertainty over the outcome of the Election lasted for only a short time—until the Hull North by-election made it clear that the Labour Government was in a virtually impregnable position. A brief spasm of anxiety about the possibility that Foley himself might lose his West Bromwich seat (brought on by what proved to be a misleading opinion poll) partly justified the nervousness of Labour members on the issue during the period of the Election; the relief with which Foley's comfortable survival and Griffiths' loss of his Smethwick seat to the actor, Andrew Faulds, were greeted was correspondingly excessive. But the moral drawn, even if formulated in exaggerated terms (the issue was 'de-fused' in one significant metaphor—'buried', in another), was helpful in opening up the situation for future constructive initiatives. On the other side, the firm refusal of the new Leader of the Opposition, Edward Heath, to countenance any exploitation of the immigration issue largely obscured the fact that his party's manifesto contained a number of provisions—particularly relating to dependants and repatriation—which could be construed as a new attempt to outflank the Government's White Paper on immigration. In brief, the conditions for a forward policy on race relations appeared to have been satisfied.

In launching this policy, there remained a number of basic conditions to fulfil. The definition of aims, choice of vocabulary, and sensitivity to political imperatives on timing, have already been dealt with above, but the strategy of the campaign for legislation also demanded a selection of priorities between the points at which pressure might be brought to bear. Heineman suggests that there were three practical imperatives for the Home Secretary: he needed to convince his colleagues of the extent of discrimination, demonstrate the appropriateness of legislation as a remedy, and face down the vested interests in industry.[11] This will serve very well as a definition of what was required within the closed society of Whitehall but it omits the important areas of parliamentary and public opinion, and in these quarters, in particular, the arguments that would be effective in cabinet might not cut ice.

'Speaking broadly,' Heineman adds, 'the industrial and economic ministers might be reluctant to further exacerbate the relations between the Government and their main constituents'[12] either by way of further legislation against discrimination or through other official initiatives. True, but the opposition might also exist elsewhere, and be a matter not so much of ministerial reluctance as of indifferent (or even mildly favourable) ministers and entrenched suspicion among advisers. In other words, the strictly constitutional attribution of departmental views to their ministers might be more than usually misleading in this instance. (We have discussed in Chapter 15 the relevance of the bounds of responsibilities to policy making.) Here, Foley's disinclination to engage in the elaborate quadrille of inter-departmental consultation, the numerical weakness of his advisory team, and the poor structural placing of his activities constituted a serious handicap. Other departments could argue that a department that had put up such determined opposition to Brockway's successive Racial Discrimination Bills was not a wholly convincing advocate for the translation of the Home Secretary's elegant formulae into hard proposals for action. Some progress was made in one direction; the 1964 election manifesto promise to provide special help for areas affected by immigration was implemented in a Local Government Bill (announced by Foley shortly before the Election) and a complex formula devised in the Home Office to provide a commitment extending to £1½ million per year to offset expenditure by local authorities on staff whose employment was attributable to the presence of immigrants locally. But by and large the objectives of policy had not been defined with sufficient accuracy to include effective action to deal with the major social problems.

Nor, by extension, had there been systematic attempts to involve the departments responsible, either in relation to the immediate imperative of extending legislation or in the longer term objectives of integration policy. The Ministry of Housing, whose minister (Richard Crossman) was personally a sceptic on legislation, was for too long complacent and even negative on the broader issues. In the Ministry of Labour, not only was the Minister himself (Ray Gunter) a persistent critic, in public and in private, of the legislative proposals, but the departmental attitude was generally hostile.

The solution to these difficulties inside Whitehall and to the Home Secretary's problems of persuasion within the Cabinet and outside lay in providing clear evidence of the extent of discrimination. From this, the need for legislation could be deduced. For a variety of reasons, this evidence would have to come from outside Whitehall. In the first place, the Home Office was not prepared to assemble it. Second, it was clearly desirable that the evidence on such a controversial issue should appear to emanate from an independent or quasi-independent source. And thirdly, the publication of the results of any inquiry conducted independently would provide the opportunity of enlisting public sympathy before officially committing the Government to take action. In order to take this next step it would be necessary to turn to the race relations agencies.

In the period after the general election of 1964, the whole configuration of the race relations scene had changed. Existing organizations were shaken up and new ones created; by the general election of 1966, these organizations were just beginning to find their feet and establish formal and informal interconnecting links. In considering the possible extension of legislation the most important of these new agencies was obviously the Race Relations Board itself—if only because this body was likely to be the principal beneficiary. The Board had been established by virtue of the Act of 1965 (whose origins we traced in Chapter 16). The form of this legislation had left the Board with limited scope (it covered only places of public resort) and an inadequate range of powers. The restriction of the scope was of course a political decision, persisted in despite heavy pressure, in the confused circumstances of the spring of 1965. Hepple, in his authoritative study of the law and discrimination in employment,[13] attributes much of the deficiency in the powers given to the Board to a confusion over the introduction into the Bill at a late stage of the principle of conciliation. He quotes Lord Stonham as justifying this change to avoid 'bringing the flavour of criminality into the delicate question of race relations', but points out that the major *raison d'être* of conciliation in the American codes, on which the revised British legislation was in part modelled, has been utilitarian—simply to provide a more efficient means of enforcement. By contrast, the procedures introduced by the Act of 1965 are 'unnecessarily complicated while, at the same time, being toothless'.[14] Conciliation should in practice involve not tempering the consequences of the discriminatory act for the discriminator but providing a speedy and informal means of satisfaction for the grievance of the victim of discrimination, without a clumsy top hamper of court proceedings. 'The lack of solicitude which the 1965 Act reveals for the complainant', he adds, 'is related to the inadequacy of the remedies provided'[15]—no civil or criminal proceedings (apart from an injunction) could be brought in respect of unlawful discrimination by any party other than the Attorney General. Finally, Section 6 of the Act amended the provisions of a Public Order Act of 1936 in relation to incitement of racial hatred, creating a new category of events leading to criminal prosecution. The inclusion of this section in a statute concerned with discrimination and providing for conciliation or civil proceedings has been a rich source of confusion and misrepresentation.

Faced with the patent inadequacy of the scope of operation of the Board and the likely difficulties of operating the Act in the areas in which it did apply, Bonham Carter made it a condition of appointment that he should be able to put the case, after a year's operation, for the extension of the scope of the Act and a revision of the Board's powers.

Initially, the clearly indicated strategy was to play from weakness—that is, while losing no time in putting effective conciliation procedures into operation, equally to lose no opportunity of exposing the inadequacy of the Board's powers and its inability to deal with the majority of complaints which came before it. In this way, the Home Secretary's need for manifest evidence for extension of the law would be met and the Board's own critics silenced.

At the same time, the Board was able to extend its range of activity by developing initiatives in other directions. First, through carefully selected appointments to the local conciliation committees which fulfilled the twin function of creating instruments for negotiation and discussion of grievances on a local plane and influencing policy formation nationally. Second, by the establishment of contacts with various interested groups which had either been affected by the 1965 Act or were likely to be involved in its extension. For example, the brewers, who had initially reacted with great alarm to the provisions in the Act dealing with discrimination on licensed premises (which they feared would im-

pinge upon what they regarded as the publican's inalienable right
to refuse to serve whomsoever he chose) were tactfully persuaded of
the advantages not only of compliance with the law but of taking
additional action to avoid future difficulty. Similarly, contact with
the insurance companies ensured that when proposals were put
forward for bringing insurance facilities within the scope of the
law they were not immediately ruled out of court, by those
affected, as commercially impracticable. In a less spectacular way,
the contacts built up in industry through local appointments
proved valuable in enabling the Board to show that the views of
employers towards the extension of legislation were by no means
as monolithically sceptical as the C.B.I. wished it to be thought in
the spring of 1967.

This approach could be seen in embryo when the Home
Secretary made his first speech on race relations to the National
Co-ordinating Conference of voluntary liaison committees on
23 May 1966. 'Some of you, I know,' he said, 'will think that
we have a better Race Relations Board than a Race Relations
Act. I would say two things on this. First, I think a lot can be
done under the present Act and, secondly, *as I have told the Board*
[my italics], my mind is far from being closed about future
changes to the Act. . . . Many, I know, take the view that discrimination in employment and indeed housing should be covered
by legislation. For the moment, I reserve judgment on the
legislative point but I am in no doubt that the employment aspect
of the matter in particular is rapidly becoming central to the
whole future success of our integration policy. The problem is now
developing with almost every month it goes by, *because we are
beginning to move from the era of the first generation immigrant to that of
the second generation immigrant* [our italics].'

The drift of the argument is clear and the position of the Board
was widely understood and even admired. From a lame duck
organization whose chairmanship had been declined by a former
Labour minister, it became the harbinger of a more effective body
yet to come. Shortly after his appointment, the *Daily Mail* had
commented with astonishment that 'Mr. Bonham Carter appears
to have been touched with the conviction that there is a great
work to be done.'[16] By the time that John Lyttle joined the Board
as Chief Conciliation Officer from a senior post at Transport
House, Bonham Carter as chairman and the Board as a body
already held a central place in the developing situation.

But the Board, in order to function effectively as front runner, needed allies. Heineman has engagingly maintained that, in the initial stages, the nature and extent of the contacts between the various official and unofficial bodies active in this field was defined by what he calls 'family relations'—that is, by the personal contacts built up by a small group which he characterizes as the 'race professionals' who:

> Do not necessarily devote [sic] full time to Race Relations, nor do they operate self-consciously in tandem [but] through close contact with one another they are able to know what others in the field are doing and complement their efforts rather than duplicate them. And in a campaign for the extension of laws this informal planning can yield activities which give an impression of strength. The 'professionals' joke about their similarity to a stage army, with its actor soldiers disappearing through one trapdoor to re-emerge from the wings.[17]

The extent to which this was true, even in the initial stages, of a rapidly developing situation, is debatable; but if there was a convergence it was on the National Committee for Commonwealth Immigrants.

The National Committee was the senior agency in the field by six months; it had had a difficult birth in conjunction with the White Paper (an association that dogged it throughout its career) and a mixed ancestry. It had been the conviction of Maurice Foley that such an agency, operating outside the restrictive structure of Whitehall, could reach the public and influence local authorities more readily than a programme devised by a central department. In the General Secretary's initial report, *The First Six Months*, the role of the National Committee was defined as threefold: 'as a general source of advice and information on all matters concerned with Commonwealth Immigrants'; for 'the examination of national and local policies and the formulation of recommendations to be made to the Government and for the prosecution and development of community activity at local level'.[18] By the time of the first Annual Report, the schedule of functions had diminished to two—advisory and community development.

The latter role stemmed from the liaison committee concept, evolved more or less simultaneously in several major provincial cities, and developed by Miss Nadine Peppard in the London area, from 1957 onwards, in her capacity as Secretary of the Immigrants' Advisory Committee of the London Council of

Social Service. In April 1964 the Commonwealth Immigrants Advisory Council had recommended the creation of a small National Advisory Committee for Commonwealth Immigrants and Miss Peppard was appointed as first secretary to supervise the development of local committees and act as a co-ordinator and clearing-house for exchange of information. This function, greatly extended by the injection of substantial financial support, was in Foley's concept to be the basis of a positive integration policy.

From the start, there was a tension between the two roles. The function of liaison demanded the holding of a very delicate balance at local level between the local authority and the members of the local immigrant community in order that mutually accepted policies could be evolved. But, simultaneously, the Committee had to discharge the function of advice giving in such a way as to command the Government's attention and support from communal organizations, without jeopardizing its conciliatory posture in local situations. And, over and above this, there was the general function of 'education in its widest sense' singled out in the first Annual Report.[19] This could be construed in a number of different ways: as directed to an elite of 'opinion-formers', or to those in direct contact with immigrants in local situations, or possibly to the immigrants themselves. Although these functions can be presented as overlapping or ambiguous, there was no necessity for them to prove mutually exclusive. But the effects of the strain of discharging them can be seen in the General Secretary's comment in the 1967 Annual Report: 'A body dedicated simultaneously to "liaison", conciliation, the eradication of injustices and the propagation of a new spirit, is constantly confronted by choices which seem impossible to make.'[20] Or, as Heineman rather more brusquely put it, 'Did the preposition "for" in the Committee's title imply that it should be putting their point of view or is it something that does things for immigrants?'[21]

But, initially, the doubts about the Committee that were later so freely expressed were not a significant element in the situation. After some hesitation, both David Pitt and Hamza Alavi decided to accept the Prime Minister's invitation to join the National Committee although they had made their view on the White Paper explicit by their joint resignations from the British Overseas Socialist Fellowship, and (in Pitt's case) the Executive of the London Labour Party. As Heineman subsequently put it:

In the Autumn of 1965, when the amendment of legislation was still a glimmer on the horizon it seemed reasonable to a majority of the CARD, to try to use the National Committee to press for the first priority, the establishment of a basic legal framework which would demonstrate the intention of the Government and the whole society not to tolerate discrimination.[22]

And Pitt and Alavi's example was followed by several members, past and present, of the C.A.R.D. executive who accepted invitations to serve on the specialist panels set up to discharge the advisory function. Martin Ennals, who as General Secretary of the National Council for Civil Liberties had helped to organize the opposition to the White Paper, resigned from that post in order to take up an appointment with the National Committee, telling readers in *Tribune* that:

Some of my friends think that this Committee should be ostracized because it was set up by the Government as an attempted palliative to the White Paper on immigration from the Commonwealth. Obviously, I do not agree. I believe that the White Paper makes race relations in the country worse instead of better; I think that it was based on prejudice and not on principle. But the job that has to be done is education towards a civilized multi-racial society and one that demands immediate attention. The Government has itself failed to meet the challenge, but by setting up an independent committee has, I hope, planted the seeds of the destruction of its own discriminatory policy. Certainly, whatever its motives, the Government has appointed a Committee which opposes its policies and has said so to the Prime Minister.[23]

This last reference was to a deputation led by the Archbishop of Canterbury, as Chairman of the Committee, which saw the Prime Minister on 1 December 1965 to protest about the restrictive sections of the White Paper. This deputation, although it found the Prime Minister 'genuinely interested', obtained no real concession, despite a lively correspondence that continued well into the next year. But the good impression created by the deputation and the Archbishop's willingness to give public expression to his doubts about the Government's immigration policy helped to encourage the previously doubtful to participate in the Committee's rapidly expanding activities. A number of immigrant organizations remained obdurate (see Chapter 25), but most of those active in what Heineman calls the 'race relations

interest' associated themselves with the National Committee in
the winter of 1965–6.

Not that these bodies necessarily determined the direction of
policy within the Committee; but it was inevitable that with the
extension of legislation in the air, those panel members who would
be concerned with the earlier Bill should press for the extension
of legislation to housing and employment, as David Pitt (for one)
did on the Committee itself. By May 1966, three of the specialist
panels, Housing, Employment, and Legal Affairs, had prepared
detailed proposals for such an extension which were submitted to
the full Committee, and the Housing panel had, in addition, drafted
an extended survey of the situation in the housing field which was
to be submitted to the Minister of Housing with a request for him
to receive a deputation.

But, like the Home Secretary himself and the Board, the National Committee found the case for the extension of legislation
needed to be carried one stage beyond the general arguments
which had proved effective in 1965 and gave detailed evidence
on the extent of discrimination. Immediately after the Home
Secretary's first major speech, discussions began on the possibility
of commissioning a study, coupled with the examination of the
American evidence and its relevance to the British situation.
By June, the decision to undertake a pair of studies and entrust
the first to the independent research organization, Political and
Economic Planning (P.E.P.), and the second to Professor Harry
Street of Manchester University had been taken and an advisory
panel assembled under the joint aegis of the National Committee
and the Board. Although for obvious reasons the Home Secretary
could not take any explicit part in the detailed negotiations, the
initiative and the responsibility for the major policy decisions
were both his.

The strategy of the Home Secretary also demanded a critical
body representative, as far as possible, of immigrant opinion,
which could both speak for the victims and act as informed critic
of the *status quo*, putting forward proposals and criticisms which
could be assimilated in a decent interval into the official wisdom.
For the time being, and in default of more effective spokesmen,
C.A.R.D. was cast in that role.

The main objectives of the C.A.R.D. Executive Committee
at this stage were to build an organization which would bridge
the gap between the majority society and the various ethnic

groups and the class divisions within those groups, and also incorporate to some degree, in a loose coalition, the major immigrant organizations. Pressure for legislation was seen as much as a means to these ends as an end in itself. By the end of 1965, members of the C.A.R.D. Executive Committee had seen their remarkable success in persuading the Government to cast their legislation against racial discrimination, in the form of providing for conciliation by an administrative agency, vitiated by the Prime Minister's White Paper and the manner in which it had been presented. The C.A.R.D. pamphlet on the White Paper, written by Alavi, was by far the most potent critique of that document and its conclusions are a classic statement of the case for looking at immigration and domestic race relations together:

So long as the National Leadership panders, or even attempts to pander, to racial prejudice and parrots the cries for tougher immigration policies, [that] prejudice will remain too powerful to be reversed by conciliation committees and marginal welfare activities, even when they are well conceived and not disturbed by racial patronage, which is the other face of racial prejudice. Those who argue that stopping immigration now will give time to 'integrate' those immigrants who are already here fail to grasp this basic fact. There can be no integration without a total fight against racialism AT ALL levels.[24]

In its approach to the task of presenting the case for the immigrant, C.A.R.D. adopted a range of different expedients. We have already touched on the tactic of permeation of views through other organizations with established positions at various points in the community; the drawbacks of this technique were that C.A.R.D., did not obtain direct credit for the views expressed by these organizations and that some members felt that a certain amount of distortion was occurring in transmission. A second, and increasingly important role, was that of stimulating complaints under the provisions of the existing Race Relations Act. Some exaggerated claims have been made for the extent and quality of the complaints stimulated by the special pamphlet drafted by C.A.R.D., and published under the title *How to expose Discrimination*, and the specially drafted C.A.R.D. complaint form. But C.A.R.D's contribution was acknowledged, in suitably cautious terms, by the Board in its first Annual Report ('Most people who suffer the humiliation of being discriminated against prefer to forget it, and groups such as the Campaign Against Racial Discrimination and the Indian Workers' Association play an important part informing those discriminated against of their rights and of the public interest at stake.'[25] Their summer project, the model for which was the activities of the still undivided Civil Rights Movement which Anthony Lester had seen in the United States in 1964 while observing for Amnesty International, served the triple function of enabling C.A.R.D. to make contact with a number of local situations, though always through the mediation of existing organizations, of providing material for further complaints (fifty-two in all) for submission to the Board, and of educating the volunteers. Finally, the most striking of these complaints were collected and published by C.A.R.D. in April 1967.

Taken together with the general activities of C.A.R.D. (in particular some of the local organizations with a rather more clear-sighted view of the deficiencies of the communal organizations with which C.A.R.D. had associated itself nationally) this performance provided good grounds for Martin Ennals' comment that, up to the end of 1966, 'C.A.R.D. has done an enormous job in shaping public opinion into a position where it accepts the facts of discrimination'.[26]

In October 1966, the Home Secretary made his second major policy speech, to the Institute of Race Relations. In it, he made further reference to the progress of the Race Relations Board (which he described as having made 'a most encouraging start') and of the forthcoming P.E.P. report on the extent of discrimination. But in this speech, Jenkins went out of his way to stress, first, the improvement in the general atmosphere—'I am glad', he said, 'that we appear to have put behind us the sterile debate about the precise level of the flow of immigration'—and, second, the necessity for advancing on the broadest possible front, combining 'individual example, community action, educational experience, industrial practice and, of course, the example of Government, locally and nationally'. The Home Secretary wound up his speech by indicating a number of specific ways in which such an example could be set, outside the scope of legislation.[27]

This theme of co-ordinated advance was taken up enthusiastically by the Home Office's Minister of State, Lord Stonham, in the Lords in the following month. Answering a motion on immigration put down by Lord Elton, he took advantage of the rules of order of the House to cover the entire front of Government activity, employing one of those ministerial briefs ranging extensively over the activities of numerous departments whose discontinuities and inconsistencies make up not so much a *tour d'horizon* as an exhausting trudge over uneven ground. After the reference to the P.E.P. report, which was becoming a ritual in official speeches at this point, Stonham referred to the National Committee's 'vigorous start', to the measures in the Local Government Act providing for financial assistance for local authorities employing staff directly related to the presence of immigrants locally and to the four full-time courses for teachers of English for pupils from overseas. But, between the growth in the provision of useful, basic welfare services and the general pronouncement of benevolent intentions, the policy gap yawned as wide as ever; in the crucial areas of housing and education the official line could scarcely be described as any advance on that in the White Paper. On housing, Lord Stonham could only say: 'There is, in fact, no immediate solution to this extremely difficult problem; only enough low-rented houses will provide the cure. So the Government is pursuing a vigorous policy directed to the building of more houses of better quality.'[28]

This, together with a glancing reference to the advantages of industrialized building and the importance of revision of policies on housing subsidies (which did not, for reasons dealt with in Chapter 17 impinge upon the newer problems of the areas of multi-occupation) apparently constituted the entire range of Government proposals in the housing field. But, taken together with the Ministry of Labour's habitual defensive account of the activities of its employment exchanges and the unfinished discussions between the Treasury and industry on non-discrimination clauses in Government contracts,* this evidently seemed sufficient to justify the manner of Lord Stonham's peroration. 'We shall make a great success of this policy—a success which, I think, will be an example to the world.'[29] This was optimism of a kind which had not been heard from either front bench for three or four years—and in the long run, optimism that could only be justified if the ultimately intangible gain of confidence were supplemented by the tangible achievements that could in turn only be obtained by public policy initiatives.

Against this favourable background, the irregulars of C.A.R.D. launched the first stage of the public campaign for the extension of legislation. Maurice Orbach, the Labour Member for Stockport

---

* Indeed these are *still*, at the time of writing, not achieved.

South, who has a long record for activity on behalf of Jewish organizations concerned with group defamation, had been successful in the ballot for private members' bills; he was prepared to put forward a bill drafted by Anthony Lester and Roger Warren Evans which would extend the Race Relations Act to the fields of housing, employment, and commercial services. The apparatus of permeation thereupon ensured that a sufficiently wide range of organizations put forward supporting resolutions; the Society of Labour Lawyers' Sub-Committee repeated their earlier commitment to extension and the National Committee itself, after considering evidence from individual panels, declared itself in favour of the principles in the bill. The main purpose of the exercise was achieved when the bill came up for debate in December; Foley, answering for the Government, indicated that the P.E.P. report would have 'a decisive effect on the Government in terms of their future attitude',[30] and Charles Fletcher Cooke, for the Opposition, suggested that a bi-partisan approach was probable in the event of extension. 'I think', he said, 'that the scope of the conciliation procedure may well have to be extended to jobs and housing'[31] (thus leaving a small enough loophole for succeeding Opposition front bench spokesmen to squeeze through). Although in terms of content the debate was disappointing (the emphasis was excessively on the side of the provisions dealing with incitement to racial hatred, and the Lord's debate—which Fenner Brockway pressed to a division— was not much better) it provided useful evidence that the pieces of the Home Secretary's jigsaw were being steadily brought together. The provision of evidence of the extent of discrimination, if forthcoming from the P.E.P. research, would in theory make up the complete picture; that the latter was still necessary became clear when Shirley Williams, answering an adjournment debate in December 1966 on immigrant school leavers, the central feature of the renewed campaign, demonstrated that extreme caution still pervaded the Ministry of Labour.[32] To some extent, this caution could be put down to the attitude of the Minister of Labour and of the T.U.C. and C.B.I. towards the prospect of future legislation in their field.

In the various stages of the negotiations that followed, the C.B.I. for tactical reasons preferred to leave the initiative to the T.U.C. And it was on the T.U.C. side that the fundamental anxiety was felt and where the entrenched opposition came—specifically among a number of individual members of the General Council. Late in 1966, it became clear to the T.U.C., both from the public activities of the lobby* and from official approaches from the Treasury (initially in the context of a non-discrimination clause in Government contracts), that something was in the air. The danger that had been averted when Fenner Brockway was persuaded to drop employment from his Racial Discrimination Bill after 1960—outside involvement ('interventionism') in what the T.U.C. regarded as essentially an internal matter for industry—had emerged again, with the additional complication that this time, as opposed to 1960 and 1965, the proposals appeared to command powerful official support. In certain quarters, this prospect did not cause great concern; Jack Jones, the Acting Assistant General Secretary of the Transport and General Workers' Union, told a Fabian Conference in November 1966 that 'even in the Trades Unions, restrictions have been operated against the immigrant worker',[33] and made it clear that he saw the solution to this problem in some form of legislation.

But generally, the official attitude, especially of senior members of the General Council and senior staff, was one of alarm and suspicion. Both sides of industry, and in particular the Trades Union movement, had, it was argued, 'already directed their efforts with success towards integration':[34] how could 'interventionism'—a suspicion of which had been exasperated by the Government's decision to take legislative powers to control prices and incomes after the July economic crises—possibly be justified? And what was the standing of the 'bodies' that now advocated it? C.A.R.D. was a mere pressure group of dubious ancestry and authority which had given hostile evidence to the Donovan Commission on Trades Unions; the Race Relations Board, an untried statutory body, headed by a former Liberal M.P. On the National Committee, the attitude was at this stage less certain; there had been discussions earlier in the year and the T.U.C. was officially represented on the Committee (to the disapproval of some members, who felt that all those appointed should serve as individuals). But even here suspicion lingered and indeed revived as the legislative campaign gathered speed. After joint consultations with the C.B.I. a statement was drafted and presented to the

* Or, as the T.U.C. subsequently put it: 'It became clear (in October 1966) that certain bodies outside industry were attempting to secure support for far-reaching legislation.'

meeting of the National Joint Advisory Committee in January 1967. In this statement, which was intended to represent the position for negotiation, the line adopted was that discrimination would only disappear 'with complete integration' and attention was drawn to past success and to the existence of voluntary machinery. Prominent officials told a *Sunday Times* investigation that there was insufficient evidence of discrimination to justify action; Lord Cooper, of the N.U.G.M.W., was 'not bothered a great deal with it, because I have never met it as a real problem'; as for legislation, Cyril Plant of the Inland Revenue Staff Association observed that 'the simple fact is that we are against it'.[35]

It was at this stage that the event that was supposed to circumvent through persuasion this anticipated opposition took place—the Conference on Racial Equality and Employment, originally proposed by Anthony Lester, and sponsored by the National Committee for Commonwealth Immigrants. Although many distinguished figures from the United States, from both sides of industry, participated in the Conference, the response from the British side was disappointing. Despite earlier discussions with the N.C.C.I., George Woodcock declined to attend the Conference, on the grounds that he had been invited in an individual capacity and not as General Secretary. A negative speech was made on the first evening of Conference by Sir Kenneth Allen for the C.B.I. who argued: 'To treat this one problem in a way which is foreign to our normal way of dealing with industrial relations problems would tend to focus attention on discrimination—and possibly exasperate it—rather than bring it into a proper balanced perspective'.[36] Allen was firmly answered by the Home Secretary, to loud applause. Jenkins' speech was clearly designed as the next stepping stone on the journey towards legislation, in his confident undertaking that 'if the results of this conference and the P.E.P. survey and the Race Relations Board report show a clear case that further legislation is needed and would be helpful—we shall not shirk the issue'.[37] But the results of the Conference were far from clear; the triple condition had to be concertinad into a double one. A solitary independent initiative was taken by Oscar Hahn, himself an employer, President of the Birmingham Chamber of Commerce, and Chairman of the Board's West Midlands conciliation committee. He suggested that independent committees established by both sides of industry in firms of more than twenty-five employees, might provide a means of voluntary conciliation within a statutory framework that might be acceptable to both sides. But this was the only move that offered any hope of constructive discussion between sides already frozen in postures of mutual misunderstanding.

In short, it was clear that the problem of the hostility towards extension of legislation on the part of the main entrenched interests in the employment field would have to be faced as a fact of the situation, that their opposition, together with the tacit sympathy of the Minister of Labour, constituted an obstacle on a scale which would require more than the blandishments of American fellow unionists to overcome. But equally, the obstacle was not immovable. Neither the content of the objections so far raised to further legislation, nor the degree of conviction and expertise with which they had been argued were such as to discourage those who knew how formidable was the charge of dynamite that was being prepared to blow it away.

NOTES TO CHAPTER 26

1. Speech given at Leicester, 12 September 1965, reprinted in *Plebs* (December 1965), p. 10.
2. Ibid., p. 11.
3. Eric Silver, 'Maurice Foley', Institute of Race Relations' *Newsletter* (February 1967), p. 16.
4. 721 H. C. Deb, c. 461, 463, 23 November 1965.
5. Roy Jenkins, *The Labour Case* (Penguin Books, Harmondsworth, 1959).
6. Ibid., p. 137.
7. B. W. Heineman, Jr., *The Politics of Race: a study of the Campaign Against Racial Discrimination* (unpublished Oxford B.Litt. thesis, 1967).
8. *Address given by the Home Secretary . . . on the 23rd May 1966 . . . to a meeting of Voluntary Liaison Committees* (London, N.C.C.I., 1966).
9. 716 H.C. Deb., c. 1056, 16 July 1965.
10. Address given on 23 May 1966, op. cit.
11. Heineman, op. cit., pp. 215, 232–4.
12. Heineman, p. 216.
13. Bob Hepple, *Race, Jobs and The Law* (Allen Lane, The Penguin Press, 1968).
14. Ibid., pp. 136 et seq.
15. Ibid., p. 141.
16. *Daily Mail*, 18 April 1966.
17. Heineman, op. cit., p. 209.
18. *The First Six Months: a report of the National Committee for Commonwealth Immigrants* (London, N.C.C.I., 1966).
19. *Report for 1966* (London, N.C.C.I., 1967), p. 8.
20. *Report for 1967* (London, N.C.C.I., 1968), p. 14.
21. Heineman, op. cit., p. 246.
22. Ibid., p. 257.
23. Martin Ennals in *Tribune*, 18 February 1966.

24. Campaign Against Racial Discrimination, *The White Paper: A Spur to Racialism* (London, C.A.R.D., 1965).

25. *Report of the Race Relations Board 1966-7* (London, H.M.S.O., 1967), p. 9.

26. Heineman, op. cit., p. 221.

27. Speech to the Institute of Race Relations, 10 October 1966, reprinted in *Race*, Vol. VIII, no. 3 (January 1967).

28. 277 H.L. Deb., c. 733, 3 November 1966.

29. Ibid., c. 735.

30. 738 H.C. Deb., c. 938, 6 December 1966.

31. Ibid., c. 942.

32. 737 H.C. Deb., c. 17–2015, 9 December 1966.

33. J. Jones *in*, A. Lester and N. Deakin (eds.), *Policies for Racial Equality* (London, Fabian Society, 1967), p.15.

34. Trades Union Congress, *99th Annual Report, 1967* (Cooperative Printing Society, n.d.), p. 268.

35. *Sunday Times*, 8 January 1967.

36. National Committee for Commonwealth Immigrants, Conference on Racial Equality in Employment, February 1967, transcript of proceedings, p. 3.

37. Ibid., p. 10.

27 Sisyphus' Stone

In April 1967 the two remaining conditions set out by the Home Secretary in his speech of February, required if the Government's consent were to be given to legislation, were satisfied. First, by the Report of the Race Relations Board, which presented a closely argued case for the extension of legislation, culminating in the conclusion that the law had a crucial role to play as a declaration of public policy, an instrument of redress for minorities and of support for those who wished to abstain from discrimination but felt unable to do so, and finally as a means for 'a peaceful and orderly adjustment of grievances and the release of tensions' and ultimately the reduction of prejudice.[1] Still more important, the report of the P.E.P. investigation provided clear evidence of widespread discrimination in housing and employment.

The contents of the P.E.P. Report have been discussed elsewhere (see Chapter 22); the chief significance of the Report for present purposes was the extent of the response to some of the material in it, particularly to the series of action tests run by Research Services as part of the investigation, using white and coloured actors. The response of the Press to the evidence was far greater than the sponsors of the Report and its advisory panel had dared to hope; the reaction in all major newspapers, even the previously hostile *Daily Telegraph,* both editorially and in the selection of emphasis for news items, was that an intolerable situation had been revealed which called for urgent remedial action. Coupled with the interpretive articles written by members of the specialist corps of race relations reporters, the extensive coverage given to the Report—which easily exceeded that given to even the most prestigious Royal Commission—provided the Home Secretary with the double benefit of the perceived support of public opinion (as it turned out, an accurate perception—see Chapter 28) and of convincing evidence to present to Cabinet colleagues. From this point onwards, opponents of the extension of legislation to the field of employment were on the defensive and the ground of opposition shifted—from the claim that discrimination was not a major problem to arguments in favour of a voluntary approach. In the potentially far more sensitive area of housing, the general mandate from public opinion could now be assumed, in the absence of any effective lobby.

At the end of April, the T.U.C. General Council arrived at the predictable conclusion that 'neither the proceedings at a conference organized by the NCCI nor the PEP report gave grounds for modifying the attitudes of the general council'[2]. However, the Council resolved to take steps to modify their previous position and to accept the C.B.I.'s proposal of further discussions on the desirability of establishing appropriate additional machinery to the voluntary machinery already existing in industry. More significantly, they conceded that 'even the most comprehensive of voluntary procedures' might leave an area where legislation might be thought necessary.[3]

Taken together with the Hahn proposals of February, this last concession pointed towards the compromise eventually reached. Although the Home Secretary and his allies in the official agencies and outside them now had a strong hand to play, there were obvious advantages in avoiding an open dispute with both sides of industry—especially if they chose to present a united front. Although in the period after the Election interest in race relations among ordinary politicians diminished sharply, a decline in the Government's general political fortunes presented an obvious opportunity for the Opposition. The indications were still that a bi-partisan front could be maintained—and the Home Secretary went out of his way to be conciliatory to his opposite number on this issue; but an open breach with the Trade Union wing of the Labour Party was obviously unacceptable. In this situation, the skills of Maurice Foley might have been an important counterpoint within the Party; unlike his successor David Ennals (see Chapter 31) he was well equipped by background and temperament to sooth the anxieties of the Congress House *apparat* and of Trade Union members of the House. But by the end of 1966, Foley had decided that the rapidly developing situation, with its progressive bureaucratization of activity, was unsuited to his particular gifts and had made his desire for an early move very clear indeed. So the risk was a real one; and such a split would provide an opportunity in which the Right Wing of the Conservative Party could hope to profit handsomely from the steady stock-piling of ammunition by Enoch Powell. In a series of speeches and articles he had been developing an analysis whose main basis was that, entirely contrary to the received view in both parties, the 'feeling of stabilization' current in early 1967 would not last but would be succeeded by 'subsequent phases where the problem will re-assume its place in public concern and in a more intractable form, when it can no longer be dealt with simply by turning the inlet tap up or down'.[4] Solutions, he argued, must therefore be sought not (as he had previously suggested) in assimilation but in repatriation and ultimately in the licensing of separate development, *faute de mieux*.

In the circumstances, although the evidence of the P.E.P. Report and the arguments in the Board's Report, summarizing the case for legislation on a basis of the first year's experience of the working of the 1965 Act, could be used to carry Cabinet colleagues and persuade Parliament, the actual machinery with which the now admitted discrimination was to be abated was not a sufficient *casus belli;* compromise was always the likely solution.

In May, preliminary discussions on the setting up of voluntary machinery were held between the C.B.I. and T.U.C., and by June these were in an advanced stage and commanded the general support of the Ministry of Labour. Also in May, the Home Secretary delivered another major speech, this time to the London Labour Party. This speech, far more political in tone and emphasis, was clearly directed towards securing the explicitly Labour Party backing for a measure likely to be a cause of nervousness to a Party whose painful memories of Smethwick had not been wholly erased by the general election of 1966. 'For a Labour Government to fall down on this', he said, 'would be a betrayal without excuse of everything for which the Labour Party has ever stood. If further legislation is necessary to deal with this issue, we should not be frightened of it.'[5] Clearly there was no doubt that a positive decision on legislation was now merely a matter of time.

On 19 June, the formal confrontation took place between ministers and the two sides of industry. The Trade Union representatives, according to their own account, referred to their statement of January, with the significant amendment that they now 'did not altogether rule out the possibility that legislation might ultimately play some residual part in the process'. Further negotiations were suggested but not on the basis that 'the Government were already committed to putting new reliance on legislation'. Was the Government not prepared to encourage a voluntary approach?

The Home Secretary's reply was apparently cautious but firm. Basing himself on the familiar second-generation argument, he explained that he 'was inclined to the view that the Government should declare discrimination illegal and that some form of ultimate sanction was necessary'. He made it clear that while it would be impossible in the new legislative proposals, on which no final decision had yet been taken, 'entirely to exclude the Race Relations Board . . . voluntary machinery established in industry should be the initial channel of settlement of cases'.[6]

This key concession obtained, the T.U.C. turned to leisurely discussion of the outlined scheme for voluntary machinery put to them by the C.B.I., in which they were overtaken by the official announcement on 26 July of the Government's decision to legislate. 'Our preliminary studies are now complete,' the Home Secretary told the House. 'Good race relations must, of course, substantially depend upon voluntary effort and a favourable climate of public opinion. But our conclusion is that by themselves they are not enough. Further legislation is therefore necessary.'[7] It would cover the fields of both housing and employment.

To all appearances, the 'bodies' whose activities had been so justified a source of apprehension to the T.U.C. had won a signal victory. But in the event, the significance of the prize was to fall short of expectations and of the subtlety and energy devoted to winning it. For this failure, there could be two categories of explanation. The first lies in circumstances outside the immediate scope of the Home Secretary's departmental responsibilities, in the progressive loss of a political authority by the Government to which he belonged. The unpopularity of the Administration was symbolized in the loss after thirty years of control of the Greater London Council in April 1967 and subsequently further catastrophic Labour defeats at the Borough Council Elections of May. But over and above this domestic unpopularity, the failures of the Administration internationally began to cast a long shadow over the domestic scene. A reservoir of goodwill which a Labour administration could hope to tap in its dealings with African and Asian Commonwealth countries was, by 1967, exhausted by the long drawn out failure of the Government's Rhodesia policy. Against such a background, constructive activity by the Government on the domestic race relations front carried less conviction than it should have done.

Beyond the British Government's sphere of responsibility grounds for discontent also multiplied. In Vietnam, a struggle, widely taken to represent the determination of expansionist Western capitalism to subdue for financial and political profit the legitimate claims of a people rightly struggling to be free, was progressively poisoning American relations with the Third World and making Britain's close foreign policy alignment with the United States a contamination by association. Further evidence for colour polarization in international affairs could be sought— and writers like Ronald Segal found it—in Cuba, in China, and even in the Middle East.[8] Domestically, the United States situation took a dramatic turn for the worse in this period, with mounting evidence that the pace of change achieved by the Civil Rights campaign, would no longer be sufficient to satisfy Negro aspirations.

The riots of Detroit broke out as Roy Jenkins was preparing to announce the Government's decision to introduce amending legislation. It has been (absurdly) suggested that the riots were a decisive factor in precipitating that decision;[9] there is no evidence whatsoever for such an assertion (as the analysis thus far presented should have made clear). But it is legitimate to point to the influence of the American situation in undermining much of the effect of the work he had put into the timing and content of his announcement. In December 1964, Martin Luther King had provided the catalyst for the formation of C.A.R.D. Malcolm X's visit in February 1965 had suggested another style of protest— though the only fruit it bore was the rotten apple of the parody campaign of Michael de Freitas. Bayard Rustin, at the beginning of 1967, had preached the doctrine of the eleventh hour, but suggested ways in which a comparatively open structure in which patterns of behaviour had not yet become fixed could still be used to obtain concessions. Stokely Carmichael on his short visit in the summer of 1967 (an attempt to return was prohibited by the Home Secretary), during which he was represented by the British Press as a kind of black bogey silhouetted against the flames of the ghetto, had no such comfort to offer. None of these visits (except perhaps King's) deserved to be recorded for their direct consequences in the United Kingdom; but the competing claims that the visitors stood for had ceased to be local American concerns and had taken on a relevance to the British situation—a relevance greatly increased with the level of attention paid to American race relations by the British Press—and their visits were effective reminders of that fact.

If the momentum were to be maintained, public opinion, both black and white, needed to be convinced not only of the need for legislation but also that tangible benefits could be expected to flow from it. The obvious line of argument for the majority was that if effective legislation were introduced in time to deal with what was demonstrably a real grievance, the kind of civil disorder that was beginning to crucify American society could be averted. 'Let us not be Bourbons', pleaded Norman St. John Stevas in the Expiring Laws Continuance Debate of 1966, 'and let us learn cheaply and vicariously from the experience of others.'[10] It can be argued—and has been—that insufficient steps (perhaps in the form of speeches by senior ministers other than Jenkins himself) were taken to bring home this point during the necessarily long delay which elapsed between the decision to introduce new legislation and the publication of the Bill. Certainly, in the interim, the debate was pre-empted by those who argued, like Powell, that such disorders were best averted not by dealing with the problems of discrimination, but by reverting to the frame of reference based on immigration and the possibility of reversing the flow altogether. This approach was greatly facilitated by the coincidental emergence of two problems associated with immigration policy: evasion of the controls by small numbers of Pakistanis (an estimated total of less than 100 by the end of 1967) crossing the Channel by small boats and the increasing concern felt both by the Government and its critics about the position of the unknown number of British citizens of Asian origin in East African countries to whom the control provisions of the 1962 Act did not apply. This was a problem to which several senior Opposition politicians, notably Duncan Sandys, whose knowledge of the problem was obtained at first hand when negotiating the Kenya independence settlement, paid increasing attention in the summer of 1967. As first one problem and then the other caught the attention of the Press, and the balance of the debate began to swing slowly back again to immigration—the sterile debate in which the Government could not help but be on the defensive.

On the immigrants' side, the arguments for legislation were also becoming less convincing. As the Home Secretary presented it, the case was based on a form of social contract argument: immigrants must be assumed to have agreed to put up with poor conditions and some discrimination on the implied understanding that their children will be admitted into British society as full citizens. Jenkins states this explicitly in his first major speech on the subject. 'Most of those who have come here in the past decade and a half are accepting an unwritten, unspoken assumption. They have come expecting to do only the most menial jobs, because they are better than no jobs at home.'[11] But this equation, by which first-class citizenship for the second generation could be purchased by second-class status in the first generation could commend itself to an audience composed largely of young adults, often with considerable skills which were, in many instances, 'transferable' only if its implications were fully worked through and explained and if some advance on the deferred gratification were provided. The positive lead which the Home Secretary had promised in the same speech to provide through non-legislative action by central government, both as employer and in placing contracts, might have been compensation but it did not materialize.

Here the Report of the Committee headed by Professor Street into the effectiveness of anti-discrimination machinery in the United States and its relevance for an extension of the law in this country might have had some influence. However, it was decided to hold back publication of the full report until the autumn. Nevertheless, the Report was widely circulated during the period of discussion and consultation that followed the Home Secretary's announcement of the decision in principle to extend the legislation.

The broad answer to criticisms that there had been failures of presentation and communication on the part of the Government was that the job of information and public education had been devolved on to the National Committee for Commonwealth Immigrants. If there were no consistent guide-lines for local and national policy on issues affecting the newcomers, then the National Committee had the duty to draw attention to the fact through the advisory function with which it had been invested. If the confidence of the immigrant community was not retained that was also the National Committee's responsibility. But by mid-1967 it was becoming clear that the National Committee in its current form was not really capable of filling this most important gap. The manner in which the Government's grant had been given imposed awkward restrictions on the pattern of expenditure; there were unfortunate setbacks as a result of staff changes at senior level, stemming broadly from the laudable aim of hiring an ethnically diverse staff. All this had not prevented the Committee from making a number of advances on different fronts. A spectacular increase took place in the number of voluntary liaison committees, many with the full-time secretary paid for from official funds envisaged in the White Paper. The effectiveness of these individual committees varied. To some extent this can be attributed to the presence or absence of a full-time worker, but as a class the local organizations suffered from a form of the malaise of their parent body. There was constant tension in their conception of their role between the desire to act on behalf of immigrants and the anxiety to retain the confidence of the local authority. This tension was only partly cloaked by the use of the vague concept of 'liaison' and by the practice of appointing non-controversial local figures to committees. Generally, the principal activities of local committees lay in such non-contentious—if useful—fields as the provision of language classes and play groups.

The Anglo-American Conference on Employment and a series of other domestic conferences were sponsored during this period, publications issued, and (perhaps most important of all) the P.E.P. Report and subsequent balancing Street investigation jointly supported with the Race Relations Board. All these were worthwhile achievements. So, by and large, was the work of the Advisory Panels. Through them there had been an unspectacular but valuable penetration into the training procedures of a number of professional groups—teachers, police, and social workers in particular—and the provision of some additional worker services, on a voluntary basis. A further extension of such welfare work was made possible when a substantial grant was obtained from the Gulbenkian Foundation in the summer of 1967. The work of the latter panels had led to a number of pamphlets and deputations, and possibly to marginal influence and the formation of policy in Whitehall. But the experience of the Housing Panel, which had argued in one report for a radical overhaul of policy towards twilight areas, and in a second, supplementary report, for the introduction of the principle of Government intervention in areas of special housing need, had not been encouraging.[12] Ministers had been polite and a conference had been called (or rather a conference which was to have been called was actually scheduled). But, this conference was diverted to the expression of grievances by local authorities against the investigators who had worked on the P.E.P. Report and the ideas in that report, and the Housing

Panel's recommendations were entirely neglected—until, suddenly, they were taken up in an emergency situation a year later. By the end of 1967, one senior member of the Housing Panel was driven to resignation.

In other circumstances, this record would have been an honourable achievement for a body set up under ominous auspices to deal with difficult conditions. But in a situation where success, as the 1967 Annual Report of the National Committee put it, 'depends on retaining the confidence of the Authorities in order that one's views will be heeded when it comes to policy-making [but] no less important the confidence of the immigrants, who may often interpret co-operation with the Authorities as condoning of what may be discriminatory policies',[13] there is clearly a serious risk that conflicting pressures will lead to evasion of the difficult issues. In the summer of 1967, Dipak Nandy argued, in a paper prepared for a new debate within C.A.R.D. on the advisability of continued association with the activities of the National Committee, that:

The truth about the NCCI after eighteen months is not, as some of us in CARD assume, that it is a stooge of the Government, but rather it is paralysed with fear, so that it can move neither to right nor to left. It cannot be a radical 'respectable' body because this would alienate the prestigious white reference group it has chosen and whose attitude it feels incapable of touching. Equally, it is debarred from being an effective welfare agency because it constantly looks over its shoulder at the immigrants, and is sensitive to the point of paranoia about their possible criticisms.[14]

John Rex also argued from the failure of the Housing Panel (of which he was a member) to press home their analysis of the deficiencies of policy with ministers that there was a basic ambiguity about the role of the Committee. He saw a division between the social work function and the political: this, coupled with weaknesses in 'the bureaucratic machinery' within the National Committee reduced it to ineffectiveness.[15]

These criticisms understate the National Committee's achievement. Nevertheless, there is enough truth in it to provide a partial explanation of the failure of the National Committee to arrest the downward trend in the general situation in the last six months of 1967. Indeed, the National Committee itself spent much of that time re-considering its own position in relation to the impending legislation and in devising expedients for evading the restrictions that its current status imposed on its activities.

Moreover, if the National Committee was increasingly attracting criticism from C.A.R.D., C.A.R.D. itself was feeling the strain of the divergence of views on the Executive Committee between those who identified colonialism as the key issue and those who wished to retain the emphasis in C.A.R.D's work on the bread-and-butter issue of discrimination in Britain. These groups had temporarily come together in coalition under the twin pressures of dissatisfaction with the capacity of the existing organizations to provide a satisfactory lead on external events and the internal race relations situation; the emphasis on further legislation had provided for a time the necessarily common aim. With its achievement, leaving only the far less glamorous task of ensuring that the form of legislation was satisfactory, and the failure of the federal structure to provide the link with the grass roots that had been vainly sought in the summer projects of 1966 and 1967, the coalition fell apart.

Heineman, summarizing the achievement of C.A.R.D. at the moment of the Government's announcement of its intention to legislate, observes: 'As the representative of a politically dispersed and powerless community [sic] C.A.R.D. has from one perspective skilfully manœuvred to obtain general acceptance of its proposals [though] dependent primarily on the goodwill and idealism of the Home Secretary.'[16]

The celebration was premature; C.A.R.D's cohesion was already under a dangerous degree of strain. In July, one of the anti-colonialists wrote in C.A.R.D's (irregular) newsletter:

The struggle of the oppressed people suffering from racial discrimination in Britain must be heightened. In addition, we must demand more realistic and positive diplomatic action and representation. Racialism is an evil that must be stamped out. It will only be stamped out by the militant struggle of the people subject to it and their friends.[17]

Those who disagreed with this analysis were divided and uncertain about ultimate ends and over-scrupulous about means. They awaited the forthcoming convention and their probable defeat in a state of near-paralysis. 'Our place now is not in the corridors of the NCCI or at the meetings of VLC's but within the community at the grass roots which we have talked about for three years and failed to reach, let alone cultivate',[18] wrote

Dipak Nandy at the conclusion of his polemic: but the time for such an alternative strategy had already passed.

The summer and autumn of 1967 saw a gradual but progressive deterioration in race relations. In a sense, this decline could be said to have started immediately on Roy Jenkins' announcement of the Government's legislative intentions, at which point Ray Gunter clearly indicated his scepticism by giving an interview to the *Daily Express* on the day of the announcement, in which he observed: 'You can't hammer men into doing what you want them to do, but you can mould them into doing it. . . . There is a general acceptance that discrimination is wrong. But how do you implement this in industry, which is not a school for lawyers? The law may possibly exacerbate these things.'[19] The doctrine of Cabinet responsibility clearly had limits for the Minister of Labour.

In July, the appearance of the report of Lord Hunt's Committee on the Immigrants and Youth Service[20] provided useful additional material for a case for favoured treatment for the second generation and the pretext for Duncan Sandys to comment: 'Instead of tackling the problem at its source, the Government has just published a report which urges us to accept a large increase in mixed marriages as an essential element in our domestic policy of integration. The breeding of millions of half-caste children will merely produce a generation of misfits and increase social tension',[21] a remark for which attempts were made to institute a prosecution against him under Section 6 of the Race Relations Act, without success. This failure contrasted rather painfully with an increasing number of prosecutions brought against black orators in Hyde Park and ultimately against Michael de Freitas, who had found an appreciative new audience as Michael Abdul Malik and unexpectedly crowned his career with the legitimation of martyrdom. The impression made in the popular mind by the use of the Race Relations Act in this context was not the happiest of auguries for the forthcoming extension of the Act.

Positive proposals for the revision of the admission procedure for immigrants, both aliens and Commonwealth citizens, and the provision of a right of appeal against refusal of leave to enter were contained in the long awaited report of the Wilson Committee[22] but passed virtually unnoticed. The Labour Party National Executive Committee working party on race relations, publishing its report in late August,[23] came out strongly for a revised immigration procedure and for comprehensive legislation covering housing and employment and providing a substantial extension of the Race Relations Board's powers—the representative of the Trades Union Congress on the working party did not sign the final report.

Some of the discontent in the Trade Union movement became briefly visible during the debate on the General Council's report at the Trades Union Congress at Brighton in September 1967. Moving remission of a resolution on legislation, Fred Hayday for the General Council referred in complimentary terms to the Ministry of Labour (who had appreciated industry's position and worked 'calmly and patiently') and in hostile terms to other departments and the ubiquitous 'outside bodies'. ('What we need is their support and not their guidance in this matter.') But there was some feeling that the General Council had, in one delegate's words, been 'dragging their feet' and the remission for which Hayday asked in order to be able to discuss 'the kind of support legislation that we would be prepared to accept to give force to the voluntary procedures which we are bringing into industry' was carried only after the Chairman had overruled a strong protest from the floor and his ruling had been challenged in standing orders committee.[24]

Supporters of legislation were luckier at the Labour Party Conference where, at a Society of Labour Lawyers' Conference, the resolution was unanimously adopted, in conjunction with the N.E.C's report on Race Relations; but none of the eleven resolutions down for Conservative Party Conference in the centenary year of the Party were concerned with legislation at all. There, the debate was directed entirely to immigration. A sizeable number of delegates clearly felt that official policy should be concerned, as Duncan Sandys put it, with a determination 'to preserve the British character of Britain';[25] an aim unlikely to be achieved, according to a new series of speeches made by Enoch Powell outside the Conference, unless the position of the British citizens of Kenya Asian origin were speedily amended to provide against the possibility of their precipitate entry to avoid the effects of the developing policy of Kenyanization adopted by the Kenyatta Government.

Powell's resumption of his campaign, and the obvious sympathy (notably warmer than in the case of his earlier analyses of the situation) with which his references for Kenya Asians were received, indicated that the impatience of the Conservative Party with the Government's policy was likely to find a sympathetic echo in sections of the Parliamentary party and make the continuation of the Front Benches mutual conciliation increasingly difficult.

At a different level, the range and content of the publicity received by Obi Egbuna for the Universal Coloured Peoples' Association manifesto[26] indicated that a focus for the opposition groups in C.A.R.D. which would attract white radical sympathy had emerged and that an explosion was not likely to be long delayed. The manifesto itself turned out to be composed of a stiff dose of rhetoric, shading at moments into flippancy ('all one needs is gumption without compunction'), coupled with a series of restricted recommendations: the setting up of advice bureaux, nurseries, and legal aid facilities. Egbuna himself reinforced the message by re-appearing on a series of public platforms, on one of which he proclaimed his allegiance to the Vietnamese people, Black Power, Che (not yet dead in Bolivia), Kwame Nkrumah, the Red Guards, Stokely Carmichael and Rap Brown, and the International Revolution; and this curiously assorted pantheon duly proved to be capable of providing just enough winds for the sails of those who by now had planned the C.A.R.D. *putsch* in some detail. At the Convention held at the end of November, the majority of the existing executive were hustled out of office by what must have been, even by the standards of British race relations, one of the most curiously assorted coalitions ever to embark on a major tactical operation, all temporarily united under the all-embracing folds of the Black Power banner.[27]

'Thus it is just at the moment when the necessity for exerting pressure on the Government to keep its nerve is greatest that the *coup d'état* in C.A.R.D. has taken place',[28] wrote Irving Reid in the Fabian publication *Venture*. And the Expiring Laws Continuance Debate in mid-November in which Jenkins made the last of his series of major speeches on race relations, suggested that, for the moment, nerve held. As a progress report on two years' activity in office, this speech is less than satisfying; Commons' rules of order, uncertainly applied by the Chairman in this instance,* were too cramping. But the tone was still constructive. The Wilson Committee Report was accepted, in principle; the

---

* David Ennals, winding up for the Government, was refused permission to discuss the question of Kenya Asians on the grounds that they were neither aliens nor Commonwealth citizens within the meaning of the 1962 Act. So anxieties on both sides of the House remained unsatisfied and no public pronouncement of policy was possible.

entry of dependants effectively defended against the growing number of critics on the right. Elaborate compliments were exchanged with Quintin Hogg, who had opened with a studiously moderate speech, celebrating the significance of a consensus on the issue. But on the Asian-British citizens in Kenya, the tone was tentative—the Government was watching the situation, which did not involve the exploitation of a loophole; 'nothing approaching an exodus' had taken place.[29] Privately, the official line was that too much attention should not be devoted to a problem which might resolve itself in time. 'We do not think that this is a matter for panic', observed Lord Stonham in the parallel Lords' Debate; but went on to add, in a notable piece of self-congratulation, that 'the present Government has tackled certain matters with far greater courage than our predecessors. We have seen the fruits of that in the fact that the net figure (of entrants) has gone down from something like 75,000 to 50,000.'[30]

By the end of the month, Jenkins had left the Home Office. Earlier it was argued that although to discuss the events of the the very recent past entirely in terms of the personalities involved would be to risk a simplistic interpretation, it is difficult not to regard official policy, laid out and planned so clearly in private and justified and analysed in public, as anything but essentially personal. Equally, to associate the admitted polarization of opinion and the end of constructive inter-party co-operation with Jenkins' successor may be to repeat the same error. But it is impossible not to contrast the constructive atmosphere in which the business of the two years of Jenkins' Home Secretaryship was conducted (increasingly overcast though the final stage was) with the alarms and partisan debates that have taken place since and to relate this contrast to the contrasting personalities of the two ministers chiefly involved.

We have argued that the choice of extension of legislation against discrimination as the principal constructive initiative of the years 1966–7 may have had its drawbacks. Not least of these lay in the fact that once a formal decision had been taken and announced, the processes of consultation were bound to take a very long time if the various interests concerned were to be adequately consulted—and that such consultations could not of their nature be conducted in the open, nor dramatic evidence of progress made public. It was therefore particularly important that once the decision had been announced the momentum should be maintained by the introduction of constructive measures whose applications had to be obvious and immediate.

In a discussion of the tactics adopted by the Home Secretary, William Deedes, a Conservative Member and himself once a junior minister at the Home Office, comments that 'as a political exercise' the 'joint operations' conducted by the Home Secretary were well executed and that they were 'timely and right'. But he adds that the evidence for a fundamental change in the law was derived from three documents, none of them sponsored by the Government, and that there had been little opportunity for debate. This is essentially a House of Commons criticism and need not detain us here. But Deedes adds that the operations were also deficient as a public relations exercise in that insufficient effort was made to enlist public support on a controversial issue. It is difficult not to agree with Deedes that there was some 'failure of political communication'.[31]

There might well have been room for a flamboyant gesture. The present Prime Minister's most significant contribution to the development of the debate on race relations in the first three years in office may well turn out to be his choice of epithet for Peter Griffiths in his first speech in office. But to ask for such a gesture from Jenkins is to ask for a different kind of politician altogether; flamboyance is not compatible with his chosen manner as a politician. Indeed, to some extent at least, the Home Secretary's cool, reasoned style had ensured that his audience would always be limited—and, on this issue, that is something of a weakness. But the role of the various agencies, once the announcement of the intention to legislate had been made, could well have been the subject of a little more attention. The standing of the Board was, of course, very high; the play from weakness was triumphantly justified.

The position of the National Committee was rather different. Under notice of basic overhaul in the legislation and restricted in its function by uncertainty over the form which the new organization would take, the Committee badly needed a prestige success. Some form of ostentatious association in ministerial announcements with the recommendations of the Wilson Committee, which after all dealt with an area within the National Committee's sphere of responsibility, might have helped to maintain confidence and avoid some of the bitterness of the following year.

Finally, there is the flaw in the strategy that was actually adopted. It was always a precondition of the success of the campaign, conceived, directed, and in part executed by the Home Secretary, in the form of a drive towards legislation directed to the needs of the second generation that neither the difficulties of the first generation (or rather their perception of their difficulties) nor the grievances in the host community over immigration should become too pressing. For a brief period, it seemed as if these twin conditions might have been satisfied; that there might have been viable solutions in the formula that had been devised. But when the public anxiety about the position of the Kenya Asians was allowed to grow, and the renewed arguments about the rate of migration again began to be heard, the 'new faulty political arithmetic' duly came into play. The price of progress was once again calculated to be concessions to the unappeasable. It is the failure to face the fact that, in the final analysis, immigration policy must be fully worked out on a consistent basis and cannot be left to chance or a temporarily favourable political conjunction that makes one reluctant to make excessive claims for this period—under which it is, in any case, far too early to draw the double lines. But it is, at least, already possible to say that the nearest we have yet come to a decent race relations policy domestically, if on a Little England basis, was reached during the Home Secretaryship of Roy Jenkins.

NOTES TO CHAPTER 27

1. *Report of the Race Relations Board 1966-7* (H.M.S.O., 1967), para. 65.
2. T.U.C., *Annual Report, 1967*, op. cit., p. 269.
3. Ibid.
4. *Daily Telegraph*, 16 February 1967.
5. A. Lester (ed.), *Essays and Speeches by Roy Jenkins* (London, Collins, 1967), p. 287.
6. T.U.C., *Annual Report, 1967*, pp. 270-2.
7. 751 H.C. Deb., c. 744, 26 July 1967.
8. R. Segal, *The Race War* (London, Cape, 1966).
9. Dilip Hiro, in *New Society*, 27 June 1968.
10. 735 H.C. Deb., c. 1252, 8 November 1966.
11. *Address given by the Home Secretary ... on the 23rd May 1966 ... to a meeting of Voluntary Liaison Committees* (London, N.C.C.I., 1966).
12. *The Housing of Commonwealth Immigrants* (N.C.C.I., April 1967), and *Areas of Special Housing Need* (N.C.C.I., May 1967).
13. *Report for 1967* (London, N.C.C.I., 1968), p. 14.
14. Dipak Nandy, *The National Committee for Commonwealth Immigrants: an assessment* (C.A.R.D. discussion paper, July 1967), pp. 11-12.

15. John Rex, 'The Race Relations Catastrophe' in *Matters of Principle: Labour's Last Chance* (Harmondsworth, Penguin Books, 1968), pp. 77–8.

16. B. W. Heineman, Jr., *The Politics of Race: a study of the Campaign Against Racial Discrimination* (unpublished Oxford B.Litt. thesis, 1967), p. 230.

17. J. James *in* Campaign Against Racial Discrimination *Newsletter*, July 1967.

18. Nandy, op. cit., pp. 12–13.

19. *Daily Express*, 26 July 1967.

20. Youth Service Development Council Committee, *Immigrants and the Youth Service* (London, H.M.S.O., 1967).

21. *The Times*, 25 July 1967.

22. Home Office, *Committee on Immigration Appeals, Report* (Cmnd. 3387), (London, H.M.S.O., 1967). Chairman: Sir Roy Wilson.

23. Labour Party, *Report of the National Executive Committee working party on race relations* (July 1967).

24. T.U.C., *Annual Report, 1967*, pp. 582–90.

25. Reported in *Daily Express*, 21 October 1967.

26. *Black Power in Britain: A Special Statement* (Universal Coloured People's Association, 1967).

27. No fully reliable account of these events has yet been produced. The only one so far published in hard covers, in *Black Man in Search of Power*, by *The Times* News Team (London, Nelson, 1968), grotesquely overestimates the role of the 'Maoists'.

28. I. Reid, *in Venture* (Vol. XIX, no. 11), p. 7.

29. 754 H.C. Deb., c. 453–73, 15 November 1967.

30. 287 H.L. Deb., c. 76, 28 November 1967.

31. W. Deedes, *Race Without Rancour* (London, Conservative Research Department, 1968).

28 The Incidence of Race Prejudice in Britain

1. THE SURVEY OF ATTITUDES *

In mid-1966 the 'Survey of Race Relations in Britain' invited five social scientists[1] to meet and consider the possibility of measuring, by means of sample surveys, the incidence of colour prejudice in the white population, the demographic characteristics of those who could be described as highly prejudiced, and the social circumstances and the psychological traits which differentiate prejudiced from non-prejudiced people.[2]

Almost from the start the members of the group were agreed that these ends could be reached by sample survey research, and that, therefore, such surveys should be carried out.

The initial approach to the problem was in terms of a probability sample of white adults drawn from the whole population of Great Britain listed in the Electoral Registers. But since it was assumed that differences in degrees of personal contact might be highly correlated with differences in degrees of prejudice and a nationwide sample would include only a handful of white natives living in close contact with coloured people, it was decided that this was an unacceptable sample design.

Various methods of 'clustering' the sample or of 'weighting' it were considered, but they were all rejected. Instead, it was decided that the study should concentrate on conditions in five local government units known to contain relatively large proportions of coloured Commonwealth immigrants, and that in each the size of the sample should be sufficient (approximately 500) to sustain a worthwhile separate analysis of the local data (see Appendix VII.1). The final selection consisted of the two London boroughs of Lambeth and Ealing and the three county boroughs of Wolverhampton, Nottingham, and Bradford (see Appendix VII.2).

In order to provide a 'control' for the intensive surveys in the five boroughs with a relatively high incidence of coloured residents, it was further decided to carry out a national survey with a sample of 2,250 white adults, but using a much more limited range of questions.

* This section has been contributed by Dr. Mark Abrams.

The field work for the intensive five-borough survey was carried out in December 1966 and January 1967; the interviewing of the national sample was done in March and April 1967. The first section is concerned primarily with the intensive survey.

(a) *The Analysis*

As a device for measuring broad trends in attitudes, it was decided to identify each respondent on a prejudice-tolerance scale and then examine the material. The method adopted was to select those attitudinal questions which provided the respondents with an opportunity to express unconditional hostility to coloured people. A numerical scale was then devised, based on four key attitude questions supplemented by ten others (scattered throughout the interview), where an unfavourable attitude to coloured people could be expressed. More details of the scale are given in Appendix VII.3, and of the questionnaire in Appendix VII.4.

(b) *The Findings*

(i) THE EXTENT OF TOLERANCE. On the basis of scores obtained on the scale, all respondents were divided into four groups:

Tolerant: those respondents who gave non-hostile answers on all four key questions.
Tolerant-inclined: those who gave only one hostile reply on the four key questions.
Prejudiced-inclined: those who gave two hostile replies on the four key questions.
Prejudiced: these who gave three or four hostile replies to the four key questions.

In each of the four groups there could, of course, be people who had expressed unfavourable attitudes to coloured people on one or more of the supplementary attitude questions.

The outcome of the analysis based on these scores divided the five-borough sample as shown in Figure 28.1.

In short, in the five boroughs, which have relatively high proportions of coloured residents, and even higher proportions of coloured children in their schools, over one-third of all white adults interviewed expressed views with no trace, or practically no trace, of hostility to coloured people; and almost another two-fifths of the sample seemed to be strongly disposed in the direction of tolerance.

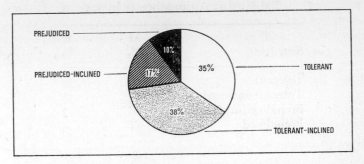

Figure 28.1. The incidence of prejudice

At the other extreme there emerged 10% of the white population whose antipathy to coloured people was almost unconditional; standing near to this one-tenth of the white population
there was another one-sixth who, while they were strongly
prejudiced-inclined, were still prepared to make exceptions and
who presumably, having once made some exceptions, could move
either in the direction of more exceptions (i.e. towards tolerance)
or fewer exceptions (i.e. towards unconditional hostility).

It is also worth noting that within each borough the pattern
of scores was broadly the same as for the whole sample. In fact, no
matter how the total sample was sub-divided in demographic and
social terms (for example, sex, age, class, tenure of accommodation, politics), the pattern of scores remained broadly constant,
i.e. usually:

30–40% obtained tolerant scores,
34–42% obtained tolerant-inclined scores,
12–20% obtained prejudiced-inclined scores, and
6–14% obtained prejudiced scores.

However, within these ranges there were some significant differences, and it is worth looking at these in detail for clues to the
concomitants, if not the causes, of high and low prejudice. (In
the following figures and tables the bottom line is arrived at by
subtracting the proportion of highly prejudiced respondents from
the proportion of highly tolerant ones. Where the balance is low
the group is above average in prejudice; conversely, where the
balance is high the group is below average in prejudice.)

First, women were slightly more tolerant than men.

Table 28.1. Attitude scores by sex

Score-types	M %	F %
Tolerant	30	39
Tolerant-inclined	41	35
Prejudiced-inclined	18	17
Prejudiced	11	9
	100	100
N =	1,136	1,358
T minus P	19	30

Second, the incidence of extreme prejudice was highest among people aged 45 to 54; it fell away on both sides of that dividing line so that the lowest levels of extreme prejudice were found among the young (i.e. under 35 years of age) and the elderly (i.e. aged 65 or over).

Within the different age-groups, women were consistently more

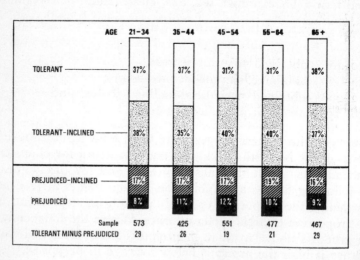

Figure 28.2. Attitude scores by age

tolerant than men: this was a little more marked among those
who had become adults in the last ten years.

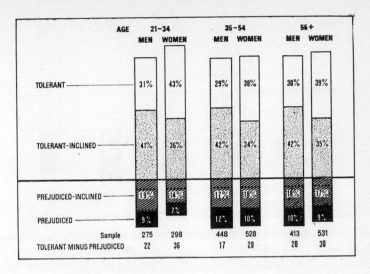

Figure 28.3. Attitude scores by age and sex

Third, as between the four socio-economic grades the highest
incidence of extreme prejudice was found among skilled manual
workers and their wives and in the lower middle class. These two
groups constituted between them little more than half (52%) of
the total sample, but they provided nearly two-thirds (63%) of
all those with the highest scores on the prejudice scale. The
lowest levels of prejudice occurred in the professional, managerial
class, and among unskilled and semi-skilled workers and their
wives.

The divergence of the skilled working class and the lower middle
class from the rest of the sample does not mean that these two
groups were top-heavy with highly prejudiced people; in both of
them almost one-third failed to give support to any of the four
main prejudice questions and subscribed to nine or less of the
supplementary prejudice-attitudes. Nor does it mean that either
the professional middle class or the unskilled working class was
completely bare of highly prejudiced people; in both these groups
one in twelve supported at least three of the key prejudice-attitudes
and a fair number of the supplementary ones.

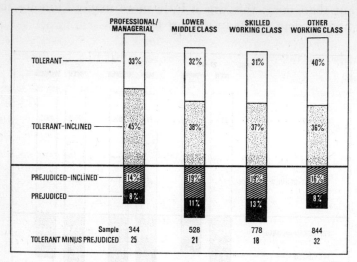

Figure 28.4. Attitude scores by social class

People whose full-time education extended beyond the minimum school-leaving age were less prejudiced than others, and (on the basis of a very small sample) this was particularly true of those with a terminal education age of 19 or later. But, only 4% of the total population fall into this last category; the great majority of the white adult population (80%) left school at the first opportunity.

Table 28.2. Attitude scores by terminal education age

Score-types	15 or less %	16–18 %	19 or later %
Tolerant	35	34	39
Tolerant-inclined	36	42	49
Prejudiced-inclined	18	16	10
Prejudiced	11	8	2
	100	100	100
N =	1,990	399	94
T minus P	24	26	37

A disproportionately high ratio of those with a background of full-time education beyond the age of 15 were still under 35 years of age, and it is this relative youthfulness which, in part, accounts for the lack of high prejudice scores among those with some higher education. If we considered as a single group all those with a terminal education age of 16 or more and sub-divided them into those aged 34 or less and those aged 35 or more, we found that only 3% of the former group received a high prejudice score, while among their elders (with the same educational background) the comparable figure was 9%. In other words, exposure to higher education seems to have had a bigger effect on the attitudes of the post-war generation than on their elders.

The findings so far indicate that the lowest incidence of extreme prejudice will be found among middle-class women under 35 years of age who have received some full-time education beyond the minimum school-leaving age, the highest incidence occurring among men in the skilled manual working class who are aged between 35 and 54 and who left school at 14 or 15 years of age.

Moving from the purely personal attributes of respondents we found that variations in prejudice were also associated with some of their social ties.

People who at the time of the survey (winter 1966–7) would have voted Conservative were more prejudiced than Labour supporters and still more prejudiced than Liberals.

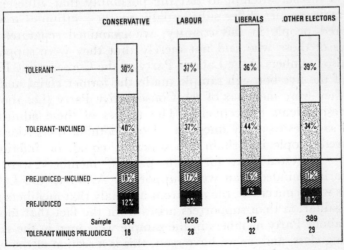

Figure 28.5. Attitude scores by voting intention

It is sometimes argued that middle-class Labour voters are much more tolerant than their working-class allies; this view is not supported by the survey where the scores of the two sections of Labour voters were almost identical. The same absence of class differences was found among Conservatives.

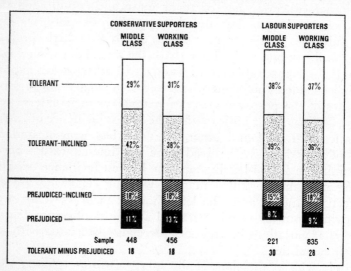

Figure 28.6. Attitude scores by voting intention and social class

In a further attempt to test the possibility that adherents of two main parties differ substantially in their attitudes towards coloured people in this country, we examined separately the replies of those who said not merely that they were supporters but also members of the Labour Party or the Conservative Party; 4% of the five-borough sample made the former claim and 5% said they were members of the Conservative Party (i.e. 100 and 125 respondents respectively). The replies of these admittedly small samples to a key question ('Do you think the majority of coloured people in Britain are superior, equal, or inferior to you?') suggested that for both parties, members were less egalitarian-minded than were supporters. As far as the Labour results were concerned, the apparent anomaly that members were less egalitarian than supporters arises from the fact that most of the Labour Party members in the sample were men in the skilled working class, and, as we have seen, this is a section of the white population more than averagely inclined to race prejudice.

Table 28.3. Attitude scores by Party membership
(Labour and Conservative)

| Coloured are | Labour Party | | Conservative Party | |
	Supporters %	Members %	Supporters %	Members %
Equal	40	32	32	20
Inferior	51	55	57	67
Don't know	9	13	11	13
	100*	100*	100*	100*

* In all four groups the proportions answering 'superior' came to less than 0·5.%

The incidence of extreme prejudice scores was highest among tenants of private landlords and lowest among owner-occupiers; council tenants occupied a half-way position. The differences between the two groups were, however, small.

Table 28.4. Attitude scores by tenure of dwelling

Score-types	Privately rented %	Council tenant %	Owner-occupier %
Tolerant	36	37	33
Tolerant-inclined	36	36	41
Prejudiced-inclined	16	17	18
Prejudiced	12	10	8
	100	100	100
N =	639	749	1,082
T minus P	24	27	25

Largely because of differences in age and sex composition people who did *not* go out to work were a little more tolerant than those in employment (80% of non-workers were women and they were mainly young women and elderly women—two groups who, as we have seen earlier, were more likely than others to express

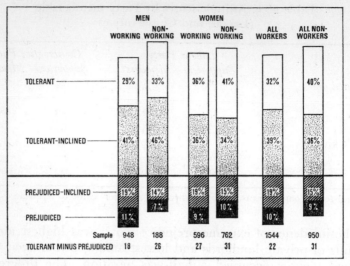

Figure 28.7. Attitude scores by sex and employment

tolerant attitudes). The incidence of tolerance was lowest among men who went out to work.

The sample contained almost a thousand working-class people in employment, and 38% of these were members of a trade union; their prejudice scores were almost identical with the scores of those who were not trade unionists.

Table 28.5. Attitude scores of workers by union membership (within working class)

Score-type	Trade unionists %	Non-unionists %
Tolerant	32	34
Tolerant-inclined	37	36
Prejudiced-inclined	20	20
Prejudiced	11	10
	100	100
N =	360	578
T minus P	21	24

There is little evidence in the survey to support the view that people who have travelled overseas are less prejudiced than those who have never been abroad. A little under half the people interviewed (46%) had at some time been outside Great Britain (for holidays, to work, or while serving with the Armed Forces). For those whose travel had been limited to Europe the pattern of prejudice scores was very much the same as for those who had stayed at home. However, travellers who had been to Asia or Africa (mainly ex-service men) were less likely than others to be in the very low prejudice category and were slightly more prone to turn in high prejudice scores. But, again, the similarities in scores between the three groups were more striking than the differences.

Table 28.6. Attitude scores by overseas travel

Score-type	Visited Asia and Africa %	Visited Europe only %	Never abroad %
Tolerant	27	35	37
Tolerant-inclined	44	39	35
Prejudiced-inclined	17	17	18
Prejudiced	12	9	10
	100	100	100
N =	348	805	1,341
T minus P	15	26	27

Respondents who, compared with their parents, had experienced upward social mobility were a little more likely to be prejudiced than those who had fallen in the social scale. (Practically all upwardly mobile respondents were in the lower middle class and the skilled working class—two groups which, as we noted earlier, are more prone than others to be below average on tolerance.) The attitudes of these people, however, were not strikingly different in general outline from those of the rest of the sample. And, as we shall see, the percentage did not change when we came to consider how respondents themselves perceived changes in their social position.

Table 28.7. Attitude scores by social mobility

Score-type	Upward %	Stable %	Down %
Tolerant	32	35	39
Tolerant-inclined	40	37	36
Prejudiced-inclined	18	17	18
Prejudiced	10	11	7
	100	100	100
N =	864	966	536
T minus P	22	24	32

The conclusion to be drawn from this review of prejudice scores by social variables is that none of them plays a decisive part in determining the incidence of prejudice. High prejudice scores are a little above average among people who vote Conservative, are tenants of private landlords, go out to work, and have visited Africa or Asia. Most of the other variables considered (for example, experience of intergenerational social mobility, membership of a trade union) failed to discriminate significantly between prejudiced and tolerant whites in the five boroughs.

At the same time, prejudice scores not much short of the average for the whole sample were recorded by other groups: Labour voters, owner-occupiers, and council tenants. We will therefore turn to another possible discriminant—differences of personality and perception of the social situation, within the white population.

Using the replies sometimes to one question, sometimes to several, respondents were assessed on six such aspects of 'sociality' or 'personality'; two of these shed no light on the identification of high prejudice, two made a marginal contribution, and two (social potency or impotence, and the extent of authoritarianism) were of considerable help. Before dealing with these two the others must be discussed, since even their non-significance is important.

First, two extreme groups were isolated in the sample—those who said that all the families living round them shared exactly the same interests and problems among themselves and with the respondent, and those who felt exactly the opposite—i.e., that their neighbours had few or no interests in common and had little or nothing in common with the respondent. Considering only these two extreme groups (between them they accounted for almost half the total sample) and ignoring the in-between replies we found that the patterns of their prejudice scores were almost identical.

Next, we examined two other extreme groups of respondents— those (19% of the sample) who said that if they moved from their present address they would miss most of their neighbours, and, on the other hand, the very much larger group of people (40%) who said that if they moved they would not miss a single one of their present neighbours, or at most only one or two of them. Our results showed that 'companionable' whites were a shade more tolerant than the isolates.

Respondents were also asked: 'Compared with the position of your parents when you were a child, would you say you've done better than them, worse, or are you in much the same position?' Over three-quarters of the respondents felt they had done better than their parents and only 7% considered themselves worse off; the balance considered themselves to be in much the same circumstances as their parents. Even between the two extreme groups (better-off/worse-off) the pattern of prejudice scores were almost identical. Whatever other emotions are generated by the feeling that one has fallen behind the material standards of one's parents, excessive colour prejudice is not one of them. And, contrary-wise, to feel that one has 'got on' does not generate any greater degree of tolerance than is shown by the less successful; if anything, the tendency is for the opposite to occur. (Just as we saw above, that those who had in fact got on were somewhat less tolerant than those who had not.)

Besides considering their past, respondents were asked to speculate about their future circumstances. The question put to them was: 'Over the next five or ten years do you expect your circumstances to change for the better or for the worse?'

Nearly 60% of the sample were optimistic about their future; only 11% felt that in five or ten years' time they would be worse off than they were at the time of questioning. The latter group, compared with the optimists, were slightly less tolerant and slightly more prejudiced. Despite this high incidence of optimism,

564 COLOUR AND CITIZENSHIP

respondents proved less confident about the degree of control they could themselves exercise over their future circumstances.

From the cross-tabulation of the answers to two questions it was possible to identify two extreme groups in terms of a sense of effective control over the socio-political environment. The two questions were as follows:

(i) 'If some problem affecting the lives of people around here came up, some people might want to get together to discuss it and take some action. How much support would you give: your full active support; your support but stopping short of taking any action; or would you keep out of it all?'
(ii) 'How far would the Authorities take account of the opinions of people around here?'

A rating of high social potency was given to those who said in reply to the first question that they would give active support and who also, on the second question, said that the authorities would certainly take account of local opinion; 15% of the sample gave such doubly positive answers. At the other extreme were the 10% of people who said both that they would keep out of any discussion of local problems, and that the authorities would take no notice or hardly any notice of local opinion.

Those with high potency ratings were appreciably less prejudiced than those who would keep out of discussion and action about local problems and who felt, additionally, that in any case local opinion would have no part in influencing the decisions and actions taken by 'the Authorities'.

Table 28.8. Attitude scores by socio-political potency

Score-type	High potency %	Low potency %
Tolerant	36	33
Tolerant-inclined	40	34
Prejudiced-inclined	18	22
Prejudiced	6	11
	100	100
N =	380	241
T minus P	30	22

However, it is likely that this finding was in part a reflection of the general effects of education and social class on attitudes, since middle-class respondents were more likely than others to express feelings of high social potency.

Finally, very early in the interview respondents were asked to express agreement or disagreement with six statements. None of the six dealt with colour or immigrants but was of the usual type used in personality scales (for example, 'sex criminals should be treated by doctors in hospital and not sentenced to prison', 'human nature being what it is, there will always be wars and conflict', 'the Authorities ask too few people before deciding what is right and wrong').

For each statement agreement or disagreement could be expressed on a five-point scale—from agree strongly to disagree strongly; and, of course, on some statements strong agreement was an indication of authoritarianism, and on others strong disagreement indicated authoritarianism.[3]

Over one-fifth (21%) of the sample qualified as consistently authoritarian and 11% as consistently non-authoritarian.[4]

The authoritarians were substantially more colour prejudiced than the non-authoritarians; they provided one-third of all those in the whole sample who gave completely prejudiced scores, and constituted only one-sixth of all those with highly tolerant scores. The imbalance of the contribution of the non-authoritarians to the prejudice scores was in the opposite direction, that is, they made a more-than-proportionate contribution to the ranks of the tolerant and a less-than-proportionate contribution to those with high-prejudice scores.

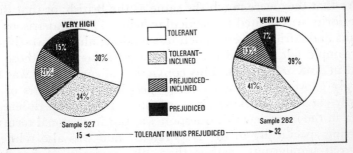

Figure 28.8. Attitude scores by authoritarianism

A comparison of the demographic characteristics of these two extreme personality types showed that the authoritarians contained more than the national proportions of men, of people aged 55 or more, of working-class people, and of those with no education beyond the minimum school-leaving age. It would, however, be rash to conclude that these are distinctive characteristics of authoritarianism. Those with high-authoritarian scores included many who were young, were in the middle class, had received some higher education, and were women. Practically everyone in the sample showed some trace of authoritarianism (and presumably this holds true of the population at large). It is merely that it is more wide-ranging, more explicit, and more intense in some people than in others; it should be remembered that on the scaling used in this analysis nearly 70% of the sample fell between the two extremes of authoritarianism and non-authoritarianism. (Further details are given in Appendix VII.5.)

(ii) ELEMENTS OF PREJUDICE. We will now turn to an examination of the responses to certain specific items in the questionnaire which throw light on general attitudes towards coloured people in Britain: the replies to these help to fill in the picture of prejudice and tolerance among white people on specific issues relating to coloured people. For this purpose we will continue to employ the five-borough sample, looking at various specific groups within the sample when that seems helpful.

One basic question the respondents were asked early in the questionnaire was how they rated British people in comparison with the majority of people in various other parts of the world. Very few considered British people to be definitely superior to Europeans and Americans; the most common attitudes here were either that they were much the same as the British, or that British superiority was limited to particular fields. The comparisons with Asians and Africans were much less modest; almost two-thirds of the sample felt that British people were superior to those who lived in Asia and Africa. This conviction of superiority was most sharply expressed by men and by people over 44 years of age; middle-class and working-class responses showed no differences. Later in the interview this question was put in personal terms (by referring specifically to the respondent) and was also related to coloured immigrants (rather than 'the majority of people' in Africa, Asia, and so on). The question ran: 'Do you think the

Table 28.9. Attitudes towards the British compared with people in other parts of the world

British people are	Africa %	Asia %	Europe %	America %
Definitely superior	33	27	8	5
Superior to some extent	32	34	28	18
Same	18	20	52	58
Inferior	4	3	4	11
Don't know	13	16	8	8
	100	100	100	100

majority of coloured people in Britain are superior, equal, or inferior to you?'

Less than 0·5% regarded coloured immigrants as their superiors and 11% felt unable to make a judgement one way or the other. The two main groups of replies were the 53% who regarded them as inferior to themselves, and the 36% who considered them as their equals—a ratio of 3 to 2. The proportion of inferior to equal responses was appreciably higher among men than among women, and among middle-class as compared with working-class respondents.

The 53% of the total sample who thought that coloured immigrants were inferior to themselves were then asked: 'Is that

Table 28.10. Reasons for regarding coloured immigrants as inferior

	All %	Men %	Women %	Middle class %	Working class %
Skin colour	5	3	6	4	5
Lack of education	44	53	35	51	40
General cultural differences	38	37	41	35	41
Specific differences: cleanliness	10	7	13	8	11
Specific differences: other	10	9	10	10	9
Lack intelligence	7	8	5	6	7
Not civilized	3	3	3	3	3
Other reasons	9	9	10	9	9

568 COLOUR AND CITIZENSHIP

because of their skin colour or for some other reason?' Not surprisingly, only 5% of the 53% justified their view on grounds of skin colour. The most commonly advanced reasons were that coloured people lacked the educational attainments of the white respondent and that their cultural and social mores were different and inferior. Age had little effect on the replies: the main variations were related to the sex and class of the respondents. Men and middle-class whites emphasized lack of education among coloured immigrants, while women and working-class respondents attached relatively more importance to cultural differences.

We wanted to discover how far, against this background of a broadly-held view of coloured people as inferior and a general ethnocentricism, respondents were able to register differences between various ethnic groups in the migration, and between the migrants and the native population as a whole. So, to see how widespread perception of cultural differences might be, respondents were asked: 'How similar to ours do you think is the way of life of the majority of people in the West Indies (in India, in Pakistan, in Cyprus or Greece)?' Nearly 30% of the sample said they knew too little about Greece/Cyprus to be able to make an assessment, but very few (10% or less) felt similarly handicapped about the 'way of life' in the West Indies, India, or Pakistan. The great majority were sure that for all three areas the similarities were either slight or non-existent, although this opinion was less pronounced when the comparison was made with the West Indies. In this pattern of replies there was little difference between the two sexes, the two age groups, and the two social classes.

Table 28.11. Attitudes concerning the similarity of the British way of life with that of the West Indies, India, Pakistan, and Greece or Cyprus

	West Indies %	India %	Pakistan %	Greece/Cyprus %
Very similar	2	1	—	1
Quite similar	15	5	5	18
Not similar	26	23	22	24
Not at all similar	49	62	63	29
Don't know	8	9	10	28
	100	100	100	100

Similarly, we were interested to see how far respondents could identify class differences within migrant groups—or whether the colour factor overrode such differences. Here an interesting contrast presented itself between the national sample and the five-borough sample. Respondents in the national sample were prepared to recognize some class differences; nearly a quarter of them thought that immigrants might be middle class or skilled working class. But in the five-borough sample the vast majority of respondents saw the immigrants as unskilled, or at best semi-skilled workers—a picture that does not altogether correspond with reality. Specifically, those who lived within half an hour's walking distance of coloured people, when asked this question, replied as shown in Table 28.12.

Table 28.12. Perception of class differences among immigrants

	%
Middle class and skilled working	8
Semi-skilled	25
Unskilled	67
	100

In other words, over 90% saw the immigrants as working class and two-thirds as unskilled. This is a particularly interesting finding since one of the classical theories of race relations is that which postulates that Britons assign the immigrants to an un-differentiated and low class category.

Another important background factor in the situation that interested us was the extent to which respondents had a realistic appreciation of the dimensions of the migration. It is often argued that fears of being 'swamped' by what is usually described as a 'flood' of migrants is a key element in forming attitudes, and that this derives from exaggerated notions of the extent of the migration and the size of the coloured population (which are compounded by the absence of reliable official statistics). By and large, our results support the view that exaggerated estimates are in circulation.

These exaggerations, however, were not correlated in any consistent way with prejudice. It is true that working-class

Table 28.13. Estimates of the size
of coloured population

	%
One million or less	27
2–5 million	23
More than 5 million	24
Don't know	26
	100

respondents (whose prejudice scores were relatively high) were more likely than middle-class respondents to give high estimates of the number of coloured immigrants in Britain; but, on the other hand, women (whose prejudice is comparatively low) were more likely than men to exaggerate the number of coloured immigrants.

The conclusion we would draw from the results so far presented in this section is that there is a great deal of widely diffused confusion, anxiety, and misunderstanding about the migration, its composition, and the background of the migrants, making up a predisposition towards rejection. In such circumstances, it is hardly surprising that hostile stereotypes, which seem to justify rejection in more specific terms, are common. We asked respondents whether they considered that immigrants took more out of the country than they put in, and asked them to make a distinction in their replies between the various ethnic groups.

At least 60% of the respondents thought that each of the three coloured groups took 'more out of the country than they put into it'; in Wolverhampton the proportion was as high as 75%. Those who held this view made little distinction between West Indians, Indians, and Pakistanis. Many of them felt that this was also true of white immigrants coming from Greece or Cyprus, but their numbers were appreciably fewer. Broadly speaking, while three-quarters of all respondents felt that *all* immigrants benefited disproportionately from the social services, a majority acquitted white immigrants of this charge.

Those who were convinced that coloured immigrants benefited unduly from the social services were asked which of the services they particularly had in mind; most of them named at least two—

Table 28.14. Stereotypes: 'Immigrants receive more social service benefits than their contributions'

True of immigrants from	%
West Indies	62
India	60
Pakistan	63
Greece, Cyprus	36
None of them	27

usually national assistance and health, with education some way behind.

Table 28.15. Stereotypes: Services 'giving immigrants more benefits than contributions'

	West Indians %	Indians %	Pakistanis %	Greeks, Cypriots %
National assistance	91	90	91	89
Health service	70	70	70	75
Education	45	46	45	53

Much of the attitudes expressed by these figures undoubtedly springs from feelings that coloured immigrants maliciously exploit the social services (e.g., 'they don't want to work', 'they come here to get all they can'), but part of it is based on the widely held fallacy that the social services are a form of insurance with a commercial actuarial basis; this presumably was the thinking of those who commented 'they haven't been here long enough to pay in', or 'we've been paying taxes all our lives'.

Similar stereotypes emerged less directly from other questions at various stages in the interviews; for example, in discussing immigration legislation many respondents justified especially stringent restrictions on coloured entry by reference to disease, 'dirt', strain on schools and hospitals, and overcrowding. We also encountered the very common view that neighbourhood decline (usually set in motion by indigenous forces) was the result of immigration.

Despite the prevalence of such stereotypes, however, there has in the past been a countervailing current of sympathy towards coloured immigrants, as victims of a biological accident for which they are not responsible, which is neatly pinned down in the common tag: 'It's not his fault he's black.' In an attempt to isolate this element in the situation respondents were placed in a hypothetical situation where they were asked to allocate sympathy between coloured immigrants and 'white people who lived in similar conditions'. A clear majority said they felt exactly the same towards the two 'underprivileged' groups; 10% of the total sample said that as between the two they had more sympathy for coloured immigrants (usually on the grounds that it was harder for them to improve their lot or because the whites by fecklessness or irresponsibility must have thrown away their opportunities); but 30% reacted in the opposite direction—i.e. they had less sympathy with coloured immigrants (the sort of comment made here was 'no one asked them to come here', or 'they're better off than they would be at home').

This suggests that although such sympathy may at one stage have constituted a significant element in the composite pattern of general attitudes it seems that it is now of declining importance.

(iii) CONTACT WITH NEWCOMERS: ITS FORM AND CONTEXT. These general attitudes, taken together with the evidence we reported earlier on the extent of prejudice in different segments of the population, suggest that in actual situations of face to face contact where a response is called for on the part of the native it is likely to be negative and rejecting and not to vary as between one situation and another—despite differences in personalities, class, and background of the two parties to the encounter and the circumstances in which they meet. In fact, on closer examination, the evidence tended to lead to rather different conclusions.

In due course, we propose to examine responses to a number of questions designed to tap not generalized prejudice but specific responses to situations which have a direct personal significance for the respondent and relate to his own pattern of behaviour; but before doing so we will examine the initial encounter between the two parties, the form of the encounter, the extent of the contact experienced, and the context in which it took place.

In total, 9% of the five-borough sample claimed to have a coloured neighbour; 47% to have coloured people living within

five minutes' walking distance; 12% to have them living within
half an hour's walk; and a third claimed not to have any coloured
people within thirty minutes' walking distance. There was considerable variation between the towns. In Nottingham over half
the respondents claimed to have no coloured people within half
an hour of them; in Lambeth only 16% claimed this.

Respondents who identified any one of the four immigrant
nationalities as living within walking distance were asked whether
they had ever talked to or had discussions with any of them. In
total, a quarter of those who had coloured next-door neighbours
had failed to talk to them at all; well over half (59%) of those who
lived five minutes' walk away had not talked to them; and two-
thirds of those who lived between five minutes' and half an hour's
walk away had not done so. Respondents who had talked with
coloured people in the neighbourhood were also asked how they
had got on with them the first few times. In all, 8% said that they
had not got on well with the West Indians, 9% with Indians, and
18% with Pakistanis. Respondents had found talking with
coloured people most difficult in Wolverhampton, Bradford, and
Lambeth. The effects of such discussions can be glimpsed in the
fact that those who said they had become more favourably disposed to each nationality had talked with them far more frequently than those who said that their attitudes had changed for
the worse. (Though it is not quite clear which is cause and which
effect.)

But there are, of course, other social contexts apart from the
neighbourhood in which contact can take place. Those who
claimed acquaintance with coloured people were asked how they
had become acquainted. The answers were as follows:

At work	37%
Living in the same house or next door	20%
In the street or shopping	17%
Through friends	11%
Through children	5%

Although the majority of encounters therefore took place at
work, in the sample as a whole less than half of all respondents
(44%) had ever worked with one of the four immigrant groups.
Although in Ealing more than half had done so and in Lambeth
exactly half, in Nottingham only just over a third and in Wolverhampton 40% had such experience. Younger respondents had

worked with coloured people more frequently than older respondents; indeed, exactly two-thirds of respondents aged between 21 and 34 had such experience. Perhaps rather surprisingly, 45% of middle-class compared with 42% of working-class respondents had worked with coloured people. All those who had this experience were also asked how they had got on; in total, 13% had not got on well with West Indians, 16% with Indians, and 23% with Pakistanis.

Despite the fact that contact through children was not a common means of striking up an acquaintance with coloured people, it was found that in all the boroughs a substantial proportion of the population said that their children shared a school with the children of at least one of the immigrant groups. The proportions were as follows:

Lambeth	89%
Wolverhampton	77%
Ealing	77%
Bradford	62%
Nottingham	49%
Average	70%

Respondents were also asked how their children got on with other children from these places and in total 13% reported difficulty in getting on with Pakistanis, 11% with Indians, and 8% with West Indians.

'Impersonal' contact was also reported to take place frequently; for example, 74% of those questioned had experience of West Indian bus conductors. The experience of waiting in a queue with coloured people or drinking in a pub where coloured customers were being served was also (as one would expect) a normal feature of life in the five boroughs.

Before considering specific situations that are linked to actual contact we need briefly to consider the social context.

The five areas were selected for study on the assumption that in all of them the incidence of coloured settlement was high and inter-racial contact correspondingly frequent. This assumption proved to be justified, as we have just seen. But, apart from this one factor held in common, there are sharp social and economic differences between the five boroughs, widely separated as they are by location and their past histories.

In two of the boroughs (Lambeth and Bradford) the amount of residential overcrowding (as measured by the proportion of persons living at densities of more than 1·5 persons per room) is well above the national rate; in Wolverhampton overcrowding is slightly above the all-Britain figure; but in two of them (Ealing and Nottingham) it is slightly below the national rate. And although in only two of the boroughs (Bradford and Lambeth) is the extent of overcrowding significantly above the national level, in three of them (Bradford, Lambeth and Nottingham) the provision of domestic plumbing amenities (indoor lavatories, hot water taps, etc.) is worse than the national average. If housing conditions are judged by a family's access to a hot water tap, a fixed bath, and the exclusive use of a lavatory, then housing conditions in Wolverhampton and Ealing are better than the average for the country as a whole, slightly worse than average in Bradford, and appreciably worse in Lambeth and Nottingham.

In terms of the Registrar-General's social class composition, in Bradford and Nottingham one-third of the male population are semi-skilled or unskilled workers, compared with only one-fifth in Ealing, at the other end of the scale. In Wolverhampton an unusually high proportion of men (nearly half) are skilled manual workers. This class composition in the five boroughs reflects to some extent the occupational structure of the local population and the configuration of local industry. In all five boroughs unemployment rates throughout the 1960s have been very low, and usually below the national average.

(iv) COMPETITION AND ALLOCATION: NEWCOMERS IN JOBS AND HOUSING. Against this background we can now turn to discussing responses to a series of questions which were intended to provide evidence of respondents' reactions when asked to take a decision on an issue with a direct relationship to real situations within their experience. Two of these questions dealt with employment, two with housing. In discussing them we will draw on evidence from the national sample survey as well as the five-borough sample.

Respondents were asked: 'Suppose there are two workers, one coloured and one white, who do exactly the same work. If one, and only one, had to be declared redundant, should it be the coloured or the white worker?'

The two samples gave identical patterns of reply. In each a

majority (56%) refused to discriminate between the two men on grounds of colour and said the decision should be based on such considerations as merit or length of service; 2% said the white worker should go (usually on the grounds that he would find it easier to find another job); and 42% of respondents thought the coloured worker should be dismissed. Occasionally this discrimination was 'justified' on the grounds that the coloured worker would probably not be as good as the white man or that any other choice would lead to trouble; but much more usually (in over two-thirds of the cases) the anti-coloured respondent went on to say that 'this is a white man's country' and that 'whites should always be preferred'.

Table 28.16. Attitudes concerning the question of redundancy

	Five boroughs %	Great Britain %
Dismiss white	2	2
Dismiss coloured	42	42
Depends, merit, service, etc.	46	53
Don't know	10	3
	100	100

However, when the data for the five boroughs were broken down some most important distinctions emerged. First, by age: in the five boroughs, readiness to dismiss the coloured worker was lowest among the younger respondents. Less than a third (31%) of people under 35 wanted to dismiss the coloured worker. Between the ages of 35 and 54, 41% advocated this course and an actual majority of respondents over 54 years of age (51%) preferred to see the coloured worker made redundant. In Wolverhampton the youngest group was significantly more prepared to dismiss the coloured worker, in Ealing they were less prepared to do so.

In the five-borough sample readiness to dismiss the coloured worker rose as the social class gradient fell. Only 30% of upper middle-class respondents supported this action. Among members of the lower half of the working class support for this course approached 50%. Two significant variations from the overall pattern were a high level of hostility in the middle class in Lambeth and a high level of hostility among working-class respondents in Wolverhampton. There were also sharp differences in the response of differing groups classified by their terminal education age. A fifth of those who had received full-time education beyond the Sixth Form wanted to dismiss the coloured worker; a third, of those with a terminal age of between 16 and 18; and approaching half, among those who left school before 16.

Trade union membership had a marginal effect upon attitudes; unionists were slightly less likely to advocate dismissal of the coloured worker. Political allegiance did not appear to have much effect on attitudes across the sample as a whole, but within the five boroughs there were two marked divergences; in Wolverhampton considerably more Labour than Conservative supporters gave a hostile response and in Lambeth precisely the opposite was true.

Nor did contact in the neighbourhood appear to affect responses materially. But respondents who had worked with coloured people were considerably less inclined to support dismissal of the coloured worker. Thirty-seven per cent of those with such experience wanted him dismissed, compared with 46% of those without. Having worked with coloured people was very strongly associated with diminished hostility on this issue. Finally, those who obtained their information about coloured people from other persons were much more inclined to support dismissal than those whose experience stemmed from personal contact—53% in the former case, as against 39% in the latter.

The second question common to the two surveys dealt with promotion, and here respondents were asked: 'Suppose there were two workers, one coloured and one white, who do exactly the same work. If one of them, and only one, had to be promoted, should it be the coloured or the white worker?'

The patterns of responses from the two samples scarcely differed from each other; in both a clear majority refused to discriminate on grounds of colour, and in both just over one-third said promotion should go to the white worker.

But, here again, uniformity at surface level concealed diversity beneath. In the five boroughs promotion for the white worker obtained least support among the younger respondents. A quarter of those between 21 and 34 years of age supported promotion of the white worker, a third between 35 and 44, 42% between 45 and 64, and 45% over 65. The preference for promoting the white

Table 28.17. Attitudes concerning the question of promotion

	Five boroughs %	Great Britain %
Promote coloured	1	*
Promote white	37	34
Depends, merit, seniority	54	63
Don't know	8	3
	100	100

*denotes under 1%.

worker rose as the socio-economic grade declined. A quarter of the upper middle-class respondents wanted to promote him compared with well over one-third of the working-class respondents. There were some variations between the boroughs, but in each case there was more working-class than middle-class hostility to the coloured worker enhancing his status at the expense of a white competitor. There was proportionately most middle-class hostility in Wolverhampton. (It is evident from these results that the five-borough sample was not homogeneous as far as the distribution of hostility among the two major social classes is concerned.)

Once more, there were wide differences between the three educational groups in advocacy of promotion for the white worker. Among those with the least schooling, 39% supported his elevation; among those who received full-time education after 19 only 16% would promote him. Conservative Party members were notably more inclined to promote the white worker than Labour Party members (41% compared with 32%); and trade union members were very slightly less inclined to support the white worker's promotion.

But once again work-place contact was most significant in modifying attitudes, though having worked with coloured people appeared to make less difference to attitudes towards their promotion than to attitudes on their dismissal. And, as in the redundancy question, those who said that their most important source of information was 'other people' were more inclined to promote the white worker than those who had experienced personal contact.

Questions were also asked about housing. In the first instance, whether the local authority should let or refuse to let council houses to members of each of four selected ethnic groups. In the sample as a whole, nearly half the respondents (49 per cent) raised no objection to the letting of council dwellings to immigrants— whether coloured or white; but over two-fifths felt they should be refused. Colour counted for little; nor were distinctions drawn between different coloured immigrant groups.

Those who opposed council dwellings for immigrants were then asked: 'Should the authorities still refuse even if the family had been on the waiting list the right length of time?' Faced with this challenge to their sense of fairness slightly over half of the initial objectors reversed their positions, and this left 20% of the total sample unconditionally opposed to the provision of council dwellings for immigrants.

Between the five boroughs there were, however, some very striking differences in attitudes towards coloured immigrants as possible council tenants; in Bradford there was very little opposition, but in Lambeth and Ealing there was a great deal.

One likely source of explanation lies in the fact that in each of the five boroughs the patterns of housing tenure were quite different. In Wolverhampton and Nottingham over a third of the households were in council accommodation; in Lambeth and Bradford a quarter; but in Ealing only 14% (the national average is 28%). However, in Ealing a half and in Bradford well over half of households lived in owner-occupied accommodation; this distinguishes them sharply from Lambeth (where half the households were in the private rented sector and only 20% were owner-occupiers) and Nottingham (where over a third were in privately rented accommodation). Wolverhampton, with almost equal groups of owner-occupiers and municipal tenants and a small private rented sector, occupied a middle position.

Table 28.18. Attitudes towards the council letting to coloured immigrants

	Bradford %	Wolverhampton %	Nottingham %	Ealing %	Lambeth %	All %
Yes, unconditionally	65	52	49	39	32	49
Yes, conditionally	17	18	23	24	33	23
No	13	18	22	23	28	20
Don't know	5	12	6	14	7	8
	100	100	100	100	100	100

In four of the boroughs the pattern of replies about Greek/Cypriot immigrants was practically the same as for coloured immigrants, but in Lambeth there was proportionately much less opposition to council dwellings for white immigrants.

Some indication of the reasoning behind the hostile attitudes, and behind the absence of discrimination between different immigrant groups, was to be found in the answers given by the unyielding 20% when they still opposed the letting of council dwellings to immigrants. Overwhelmingly the attitude expressed was that access to council dwellings should be limited to 'our own people'—that it was part of the benefits of the Welfare State that should not be shared with people who had not contributed adequately to the costs of these benefits. Only very rarely was the objection supported by the argument that the presence of coloured tenants would adversely affect the quality of the property.

Table 28.19. Reasons for refusing council dwellings to immigrants

	Coloured %	Greek/Cypriot %
Preference should be always for our own people	74	76
Bad effect on property	8	5
Dislike them	7	7
Should be segregated	4	4
Other reasons	8	9
Don't know	3	2

The overall impression that these findings give of a guarded willingness to allow coloured entry into the fortress of working-class privilege was also reflected in the results obtained when respondents were asked to consider whether coloured people should be allowed access to property owned and let by private landlords.

In this situation nearly 60% of respondents considered that there should be no withholding of tenancies from either coloured or Greek-Cypriot immigrants, and half of those who initially objected reversed their position when they were asked if they would still refuse if the landlord knew that the immigrants would look after the accommodation properly. Thus, only 10% of the sample were unconditionally hostile to the idea of private letting to immigrants. And, again, this hostility did not differentiate between the four specified immigrant groups.

Between the five boroughs the main difference was between the 'openness' of the Bradford respondents and the comparative restrictiveness of whites in the two London boroughs (where the pressure on housing—both municipal and private—is greatest). However, even in London the outright opposition amounted to little more than 12%; in both boroughs a majority of those who failed to give a positive reply did not express a completely negative attitude; instead, their position was rather that behaviour in the private market place was no business of theirs, it was 'up to the landlord' to decide who should or should not be his tenants.

Table 28.20. Attitudes towards private landlords letting to coloured immigrants

	Bradford %	Nottingham %	Wolverhampton %	Lambeth %	Ealing %	All %
Yes, unconditional	71	59	56	54	50	59
Yes, conditional	9	15	8	10	9	10
No	7	9	14	12	13	10
Don't know	13	17	22	24	28	21
	100	100	100	100	100	100

In sum, these findings suggest that despite some discontinuities and contradictions, there are two major factors which may modify attitudes: the extent of realistic competition for scarce resources, which accounts for the fluctuation in response on the housing question; and in relation to jobs, face to face contact at the workshop or office—particularly in the younger age group.

We should add that not all the evidence on contact pointed in the same direction. Earlier in the interview, respondents were asked to assess the effects of contact in relation to their own personal experience in specific situations. In this instance, as we have reported above, experiences seemed on the whole to have been favourable. But when respondents were asked to reflect generally on the consequences of contact with different ethnic groups the picture became rather more complicated. Here we should remind readers that the experience of each locality has been different: Table 28.21 shows that ethnic groups which are strongly represented in one area are not present in others (this diversity of experience was, of course, one reason for selecting different towns for study).

Table 28.21. Percentage of coloured immigrants in each of the five boroughs, by place of birth at 1966 Census

Borough	Per cent of population from West Indies	Per cent from India	Per cent from Pakistan	Per cent from West Indies, India, and Pakistan
Ealing	1·5	3·0	0·2	4·7
Lambeth	5·2	1·1	0·1	6·4
Nottingham	1·6	0·6	0·3	2·5
Wolverhampton	2·2	2·5	0·2	4·8
Bradford	0·6	1·2	2·4	4·2

Generally, both middle-class and working-class groups felt that experience had made them more favourable rather than less favourable to West Indian immigrants, but this feeling was much more common among middle-class respondents.

The most striking variations, however, were between the boroughs; in Nottingham and Wolverhampton the numbers reporting more favourable attitudes were roughly the same as those reporting less favourable attitudes; but in Ealing and Bradford (where the incidence of West Indians is comparatively low) favourable reactions greatly outnumbered unfavourable ones; and in Lambeth (where contact with West Indians is highest) unfavourable shifts in attitude greatly outnumbered favourable ones.

In the case of Indians only slightly more respondents reported favourable results of contact than reported unfavourable; this adverse balance was particularly marked among working-class people, among men, and among those under 45 years of age. Among the five boroughs Wolverhampton and Lambeth stood out: the former because of the strong negative reactions to contact with Indian immigrants and the latter because, uniquely, favourable reactions to Indian immigrants substantially exceeded less favourable views.

In the case of the Pakistanis the unfavourable responses outnumbered favourable ones substantially. This outcome not only contrasted strongly with the favourable balance of reactions to contact with West Indians—it was even more adverse than the comments on contact with Indian immigrants. As with the unfavourable balance on the latter, negative reactions were most strongly expressed by working-class people, by men, and by those under 45 years of age; but this time there was also a substantial unfavourable balance among middle-class people, women, and older people. Among the boroughs Bradford (with a relatively high incidence of Pakistani residents) joined Wolverhampton as registering the highest unfavourable balance.

Generally, the ethnic group *not* represented locally was the most popular one and this result was repeated when respondents were asked which group they would prefer to have (if they had to select one) as new neighbours.

(v) CLUES FOR ATTITUDE CHANGE. After considering the distribution of prejudice among groups within the population distinguished by social and demographic characteristics and personality types, the reactions of respondents to the experience of contact and their attitudes towards situations in which decisions on the allocation of scarce resources (which bring together predispositions and experiences) were requested; what clues can we draw out for the future development of opinion on this issue?

First, we should consider the replies given to a series of questions designed to test the respondent's perception of attitudes in other sectors of the host community. It has been suggested in the past that individuals usually tend to overestimate the extent of hostility generally and that if they can be brought to see that tolerance will not isolate them there may be some prospect of behavioural change. But in this case nearly 50% of respondents in the five boroughs thought that local attitudes to coloured people were either much the same as would be found among white people in the rest of the country or were even more favourable; in other words, those expressing anti-coloured attitudes were likely to feel that they were in line with national norms. Only in Lambeth and Wolverhampton was there a widespread acknowledgment of the possibility that local attitudes to coloured people were less favourable than in Britain as a whole.

In another attempt to probe this question of how white respondents in the five boroughs perceived the attitudes of various groups and institutions they were told: 'There are some sections of the public which are more favourable towards coloured people than others.' And were then asked: 'As I read out some groups would you say whether, on the whole, they are favourable or unfavourable to coloured people?'

Substantial majorities identified the Churches and the Labour Party as well disposed towards coloured people; most respondents considered the mass media to be either neutral or favourable. But when they were asked about specific types of people (for example, old people and people living in new houses) the most common response was that such people were unfavourable; the only exception to this was when they were asked about young people: a majority considered young people to be either favourably disposed or else neutral.

The pattern of replies was very much the same for all sections of the sample. The main exceptions to this uniformity were that a substantial majority of Bradford respondents felt that their local newspapers were favourably disposed, and in Lambeth and Wolverhampton more people saw the Conservative Party as against rather than for coloured people.

It is sometimes argued that hostility towards coloured immigrants is based primarily on the fact that they are immigrants and that there is much more acceptance on a basis of equality for coloured people born in Britain. In order to test this the 30% of the sample who said they had less sympathy for coloured immigrants than for whites living in similar conditions were asked if they would still feel this way towards coloured people born and brought up in this country. This proviso did, in fact, substantially shift people's views; only one-third of the original 30% persisted in their initial attitudes, while slightly over half (52%) felt that then their feelings towards the two underprivileged groups would be the same; in other words, only 10% of the total sample carried their hostility to coloured people to the point where they felt able to dismiss place of birth or upbringing as irrelevant.

As for the first generation, respondents were asked (at the end of the interview) to suggest any actions which coloured people in Britain could undertake to improve their position. Some of the answers were defeatist or negative (e.g. 11% of the sample said they could not think of anything that would help, 7% that they should go back to their own country, and 3% that there was nothing coloured people could do—any improvement depended upon a change in the outlook of white people). However, most respondents readily offered advice. The most frequent suggestions were that they should adopt a more English way of life, they should be cleaner, they should work harder, give up living in overcrowded conditions, and spend more time educating themselves.

In an attempt to find out what was meant by 'adopt a more English way of life' the 25% respondents who gave this reply were then asked: 'In what ways do you mean?' Some of the supplementary answers were not very enlightening; for example, one-half of the 25% merely said: 'They should live the way we do', or 'They should raise their standards of living'. Most of the other half explained that what they had in mind was that coloured immigrants should adopt English moral standards ('moral' was used in the context of both washing and sexual behaviour), eat English food, and wear English clothes.

But conformity does not guarantee acceptability, at least as far as respondents' attitudes towards the processes of immigration were concerned. Slightly over half of the white respondents thought that there should be different conditions of entry for white as opposed to coloured immigrants and this tendency was particularly marked among working-class people and those aged over 45.

Those who felt there should be special regulations for coloured immigrants were asked for their reasons. Answers to earlier questions might have led one to expect that the advocates of such distinctions would ask for educational tests or an understanding of British culture. A few did, in fact, reason along these lines, but the great majority of them wanted special regulations on the grounds that coloured immigrants (unlike white immigrants) strained the social services, brought in disease, were dirty, or competed for jobs.

In Lambeth the threat of overcrowding and the competition for jobs dominated the replies. Neither of these was of outstanding importance to Bradford respondents; instead, they dwelt on the diseases brought in by coloured immigrants.

Finally, a number of questions were asked which were designed to test the respondent's subjective appreciation of the significance of the situation and the extent to which he felt personally affected.

We consider this second question particularly important since it is commonly argued that a sense of betrayal and overwhelming concern is endemic in all areas into which migration has taken place. We were interested to find that only 14% of the total sample in the five boroughs said they regarded it as a very important part of their problems and that over two-thirds of the sample said, with varying degrees of emphasis, that it was of no importance.

Table 28.22. Attitudes towards the presence of coloured people as affecting personal problems

	Five boroughs %	National sample %
Very important	14	9
Quite important	18	16
Not important	38	37
Not at all important	30	37
Don't know	—	1
	100	100

The 32% of the five-borough sample who said that this was one of the important problems facing them were then asked to specify in what way it was important. Three main worries were expressed: that the presence of coloured people was bad for the neighbourhood (31%), that their presence would lead to intermarriage (25%), and that they would become a local majority (22%).[5] Sixteen per cent considered that the newcomers presented a problem because they were likely to place a strain on the local social services. In this case, the pattern of responses was not affected by age, except that those over 55 were less inclined to see this as a personal problem—though the older group were more inclined to worry about the deterioration of the neighbourhood than the younger respondents and anxiety about the competition for scarce social resources was felt almost exclusively by those under 45. But, although there was no difference between respondents who had coloured neighbours, those who lived within five minutes' walk, and those who lived within half an hour, there were very sharp differences between one town and another. In Wolverhampton, where 75% of respondents claimed to live within walking distance of coloured people, over half of all respondents also said that they found the presence of coloured people an important problem. The proportion of Lambeth respondents living near coloured people who found their presence important approached this level, but in Nottingham less than a quarter of respondents with coloured people within walking distance found that their presence presented a problem, and this was fewer than the percentage of Nottingham residents not living near them who found their presence worrying. It is clear that the total five-borough percentages give a misleading picture of the relationship between proximity and hostility; social and geographical distinctions between towns are stronger determinants for attitudes than proximity.

Asked to estimate the future importance of colour 'in the way people feel about each other', nearly 60% of the five-borough sample thought that colour *would* remain important. This percentage was nearly identical with that obtained in the national sample. Again, there was some local variation. Wolverhampton respondents tended to be most pessimistic, working-class respondents were also likely to be pessimists, and respondents who had worked with coloured people thought that colour would become unimportant more frequently than those who had not.

(c) Conclusions

But does the evidence from this study, taken as a whole, justify us in being as optimistic as some of the responses to our questionnaire were? There are a number of items on both sides of the balance sheet which we need to take into account when weighing the issue up.

On the criteria used it would seem that in the five boroughs the adult white population contained two extreme groups: 10% whose attitudes towards coloured immigrants were highly prejudiced, and a much larger minority, 35%, whose attitudes were almost or entirely free of prejudice. The 10% of highly prejudiced whites were flanked by a further 17% who stopped short of unconditional hostility, while the 35% of tolerant whites were supported by a further 38% of the population whose views were predominantly free of colour prejudice.

On the variables studied in this survey it would appear that the

10% registering extreme hostility was spread through all sections of the white population—men and women, young and old, middle class and working class, Conservative and Labour supporters, council tenants and private tenants, and so on. There were some marginal differences between the various groups and one can feel reasonably certain that the incidence of prejudice is below average among women, among the young, and among those who have received full-time education at least to a Sixth Form standard.

The most striking differences, however, between the 10% and their fellows was found in the psychological field; the highly prejudiced minority turned out to be people much more prone than others to an authoritarian approach to life. The two distinctive characteristics of this approach are an exaggerated need to submit to authority and acute hostility towards any outgroups; both attitudes 'spring from underlying hostility towards ingroup authorities, originally the parents. The individual strives to keep this hostility in check by overdoing in the direction of respect, obedience, gratitude towards the ingroup authorities and by displacing the underlying hostility towards these authorities on to outgroups.'[6]

If this theory is accepted then the findings of the survey have various policy implications. Perhaps the most important of these is that attempts to improve race relations, while they must not ignore the views of the 10% minority, should see them for what they are—irrational 'solutions' to personality inadequacies which would persist without regard to the policies adopted.

Real concern should be with the 55% of the population whose criticism is specific and limited. In some cases this springs from error or misunderstanding—for example, that there are already over five million coloured immigrants in the country, or that coloured immigrants as a group are abnormally high beneficiaries of the Welfare State. In other instances, criticism is generated by a relative assessment of the environment—the competition for, for example, decent housing, school places, hospital beds. A reduction in this competition might lead, at least among the 'in-between' 55%, to a lessening of white criticism.

2. THE FINDINGS IN PERSPECTIVE

Before going on to relate Dr. Abrams' findings to the conclusions and recommendations for further action with which this report will end, it might be useful to try to place his findings in the context of the broad outline picture given in Part I of British society and the dynamic elements in its response to newcomers, to relate them to previous findings about attitudes towards coloured people in Britain, and finally—but very briefly—to some relevant evidence from the far more extensive investigations that have been made in the United States.

A favourite simile for the sample survey of attitudes is the snapshot: by which those who use it imply that it discloses attitudes frozen at one point in time and thus may be chiefly of historical value. An additional objection is that attitudes expressed in the interview situation cannot be related to behaviour; what the harassed housewife on the doorstep says to the plausible lady in the pretty hat does not correspond with what she does once the door is shut.

This drawback has been documented in a series of studies: LaPiere and his Chinese couple are too well known (and too dated) to bear quoting again; a similar effect has been described more recently by Kutner, Wilkins, and Yarner, using telephoned and written requests for bookings.[7] In this case restaurant owners who declined to make reservations for racially mixed couples had in fact in most cases already served them.

But to point to these deficiencies is not to suggest that the findings of surveys of opinion (like snapshots) should be shut in an album and forgotten. On the contrary, once their strength and weaknesses are understood better use can be made of the findings— and this involves first establishing the nature and components of the phenomenon that is being examined.

As Dr. Abrams has hinted, several disparate elements are subsumed under the label prejudice. It is common practice to distinguish at least three dimensions.[8] First, the element that derives from the personality system of the individual concerned—or, in terms of the approach employed in its study, the psychological aspect. Particular emphasis was placed on this approach in a number of investigations conducted immediately after the Second World War; T. W. Adorno's study, *The Authoritarian Personality*, is the best known example.[9] Ideally, an approach which proposes an examination of the individual's childhood, his relations with his family, his frustrations, and the factors which might lead him to displace his aggression on to a scapegoat group demands extensive unstructured interviewing over a long period. And this technique has been employed on a number of occasions—by Bettelheim and Janowitz[10] in the United States and by J. H. Robb in his pioneer study of working-class anti-Semitism in Britain.[11] But there are drawbacks to this technique; the depth interview cannot be applied to large samples and the subjective element in the interviewing means that it is difficult to repeat the study. In the circumstances the single straightforward interview with standardized schedule can, as Dr. Abrams has shown, elicit valuable information about the broad contours of personality configuration and relate them to expressed attitudes—even if it is too generalized and unsubtle an instrument to elucidate the underlying processes of personality formation and development.

But the value of studies addressed to the personality system is ultimately limited, for present purposes: in their Sparkbrook study Rex and Moore concluded that this approach was inadequate for their purposes:

because we were concerned to explain the behaviour not of a minority but of the majority of the host community. Moreover, we had to explain why people who had not in the past shown racial prejudice began to do so in a new social situation. We therefore thought it necessary to explain this prejudice not in terms of the personality system but in terms of the social system, that is, in terms of a structure of social relations.[12]

The focus of this approach through the relationships between people performing roles within social institutions tends to fall particularly on the relationship between attitudes and behaviour, and here, as we have already suggested, the survey of attitudes may have limitations. The evidence from other studies suggests that expressed attitudes predict behaviour only to a very limited degree and that changes in the social situation or the roles that individuals perform override the predispositions which may be expressed in answers to questions about opinion.[13] For example, trade unionists who accept integration in their capacity as workers may simultaneously resist it as householders.

These hypotheses are susceptible of measurement by survey techniques, and it seems clear from a number of studies that the location within the social structure of the individual, whether measured in straightforward class terms, or in a status hierarchy— for example, one derived from educational achievement—is one powerful factor in changing attitudes[14] and that attitudes are substantially modified when the class standing of subject and object are similar.[15] This last finding has particularly important implications for integration programmes.

The final dimension of prejudice that we need to consider is the cultural. By this, we mean the set of values to which every individual in society subscribes, to some degree; which are inculcated by education and upbringing; and which implicitly affect behaviour in certain social situations. The most relevant elements in this context derive from Britain's imperial past and from certain linked assumptions about the biological and cultural superiority of the white man (which were discussed in Part I). But other culturally-transmitted values—for example, about the proper degree of contact with neighbours or strangers, about child upbringing, and about the existence of a class hierarchy and the individual's place within it—can also be relevant in determining what attitudes are expressed towards newcomers about whom there is uncertainty or anxiety. These have been drawn upon to support a theory of race relations derived from a historical perspective based on immigration, rather than race relations.[16]

In this area the questionnaire approach is particularly relevant, since what is being measured is beliefs; but, with the important exceptions of a comparative study of anti-Semitism[17] and Dr. Abrams' investigation, less work than might be expected has been done in this field.

Finally, it is important to stress that although it is possible to distinguish a number of different elements within the general phenomenon of racial prejudice, these strands are overlapping, mutually reinforcing, and often find expression in a single action. For example, stereotypes about coloured newcomers which are essentially culturally derived become embedded in the individual's own system of values, may play an important role in the development of his personality, and will then be employed as a rationalization of the treatment he gives to a coloured man in an encounter. So if the concepts are in theory distinct, operationally they often merge. However, it is the experience of American investigators that it is the social dimension which exercises the maximum influence over behaviour and it is on this sector that remedial action needs to be concentrated. For example, culturally-derived hostility among Americans from the Deep South towards working on equal terms with Negroes in the Armed Forces disappeared when such work became part of their military duties.[18] And individuals predisposed towards hostility to Negroes for personality reasons (authoritarianism) express that hostility when the social situation permits it, but suppress it in situations where it is unacceptable.[19] In this sense, the old saying is quite untrue: men's hearts *can* be changed by passing laws. Evidence over time from opinion polls shows that in the Deep South attitudes towards Negroes have become consistently more favourable as Civil Rights legislation has broken down discriminatory barriers between the races. As Robin Williams has commented, prejudice may be endemic in American society but most individuals carry it at low temperature.[20]

Against this background, what other evidence can we draw on for clues to the development of attitudes on this issue in Britain? Two studies exist from before the Second World War;[21] they are now of historical interest only, but it is worth mentioning that they both revealed marked degrees of ethnocentrism and aversion. A once famous study conducted for the C.O.I. was initially interpreted to suggest that a third of the population were actually prejudiced against coloured people;[22] but the data are patchy and the situation in which they were gathered bears no resemblance to present circumstances; for respondents immigration was a hypothetical not a real proposition.

Apart from Robb's study of anti-Semitism the systematic investigation of attitudes towards coloured people began with Banton's *White and Coloured* (the fieldwork was carried out in 1956).[23] Banton found a widely-diffused norm of tolerance, and explained such discrimination as occurred in terms of the uncertainty generated by the arrival of the immigrants. Culturally-derived stereotypes certainly existed, but 'they are not articles of faith'. Banton's findings suggest that those reactions deriving from the social structure had not yet come into play (and in fact, his sample was drawn chiefly from areas which had not yet experienced contact with coloured people). But it is interesting that his findings suggested that a residue of 10% of respondents existed who rigidly adhered to belief in the inferiority of coloured people. We shall meet this untalented tenth again.

In 1958 the disturbances in Nottingham and Notting Dale stimulated the Gallup organization into conducting a survey of attitudes, and these data were dexterously re-analysed by Mrs. Glass.[24] The basic findings on the extent of prejudice, with Dr.

Abrams's findings given for comparative purposes, are shown in Table 28.23.

Table 28.23. The extent of prejudice, 1958 and 1968

	1958 Glass: Gallup %	1968 Rose: Abrams %
Tolerant	19·4	35
Tolerant-inclined	31·2	38
Prejudiced-inclined	36·8	17
Prejudiced	12·6	10

It will be seen that the proportion of those found to be prejudiced is surprisingly similar. Mrs. Glass also isolated a number of variations within the overall sample: there was a strong association between tolerance and contact; young women were the most tolerant group of all (young men the least) and the Midlands displayed the greatest regional incidence of intolerance. Some of these findings still held good ten years later.

It is also possible, using the 1958 data as a baseline and drawing on information from subsequent polls, by the Gallup organization, other opinion research bodies, and independent investigators, to look at the evolution of attitudes on certain issues over time. Some topics have persisted in importance throughout the decade; they could be roughly divided into three categories—those that tap general attitudes on various aspects of the question, those that measure response to issues that affect the individual personally, in one capacity or another, and those that ask for respondents' opinions on policy issues or matters of fact, and predictions for the future. In the American evidence there are clear signs that respondents are prepared to accept for others developments which they are not able to contemplate for themselves. This gap is, of course, another glimpse of the famous American dilemma, the existence of which has been confirmed (in a modified form) through tests using attitude survey data.[25]

Unfortunately the British data are rather uneven; different questions were asked at different times and rather different approaches seem to have been employed. Nevertheless it is possible to assemble sufficient data to enable us to look at a number

Table 28.24. Changing attitudes on race relations, 1958–68

		Banton 1958	Gallup 1958	Gallup 1961	Gallup 1964	Hill 1964	O.R.C. 1960	Gallup 1968
A. Situations (personal and impersonal)								
1. Do you object to working with a coloured man?	Yes	29			29	22	17	17
	No	71			61	76	79	72
	D/k				10	2	3	11
2. Should coloured people be allowed to compete for jobs?	Yes		48	60				57
	No		37	29				33
	D/k		15	11				10
3. Would you move if coloured people moved in next door?	Yes		9	11				19
	No		70	50				31
	Might		21	33				43
	D/k, etc.		—	6				7
4. Should coloured people be allocated council housing?	Yes		34					44
	No		54					46
	D/k		12					10
5. Do you object to the idea of coloured children at your child's school?	Yes	7	9					12
	No	81	84					80
	D/k	12	7					8

Table 28.24. (cont.)

B. Policy	Banton 1958	Gallup									
1. What kind of immigration policy?		1958	May 1961	Oct. 1961	Nov. 1961	1963	1964	1965*	Mar. 1968*	Apr. 1968†	Apr. 1968†
Free entry	37	21	21	12	21	19	10	5	6	3	1
Control	53	65	73	76	62	70	88	88	90	91	95
D/k	10	14	6	12	17	11	2	7	4	6	3

	Gallup					
2. Is the situation getting better or worse?	August 1964	November 1965	December 1965	January 1966	August 1967	April 1968
Better	24	14	18	19	13	6
Worse	26	43	39	33	45	55
Same	41	31	33	37	33	32
D/k	9	12	10	11	9	7

* Do you agree with proposals for further control?
† Are controls too stringent?

Source:
We wish to acknowledge the courtesy of National Opinion Polls, the Gallup organization, and Opinion Research Centre for making available material for this table and Table 28.25.

of topics under the three main heads given above over time. These deal with work, neighbourhood, school, immigration policy, and predictions. (See Table 28.24.)

Although it is not spectacular, there seems to be a trend for general views on major policy issues affecting the individual to become more favourable: but when respondents are asked to consider situations in which they are personally concerned they have been inclined over the ten years to express less favourable views— with the important exception of workplace association. Respondents are also becoming increasingly apprehensive about the future of race relations, and inclined to support stricter immigration policy.

It is interesting to compare this evidence with similar findings from the United States. Relevant material for the period up to 1965 has recently been collected:[26] it shows that both where values are concerned and where social contact is involved opinion has become steadily more tolerant over the past twenty years on every issue—homes, jobs, and civil rights generally. This holds good for all regions, age groups, and levels of education, and it has persisted in spite of growing apprehension about the future of race relations and resistance to the increasingly hard line taken by Negro protest groups.

This increased pessimism, which also seems to be gathering speed in Britain, after some fluctuation—and even a turn for the better during Roy Jenkins' Home Secretaryship—is obviously a reflection of events and the publicity given to them (although we have suggested earlier that there were also other factors at work). It relates directly to one of the main objections that can be raised to the use of the results of such studies for predictive and policy purposes: namely, that the situation that is being measured is so volatile that the findings can only be applied in the immediate context to which they relate—or, to continue with photographic metaphor, that surveys 'freeze' a scene which is in a state of continuous flux, within which there are numerous short-term variations created from day to day by public events.

Fortunately, the opinion poll material can help us again. The greatly increased interest in domestic race relations in 1968 led to the taking of a considerable number of polls, both before and after Enoch Powell's speech (see Chapter 31). For policy issues and predictive questions it is possible to trace changes in opinion over weeks, rather than months. In this instance, the issue concerned is that of legislation against discrimination and the areas to which it should apply.

Table 28.25. Attitudes towards legislation against discrimination

		O.R.C. 1967	Gallup early April 1968	O.R.C. 1968	Gallup late April 1968	N.O.P. May 1968
1. Do you approve of legislation against discrimination?*	Yes	58	42	53	30	44
	No	31	29	36	46	44
	D/k	10	29	11	24	12
2. Should it affect jobs?	Yes	48	40	44		58
	No	44	47	51		34
	D/k	8	13	5		8

		O.R.C. 1967	Gallup early April 1968	O.R.C. 1968	Private	Council
3. Should it affect housing?	Yes	44	34	39	41	51
	No	45	49	53	51	40
	D/k	10	17	8	8	9

		Gallup 1967	Gallup early April 1968		Gallup late April 1968	
4. How much danger do you think there is of race riots?	Serious	15	23		22	
	Some	41	48		52	
	None	36	22		21	
	D/k	9	7		5	

* After April 1968: Do you approve of the Race Relations Bill?

These findings certainly show that opinion is subject to modification in the light of events, but not that it is spectacularly volatile. But these questions in themselves, although useful in explaining the general profile of opinion, do not enable us to examine specific elements within the profile: it is true that by aggregating the answers to questions asked at this time it is possible to derive some indication of the level of prejudice—and here it is of particular interest that National Opinion Polls found a 'hard core' of 12% who expressed hostile views on all the attitude questions—but to establish whether changes in the political atmosphere have now given cause to question Dr. Abrams' findings it would be necessary to look more closely at the individual components of prejudice.

Fortunately, the Gallup Poll taken immediately after Enoch Powell's speech (of which 96% of respondents had heard)

employed a schedule sufficiently elaborate to enable this to be
done. Four variations that proved to be significant in the Abrams
investigation can be isolated: age, class, educational level, and
contact, or friendship, with immigrants. A further variable
(political loyalty) does not yield results of any significance; instead
we will look at another—respondents' assessment of the likeliness
or improbability of race riots in Britain (we have labelled these
groups 'pessimists' and 'optimists' respectively). These variables
can be examined in turn, in relation to their effect on answers to
four questions: an assessment of the benefits or disadvantages of
immigration and reaction to contact in the neighbourhood, workplace, and school. We should add that in the sample as a whole
three-quarters agreed with Enoch Powell's speech but two-fifths
(and an absolute majority among Labour supporters) supported
the Race Relations Bill as drafted, and a majority favoured some
form of legislation against discrimination.

The results show that age, class position, and level of education* had a significant effect in most cases on views expressed on
general issues—but not on the reaction to the prospect of coloured
neighbours, and in the case of coloured children in school only
among the old (to whom the issue is presumably least relevant).
Also, that workplace (but not neighbourhood) contact also
modified attitudes in a favourable direction and friendship did so
more decisively. But by far the most clear-cut association is
between a tolerant attitude and 'optimism' about the future. It is
not quite clear why this should be so: an examination of the
'optimistic' group shows that they are rather more educated,
younger (they are likelier to be found in the 21–35 age group),
and slightly more prone to be drawn from the white-collar end of
the class spectrum. They are also likelier to have coloured friends.
They are *less* likely to be Conservative supporters and (possibly)
more likely to be Liberals. But none of these characteristics are
very marked: in all these directions the group is near average.
They also differ from the most educated (taken as a group) and
the white-collar respondents as a whole on other political issues—
they are far more prone to support a strong line by the Government on Rhodesia and to advocate a bombing pause in Vietnam.
The possibility is that this question may have tapped what is

* It is likely that three different aspects of the same phenomenon are being measured
here—in other words, the very poor have least schooling and are also likely to be
largely made up of old people.

Table 28.26. Attitudes towards the benefits or disadvantages of immigration and contact in the neighbourhood, workplace, and school

		All	Selected Comparisons		
			ABC1 class	'Pessimists'	Some coloured friends
	N =	928	297	207	148
1. Do you think that on the whole this country has benefited or been harmed through immigrants coming to settle here from the Commonwealth?	Benefit	16	24	6	33
	Harm	61	54	81	49
	No difference	14	16	8	13
	D/k	9	7	5	6

		All	'Optimists'	Neighbourhood contact now
	N =		194	155
2. If coloured people come to live next door to you would you want to move away or wouldn't you mind?	Yes	19	8	13
	No	31	49	34
	Depends	43	33	40
	Other answers	8	9	13

		All	Educated beyond 16	'Pessimists'	Workplace contact now
	N =		242	207	148
3. If your employer took on coloured people to work with you would you mind or not?	Yes	17	12	32	14
	No	72	78	59	83
	D/k	11	10	13	3

		All	Aged over 65	'Optimists'
	N =		148	194
4. Would you object, or wouldn't you, if there were any coloured children in the same class as your own children at school?	Yes	12	21	3
	No	80	66	89
	D/k	8	13	7

essentially a function of personality rather than social position; 'optimists' may be better capable of rational* assessment of the situation and of containing anxiety and keeping it in perspective. One cannot help recalling here Stouffer's finding in his major

* Though we must not exclude the possibility that there are passive as well as active optimists—whose optimism reflects lack of information.

study of attitudes towards civil liberties and communism, that those both best informed and best disposed towards the maintenance of civil liberties showed least anxiety about the 'Communist conspiracy'.[27]

But the main conclusion to be drawn from the Gallup material is that the wide area of middle ground that existed when Research Services conducted their fieldwork in the winter of 1966–7 still exists. The general concern about the future (shared with their transatlantic confrères) has led respondents increasingly to support restrictive—and if necessary discriminatory—immigration policies. But this anxiety is not necessarily carried over into hardening attitudes towards minorities within our society, though there is a trend towards slight additional avoidance in the neighbourhood.

The final question that we need to ask is whether there are any *broad* explanations, combining all the various elements discussed at the beginning of this chapter, which will explain the various trends exhibited in these findings (both for opinion polls and other survey research) and Dr. Abrams' research.

As we suggested earlier, explanations based purely on the personality structure of individuals are not likely to provide satisfactory overall explanations of the state of race relations—and especially of changes in the social or political situation. Nevertheless, Tumin's findings on the widespread prevalence of authoritarianism and its relationship with rejecting attitudes towards Jews and coloured people are obviously important. And, as we have seen, Dr. Abrams also found a relationship—though not a very strong one—between prejudice (as determined by his P-scale) and authoritarian attitudes.

A second and possibly more promising area of search for hypotheses lies in the social situation and the way in which the newcomer is identified and 'placed' (which may in turn lead to avoidance). Richmond's contention[28] that the coloured man has no assigned place at all in the English class sytem now commands little support: the notion of the immigrant as 'the archetypal stranger', though obviously once of value, also seems less relevant; most respondents now have a clear, if undifferentiated, notion of what kind of a person he is. As we saw, there is some support in Abrams' findings for the view that immigrants are assigned a universal and low position in the class hierarchy: but a more promising approach is the one that splits up the reaction to the newcomer between the various roles he performs. This, essentially, is the technique employed by investigators using the well-tried social distance approach which sets out to measure the degree of proximity which respondents will allow a stranger to attain. In Tumin's investigation, as in the classic American studies, a clear progression was found, ending in almost total rejection of the entry of newcomers into the family unit through marriage. Moreover, it was clear that the extent of rejection was far greater in the case of West Indians than for other minority groups. Further data from the opinion polls, taken together, support a general picture of considerably greater acceptance in one social sphere than in others; as Banton put it: 'integration appears to be proceeding at different rates in diverse social spheres'.[29]

Another line which might turn up explanations is concerned with the actor's own standing in the social system. It has long been a theory among American students of race relations (the evidence for which is comprehensively reviewed in Bettelheim and Janowitz)[30] that those who have experienced rapid change in their social class position, either upwards or downwards, are more liable to hold hostile views towards minority groups than those in a stable situation. In contrast, Dr. Abrams found that those who assessed themselves as having moved upwards did not differ significantly in their attitudes from the rest of the sample.

Another approach singles out those whose subjective identification of their class position differs from the objective reality.

A large literature has grown up around this theme; one major point of departure is the finding that working-class individuals who rate themselves as middle class are more inclined to support the Conservative Party. By extension, it is suggested that these 'status seekers' are more liable to subscribe to a constellation of punitive and authoritarian attitudes.[31] Careful re-examination of the evidence by Nordlinger softened this picture somewhat; he found that strongly-held patriotic and nationalistic attitudes tended to be a characteristic of the group he describes as 'deferentials'—working-class Conservatives who accept their position in the class hierarchy.[32]

Another form of subjective assessment that may affect attitudes towards minorities is the anxiety aroused by the perception that others may have been doing better than one has oneself. This sensation of 'relative deprivation' has been extensively explored by Runciman,[33] and further analysis of the data gathered during his investigation shows that a majority of respondents were inclined to include immigrants in this category of those doing well at the respondent's expense. The age and class profile of those who were particularly insistent on this proportion conforms with that of those inclined to express greater prejudice in the present study.[34]

Finally, there is the respondent's perception of his status in various different social dimensions, and the suggestion that if there is a marked disparity between the levels he has achieved (or to which he is consigned), in differing dimensions this may lead to hostility directed against an out-group or the majority. This phenomenon was labelled by Everett Hughes 'status incongruence';[35] subsequent investigations have evolved the concept of 'status crystallization' to explain the situation that arises when the various dimensions of status are in equilibrium. It is suggested that tensions and hostility that arise when crystallization has not taken place may be displaced on to ethnic minorities.[36]

The final area in which we could look is the general cultural background. Here Tumin's findings on notions about cultural superiority and the persistence of explanations of the 'inferiority' of coloured people in terms of heredity are very suggestive; it argues that these concepts are deeply rooted in our culture and may require extensive action by way of remedial educational programmes to root them out. There is also additional evidence in his study on the prevalence of hostile stereotypes of different ethnic groups, notably Jews and coloured people. One of the most striking findings of Dr. Abrams' study was the persistence of such stereotypes; and on two separate occasions (1961 and 1967) Gallup have established that they are widespread and show little change in the order of importance attached to them. It is of particular interest that these stereotypes cluster round the use made by the newcomers of the welfare state: although 70% of respondents, when questioned by Opinion Research Centre in 1966, were prepared to agree that immigrants should enjoy full rights, their existence suggests a tension between received ideas of 'fairness' and estimates of what is involved in equality at a practical level which might be held to correspond in some respects to Myrdal's 'American Dilemma'.[37]

If there is no single explanation which can satisfactorily account for the dimensions and distribution of prejudice there are obviously several which have helpful elements. Most of these have implications for future policy and for individual conduct: we will revert to them when we come to examine the policy alternatives and make recommendations in our final section.

NOTES TO CHAPTER 28

1. Professor M. Jahoda, Professor M. Banton, Professor J. Gould, Professor H. Tajfel, and the present author.

2. Not all negative, unfavourable attitudes towards a group and its individual members necessarily constitute prejudice. The essence of prejudice lies in the fact that the hostility has its origins not in any realistic assessment of the actual behaviour and the attributes of the group in question but results rather from processes within the bearer of the hostile attitude.

3. Briefly, the authoritarian believes that social problems are created by the intractable malice of anti-social individuals and should be resolved by the firm use of established power.

4. It was found that answers to four of the six statements gave practically all respondents the same authoritarian rating as when replies to all six were used. We therefore drew two types of respondents on these four statements—those who *strongly* agreed with all four authoritarian views, and those who *strongly* disagreed with all four.

5. Compare with 'Enoch Powell's Postbag', *New Society*, 9 May 1968.

6. Nevitt Sanford, 'The Approach of the Authoritarian Personality', in *Psychology of Personality*, J. L. McCary (ed.) (Grove Press, New York, 1956).

7. B. Kutner, C. Wilkins, and P. R. Yarrow, 'Verbal Attitudes and Overt Behavior Involving Racial Prejudice', *Journal of Abnormal and Social Psychology* (July 1952).

8. G. W. Simpson and J. M. Yinger, *Racial and Cultural Minorities: an analysis of prejudice and discrimination* (3rd ed.) (New York, Harper and Row, 1965).

9. T. W. Adorno and others, *The Authoritarian Personality* (New York, Harper, 1950).

10. B. Bettelheim and M. Janowitz, *Social Change and Prejudice, including Dynamics of Prejudice* (1st ed.) (New York, Free Press of Glencoe, 1950).

11. J. H. Robb, *Working Class Anti-Semite* (London, Tavistock Publications, 1954).

12. John Rex and Robert Moore, *Race, Community and Conflict: A Study of Sparkbrook* (London, Oxford University Press, for Institute of Race Relations, 1967).

13. J. D. Lohman and D. G. Reitzes, 'Notes on Race Relations in Mass Society', *American Sociological Review* (November 1954).

14. C. H. Stember, *Education and attitude change* (New York, Institute of Human Relations, 1961).

15. F. R. Westie, 'Negro–White Status Differentials and Social Distance', *American Sociological Review* (October 1952).

16. M. Banton, *White and Coloured* (London, Cape, 1959), and S. Patterson, *Dark Strangers* (London, Tavistock Publications, 1963).

17. M. Tumin, *Ethnocentrism and Anti-Semitism in England, France and Germany* (Forthcoming).

18. S. A. Stouffer et al., *The American Soldier: adjustment during Army life* (Princeton University Press, 1949).

19. T. F. Pettigrew, 'Personality and Socio-cultural Factors in Intergroup Attitudes: a crossnational comparison', *Journal of Conflict Resolution* (Vol. II, 1958), p. 29.

20 R. M. Williams, *Strangers Next Door: Ethnic Relations in American Communities* (Englewood Cliffs, Prentice Hall, 1964).

21. R. T. La Piere, 'Race Prejudice: France and England', *Social Forces* (Vol. VII, 1928), p. 106; and S. P. Adinarayan, 'The Psychology of Colour Prejudice', *British Journal of Psychology* (1941).

22. Central Office of Information, 1951—referred to in A. H. Richmond, *The Colour Problem* (Harmondsworth, Penguin Books, 1955), p. 240.

23. M. Banton, *White and Coloured*, op. cit.

24. Ruth Glass, *Newcomers: the West Indians in London* (London, Allen & Unwin, for Centre for Urban Studies, 1960).

25. F. R. Westie, 'The American Dilemma: an empirical test', *The American Sociological Review* (Vol. 30, no. 4, August 1965).

26. M. A. Schwartz, *Trends in White Attitudes towards Negroes* (Chicago, University of Chicago National Opinion Research Center, 1967).

27. S. A. Stouffer, *Communism, Conformity and Civil Liberty* (New York, Doubleday, 1955).

28. Richmond, op. cit.

29. M. Banton, *Race Relations* (London, Tavistock Publications, 1967).

30. Bettelheim and Janowitz, op. cit.

31. A. Silver and R. McKenzie, 'Conservatism, Industrialism and the Working Class Tory in England', in R. Rose (ed.), *Studies in British Politics* (London, Macmillan, 1966).

32. E. Nordlinger, *The Working Class Tories* (London, McGibbon & Kee, 1967).

33. W. G. Runciman, *Relative deprivation and social justice: a study of attitudes to social inequality in twentieth-century England* (London, Routledge & Kegan Paul, 1966).

34. W. G. Runciman and C. Bagley (to be published in *Sociology*, 1969).

35. Everett C. Hughes, 'Dilemmas and Contradictions of Status', *American Journal of Sociology* (Vol. L, 1945), pp. 353–9.

36. C. Bagley, 'Relative Deprivation and the Working-Class Racialist', Institute of Race Relations *Newsletter* (June 1968).

37. G. Myrdal, *An American Dilemma* (New York, Harper, 1944).

29 The Descending Spiral

The picture given in Part VII of the climate of opinion on race relations in England in 1967 and 1968 might suggest that considerable room for manœuvre existed for policy-makers—especially in the field of employment. In practice, the politicians have perceived themselves as men hemmed in by pressures almost too great to withstand. The perception of undifferentiated hostility is almost universal and extends to all shades of opinion. Opponents of continued immigration justify their advocacy of extreme—even desperate—measures by claiming that the patience of the British people has worn too thin for endurance. And the Government argues, in defence of the Commonwealth Immigrants Act of 1968, that the situation has become dangerously overheated and needs to be cooled down by the application of new measures of control.

In Part VIII we first propose to chart and as far as possible assess these and other developments in policy after the change of Home Secretary at the end of 1967 (Chapter 29). But although the policies adopted by central government are a crucial determinant in the evolution of race relations, they are not the only element in the situation. Other factors need to be considered, some of whose effects are more open to objective (even quantified) assessment than the activities of politicians. We have chosen to examine two: the projected growth of the coloured population of this country (Chapter 30) and the progressive effects of immigration on the economy (Chapter 31). The first has been elevated into the main determining factor in the situation by some politicians: for this reason, and also because the estimates given vary so very widely,* we have thought it right to provide our own estimates. But this should not be taken as an endorsement of the view that the mere numerical proportion among us at the end of the century who possess coloured skins will be in itself the crucial—or even a major—factor in the total situation. Secondly, we will provide an assessment of the economic consequences of immigration—a topic on which there has been a good deal of dispute, and which has also been presented as crucial to future policy on this issue. Finally,

---

* Those given by Enoch Powell, for example. Between April and November his estimate shrank by no less than two million.

in Chapter 32, we will try to summarize and evaluate the significance of those and other elements in the situation and offer a synthesis of the various relevant features in the current debate on the eradication of inequality in our society generally. In doing so, we shall be trying to rediscover the lost freedom of manœuvre and to provide a secure footing from which constructive recommendations for future policy on race relations can be launched.

In the four years, since 1964, for which immigration and race relations have been accepted as one of the range of policy issues occupying a permanent place in political debate, the terms on which discussion of the issue has been conducted have radically altered. 'All I know', said Enoch Powell, ending his notorious speech of April 1968, 'is that to see, and not to speak would be the great betrayal.'[1] Since 1964, at any rate, the right to speak (though perhaps not the capacity to see) has been generally conceded to politicians and publicists. The doubts about the legitimacy of public discussion of the topic which were widely felt—mainly by Conservative politicians—before the general election of 1964 have evaporated. But, granted that such discussion is permissible—even essential—on what terms is it to be undertaken? The significance of the 1966 Election campaign seemed at the time to be that genuine differences of opinion over policy on a difficult and controversial topic could be debated within certain understood limits. And, as we have seen, this *de facto* consensus was still in working order when Roy Jenkins left the Home Office at the end of 1967. The breaking down of this tacit understanding, which occurred during 1968, was not merely the reflection of increased concern about the subject. In addition, a willingness emerged to abandon restraints on the manner in which the debate was to be conducted. It was not merely that the solutions now proposed were those that had only previously been heard from street-corner orators; the style in which they were advocated was also one previously the prerogative of Sir Oswald Mosley. If the policies and practices of politicians have been one important determinant affecting the development of race relations, the immigration may in turn have left a mark on the manner in which politicians carry on their business.

One parallel suggests itself straight away. By 'playing the Orange card'—that is, by deliberately inflaming the anxieties of Ulster Protestants over the Home Rule issue—Lord Randolph

Churchill helped to precipitate a process which led to the dislocation of British political life and finally to violent conflict. His successors, in broadening the area of debate, in the way which has been seen in the last year, profess concern with a similar objective —the preservation of the British polity. In doing so they may have precipitated a similar process. Thus, through a phenomenon well known to social scientists, the self-fulfilling prophecy, the prophets of doom achieve precisely the object they wish—consciously, at least—to avoid. The Tiber may indeed flow with blood—but its source will first have been polluted.

But if the manner in which renewed debate on race relations in 1968 was conducted exhibited some striking new characteristics, the content of the debate remained much the same. The change lay chiefly in the balance of emphasis within the discussion. All the themes whose development we have traced in earlier chapters still preoccupied politicians: the place of the coloured minorities in our society and the terms on which they are to be admitted to it; the extent to which the Government is justified in intervening on their behalf and the rationale and technique of such an intervention. But the shake given to the kaleidoscope by the events of the spring of 1968 caused these pieces to fall into a different pattern. And although most of the arguments were familiar from earlier stages in the debate some of them took on a fresh significance in their new context. A specific example concerns the proposals in the Conservative Manifesto of 1966. In the context of the Election campaign and the manner in which it was conducted, these proposals lent themselves to rational debate on immigration policy. After April 1968, they assumed a quite different significance, in terms of the way in which the debate was then being conducted.

The argument on policy is still working itself out at the time of writing, but these realignments make it essential to consider events over the past year in some detail. This will involve journalism rather than considered analysis, with all the fallibility of perspective that this implies. But these events are necessary evidence, taken together with the background information already presented, if we are to reach any conclusions on the interaction between race relations and the political process.

These further developments still lay in the future in January 1968 when the new Home Secretary, James Callaghan, delivered a lengthy analysis of policy on race relations to an audience convened by the Institute of Race Relations. In an extended preview of the forthcoming Race Relations Bill, he reaffirmed the Government's intention to introduce a measure which would be comprehensive in scope, but indicated that voluntary machinery would be given a substantial role to play in the employment field. Housing, though a field which 'lends itself more readily to conciliation than to enforcement', was a proper area for intervention by the law, whose chief function was to ensure 'that these citizens who are now part of this country, but who are readily identifiable as a minority group should be given clear evidence of the basis on which our society is founded'.[2]

This section of the Home Secretary's speech was in direct line of descent from those of his predecessor; as was Callaghan's relative lack of emphasis on the question of immigration as such. He also emulated his predecessor by attempting to lay down a formula for future policy; his aim would be to create a society in which 'every citizen shares an equal right to the same freedoms, the same responsibilities, the same opportunities and the same benefits'.[3] Only one month later the same Home Secretary, in tacit coalition with the Shadow Cabinet, introduced into Parliament on an emergency footing an illiberal and arguably irresponsible and opportunistic measure intended to remove from one identifiable minority a basic benefit of British citizenship. As evidence of the basis on which our society is founded the Commonwealth Immigrants Act of 1968 could not have been more damning.

The explanation of this apparent *volte face* lies in part in processes which had already been set in motion before Callaghan became Home Secretary. We have examined some of them in Chapter 27. The commitment to the extension of legislation against discrimination entered into by Roy Jenkins in the summer of 1967 had been followed by an elaborate exercise in consultation, involving both the official agencies—the Race Relations Board and the National Committee for Commonwealth Immigrants— and the voluntary agencies and immigrant organizations. This process, which necessarily involved a good deal of confidential discussion, was later the subject of a certain amount of misunderstanding.*

The immediate effect was to transfer the debate on legislation to a different plane where progress was measured in terms of

* This involved a confusion over whether the Conservative Opposition had been formally consulted and if so, the status of the person consulted.

amendments to drafts and could of its nature receive little or no publicity. And in the interim, proposals for action in fields related to but not covered by the draft bill—for example, suggestions that the Government should intervene directly in certain aspects of local authority housing policy—tended to be shelved on the grounds that the outcome of the consultations on legislation must not be anticipated. To put it in terms of an analogy drawn from urban environment, there was a form of planning blight. This is not to suggest that the consultations were fruitless. On the contrary, considerable progress was made by way of eliminating proposals in the original draft which might have proved unsatisfactory in practice—for example, the continued presence in the legislative procedures of the Attorney General, the necessity for whose consent to prosecutions under the 1965 Act had proved to be an awkward stumbling block. But these concessions could not be publicized; and lack of visible progress meant that the element of increased confidence which might have resulted from an important initiative in the area of racial discrimination could not come into play.

At the same time, the pressure for further action on the other main front, that of immigration, was steadily increasing. At the end of 1967, *The Times* began to intensify its campaign for a form of exemption from control to be conferred on citizens of the white Dominions—Canada, Australia, and New Zealand. And on 9 February Enoch Powell made another major speech on the subject, in Walsall. He told his audience, in a significant phrase, that 'you and I might as well be living in Central Africa for all they know about our circumstances'.[4] This image of remoteness was only one metaphorical illustration of the theme he and others were later to develop further: the notion that the legislators and the liberals were remote and uncaring in a situation arriving rapidly at crisis point. The other persistent front runner in this campaign, Duncan Sandys, took a further practical initiative. He announced that he intended to introduce a private member's bill containing provision for far tighter restrictions on the entry of immigrants. And when the Shadow Cabinet persuaded him to postpone this step, he was able to obtain ninety signatories to a motion in the same sense and a further half-dozen, all Labour, to an amendment in broadly similar terms.

The main motive force behind this renewed activity was the rapid growth in the number of British citizens of Asian origin entering this country from Kenya as a result of the Kenyanization policy of the Kenyatta Government. Unlike other African governments, the Kenya Government had applied a time-limit of two years from Independence within which aliens had to make their application for citizenship. Legislation passed by the Kenya authorities in 1967 created a situation in which those aliens who had not opted for Kenyan citizenship were permitted to work and live in Kenya only on a temporary basis. Six thousand Asians possessing British citizenship, who were not subject to immigration control, had entered the U.K. in both 1965 and 1966. After the Kenya legislation this figure rose to 1,500 in the month of August 1967 alone, and to 2,661 in September, dropped to 1,334 in November, and built up again to 2,294 in January 1968. The initial reaction in the Home Office, as we have seen, was to watch the situation without commitment.

But the increase both in the numbers entering and in the attention paid to the subject by Sandys and Powell—almost certainly mutually reinforcing factors—compelled a reassessment. Malcolm MacDonald, the Government's Special Envoy to East Africa, was sent to see President Kenyatta and ask for a slackening in the scope and tempo of Kenyanization. He returned empty handed; and although as late as 15 February Lord Stonham was assuring the House of Lords that legislation to control the entry of the Kenyan Asians was unlikely as 'it would remove from them their right to U.K. citizenship and under the U.N. Convention of 1961 we are pledged to avoid any further statelessness',[5] the Cabinet at two meetings on the 20 and 22 February decided to act. They did so by spatchcocking into a bill prepared some time previously, when Jenkins was still Home Secretary, to deal with what the Home Office considered to be anomalies arising in the operation of the Commonwealth Immigrants Act of 1962, a new clause. This extended the operation of that Act to those possessing citizenship of the U.K. and Colonies without a substantial personal connexion with this country—defined in terms of birth-place, of parents or grandparents.[6] The provisions of this bill were announced to the House by the Home Secretary on 22 February and received with general assent on the part of the Opposition, the Shadow Cabinet having met the day before and agreed that some phasing of the entry of Kenya Asians must be introduced. The Parliamentary Labour Party, preoccupied with the third London airport at Stansted, paid little attention to the Government's proposals, and opposition in the Cabinet was apparently confined to three members and not sustained. If the Government misjudged the likely effects of the action they proposed to take, they had some warrant for their myopia in the initial response at Westminster.

The debates that followed were concentrated into three days and notable for their growing bitterness and mounting disapproval of the Government's action. From the outset, there was a great deal of confusion about what was involved. In the first place, there was misunderstanding about the technical aspects of the citizenship element in the situation. The Kenya Asians had in fact already been subject to control between the passage of the Act in 1962 and Independence: their change of situation derived from the Kenya Independence Act of 1963 and was a function of the fact that their passports were subsequently issued by the British High Commissioner, not the Colonial Government, which had ceased to exist. The Home Office took the view that to subject them to control again was merely to extend the principle, already introduced in 1962 and tested in the High Court in 1967, by which United Kingdom citizens with passports issued in the colonies were brought under immigration control.[7] To illustrate this distinction the terms 'belongers' and 'non-belongers', already familiar in nationality law, were employed. This gave a good deal of offence to those who saw the issue in terms of an ideal of British citizenship and did not appreciate that a wedge had already been driven in it by the Act of 1962. The 'grandfather clause', with its unfortunate overtones of segregationist legislation in the American South, also provided a focus for a good deal of resentment. But the important factor was that which distinguished the Kenya Asians from other U.K. and Colonies citizens subject to control—the fact that they had no other form of citizenship to fall back on and would in effect become stateless if deprived of their right of entry to the United Kingdom. This, together with the Government's failure to introduce any provision for an appeals machinery, despite the fact that they had accepted in principle the recommendations of the Wilson Committee as long ago as the previous November, provided the main grounds for informed opposition to the Government's action.

A second school of critics concentrated on the pledge which, it was maintained, had been given to the Kenya Asians at or before the time of Independence when Duncan Sandys was himself

Commonwealth and Colonial Secretary. In an open letter to Sandys, Iain Macleod, who had also served as Colonial Secretary, set out the position quite unequivocally. 'We did it. We meant to do it. And in any event we had no other choice.'[8] This declaration was reinforced by Hugh Fraser (at the Colonial Office in 1960–2) who wrote to *The Times* in the same sense, and by Lord Lansdowne also a former Colonial Office Junior Minister, who assured the Lords that 'I understood, as Mr. Iain Macleod understood, what we were doing. I understood we were making a solemn undertaking to these people.'[9] It is fair to say that these impressive declarations were never satisfactorily refuted, in spite of Duncan Sandys' attempts to prove that there was no specific undertaking given to Parliament or in the legislation. The Home Secretary himself admitted that a tacit understanding existed (even if it had not been spelt out in terms in the Kenya Independence Act—a point which itself attracted criticism) and pleaded *raison d'état*.[10] This caused Lord Foot to reflect that British passports carried the significant phrase 'not to be altered in any way, except only by the British Government'.[11]

The third line of criticism related to the Kenya Asians themselves. It was widely argued that these potential migrants were particularly well adapted to settlement in the U.K.: they were literate, educated, and possessed skills and capital. The implication of this line of argument lay not so much in its rather patronizing suggestion that middle-class migrants should be given priority (which stuck in several radical gullets)[12] as in its relevance to the arguments subsequently advanced by the Government about the strain that they were likely to cause on the social services, and in particular on education. The special status of the Kenya Asians did lead to some suggestions on both sides—notably by Reginald Maudling winding up for the Opposition at Second Reading—that they should be given some form of priority over migrants from other parts of the Commonwealth.

These disparate lines of criticism—the lawyers' concern about statelessness, libertarian anxiety over immigration procedure, sentiment about British citizenship, traditionalist anxiety over broken pledges, and specific concern for the Kenya Asians as such—combined to produce a situation in which the Government barely managed, despite the Opposition front bench's support, to push its legislation through Parliament. In the Lords, where all these streams of criticism flowed together unchecked by the Whips, the Government's Second Reading majority was only twenty-four. The reaction of the press, at first confused and muted, swelled to a crescendo until, at the week-end immediately following the passage of the legislation, *The Times* delivered itself of a thunder-bolt reminiscent in scale and tone of those of 1961. Both major parties were excoriated. 'The Labour Party', *The Times* said, 'now has a new ideology. It does not any longer profess to believe in the equality of man. It does not even believe in the equality of British citizens. It believes in the equality of white British citizens.' And of the Conservative Party *The Times* commented that its great failure was that it had 'failed to stand by the interest of the Constitution'.[13]

In self-defence the Government and its back-bench supporters resorted to three lines of argument. First, it was suggested that the Kenya Asians were merely the tip of an iceberg and that large numbers of other British passport-holders were likely to enter if further controls were not introduced.* The precise figure, cited initially as a million, grew to a million and a quarter and sub-sequently to two million during the course of a week, only to shrink again to a million and a quarter. Secondly, the suggestion was made by the Home Secretary,[14] and reinforced in official briefings, that a grave situation had developed in the country at large, which was now trembling on a knife edge from which it could only be retrieved by an act of major surgery—the amputa-tion of the cause of infection. This argument was supported by no respectable evidence, although a number of *ex parte* statements by local authorities could be and were cited. But it was revealing, in that it provided—by implication at least—an alternative official assessment of the work of the Government's agencies over the three years since they had been established. At times the matter went further; to the fascinated horror of many who heard them, Government back-benchers, urged on by their front bench had by the end of the Lords debate reached a stage of fully fledged advocacy of a white Britain policy.[15] By this, they meant a policy which, in Lord McLeavey's words, involved being 'prepared to stand on our feet and say at least "Britishers come first" '.[16] It was strongly and repeatedly denied during the passage of the legislation

---

* The real significance attached by the Government to the presence of large numbers of potential British passport-holders in the Far East—to whom spine-chilling reference was made by the Lord Chancellor in February—was revealed in November 1968 when the Government declined to review their dual citizenship on the ground that they had no intention of coming to the United Kingdom.

that the control was based on racial grounds. David Ennals informed the House of Commons that 'there are many people who will be entitled under this Bill to admission and who are not white-faced', only to be told by Jo Grimond that this was 'humbug. Anyone who believes that the Bill has been brought in for any other reason than against coloured people coming to this country is really beneath contempt."[17] The Prime Minister told the Archbishop of Canterbury in a long and reasoned defence that 'the criteria for exemption from immigration control are geographical, not racial. The fact that most of those who are exempt from control will be British is simply a consequence of the fact that most of the inhabitants of the U.K. are British.'[18] This statement is only intelligible if the term 'British' is understood to be synonomous with the term 'white'.

In the course of a further defence of the Government's policy later in the year, David Ennals told an audience in Wimbledon that 'successful handling of race relations depends upon three aspects of national policy. First, a positive programme of community action. . . . Secondly, a clear determination by the Government to act administratively and by legislation to ensure equality of treatment. And thirdly, a decisive yet humane approach to immigration control.' The events of February, however, set off a process of cross-infection. The corruption of the Government's judgement in the third area of policy severely limited its capacity to take effective action under the second heading and revealed the inadequacy of action so far embarked upon under the first head.

In personal terms, the passage of the Commonwealth Immigrants Act gravely compromised the position both of the Home Secretary and Ennals himself and hence the credibility of the Government's whole integration programme. A former Liberal parliamentary candidate before entering Parliament as Labour M.P. for Dover in 1964, Ennals had been Chairman of the Executive Committee of the Anti-Apartheid Movement, Treasurer of the South African Freedom Group, a member of the Executive Committee of the Freedom From Hunger Campaign, and a former secretary of the United Nations Association. He had been one of the Labour back-benchers who had openly opposed the Government's White Paper of 1965 and was a signatory to a letter to *The Times* on the subject. But in office, he had displayed the capacity for inter-departmental manœuvre which his predecessor had lacked and found no little difficulty in sustaining the role of spokesman for the Government's immigration policy. The increasing tension between this role and the other task of co-ordinating the various elements in the integration programme strained his adaptability to the limit and increasingly alienated him from his former associates in the Labour Movement. By the time he was moved from the Home Office in October 1968, his position had become increasingly isolated and he had been subjected to attacks from a wide variety of sources, ranging from immigrant organizations to academics. Hostility had reached such a pitch during the passage of the Race Relations Bill that the Home Secretary felt it necessary to intervene directly on his behalf. He said in Committee that Ennals had been 'the victim of a particularly nasty, vicious and mean campaign. People do not realize that he is a true friend to everybody who believes in race relations.'[19] Ennals himself energetically defended his record and that of the Government both in speeches and articles.[20] But after the Kenya Asian episode it was a case of 'never glad confident morning again'.

This alienation was only one of the by-products of the events that scattered the coalition which had come together during the period of Roy Jenkins' Home Secretaryship to link official and voluntary organizations with the Government. The National Committee for Commonwealth Immigrants took most of the strain, since it was in many ways the incarnation of the coalition. The Committee itself, which had at no stage been consulted by the Government despite its official consultative role, teetered on the brink of resignation after the Archbishop of Canterbury had paid two visits to ministers to protest against the terms of the legislation. Eventually, the Committee as an institution decided to remain in operation but individuals on the Committee, on the staff, and on the advisory panels resigned. Some of the latter then came together to assist a new lobbying organization, Equal Rights, which had been set up in the previous December by three members of the N.C.C.I. housing panel and was chaired by the West Indian law don, Roy Marshall. The intention was to mobilize expertise to ensure that the forthcoming legislation against discrimination was as effective and far ranging as possible. A final and equally important element in the situation was the impetus that these events gave to the growing cynicism in immigrant organizations about the intentions of the Government. Informal collaboration had ended with the collapse of C.A.R.D. at the end of the previous year; now benevolent neutrality changed successively to critical abstention and outright hostility.

But the most important immediate effect of the Kenya Asian episode was to provide the opportunity for which Enoch Powell had been waiting. In a situation disturbed by the publicity that these events had received and into which the Government had injected a further element of uncertainty and anxiety about the consequences of immigration, Powell's third major attempt to obtain wide attention for his views was a triumphant success. There was very little in this third speech which differed from the previous two, except in the anecdotes—and even these were only new in the sense that Powell was using them for the first time.[21] The key lay in the timing.

Powell's speech, delivered on 20 April in Birmingham, effectively blanketed in terms of publicity and public attention the introduction of the Race Relations Bill on 9 April. This process illustrated in the most striking way possible the submergence of constructive initiatives by the reimposition of the immigration frame of reference. The Government, in introducing the Commonwealth Immigrants Bill, had recognized that the Race Relations Bill was *en cause* and had at first indicated that it would provide the balancing item in the scales. When critics were not prepared to accept this interpretation, David Ennals had appealed to them not to press their opposition to the Government's action beyond the point of the passage of the Commonwealth Immigrants Act.[22] His intention in doing so was clearly to avoid compromising the legislation to follow. But even if they had been able to do so, the declaratory effects of the Race Relations Bill, on which the Home Secretary set so much store, were already compromised by the processes the Government had themselves set in motion.

The new Bill was in any case something of a disappointment to those who had been involved in the processes that had led up to its introduction. Although courageous in scope—both employment and housing were included, together with all commercial and public services—the enforcement procedures left a good deal to be desired, especially in the field of employment where specific provision was made for voluntary action in advance of statutory consultation. More generally, the Bill contained unsightly clauses permitting employers to operate undefined racial quotas and permitting shipping companies to provide racially segregated cabins and to discriminate against coloured seamen. Moreover, in view of the elaborate consultation that had taken place and the clear advice submitted in the Street Report, the Bill was surprisingly slackly drafted. In the circumstances, the lawyers and other critics who had gathered in the Equal Rights lobby were faced with an elaborate technical exercise in attempting to amend the details of legislation. On the general points of principle their room for manœuvre was severely limited by the changed atmosphere deriving from the events of February. The Government was able in most instances to reply to their criticisms by suggesting that in the current state of public opinion such concessions would be impossible to justify and that the main task was to prevent the Opposition from making inroads on the ground already gained. These political considerations led the Race Relations Board to swallow its private doubts about restrictions on the powers which were to be conferred on it and to issue a public statement in which the new legislation was warmly welcomed. And indeed it was inconceivable that any of those who had been concerned with the preparations for the legislation should now repudiate the results of two years' systematic preparation and lobbying.

The Bill was also the subject of some embarrassment for the Conservative Shadow Cabinet. There were those on both wings of the party who wished to take a clear-cut line. Ronald Bell and a number of right-wing critics argued that the party should reject the new legislation outright; Sir George Sinclair, Nicholas Scott, and a few supporters among liberal Tories argued for conditional acceptance. Ultimately, the Shadow Cabinet decided to move a reasoned amendment accepting the principle of legislation but rejecting this specific Bill. Although this represented a smart step backwards from the line that Quintin Hogg had taken in the expiring laws continuance debate of 1967, this could still be represented as generally consistent with past Conservative policy.

The extent of the impact of Enoch Powell's speech and of his subsequent dismissal from the Shadow Cabinet at the hands of Edward Heath were fully revealed when the Race Relations Bill received its second reading on 23 April. This occasion was dominated by Powell, despite the fact that he did not himself speak. In what was by all accounts a brilliant debating speech Quintin Hogg taxed his colleague with 'flicking cigarette ash in an explosives store' and emphasized that it was the manner rather than the content of the speech which had incurred the disapproval of the Shadow Cabinet. The Conservatives divided the House at the end of the debate but a number of radicals, led by Sir Edward Boyle, did not vote with the Opposition. The general upshot was to throw the Government once more back on the defensive and the debate on the means of relieving discrimination was jeopardized before it had been properly launched by the renewal of the sterile argument on immigration.

There is no space here to trace the details of the passage of the Bill through Parliament, which occupied the House from April to October, and involved thirteen sittings of the Standing Committee and 400 amendments. The Government's critics, acting in part with the assistance of briefings provided by Equal Rights, were able to secure a meagre handful of concessions. The Crown was brought within the scope of legislation and the defence of good faith, in cases where discrimination is practised to promote integration, was deleted. A new general definition of the act of discrimination was also introduced in response to criticism but the last state was in many ways worse than the first. Minor concessions were made in relation to housing and the machinery for investigating complaints of discrimination. On other clauses the concessions were in the opposite direction, notably in the field of employment; Quintin Hogg argued in the intra-party debate still tormenting the Opposition that the Conservative front-benchers had gained sufficient ground in committee to justify not opposing Third Reading. But no less than forty-five Conservative back-benchers disagreed with him and divided the House with the approval of senior members of the back-bench 1922 Committee, to provide an ill-tempered end to the lengthy passage of the Bill through the Commons.

In general, there is no reason to question the sincerity of the Government's intentions in introducing this legislation nor to suppose that the Race Relations Board, which has made good use of its existing inadequate powers, will not be able to make further progress in dealing with discrimination in its new extended capacity. In this respect, John Rex's criticism[23] that the Bill is not only not half a loaf but is barely a crumb seems misjudged. But it is equally clear that an initiative which was intended to provide a sound basis in law and practice for a constructive programme of community action has misfired. By its failure to devise and maintain a credible immigration policy the Government forfeited confidence on every side.

One sign of this lost confidence lay in the re-emergence of a series of extremist organizations which have been briefly discussed in Chapter 21. They had little significance in themselves—and the press who, as in 1964, went hunting for Neofascist affiliations were barking up the wrong tree. In fact, these organizations reflected in a much exaggerated form a generalized anxiety about immigration and its consequences. The Government had apparently contemplated for three years with no intention of taking action the prospective admission of two million (or one million, or one and a quarter million) migrants from all parts of the Commonwealth. Then, in February their presence suddenly became sufficiently threatening to justify rushing through discriminatory legislation. This was clearly not the action of an Administration in control of the situation. It is true that some of this anxiety was sub-rational; there were those who wrote to the *Observer* from Pinner complaining that no one concerned with this subject had personal experience of its consequences, and correspondence was published in other papers with views which were clearly based on those stereotypes we have described in our data on attitudes in Chapter 28. But their anxiety was shared by others who accepted the necessity for fair treatment for coloured Britons—that is, by the majority who supported some form of legislation against discrimination. To have forfeited the confidence of this group was a considerable achievement on the part of the Government. It should be added that anxiety had received legitimation outside the ranks of the Government in speeches such as that of Sir William Carron, shortly to become Lord Carron, who gave his imprimatur to the backstreet anecdotes on exploitation of the Welfare State in the farewell speech as Union Secretary quoted in Chapter 19.

The immigrant organizations, as we have seen, were severely shaken by the introduction of the Commonwealth Immigrants Act. Once it had been passed, it was easy to say that the Government had never meant business when it talked about not permitting second-class citizenship and easy to argue that there was a cyclic pattern of reaction in the Labour Movement from the compromise of 1963 to the White Paper of 1965 to the 1968 Commonwealth Immigrants Act. Labour leaders' judgement seemed in pawn to the prejudices of their followers. In this atmosphere the Race Relations Bill could hardly be expected to recapture lost confidence, particularly since its declaratory effect was already weakened. Moreover, the failure to prosecute Duncan Sandys and Enoch Powell for their speeches, where Michael de Freitas had received a stiff prison sentence, gave rise to a good deal of cynical speculation about the basis on which prosecutions were made. The fact that prosecutions for incitement were undertaken under Section 6 of the 1965 Act, which is concerned with incitement and not discrimination, and that the 1968 Bill did not concern itself with this side of the law, was a point lost on most critics. Coalition tactics had in any event largely lost their appeal with the collapse of C.A.R.D. and in the last year of C.A.R.D.'s activities several individual organizations had been developing a line strongly critical of the Government. West Indian Standing Conference in particular had been broadening its line of criticism from the specific complaints against the police and London Transport to a thorough-going critique of the basis on which they were being invited to participate in British society and the nature of the citizenship offered to them. In a long statement issued after Powell's speech, Standing Conference's Legal Panel argued: 'We are not British; we are citizens of the Commonwealth, not of the British Commonwealth which does not exist.' The Panel added that 'the fiction of the "Mother Country" is to be blamed for the failure of both the British Government and the High Commissioners to respond to their respective duties to black people in Britain at the height of racialist violence and threats'. This broader critique led Standing Conference into temporary alliance with the Indian Workers' Association of Birmingham, representing the Left-Communist Party fraction, and with individual Pakistani militants to form a Black People's Alliance—though at the date of writing this alliance does not seem to have developed a coherent programme for action. Another style of protest was provided by the Indian Workers' Association of Southall. After going through another of the periodic cycles of upheaval caused by internal disputes, the Association were able to mobilize sufficient voting support to ensure the election of a former president, S. S. Gill, to Ealing Borough Council as a Labour representative. This communal intervention in host community politics represented an interesting exception to the general trend of separation from the mainstream of host community politics. The Joint Council for the Welfare of Immigrants, a coalition body set up to oversee the

interests of immigrants arriving at airports and other points of
entry in the British Isles, also broadened its functions to include
participation in the protests against the Government's action in
February. However, the Joint Council's most important function
was to devise a means of implementing the welfare recommendations in the Wilson Committee Report. These were actually being
discussed with the Government at the point when the restrictions
on the Kenya Asians were introduced.

A parallel stream of protest was that directed to certain provisions in the Race Relations Bill. Under the Bill, the National
Committee for Commonwealth Immigrants was to be dissolved
and replaced by a Community Relations Commission. A group of
local liaison officers, led by an Anglican clergyman from the West
Indies, Wilfred Wood, came together to draft a series of proposals
which would have the effect of investing the main responsibility
for the expenditure of official funds in local bodies, not with a
national organization. This initiative, which reflected the disillusionment of many individuals with the notion of direction by a
quasi-official agency, failed to convince the Government. In view
of the strength of the case deployed, this failure reflected the
absence of effective channels of protest with particular clarity. But
official provision was made in the administrative arrangements for
the constitution of the new commission for the inclusion of
representatives of local committees in the new governing body.

Broadly, the attitude of the immigrant leadership towards the
events of 1968 was that they had demonstrated that the organizations would have to devise their own solutions and could no longer
rely on the benevolence of the host community. But the obstacles
in the way of such organizations remained the same as before; the
practical difficulties facing West Indian leadership in particular
had not disappeared. A study conducted on behalf of the United
Nations Institute for Training and Research (U.N.I.T.A.R.)
suggested that the same hostility to the whole concept of leadership
and scepticism about its function in the British situation still
existed. Moreover, those who did exercise such functions oscillated
between various styles of leadership, uncertain of the response both
of their constituents and of the majority.[24]

Nor were the doubts on all sides stilled when the Government
eventually produced proposals for positive intervention from the
centre in the problems of under-privileged inner city areas—the
so-called 'Urban Programme'. This consisted in essence of a

gathering together of various threads in existing Government policy: the educational priority areas (E.P.A.s), introduced as a result of the recommendations in the Plowden Report, the housing priority areas, designated as a matter of administrative practice by the Ministry of Housing and Local Government, and the fifty-seven local authorities receiving grant aid on the basis of the presence of immigrants under Section 11 of the 1966 Local Government Act, amounting in 1967–8 to £1·9 million. These criteria were combined into a new description of 'special social need' applied to the areas affected. In conception, the programme represented the culmination of a series of lines of argument urged on the Government with increasing force throughout its period of office, which were all based on the concept of relieving need rather than defining groups by ethnic origin or other special character-istics.

Yet here again the impact of the programme was blunted. First, by the timing. By launching this new development in the back-wash of the Powell debate, the Prime Minister ensured that it would be seen as a straightforward programme of assistance to immigrant areas, in which the problem to be relieved derived quite simply from the presence of immigrants in those districts. This confusion was worse confounded by the actual terms of the Prime Minister's speech, delivered in Birmingham on 5 May. He said: 'The problem of integration has aggravated many of our inherited difficulties; and all the adjustments necessary to cope with the problem of immigration to assimilate and integrate, are painfully limited by our economic resources.' Hence, 'the load on our education system to say nothing of housing, health and welfare is such that the strictest control is now necessary'—'irrespective of race, colour or national origin', naturally. This 'social problem is presented for nearly sixty of our towns and cities, where the prob-lem of immigrants and their families has made a great social impact': thus, 'a comprehensive examination to find out what additional help is required with particular emphasis on education' will be carried out. Such need as was established might have to be satisfied by 'contribution by more favoured areas to meet the needs of those where the strain of inadequate education and housing provision is greatest'.[25] Local authorities, who had already used the opening provided by the Government's action over the Kenya Asians in February to suggest that Whitehall should step in and relieve them of all responsibility for services affected by or

affecting immigrants, had some ground for hope in this pronouncement. As a result of the further series of Labour defeats in
the May local elections, virtually all the local authorities affected
became Conservative controlled and an element of political
calculation was now added to the other motivations for pressing a
Labour Government to embark on a massive intervention in this
field.

The disillusionment of local authorities was correspondingly
greater when the Home Secretary made his announcement about
the detail of the Urban Programme on 22 July. After a sharp
internal struggle Callaghan had succeeded in retaining the
responsibility for the Programme at the Home Office. In announc-
ing that the Government were prepared to commit £20–£25
million—in additional funds, not (as the Prime Minister had
hinted) in grant aid diverted from other recipients—over four
years to such a programme, he made it clear that they had no
intention of defraying the accounts which had been industriously
cobbled together by local authorities like Birmingham. New
legislation would be introduced to supplement the provisions of
Section 11 of the Local Government Act of 1966. But such a
programme would be based on the extent of need, as defined by
three criteria—the existence of strain on educational and housing
facilities and the presence of immigrants. And only twenty-three
local authorities proved to qualify under all three heads—less than
half of those who receive grants under the 1966 Local Government
Act provision. In the circumstances, Conservative-controlled local
authorities, particularly those in the West Midlands who had
received visits from the Leader of the Opposition immediately
after the Powell speech, turned to him for reassurance.

But when Edward Heath came to deliver his major speech on
Race Relations at York on 2 September,[26] it emerged that the
immigration issue was for him too the decisive factor. Heath's
main theme was that the procedures for controlling the entry of
aliens and those governing Commonwealth citizens should be
combined. His chief proposals were that entry to the United
Kingdom for immigrants coming for employment should be
conditional and related in all cases to a specific job, negotiated
before departure. The unconditional right to reside would be
conceded only after four years' satisfactory residence. In the
initial period, permission would have to be obtained for any
change of employment. U.K. citizenship, by a logical progression,

would cease to be granted of right after five years (as at present) but conferred through an application procedure similar to that already existing in the case of aliens. Heads of household intending to bring over dependants would have to register their intention before departure: the implication being that this would reduce total numbers. Repatriation of those immigrants who had failed to settle down would be encouraged.

The stress Heath laid on the distinctions between the policies of the two parties in this speech was comprehensible in terms of political tactics—although there was in fact a good deal of truth in David Ennals' assertion to the House of Commons in July that very little separated Government and Opposition on this issue. Once again, it was a matter of style and manner rather than content: and in this new atmosphere Heath's proposals, although some had indeed appeared in his party's Manifesto of two years previously, assumed quite a new significance. Ultimately, however, it was not the lack of emphasis on the civil liberties aspect of immigration control or the impractical nature of the control procedures to which objection might be taken. It was the tentative and unthought-out nature of the proposals for integration, at best a smudged carbon of the Prime Minister's proposals of May. All this is not to make a political point. It is merely that the pace is set and the terms defined for Opposition, as for Government, by those who can present the case in terms of stringent control and rigorous supervision. The notion of first-class citizenship for all Commonwealth citizens in Britain has become, like earlier politicians' slogans, an empty phrase.

This analysis suggests that the Government's handling of the Kenya Asian episode lies at the root of the deterioration in the situation which has followed. To argue this is not to deny that the Government had an extremely awkward problem on its hands. It is entitled to ask its critics what they would have done, confronted with a similar situation. The answer is not a straightforward one, but what is clear now is that any decision had to satisfy the test that it did not disturb confidence, either in Kenya or in the United Kingdom. The Government's line of action failed this test. In fact, there is now evidence to suggest that had the Government been prepared to guarantee the right of entry, few of the Kenya Asians, even in the atmosphere of 1967, would have chosen to exercise it. An independent inquiry conducted by Martin Ennals, former Information Officer of the National Committee for

Commonwealth Immigrants and brother of the Minister responsible for integration, indicates that most of the Kenya Asians would have preferred to return to India or Pakistan rather than enter Great Britain.[27] And in July a compromise agreement was in fact reached between the United Kingdom and Indian Governments, enabling United Kingdom citizens of Indian origin to enter India with a special passport endorsement. Those who did come here might well have come less precipitately; Peter Marris, who recently conducted an extended investigation in Kenya argued that:

without any restriction on entry to Britain, these pressures [that is, the pressure to leave in the aftermath of the Kenya Government's legislation] would, almost certainly, have resulted in reasonably gradual dispersal and diversification. Secure that they could come here whenever the situation in Kenya became unmanageable, there would have been no rush to leave while commercial and employment opportunities remained. But by imposing a quota the British Government have created a much more dangerous situation. In the rush to beat legislation many businessmen and skilled craftsmen . . . left because they had resources . . . the result is probably a loss of skills that Kenya still needs, while those most likely to be debarred from earning their living in Kenya are now unable to escape.[28]

One other important element in this situation was the Government's uncertainty about the numbers of those likely to come; as Elizabeth Burney succinctly puts it: 'the last thing the Government knew for certain when it published the 1968 Commonwealth Immigrants Bill was how many people were going to be affected by the now notorious Clause 1.'[29] There are good grounds for supposing that official sources had grossly overestimated the numbers of those likely to come: indeed, the Government rather gracelessly admitted as much during the expiring laws continuance debate in November 1968. This is perhaps not surprising, in view of the inadequacy of the existing arrangements for assembling information. In many ways this episode was the clearest possible illustration of some of the continuing deficiences in the official apparatus: the absence of any form of planning machinery equipped to determine the scope of the difficulties and the action to be taken in the event of a situation arising within the Commonwealth involving the possible movement of population. It is not that British civil servants are incapable of taking emergency action to deal with the sudden arrival of newcomers in Britain: the

Hungarian episode proved that. Rather, it is that the notion that planning of population movement is illegitimate if applied to Commonwealth citizens has sunk in so deeply that it has discoloured official thinking on the whole topic.

Ultimately, argument about alternative policies open to the Government on this occasion must be based largely on speculation; it is conceivable that David Ennals is right in arguing that the Kenya Government would have been stimulated to further action designed to accelerate the exodus; although he cannot be correct in equating the Kenya Asians with 'those in similar citizenship situations in other parts of the world'.[30] In the latter case, the possession of alternative citizenship means that the dilemma is not likely to be presented to them in as sharp a form.

Of the general effects of the legislation within the Labour party there is no doubt.

The pretended neutrality of obeying a consensus in Parliament and a supposed majority outside will not savour the reputation of the politicians who have supported the Commonwealth Immigrants Act of 1968. In questions merely political an honest man may stand neuter; but the laws and constitution are the general property of the subject; not to defend is to relinquish.[31]

Anthony Lester's words are a parody of Junius; but behind the satire the feeling is bitter. On what Paul Foot calls 'the principled right', numerically insignificant in the Labour Movement but in the past an influential element in forming policy, the revulsion was particularly marked. It is too early to say whether this will have any long-term significance but there is no doubt that the Government's reputation with its own followers has been seriously damaged.

We have already dealt with the broader implications: the significance for the white majority, in terms of the reinforcement of existing anxieties and prejudices and the providing of the opening for Powell's attempt to ignite the issue. The last was of particular significance, since once Powell obtained the response he had failed to arouse in his speeches before the Act, he was able to develop and consolidate his root and branch case against immigrants—notably in his November 1968 speech at Eastbourne, with its proposal for a Ministry of Repatriation. But for the coloured minorities the direct effects were even more serious. What had once seemed secure was now seen to be at risk; equality under the law could no longer be taken for granted. But the Act of 1968 did not only do damage to the concept of equal citizenship and reduce the structure of British nationality law to a heap of rubble. It also gave the quietus to the argument that a gatekeeping policy of increasing severity could be undertaken without regard to the consequences for the integration programme. The damage to the confidence both of minorities and majority, which must be based upon certain stable assumptions, was too great. And since, as we have argued earlier, the factor of confidence is a decisive element in the formation of policy, this psychic wound will, like that of Philoctetes, remain festering, a permanent limitation on the Government's freedom of action in this field. Whether the infection is more general and more lasting it is too early to tell.

NOTES TO CHAPTER 29

1. The Rt. Hon. J. Enoch Powell, M.P.: text of speech delivered at the Annual General Meeting of the West Midlands Area Conservative Political Centre at the Midland Hotel, Birmingham, 20 April 1968. Reproduced in *Race* (Vol. X, no. 1, July 1968).

2. Speech by the Home Secretary to the Institute of Race Relations, 8 February 1968. Reported in the Institute of Race Relations *Newsletter* (February 1968).

3. Ibid.

4. *The Times*, 10 February 1968.

5. 289 H.L.D., c. 203, 15 February 1968.

6. There are a variety of accounts of the genesis of the Bill. The most reliable is probably that given by the *Sunday Times* (3 March 1968).

7. *The Times*, Law Report, 12 August 1967.

8. *Spectator*, 23 February 1968.

9. 289 H.L.Deb., c. 1089, 29 February 1968.

10. In his statement to the House of Commons; 759 H.C.Deb., c. 662, 22 February 1968.

11. 289 H.L.Deb., c. 1007, 29 February 1968.

12. See particularly an otherwise ill-informed polemic: Ann Ward, 'Race and Immigration; the hysteria of the intellectuals', *Plebs* (April 1968).

13. *The Times*, 2 March 1968.

14. Both in his television appearances on 22 February and in his announcement in the House the same day, in which he referred to the risk of 'racial disharmony and explosions' (759 H.C.Deb., c. 662).

15. Labour peers were apparently told this at their weekly meeting (private information).

16. 289 H.L.Deb., c. 1021, 29 February 1968.

17. 759 H.C.Deb., c. 1050, 28 February 1968.

18. Letter of 25 March 1968.

19. *Official Report*, Standing Committee B, c. 827, 25 June 1968.

20. See, for example, *Venture* (November 1968).

21. Powell, April speech, op. cit.

22. 759 H.C.Deb., c. 1359, 29 February 1968.

628   COLOUR AND CITIZENSHIP

23. In *Matters of Principle: Labour's Last Chance* (Harmondsworth, Penguin Books, 1968).

24. R. Manderson Jones, 'Report on Leadership in the West Indian Community in Britain', prepared for United Nations Institute for Training and Research by Institute of Race Relations (unpublished).

25. Transcript of speech by the Prime Minister, Birmingham, 5 May 1968 (Labour Party).

26. The complete text of Heath's speech was published in *The Times*, 3 September 1968.

27. M. Ennals, *U.K. Citizens of Asian Origin in Kenya: an independent survey* (London, Committee on United Kingdom Citizenship, July 1968).

28. P. Marris, 'The British Asians in Kenya', *Venture* (Vol. XX, no. 4, April 1968).

29. Ibid.

30. 759 H.C.Deb., c. 1358, 28 February 1968.

31. A. Lester, 'The Race Relations Bill', *Venture* (Vol. XX, no. 5, May 1968).

30 The Future Coloured Population of England and Wales*

In the previous chapter we have shown that throughout the year 1968 the focus of political discussion shifted from integration policies back again to immigration and the question of numbers. The most significant decision taken and the policy pronouncements by both the Government and the Opposition were about the numbers and kinds of immigrants to be admitted, whether voucher holders or dependants. Mr. Enoch Powell gave a new twist to the discussion by making a variety of forecasts of what the size of the coloured population would be by the end of the century. In this chapter, relying on the evidence available and making certain explicit assumptions, we will make our own estimates of the size of the coloured population at five-year intervals from the 1966 Census until the year 1986. It is the fate of most population projections to be proved wrong within a fairly short time and if we make our own projections it is not because of their absolute value but for their relative importance as one element in the discussion.

In Chapter 10 we estimated the total coloured population at census date 1966 to be 924,000 persons, including persons not enumerated accurately and coloured children born in the United Kingdom. Since the 1966 Census, the number of dependants arriving has been considerable. At the end of Chapter 10 we suggested a total coloured population of 1,113,000 persons at mid-year 1968, an increase of 189,000 persons (new babies and new immigrants) in a little over two years.

The future coloured population will clearly depend to a large extent on the number of children born here. However, we have to take cognisance of the number of remaining dependants eligible for residence in the United Kingdom. In addition, there is a small but continuing flow of new primary migrants, men and women with Ministry of Labour employment vouchers, and they too are allowed to have their dependants join them in the host country. In sum, an estimate of the total coloured population at future

* This chapter has been contributed by Mrs. Valerie Jackson.

dates demands consideration of these three kinds of immigrants and their offspring:

(i)   persons already resident at 1968;
(ii) persons who are eligible to enter the country as forming part of incomplete families at that date; and
(iii) voucher holders admitted from 1968 onwards, and their permitted dependants.

Each of these groups will be growing by a process of natural increase during their stay in the United Kingdom. Since the immigrants are still predominantly young, there will be few deaths in the next twenty years. But the number of new births is a significant feature for which we can have no sure answer. A second source of uncertainty is the number of eligible dependants who were resident in the immigrants' home countries in 1968 and the proportion of them who are likely to take up residence in Britain. Thirdly, the future flow of primary migrants (voucher holders) is obviously unknown, as is the likely rate of return of coloured persons to their homelands.

1. THE METHOD OF PROJECTION AND THE ASSUMPTIONS

Our calculations have been confined to the five major immigrant groups for which special census information is available. Estimates have been made in detail for persons of Indian origin, excluding white Indians, for Pakistanis, Jamaicans, other Caribbeans, and West Africans. These groups contained 92% of the coloured population in 1966. Projections have been made for five-year points in time until 1986. Throughout, the three major population sectors indicated above were kept separate. Thus, we are able to indicate that proportion of each immigrant population in 1986 which may be attributed to persons already resident in 1968, and to persons arriving after this, either as dependants of the 1968 population, or as new voucher holders with their families.

(a) Assumptions about Fertility and Mortality

The number of coloured children born in the next twenty years will depend primarily on the number of coloured married women and their fertility rates. The total number of women in each racial group is not difficult to estimate and we have attributed the degree of marriage on the basis of the 1966 Census data and how we think this will change as British cultural values are assimilated. Within marriage, two levels of fertility assumptions have been made. In the low fertility model, which we consider the more likely outcome, for each age group under 25 years, immigrant birth-rates mirror those in the population at large; above this age, immigrant rates are double those experienced by the English population on the experience of the years 1964 to 1966 inclusive. In the high fertility model, fertility at all ages is twice that according to the English pattern. But, since skin colour is a dominant trait, we have to account in some fashion for the number of children born to coloured fathers and white mothers. The degree of inter-marriage, even currently, is difficult to estimate. For cultural and language reasons, we expect more inter-marriage of whites with West Indians than with Asians, but it is precisely these latter groups for whom the degree of sex imbalance is most severe. Anxious not to under-estimate the future number of coloured births, we have calculated the total births attributable to married coloured women and then increased this number by 10%. This figure seems to us a generous allowance for the effect of births to coloured fathers and to illegitimacy.

Mortality is subject to less uncertainty. Outside infant mortality, there is now little international variation in death rates. We have assumed that immigrant mortality will be exactly the same as that experienced by the English population from 1964 to 1966 inclusive, except that infant mortality will be almost twice as high as the general level, at forty deaths per 1,000 births. This assumption is based on the poor living conditions revealed by our housing analysis.

Throughout the projections constant vital rates have been assumed. By 1986, it is quite likely that infant mortality will be lower than estimated, though the number of births may also be smaller than even the low fertility model suggests.

(b) The Flow of Dependants

This is a complicated as well as a controversial issue. Our demographic analysis revealed a significant proportion of married Indians and Pakistanis whose wives were clearly not resident in England and Wales at the time of the 1966 Census. We may thus regard the population enumerated as comprising some complete and some incomplete families. The incomplete families may be composed of a father and mother who have left some of their earlier children in their home country, or the father may be living alone.

The precise estimate of how many dependants we think were eligible at mid-1968 to join their families is set out in Appendix VIII.1. On the basis of the flow of dependants since 1962, it seems highly unlikely that all those eligible to migrate to the United Kingdom will do so. For example, children are only admitted while they are under 16 years of age. The lone husband who, by 1968, may have been separated from his family for seven or eight years has probably become accustomed to his altered domestic circumstances. The expense of adequate housing accommodation may be an additional deterrent.

Basically, the estimate of eligible dependants stems from a careful analysis of the 1966 Census.* Appendix VIII.1 sets out the estimated number of eligible dependants within each ethnic group. The material has been updated by the number of new primary migrants from the 1966 Census to mid-year 1968, and we have allowed for the number of dependants who have arrived during this period. We also indicate how many dependants we expect to arrive in the years before 1976. For the reasons given above we have assumed that beyond that date there will be no further arrivals of dependants of persons resident in England and Wales at mid-year 1968.

(c) Future Voucher Holders and their Dependants

Since 1966 the number of new entrants with employment vouchers has been small, less than 5,000 vouchers were issued to all Commonwealth immigrants in 1967. It is clear from the kind of persons who are now admitted that the current trend is for vouchers to be allocated primarily to artisans and professionally qualified persons. Assuming that marriage rates and fertility levels are lower in these strata of the immigrant societies, we have calculated that each new primary immigrant will have just over two dependants when he arrives, though of course there may be further natural increase over the years. Our projection is based on the assumption that the current rate of issuing new vouchers will be continued throughout the projection period. This means that

---

* The work relies heavily on an extensive monograph on the likely number of dependants arriving: David Eversley and Fred Sukdeo, *The Coloured Population of England and Wales and their Dependants* (London, Institute of Race Relations, Special Series, 1969).

before 1986 there will be about 41,400 voucher holders arriving from India, 13,800 from Pakistan, and a further 13,000 from the West Indies. There were less than a hundred vouchers issued to West Africans in 1967. We have assumed no further voucher holders will arrive from these territories, though the model allows for a revolving student population.

2. PROJECTIONS

The five population groups we have considered contained 848,000 persons according to our interpretation of census and other information at April 1966. Our projections indicate that they will have increased to a total of 2,074,000 persons by 1986, by a process of natural increase and migration. Table 30.1 shows the progress of growth between 1966 and 1986. The significant increase during the last five years of this period reflects the importance of births occurring to coloured parents themselves born in the host country. By 1986, the high fertility assumptions inflate the total estimated population by almost 14%. But the evidence of current fertility patterns in Birmingham and Notting Hill makes us doubt that these high levels will be reached. We shall proceed on the assumption that the lower fertility model is more likely to be achieved.

Table 30.1. Estimated future populations, five major immigrant groups, 1971–86

Country of origin	1966*	1971†	1976†	1981†	1986†	1986‡
India	223,600	377,000	510,000	579,000	768,000	890,000
Pakistan	119,700	211,000	290,000	306,000	408,000	485,000
Jamaica	273,700	343,000	383,000	411,000	474,000	529,000
Rest of Caribbean	180,300	229,000	265,000	293,000	341,000	375,000
West Africa	50,800	68,000	74,000	80,000	83,000	94,000
Totals	848,100	1,228,000	1,522,000	1,669,000	2,074,000	2,373,000

Source:
Census and projections.

* Census, amended, see Chapter 10.
† Low fertility projection.
‡ High fertility projection.

We have indicated that the degree of future migrations is a major unknown feature of these calculations. Table 30.2 shows the composition of the estimated 1986 population of each country in terms of those resident with their children in this country at mid-1968. For example, only 492,000 of the total population of Indians originate directly from those resident in England and Wales in 1968; a further 186,000 result from future migrations of voucher holders, their children, and grandchildren. On the current pattern it is only the Indian population which will grow significantly as a result of new primary migrations. We should also remember that if these are predominantly professional people, for some of whom the stay in Britain is seen as part of a training programme, then their migration may be only a temporary phenomenon. Whatever proportion of the total assumed primary migrants (voucher holders) eventually returns home with their families, by that proportion we should also reduce the figure of 186,000 persons allowed to new initial migrations from India.

The matter of dependants of the 1968 population is only of numerical significance among the Indian and Pakistani groups. Dependants loom large in the total population estimate for Pakistan, because this is the group which currently has the largest sex imbalance. We have assumed that a high proportion of all Pakistani immigrants were legally married at the time of leaving their homeland because of the low age of marriage under Islamic law. The total population emanating from the dependants group is considerably larger than the number of initial dependants, simply because a high proportion of the dependants are women and we are assuming that those women who come to join their husbands will still be of fertile age, and will resume child-bearing after their arrival in England. In addition, many of those children admitted before 1971 will, by 1986, be married and bearing their own children. Many of those features are difficult to estimate, in particular the likely arrival rate of Pakistani wives. In fact, although Table 30.2 shows that Pakistanis are particularly important among the total arrivals of dependants, we have assumed that only 50% of the eligible Pakistani wives will make the journey to join their husbands.

The significance of the coloured population within the total population of England and Wales depends to some extent upon the rate of natural increase of the indigenous population. We have estimated in Chapter 10 that in 1966 the census enumerated coloured population amounted to only 12·6 persons per 1,000, though our amended calculations indicate a concentration, including children, of almost 20 per 1,000 total population at that date. An exactly comparable calculation, including estimates of persons from Ceylon and the Far East within the total coloured group, suggests the position shown in Table 30.3.

We thus envisage something over a 100% increase in the proportion of coloured persons if further immigration continues as projected. Without any further migration, the proportion will increase by about 50% in 20 years. We have assumed that the

Table 30.2. Sources of the estimated 1986 population

Area of origin	1968 residents and their children	1968 dependants and their children	New migrants and their children	Total
India	492,000	90,000	186,000	768,000
Pakistan	248,000	102,000	58,000	408,000
Jamaica	433,000	23,000	18,000	474,000
Rest of Caribbean	289,000	19,000	33,000	341,000
West Africa	87,000	−4,000*	—	83,000
Total	1,549,000	230,000	295,000	2,074,000

* We assume the current practice of returning children to the homeland is continued.

Table 30.3. The proportion of the coloured population in 1986 (coloured persons per 1,000 total population)

Indigenous population growth	1968 residents and their children	Dependants and new voucher holders included
5 per 1,000 per annum	31·8	43·8
8 per 1,000 per annum	29·7	40·9

indigenous rate of growth will be between 5 and 8 per thousand (the present rate being about 6 per thousand). But it is clear that the indigenous rate of natural increase is not very important in the eventual outcome.

We have shown that in 1966 the major demographic features of the immigrant populations were a severe imbalance of males over females among Indians and Pakistanis, and a relative youthfulness of all ethnic groups. A composite age structure and individual sex ratios at 1986 are shown below in Tables 30.4 and 30.5. Again we quote two models, with and without any further migration after mid-year 1968, and comparative material for 1966 is added for reference.

Table 30.4. Age structure, 1966 and 1986, five immigrant groups combined

Composite age structure: % of total population	1966	1986 1968 residents and their children	1986 1968 residents, new migrants, and children
Under 15 years	34	29	32
15–24 years	13	21	22
25–44 years	42	20	23
45–64 years	10	28	21
65 years and over	under 1	2	2

Table 30.5. Sex ratio, 1966 and 1986, males per 1,000 females

	1966	1986 1968 residents only	1986 1968 residents, new migrants, and children
Indians	1,479	1,128	1,087
Pakistanis	4,231	1,745	1,180
West Indians	1,051	1,008	1,001

In the long run, the imbalance of males and females will disappear, since it is to be expected that among new births male and female will be in about equal numbers: further immigration of dependants will merely hasten the process. A surprising feature is that the youthfulness of the immigrant population will be reinforced rather than reduced. The model which excludes further immigration after 1968 clearly indicates the ageing of the original migrants; by 1986, the number of people between 45 and 64 years of age is larger than the younger age group, 25 to 44 years. Further immigration after 1968 would tend to normalize the age structure by 1986.

We have confined our attention throughout this later analysis to the low fertility model, and feel confident in our judgement that this is the more likely outcome. We have indicated that the 1986 population in these five major coloured groups will amount to just over two million people. It is perhaps wise at this point to review the basic assumptions that form an integral part of the calculations on which this figure is based. We have assumed:

(i)   that fertility in immigrant women over 24 years of age is twice that currently applying in the English population;

(ii) that there will be a considerable inflow of dependants from India and Pakistan;

(iii) that the current rate of voucher issues will be continued;

(iv) that for every ten babies born to coloured mothers, there will be one coloured baby born to a white mother; and

(v)   that there will be no return migration.

Thus, there are several reasons to question whether the estimate we have given is not too large. For example, the new trend in issues of vouchers since 1965 suggests that newcomers will be professionally qualified in a way that will make them highly favoured in their own labour markets. If half those persons newly admitted with vouchers in fact return to their home countries, our total population estimate of 2,074,000 persons will be too large by 150,000 persons. The rate of achieved family reunion may be slower than what has been assumed. The number of births by white mothers to coloured fathers is also very difficult to estimate in the long run, since it depends upon the likely degree of intermarriage and illegitimacy; our ratio of one in ten may be generous to the eventual number of births of this kind. Finally, the assumption of no return migration is an extreme one, particularly in the light of the present return flow to India, Pakistan, and the West Indies, which ran at an average of 14,000 a year in 1966 and 1967. Clearly, the degree of return migration will depend to a great extent upon economic and social conditions in this country and, in particular, upon the success of government policies with respect to racial integration. But if the present rate continues, our total population estimate will certainly be too high. Balancing out possible combinations of errors in our assumptions which tend to over-estimate the future coloured population, it seems relatively safe to assert that the coloured population at 1986 will be between 2 and 2¼ million people, including the minority coloured groups;* we further think it likely that the figure will in fact be close to the bottom end of this range even if current admission policies remain unchanged. In the event of a total ban on future arrivals of Commonwealth coloured immigrants in the near future, it is unlikely that the total population at 1986 would exceed one and a half million persons.

However unlikely such a ban might be, any decision to make a radical change in immigration policy would be based not merely on demographic calculations. There would be many other considerations including the social as well as the economic effects of such a policy. In the next chapter we turn to a discussion of the economic effects of the immigration and of the costs and benefits which it has brought to the British economy.

* About 130,000 persons added in 1986 to cover persons from Ceylon and the Far East.

31 Effects on the Economy*

Immigration is not a phenomenon which has been of central concern to the economist. A perusal of the standard textbooks, which may be expected to reveal what is the main subject matter of economics, will find few references to the international movement of labour. Indeed, it is a crucial assumption in the pure theory of international trade that while commodities are exchanged between countries the labour force stays where it is. In other words, the economist assumes that in general at most times the international movement of labour is so small as to be approximately zero.

There have, of course, been some studies of immigration by economists, and economic historians have not neglected the subject. Even here, however, the main interest seems to lie in the causes of immigration rather than the consequences, and little emphasis is laid on the costs and benefits either in the country which loses labour or in the country which gains it. A quantitative evaluation of the effects of immigration to any particular country has yet to be carried out.

This is puzzling for two reasons. First, immigration has been a noticeable phenomenon in history, and has not been negligible in modern times. It is certainly a major jump to go from the true statement that the internal mobility of labour is much greater than the international mobility of labour to the false one that there is no international mobility of labour at all. Secondly, in most countries of the world there are restraints on the free entry of labour. These would surely be irrelevant if labour did not have a propensity to move from country to country. It is worth asking, therefore, what is the economic rationale of immigration controls, bearing in mind that they are also likely to have a social and political rationale as well.

This essay stems from a concern with the costs and benefits of labour as they affect the United Kingdom. Because of the lack of appropriate empirical studies it has to be mainly analytical and speculative. Its purpose is, therefore, chiefly to consider various possibilities and to put current discussion into some sort of

* This chapter has been contributed by Professor Maurice Peston.

perspective. An attempt is made to show that certain simple views of the economic effects of immigration are probably untrue, but whilst it is easy to show that the effects of immigration on the United Kingdom are neither necessarily advantageous nor disadvantageous, it is much more difficult to estimate what may have been the actual net benefits or disbenefits during the past two decades.

Our plan will be to consider some simple hypotheses concerning the economic effects of immigration. In addition, we will discuss broadly the sort of conditions under which it is likely to be advantageous for the home population to permit the entry of labour from other countries. Before doing that, however, it is useful to mention briefly the economic causes of immigration.

Immigration can occur for a variety of reasons, many of which will be extraneous to the economic system. But the economist will emphasize that immigration is determined partly by the comparative economic conditions in the giving and receiving country and partly by transport and similar costs. In addition, however, there may be an income effect in the giving country, namely, that up to a point as incomes rise in that country immigration may *increase*, because at high income levels immigrants may be able to afford to move where previously they had been unable to do so. (There may also be increased knowledge of immigration possibilities connected with rising income.) It is also possible that up to a point immigration is self-increasing, the earlier immigrants pulling others after them.

There are certain hypotheses that have been put forward concerning the economic consequences of immigration which are worthy of consideration, either to show that they are false, or that their significance is much less than might be imagined. These are as follows:

(i)   immigration causes unemployment;
(ii) immigration reduces the rate of economic growth;
(iii) immigration reduces the rate of technical progress;
(iv) immigration leads to a deterioration in the balance of payments; and
(v)   immigration causes inflation.

These hypotheses are of course inter-related and are here separated out for the sake of analytical convenience. Also, in so far as they are intended to be empirical, ultimately their truth or falsity will depend on appropriate testing. This, it must be emphasized, has not yet been carried out on a large enough scale or in enough detail to decide the matter, but it does not mean that no serious discussion is possible in this field or that the issue can be regarded as entirely open.

One topic which is frequently discussed is the relationship between immigration, the tax system, and expenditure under the social services. We shall consider this chiefly under the heading of immigration and inflation, although it is, of course, true that it is somewhat broader than that.

Let us start with the question of unemployment. It may be expected that, especially in conditions of comparatively free entry to a country, immigrants themselves may expect to experience unemployment in the initial stages of looking for a job or in deciding whether a particular job is suitable. It is also likely that immigrants, as the latest arrivals, might expect to be amongst the first to be laid off in any slack conditions of trade that arise in most countries from time to time. Also, there is a tendency for immigrants to enter those occupations which experience large amounts of unemployment anyway. Putting these three factors together there is a considerable likelihood that the immigrant population would on average experience more unemployment than the population in general, and also that within the immigrant population those who arrived the longest time ago would experience less unemployment than the average. (This is, of course, not to say that *all* immigrants necessarily experience more unemployment than the population on average, but rather that the spectrum of unemployment experience of immigrants lies to the right of the spectrum of unemployment of the home population where these two are measured on a scale of increasing unemployment from left to right.) In this connexion two points emerge from the examination of immigrant unemployment in Chapter 13: first, that the cyclical pattern of the immigrant population is much the same as that of the total population and, secondly, that immigrants form an increasing share of unemployment in the downswing.

Further evidence on unemployment among immigrants is provided by Eric Butterworth in *Immigrants in West Yorkshire*.[1] While the data is not absolutely clear cut, it is certainly compatible with the view that immigrants experience relatively more unemployment than the domestic population, and that economic fluctuations tend to affect them disproportionately. What is not apparent from Butterworth's data, but would repay further study, is whether there is a 'settling-in effect', so that after a point the unemployment experience of the immigrant becomes the same as that of the domestic population.

The fact that immigrants may experience more unemployment than the home population is not the same as saying that unemployment among the home population will rise as a result of immigration or even that unemployment among the total population will rise. This may be seen in a variety of ways. First, it has been argued that for an economy to work effectively in the short run, it must have a degree of slack, made up partly of physical capacity and partly of human capacity. It is likely that, to the extent that this slack is made up of immigrants, it will not be made up of the home population. As a result the effect of immigration is not to increase unemployment but merely to take over the burden of unemployment from the home population. Secondly, in the case of some countries, notably West Germany, the flow of immigration may be extremely responsive to pressures in the domestic labour market so that the pool of unemployment does not even occur in the domestic economy itself. Ceri Peach has shown that in the 1950s there was a similarly close relationship between the demand for labour in the United Kingdom and West Indian immigration.[2]

Thirdly, economic efficiency requires to some degree a willingness of the labour force to be mobile. While this mobility is partly occupational and industrial, it is also partly geographical. If the immigrant population is more mobile geographically (and that is certainly the general impression of, for example, Pakistanis given in the earlier parts of the present Report), it will happen that the same shifts in the structure of economic activities will take place with less disruption both of the home labour force and of the labour force as a whole. If the immigrants are more mobile, this enables the domestic population to be less mobile. Moreover, immigration may be partially a substitute for inter-regional migration, and may help to offset the alleged costs of inter-regional migration.

Fourthly, and this refers also to the last hypothesis on the list, some unemployment results from the central government's attempts, not always successful, to deal with the problem of inflation. If it happens that the net effect of immigration is anti-inflationary, this too may help to reduce the overall unemployment in the economy. In sum, I am not arguing that immigration necessarily leads to lower unemployment, or that it would be impossible for any person or group in the home labour force to suffer from more unemployment as a result of immigration. My point is that the view that immigration inevitably leads to more unemployment is easily criticized on theoretical grounds and is not in accordance with the facts. To take the two obvious cases: West Germany for two decades did not experience increased unemployment as a result of immigration, and United Kingdom unemployment does not correlate with immigration (indeed, Peach tends to argue that there is a positive correlation between unfilled vacancies in the United Kingdom and immigration from the West Indies— see Chapter 7).[3]

Turning now to the problem of economic growth, one difficulty is that there is not general agreement on the causes of economic growth. This, however, will not prevent us establishing the negative point that immigration is not necessarily deleterious to growth. Again, it is worth mentioning that as far as empirical work is concerned not a great deal has been done, and there are difficulties lying in the way of the potential researcher. The most obvious of these again concerns cause and effect—any positive connexion between immigration and growth might be that the first is conducive to the second, or that the second is conducive to the first.

On the theoretical side, it is possible that an economy may grow at a slower rate than otherwise because of shortage of labour in general or shortage of a particular kind of labour. This point is obviously relevant in situations of increasing marginal product of labour or where (as is remarked below) the rate of technical progress is an increasing function of the rate of growth of the labour force. While it is highly controversial, it is worth noting that Professor Kaldor's inaugural lecture, 'The Causes of the Slow Rate of Economic Growth of the United Kingdom', would support this view as far as the United Kingdom economy is concerned.[4] If we set aside the problem of the marginal product of labour, before looking at technical progress, it is worth paying a little attention to the propensity to save.

It is usually accepted that physical capital accumulation has a positive connexion with the process of growth and at full employment can be undertaken only if firms, households, or the Government saves. Saving depends partially on the distribution of income, which aspect of the subject we shall deal with later on. At this point, we are only concerned to ask whether there is any reason to believe that the propensity to save of immigrants will be lower than comparable people born in this country. This is to some extent a psychological or sociological matter and outside the compass of a purely economic article, but it is worth mentioning that there is nothing in those other social sciences which leads to the conclusion that immigrants have a lower propensity to save. Within economics itself there is one positive point that may be noted, namely that immigrants may well own less capital than people in the home population with similar incomes, which would act as an incentive to save more. Evidence on immigrants to the United States or the United Kingdom certainly does not support the view that they have an unduly low propensity to save. In fact, it is apparent from Radburn's and Vanags's investigations (see Chapter 14) that West Indians and Pakistanis in Birmingham have a higher propensity to save than the comparable domestic population, even when allowance is made for their remittances home.

As far as technical progress is concerned, it could be argued that this will be determined partly by the resources available for it, so that if immigration is conducive to growth, it is equally conducive to technical progress and thus to further growth. It is sometimes argued, however, that technical progress is increased in conditions of labour shortage, making it imperative to develop and employ new labour saving techniques. This would be slowed down by an easier availability of labour which would encourage employees to go on using old-fashioned labour intensive methods. There are two arguments to be set against this. One is that technical progress means change, and an immigrant labour force may be less well entrenched and more willing to change than the domestic population. Secondly, technically advanced equipment may be situated in unattractive places or may need to be worked continuously through the day and on every day of the year. Again, an immigrant labour force, especially if it has fewer family ties, may be more willing to work in this way. As far as the facts are concerned they do not show that those countries which have experienced the greatest labour shortage have also made the most technical progress. It is equally not true that as immigration has increased in the United Kingdom in the past fifteen years, the rate of technical progress has fallen.

It may be expected that technical progress is related not simply to the aggregate labour force but also to its structure. There may be certain sorts of labour which are conducive to technical progress because it is comprised of the kind of people who carry it out, either inventing new techniques or helping to put them into practical use. In this category would come scientists, engineers, and certain sorts of managers or entrepreneurs.

Another sort of labour may be conducive to technical progress because it is willing to work the technically advanced machines or is complementary to the labour force working on those machines. This sort of labour may not itself need to be particularly advanced, but, as has been remarked above, it may have to be sufficiently flexible to be willing to work under all sorts of adverse conditions. It should also be remembered that, for example, there may not only be a demand for multi-shift working directly on the advanced machines, but for all the other activities of the factory, including all the managerial and office staff who may have to be continuous around the clock. A person who is willing to make tea, drive a vehicle, or answer the phone at any time of the day or night is just as vital to continuous working as an actual operative.

There is ample evidence that in many industrialized countries, including the United Kingdom, immigrants have been a significant source of supply of both these types of labour. A pool of cheap immigrant labour may well have played a vital part in the technical progress of the United States or, more recently, Germany and Italy. (In the case of Italy there is every reason to treat the population movement from the extreme south to the north as a special case of immigration.) Similarly, at the top end of the spectrum, in both the United States and the United Kingdom, technically advanced industries such as chemicals have developed on the basis of immigrant labour. Once again, therefore, the conclusion must be that the hypothesis that the recent comparative technological backwardness of the United Kingdom is attributable to immigration and would be reversed by immigration control is unproven, and certainly cannot be substantiated beyond doubt by existing economic theory.

Indeed the available evidence does allow one to go considerably further on this subject. In his work, Butterworth states:

The night shifts of many woollen mills in West Yorkshire depend on immigrant labour, illustrating that migrants are to be found in jobs which involve a good deal of disruption of normal patterns of life. The economic motivation with which migrants come makes them look for ways of supplementing income, particularly as they have been much more mobile than the bulk of the labour force, and the woollen industry provides plenty of opportunities for overtime.[5]

In their extremely important article in *Race*, Cohen and Jenner reach the following conclusion:

The degree to which new capital investment and the employment of immigrants go together is surprising, and it would be fair to conclude that the employment of immigrants has facilitated new capital investment in the sample of firms under study. This is because new machinery is too expensive to be worked only forty or forty-eight hours a week and it must be employed as intensively as possible thus necessitating shift work. This is a trend not confined to the wool industry and may well, in the future, make headway into more white-collar occupations. It is well recognized that there is a general disinclination to work nights or changing shifts, and higher rates of pay are the general rule. The immigrant (Pakistani) workers are usually more willing to take this work than local labour. . . .[6]

It may be remarked that in this respect the domestic population are akin to the latter day Luddites whose restrictive practices and antipathy to new equipment may be undermined by the immigrants. There is, however, another side to this question of technical progress which must be mentioned. It is possible that immigration may benefit the receiving country; it is equally possible that the equivalent emigration will harm the losing country. This is particularly likely at the top end of the skill spectrum. In so far as such people flow from poorer countries to richer ones, the technological backwardness of the former and the technological advance of the latter may both be accentuated. This possibility applies to the United Kingdom as a loss of high level manpower to the United States and the rich Commonwealth and to the poor Commonwealth as a loss of manpower to the United Kingdom. Immigration restrictions on such people may well, therefore, benefit the losing country and could be advocated on those grounds, but for the same reason they would harm the receiving country.

The effect of immigration on the balance of payments turns partly on whether the free movement of labour into the economy is inflationary. It is easy to show that it is not necessarily inflationary, and may even be anti-inflationary. It is agreed by most economists that some or all of the rise in prices and money wages that occurs from time to time (and has occurred pretty continuously in the United Kingdom for the past thirty years) is attributable to the excess pressure of demand in the labour market. The greater the shortage of labour, the more a particular demand pressure will be inflationary. The effect of immigration is to provide one additional source of supply of labour and, therefore, the outcome will be to reduce inflationary pressure rather than increase it. To quote the obvious example, the ability of West Germany to grow at an extremely fast rate with little or no unemployment and minimal price inflation is attributable in large part to the availability of immigrant labour. Inflation is also sometimes attributable to the cost pressure of trade unions. Although this is a more controversial matter, it can hardly be argued that increased immigration will add to that cost pressure. If anything, the expectation must be that it will be reduced.

A particular argument that has been presented on the subject of immigration and inflation is based on the view that immigrants typically place a greater burden on the social services than they pay in taxes. This view has been associated with E. J. Mishan and L. Needleman, although it is not unique to them and their analysis of the macro-economic effects of immigration covers a much wider field. The general idea involved here is that immigration adds less to supply than to demand, causing the general level of prices to rise, or in crude terms, that immigration has an expenditure multiplier greater than its output multiplier, both measured in approximate terms. To quote Mishan and Needleman:

If net immigration added to the natural product without increasing effective demand, or if it increased effective demand in smaller proportions, then, whatever the other economic effects, it would contribute in the short run to a reduction of the pressure of excess aggregate demand however caused.[7]

Although the public sector side is only part of the story, the result of an excess demand for social services over tax payments would be either a decline in the quality of the social services provided or, if quality is maintained, an increase in the budget deficit which at full employment is inflationary. This argument may be criticized partly in terms of its assumptions. It is not necessarily the case that all immigrants place a greater burden on the social services than they pay in taxes, even in the short run.

Secondly, even if this aspect of immigration were inflationary, it would have to be set against other aspects which may be non-inflationary. Thirdly, the point is often made that many of the social services in the United Kingdom are staffed to a considerable extent by immigrants. If those immigrants were barred from the United Kingdom, the cost of the social services would be higher, and that is certainly inflationary. A crucial piece of evidence in all of this was presented by Mrs. K. Jones in 'Immigrants and the Social Services'.[8] It seems to follow from her investigations that, presumably partly as a result of the different demographic structure of immigrants and their higher participation rates, the pressure of expenditure on the social services is less than that of the domestic population.

It is also worth noting that it is not true that the immigrants' needs are met solely by the provision of new social capital. Instead, they move to a considerable extent into the old and obsolete social capital vacated by the domestic population. A recent report from Birmingham has the following to say:

It is difficult to give an accurate estimate of the cost of school building necessitated solely by immigration. For instance, probably, a large number of English families have moved from the city to such places as Sutton Coldfield, Milfield, Solihull, etc. which has freed places in Birmingham schools for immigrants, but it is estimated that seven schools would not have been required had there been no immigration at a cost of £991,421. In addition, two other schools would probably have been much smaller in size had it not been for immigration. Twenty three minor works at a total cost of £110,470 are attributable to immigration. The cost of school building for immigrants on this basis to date is approximately £1,376,235.[9]

It is difficult to determine how many children are to be counted against this expenditure, but for 1962–8, the number of so-called non-European children in Birmingham schools has increased by 12,500 approximately. This is a capital cost of £110 per child or, as an annuity over thirty years at 8% per annum, slightly more than £10 per year per child. To put this into perspective, it is worth noting that a family with two children earning the average industrial wage will pay some ten to fifteen times this in rates and taxes in a year. The point may be put in another way. Studies of the incidence of taxes and social service benefits (for example, in *Economic Trends*, August 1966) show that these are redistributive towards people with lower than average incomes and larger than average families. If immigrants fall into these categories there will be a redistribution in their favour. This redistribution, however, will be mitigated in the short run at least by the lower pressure on social services of the sort indicated by Mrs. Jones. (We do not have a great deal of evidence on taxes, but note this remark of Davison: 'There were also a large number of cases where there appears to be quite genuine hardship and overpayment of tax.')[10]

It is by no means unlikely, therefore, that the efficiency of some or all the economy may rise as a result of immigration, and it is possible that inflationary pressures will be reduced. It follows that it cannot be argued with certainty that immigration will lead to a deterioration in the balance of payments. It may well lead to an improvement in the balance of payments, and in the case of West Germany most certainly has. There is, however, one special aspect of immigration which might be presumed to have a deleterious effect on the balance of payments. That is, that it is not unreasonable to argue that immigrants coming from foreign lands may have a high propensity to import compared with home-born citizens with the same incomes, and, in particular, they may have a high propensity to remit sums to their original homeland, either to raise the income levels of their poor dependants left behind or to help them meet the cost of becoming immigrants themselves. The obvious example here concerns the sums sent from the United States to Italy which, while they have been a great help to the Italian balance of payments, have been an equal hindrance to the United States! There is no doubt that West Indians, Indians, and Pakistanis remit significant sums home, although it is worth noting that these financial flows are to the Sterling Area. Even here, however, the matter is not quite as simple as all that because in these days of foreign aid it is not inconceivable that now or in the future these remittances may take the place in part of aid that would have been given by the richer country to the poorer. In other words, although there is every presumption that from this point of view the effect of immigration would be to worsen the balance of payments, the net effect may be less than the sum remitted.

If we now summarize the arguments on these major macro-hypotheses, they amount to the view that from a purely theoretical view there is no presumption that overall immigration is harmful in the sense of causing unemployment, lowering growth, adding to inflation, or worsening the balance of payments. Immigration may be benevolent, reducing unemployment, increasing growth, diminishing inflation, and even improving the balance of payments. These general considerations may, of course, be regarded as secondary to the particular conditions of the United Kingdom economy in the post-war period. On this it is impossible to pronounce with any confidence because of the lack of empirical knowledge. None the less, there is no strong evidence to support the theory that overall immigration is harmful and there are small pieces of evidence, varying from the willingness of immigrants to work in bad conditions to their staffing of the social services, that immigration has been positively beneficial to the economy. My own view on this appears at the end of this chapter. A fundamental analysis of the costs and benefits of immigration would need to consider both of these as flows over time firstly in conditions of zero or restricted immigration. Whether immigration itself has a beneficial effect is too open-ended a question; the correct approach is to compare more immigration with less and to specify all the other relevant events that would occur. In this chapter it is impossible to carry out an analysis in such fundamental terms, especially as far as its dynamic consequences are concerned. Apart from shortage of space, there is also the point that there is within economics little realistic analysis of the alternative future development paths open to an economy, especially when alternative population and manpower developments have to be taken into account. It must be appreciated, therefore, that the elementary view that we present may have to be modified later on as a result of a more sophisticated study of the subject.

The domestic population will gain in economic terms from a higher rate of immigration compared with a lower if the flow of benefits which it gains from that immigration is greater than the flow of costs. In emphasizing the flow side it is accepted that the fact that in any year the costs may exceed the benefits is not a sufficient condition for restricting immigration, or the fact that in any year the benefits may exceed the costs is equally not a sufficient condition for encouraging immigration. We also emphasize economic terms to mean that while economics is in principle an all embracing subject, what would normally be included in a cost-benefit analysis, and what is most likely to be quantifiable, might take no account of the social aspects of the matter which might be decisive in determining the total net benefits in any real case.

The net gain to the domestic population may be measured by the change in the flow of disposable real income plus the change in the flow of public consumption goods (including in these such aspects of environment as congestion, noise, smoke, and so on) accruing to them. The effect of immigration, therefore, will be economically beneficial if the increase in the flow of real national income plus the flow of economic goods not measured by real national income increases by more than the immigrants' share. This means that it is not a sufficient test of the value of immigration from the economic standpoint to inquire if real national income rises. On the one hand, part of all of the increase may accrue to the immigrants; on the other hand, economic welfare is measured only imperfectly by real national income.

In strict economic terms (which the general reader may prefer to ignore) this seems to mean that if there were diminishing marginal product of every factor of production, a given technology, no external economies and diseconomies of production or consumption, and the economy were in a state of perfectly competitive equilibrium, there would be no advantage to the domestic population from allowing immigration to occur. If, however, technical progress is speeded up, if net external effects are increased, if there are unexploited returns to scale and increasing marginal product of labour, if the frictions in adjusting to economic change are diminished, and if there already exist monopoly elements, restrictive practices, and imperfect markets, immigration could be economically beneficial to the domestic population.

Technical progress and the problem of economic adjustment have been referred to already, and it has been argued that these could well be helped by immigration, either generally or of specific kinds. As far as external economies or diseconomies are concerned, immigrants may obviously have a direct effect in so far as they add to congestion or noise. They may, however, also represent a supply of labour to certain occupations which might cut down the costs of mitigating these external economies. For example, public transport might fall in price relative to private transport as a result of immigration. (It is indeed the case that immigrants do tend to work to a disproportionate extent in transport.) In certain countries at certain times, with labour comparatively scarce compared with land and physical capital, there may be unexploited returns to scale due to shortage of labour, and increasing marginal product of labour. It is, perhaps, unlikely that this is characteristic of the United Kingdom today. At the same time, the markets for commodities and for all sorts of labour are imperfect and contain strong monopoly elements.

These phenomena are all interrelated, especially the neighbourhood effects, economies of scale, and market imperfections. To the extent that they exist in a country such as the United Kingdom, their effect will be to enable the domestic population to gain some of the increase in output resulting from the immigration. This is not to argue that an economy *must* gain from general immigration. Obviously, the closer an economy corresponds to the static perfectly competitive model mentioned earlier, the less likely the domestic population will gain. Speculation on the United Kingdom position at this point is dangerous. It would certainly seem unlikely, however, given the monopoly power of many firms and of organized labour, that the full value of their marginal product would automatically accrue to immigrants. Thus, apart from the benefits connected with the technical progress and economic adjustment, it is quite possible from the theoretical standpoint that overall the domestic population in aggregate would gain from further immigration.

This gain overall, of course, would not imply that everybody actually did benefit from immigration or that no section of society would lose. Thus, in considering the economic impact of immigration, it is important to consider what the immigrant consists of. In the simplest analysis one might assume that he consists simply of a unit of labour, and, indeed, that might have been a satisfactory assumption to deal with some of the immigration of the nineteenth century. For analysis of contemporary phenomena, however, something more sophisticated is called for. One thinks in terms of a unit of human capital, possessing a certain general education, certain particular skills, and a given expectation of working life. (He may also be accompanied by savings, i.e. command over physical capital.) As such, on arrival the immigrant will represent an addition to the supply of labour to many different occupations. He may also represent a supply of entrepreneurship to various trades and markets.

It follows that to some types of domestic labour an immigrant representing a good substitute will weaken their market position and cause their income to be lower than it otherwise would be. This substitution effect from immigration is not a trivial matter, and it will only be in extremely special cases that the immigrant does not represent a threat of this kind to somebody. An immigrant doctor or teacher is a substitute for a domestic one; an immigrant labourer is a substitute for a domestic one. More generally, immigrant labour overall is a substitute for domestic labour. At the same time, immigrant labour is complementary to some sorts of domestic labour, enabling them to carry out their function more effectively and remuneratively. An immigrant medical auxiliary will be of help to a domestic doctor, an immigrant research assistant to a domestic researcher. More generally, there may be all sorts of activities which are not carried out at all and occupations left quite empty because no one could afford them at the prices required if they were staffed by the domestic labour force. In this case, of course, the immigrant labour would be complementary to the domestic labour force.

Reference may also be made here to the upgrading of the domestic labour force as immigrants appear to take over certain low level occupations. The labour market may, indeed, be administered so that generally the existing population moves up as immigrants arrive. It should be emphasized, incidentally, that this is not necessarily a discriminatory phenomenon. On the one hand, it seems to be characteristic of immigrants all over the world, and on the other, immigrants may have less capital invested in them; in addition to which further investments in human capital may require them to move through the occupational hierarchy from the bottom up. What is true of labour is also true of capital. It has already been argued that the productivity of capital could be higher as a result of immigration. Equally, however, in certain cases it could be lower. The obvious cases concern the substitution of capital for labour because the home labour force is so expensive. Cheaper immigrant labour may in turn be a substitute for this capital. Examples would be domestic servants in place of household equipment, kitchen staff in place of kitchen equipment, teachers in place of teaching machines. It certainly does not follow *a priori* that because the immigration is of human beings the net effect will be to raise the return to capital and lower that to the home-born labour force. (Incidentally, to recall an earlier remark, it would also be necessary to state what is happening to the flow of capital anyway. It is possible that the flow of immigration would be going on at the same time as an influx of physical capital from overseas complicating the analysis still further.) Having said that, however, it would certainly be surprising if workers in the home country did not scrutinize the economic effects of immigration most carefully and did not at least start from the position that a new supply of labour, as of anything else, is a threat to the existing supply.

On this a further point can be made. In certain cases, the domestic population may decide through their elected representatives that the entrenched position of certain local workers is anti-social, anyway, and far from giving them protection from the competition of immigrants may welcome this competition. In other cases, as long as the gross domestic product rises in aggregate, the Government can adjust the tax system so as to reduce the gain of certain sections of the population to offset the loss of others. To take the obvious point, it has been alleged that immigration bene-fits the rich and the owners of capital. If this turned out to be true, it could be possible to modify the tax system to take at least some account of such untaxed gains.

In this brief essay I have examined a number of arguments that are usually put forward in connexion with the economic effects of immigration. I have also taken into consideration whatever empirical studies have been made in this field, bearing in mind that it is early days yet and there is a great deal more sophisticated research that needs to be done before it would be possible to regard the subject as exhausted. My intention throughout has been mainly negative—to show that a number of opinions that have been expressed do not stand up to analysis and are at variance with the facts. In that way it is possible to come to the negative conclusion that it cannot be established that immigration in general or the immigration of the past decade or so has been disadvantageous to the United Kingdom economy. It, therefore, remains for those who are opposed to immigration on economic grounds to explain further what their arguments are, or to invent new arguments, or to discover and present new relevant facts.

Having reached this point, it might well be argued that as an academic one should and can go no further. One has helped to clarify the issues, and it is now up to the politicians to decide, and it is, anyway, likely that they will decide chiefly according to non-economic criteria.

My own view, however, is that one can legitimately go further than this, without offending against the tradition of pure scholar-ship. What follows is admittedly largely a matter of judgement, but

I cannot help but conclude from my own interpretation of the available material, both theoretical and empirical, that on balance immigration has been economically beneficial to the economy, and I would add that excessive restraint on immigration might have adverse effects on the economy at large and on particular sectors. Although neither I nor anybody else has done the cost-benefit analysis which would enable us to place a precise figure on the net benefit to the domestic population, there are certain phenomena which are outstanding and tip the balance in the positive direction. I am particularly impressed by the greater mobility and flexibility of the immigrant population, the fact of its providing a pool (however temporary) of spare capacity in the labour market, its propensity to save, and its propensity to work in the social service sector of the economy while imposing a disproportionately small burden on public expenditure. For these reasons my conclusion is that immigration has been conducive to growth and has been anti-inflationary. It is reasonable to infer that it has led to a rise in the standard of living of the domestic population, and an up-grading of the domestic population in the occupational hierarchy. Even where, as in the case of dock workers, it could conceivably be a threat to the existing labour force, this is mainly because of the restrictive practices that exist and might be broken down by an alternative supply of labour.

My final conclusion, therefore, is that not only must the opponents of immigration base their case on grounds other than economic, but also they must show that the non-economic disadvantages, to the extent that they exist, offset potential economic benefits.

NOTES TO CHAPTER 31

1. Eric Butterworth (ed.), *Immigrants in West Yorkshire* (London, Institute of Race Relations, Special Series, 1967).
2. G. C. K. Peach, 'West Indian migration to Britain: the economic factors', *Race* (Vol. VII, no. 1, July 1965).
3. Ibid.
4. N. Kaldor, 'Causes of the Slow Rate of Economic Growth of the United Kingdom' (inaugural lecture, published by Cambridge University Press, 1966).
5. Butterworth, op. cit.
6. B. Cohen and P. Jenner, 'The Employment of Immigrants: a case study within the wool industry', *Race* (Vol. X, no. 1, July 1968), p. 54
7. E. J. Mishan and L. Needleman, 'Immigration, Excess Aggregate Demand and the Balance of Payments', *Economica* (May 1966).

8. K. Jones, 'Immigrants and the Social Services', *National Institute Economic Review* (No. 41, August 1967).

9. Report from the Finance and General Purposes Committee of the City of Birmingham, May 1968.

10. R. B. Davison, *Black British* (London, Oxford University Press, for the Institute of Race Relations, 1966), p. 100.

In this chapter we shall begin the process of pulling together the threads of the discussion so far. In order to do so, it is essential first to establish the basis upon which the evidence is to be considered and evaluated, and for this we need a frame of reference within which to examine the evidence and on which the recommendations for action with which this Report will conclude can be securely based.

Oscar Handlin, the American social historian, has suggested three overlapping ways in which the evidence of the effects of the process of migration on a substantial scale can be examined. The first is the demographic. That is, one can consider the consequences of population change and the situation of the newcomer in purely statistical terms. The evidence presented earlier in this Report on the situation of the coloured man in Britain in 1968 reveals a substantial degree of inequality over quite a wide range of areas—housing, jobs, and, to some extent, educational facilities. Moreover, it is clear from the investigation of immigrant attitudes carried out as part of the P.E.P. Report that this inequality is perceived and resented by the majority of coloured people in this country—although there is evidence of sharply differentiated responses between one immigrant group and another. In this realistic experience of deprivation, and the perception of deprivation that results from it, lies one basis for action, and a precise one, too, in that it suggests where remedial action can immediately be applied. But this evidence by itself, valuable though it is, cannot be regarded as sufficient. Such an assessment provides items for only one side of a balance sheet. Remedial action directed to the material needs of the minority, although indispensable to satisfy their grievances, does not cater (except indirectly) for those of the majority. It may even be that the processes of satisfying one set of grievances may cast an additional strain on the majority—either because they resent the process of satisfaction or because it affects them directly and materially. One of the first coherent statements linking the two sets of grievances and attempting to reconcile them was that of Philip Mason's, and the field in which he argued that a concession to majority feeling is necessary was that of immigration. He suggested, at the beginning of 1965, that the aim of official policy should be defined as follows:

We are determined to treat those immigrants who are here as kindly as we treat our older citizens; we are determined to cut down sharply the number of fresh entries until this mouthful has been digested.[1]

It is a prescription which has since become the political orthodoxy. Whether this separation is satisfactory in concept or practical in execution is another matter; but the notion that stringency in control could be justified by reference to a forward policy in domestic race relations has had an enormous influence on the evolution of policy generally, as we have seen in Chapters 26 and 27.

But, with immigration policy, another set of considerations comes into play, including the second criterion for the determination of policy suggested by Handlin—the economic. It is possible to evaluate the entry of newcomers into our society purely in terms of economic costs and benefits and this process has been attempted by Professor Peston in Chapter 31. He concludes that immigration has been economically beneficial and that excessive restraints upon it might have adverse affects on the economy at large, especially in particular sectors.

Clearly these findings have important policy implications for the numbers and composition of immigration alike. Some of Professor Peston's other findings are also relevant for internal social policy—for example, in relation to the deployment of skills and the relevance of retraining programmes. Yet, as he himself is the first to accept, these considerations cannot in themselves be decisive for the formation of immigration policy. Other calculations must enter the picture—in particular, the capacity of the social structure, as distinct from the economic system, to absorb newcomers. This introduces the third of the categories devised by Handlin, the socio-cultural, and it is this perspective with which we will now be chiefly concerned.

However, this cultural dimension, unlike the economic, does not lend itself to precise calculations. It is true that in the rationalizations for the restriction upon numbers and rate of entry advanced by politicians, the restrictions are conceived of and justified directly in terms of material stress upon social services. Strain, that is, placed either on existing resources—housing stock educational facilities, provision of health services—or on the capacity of the natives to accept the arrival and settlement of the newcomers. This argument from stress was the chief plank on which the case deployed in the Labour Government's White Paper of August 1965 rested. It is implied in a formula subsequently devised by Roy Jenkins: that 'immigration should not be so high as to create a widespread resistance to effective integration policies [nor] so unreasonably low as to create an embittered sense of grievance in the immigrant community itself'.[2] But it is significant that neither at the time nor subsequently has any attempt been made to explain the basis on which the detailed calculation of the numerical quota was made. As we have seen, Ray Gunter (as Minister of Labour responsible for the employment voucher system, which serves as regulator) declined to do so. Indeed, it is doubtful whether any precise calculation could ever be arrived at. Once the concepts of cultural assimilation or psychological stress enter the picture, precision is inevitably lost. Nor is it possible to devise a formula in relation to the outflow of emigrants from the British Isles, since the composition and basis of the emigration is necessarily quite different from that of the immigration.

Moreover, the already insuperable difficulty of deriving objective measurements of stress multiply when subjective criteria come to be considered. The former are to some extent quantifiable, in so far as they are related to levels of effectiveness of services and amenities locally. But when we come to consider the effects of the changes in use which frequently take place with property in areas of immigrant settlement and the effects on amenity of the differing life styles of the newcomers, we are moving into an area where objective assessment is impossible.

Furthermore, anxiety about the extent of immigration and its consequences is based very largely on irrational—and consequently unquantifiable—factors. The point of focus derives from an element which is objectively irrelevant—the colour of the newcomers' skin. That the roots of the attitudes which make up the main element in the public reaction are irrational is indicated by the findings of the survey of attitudes reported in Chapter 28. Distorted information and the misleading stereotypes now in wide circulation play a major role in attitude formation: actual experience of migrants often substantially modifies the individual's response.

The fact that anxiety is often irrational does not mean that it is irrelevant. But it poses a problem of evaluation and weighting and the implications for policy are not clear. Edward Heath has stated—and there is truth in his assertion—that current public anxiety derives largely from the ordinary voter's fear that the Government has lost control over the phenomenon that affects him personally. The moral that Heath draws is that he himself must immediately be seen to be advocating the most stringent possible control of immigration; but the conclusion that this is the only way to recover confidence is a *non sequitur*. One cannot base policy indefinitely on conciliating opinion as such, regardless of the justice of the demands that are made. Most politicians realize this, and their repeated demands for stringency of control are a platform device in which the importance lies in the gesture struck and not the practical consequences. But such gestures have the effect of reinforcing the anxiety, not of relieving it—and hence intensifying the demands which must in turn be satisfied with further gestures *ad infinitum*. In short, public confidence is an even less reliable guide to the formation of policy than the evidence on stress.

While all the factors we have discussed must be taken into account when policy decisions are taken, they are not necessarily the decisive ones—important though they are in many ways in their implications for the quality of life in this country. There are other perspectives in which the issue can be viewed.

At the outset, it was generally considered, as we have seen, that the external factors deriving from Britain's relationship with the outside world decisively overrode all domestic considerations. Julius Isaac wrote in 1955:

Their presence must be welcomed from an international point of view. They are a challenge to those who regard racial prejudice, discrimination and the colour bar as unjustified, immoral and incompatible with the ideal of mutual aid and the common destiny of mankind. By fighting symptoms of deep-rooted racial prejudice, such people help to create a climate conducive to friendly international relationships. They have a powerful and less emotional argument to support them: the importance of this immigration for the cohesion and survival in its present form of the British Commonwealth.[3]

This kind of statement derives from assumptions about the relative significance of international and national policy objectives and has gradually lost significance as the one has diminished in importance and the other increased. We have described the process by which a Labour Administration came to adopt first what we have called a 'Little England' policy on race relations and then, in the throes of rejecting a last post-imperial responsibility, lapsed into a 'White Britain' posture. But it was a Conservative leader of the Opposition, Edward Heath, who was the first major political figure to argue that the semi-dismantled structure of Commonwealth preference in immigration procedures should be finally demolished. From the assumption that any form of control would infringe inalienable rights to an equal status, there has been a rapid decline to the complete dismissal of the notion that the Commonwealth connexion imposes obligations that should remain binding.

But whether the British Government chooses to concern itself with these considerations or not, British policy has implications both for the Commonwealth countries and internationally. The perspective exists, even if it is not employed. Robert Gardiner, reviewing the problems of international race relations in the 1965 Reith lectures, concluded that:

It seems to me that problems of migration and the treatment of settlers, which are now within the exclusive jurisdictions of individual countries, will eventually have to be examined collectively in a world organisation.[4]

Such a voluntary surrender of an admittedly important aspect of national sovereignty would certainly have important implications and might well be impractical in practice: that it is not totally a fantasy has been shown by the success of the E.E.C. countries in abolishing all restrictions on the movement of immigrant workers and their families within the European Community. But it is not, in the present climate of domestic opinion, practical politics. Nor, in present circumstances, are arguments (like those of Dr. Isaac) deriving from a discarded view of the significance of the Commonwealth connexion. To the extent that they still persist among politicians, these attitudes—like those expressions of the Christian perspective on the issue still frequently heard at moments of crisis—are no longer regarded as relevant for policy.

In any discussion conducted upon the terms so far outlined the individual is largely excluded. Arguments on broad grounds of principle employing purely symbolic terms are justly suspect when applied to social problem issues in which questions of human suffering are involved. They may also embody assumptions which have never been put to the test of free consent.

Policy-makers in the past have proceeded from the assumption that the act of migration implies a willingness to accept not only the material conditions obtaining in the new surroundings but to take on the values and customs prevalent in that society. Migration has, since the nineteenth century, implied the entry of future citizens. And, although the increasing recognition given to cultural diversity has modified this assumption in the case of the migrant himself and restored a degree of identity to individuals who were once regarded purely as objects on a totem pole, it has been transferred, often in an intensified form, to their children—the second man on the pole. There is a feeling, to which one cannot help applying religious metaphors, that the 'Black British' will redeem our sinful society: that by making them first-class citizens we will wipe out the sin of the second-class status of their fathers. In short, what one could call a new social contract. In one version, they will become the simulacrum of Englishmen—their skin colour, a constant reminder of our virtue in their equality, in another, the less patronizing, there will be a new mixed youth culture, with multi-racial and multi-cultural characteristics. Norman Bentwich has written of the generation of German Jewish refugees who came to this country at the end of the 1930s, that their children 'may yet produce the best fruit from the meetings of the two cultures . . . the return which the new citizens have already made is a rich reward for the virtues of tolerance and the asylum that Britain signally offered'.[5] This notion of cultural amalgamation is clearly a stage beyond the crude assumption of Anglo-conformity with which their parents were confronted and with which coloured newcomers are still confronted by the host population generally. But it is still based on the presumption that a contract which for one party has not been offered on a footing of free choice has already been entered into. In most of the policy decisions taken in the past on race relations the consent of the minority has been assumed. The possibility that it can no longer be taken for granted has not been subjected to any serious scrutiny and the flippant rhetoric of those few black men who have so far questioned it has not encouraged such scrutiny.

American Negroes, it is often suggested, have ceased to be prepared to accept the overdue concession of justice if it is offered as an act of charity. What hasn't been given of right isn't worth having. The same might come to be true of the equal citizenship offered to the coloured Briton by British politicians. For instance, it may be that some of the inducements offered to him may not be as attractive as the white majority have assumed them to be. To be a visible example of British tolerance may not be a very satisfying role to perform. To take an obvious example, for a white house-owner, the arrival of a black neighbour, according to the unshakeable folk-lore, will diminish the material and hence the psychological value of his property. A contrary assumption is no less tenaciously subscribed to; that for a coloured man, white neighbours confer vastly increased social status. But, like the American Negro—or rather the American Negro who listens to the advice given to him by the Carmichaels and Hamiltons—a coloured Englishman might decide that concentration would mean not only increased security but a basis for future political power.

Faced with a challenge to the cultural imperialism which has been unthinkingly accepted for so long, what degree of pluralism can our society, its homogeneity already under attack from other directions, tolerate? The separatism of the Indian and Pakistani communities has been the subject of both criticism and defence: criticism, on the grounds that it constitutes an impermissible degree of communalism, and defence on the grounds that the phenomena involved are of a temporary nature and have a certain exotic value in terms of style of life. In neither case has the problem of the evolution of separate institutions and the extent to which they can be conceded parity of esteem been considered. The idea has rarely been entertained that British society might move, like American society in the model devised by Milton Gordon, towards a chequer-board pattern in which class and ethnic differences divide society horizontally and vertically. And the problems of keeping the way open for those who decide to leave one system for another has therefore not been examined, although the experience of previous migrations suggests that this transition is far more painful and difficult than the process of migration itself.

One difficulty about charting a secure passage through these rocks is that the debate on cultural diversity has so far taken place on such a superficial level. Because discussion has concentrated on a limited number of manifestations of different life style, there has been a general tendency to mistake temporary fringe phenomena for the more significant differences that they reflect. Many justifications of the migration have been mounted on the rickety platform of these transitory, lower order, differences. One can classify these briefly in terms of the senses which register them. The visual variety, such as the differences in skin pigmentation, dress, and styles of decoration, makes up the image of cosmopolitanism which many people consider appropriate to large cities; as does diversity of cuisine, which is perhaps where the notion of cultural amalgamation has been closest to realization; and, in the case of the young, musical tastes which reflect all kinds of diverse influences—American Negro, West Indian, Indian. Furthermore, distinctions in use of the English language, dialect, slang, and, on a more serious level, special contributions of African and Caribbean novelists, are an important element in the development of fiction in post-war Britain, but one possibly exaggerated in significance.

In all these directions, and in others, there has been an assumption that the behaviour and style of the newcomers will make a special contribution to modifying the Englishman's own style of life. Thus, he will exemplify the virtues of relaxation, persuade the Englishman of the value of living in the present, and communicate the notion that the enjoyment of sex is a legitimate and important part of life. Sporting life, both in the sense of the high definition performances of cricketers like Constantine and Sobers and in the other sense of guilt-free indulgence in sensual pleasures, is the contribution that the immigrant, in this interpretation, has to make. Professor Rex has urged that he has another function, as an ingredient in 'some kind of Latin Quarter, with students, unmarried people and deviants of all sorts'.[6] It may well be that this kind of interpretation of the position of the immigrant in our society contains as much cultural patronage as the earlier assumption that all migrants were instant Englishmen. But the most serious criticism of this attitude is that it overlooks the intense puritanism of most West Indians, who would reject the 'students, unmarried people and deviants' and the life style with which they are associated with far more vehemence than the white middle class. Although amalgamation in a multi-cultural and inter-racial setting is possible, this is not the kind of footing on which it can be launched, except by foot-loose under-25s. If we are to evaluate the prospects for pluralism satisfactorily, it will have to be done on a more systematic basis than this.

Not merely should discussion extend beyond the purely exotic aspects of the migration: it must transcend the limitations implicit in the politicians' definition of the issue as 'the immigration problem'—a concept implying equally restricted views of causation and the aims of future policy. For, in practice, the issue has not been an isolated feature in the political landscape. By throwing light on a series of major social issues, culminating in the whole debate about the relief of poverty and maldistribution of resources to which the Urban Programme is to be directed, the immigrants illuminate the strengths and weaknesses of our social system and indicate the surgery which it requires. For the effects of the deprivation of rights cannot be viewed in isolation: the perspective in which it must be placed is ultimately that of the debate about these concepts in the wider society. Equally, the implications of pluralism relate to the basic structure of that society and the basis on which certain facilities are provided within it. In short, our society is in important respects an unjust society organized in such a way as to perpetuate these injustices. Immigration, by stimulating a concern for social justice, may also provide the solvent for the inflexibility which helped to produce the symptoms now ascribed to the presence of immigrants.

This perspective has provided the focus for the diagnosis made by a number of eminent social diagnosticians. Professor Peter Townsend, in his discussion of the social policy of the Labour party in office, wrote:

There has been a marked shift of emphasis away from social equality as a national objective. The White Paper on Immigration from the Commonwealth in 1965 (together with the later failure to promote integration) can now be perceived as representing a major retreat from universalistic values, which inevitably sapped the moral authority of the Government in other social spheres and affected the whole delicate structure of community services. . . . The interdependence of institutions and values [ensures] that changes in one part of the social structure are bound to affect other parts of that structure. The restrictive policies reflected by the White Paper and by measures like the Kenya Asians Act [sic] were bound to make racial equality harder to achieve. But they make social equality harder to achieve too. . . . After the White Paper of 1965 the term 'equality' could no longer be used unselfconsciously by members of the Labour Party. Much more important, the concept could no longer lend coherence and simplicity to the Government's long-term objectives.[7]

This view, that the official attitude towards the social rights of minority groups is inseparable from the values articulated in

Government action over the whole field of social policy, is illustrated, in the least attractive possible form, in the punitive gestures made towards stigmatized or powerless minorities. It might, for example, explain the simultaneous announcement, on 26 July 1968, of new measures to prevent the fiancé(e)s of immigrants from entering this country and new methods of scrutinizing claims for supplementary benefit in order to screen out 'layabouts'.

This perspective is also crucial at a time when the whole functioning of the Welfare State and the provision made for those who fall below the minimum subsistence level have come under close and critical scrutiny. Douglas Houghton has pointed out that the entire structure of the Welfare State has come into existence in one lifetime: 'Everyone now over pension age was born at a time when the only institutional care provided by the State was the Workhouse and the Lunatic Asylum.'[8] Yet the institutions are already displaying the signs of stress and wear and tear appropriate to a far older structure. The governing assumption of the 1950s had been that the minimum living standard envisaged by Beveridge had been achieved; a safety net was presumed to exist which symbolized society's commitment to ensuring that individuals would not find themselves living in poverty. Against this background, the selectivist argument gained ground. Certain services need no longer be provided by the State and could be more efficiently met out of private resources. The ecstatic view that the class system itself was dissolving in the solvent of the new prosperity was widely heard: it was based, in part, on the evidence of increasing embourgeoisement in the new prosperous section of the working class, whose possession of a wide range of consumer goods and taste for continental holidays attracted a great deal of attention at the end of the 1950s. Evidence to support this assertion was also derived from the Conservative election victory of 1959 which was held to reflect a shift in the social class basis of British politics.

Yet the evidence for the wholesale abolition of poverty in our society was never satisfactory and on closer examination it became clear that the increased prosperity of a large section of the working class had left behind it substantial pockets of poverty, made more visible and painful to those who endured it by the relative success of the majority. Galbraith's famous use of the Latin tag about private affluence and public squalor underlines the important element in this residual poverty—the poor quality of the services

THE BALANCE SHEET 667

which were available to a substantial section of the population in
the inner areas of great cities. The 'cheerful' school could point
with justice to the enormous changes in life style and access to
amenities enjoyed by a large section of the population. We have
quoted one such analysis, that of Dr. Abrams, in Chapter 3.
Professor Titmuss has put the other side of the picture:

In Britain, in 1951 there were few who would have thought that in the
years ahead the proportion of children and old people considered to be
living in poverty would increase; that incomes would become more
unequal; that the distribution of personal wealth would be found to be
more highly concentrated in the top 5 per cent of the population; that
there would be no narrowing of the differentials between working
class and middle class children in the higher reaches of the educational
system.[9]

And there is solid evidence of the diversion of the increased
resources available away from those who needed them most—for
example, in the proportion of the gross national product spent on
social welfare services.

The rediscovery of poverty, that endless cyclic process through
which every generation passes, had this much in common with
earlier revelations: the quite unexpected extent of the suffering
revealed had an electric effect on the social conscience of the
nation. But there is a distinction which sets this process of discovery
apart from previous ones—the complicating and illuminating
presence of an element of coloured immigration. The newcomers,
caught like their white peers in the narrowing walls of the private
rented sector of major cities, were subject to the same material
deprivations; but too often they became the scape-goats for them.
Yet there was another distinction which may in the long run prove
to be more important. The poor, in the mid-twentieth century, are
not conceived of as constituting a physically or socially separate
section of the community. They are not separated from the body
of society, as the nineteenth-century pauper was, by formal
deprivation of social rights. Nor are the areas of poverty remoter,
as C. F. G. Masterman portrayed the Edwardian slums, than
China or Peru. The mass media see to that. As Professor Townsend
has put it: 'The extent of poverty and the current methods of
treating the poor are inescapably linked to the prosperity and
expectations of other sections of society.'[10] And the responsibility
for remedial measures has been by and large accepted, once the

diagnosis was admitted to be sound. This distinction derives largely from the historical processes which we have described in Chapter 3. The access of the working class to sources of power has been considerably improved; to the civil rights gained in the nineteenth century has been added the effective enjoyment of a substantial degree of political leverage derived from the rise of the Labour movement. Nevertheless, the deprivation of social rights suffered by those whose income or family size confined them to the rented accommodation in the inner areas of large cities and forced them to accept unskilled work for themselves and poor educational facilities for their children cast a shadow over these other rights. Professor Townsend goes on to comment: 'It is not surprising that they [the poor] *feel* stigmatised. To a large extent they *are* stigmatised.'[11] Or, at best, the processes of exercising those rights are clogged by the complexities and inefficiency of the machinery devised to satisfy them. And the coloured poor, suffering in common with their neighbours this deprivation, have additional disadvantages deriving both from discrimination and from the neglect deriving from the *laissez-faire* integration policy of the 1950s, which embodied a failure to recognize the need for separate facilities to cater for their needs.

Professor Titmuss has suggested that there are three ways of classifying the benefits or uses of social security and social service provision. It can be regarded as a form of investment on the part of society or the individual; or it can be seen as a method of distributing income or command over resources; or, finally, it can be seen as a form of compensation for deprivation—for example, inadequate access to existing services or welfare provisions. The means to achieving these ends, he argues, lies in the provision of a range of benefits on a universal basis. He concludes that 'there can be no answer in Britain to the problems of poverty, ethnic integration and social and educational inequalities without an infrastructure of universalist services'.[12] This is, of course, a view that has been strongly criticized by those who feel that if need can be accurately identified it can be satisfied in a less wasteful way than by the provision of benefits on a universal basis.

It is not part of our purpose here to suggest that universal benefits, at least as provided at present, are necessarily always the most efficient way of dealing with all the needs of the minority with which we are particularly concerned. This argument was advanced by the Government in the White Paper of 1965 and we have described it elsewhere as 'weak' universalism. In the case of a minority differing in age structure and family size from the population at large, there may be objective arguments for a degree of variation in the provision of services. The time scale of need may also be different; there are additional—but temporary—needs arising from the migration process which have to be satisfied in the short term but whose satisfaction should not be built into any long-term solutions. The deprivation for which compensation is necessary may also need to be satisfied in different ways. And some services provided for the population at large may at present not be relevant for the needs of this minority: for example, there is very little use made of the geriatric services by immigrants, both for cultural reasons and as a result of their age structure. But none of these propositions is inconsistent with the general case for the provision of the kind of reinforcement of the universal infrastructure for which Professor Titmuss is arguing.

A programme which involves, even in a partial way, distinguishing a particular group and giving them access to benefits not provided for the population at large presents formidable political and practical difficulties. As Professor Titmuss comments, the problem of redistribution presents such a formidable challenge precisely because 'it is inextricably mixed up with the change of social rights as well as civil rights for coloured citizens'.[13] This is in many ways the crux of the whole issue. One strategy already proposed would go a long way towards surmounting this obstacle. It is one which will already be familiar from discussion of policy and its evolution—the application of the principle of territorial welfare justice. That is, the identification for action of the geographical areas in which the burdens of underprivilege bear particularly hard on inhabitants of all colours. This is the policy adopted in defining the Plowden educational priority areas (E.P.A.s) and the Milner Holland areas of special housing need. The rationale for this approach is that the handicaps of poverty are cumulative: a disproportionate amount of the social cost of change is concentrated on certain social groups occupying certain geographical areas and the burden of unemployment deriving from technological change will fall particularly heavily on this group. It is also this group that will feel the impact of urban renewal and has to put up with poor quality services and a poor quality environment in the inner urban areas. Ultimately, effective community services, preventive in outlook and of a high quality (both in terms of facilities and personnel), should provide the main answer for the problems of this group, but in the interim there must be a redistribution of resources to compensate for what Titmuss calls the 'diswelfare' imposed by the factors detailed above. Such a programme must be directed to the needs of all those who are affected by these processes; such a policy of 'strong' universalism would represent something of a revolution in social priorities. And even if such a revolution left certain specific needs of coloured minorities unsatisfied it would still represent, for them as for their white neighbours, an enormous advance on the present position. Furthermore, it could provide the context within which any additional special measures could be set in perspective.

In any programme involving positive discrimination, whether it is in favour of a group defined by area of residence or one distinguished by ethnic origin, the major justification for action must be past negative discrimination. Such discrimination must be recognized as existing, and accepted for what it is. As the evidence from the attitude survey suggests, the average Englishman recognizes no responsibility for the immigrants who have entered his society. Like Lord Carron, he feels that they have not made sufficient contribution to justify permitting them to obtain benefits on a scale equivalent to that to which the population at large is entitled, let alone to benefits over and above these. However, a degree of responsibility is admitted in the case of those born here— who are sometimes called the 'Black Britons'. This group appears to have crossed the boundary line between 'them' and 'us' (though whether this acceptance is a temporary or permanent phenomenon it is hard to say). Their situation provides a basis for action—because their title to access to the civil and social rights we discussed in Chapter 3 is not clouded by recent arrival or, at least so far, by uncertainty about which society they belong to. The obligations should be clear—both on their side and that of the majority. If the latter acknowledge their responsibilities, there is a better chance that the minority will accept the full implications of citizenship. Action on their behalf could take the form of corrective legislation to restore the social rights which they are unlikely to be permitted to enjoy in present circumstances or through administrative action to enable them to exercise them adequately. It is important to emphasize that these rights are available to them as citizens: there should be no implication of a special contract entered into between them and the State which differs from the reciprocal rights and obligations which apply in the case of all British citizens. Providing access to services and amenities of right should not involve the narrowing of their area of choice and personal behaviour—the friends they choose, the places they live in, their tastes in food and clothing. They must not be expected to be more British than the British.

The broad principles for special programmes are hard enough to devise, even in the case of the Black Britons: in practice, their application presents even more formidable difficulties. Such programmes are hedged round with the psychological problems of identifying need without ascribing responsibility for its existence. We have argued in Chapter 29 that in the new Urban Programme the Government has fallen into this difficulty; by exaggerating the importance of immigration as a cause of difficulty, they have made it more difficult effectively to relieve the disabilities of immigrants.

The suggestion that the presence of immigrants has a universal rather than a relative significance has been the main source of difficulty. Poor housing conditions and inadequate educational facilities are adequate indices of social deprivation; the presence of immigrants can mean any number of things, depending on local circumstances and one's perspective, but there is no one-to-one relationship between the fact of an immigrant residing in the area and the existence of a material problem—indeed, the individual migrant may find himself deprived even within an area in which there is overall prosperity. By encouraging the view that immigrants were in themselves one form of natural disaster (as Elizabeth Burney puts it), the initial ministerial explanation of the Urban Programme nourished the illusion that the problems of areas of settlement would disappear if the immigrants departed—either voluntarily, through dispersal, or compulsorily, through repatriation—and impeded the formulation of realistic objectives for central and local government.

We have already suggested that part of the difficulties involved lie in the structure of central Government. The proposals in the Seebohm Report for the co-ordination of local authority services may point the way to a solution to some of these structural difficulties, but it is imperative that the task of defining the scope of the special needs of coloured citizens and the most effective means of relieving them is entrusted to a department capable of making a realistic appreciation and well equipped to devise remedial measures. The deployment of personnel and resources, the organization of the services, and the access to information has in the past been wholly inadequate to those needs. The significance of these themes has already been touched upon but it has an increased significance in the aftermath of the announcement of the Urban Programme and the confusion caused by the imprecise definition of the aims of policy.

Finally, Professor Townsend has commented that poverty should not be regarded as an absolute but as a relative condition and 'for it to be alleviated there has to be a complex reconstruction of the systems of reward in society, as between those at work and those who are not at work, those with and without dependants, and those who live in depressed and prosperous regions'.[14] We cannot urge that the significance of race relations is such that the entire reconstruction must be undertaken with a view to resolving this issue alone. Nor, even in the broader context of meeting the needs of the under-privileged as a whole, can the necessity for such a reconstruction be completely decisive for the evolution of policy. It is attractive to see the focus of government action purely in terms of 'social growth', but, as Douglas Houghton, himself once Ministerial Coordinator of Social Services has pointed out, there is a problem in reconciling unimpeded rises in social expenditure with the severe curbs on personal consumption and minimal rise in economic growth which are a feature of the British economy in the mid-1960s. At this point other factors come into play and involve us in issues beyond the scope of this Report. But the touchstone by which our proposals must be measured is the extent to which they contribute to a situation in which a redistribution of resources can be undertaken on a socially just basis, between citizens with full and secure access to social, civil, and political rights, employing means which permit the exercise of the maximum degree of choice compatible with these overriding aims.

NOTES TO CHAPTER 32

1. P. Mason, *Guardian* (23 January 1965).
2. In a speech to the National Committee for Commonwealth Immigrants, 23 May 1966.
3. Julius Isaac in *The Positive Contribution by Immigrants* (Paris, UNESCO, 1955), p.62.
4. *A World of Peoples* (London, B.B.C. Publications, 1966), p. 23.
5. Quoted by Isaac, op. cit., p. 65.
6. In a speech to the Summer School of the Town and Country Planning Institute, quoted in *The Times* (9 September 1968).

7. Peter Townsend in *Social Services for All?*, Part One, Fabian Tract 382 (London, Fabian Society, 1968), p. 2.

8. Douglas Houghton, *Paying For the Social Services* (London, Institute of Economic Affairs, 1967), p. 7.

9. R. H. Titmuss, *Commitment to Welfare* (London, George Allen & Unwin, 1968), p. 161.

10. P. Townsend in *Social Services for All?*, Part Four, Fabian Tract 385 (London, Fabian Society, 1968), p. 110.

11. Ibid., pp. 110–11.

12. Titmuss, op. cit., p. 123.

13. Ibid., p. 114.

14. Townsend, Fabian Tract 382, op. cit., p. 6.

33 Findings and Recommendations

INTRODUCTION

The recommendations which follow spring from the analysis in the rest of the Report and are based on the diagnosis which we have made of the state of race relations in this country. In our analysis we have tried to isolate some of the causes of past failures in policy. The greater part of our analysis has been concerned with the British reaction to immigration and the greater part of our prescriptions are for programmes for which British society—still overwhelmingly white—would have the responsibility. We are not as sceptical as some about the prospects of persuading the majority to assume that responsibility.

From our survey of British attitudes to colour we have evidence that, contrary to the general view, the majority of the population are tolerantly inclined and that there is more tolerance among those who live near coloured people than among those who live in areas of England where there are no settlements of coloured immigrants. We have also learned that tolerance is greatest among those under 35 years old and especially among those who have had contact with coloured people at work. To find the greatest tolerance among this age group is encouraging because this is the section of the population who have spent the greatest part of their lives in a multi-racial society.

While our findings show that there is still room for manœuvre, given constructive policies and firm leadership, the evidence also shows that there are variations in the levels of tolerance in different regions of the country. The response is not at all uniform: it varies with the availability of a scarce resource like housing, but even more with the character and make-up of the local population and its past economic and social history. To speak very broadly, there are great differences between the North of England, the South-east and the Midlands. It is a mistake to think of English society as monolithic or even to assume that within a given region the response will be uniform. There are, for example, noticeable differences between the East and the West Midlands. The evidence suggests that in some situations there is more room for manœuvre than in others. Local attitudes affect the policies of local authorities which in turn reinforce the attitudes of their electors. A situation in which such a wide variety of responses is possible demands that any policy introduced should have a strong element of flexibility: but it also implies that policy makers need not be necessarily deterred by hostile responses in one particular area, which need not be taken as typical. We are therefore encouraged by these findings to put forward our recommendations, since they seem to us to provide solid ground for expecting a favourable response to positive policies.

Our recommendations are put forward as part of our concern with the disadvantages of the coloured minorities which in the previous chapter we have set within the general context of poverty and of the crisis in the inner city. Our proposals are designed to equip members of these minorities to be equal citizens as well as to be equal under law. We accept that equality does not mean uniformity; we agree with the Hunt Committee that the preservation of different cultures can enrich the quality of the whole society. The measures that we propose are designed to compensate these minorities for disadvantages which are peculiar to them and not to coerce them into abandoning their identity, culture, or customs. Such action is imperative to prevent a feeling of alienation from growing within the coloured communities and to ensure that individuals are able and willing to exercise their rights as citizens.

To say that these immigrants have decided to adopt this society as their own masks an assumption about their intentions. But on all the evidence which we have reviewed in Parts II and V of this Report we are satisfied that we are dealing with minorities who are here to stay and that they and their children will be part of the future of this country. This is not a situation which can be altered by anything short of deliberate coercion of these minorities into departure. To advocate a policy of *voluntary* repatriation is an evasion which is in essence the counterpart of the *laissez-faire* policies of the 1950s. Only economic aid to the countries of origin on a scale which would offer the prospect of an adequate standard of living there could make voluntary return attractive as a realistic proposition, and aid on this scale is out of the question. It is perfectly true that, regardless of economic circumstances, nostalgia may induce a good deal of talk about return. But nostalgia involves no action; it is the stock-in-trade of all exiles, and fades with the passing of time.

Previous migrations to this country have been allowed to work out their own salvation at their own pace. They have endured varying degrees of hardship from discrimination and hostility at the hands of the native population and the frictions engendered have resulted in local conflicts. But in the end, whatever the cost in suffering, the immigrants and their dependants have moved away from the areas of initial settlement into the wider community and up the economic ladder. Hence the unspoken assumption behind the *laissez-faire* policies which we have described—that no special measures are needed to assist the postwar coloured immigrants. But there are signs that these new communities will not follow the paths of economic and geographical dispersal of previous immigrants: the second generation, instead of progressing, remains stationary or even falls back. Instead of moving outwards, they are encountering barriers; and behind these barriers pressures are building up. And what finally distinguishes this from previous migrations and calls for some measures of intervention by the Government through administrative action and the law is the factor of colour. The evidence for the existence of discrimination based on colour is overwhelmingly strong. And this discrimination against coloured citizens is not to be equated with discrimination against foreigners who are white. Furthermore, coloured people in one country cannot be insulated from the sufferings of coloured people at the hands of white people elsewhere; the second generation of coloured children are going to feel the pressures of the Third World's struggle to achieve parity. For all these reasons colour changes the time scale; even if there were no special barriers in the way of these communities, our society could not afford to wait for these migrations to run the course of their predecessors.

In our recommendations we are trying to show a way through this situation. We are concerned with the next ten years, which will be decisive for the future course of race relations. Our recommendations are therefore mainly for the short term and can for the most part be put into operation immediately by administrative action. This emphasis is not because we think that more radical policies are not required—we would like to see our recommendations carried out against a background of broader measures of social reform, some of which we have sketched in. Rather, it is because we want our proposals to be taken seriously as a basis for early action. Given the prevailing economic climate, we have therefore confined ourselves to recommendations which will not involve much, if any, capital expenditure.

Dispersal

There are a number of subjects which are central to nearly all our recommendations and which recur as a common theme in the discussion of policies. These subjects are: first, the special training required by all those whose duties give them some responsibility for the lives of people of another culture; secondly, the need for information and for systematic standardized records; and finally, and most important, the causes and consequences of concentration and the extent to which a policy of dispersal is desirable.

The Kerner Report defines a ghetto as 'an area within a city characterized by poverty and acute social disorganization, and inhabited by members of a racial or ethnic group under conditions of involuntary segregation'.[1] By this definition, there are few, if any, coloured ghettoes in this country, but many cities have coloured quarters where coloured people may be in the majority. Moreover, from the evidence of the 1966 Census, it appears that these concentrations increased in the five years since the previous census was taken in 1961. They are reflected in the changing composition of the school population in the areas concerned. There are already a number of primary schools with a majority of coloured pupils. The Secretary of State for Education has recently dealt in public with the question of all-black schools which are likely to appear if the concept of the neighbourhood school is retained. He concluded that he would very much regret the emergence of such schools, as they could not make any contribution to integration. We would agree with him. He added that he did not think it was the policy of any local authority in Britain to create all-coloured schools. While this may be true of local education authorities, the matter may be beyond their control as concentrations may result from an authority's housing policy. In any discussion of whether concentrations are undesirable, it is necessary to distinguish the factors which have brought these concentrations about. It is one thing if they occur in response to the cultural needs of a community: it is quite another if they are involuntary, in the sense that the inhabitants can find no way out. It is different again if people cluster together for security and are afraid to move outwards into what they fear to be a hostile environment.

We address ourselves to the question of dispersal before we set out any of our policy recommendations because it is fundamental to the future of race relations in this country and because the question 'to disperse or not to disperse' will increasingly confront planners as the coloured quarters of our cities come to be cleared and redeveloped. Moreover, if central government is increasingly to intervene, it is essential that the goals of policy should be entirely clear. In the past, the assumption, shared by all concerned, has been that the aim is the dispersal of the minorities. By analogy with previous migrations, it has been assumed that social problems will cease to exist as the minorities break out and assimilate themselves to the majority society. Nevertheless, we do not believe that dispersal is always the right policy to follow. This is not to say that there are not dangers in leaving things as they are. A danger exists that in some cities the twilight areas may be left out of development plans because they contain a large number of coloured people, and that in twenty years' time they will have become coloured enclaves. There is no virtue in the continued concentration of coloured people in overcrowded housing, in the poorer quarters of our cities. On the contrary, there are great dangers, and the dangers seem to us to be greatest in the case of West Indians. There is the danger of the growth of separate communities, alienated from the majority society and demoralized by the low status accorded to the area in which they live. There is the danger of perpetuating their present disadvantages. There is the risk of a flight of white teachers from all-coloured schools, of poor performance by pupils unqualified for any but unskilled work. There is a danger of a different kind of policing in these areas.

Despite all these dangers, we would not feel justified in recommending the introduction of the more drastic measures that would be necessary to promote wholesale dispersal—the regulation of settlement of newcomers, the wholesale breaking up of immigrant settlements, and the rigid restrictions on residence in close proximity in public housing.

We would not feel justified because there is no prescription that can be universally applied. In our description of the cultures of the immigrant communities in Part II of the Report and in the analysis of their response to the British situation in Part V, we have tried to show the great differences that exist between these communities and also within them. We have shown, for example, that among Pakistanis the reasons for clustering in all-male settlements (and for refusing council tenancies) were largely economic, while cultural imperatives have caused families to disperse when wives come to join their husbands; in the next stage, the gradual concentration of Pakistani families in the dispersal areas provides support for women cut off by religious restrictions from full association with their neighbours. In general, communal institutions afford protection for newcomers confronted with a double problem of adjustment to an urban society and to the idea of being categorized as coloured in a white man's world. Thus, for the Sikhs, the temple (*gurdwara*) provides a cultural and social centre which is indispensable in the early stages of settlement and dispersal is likely to take place to areas that are within easy reach of these centres.

There are already many Indian communities which are becoming well established, as families have been reunited and are grouped together by kinship or village ties. Their members have bought property, started their own enterprises, founded welfare associations, and in many other ways are mutually supportive. In some cases they have entered local politics. These communities are putting down roots and there is no case for an active policy of dispersal, but it is desirable that Indians should not be involuntarily confined to particular areas of any town. Wherever the housing market is not artificially restricted, it is likely that some thinning out of the areas of settlement will take place naturally. Aspiring members of these communities are already making their way into suburbia and if anti-discrimination legislation is effective this process will accelerate. However, it could be arrested by open hostility or by the continuance of the kind of propaganda which warns us against the danger of 'foreign' areas being established in certain towns. The answer is not to arrest the movement but to abate hostility.

The situation of the Pakistanis is likely to be analogous to that of the Indians, but the development has been far slower because of the demographic imbalance in the immigration. Some West Pakistani settlements have already formed on the Indian model and we expect that this pattern will spread as more families are established in this country. This process is likely to be accelerated by the effect of the 1968 Commonwealth Immigrants Act which requires both parents to be present before dependent children can be allowed to enter. The communities will perhaps be more tightly grouped because of the seclusion of wives and possibly of daughters when they leave school. In many areas where Pakistanis have settled, particularly in the North of England there is no shortage of houses, and therefore any clustering that occurs is likely to be voluntary. The all-male settlements will remain but will naturally be reduced as families are formed over here. It is unlikely that a policy of dispersal would break down the insulation of their inhabitants who, like the Irish labourers before them, will continue to live co-operatively, sacrificing amenities to their economic goals. Any change in the current regulations which would lower the age for dependent children permitted to join their parents would almost certainly deter many wives from joining their husbands in this country.

The position of West Indians is different and more complex. In some places, there are communities that have established themselves and, despite poor housing, prefer the neighbourhood because it is near to their work and, as in Brixton, has a market which supplies the food they prefer. In Elizabeth Burney's words, 'there is a great deal that is warm, sociable, and attractive about central Brixton as its West Indian inhabitants have made it; a great potential for planners to build on.' There are many other West Indians who live in twilight zones or in slum areas with nothing in common but poverty or their shared experience of wretched housing, but they are not a community. We have shown in an earlier chapter that the Birmingham and London West Indians often pay more rent than their white neighbours for accommodation with poorer amenities. Because of the colour tax, many cannot afford anything better; but it is often forgotten that many more West Indians who live in the under-privileged areas of our cities are not there by choice and could pay for better housing if only they could get it. They and their families are at present condemned to bad material surroundings by the critical shortage of housing in these areas and by discrimination. Many West Indians are the archetype of the council house tenant—skilled artisans whose wives are prepared to go out to work to add to family resources. If the present obstacles are removed it seems to us likely that they will follow the Irish into acceptance in the public sector. That others would willingly buy houses if credit were available is shown by the extent of home ownership among West Indians, which is far higher than in the English working class. All these people need to be helped to get out of the areas in which they are so often involuntarily segregated. They need information on the options available to them. Above all, they need to be given a choice. It does not follow that because they wish to get out of overcrowded housing in their present neighbourhoods they would choose to be dispersed in isolation, for there is much security and comfort in familiarity. Nor is there any virtue in isolating them from one another; if families or friends wish to stay together it should be possible to offer them rehousing in the same neighbourhood on an estate. There is equally no need for planners to reproduce the large groupings that have grown up often by accident or necessity in the inner city. Among West Indians there is not the same pattern of the extended family or the village network that is found in Indian and Pakistani settlements. It is true that some small islanders, like the Montserratians, have clustered together in one or two places, but this is the exception.

However, there are West Indians who will not want to leave the concentration in the inner city, either through fear of the unknown or because they do feel threatened by the hostility of the majority who may reject them. For them, and for the established communities who do not want to be moved, the alternatives will ultimately be rehousing within the area those who are displaced by redevelopment schemes, or assisting property owners to rehabilitate their houses. But if these alternatives to dispersal are to be justified, two essential preliminaries must be satisfied. First, exit from areas of coloured settlement must be safeguarded and entry of newcomers of all colours (which still takes place more frequently than many people realize) must be assured. Secondly, the link between colour and squalor which is firmly cemented in the public mind by conditions in the twilight areas must be broken. In fact, such an association existed for Jewish immigrants while settlement was concentrated in the East End and the inner areas of Northern cities; it has been broken by the diaspora of Jews from these areas to the middle-class suburban communities in which the majority now live. If these conditions are to be satisfied not only must housing conditions be improved, as current policy may perhaps achieve, but educational facilities and environment must be brought up to a level at least equal to that of suburbia. Parity of esteem must as far as possible be assured. In these circumstances, a degree of concentration can be acceptable. It provides a bridge for the second generation to cross into the wider society without repudiating too abruptly the culture of the parents, by association with the poor conditions in which the children knew it, and it will provide some form of security for those who feel threatened by the hostility they have increasingly perceived among the majority.

1. MACHINERY OF GOVERNMENT

If there is one allegation that is more frequently made than any other it is that the Government (by which is meant both Parliament and Whitehall) has lost control of the race situation—if, indeed, it ever had such control. As our analysis would suggest, we do not accept the view that successive governments have entirely overlooked this question, or that there was a basic failure of intelligence, in the military sense. Rather, our view is that many of the decisions taken during the early stages of the migration were sins of commission and not omission (that is to say, the failure to intervene was an act of deliberate policy). But, having said this, we would agree that there has been a failure of forward planning; no consistent attempt has been made to deploy available resources with clear aims in mind. This failure, which extends up until the recent past, has stemmed partly from the placing of the responsibility for race relations within the structure of government and partly from the attitudes of those in authority on the legitimate aims of policy on this issue.

In our view, the key to reform lies in clearly distinguishing policy on race relations from policy on immigration. Each demands a different approach; each the deployment of a different range of resources.

Problems of race relations in this country are closely linked with a whole series of difficulties arising from the problems of the inner city and can only be tackled in the context of a broader attack upon these problems, involving a wide range of agencies and government departments. Immigration policy lends itself more easily to consideration as a separate element and the considerations that need to be brought to bear are more easily susceptible of being quantified. Nor is the prime need to devote substantial additional resources to the solution of difficulties; the main aim must be to devise an effective and humane policy in which all parties can have confidence. All this is not to say that the two problems can ever be considered in complete isolation from one another: it is the suggestion that they must be indissolubly linked for administrative purposes that is untenable.

In Chapter 32 we argued that in the long run efficiency and

social justice both demanded that the solutions to the main problems associated with immigration should be sought within a broad strategy directed towards the urban situation and based on need, and not race. We called this a policy of 'strong universalism'. If such a strategy were to be introduced, the logical point from which it could best be directed is the office of the Secretary of ▌ State for Social Affairs. We therefore recommend that the responsibility for integration policy be transferred to the Department of Social Affairs (that is, the new department made up from the amalgamation of the Ministries of Health and Social Security).

It may be argued that this is not a feasible step at this stage, while the new department still consists merely of an unconsummated union between the two existing bodies. But this does not seem to us a sufficiently weighty reason to prevent the Government from taking a decision in principle, and planning a transfer when the amalgamation has taken place and the Department has assumed its full responsibilities.

Such a reform has a number of implications both for the structure of the machinery of integration and access to official resources. Within the Department, we recommend that a junior minister should be made responsible for the subject and that a branch of the Department under an under-secretary should be established. This branch should form part of the Department on the same footing as those concerned with other aspects of social policy. Further, we recommend that the present inter-departmental arrangements for co-ordination of policy at civil service and ministerial level should be continued, but with the responsibility for co-ordination vested in the Secretary of State. Thirdly, we recommend that the responsibility for co-ordinating the existing official agencies set up to promote integration should also be transferred to the new Department. In fact, this would mean that the Community Relations Commission, with its responsibilities for public education and integration at a local level, will cease to be the responsibility of the Home Office.

But more important is the responsibility for the planning and execution of the Urban Programme. It is in our view inappropriate for a department with a regulatory rather than a social policy orientation (that is, apart from the historical accident of the Children's Department) to be responsible for such an important new initiative. The role of the social services in tackling the

▌ This symbol marks principal recommendations.

problems of areas of severe social deprivation—the declared aim of the Urban Programme—is clearly best considered by a minister with an overview of social policy departments. And to the extent that immigration has been singled out as 'an important factor, though not the only factor, in determining the existence of special social need', it seems clear that the race relations aspects of policy should also fall within the new Ministry's responsibility. Hence, we recommend that the grant giving function in Section 11 of the Local Government Act of 1966 and the Local Government Grants (Social Need) Bill should be entrusted to the Secretary of State for Social Affairs.

Almost equally important is the question of the relationship between central and local government in this field. In our earlier analysis, we traced a number of weaknesses in policy deriving from the failures of communication and maldistribution of responsibility between centre and periphery. The organization of local government and the calibre of local government representatives are clearly of immense importance in this connexion. However, these are matters already under consideration, which are too broad to be considered here. Nevertheless, pending local government reorganization, it seems to us desirable that there should be a reserve power for central government to intervene in cases in which the resources or the capacity of local government are inadequate to a local situation. The context in which intervention could take place is a question that we will consider when dealing with individual subjects; but we feel that the principle needs to be stated here.

Finally, we attach great importance to the role of research in the formulation of policy. The Home Office has taken powers under the Race Relations Act of 1968 to conduct and commission research in this field. We welcome this important step forward, although we have reservations about the methods by which research has sometimes been organized in the past by government departments. In any reorganization such as we propose, it will be logical to transfer the research function to the new Department. If this is done, we would hope that there could also be a close look at the ways in which research funds could most productively be disbursed.

It should be made clear that in the previous recommendation on functions we would not wish to make any change to the present status of the Race Relations Board. This is in any case an independent body, established by statute to exercise a semi-judicial function. In so far as there are residual ministerial functions (for example, in connexion with the presentation of the annual report), these are exercised by the Home Secretary, and there seems to us to be no reason to disturb this arrangement.

In conclusion, we would stress that reform of the structure of integration machinery is only half the battle. The style in which the machine is operated is of almost equal importance in a situation where confidence is so vital. The new structure must be 'open' to outsiders: access as a matter of course to all levels where required should be routine, there should be interchange of personnel between the agencies and the Department—and if possible between immigrant organizations and the Department—and full advantage should be taken of the recommendations in the Fulton Report about the exercise of responsibility by officials. This is a field in which the willingness of individuals to emerge from behind the departmental parapet could be of particular importance.

Immigration policy involves different imperatives and we will consider them in a later section.

2. THE LAW

(a) General

We observe as we look at the 1968 Race Relations Act that the law is neither wholly criminal nor wholly civil. It is not criminal, for proceedings are to be brought in the civil courts for damages or an injunction. Yet it resembles criminal rather than civil law in that the individual complainant is denied direct access to the courts to seek a remedy on his own behalf; only the Race Relations Board is entitled to bring proceedings under the Act. This exclusion of the individual complainant from direct access to the courts for the wrong done to him is most unusual and may have the unfortunate effect of diminishing confidence in the efficacy of the law. The danger would be less if the Board had been given all the powers of enforcement which are usually available either to a party to civil proceedings or to a public agency like the Monopolies Commission. For example, unlike a party to ordinary civil proceedings, the Board cannot seek interim relief or mandatory injunctions, and, unlike other public agencies, it has no power to subpoena witnesses or documents in the course of its investigations.

There is therefore a danger that the individual complainant will sometimes resent the fact that he has no direct access to the courts or any power to decide on the conduct of his own case; and that he will translate that resentment and any dissatisfaction with the handling of his complaint into hostility to the Board or suspicion about the value of legal remedies in combating racial discrimination. By contrast, in the United States, the equivalent legislation usually enables the individual to resort to the ordinary courts at some stage in the proceedings, and also confers a wider range of powers upon the statutory enforcement agency.

We make these general observations not because we recommend any specific amendments to the Act (this would be impractical so soon after it has come into force), but because we fear that although the new Act is liberal in intention and broad in range it contains weaknesses which may well result in a loss of confidence in the efficacy of legislation of this kind. In our proposals on housing we point to further weaknesses in the enforcement procedures which may make it difficult for the Board to ensure compliance with the law. Even if it is politically out of the question to expect any amending legislation in the foreseeable future, the existence of the new Select Committee on Race Relations and Immigration offers an opportunity for reviewing the effectiveness of these and other provisions in the Act.

(b) *Race Relations Act 1965: Section 6*

There is, however, one provision of the Race Relations Act 1965 about which we do wish to make a specific recommendation: namely, Section 6, which makes it a criminal offence by speech or writing to incite others to racial hatred.

In our view, this provision suffers from serious disadvantages. First, by penalizing not only speech or writing which is likely to result in violence but also speech or writing which incites racial hatred, Section 6 comes close to encroaching upon freedom of expression. Secondly, in view of the existing law relating to public order, sedition, and criminal and obscene libel, it is doubtful whether Section 6 was a necessary or desirable extension of the criminal law.

Thirdly, Section 6 may actually arouse public sympathy for those who are threatened with prosecution or in fact prosecuted under it. Fourthly, when a prosecution is brought under Section 6, it may give far wider publicity to racialist views than they would otherwise receive: the trial itself becomes a platform for racial incitement. Fifthly, Section 6 will lead to the prosecution and conviction of those who use crude, flamboyant, vulgar speech, but it will not touch those who express highly prejudiced opinions in a more sophisticated style. As a result, the law will appear to be unequally applied.

Finally, the inclusion of Section 6 in legislation concerned with race relations creates a false impression that the race relations legislation as a whole is penal, whereas in fact this is the only provision that is so. It also encourages the public to conclude wrongly that racial discrimination and racial propaganda are closely connected and, similarly, that the law against racial discrimination is a curtailment of freedom of expression. And, by encouraging the mistaken view that the Race Relations Board (rather than the Attorney-General) is a prosecuting body in cases of racial incitement, Section 6, which lies entirely outside the Board's jurisdiction, seriously impairs the Board's real functions in dealing with cases of racial discrimination.

For all these reasons, we recommend that Section 6 should be repealed. However, if the obstacles are too formidable, then it should at least be incorporated into a statute where it will create less damaging confusion, such as the legislation relating to Public Order.

3. HOUSING

It is generally agreed that if any one problem lies at the root of the complex knot of difficulties which face the inhabitants of the inner city, it is housing. Worse, there exists in the housing field a particularly painful form of poverty-in-affluence. While in the mainstream, steady progress towards better conditions has been made since the war, in what Hilary Rose calls the 'backwaters',[2] conditions have remained stagnant or become worse. These areas, the 'twilight zones', are not identical with the 'classical' slums— the Industrial Revolution back-to-backs, the Victorian tenements —which successive governments have tried since the war to clear. They are the areas of multi-occupation and poor environment; and to these areas the immigrants are the latest comers, suffering from the double handicap of recent arrival and racial discrimination.

There are two elements in the situation to which we would

especially draw attention. These are the pace at which the private rented sector is shrinking and the increasing importance of the local authority and of local authority housing. In the twilight areas some houses are passing into the hands of the local authority to be either patched or cleared away, others are reverting to owner-occupation via a process which Ruth Glass pejoratively calls 'gentrification' and others, more flatteringly, unslumming. As a result of these processes it has been estimated that the private rented sector will shrink from 29% of the housing stock in 1960 to 8% in 1982 (in Greater London from 35% to 16%). These changes in tenure will in many cases aggravate tenants' problems; especially since change is often at the expense of poorer tenants, who see the stock of accommodation available within their financial resources diminishing more rapidly than the remainder, and cannot count on obtaining a council tenancy.

(a) The Role of Central Government

Against this background, it is important that the Ministry of Housing should have embarked upon a general revision of policy towards twilight areas which does not involve their wholesale clearance. In the White Paper *Old Houses Into New Homes*, the Ministry took up a series of suggestions—in particular those in the Milner Holland Report—and set out a generic strategy which involves the rehabilitation of housing in poor condition and the preservation of settled communities in inner areas. We welcome this White Paper, and in particular its proposals for making information more readily available (para. 5), the willingness shown to give positive direction to local authorities (para. 7), and the proposals for working with rather than against landlords in the rehabilitation process.

These proposals mark a new departure in official policy; but they will not provide solutions unless there is a major reallocation of resources to help the under-privileged in these areas. We should stress that we are here considering the problems, not of an ethnic minority but of a minority defined by membership of what John Rex calls a housing class. That is, those who by virtue of their income level, family size, recent mobility, or other factors have no alternative recourse to accommodation except in the inner areas of major cities. As we showed in Part III the majority of immigrants fall into this group—which is not to say that the majority are immigrants. Their problems may be considered under two heads. First, the situation in the shrinking private rented sector, and secondly, the difficulties they encounter in attempting to pass from one class to another and enter either the security of local authority housing—as Rex puts it, become part of the 'public suburban class'—or, alternatively (like a substantial minority of immigrants) embark on house ownership.

In the private sector the incoming Labour Government took action which was intended to provide security of tenure and a guarantee against the charging of excessive rents. The Furnished Rent Tribunals which fix rents and can grant security of tenure in furnished lettings have had their powers expanded; a nationwide network of rent officers and committees has been set up to fix 'fair rents' for unfurnished tenancies. But in practice, the system has not functioned in a way that assists the under-privileged. Of the 34,000 fair rents fixed in the eighteen months since January 1966, more than half were an increase on the previous figure. Perhaps more important, very few people know what their rights are under the legislation. Michael Zander found that only half the sample of tenants had even heard of the Rent Acts—despite the fact that half were, on an objective assessment, paying too much rent.[3]

We consider that the scope and provisions of the Rent Act should be more widely publicized and that power should be conferred on local authorities to establish a fair rent, or otherwise the Supplementary Benefits Commission will have to act on behalf of tenants reluctant to seek their rights. Only under these circumstances should the older controlled houses be brought into the fair rents scheme, as the Conservative party suggests. Such a programme would of course benefit from the Government's proposals to give further assistance to landlords in such areas.

(b) The Local Authorities

Increasingly, however, the needs of the under-privileged will have to be satisfied by the public sector unless radical overhaul of the system of housing finance is seriously contemplated; and in relation to the public sector the under-privileged are still at a disadvantage. In fact, the local authority's role begins before the tenant actually attempts to obtain housing. Its existing powers in relation to areas of multi-occupation—public health and, in particular, management aspects—makes the local authority a key figure in the problems of the inner city, especially in view of the high proportion of property in local authority ownership and the considerable competition for entry to local authority housing (a situation unlike that in the United States, where the proportion of public housing is vastly smaller and local authority housing is held in low esteem).

In the circumstances, we consider that as a basic strategy local authorities should be prepared to assume a far greater responsibility for housing in their area and its inhabitants. The adoption of such a strategy would start with a radical overhaul of the method of organization of local authority housing departments. The Minister should urge on local authorities the desirability of creating unified housing departments, combining the housing functions at present exercised by public health and welfare departments. This measure would be in line with the current movement towards the closer grouping of related functions, exemplified in the recommendations of the Seebohm Committee. In such a revised structure the role of the policeman of twilight zones, exercised in the past by public health departments, should be dropped. Such control of excessive multi-occupation as is necessary should be more closely related to the other responsibilities of local authorities—rehousing, rehabilitation of property, and the granting of mortgage facilities. In this connexion, we recommend that the decision to extend the power to refuse registration to persons or in areas considered by the local authority unsuitable should be revised (para. 34 of the 1968 White Paper). Such a power should only be made available generally if there are effective means of ensuring (perhaps through Departmental review) that the powers are not being exercised negatively to keep coloured people out of certain areas.

Within the private sector in the inner city the local authority should take all possible steps to assist individuals who wish to find accommodation outside the twilight zone but who do not immediately qualify for local authority housing or prefer to buy their own houses. The impact of the Government's change of policy on inner areas, embodied in *Old Houses Into New Homes*, will take some time to take effect, and the results may be uneven. In the meantime, people are mobile where houses are not and steps should be taken to help them to break free of the cycle of deprivation which is the crux of the problem. This is why the drying up of the mortgage funds available to local authorities is a serious setback to those citizens attempting to struggle free of poor conditions in the twilight zones of major cities. We recommend that the severe limitation on home loans now in force* should be lifted, as soon as this is economically possible.

(c) The Problems of Coloured Immigrants and the Private Sector

Changes in policy along these lines would in themselves go a good way towards meeting the difficulties of coloured inhabitants of the inner city. But not all the way. Coloured tenants suffer additional difficulties over and above those of their white neighbours, some of which continue to exist even when they have escaped from the physically worst conditions. These difficulties bite hardest in three ways: first, in the situation faced by the newcomer attempting to find accommodation in the private rented sector; secondly, when the immigrant attempts to buy property; and thirdly, when the immigrant comes into contact with the public sector.

Discrimination is overt under the first two heads and recognition of its existence produced the recent legislation (the Race Relations Act 1968) which covers the housing field. It is too early to say how effective this will be, but it is clear that close attention should be paid to several aspects of the new law. First, the effectiveness of the machinery set up to deal with cases of discrimination. Although the scope of the legislation was wide, especially in the field of housing, where exemptions were few, considerable anxiety was expressed during the passage of the Bill about the limited powers of local conciliation committees and the Race Relations Board; in particular, the lack of any provision to 'freeze' a transaction involving property when an accusation of discrimination has been made. It will also be necessary to ensure that there is no evasion (for example, through sales by private transaction in place of those through estate agents, to avoid the provisions in the new Act) or intimidation of complainants. In some areas enforcement may prove particularly difficult, as for example in the important matter of the granting of credit facilities to house purchasers.

In view of the evidence we have already cited about the public's ignorance of their legal rights, we recommend that all possible measures are taken by both statutory and voluntary bodies to ensure that publicity about the Act is widespread and the limitations on the Board's powers understood.

* Since this was written further restrictions on home loans have been imposed by the Government.

Estate agents, despite the fact that they have now voluntarily embarked on a system of regulation and certification, have in the past been a source of considerable difficulty for immigrant house purchasers—both directly, in that there have been cases of misappropriation of deposits and inflation of prices, and indirectly, in that they sometimes intervene in order to direct immigrants to areas which they consider suitable. Many of the abuses occur because the immigrant is ignorant of the housing market and is not considered credit-worthy by conventional lending institutions. Malpractices like misappropriating deposits should be eliminated by legislation similar to that applying to solicitors. Building societies and other companies granting mortgage facilities should re-examine their policies towards immigrant house purchasers.

(d) The Local Authority and the Immigrant

The immigrant, like other inhabitants of the twilight area, may encounter particular difficulties in relation to the public sector. Local authority housing is included in the scope of the anti-discrimination legislation and we understand that the Ministry of Housing will issue directions to local authorities on the operation of the Act in a forthcoming circular. But the difficulties encountered in this sector are not so much of overt discrimination but arise from practices whose intentions may be benevolent but whose results are damaging. The rigid application of the residential qualifications and the shying away by local authorities from the problems of the twilight zones have borne particularly harshly on immigrants, few of whom have become tenants of major local authorities—despite the P.E.P. finding that many West Indians would consider such accommodation and the Bristol evidence, cited in Chapter 23, that integration on new council estates need not present any major difficulties. Some local authorities may have a tougher job, but there is evidence that a policy of integration firmly, fairly, and humanely pursued will meet with success.

Eligibility for rehousing in local authority accommodation arises either through clearance or redevelopment schemes, or through the working of the existing housing list. Confusion exists about the rights of inhabitants and the responsibilities of local authorities. We recommend that in the case of clearance schemes, the basis for qualification should be made clear to all involved when the scheme is first announced, and further, that local authorities should be obliged to see that everyone displaced has somewhere to live, though not necessarily in local authority housing.

In general, the qualification for the housing list should be need. At present, however, the list is, in the last resort, a clumsy compromise between claims of local residence and the reality of housing conditions. The Ministry has several times urged on authorities (for example in Circular 2/67) the desirability of placing greater emphasis on need. We recommend that powers be taken to introduce a uniform system of allocation extending to all local authorities, at least within a region if not nationally. If such a reform were to be effective it would have to be coupled with an effective system of collecting and processing of information about the housing conditions of all residents. Such a system, which should employ modern techniques of data processing, would provide local authorities with an up-to-date profile of housing need in their area, as a basis for action.

Clearly, a substantial change in the attitudes of many local authorities towards the specific problems of immigrants is also desirable. Local authorities should set out to obtain more information about the needs of local coloured citizens and how they can best be satisfied and to convey information about the council's policy. This involves a recognition of the cultural diversity within the immigration, and a willingness to discuss the issue with local leaders—either directly or through the existing machinery of the voluntary liaison committee.

Too often the preconceptions of local officials or councillors are reflected in a blanket policy of dispersal, or a system of allocating to certain types of housing (large pre-war accommodation or patched housing bought by the local authority in the course of clearance schemes) or to certain estates which are thought desirable. We deprecate these practices: special policies of this kind can only be justified if special circumstances exist locally, and if they have the consent of the minority concerned.

Restrictions on the availability of certain types of housing to coloured newcomers are sometimes not deliberate policy but the result of the stereotyped thinking on the part of those responsible for interviewing candidates for accommodation. The present system of interviewing prospective tenants and allocating them to local authority accommodation leaves a good deal to be desired. There is evidence to suggest that various categories of tenants are unlikely to be allocated to the best housing and that some staff approach their task with marked preconceptions. We recommend that housing visitors should receive further training which will enable them both to exercise their function on a basis of relevant information and a proper background knowledge, and to know when to refer families to social workers. Such training should include detailed instruction in the cultural and social background of coloured minorities.

Some of the practices we have described might well fall within the scope of the Race Relations Act of 1968. If local authorities are to satisfy the Board's local conciliation committees that they are not practising discrimination, they will need to undertake the keeping of statistics which distinguish by ethnic group. (It is desirable that a uniform formula for doing so be agreed between the Board, the Ministry, and the local authority associations.) This will not merely have the negative function of enabling local authorities to comply with the law, but the positive one of enabling measures for meeting the specific needs of immigrants to be effectively devised and efficiently executed.

Finally (and in many ways most important), we recommend that local authorities be encouraged to take a more positive attitude both towards applications from immigrants for mortgages, and to requests from immigrant house-owners for improvement grants. The impulse towards house-ownership in the new minorities is one of the major factors that distinguishes them, both Asian and West Indian, from the majority of inhabitants of the twilight zone. It is essential that it should be built upon as a means of allowing those who wish to leave the inner areas to finance the operation, and those who remain to improve the conditions under which they are living. In either case, the link between colour and squalor which is at the root of so many difficulties can be broken.

(e) Housing Associations

Local authorities can also assist indirectly through a more positive attitude towards housing associations by helping to make land available for purchase and by providing mortgage facilities. In our analysis we tended to be less than enthusiastic about the work done so far by associations. Some (by no means all) have been more a vehicle for the surplus energies of local voluntary committees than a positive contribution towards the housing needs of immigrants; almost all have operated on too small a scale to make a significant impact on the problems of the inner city. As a first step towards becoming effective there should be amalgamations or joint management of small associations. Moreover, with funds becoming more freely available, both from the Housing Corporation and through funds channelled by organizations like Shelter, the situation becomes rather different. In collaborating with local authorities—as the Mulberry Housing Assocation have collaborated with Westminster Borough Council—housing associations can make a significant impact on these problems, if they are not employed as a safety net by local authorities into which borderline or particularly difficult cases can be allowed to tumble.

Consideration might be given to training staff to work either in associations or in the Housing Corporation with a specific brief to consider the special needs of immigrants, as consumers of housing. Furthermore, private developers might well think it worth their while to investigate the possibility of meeting the special housing requirements of certain categories of migrants—especially Asians.

(f) Some Broader Perspectives

All these proposals are made within the existing framework of housing policy. We have not so far considered broader recommendations involving significant departures from present procedures, which might none the less have great importance for race relations. For example, we have not discussed the possibility of a drastic change in the system of subsidies, like that proposed by Della Nevitt.[4] Her scheme for national housing allowances, to be provided for all those at a certain income level, might, if it could be combined with more effective operation of the provisions of the 1965 Rent Act, provide a viable solution to the problems of the privately rented sector—quite apart from its impact on the public sector.

Nor have we discussed the New Towns. The concept, first defined by John Barr in *New Society*,[5] of New Towns as 'antighettoes' is attractive but has not so far been worked out in practice. An inconclusive experiment by the Housing Panel of the National Committee for Commonwealth Immigrants showed that, for both coloured and white applicants for entry to the industrial selection scheme, one of the major difficulties was maintaining contact while the applications were processed and passed between the local authority and the New Towns authorities. These practical difficulties apart, it seems at first sight as if immigrants might well be very suitable tenants for New Towns and could provide relevant skills. But if they are to be encouraged to make the move, the operation needs to be planned in advance and co-ordinated with both immigrant organizations and employers. We recommend that development corporations should consider at an early stage in their planning the possibility of actively recruiting for certain occupations from among immigrant groups and take steps to open negotiations with other interested parties.

Finally, the Urban Programme. Although the areas which are to receive aid—£25 m. over the next four years—are at present to be identified partly on the basis of housing need, the main emphasis of the Programme is at the moment on compensatory facilities for children—nursery schools in particular. The method of identification employed is clearly superior to one based purely on the presence of immigrants, as the Conservative party's rather vague proposals have so far been; there are obvious pitfalls in treating immigrants as some form of natural disaster. But we strongly recommend that the narrow range of services for which funds have so far been made available be expanded in the course of the Programme. It is not enough to say, as ministers have so often done, that existing building programmes—or slum-clearance schemes—are adequate to meet the pressing needs of the inner city. Welcome new attitudes in Whitehall and Westminster will not mop up the pockets of poverty and underprivilege overnight.

No dramatic proposals, such as have been made in several quarters, for full-scale central intervention, have so far been generated by the Urban Programme. Yet the very fact of the Programme is eloquent testimony that the problems of the inner city are outside the scope of local government resources. We consider that it is essential for a reserve power to exist which enables central government to intervene in cases where local authorities are clearly unable to discharge their responsibilities. This cuts across the whole debate on the reform of the machinery of government in this country; it may be that the most satisfactory solution will in the long run be found if a system of regional government is established as a result of the Report of the Redcliffe-Maud Commission. Where a local problem is intractable, solutions may be found in the creation of special agencies, analogous to the New Town development corporations. But whatever solution is preferred, our examination has convinced us that in the last analysis the problems of the inner city are now too pressing for local authorities to be entrusted with sole responsibility.

XI

4. EDUCATION

(a) General

We preface our recommendations with two quotations from 'The Education of Immigrant Children', a document issued in November 1968 by the National Association of Schoolmasters.

It must be clearly understood that the neglect of school opportunities and educational provision both between the wars and since was a scandal in some areas which now have large numbers of immigrants.

It is also essential to make clear that, in spite of all the discussions on the 'immigrant problem' in our schools the socially deprived native children are a greater problem in educational terms than the immigrant. The stresses put upon a native child which cause him to become a social and educational misfit are probably more difficult to cure than those which cause the immigrant to be a difficulty in the school.

While the children of immigrants share the needs of all other children in the Educational Priority Areas (E.P.A.s), and in the long term the problem of the deprived native child may well be greater, in the short term the children of immigrants have special needs which either have to do with language or with the problems of adjustment to a totally new environment and to an alien culture. We shall be concerned here primarily with these short-term needs, which may persist for the next fifteen years. Because of the state of the national economy, we shall confine our recommendations to policies which do not involve the investment of much social capital.

(b) A Major Limitation of the Education Service

An important limitation of the education service is that it can, of itself, do little if anything to correct major defects in other fields of social welfare. The Department of Education and Science (D.E.S.) recognized this, in respect of the Youth Service, in Circular 8/67 introducing the Hunt Report, but their statement could just as suitably have applied to the education service as a whole: 'It may be', para. 6 reads, 'that the overriding factors which will affect the success of racial integration in this country lie outside the Youth Service—factors such as town-planning, housing and employment.' In other words, residential concentrations of immigrants, and therefore of their children, must be tackled as such. As it is, some local education authorities have attempted to correct the effects of residential concentration by dispersing school children. It is time now to re-examine the position, particularly of the younger children, and to ask whether the money-consuming arrangements involved are really bringing proportionate educational benefits to the children concerned.

(c) The Department of Education and Science

The Department should set up an inquiry into the effectiveness of dispersal policies in the few areas in which they have been adopted. They should be compared with the results obtained in matching areas where there has been no dispersal and where other policies have been tried. Priority in the inquiry should be given to primary schools and a distinction should be made between dispersal of non-English speaking children and others. Although the principal criterion of effectiveness should be educational attainment, this should be weighed against other considerations, the basic question being the extent to which policies benefit or harm the children involved. In this connexion, Chapter 4 of the Plowden Report, 'Participation by Parents', with its strong emphasis on the important community role of the primary school —as a 'genuinely neighbourhood school' to which 'parents do not have far to travel'—might be presumed to apply *a fortiori* to immigrant parents and their children. But, however logical such a conclusion might seem, it is one the Report itself fails to draw.

We have shown in our analysis of education policy that in the absence of a lead from the D.E.S., the responsibility for tackling the educational problems of immigrant children was left to local education authorities and to individual teachers. Some authorities produced excellent schemes, some teachers improvised with courage and skill, but there has been no co-ordination except through teachers' associations and in many authorities little was done.

(i) THE INSPECTORATE. The members of H.M. Inspectorate have, by tradition and policy, been confined to an advisory role in immigrant, as in other, education and even then have been hampered by the confusions of Circular 7/65 (on dispersal). For both reasons they have been less helpful to L.E.A.s and others than they might otherwise have been. It is suggested, therefore, that the

D.E.S. should now consider taking a new initiative somewhat on the following lines.

▌ It should create a small new special branch for immigrant education headed by a Staff H.M.I., released from other present duties to concentrate on immigrant education, and with adequate professional and clerical staff to facilitate his work. In areas of immigrant concentration, local H.M.I.s (willing and with special interest) should be similarly released to work as field-officers in co-operation with the central team.

This new branch should examine the situation in the light of experience and knowledge now available (as well as of any new investigations that might prove desirable) and advise and help L.E.A.s, schools, and colleges, including colleges of education, in developing effective measures.

Part of the duty of the new branch would be to assist the Statistics Branch in producing statistics with greater speed, and of greater practical utility to those responsible for immigrant education than is the case at present. In addition, the new branch should use the various channels of publication open to them to make more freely available knowledge of local experiments and developments likely to be of help to others.

A further part of the work of the new branch would be to help and encourage the work of bodies such as the Schools Council and the National Foundation for Educational Research, as well as universities, colleges, and teachers' organizations, in undertaking practical investigations into educational methods best suited to the needs of immigrant pupils.

(ii) TRAINING. We welcome the initiative of the D.E.S. in organizing short in-service courses on teaching English to immigrants. Twelve one-week courses are to be held over a period of two years from the beginning of 1969. We consider that this period is too short and that three-week intensive courses would be preferable. This is probably the shortest effective period to replace the one-term full-time courses which have been tried and appear to have failed, in some instances through lack of support from the L.E.A.s who are reluctant to release teachers. The three-week course should also include some instruction on the cultural background of immigrants. It is desirable that one-term courses on the education of immigrant children should not be abandoned and that L.E.A.s should support them. They should be devised for the training of key people in the educational system, for example lecturers for teacher training colleges. They should embrace the teaching of English as a second language, the cultural background of immigrant communities, and studies of prejudice.

(d) Local Educational Authorities

L.E.A.s which are large enough and have a large number of immigrant pupils should consider the appointment of an adviser or organizer for immigrant education. The adviser should be chosen for his organizing ability and on the basis of long experience, preferably in both primary and secondary schools, and with immigrant children. He should be a member of a team of advisers concerned with other aspects of education within the authority and he should be prepared to offer advice and guidance to those colleagues. Given the special remedial problems of some immigrant children (which are the subject of other recommendations below), the adviser should closely involve the various branches of the Educational Guidance Services in his work.

His special responsibilities should include the in-service training of teachers who are dealing with immigrant children, the provision of materials and teaching aids; his office should be a clearing house for up-to-date and relevant information. He should advise on reception policies and on the placement of immigrant children. His duties would require that he be given power to take certain decisions and to carry his policies through and he should therefore have the full support of his superiors, with whom ultimate responsibility lies.

Whether or not the L.E.A. employs a local adviser or organizer for immigrant children, chief and borough and divisional education officers should take a direct personal interest in the educational problems of immigrant children to a greater extent than some of them have previously been able to do. They might also make greater use of their own professional organizations, as well as local authority associations, for the exchange of views and information.

L.E.A.s not already doing so should establish teaching centres, as advocated by the Schools Council, to assist the development by practising teachers of new ideas and methods in various aspects of teaching and learning, including those particularly appropriate to the needs of immigrant children.

L.E.A.s should be more active in arranging courses and in

devising means of releasing a greater number of serving teachers for training courses in the teaching of English to non-English speaking pupils, and to West Indian pupils. This applies to teachers of children in all age groups—nursery to secondary age.

▌ In addition, part-time courses should be arranged for nursery and infant teachers and for other teachers, not English-language specialists, on immigrant backgrounds and on the follow-up remedial approaches needed for immigrant pupils no longer attending special language classes.

▌ As so few teachers at present receive any special preparation for teaching immigrant children and feel at a loss when they are confronted with their educational and cultural problems, L.E.A.s should organize one-week crash induction courses for probationers on the lines of those which have been started by the I.L.E.A. and by Bolton L.E.A.

▌ Teachers who have had at least one year's special training, whether pre-service or in-service, should receive an appropriate salary addition.

We welcome the limited acceptance by the Secretary of State for Education of the Plowden recommendation of a special salary addition for teachers sharing the general extra burden in E.P.A. schools, but we consider that a larger increment is required to attract staff to the schools which have the greatest need.

(e) Colleges and University Departments of Education

The University Council for the Education of Teachers should examine syllabuses of training establishments to see how far they are adequate to prepare students for the education of our children in a multi-racial society. Following the inquiry, we recommend ▌ the preparation of a general syllabus for introduction into teacher training programmes in both colleges and university departments of education. This should, we suggest, include instruction in what has been established about inheritance, cultural variation, and the sources of prejudice. This should help students recognize and come to terms with their own racial prejudices and equip them for their responsibility in the shaping of children's attitudes.

Colleges and university departments of education, wherever located, should realize that some at least of their students are likely to have to teach immigrant children. The colleges should, therefore, take steps to provide suitable courses to help such students. Where colleges are in areas of immigrant concentration, they should co-operate with teachers' and other local organizations in exchanging ideas and experiences. Even closer links might be developed between colleges and schools in E.P.A.s. It might be possible for a part of the college to be located in the area near the schools chosen for teaching practice. The training unit would then be the college and school combined and would bridge the gap between the lecture hall and the classroom. Financial and career prospects of teachers could be linked to work in the E.P.A.s, by means of special increments or accelerated promotion for such special services. Colleges situated away from such areas should ensure that specially interested students can undertake some of their teaching practice in schools with a considerable proportion of immigrant pupils.

(*f*) *Nursery Education*

The need for pre-school provision in E.P.A.s has been amply stressed in the Plowden Report and has been given priority in the Government's Urban Programme. While we recognize that even when this Programme is under way there will still be a great shortage of places, we would stress the special benefit that children of immigrants can derive from nursery classes or other pre-school experience. At present they are under-represented in existing L.E.A. nursery classes, partly through the ignorance of their parents. Here, as with most local authority services, there is a need for more information. The Community Relations Commission will no doubt provide literature in the necessary languages and the Community Relations Councils should enlist volunteers to visit homes in areas where pre-school provision is available.

Where possible the schools should make contact with child-minders and should explain to them the needs of the pre-school child. For this purpose Community Relations Councils might also serve as a useful link: child-minders could gain much practical help in the care of children from trained play-group leaders.

(*g*) *Primary Education*

(i) INFANT SCHOOLS. The problems that arise are not confined to non-English speaking children but affect many West Indian children who are either immigrants or, more likely, have been born in Britain. There are problems of social and cultural differences, but language and speech should be given the highest priority. If they are not tackled in the infant school they will

continue to pose even greater problems in the junior and secondary school. The development of language is central to the educational process. To quote the Plowden Report: 'Children who are
brought up in a home background where the forms of speech are
restricted are at a considerable disadvantage when they first go to
school and may need to have considerable compensatory opportunities for talking if they are to develop verbal skills and form
concepts' (para. 55). The Plowden Committee was gravely
concerned about 'those [English] children who get to the top of
the infant school and even more the lower reaches of the junior
school, before they have become fluent in speech' (para. 581).
These principles and these concerns apply *a fortiori* to the children
of immigrants.

And yet a survey of primary schools conducted in the autumn of
1967[6] discovered that in infant schools there were almost no
teachers who had any training in specialized language teaching;
and very few teachers realized that non-English speaking children
and children who are linguistically deprived need special instruction. Unaware of the importance of spoken language, teachers
often introduce the child to reading before he has a sufficient grasp
of oral English.

Teachers need special help in this field. If it is not possible for
L.E.A.s to release them for in-service training courses we suggest
that schools should be visited by small peripatetic teams of teachers
who could conduct in-service training in the schools themselves.
They could discuss their problems with the teachers and introduce
them to new methods, materials, and techniques.

There is an urgent need for new teaching materials and we hope
that the Leeds Centre (see below) will be given the resources to
produce them for teachers of infant 'immigrant' children. In the
meantime, there is an interim need for pamphlets which could
'draw the attention to the ways in which teachers can develop the
child's control of language and at the same time enlarge and
enrich the language of the English children in the same class'.

Teachers in multi-racial classes need full-time assistants in the
classroom. We endorse the Plowden recommendation of at least
one aide to every two classes in infant schools in E.P.A.s. It should
be possible to enlist volunteers for this work who might be
provided with short training courses. We recommend that parents
be encouraged to help and that in many areas volunteers be
drawn from the sixth forms of local secondary schools.

(ii) JUNIOR SCHOOLS AND THE PROBLEM OF TRANSFER. The problem of transfer from one system of education to another can be acute for children for whom the transfer comes too soon in their 'learning' age: it is particularly acute for non-English speaking children and children of immigrants with poor speech. It is not uncommon for some children to have passed right through primary education and to enter secondary schools without being able to read.

Many children still need much individual attention by the time they reach junior school age, but few junior teachers have experience in teaching the beginnings of reading and a non-English speaking child needs specialized help. This problem of learning to read is of a different order from that of the Remedial English child and the two problems should not be confused, yet many immigrant children are put into Remedial classes with disturbed English children.

There should be more consultation between infant and junior teachers so that a smooth transition can take place, but more radical solutions seem to be required.

(iii) MIDDLE SCHOOLS. If there is a problem of transition from primary to junior schools the problem is even more acute for the child who may be one or two years behind his contemporaries and has to move to the more formal subject teaching in the secondary school. A more flexible approach is required from L.E.A.s to the problem of transfer. Deferments should be met on the recommendation of the head teacher together with the advice of the educational guidance services. The child may need an extra year in the primary school and he may also need a full four-year course in the secondary school. We recommend the withdrawal of these children in small tutorial groups for a part of their school day and the appointment of teams of peripatetic teachers to give them extra tuition on the lines pioneered in Huddersfield.

But we think that the problems of premature transfer could best be met by the introduction of the Middle School to cater for the age range from 8 to 12, as was recommended in the Plowden Report* and made possible under Section 1 of the 1964 Education Act. This would mean that children would have three years in

* The arguments for and against raising the present age of transfer to secondary education are set out in paras. 365–78.

infant schools and four years of junior school before transferring to secondary education. Great care should be taken that the curriculum in these schools is not dominated by secondary school influences and that they retain what is best in primary education. To meet the needs of immigrant children the system must be flexibly applied. Allowance would have to be made for earlier transfer to secondary education for children who mature early.

(h) Secondary Education—Remedial Groups

Whether or not the problems of transition are mediated by the introduction of Middle Schools, the transfer from a fourth-year primary to a first-year secondary class represents a very great change; it is the change from informal class teaching to more formal subject learning. The stress is particularly acute for immigrant children who have entered primary education at junior school age. Schools can help these children in their first year by organizing small tutorial groups and by a class teacher approach. Some schools have found it helpful to abolish streaming in their first year with setting in English and mathematics.

(i) Further Education

Colleges of further education, with young immigrant students, whether part or whole-time, have an important role to play, both in their own right and in co-operation with the schools and the youth service. Their importance has been enhanced by the decision to postpone the raising of the school-leaving age. We consider that many immigrant children who now stay on an extra year at school, often in the lower stream of a fifth form, would be better served by attending a local college of further education at least for some part of their course or else full-time. (See also below under Employment.)

We recommend that immigrant teen-agers who are too old to fit in easily with school arrangements and know too little English to attend ordinary further education courses should have special tuition in English. The Pathway Further Education Centre in Ealing is doing pioneer work in this field.

(j) Parents and the Link with the Home

The conclusions of Chapter 4 of the Plowden Report, 'Participation by Parents', should be regarded as applying with not less equal force to the parents of immigrant children than to other parents. The recommendation of Chapter 29 of the Plowden Report that 'parents of children attending the schools should be represented on the managing body' would also, if adopted, carry equal rights for immigrant as for other parents.

The role of the education liaison officer, who may be a teacher or a non-teacher, has proved to be of great value in some areas. In schools with non-English speaking children a liaison officer who shares a common language, might act as an interpreter between the parents and the school authorities. In schools where the problems are not those of language but of behaviour or of cultural deprivation, the liaison officer might be appointed to make contact with the parents and generally to find out about the effect of the child's home upon his work. The liaison officer would also help the parents to understand what the school is doing and to involve them in the process of education and the work of the school.

The conclusion of recent educational research in Britain and the United States shows the overwhelming importance of the home as an influence on the achievement of the child. It has been shown to be more important than school amenities, pupil teacher ratios, and even than the influence of the teacher. More attention needs to be paid to measures for establishing links with the home at all levels of education. The D.E.S.'s recent survey, 'Parent/Teacher Relations in Primary Schools' (H.M.S.O., 1968), shows that there is much good practice. In secondary schools in areas of social stress the best link may be through the appointment of a counsellor or teacher-social worker, who can help parents unable to give articulate expression to their problems and their aspirations for their children. Some knowledge of the background of immigrants is clearly desirable.

(k) *The School Psychological and Child Guidance Service*

John Triseliotis outlines very clearly the kinds of special psychological difficulties in immigrant children which educational psychologists and others in this branch of the service may meet.[7] He stresses the importance of making help available at an early stage 'to forestall the possible development of emotional complications later on'.

Psychologists, psychiatric social workers, psychotherapists, and psychiatrists, like teachers, need some measure of special training if they are to handle successfully the difficulties of immigrant children. Teachers need help also in recognizing signs in the behaviour of immigrant children which make early psychological referral advisable.

A major obstacle in some localities to developments on these lines is that the school psychological and child guidance service was inadequate even before the arrival of immigrants. In those areas the expansion of the service is even more urgent now.

(*l*) *Reports*

We welcome the research that has been started on diagnostic testing by the National Foundation for Educational Research and we are glad to learn that research on proficiency tests is to be undertaken at Birmingham University.

Until these tests are perfected, schools are faced with the problem of assessing the ability of immigrant children, classifying and placing them. Children from Caribbean islands who arrive here after long separation from their parents frequently suffer from shock and cannot do themselves justice in their first weeks at school. We recommend that a report from their headmasters in the Caribbean should be brought by the children or preferably should be sent to the D.E.S. for onward transmission to the L.E.A. in which the child's parents are living. Once the child is registered the authority would send the report to the school. All that is required is that the D.E.S. should act as a clearing house. This recommendation has been put forward by the Education Panel of the N.C.C.I. but has met with little success. We know that the Jamaican Education Authorities are prepared to operate the scheme. If successful it could be extended to other West Indian islands. Once again we cite the authority of the Plowden Report in support of this recommendation: 'Record keeping is especially necessary for teachers in schools in deprived neighbourhoods. . . . A child's progress may depend very much on the amount and quality of information that can be sent with him from school to school' (para. 137). If this is true of native children, it has even greater force for immigrants.

(*m*) *Schools Council Project in English for Immigrant Children*

The Schools Council Project in Leeds has produced an introductory course in English for non-English speaking children within in the age range 8 to 13. As we showed in Chapter 18, the Project has met a need for standardized materials and teaching aids which was being satisfied from no other source. But much more needs to be done. Teachers need materials for adolescent non-English speakers who have only two or three years to spend in school and need to be equipped to compete in the labour market; they also need materials for infants. It will also be necessary to provide continuation material for children who have worked through the Project's introductory course: they will have received an elementary grounding in English but will not be able to participate in subject lessons, least of all in the secondary school. Many children may in fact regress after this initial grounding, unless they receive further instruction.

The Project is due to come to an end in 1970: there is very much to be done on work for adolescents, for infants, and for continuation of the introductory course. We recommend that the Project be enlarged and its life extended.

(n) The Problems of West Indian Children

The specific problems of children from the Caribbean have been described in Chapter 18. They were not generally recognized until 1967 when the Schools Council set up a three-year research project at Birmingham University. The research is concentrating on the educational problems of West Indian children and their teachers, mainly in junior schools. It is concerned with children who have newly arrived and with the children born to immigrant parents in this country. We welcome this belated approach to the problem and urge that pending the findings of the project more attention be paid to the educational and behavioural problems of children who have been reunited with their parents.

(o) Church Schools

The Churches can exert a strong influence on educational policy on racial issues through the denominational schools. The record shows that in the West Midlands the percentage of immigrant children in Church of England schools is comparable with the proportion in the State schools, but that Roman Catholic schools have a consistently lower than average percentage, especially in Birmingham. We welcome the initiative of the Roman Catholic Bishop of Birmingham in asking his school managers to give places to Asian pupils and we feel that this practice should be followed in other dioceses.

Many history and geography textbooks in use in schools perpetuate the image of the coloured man as a primitive or noble savage and, by giving support to outdated views on race, religion, and cultural differences, instil attitudes in young children whether white or coloured which can be harmful to race relations. There have been proposals for a review of textbooks in our schools and for enlisting the support of publishers in commissioning authors to provide textbooks which would encourage racial understanding.

We recommend that the Churches should conduct their own inquiry, particularly in their primary schools, to find out what textbooks are in use and should publish their findings on their suitability for education in a multi-racial society and recommend a list of suitable books, for the guidance of headmasters. This would serve as an important model for the State schools.

5. EMPLOYMENT

(a) *General*

The passing into law of the 1968 Race Relations Act has introduced an entirely new element into the field of industrial relations. The Act, with certain exceptions, outlaws discrimination in employment. While there are certain weaknesses in the law, mainly in the field of enforcement, we have said earlier that we will not make any recommendations for amendments as it would be quite unrealistic at this stage to do so. We observe that the successful implementation of the Act will depend to a large degree on the effectiveness of the voluntary machinery within industry and therefore many of our recommendations are addressed to both sides of industry.

It is still too soon to tell how the Act will work in practice. However, enforcement relies to a great extent on individual complaints. While it is important to provide redress for aggrieved individuals, it is equally important that the Race Relations Board should make full use of its power to initiate investigations. There are three reasons which may make this imperative. First, the individual may not know that he is the victim of discrimination: this has been demonstrated by the P.E.P. Report. Secondly, even if he does know he may be reluctant to come forward. Thirdly, there is a danger that the worst cases of discrimination may escape the impact of the law because members of minority communities will tend to avoid those firms which have a reputation as discriminators, and therefore no specific complaints will be lodged against them. It would be regrettable if the Board were to allow individual complaints to monopolize its resources so as to prevent it from investigating large concerns where there may be a pattern of discrimination.

Most of our proposals are for the short and medium term and can be put into effect without great expenditure of money. Many would provide opportunities for wide ranges of the population and not just for members of the coloured minority groups. There are, however, other fundamental problems in the sphere of employment which call for more far-reaching solutions. One example is the whole question of redundancy, re-training, and mobility. In the long term, these problems will have to be tackled if we are to achieve technical advance with good industrial relations. If they are not tackled, growth in racial prejudice and discrimination will be one of the inevitable consequences.

(b) Record Keeping

It is an essential for a non-discriminatory employment policy that records be kept which distinguish employees by ethnic origin at all levels of employment. Some employers have argued that to differentiate by colour or racial origin is in itself discriminatory, but there is no other way to determine whether minorities are being accorded equal employment opportunities or to gauge whether progress is being made over time.

There should be no difficulty for Government departments to keep such records and indeed many do so, but as we have shown in Chapter 19, others do not. It is desirable that there be uniformity in this field.

The local authority as an employer should also keep similar records if it is to ensure that it is complying with the Race Relations Act.

There is nothing in the Act which requires an employer to keep such records but for the reasons given it is desirable that he should do so, and in fact employers who wish to offer equal opportunity to coloured citizens will find it essential; others, if they should have to justify their policies to the Race Relations Board, will need to produce evidence.

Moreover, if, as we recommend below, the Government introduce a non-discriminatory clause into all their contracts, any contractor could be required to keep such records.

(c) *Government*

(i) CONTRACTS. Of all those involved in the field of employment the Government has the greatest power to ensure equal opportunity. In the words of the Street Report:

> The Government are such huge customers of industry that they have a unique opportunity through the medium of their contracts to control racial discrimination. . . . We believe that through the medium of government contracts the opportunity should be taken of controlling discrimination by methods which would not at present be feasible in other areas of employment.

▌ We endorse this opinion and therefore recommend that the Government amends the Fair Wages Resolution of 1946 to include a non-discrimination clause in Government contracts.

The London Borough of Camden has amended its standing orders so as to demand a written undertaking from firms supplying goods or services to the Council that they will not discriminate. We recommend that other local authorities follow this example.

▌ American experience has shown that if there is no agency with power and responsibility to ensure compliance with a contract clause, it will have no effect. We accordingly suggest that if such a clause is added to Government or local authority contracts, responsibility for ensuring compliance be given to the Race Relations Board, to which complaints could be referred and which could make its own investigations.

▌ It should also be made a condition for the grant of licences (and subsidies) by Government that those in receipt of such grants follow fair employment policies: this may in some cases involve amending the Acts under which such licences are granted.

(ii) EMPLOYMENT EXCHANGES. Since 1964 the Department of Employment and Productivity (D.E.P.) employment exchanges have been empowered to withdraw their facilities from certain categories of discriminatory employers. This power has rarely been used, largely through fear that employers would look for their labour elsewhere. At present many vacancies, especially of higher status, are not notified to employment exchanges and opportunities available through these exchanges are therefore needlessly restricted. We think it desirable that employment exchanges should be able to offer a full range of employment opportunities and we therefore recommend that it should be compulsory for all vacancies to be notified to employment exchanges, as was the case until 1956. Compulsory notification would also make it easier to detect patterns of discrimination.

We also recommend that private employment bureaux should be registered and that their records should be open to inspection.

(iii) YOUTH EMPLOYMENT SERVICE. The Youth Employment Service (Y.E.S.) has been and will continue to be an important resource for the coloured school leaver; as the numbers of coloured school leavers greatly increase in the next few years it will be necessary to expand the Y.E.S. if it is not to be swamped. Arguments have been advanced for transferring the Y.E.S. from the local education authority to the D.E.P. (which meets 75% of the cost of the Service) on the grounds that this would give youth employment officers (Y.E.O.s) a greater knowledge of the labour market and a better career structure. However, we consider that there are drawbacks which may outweigh these advantages. The Y.E.S. must have very close links with the schools, and the Y.E.O. needs to have qualifications for working with young people, including training in vocational guidance. He also needs to be fully acquainted with the area in which he is working. There is a danger that a career in the D.E.P. may not attract the same kind of person and that frequent posting may break the essential links with the area.

Whatever the structure of the Y.E.S., we consider that Y.E.O.s need to receive more training in vocational guidance. The recent development by the D.E.P. of an occupational guidance service for adults may point the way for an integrated vocational guidance service which would cover all ages and embrace the Y.E.S. Any development along these lines would benefit the whole population.

We recommend that the D.E.P. and the Y.E.S. in conjunction with the local education authority should consider the introduction of a system which would allow schoolchildren in their last year at school to take temporary supervised placements for periods of up to four weeks with employers.

(d) Workshop Bargaining

The Donovan Commission recognized the great importance of workshop bargaining in industrial relations. We have shown in Chapter 19 that whatever the external sanctions against discrimination and whatever industry-wide agreements may be negotiated, factory floor procedures may lead to evasion of these agreements. We therefore support the proposal by the Donovan Commission that agreements be registered with the projected Industrial Relations Commission, and we also recommend first, that the Commission refuse to accept any workshop agreements that do not affirm racial equality in employment, and secondly, that the Commission in consultation with the Race Relations Board encourage the setting up of effective workshop procedures for dealing with individual complaints of racial discrimination in employment, including engagement, promotion, training, and dismissal.

(e) Management

The existence of an anti-discrimination law should now make it easier for managements who do not wish to discriminate but who have hitherto feared pressures from employees or customers. In other cases, the law may bring about a change in policy either before or after a complaint has been investigated and upheld. But equal opportunity in employment cannot be obtained by legislation alone and voluntary action has a vital part to play. Real progress in breaking patterns of discrimination will only be made if management is committed to making equal opportunity a reality. We agree once again with the comment in the Street Report: 'In employment we attach more importance ultimately to affirmative action which stamps out discrimination than to the processing of individual complaints.' By affirmative action we mean that management should bring to a policy of equal opportunity the same determination and equivalent techniques and controls that it would apply to any other programmes which it wishes to succeed.

We suggest that companies should:

Issue a declaration of policy on equal opportunity which should be communicated to every employee and to trade unions and employment agencies and the community at large.

Make one executive responsible for the implementation of this policy, who should require regular progress reports from all departments to ensure compliance with the company's directive.

Include in agreements (with trade unions) non-discrimination clauses and also special procedures for dealing with workshop complaints.

Widen the sources from which labour is recruited if it appears that the normal channels are excluding coloured applicants.

Ensure that the promotion system is being operated fairly and that coloured employees are gaining the experience necessary to qualify them for promotion. This involves their participation in the company's various training programmes.

Ensure that where tests are used to select employees for engagement, transfer, or promotion, these tests are fairly applied and are relevant to the requirements of the job. In particular, they should ensure that language or dress (for example, the wearing of turbans) are not made a bar to employment where an imperfect knowledge of the language or standard clothing are not essential to the requirements of the job.

(f) Trade Unions

If affirmative action on the part of managements is to be successful, it will require a corresponding commitment from trade unions, particularly in respect of training, acquisition of skills, upgrading, and promotion.

We therefore suggest that trade unions, as distinct from the Trades Union Congress, should:

Issue a declaration that the union is committed to a policy of equal employment opportunity for coloured citizens and communicate this to all its members.

Appoint a senior official with responsibility to see that this policy is carried through at all levels. This official should be empowered to communicate the policy of the union to all paid officials, to elected officers at national, regional, district and branch level, and to representatives of the unions who sit on various bodies, whether at a national or local level. He should call for reports to be submitted through the various levels within the union structure on the way in which the policy is working, and see that there is available at union headquarters and in the regions officials and leading members of the union with specialist knowledge to come to the help of any section of the union where friction may be anticipated or may be occurring. For this purpose he will need to organize training courses for officials, elected officers, and other members. We have shown in Chapter 19 that discrimination has often worked against the interests of the white workers. The training course should therefore not merely include instruction on the special needs, customs, and cultural backgrounds of ethnic minorities, but should emphasize the importance of equal treatment, if the best interests of the union are to be served. Courses on the practices of industry should also be provided for members of minority groups.

Encourage coloured members to participate more fully in the activities of the union at all levels, and particularly to attend union conferences and courses.

Include non-discrimination clauses and special procedures for dealing with workshop complaints of discrimination in agreements with management.

Agree, in consultation with employers and with the Government, to the provision of realistic trade tests as an entrance to skilled crafts for persons who have not completed an approved apprenticeship.

Make the rules over the age of entry to apprenticeships more flexible.

The T.U.C. should also advise local trades councils on official policy and request periodic reports.

Smaller trade unions may find it beyond their resources to follow some of these recommendations. They may find it preferable to request the aid of the T.U.C. or the co-operation of other unions.

(g) Training

The Industrial Training Act should be operated in a way which ensures that employees have an equal opportunity to acquire trade skills. We recommend that to qualify for training grants under the Act, employers should be required to show that they are not discriminatory either in their employment policies or in the provision of training.

Companies who employ non-English speaking workers should provide these employees with opportunities to learn English, whether by organizing instruction at the place of work or through day release.

With the increasing pace of technological change and the spread of industrial mergers, new jobs are appearing and old ones disappearing continuously. In order to meet the needs of this situation and to capitalize on the economic potential which such changes hold for the country, there is a growing demand for retraining. We recommend that the present Government retraining schemes be expanded greatly and that training centres be situated in all the major centres of population and be more flexible in the type of course offered. Such an expansion would be beneficial to the whole labour force and especially to coloured workers.

6. SOCIAL WELFARE

The social circumstances which are common to all those living in areas of social deprivation are more important than the countries of origin of those affected and we repeat that any solution of the difficulties that arise must be applicable to all inhabitants of those areas. At the same time, within the services available special provision should be made for those needs of the immigrant communities which are specific to those communities.

The increasing complexity of social welfare provisions over the past years and the growing number of specialized social workers may tend towards the fragmenting of services to the family rather than an understanding of the needs of the family as a whole.

Further, the complexity of structure makes it difficult for a client in need to know which is the relevant agency or department able to help him. If he is redirected from one officer to another he may well feel rejected and unwilling to repeat the same painful process of formulating and recounting his needs to another social worker. This common problem is even more true of newcomers to the society who may have difficulties in communicating in English and who may be altogether ignorant of the statutory services and in particular of the professional counselling available. This need for information and advice is felt by many sections of the native population, but even more intensely by those persons who come from societies with a different social structure and administration.

We therefore welcome the proposals contained in the Report of the Committee on Local Authority and Allied Personal Social Services (the Seebohm Report) for a unified social service department within each local authority area, and in particular for the setting up of area offices in large urban areas which would provide easier access for families in need.

While many local authorities have information available on their services, this may be in a form or language which makes it of little help to newcomers. Some voluntary liaison committees have produced useful brief guides to the local services and facilities, but publicizing the statutory services should be the responsibility of those who provide the services and we note the opinion of the Seebohm Committee that 'those who may require the help of the personal social services, for instance the welfare and children's services, encounter little encouragement to use them, nor is there a ready flow of simple information about their nature and how they can be obtained' (para. 145). The Committee went further and maintained that historically the aim has been to deter people from seeking help and that consequently a stigma attached to those who did so.

Newcomers need information and they also need advice and guidance on the use of the services available to them. With an integrated service, publicity and comprehension would be considerably simpler. We recommend that the local authority should assume the responsibility for an advisory service on the lines of centres for housing advice which are recommended in the Seebohm Report (para. 391). But whatever advisory services are set up we consider that there will still be a need for an independent source of advice and information, at present provided by Citizens Advice Bureaux who are called on to advise on a wider range of problems than the local authority. We therefore recommend that local authorities should continue to give financial support to the Citizens Advice Bureaux.

The reorganization of personal social services into a simple and comprehensive 'one-door' service, available locally to a community and with adequate publicity, would make it easier for a client in need to ask voluntarily for help at the first symptom of a problem rather than at the point of breakdown. It would also make it easier to identify needs and thus lead to preventive action through the provision of service to families or whole areas which show risk of breakdown.

(a) Training

The identification of need calls for special training for all social workers who come in contact with immigrant families. They need to understand the cultural backgrounds of the immigrants, differences in family structures and child-rearing patterns, and attitudes towards officials and towards services provided by society. Such understanding is relevant not only to the professional social worker but to many other officers whose work is of such vital importance in the process of integration: education welfare officers, health visitors, and housing visitors (who play a key role in the allocation of local authority housing), and the officers of the Supplementary Benefit Commission.

We therefore endorse the recommendations arising out of the International Social Service Report, *Immigrants at London Airport*, that there should be special in-service training for professional workers who are now offering services to immigrants and that this training be organized locally to ensure its relevance to the local situation.

Training should include some discussion of the policy issues involved in the provision of services to immigrant groups, issues which underly the concepts of pluralism and parity of esteem.

We also recommend that wherever possible both pre-service and in-service training courses for all branches of social work should include, in the study of human relations, the psychology of prejudice and the effects of prejudice in the community. We further recommend that cross-cultural studies will be included in all courses, so that students may acquire some knowledge of a society and customs which differ from their own, and may be prepared for living and working in a multi-racial society.

We further suggest that there is a need for training courses for those who will be responsible for training social workers for their work with immigrant communities.

(b) Day Care

As our economy relies increasingly on female labour, so the need for further provision for young children becomes more apparent. The insufficiency of day nurseries, nursery schools, and play groups affects the community as a whole, but the need is particularly acute among immigrant families where the mother is working and there are no relatives to take care of the children. Unregistered child-minders will continue to be used if the working mother cannot find alternative provision for her child. We have pointed in our education proposals to the risks to the child in such situations and we have recommended that families with these special needs should receive special consideration in the provision of day-care facilities.

An integrated service which is based on a fairly small area and is in touch with the community would supervise the play groups in the area, would be aware of the need for further groups, and would stimulate voluntary workers to organize them. The service could also provide the link between the nursery school, the child-minder, and the play group which we recommended in our education proposals.

(c) *Local Authority Care*

A further series of problems arises from the pattern of domestic relationships in the West Indian community which result in the existence of substantial numbers of families in which the mother is the sole support. The historical origins of this pattern have been discussed in Chapter 5, where we also examine the evidence of an increasing trend towards marriage in this country. However, this process is bound to be slow and meanwhile there is a need for flexible services for these families, especially since it is becoming increasingly difficult to find foster parents or adoptive parents for coloured children.

A distinction must be drawn between short-term needs, for example during the illness or confinement of the mother, and long-term care. The case for temporary child care need not be argued, particularly as there are very few three-generation families in West Indian communities in England. As an alternative to with-drawing the child from the home, it is worth considering a system operated by the London Borough of Camden whereby peripatetic staff live in the house and take charge of the family while the mother is away. This might also be a field in which the statutory authority and voluntary workers might combine.

Long-term care is another matter. The reasons why children are received into care or remain in care need to be closely examined. In some cases, family breakdown makes it inevitable, but in others, children are kept in care because their homes are deemed to be overcrowded. As institutional care, which is no substitute for the family, may have particularly harmful effects on coloured children, we feel that there should be greater flexibility in applying statutory standards. More community provision in the field of day care would further lessen the need to withdraw children from their homes.

It has been suggested that some West Indian mothers are too prone to ask for their children to be received into care when they could find a solution within their own community. Many mothers, unaware of the dangers, feel that their children will benefit from being brought up with white children. For many others there is no other solution to their problem. This underlines the importance of special preparation for social workers who will need to distinguish preferences which may be culturally based from those which are imposed by circumstances. Given the tensions that can be set up in coloured children who are brought up by white workers in children's homes, we recommend that staff for these homes be recruited from among the coloured communities. It is important that children in care should not be led to reject their colour.

(d) Social Work in Schools

In our education proposals we have stressed the importance of building links between the home and the school and we believe that one way of achieving this link would be to transfer the welfare duties of the education welfare officers to the new social service department, as the Seebohm Committee recommends (para. 226). This should benefit all children, but it would be particularly helpful to immigrants and their children because the cause of the problem which the child presents at school is so often to be found within the family. Once a problem is detected in the school, the social worker, who should be based on the school, would visit the home and, if a member of the social service department, would be able to deploy the services of the department to deal with the problems of the family. In this way immigrant families might be brought into contact with a number of people from the same office and with voluntary workers.

(e) The School as a Community Centre

A family service for children and for families with children which would embrace education welfare work and the youth service could be greatly reinforced in under-privileged areas if schools were to be developed as community centres, providing evening activities both for parents and for adolescents. It has been found in some areas that where youth groups have been based on schools they have attracted immigrant children from all the communities, who feel an attachment to their school and know that this is one place in the neighbourhood where they are sure of a welcome. We therefore recommend that wherever possible school buildings be opened in the evenings as community centres offering classes for adults and for adolescents and recreation. They would provide a centre for the whole community and would help to resolve the tensions within immigrant families that arise between the generations.

7. THE POLICE

The problems that confront the police and coloured immigrants in their mutual relations are frequently the problems of the area in which they meet. Many of our recommendations would therefore apply to police work in cities generally, but there are others which arise from the nature of race relations and take account of specific problems which the police face in dealing with coloured people.

While difficulties certainly exist and relationships require very careful management, we do not think that the problems are yet of the same dimension as others which arise, for example in the fields of housing, education, or employment. However, any deterioration would be so damaging to the process of mutual adjustment that we have treated this subject at considerable length.

The police are themselves a minority group and by the nature of their organization tend to be isolated from the communities they serve. This isolation is most marked in the areas where the majority of coloured immigrants are living. We believe that current training programmes fail to do justice to the complexity and importance of the role of the police in urban areas and that the sense in which they are a minority group means that they are too isolated from sources of opinion, information, and knowledge which could help them to adapt themselves to the changing situation in which they must function. Many of our recommendations are therefore addressed to questions of training and of community relations.

(a) The Training of Police

We recommend that the Home Secretary should appoint a committee of inquiry to assess the adequacy of current methods and content of police recruit and in-service training. The membership of the committee of inquiry should be drawn from the police forces and from laymen.

As an indication of where we consider the need for reform to be most urgent, we recommend the inclusion in training programmes, to a far greater degree than at present, of courses which pay particular attention to the needs of policing in urban areas. These courses would relate to the structure of poorer urban areas, the causes and effects of social and cultural deprivation, crime, and delinquency in relation to other aspects of social disorganization, and the role of voluntary and local government agencies in helping 'problem' families.

Courses should also be included in training programmes which focus on controversial or problematical aspects of policing as they relate to the social role of the police and to relations between police and the community: such aspects include complaints against the police; the police use of force; discretionary decisions by individual police officers and police forces; civil rights; public attitudes to policing; the accountability of the police to local and national political structures.

In training it should be recognized that community relations— and the work of liaison officers—is a specialized police function similar to other specialized functions like detection, traffic, and crime prevention, and that during any probationary period the new recruit should become thoroughly familiarized with such work.

In-service training should be seen to be as important as recruit training; and the experience of the new recruit fresh from training school should be regarded as an integral part of any training scheme. Thus, the experienced officers who work with new recruits need to be apprised of the goals of training if in the light of experience training is not to be thought of by the recruit as irrelevant and forgettable. Training officers at a local level can play a vitally important role in this respect.

To provide high calibre staff for police training schools at district and local level, there is a need for specialized courses, perhaps in universities and colleges, which will provide adequate broadly-based training for the training officers. Police training at all levels would benefit if greater use were made of specialists from outside the ranks of the police.

To help the police to operate in multi-racial communities and to understand the needs of coloured communities in our cities, we recommend the inclusion in police training of lectures on race relations, on the cultures and customs of minorities, on the nature of prejudice, and on the legal and social background to recent race relations and immigration laws. The present arrangement of including occasional lectures in a term cannot be considered in any way adequate.

(b) Recruitment

In a multi-racial society it is desirable that all sections of the community should be represented in the police and should be seen to be represented. It is only recently that there has been an active policy of recruitment from among coloured minorities and this policy has not yet been universally followed. That the response has been disappointing may be due to a lack of confidence on both sides which expressed itself initially in opposition from serving policemen and was then translated into disappointment and resentment among members of the immigrant communities. The problem may be compounded not only because of the deterioration in police-community relations but because in some of the countries of origin the reputation of the police is not very high.

▌ To overcome some of these difficulties we recommend that there should be a declaration of a firm policy on the recruitment of police officers from among the immigrant communities and there should be special recruiting programmes—using liaison officers, local community committees, and immigrant organizations—to advertise the opportunities existing throughout the police service for suitably qualified coloured citizens. A special emphasis might be placed here on the police cadet scheme.

▌ We also recommend that special pre-training programmes should be devised to prepare immigrant applicants for qualification, through language classes and introductory 'social orientation' courses. Recruiting criteria should be reviewed to see if present standards set an unreasonable barrier to immigrant recruitment.

Consideration should be given to developing the role of the special constabulary and establishing a volunteer or part-time force of 'sub-professionals' with a particular task in community relations within which coloured citizens could play a valuable part.

(c) Community Relations

A contribution to improved race relations and police-community relations can be made by local police liaison officers. They have two distinct roles to perform. The first is to establish contact with local communities through local voluntary committees and immigrant associations, and to approach and advise members of local committees as individuals and in groups about matters of common interest and concern.

The second function is to develop a sensitivity within police forces on questions affecting race relations. This function will be served through developing training programmes which should include information for serving officers of all ranks on local issues, local immigrant communities, and local criticism of the police.

Through means of lectures, seminars, conferences, and group sessions members of local forces can be helped to appreciate how individual attitudes may be detrimental to good policing. To promote positive attitudes on which good policing depends may be the most important aspect of a liaison officer's work. The work of a liaison officer is so important that it should be a full-time occupation.

To support and systematize the work of liaison officers we suggest that a community relations department be set up within the police service, which would prepare resource materials and guidelines, devise training programmes, and organize conferences and seminars.

(d) Complaints Procedure

There is no more crucial area for immediate action than to review the mechanism for handling complaints against the police; any lasting improvement through training, recruitment, and improved structures for community relations will wait upon action in this field. We have argued in Chapter 20 that a system of internal review, regardless of its fairness, cannot generate sufficient confidence; and confidence is fundamental to good relations with the coloured communities and with the community at large. If the complainant sees only that the police are judge and jury in their own case, he will not feel that effective channels exist for the redress of complaints. We recognize that there are practical difficulties in operating a system of external review and that the morale of the police must be considered as well as the confidence of the immigrants in the fairness of the system. Nevertheless, we repeat that what is needed in a complaints procedure is not so much to prove or justify behaviour as to reassure an offended person. We therefore recommend that a select committee of inquiry be appointed to examine procedures for the handling of complaints against the police, and that it be empowered to authorize and conduct on an experimental basis one or more alternative procedures in selected areas, which would introduce the element of external review to complaints procedures.

We also recommend that the Home Secretary should revert to his original decision to include in police disciplinary regulations a special category of offence of racial discrimination. This would officially recognize that prejudiced behaviour undermines the basis of trust and integrity upon which good policing depends, and declare within and without the police force that discriminatory behaviour is not to be tolerated.

We understand that it is now the policy within the Metropolitan Police Force that if an officer is the object of persistent complaints which reveal genuine friction, misunderstandings, or conflict, he may be transferred to other duties or to work in another area. We feel that, subject to proper safeguards, this policy should be adopted elsewhere.

(e) Information and Research

There is a need for more public information on police matters and for further research and development of new programmes.

■ We therefore recommend that the methods of collecting and presenting data be improved to allow accurate assessment of rates of crime and delinquency among ethnic and other minority groups; and that data and information be available about complaints against the police, about applications, recruitment, and promotion from among coloured minorities so that important issues on race relations can be examined with some precision.

■ We also recommend that establishment of a specialized institute be considered—on the model of New York's Vera Institute of Criminal Justice—to develop and plan, in conjunction with police forces and the Home Office, a continuing experimental programme of measures to develop the community relations function of the police service.

(f) Rights and Obligations of the Citizen

In the present state of relations between coloured immigrants and the police the suspicion is widely held that a coloured man is liable to arbitrary arrest and unfair treatment at the police station.

■ It is therefore important that the police should be reminded of their responsibilities under the Home Office Rules embodied in Circular no. 31 of 1964, and that coloured citizens, like all citiziens, should be properly informed about the rights of a police officer, particularly in the Metropolitan Police Area, and the positive duties of a citizen in assisting the police in the detection of crime and the apprehension of offenders.

■ Routine police station procedure is vitally important. It is in the comparative privacy of the station that the confrontation with the police, with all its overtones and complexities, is most acute. Police procedure should therefore be beyond all reproach. The task is not to devise new principles of procedure: Circular 31/64 is wholly satisfactory. The challenge is to ensure that it is put into practice. It provides, for example, that prisoners should be informed orally of their rights in custody.

We recommend that this provision should be implemented by the introduction of a standard verbal formula, covering the prisoner's rights to consult solicitor, friend, or relation, to make telephone calls or send telegrams, and to receive writing materials; and we further recommend that the use of the verbal formula should be compulsory, just as the oral caution is compulsory under the Judges' Rules. Reliance should never be placed on written notices or posters; in so far as standard procedure at present permits this to happen, it should be changed.

Secondly, a programme of public education is needed on the role and powers of the police. It is not for the police to undertake this work: however well-intentioned, police initiative is likely to be misconstrued. The work is best undertaken by community relations councils, the schools, the National Council for Civil Liberties, and other voluntary bodies including immigrant organizations. Much needs to be explained: the duty of the citizen to assist in the investigation of crime and the apprehension of offenders, and the conventional refusal of the English police to become involved in domestic 'civil' disputes, outside the scope of the criminal law. And above all, police powers of arrest must be fully, and repeatedly, explained; it is particularly important that the special powers of arrest and search possessed by the Metropolitan Police should be thoroughly understood, as well as police powers under the Dangerous Drugs Acts.

In making these recommendations, we repeat that in many countries from which the immigrants have come the police have wider and more arbitrary powers than the police in England and are often suspected of bias against the poorer classes. Scrupulous police procedure, external review of complaints, and a programme of public education conducted by independent bodies could do much to improve a relationship which is at present deteriorating.

8. COMMUNITY RELATIONS

(a) The Community Relations Commission

The new Community Relations Commission (C.R.C.), which was set up under the 1968 Race Relations Act, has taken over the apparatus of the National Committee for Commonwealth Immigrants including the structure of voluntary liaison committees (now to be called community relations councils) to which it will continue to grant the salary of the liaison officer (now community relations officer), presumably on the same conditions as were laid down in the 1965 White Paper. The C.R.C. will wish to make its own definition of community relations work and will no doubt formulate the 'comprehensive body of doctrine' which the White Paper expected from the N.C.C.I., and which 'could be flexibly applied to a variety of local situations'.

As a contribution to this process we make the following suggestions:

The pivot of the system is the paid liaison officer. He has suffered in the past from many grave handicaps. In the first place, there was ambiguity about his operational subordination. The local committee was his employer but his salary came from the National Committee, which had to be satisfied about his competence for the job and assisted the local committee in recruiting and training him. Once employed, he was the servant of the local committee although he looked to the National Committee for training, guidance, and support. But in fact, once the grant was made, the National Committee which was responsible for the expenditure of public funds no longer had any but a permissive power to influence the policy of the committee or the conduct of its officer. The guidelines had to be very flexible indeed. If anything went wrong the only sanction it possessed was to withdraw the grant.

The Government hoped that the National Committee's grant would be matched by the local authority which would supply accommodation; local authority support was generally, but not always, made a condition of the grant. This made the officer very often dependent on the local authority and identified him in many cases with local officialdom when his job was to involve the whole community. It made him appear less accessible to the rank and file of the immigrants who might be doubtful about his independence of the statutory authority.

We suggest that it would be better if there were a corps of liaison officers recruited and trained by the Community Relations Commission and seconded to serve the local community relations councils. No one would be assigned to a committee until he had been fully trained. Once working for the committee he would be operationally subordinate to the chairman of the committee and

and his executive but he would also report to the C.R.C., preferably through regional officers whose function would be to support him and interpret C.R.C. doctrine. This would enable the C.R.C. to transfer officers if for any reason relations with the local committee did not prove satisfactory. It would also provide some form of a career structure, however slight, for officers, who could hope for promotion to a regional supervisory post or to headquarters. In this way the C.R.C. could build up an elite corps of highly trained and highly regarded workers.

If this were to be done, it would be indispensable to define the role of the officer and erect standards for selection. The definition of role would not only determine the qualfications required but the type of training needed.

Given this structure, it would then be important to have regional development officers of a high calibre, paid at appropriate rates. One of the weaknesses of the N.C.C.I. was that very few liaison officers had received any training before their appointment and this was understandable considering the speed at which committees were formed and staffed. A second weakness was the small number of development officers, who were based not in the regions but at headquarters.

There were two main assumptions behind the Government's policy in promoting voluntary liaison committees through the N.C.C.I. A harmony of interests would develop if a range of views was represented and policies could be formulated by people brought together on a representative basis. The committees must therefore involve the whole community, including private individuals drawn from the host and immigrant communities as well as representatives of both statutory and voluntary organizations. A high premium was placed on consensus and it was generally assumed that a benevolently paternalist approach fitted a situation which was relatively satisfactory. This policy had two basic weaknesses: local decisions are not made in this way and the situation was changing very rapidly. The relationship between benevolent hosts and suppliant immigrants could no longer be maintained, but the committees were not equipped to anticipate social changes in the structure of the immigrant groups and in their relationships with the wider community. There was a desire to embrace the shadow of consensus about relatively unimportant matters rather than the substance of conflict which would arise given the true expression of group feelings.

Where situations are unsatisfactory it has been difficult for the liaison committees to come to grips with them. A large section of the committee often represents a power to block controversial action. Many committees have been dominated by political representatives who do not wish to have their policies questioned. In many areas the weakness of immigrant organizations and the lack of effective leadership has also been a serious handicap. Too often the immigrant communities have been represented by prestige leaders who have no roots in the community, and the immigrants have remained unaware of the committee whose activities have been conducted over their heads. The crisis within C.A.R.D. (Campaign Against Racial Discrimination) and the absence in most areas of an effective protest organization also handicapped the N.C.C.I. because it left a vacuum which many liaison officers felt should be filled by their committees. This has led at times to a conflict of aims between the officer and his committee which the N.C.C.I. was in no position to resolve.

Should an effective national civil rights organization arise on the flank, the conflict would be much reduced and the benefits of an improved structure and thorough training could be more fully realized. But at present the vacuum remains and it cannot be filled by the C.R.C. or the local councils who cannot represent merely one side of the community. None the less, their principal concern will presumably continue to be with the integration of the various immigrant groups and to perform this role they must be able to assess the needs of the community, and organize effective programmes to meet those needs. It follows that they must involve not only the people in the area who can take decisions, whether through their official positions or through membership of other relevant voluntary organizations, but also the people whose problems require a solution. They must therefore be more accessible to the rank and file of the immigrants and should be seen to be a channel through which immigrant groups can have access to local sources of power. This will mean more than providing an efficient link with relevant departments; it will require a change from a preoccupation with welfare to an increasing concern with such questions as opportunities for school leavers and the policies of the local authority. It will mean that the local community relations council and its officer cannot remain indifferent to allegations of discrimination or prejudiced behaviour on the part of local officials or the police. They may have to be critical of local policies and this makes it all the more desirable that the paid officer should be independent and should be seen to be independent of the local authority.

(b) Civil Rights and Immigrant Leadership

In practice, the likelihood of a civil rights organization emerging which would embrace all the immigrant communities is remote. There are many factors which militate against it. In the first place, the rank and file of the immigrants are still concerned with establishing themselves in this country and with getting a living and so they keep their heads down. Secondly, the different immigrant communities have little in common except the fact of being migrants and the shared experience of discrimination. But, as we have seen, and as the P.E.P. evidence shows, discrimination is felt differently by different groups and many immigrants avoid situations where they might encounter it. Thirdly, the diplomatic and consular role of the High Commissions perpetuates uncertainty in the minds of the immigrants (and among the British) about their status. Some of the missions are more concerned with the welfare of the immigrants than others who tend to emphasize cultural separatism and obligations to their country of origin. In the initial stages of a migration it is beneficial, though it may be quite unusual, to have consular representatives of the sending country who will ease the entry into the receiving society. Before the break-up of the West Indies Federation the Migrant Services Division of the Federation performed this function, but as we have shown in Chapter 25 this kind of paternalism, although it had fruitful consequences in terms of communal organizations, was in some ways inconsistent with the development of independent immigrant leadership.

No one from outside the immigrant communities can create a civil rights organization and it is not for us to recommend what can only occur spontaneously. We can merely state our opinion that whether there are vigorous civil rights groups or not it is in the interests of good community relations that effective representative immigrant organizations should emerge and that their leaders should be given every opportunity to be of service to their own communities.

We recommend that as leaders are identified they should be consulted by government departments, by local authorities, and by the police and that they be invited to be members of local bodies such as regional hospital boards and education and housing committees of local authorities, which serve the community as a whole. This is all the more important since the structure of the Community Relations Commission does not include representatives from functioning immigrant organizations.

We also recommend that there should be a sensible and balanced response to the emergence of civil rights leadership and that the lines should be kept open to them. To take alarm on hearing the words 'Black Power' helps no one. It is important to understand the reasons that lie behind it. Black Power is as yet a small minority movement, but it represents in an extreme form something that we have charted in our analysis, namely a progressive disillusionment which has become so strongly felt that colour transcends cultural differences. Black Power enshrines a real emotion based on real grievances; it should be recognized as a serious symptom of a pervasive malaise.

(c) The Role of the Churches

The Churches have an important role to play in the field of community relations. In our analysis we have noted the decline of the hold of the Church of England in the central areas of our cities, and the inadequate preparation of many ministers who are unaware of the social forces which shape society and who are ill-equipped to face the problems of the communities in these areas. We have expressed the view that with the decline in congregations the concept of pastoral care which is concerned with the individual church member in distress is losing its relevance.

We therefore recommend that the training of ordinands should include some instruction in the social issues which affect the lives of communities in the inner city.

We further recommend that closer links be forged between the clergy, social workers, and other officials: to this end ministers in their training should be made familiar with the range of welfare services available to the community.

Many promising community projects are frustrated for lack of premises in underprivileged neighbourhoods. At the same time, many church buildings are under-used. In some areas where parishes are being amalgamated, redundant properties are left largely empty or else they are sold. Simultaneously with the decline in congregations there has been a welcome growth of the spirit and practice of ecumenism, which has brought about an increasing use of buildings by two or more denominations for joint or consecutive services. This should lead to more church property becoming vacant which could be made available for community activities. We agree with the authors of *Vicious Circle* that 'a multi-racial playgroup in the church hall may do more for race relations than fifty-two sermons per year on the subject'. A model of what can be done is the Ecumenical Centre provided by the Methodist Church in Notting Hill.

▎ We recommend that within each denomination, where there is duplication of buildings in an area, some should be released for community activities, and that in order to make more buildings available others should be shared on an ecumenical basis. If church property has to be sold, we hope that it will be offered in the first place to the community on a mortgage at a minimal rate of interest.

▎ We further recommend that church buildings be made available to West Indian sects and to members of other faiths for the holding of religious services.

There are many possibilities for action open to the Churches in areas of the cities where coloured immigrants live. Because of their authority and their central location, the Churches can inform themselves of the disabilities which immigrants suffer from discrimination in housing or employment and they can bring pressure to bear on the local authority or on employers to remove some of these disabilities. They can also make representations to the local press if they detect signs of bias in reporting or in the treatment of news stories. They can perform a most valuable service in mediating between the local police and the immigrants in areas where relations may be deteriorating. In making these suggestions we realize that we are proposing a role for the Church which is perhaps more militant than many believing Christians would wish it to perform. We also recognize that in an increasingly secular age, the minority of believing Christians can have only a limited influence and that a fair proportion of them, though by no means a majority, may coincide or overlap with other groups who are playing their part to improve community relations. The clergy may often find that their most effective contribution can be made in association with others who are working to the same end, but they have special responsibilities and opportunities for leadership.

(d) The Neighbourhood Project and the Individual

Whatever the type of institutional structure and whatever the qualifications required in a paid officer, community work depends for its success on attracting the support of the individual voluntary worker and thereafter on sustaining the enthusiasm of the volunteer. There is a dual problem, particularly in deprived urban areas. Initiatives may fail because they do not appeal to the community which they are designed to serve; at the same time there may be many people in these areas who care very deeply about the decline of their neighbourhood but feel impotent to do anything about it. This feeling of impotence may turn into resentment against coloured immigrants who will be held responsible for the decline. The old established residents who are potentially valuable allies are not likely to be interested in programmes which have the expressed aim of integrating the immigrants, but their energies can be enlisted for projects which are designed to improve the amenities and morale of the neighbourhood as a whole.

Local associations which are formed to cater for the welfare of all the people in an area, irrespective of their origins, can arouse a response from old and new residents alike. They are effective if they can create a sense of purpose and make people believe that it is possible to get things done to improve the conditions in which they are living. The most disparate elements in a neighbourhood, who would not otherwise feel any sense of community, can be brought to co-operate in projects which are seen to be needed. These associations have a double value. They preserve the morale of the native, by providing an effective channel of action for people who might otherwise have found no outlet for their frustration except in some anti-immigrant organization, and, as Rex and Moore have said of the Sparkbrook Association, they declare racialism to be an illegitimate response and offer alternative solutions to the problems which it purports to solve. They also draw on the congregations of different denominations within the area. Where there is a shortage of voluntary workers and the clergy are hard pressed, the Church can often make its most effective contribution by joining in the work of these associations either through group ministries or on an ecumenical basis, and by offering church premises for the use of secular groups.

(e) A National Community Service

We have so far been discussing a range of community activities which depend for their success on enlisting the support of adult members of society. They are a necessary complement to the work of the statutory services and can very often succeed in attracting welfare facilities for the areas which they serve. Where they are effective they can help to arrest the growing demoralization in underprivileged neighbourhoods. But whatever the achievements of the voluntary system, it does not appear to be adequate for the needs of youth. The nation is faced with the problem of harnessing the energies of its young people, who have more money and more leisure than ever before and who are bored. That there exists in the youth of this country a reservoir of latent idealism is attested by the success of organizations like Community Service Volunteers, International Voluntary Service, and Voluntary Service Overseas. At the same time, there is ample evidence that the Youth Service is failing to attract young people in sufficient numbers to counter the feeling of aimlessness which is reflected in the disporportionate increase in juvenile crime. The voluntary principle does not seem to provide a solution.

It has been aptly said that the abolition of National Service removed a watershed between youth and adulthood from the lives of young men. The transition from the protection and disciplines of the school to quasi-adult freedom is abrupt and young people find themselves with freedom before they have the maturity to make full use of it. But National Service offered more than a bridge between school and the outside world. Whatever its frustrations, it often provided a means for promoting social cohesion which is sorely missed today.

We believe that some form of expanded and diversified National Service is well worth considering. The obligation might be discharged in a variety of ways and the range of options could be as wide as possible embracing a large number of civilian occupations, various forms of community service at home or in developing countries, and service in the Armed Forces.

Compulsory service could be an instrument of social progress. It would enable young people to make a positive contribution to their country; it would bring together young people from all classes and from all ethnic groups; and it would also give an added meaning to the obligations of citizenship. In our recommendations for a new immigration policy we urge that full citizenship should be available, after a qualifying period, to all who are admitted for settlement. If citizenship entailed an obligation to national service, anyone who applied for permission to settle in this country in preference to entry for temporary employment would be accepting a definite obligation, for himself or his children, in return for the right to qualify for citizenship.

9. PUBLIC EDUCATION

The four most important findings of the attitude survey are:

(i) The degree of prejudice in the population is quite considerable. Using a fourteen item scale, one-tenth of the sample were found to be extremely prejudiced and unconditionally hostile, while another one-sixth were strongly inclined towards prejudice.

(ii) The degree of tolerance in the population is even higher. Over one-third of all white adults in the sample 'expressed views with no trace, or practically no trace, of hostility to coloured people'; nearly two-fifths 'seemed to be strongly disposed in the direction of tolerance'. Together they account for seven out of ten of the sample in the five boroughs with heavy immigrant settlement.

(iii) Two of the most important factors underlying the amount of prejudice a person displays are his age and the amount of education he has received. These two factors are independent of one another, so that educated, middle-aged people are less prejudiced than people in this age group without further and higher education, and young people with further and higher education are less prejudiced than young people without such education; and educated young people are less prejudiced than educated old people.

(iv) 'there is a great deal of widely diffused confusion, anxiety and misunderstanding about the migration [of coloured people], its composition, and the background of the migrants, making up a predisposition towards rejection.'

These findings prompt us to underscore Dr. Abrams' basic recommendations that 'attempts to improve race relations, while they must not ignore the views of the 10% [prejudiced] minority, should see them for what they are—irrational "solutions" to personality inadequacies which would persist without regard to the policies adopted. Real concern should be with the 55% of the population whose criticism is specific and limited.'

On this basis, the main guideline for policy must be to dispel confusion, to remove misunderstanding, and to allay anxiety.

There is first of all an unquestioned need for an extensive, varied, and authoritative attempt to publicize the actual facts concerning immigration, and, in particular, the real characteristics of the coloured population.

The exaggerated estimates of the size of the coloured population, the prevalence of the stereotype of the coloured immigrant as an unskilled working-class person lacking education and culture, and the widespread belief that coloured immigrants 'take more out of the country than they put in'—these suggest the extent to which ignorance or misinformation lie at the root of the anxiety and confusion on this issue. Correcting these misconceptions is a necessary part of any effort to improve race relations.

While the survey found a clear majority (73%) who were either tolerant or inclined towards tolerance, it noted at the same time that 'those expressing anti-coloured attitudes were likely to feel that they were in line with national norms'. This paradox highlights the way in which it has simply come to be assumed in recent years that the population is more likely to be ill- rather than well-disposed on the question of race; and it prompts a dual foundation for policy.

First, the extent of tolerance in Britain cannot be stressed too often and is indeed one of the major facts of the actual situation which has to be communicated to people whose anxieties on this score may stem in part from the mistaken view that there is not only widespread anxiety about coloured immigration but widespread hostility towards coloured people as such. What is needed in short is not an effort to make people unprejudiced, but rather to remind them that they *are* unprejudiced.

Secondly, there seems to us a need now to define explicitly what our national norms are on issues of race and colour. The fluidity of the situation and, more importantly, the extent of the basic inclination towards tolerance suggests strongly that forthright, unequivocating leadership would be a powerful factor in allaying unfounded anxieties. Such leadership must be expected not only from the major political parties, but also from the major public institutions in the country—the Churches and trade unions—and from people of influence at national and local level. Conversely, there is a danger that in the absence of leadership, anyone who wishes to play upon the anxieties of the majority who lie between the extremes of tolerance and hostility can move them towards prejudiced attitudes.

The findings concerning the effects of education suggest that an increase in the educational level of the population would reduce the amount of prejudice, other things being equal. Even a single year's further education beyond the present school leaving-age of 15 would have a valuable return in decreased levels of prejudice. Even if there were no other compelling reasons, this in itself would constitute the strongest argument for raising the school leaving-age. The more education the population receives, the more this effect is likely to be felt. The most tolerant group of all, in the national study, were those who had been educated beyond the age of 18; while these comprised only 4% of the population the majority are still under 40 years old. The continued and further expansion of higher education at all levels would, on this evidence, be associated with a valuable reduction in prejudice.

Not only would an increase in general levels of education be highly likely to increase tolerance, but also an increase in specific forms of education relating to race relations would be particularly likely to have a valuable pay-off. In particular, the widespread equation of cultural *differences* with cultural *inferiority* demands an effort on the part of educationists to stress the extent and value of *diversity* in Britain as well as in the world at large. Teachers and educationists cannot tell people to be tolerant, but by promoting knowledge and understanding they can contribute towards an intelligent and tolerant society. At the source of teacher supply, in teacher training colleges and colleges of education, there should be a national agreement on the introduction of a course at both an academic and a practical level as we have suggested in our recommendations on education. In both further and higher education (colleges of further education, commerce, and technology, polytechnics, and universities) the introduction or greater emphasis on social studies courses having race and group relations as a core component would bring rewards, both in respect of the greater tolerance of the individuals concerned, and also in respect of the potentiality of such students as teachers and as business and professional people themselves. It is, however, of great importance that such efforts should not mistake the generalized preaching of good-will for a firmly based grasp of the principles of cultural variation and of race and group relations, nor should there be any suggestion of an official 'line' which only permits approved views to be expressed and discussed.

With the growing concern with further education for adults (as expressed, for example, in the Open University), a general alertness on the part of those involved in such developments would provide new channels for the provision of information and new methods for the promotion of education in this field which were not available hitherto. The considerable development of research in education now backed by government and private foundations could be effectively utilized both in the development of projects for educational institutions and the formulation of new strategies in further education and adult education.

Other agencies in society can usefully reinforce the efforts of education by undertaking an educational effort of their own. There is no reason why trade unions, churches, and even political parties should not attempt to influence and educate their members towards greater understanding and tolerance. Given the enormous segment of the population whose formal education ceased at 15, the educational effort of these agencies could be crucial.

The findings of the national as well as of the five-borough survey on the effect of contact with coloured people in diminishing hostility suggest that measures which promote such contacts can be educative in themselves. One of the most encouraging findings of the national survey was that the people who were least prejudiced tended to live near to coloured people; getting to know a coloured man as an individual, as a human being, is associated with a reduction in prejudice. On this evidence, the dispersal of coloured minorities through the availability of housing would be an additional factor leading to a reduction in prejudice. The evidence also suggests: first, that the effective operation of the Race Relations Act 1968 will tend to bring white people into contact with coloured people in new roles and capacities. To the extent that this actually occurs, the Act will lend support to other educational efforts. Secondly, voluntary community organizations of a multi-racial character (such as those established by the N.C.C.I., though not only those) can play a crucial part in bringing more people into contact at a community level.

To the extent that those who feel socially helpless are more likely to hold hostile attitudes, constructive programmes of community action which involve citizen participation and which focus attention on the real problems of the community may lead to the dispelling of unfounded anxieties and perhaps even to a lowering of hostility.

Our principal recommendation is that those who are in positions of authority and influence should take heart at the extent of support that can be found for tolerant attitudes.

The Mass Media

The role of the press and of the broadcasting authorities in all this can be crucial. In the last five years immigration and race relations have rivalled almost any other subject except natural disasters for prominence in newspapers and on television. They have an irresistible appeal for news and feature editors and for those who produce discussion programmes. They bulk largely in the cockpit of the correspondence columns, especially in local newspapers. Whenever a politician speaks on this subject he knows that he will almost certainly be reported; some do not even trouble to speak: they pick up the telephone and dictate a statement to the Press Association.

We are not questioning the professional judgement of those who decide on news values or on what will interest the public but there are certain matters of taste and procedure which do concern us and which we feel should concern the professions of journalism and broadcasting. The law of libel already provides safeguards for a man's reputation and if he is on trial the law of contempt ensures that nothing shall be published which would prejudice his defence. But the law cannot protect a group from being libelled unless it can be shown that the libel will lead to violence against members of the group. We have already stated that in our view section 6 of the 1965 Race Relations Act encroaches on freedom of speech and freedom of expression and that we would like to see this section of the Act repealed. We cannot therefore be suspected of wishing to abridge freedom of the press if we suggest that the press and the broadcasting authorities should abandon certain practices which may do harm to minorities or worsen group relations.

Our attitude survey shows that the great majority of the public are poised somewhere between the extremes of tolerance and irrational hostility and that they can be moved in either direction by argument or by appeals to their emotions or to their fears. The survey also shows that there is a widespread tendency to hold stereotyped views about minority group members.

Editors, who have a sense of responsibility to the public, will not want to excite the prejudices which are latent in most of us. And yet some of the practices in newspapers have this effect. In reports of crimes or of criminal proceedings or in court reporting it is harmful to identify a defendant by his racial or ethnic origin unless this identification is an essential part of the story. And yet defendants are constantly identified either in headlines or in lead paragraphs, and in some cases, on conviction, by the publication of a photograph.

The 1949 Royal Commission on the Press examined the way news stories became distorted through their treatment in different sections of the press. If one considers the treatment of stories on race or immigration the analogy is not so much with a distorting mirror as with a variety of prisms through which the light of a news story is broken up into different colours before it is refracted from the page. The headline treatment and the play of a story depends on the judgement of the sub-editor, but it often reflects the editorial position of the newspaper. From a reading of the headlines and the opening paragraphs in different newspapers, it is sometimes impossible to realize that they are dealing with the same story. There is a tendency to sensationalize, to pick out the most prejudicial elements in a story, and to print scare headlines. Some newspapers appear to be following Lenin's precept of agitating through their treatment of the news: news headlines are read, editorial columns are not.

Many editors print letters which are hostile to coloured immigrants: they do so on the grounds that they are of public interest and that in allowing readers to give vent to their prejudices the newspaper is acting as a safety valve. Some editors print these letters over pseudonyms. The tone and content of many letters is very prejudicial and must undoubtedly seem threatening to immigrants and their children. The fact that the newspapers also print replies from immigrants or their champions does not absolve them from all responsibility.

In the fifteen years of its existence the Press Council has had something to say on these practices. It appears to have adjudicated on seven complaints concerning the treatment of religious or ethnic minorities. Three of these cases concerned coloured people (one of which was upheld), four concerned anti-semitism (two of which were upheld and one did not call for a special adjudication). Two complaints, which were upheld, were about tendentious reporting. In the first case (1956), the Press Council censured the editor of a London weekly paper for refusing to publish a correction from the Minister of the local synagogue and it deplored the exaggerated tone of the article. In the second case (1965), involving a story about a possible colour bar, the Press Council found that a local evening paper 'turned a trivial incident of a domestic nature into something sensational, *disregarding the harmful social effects* [our italics]'.

One complaint (1958), which was dismissed, concerned the wrongful identification of a man, later hanged for murder, as of Polish-Jewish extraction. The paper had in fact amended the description the following day. The Press Council in dismissing the complaint declared that there was no substance in the implied suggestion that the publication of an admitted error showed anti-semitic motives. It would be wrong to deduce from this ruling that the Council held any views on the desirability or otherwise of this sort of identification.

In 1959, the Press Council severely condemned a local London weekly newspaper for publishing an anti-semitic letter over a signature (G. A. S. Chambers) 'which should have put the Editor on his guard as to its purpose'.

In 1960, the Council published a letter in its Annual Report in response to a request for help from the General Secretary of the Council of Christians and Jews. The letter called attention to the occasional appearance in children's papers of articles or pictures calculated to stimulate prejudice or hostility to minority groups.

On the evidence of these few cases it would appear that the Press Council's position has been consistent and unambiguous. But its adjudication in two other cases makes its record inconclusive. Both were concerned with cartoons, in each case by the same cartoonist. In 1965, a complaint was made against a cartoon on the grounds that it was a 'calculated insult to coloured people both in Britain and in the U.S.A.'. The Council rejected the complaint without explanation. In 1968, in rejecting a similar complaint, the Council did give a ruling. The cartoon was referred to it on the grounds that it was offensive to coloured immigrants and to Englishmen concerned with improving race relations, and that it was 'crass, gross and a blatant incitement to race hatred'. The Press Council's adjudication was: 'to censure a publication simply on the ground that it is or may be offensive to a part or even the majority of the population would be quite inconsistent

with the freedom of the Press.' This seems to us to be confusing
the Council's duty to censure bad taste with its obligation not to
censor opinion. If the doctrine were to be pursued to its logical
conclusion it would appear to mean that the Press Council must
stand neutral should a newspaper pursue editorial policies which
may be socially disastrous in a developing race situation. And yet
this was not the view that it formed of its responsibilities when in
its 1965 ruling on the 'colour bar' complaint it took into account
the harmful social consequences of a newspaper's treatment of a
story. In upholding a paper's right to comment on matters of
public interest there is surely a legitimate distinction to be made
between the expression of an opinion which may be offensive to
the majority (who have some protection) and of one which may
injure a minority (who, *ex hypothesi*, have little or none).

The press and broadcasting authorities have a preponderant
role in public education and in performing this role they are
confronted with many professional problems. We know that many
of those in responsible positions are already fully aware of these
problems, which cause them some anxiety. We suggest that it
would be an advantage to have frequent discussions through their
professional associations and that in particular the Press Council,
which through its rulings over the years has begun to establish a
kind of case law or code, should address itself to some of these
questions and perhaps lay down certain guidelines for professional
practice. It established a precedent in 1966 when, after consulting
newspaper editors, it issued a Declaration of Principle on the
practice of payments to witnesses in criminal proceedings and on
cheque-book journalism.

There may be a feeling that the existence of a law against
incitement absolves the Council from setting standards for the
press in this field, but this would imply that the law provides a
licence for the press to sail as near to the legal limit as it can. Any
such position would be wholly inconsistent with the objects of the
Council, which include not only preserving the freedom of the
press but also the maintenance of 'the character of the British
Press in accordance with the highest professional and commercial
standards'. One of the most encouraging items in the 1968 Report
of the Press Council shows how much journalistic standards can
be raised within a very short period. A witness whose conduct of
an interview in 1964 was the subject of a complaint contended that
the complaint was being considered by 1968 standards, whereas

since 1964 there had been a dramatic change in interviewing: a reporter would not in 1968 be assigned to cover the kind of story which had given rise to the complaint. The Press Council agreed with this view. There is no doubt that the Council has had a considerable influence on the standards of the Press and in some respects on the press' conception of its role in society.

There is a danger peculiar to broadcasting, in the field of current affairs. We refer to the discussion programme. Through a desire to avoid the charge of partisanship both the B.B.C. and the commercial television companies appear to feel that in their treatment of a controversial subject like immigration, race, or race relations they must preserve neutrality by giving equal prominence to opposing points of view. This often leads them to select as protagonists those who hold extreme positions on either side. The discussion then becomes a gladiatorial show. This may make good television, but it can have disastrous effects on race relations. In these matters we suggest that neutrality does not consist, in the apocryphal words of the colonial judge, in maintaining a balance between impartiality on the one hand and partiality on the other. We are not suggesting that there should not be free discussion on matters of public importance but that there are ways of promoting discussion without giving prominence to expressions of irrational prejudice.

There is one further danger, which confronts all the mass media. By giving prominence to the views of extremists they may appear to sanction them and to confer a respectability and importance on their holders which they could not otherwise achieve. A chain reaction is then set in motion. Prominence in one medium leads to attention by another. By this kind of cross-fertilization between newspapers and broadcasting the demagogue becomes a public figure.

10. IMMIGRATION POLICY

As our analysis so far should have suggested, it has been the want of a coherent immigration policy that has been one of the main factors in the deterioration of race relations in Britain. The anxieties provoked by uncertainty and by the anomalies of the present patchwork system are a standing invitation to exploitation for political gain by the unscrupulous of all shades of opinion and skin colour. And even if the political climate were different, the objective case for reform would be strong—there is a pressing need to consolidate the practice on immigration from all sources. This can only be achieved by legislation, and the present Home Secretary has declared that he is not at present prepared to embark on a consolidation. However, this need not prevent us from sketching out a broad programme for reform. In doing so, it is not our concern to provide a blueprint for legislation but to indicate guidelines for policy.

We consider that four broad considerations need to be kept in mind in framing a revised policy. First, the view that in the case of movement of population to the United Kingdom our national interests should ultimately take first pace is a reasonable one, under present circumstances—that is, as long as population policy is the responsibility of national states and while effective machinery for consideration on an international basis does not exist. However, the absence of international agreements which could be enforced without detriment to national sovereignty is a regrettable situation and the long-term aim should be to negotiate them.

In considering the national interest there are certain different aspects which need to be taken into account. There are the economic interests of this country and the effects on the economy of the numbers and composition of migration. There are the effects on the efficiency of the social services. There is also the less tangible factor of confidence—that of the majority (who have been led to fear 'sweeping' changes in the 'national character') as much as that of the minority. Immigration policy must not only operate fairly and efficiently, but be seen to operate fairly and efficiently. Finally, policy must not damage our interests internationally. A programme which is either patently inhumane or racially discriminatory (as a repatriation policy or a system of preference based on colour would be) could do serious damage to our interests abroad.

Secondly, there must be a recognition that migration is a process that does not solely affect the country of reception. It also involves the sending society, and often third parties—as in the case of the Kenya Asians episode, where the interests of the United Kingdom, Kenya, and India were involved. Policy must therefore not be devised purely on the basis of the interests of the receiving country but should take into account the legitimate concerns of the other partners to the process. This is a factor which we in this country, who export more emigrants than we take in immigrants, particularly need to bear in mind. It should be framed not on a unilateral or even a bilateral basis but through multilateral negotiation.*

Thirdly, it is important to devise an efficient administrative structure for operating an immigration (or rather migration) policy which will serve all these ends. The different aims are at present too often in conflict. Thus, one needs a structure which will take account of our international and Commonwealth connexions, which will cope with needs arising from political or economic emergencies; a system which will utilize the best departmental advice and promote effective forward planning, and one which will offer the best guarantees for the civil liberties of newcomers by providing a right of appeal against exclusion and freedom from harassment while in this country.

The fourth and final consideration is that policy must be linked to a fair and coherent system of citizenship. At present, the system of United Kingdom citizenship deriving from the British Nationality Act of 1948 is in a state of total disrepair. It is an essential cornerstone of any reform of immigration policy that our citizenship should be restored to some degree of consistency even though this would also require legislation.

Let us now consider details. We need to recognize at the outset that the era of mass population movement, composed largely of the unskilled, is probably over. As Richmond puts it:

Although there is still a residual movement of people from rural to urban areas major population movements, both within and between post-industrial societies today, are from one large city or metropolitan area to another. . . . Migration now is more highly selective and contains a relatively small proportion of unskilled workers.

And although the greatly increased facilities for travel still make large-scale movements of unskilled populations feasible, in practice, political restrictions, often selective in economic terms, have created a situation in which migrants are likely to be drawn from limited groups—the young, the highly skilled, and those from a culture with a tradition of migration. In this country we have a relic of the earlier large-scale migrations in the continued entry of

---

* This paragraph was written before the Prime Minister's announcement in the House of Commons on 21 January 1969 on the outcome of the Commonwealth Prime Ministers Conference. In this statement he indicated that the Government 'propose now to seek bilateral discussions with the Commonwealth countries most closely concerned. We shall, of course, also participate in the studies of the wider problems of Commonwealth migration which the Secretary-General (Mr. Arnold Smith) was asked to undertake.'

dependants of migrants from the Commonwealth who entered this country before the Act of 1962. But this movement is already 'on a plateau' (as the Home Secretary put it):* in the future it is likely that the only substantial movement of unskilled labour will be in certain restricted categories, notably seasonal workers coming, like the Irish, to work for a strictly limited period.

Additionally, we would urge a recognition that the needs of the country of emigration may also have changed and should be borne in mind when policy is determined. The principle that the economic needs of certain territories entitled them to different treatment was recognized when an extra quota of 1,000 employment vouchers was made to Malta in 1965. Similarly, the needs of another special situation in which political factors created an emergency was provided for when an allocation of 1,500 additional vouchers was given to the Kenya Asians in 1968. In framing policy provision should be made for satisfying such needs.

These considerations point to a policy in which there is a greater degree of flexibility than under the present system of control. This will not be achieved by assimilation to the present system of aliens control, as the Conservative Opposition suggests. Although this system is based on different criteria, it is in its way nearly as rigid as that which applies to Commonwealth citizens; more important still, it is based on an excessively restrictive view of the rights of the individual while in this country. Finally, it is in any case likely to undergo substantial modification if Britain enters the European Community (within which full freedom of movement for Community workers applies). We would prefer an integrated system in which admission of newcomers takes place within a series of broadly defined categories and where certain rights are explicitly assured to the newcomer. Detailed decisions on the numbers to be admitted within each category should in general be a matter of administrative discretion, as should be decisions to admit in individual cases. The safeguards against abuse of discretion would be a greater degree of Parliamentary scrutiny employing the resources of the new Standing Committee on Immigration and an effective independent machinery for appeals against decisions in individual cases (as is proposed in the Immigration Appeals Bill published in November 1968). Although we recognize that the treatment of Commonwealth citizens and aliens

* Eversley and Sukdeo (1969) demonstrate that the number of dependants to come is less than 250,000.

on the same footing within such a system may cause a degree of concern to those who feel that preferential treatment is still justified, we are inclined to accept the argument that the accidents of imperial geography should no longer determine policy. Nevertheless, it is important to insure that those rights legitimately enjoyed in the past by Commonwealth citizens—in contrast to aliens—are not lost in any revised system.

■ We therefore recommend that admission to this country is in future permitted on the following basis, to be applied equally to aliens and Commonwealth citizens. (Whatever logic may suggest, for practical reasons we consider that no control is possible in the case of the Irish.)

(i) Admission to temporary skilled employment.
(ii) Admission as seasonal or temporary workers.
(iii) Entry for settlement.
(iv) Admission as students.
(v) Admission as visitors.

No numerical limit should be laid down in legislation but the numbers admitted would be subject to annual review by Parliament. There is no magic formula on which to base a quota: the choice of a ceiling must be a matter of exercise of judgement—subject to the scrutiny of the legislature.

The first category is intended to replace the present category B vouchers as they apply to Commonwealth citizens and to cater for the professional and highly skilled personnel who make up that category. Entry would be linked to a specific job and would be for two years in the first instance, extendable for a further period on application. Separate application would generally be required for transfer to the category of 'settler'. During the first two years' residence on a temporary skilled employment permit, application would have to be made for permission to change employment and to bring dependants; but subsequently, the only condition would be that the authorities should be informed of changes of residence and employment. The intention is to permit professional people, especially Commonwealth doctors, to continue to enter this country and make their crucial contribution to the Health Service while acquiring additional professional skills, but at the same time to encourage ultimate return to the country of origin, except in a residue of cases. The numbers to be admitted will be a matter of administrative discretion. We recognize that these proposals will involve some deterioration in the position of aliens, but we consider that this is justified in view of the importance of checking the exodus of talent from the Third World.

Entry under the second category, which would also supersede the present category A, corresponds roughly with current provision for the admission of short-term workers (for example, *au pair* girls) to the United Kingdom and should normally be confined to a time limit, of one or at maximum two years—although subsequent separate stays of up to the same period would be permitted. Dependants of such workers will not usually be admitted. This proposal is intended to serve two ends. First, it will satisfy the needs of the economy for unskilled labour in certain industrial categories. The rigidity of the present system of control over Commonwealth citizens contrasts unfavourably in this respect with the aliens' procedure, which is effectively linked to the needs of the economy. Second, it will provide workers from less developed countries (for example, some smaller West Indian islands) with an opportunity to come to this country to acquire skills that are scarce in their country of origin and can profitably be applied there. Here we envisage two different categories of entrant—first, the sponsored emigrant completing a technical course or apprenticeship or acquiring certain defined skills in industry. He would normally be supported—at least to the extent of having his passage paid—either by the sending government or by the Ministry of Overseas Development. The second category would be a form of contract labour, for whom employers would assume a degree of responsibility (for example, they would be expected to obtain accommodation for the new arrival). In order to make such a scheme viable, especially in the case of workers from the Indian sub-continent, the period for which they are admitted should normally be two years.

Admission for settlement should be once-for-all and not linked to any particular form of employment. It should extend to the families of settlers on the principle that future citizens should be entitled to maintain their family unit intact. Families should normally mean wife or wives and dependent children or elderly parents, but discretionary power to admit other dependants should also be introduced: in the case of any dispute, the onus of showing that any individual is not a *bona fide* dependant should rest on the authorities. Dependants should be admitted up to a limit of five years from the entry of the head of household. Consideration should be given to requiring the head to give notice of the number of dependants likely to follow him, but their number, as such, should not be a material factor in deciding whether he should be admitted.

Two broad criteria could be applied in selecting applicants for settlement. First, that as individuals they are likely to make a positive contribution to our society. Second, there may be circumstances where a class of persons should for one reason or other be granted entry as a group—the dependants of migrants already admitted for settlement, for example, or inhabitants of certain territories who for economic or political reasons are in a special situation. In the case of dependants of those admitted under the term of the present legislation, all the evidence available to us suggests that any interference with their existing right of entry would be highly undesirable. The other example is not intended to imply that certain countries should receive special treatment—either more or less favourable—because of the ethnic composition of their populations. It is when pressure on the population of any country reaches an intolerable level that the safety valve of emigration may need to be opened. (Political pressure in the case of Gibraltar, and economic pressure in the case of some smaller West Indian islands might be examples within the Commonwealth.) In general, allocation ought to be on a first come, first served basis, but with a fixed limit overall for any one territory. Finally, there should be provision within the global figures for a quota for applicants wishing to transfer from the second category.

In all the first three categories the entry procedure would involve obtaining entry certificates before departure from the country of origin. (We do not propose any changes in the present procedure for the last two.) There would be a right of appeal both against the refusal of a certificate and the exclusion of a person at the port of entry. In this connexion, we welcome the Government's acceptance of the Wilson Committee's recommendations on welfare facilities at points of entry, although we would prefer to see a specific commitment to the existing Joint Council for the Welfare of Immigrants.

Deliberate evasion of the conditions imposed or conviction for certain specified offences should result in deportation, as now provided for in Commonwealth Immigrants Acts and the Immigration Appeals Bill. But deportation should, as proposed in the Bill, be subject to review by an independent tribunal. It is in our judgement essential that the law should be not merely clear but consistently and fairly enforced.

It should also be clearly recognized that these proposals—although they are in our judgement a necessary rationalization of a confused situation—may have to be drastically amended, in the event of entry into the European Community. The agreement reached in July 1968 under the provisions of the Treaty of Rome is a conspicuous exception to the rule we earlier stated that no viable international agreements on free movement of population has yet been reached—although it is interesting that in the case of one member country it has already had the effect of sharply intensifying the degree of control exercised over workers from outside the Community. The situation of European preference which will result from the acceptance of the Treaty may have to be corrected by bilaterally negotiated concessions to Commonwealth countries.

Our second major recommendation is an overhaul of current citizenship law. We recommend that discussions be initiated as a matter of urgency within the Commonwealth, with a view to legislation being introduced to redefine U.K. citizenship and the rights and obligations deriving from it. The present system of a combined U.K. and Colonies citizenship, already undermined in practice by successive Commonwealth Immigrants Acts, should be abandoned. The remaining colonies should introduce their own citizenship provisions, and a separate U.K. citizenship should be instituted, based on birth in the U.K., marriage to a U.K. citizen, or continuous residence in the British Isles for five years or more. Qualification in the last category should be automatic: citizenship would be made available on formal application, the sole condition being residence for the specified period without conviction in a court of law. The possession of U.K. citizenship should guarantee free entry and departure from this country under all circumstances and possession of a passport as of right. It would not be capable of being revoked. Certain rights and duties —for example, the right to vote in Parliamentary or local elections or to stand for elected office—should be confined in the first instance to citizens (though the possibility of opening them to citizens of other countries by bilateral negotiation should not be excluded). In order to avoid the ambiguous situations to which attention was drawn during the passage of the 1968 Act, we would also recommend that dual citizenship be phased out (perhaps by an exercise of choice at 21) and that ultimately the holding of U.K. citizenship should be inconsistent with possession of any other citizenship and with permanent residence outside the United Kingdom for longer than a certain period.

It might reasonably be asked in what way our proposals differ from those advanced by the Conservative Opposition in their 'mid-term manifesto' of 1968, *Make Life Better*. There are four main differences. First, our proposals are based on the proposition that those whom we decide to admit are future citizens, and that no unnecessary obstacles will be put in the way of those of them who genuinely wish to make their home here and observe certain basic conditions. This is reflected in the proposal to make citizenship automatically available to those who complete a period of residence without abusing conditions of entry or getting into serious trouble with the law. Secondly, although the situation of aliens over conditions of entry may in some respects become less favourable under these proposals, by way of compensation we propose to extend to them rights previously available only to Commonwealth citizens. Equally, we intend to invest entry from the Commonwealth with the flexibility that it conspicuously lacks, and open the door to the ambitious unskilled worker who can be such an asset to the economy and who has been excluded for the past four years. Thirdly, we attach great significance to instituting negotiations on policy within the Commonwealth. We strongly endorse proposals that the Commonwealth Secretariat, suitably strengthened, should function as a means to this end. And finally, we also set store by meeting the international obligations this country has already entered into, by way of European and United Nations Declarations and Conventions—the majority of which were breached by the Commonwealth Immigrants Act of 1968—and widening the scope of such agreements, as a preliminary step on the long road towards bringing the movement of population under some form of international control.

Finally, we recommend that the machinery of administering immigration policy should be overhauled. A demographic policy branch should be set up within an economic department—preferably the Board of Trade. This branch should have two functions:

First, the forward planning of population policy, employing the machinery recommended in the Fulton Report and drawing on the services of technical advisers. All aspects of population policy—birth control, population growth, and emigration as well as immigration—should be considered in the course of this process.

CONCLUSIONS 753

Secondly, the co-ordination of immigration policy and the administration of the system outlined in the previous recommendations. In order to achieve this, an inter-departmental committee should be established bringing together representatives from the following departments: the Home Office, as the department responsible for the administration of the control machinery and nationalization procedures; the Department of Social Affairs, responsible for integration policy and aspects of population policy; the Foreign and Commonwealth Office, for its interest in the international implications of immigration control, and for relationships with Common Market countries; the Department of Employment and Productivity, for the economic aspects of policy; and representatives of the Commonwealth Secretariat, in which a unit should be established to co-ordinate policy on the movement of population within the Commonwealth.

The new department should publish an annual report, to be submitted to Parliament, and should be subject to the scrutiny of the Parliamentary Select Committee on Immigration and Race Relations.

NOTES TO CHAPTER 33

1. *Report of the National Advisory Commission on Civil Disorders* (Kerner Report) (New York, Bantam Books, 1968).
2. Hilary Rose, *The Housing Problem* (London, Heinemann Educational, 1968).
3. Michael Zander, 'The Unused Rent Act', *New Society* (12 September 1968).
4. D. A. Nevitt, *Housing, Taxation and Subsidies* (London, Nelson, 1966).
5. John Barr, 'New Towns as Anti-Ghettoes', *New Society* (1 April 1965).
6. 'The Education of Infant Immigrants', a survey conducted by Mrs. Diana Stoker for the Schools Council Project in English for Immigrant Children.
7. In *New Backgrounds*, edited by Robin Oakley (London, Oxford University Press, for Institute of Race Relations, 1968).

Conclusion

The aims of this Report are very simple—to put into circulation information which might serve as a basis for policy making. In doing so, we cannot claim the authority of a Royal Commission or the impartiality of pure social science. Our authority is the combined weight of the studies undertaken during the lifetime of the Survey, coupled with the personal concern of those who drafted this Report for the future of the society they live in.

Our recommendations spring from a profound conviction that some form of additional official intervention is essential and that the policies so far undertaken have not proved adequate to the situation. In the case of some of the areas we discuss we realize that we are pushing at an open door. We are very much encouraged by the constructive action taken in some fields in the course of the last year, while this Report was being written; we are also encouraged by the existence of new agencies with the capacity to intervene constructively. But in other directions the situation seems profoundly disturbing. We refer here particularly to the open sore of immigration policy. While this wound remains unhealed, the basis for constructive action in other directions is constantly undermined. Like nineteenth-century British governments in their Irish policy, contemporary administrations have followed a policy of 'kicks and kindness'. It is the kicks that those at the receiving end tend to remember.

We do not wish to imply that without the constant debate on immigration policy, with its progressive degeneration in tone, the situation would have resolved itself without difficulties. Some problems of adjustment are inseparable from all situations of immigration. The factor of colour is bound to induce additional insecurities at a time when the black man the world over is struggling to reassert himself after centuries of oppression. The legitimate element in the aspirations of the Black Power movement derives from this struggle and its legitimacy must be accepted by the majority society. But these endemic uncertainties do not lead us to the all-too-common view that no intervention can now assure the stability of a multi-racial society. On the contrary, we are convinced that the room for manoeuvre remains wide. Our recommendations are framed with this in mind; they are a realistic programme for action, not a statement of impractical liberal aspirations.

Ultimately, in the words of Roosevelt in his first inaugural, our society has nothing to fear but fear itself. If this Report has any message it is that the decision-makers must recover the confidence necessary to take initiatives of the kind that we have outlined here. Not merely because justice for new citizens is a necessary measure if we are to avoid the disasters that have overtaken other societies struggling with far more intractable problems, or even because injustice disfigures our society as a whole, but because ultimately this issue involves even more than the future health of our society.

The dominant question of our century is whether men of all races and colours whom advances in science and technology have made near neighbours, can live together in harmony. We are apt to depreciate our own country's past achievement and to deplore the present decline in its influence in the world. But influence is not measured only in material terms. A society which has provided the model for other societies by evolving democratic forms that respect the individual, and which has known how to combine tolerance with dissent, now has the chance to set a further example by proving that men of many races can live together in justice and harmony.

It is thirty years since W. H. Auden, at the end of 'a low dishonest decade' which saw the shipwreck of so many ideals, proclaimed the paramount necessity to 'love one another or die'. We who believe in the future of our own society urge all our fellow citizens not to let this opportunity to translate love into practical reality pass us by.

Appendix I.1.   A Note on the Survey of Race Relations in Britain

When the Survey of Race Relations was set up in the autumn of 1963 we knew of no research in progress except under the auspices of the Institute of Race Relations, and apart from some post-graduate students there had been no one working in the field since 1959. Distinguished work had been done in the 1950s by a handful of social scientists and it had been mainly concerned with Negroes from West Africa or the West Indies. This was not surprising as the emigration from India and Pakistan had not reached any proportions and the main settlements were still in the port towns. The literature on race relations in Britain was therefore fairly small and there had been surprisingly little study of other migrations, particularly the Irish, by far the largest in our history and so there was little evidence which would help to gauge the progress or the prospects of the post-war migrations from the Commonwealth. No Government department had conducted any research and apart from the evidence of the census there were practically no records anywhere in the country which differentiated white and coloured.

It was against this background that the Institute of Race Relations obtained a grant from the Nuffield Foundation for a five-year survey of race relations in Britain.

Where so little was known we decided that the research plan would have to be extensive—at the risk of some loss in depth—and that it must involve the skills of many disciplines. It would not be practical to form our own research unit and we would therefore commission research from the universities and elsewhere. Four years would be the minimum period needed for planning, discussion with the Universities, and completion of original research.

With the help of a distinguished panel of advisers an overall plan was drawn up and presented to the universities. While the Survey would have to concern itself with the cultures and values of the receiving and sending societies, the main weight of the research was to be directed to studying their interaction and the response of each side to the other when they met in this country. A central feature of the plan was a series of area studies, loosely linked together and conducted in areas of heavy immigrant settlement. The first of these studies to be commissioned was a research in the twilight zone of Sparkbrook in Birmingham by Professor John Rex and Robert Moore, which was published as *Race, Community and Conflict* in February 1967.

The second area study was conducted by Professor Anthony Richmond and Michael Lyon in the St. Paul's area of Bristol, a twilight area with a dense Jamaican settlement and a fairly large Irish population. There were some resemblances between the St. Paul's and Sparkbrook studies but the Bristol research also included an inquiry on council estates among dispersed West Indian families and their neighbours.

While these two researches in Bristol and Birmingham were about the relationships of groups of native English and immigrants in the decaying area of the city, the third study—conducted in Bradford by Eric Butterworth—was more concerned with the municipal response of a city to a non-English speaking, largely illiterate, and almost wholly male settlement of Pakistanis. Housing and housing policies are a central preoccupation of all three area studies and it soon became clear to us that discrimination against immigrants in the allocation of housing was going to be the single most critical factor in the development of race relations in the next few years. We therefore commissioned Elizabeth Burney to make a comparative study of municipal housing policies in six areas other than those already covered. Her book *Housing on Trial* was published at the end of 1967.

An earlier study of the British response centred on political behaviour. This was published in 1965 as *Colour and the British Electorate*, edited by Nicholas Deakin, Assistant Director of the Survey. It consisted of an examination of the 1964 electoral campaigns in six constituencies with a relatively large immigrant settlement. A complementary study was carried out during the 1966 General Election and published in *Race*. The most ambitious approach to the study of the British response was the survey of attitudes to colour which we entrusted to Dr. Mark Abrams and Research Services. An analysis of the findings forms Part VII of the present Report. This may prove to be the most important study of prejudice yet conducted in this country.

The immigrant response was to be studied in a number of ways, but principally through observation by social anthropologists working within the immigrant communities. We commissioned a number of studies: of Sikhs in Southall and in Gravesend, of West Indian families dispersed in an area of secondary settlement in North London, of changing West Indian family patterns in South London, of an all-male Yemeni settlement in Birmingham, and of Pakistanis in Bradford. Most of this research was concerned with the processes of adjustment of a first generation to a new environment and the immigrants were observed in their homes. To these studies we later added an inquiry by DeWitt John into the Indian Workers' Association. Published in 1969 as *Indian Workers' Associations in Britain*, it is a study of leadership and factionalism within a community associating together initially for welfare and later to meet the pressures of a developing situation.

In the first stages of a migration people tend to come in along a chain that extends from their village or parish and thus the initial settlements are swollen by the arrival of kin and village members who keep together for mutual security and support in an unknown land. In this way clustering occurs, which may be reinforced by the attitudes of the receiving society and by administrative policies which limit the choice of housing. At a later stage of resettlement migrants will begin to disperse and the extent to which members of different ethnic groups keep together or separate as they move along this cycle may be an indication of their rate of adjustment. To discover how this process might be working we commissioned a study of settlement patterns within the various ethnic groups in different parts of the country.

The primary source for statistical evidence on the immigrant communities are the censuses taken in 1961 and 1966. Special tabulations from the 1966 Census were commissioned for the Greater London and West Midlands Conurbations, which contain over 60% of all coloured immigrants in England and Wales. In order to assess the changes that have taken place in the five years between 1961 and 1966 further tabulations were commissioned for inner areas within these conurbations which had been the subject of special analysis by Dr. R. B. Davison and Valerie Jackson following the 1961 Census. From this material Valerie Jackson prepared the demographic analysis and the studies of numbers, distribution, and housing conditions, and Brian Cohen the employment study of the immigrant population which form the basis of Part III of the Report.

At a late stage in the life of the Survey, when the number of wives and children entering the country was outnumbering voucher holders by nearly ten to one, the Social Research Unit of Sussex University made a study for us of the probable number of dependants of Commonwealth immigrants who were likely to join their husbands or parents present in Britain at the end of 1967. This was published in 1969 as *The Dependants of the Coloured Commonwealth Population of England and Wales.*

The use to which earnings are put, whether by saving, house purchase, or in remittances to the home country, is an indicator of a changing response to the new environment. A study of the earnings and family budgets of 1,000 Indians, Pakistanis, and West Indian families in Birmingham was carried out as part of a planned inquiry into the economic costs and benefits of the immigration. The results of this inquiry have been drawn on by Alfred Vanags and Professor Maurice Peston for the chapters (14 and 31) which they have contributed to the Report.

One of the most successful operations in the employment of Commonwealth immigrants appeared to be conducted by London Transport. We therefore gave a grant, jointly with the Department of Scientific and Industrial Research, to the Acton Society Trust to study this experiment, starting with the recruitment and training in Barbados and following through their employment both on the buses and the underground system.

As immigrants settle initially in areas of cities with the highest crime rates, it was to be presumed that the Commonwealth immigrants might well be affected by these conditions, and by the strain which these conditions impose on the police. John Lambert, a Cambridge criminologist, was commissioned to study the extent and pattern of immigrant crime and the relations of police and immigrants in the F Division of Birmingham which includes Sparkbrook and Balsall Heath and has the highest crime rate in the city. Lambert soon established that the rate of immigrant crime was low and shifted the main emphasis of his research to the problems facing the policeman on the beat in an area under social stress, the training needed for this work, and the relationships of police and immigrants in such an area.

In our original plan we assumed that we must concentrate research on the first generation of immigrants rather than on their children, who were still in our schools when they were not, as often, left behind. The young people seeking employment were themselves first-generation immigrants and none had passed right through our educational system before entering the labour market. However, we were fully aware that this country would fairly soon reach the stage where the main questions would not be about the reception of immigrants and their adjustment but about attitudes to coloured Englishmen and the future of a second generation. We therefore accepted a proposal from a social psychologist, Leonard Bloom, for research in Bute Town, Cardiff, where there has been a coloured settlement for the last fifty years. He was to observe how far the children and grandchildren of coloured and European immigrants perceived themselves to be Welsh and how far they felt themselves accepted or alienated from the rest of Cardiff. We also commissioned from Peter Figueroa a study of West Indian school leavers who were interviewed in their last term at their North London schools and then followed up six months later once they had entered the market. Assistance was given for another but less extended research among school leavers, in Birmingham, which the Institute published in March 1968 under the title *Immigrant School Leavers and the Youth Employment Service in Birmingham*, by David Beetham.

In any research programme of this scope some of the projects do not come to fruition; but the failure rate has been remarkably low and where a research has had to be abandoned the reason has in every case been a change in the personal circumstances of the research worker whether through marriage or, in some cases, ironically, due to emigration. The chief casualties have been among the anthropological studies but most of the commissioned work survives and is listed below.

Research Completed

Nicholas Deakin (ed.), *Colour and the British Electorate 1964* (London, Pall Mall Press, 1965).

John Rex and Robert Moore, *Race, Community and Conflict* (London, Oxford University Press, 1966).

Elizabeth Burney, *Housing on Trial* (London, Oxford University Press, 1967).

David Beetham, *Immigrant School Leavers and the Youth Employment Service in Birmingham* (London, Institute of Race Relations Special Series, 1968).

David Eversley and Fred Sukdeo, *The Dependants of the Coloured Commonwealth Population of England and Wales* (London, Institute of Race Relations Special Series, 1969).

De Witt John, *Indian Workers' Associations in Britain* (London, Oxford University Press, 1969).

Anna Craven, *West Africans in London* (London, Institute of Race Relations Special Series, 1969).

Klim McPherson and Julia Gaitskell, *Immigrants and Employment in East London and Croydon: two case studies* (London, Institute of Race Relations Special Series, 1969).

Main journal articles:

Narindar Uberoi, 'Sikh Women in Southall', *Race* (VI, 1, 1964).

Nicholas Deakin, 'Residential Segregation in Britain: a comparative note', *Race* (VI, 1, 1964).

Nicholas Deakin, Daniel Lawrence, Jonathan Silvey and M. J. LeLohe, 'Colour and the 1966 General Election', *Race* (VIII, 1, 1966).

Beryl Radin, 'Coloured Workers and British Trade Unions', *Race* (VIII, 2, 1966).

Vic George and Geoffrey Millerson, 'The Cypriot Community in London', *Race* (VIII, 3, 1967).

Graham Thomas, 'The Integration of Immigrants: a note on the views of some local government officials', *Race* (IX, 2, 1967).

Betty Davison, 'No Place Back Home: a study of Jamaicans returning to Kingston, Jamaica', *Race* (IX, 4, 1968).

K. Hylson-Smith, 'A Study of Immigrant Group Relations in North London', *Race* (IX, 4, 1968).

Nicholas Deakin, 'The Background to the Commonwealth Immigrants Bill (1962)', *The Political Quarterly* (XXXIX, 1, 1968).

Nicholas Deakin, 'Racial Integration and Whitehall', *The Political Quarterly* (XXXIX, 4, 1968).

Brian Cohen and Peter Jenner, 'The Employment of Immigrants: a case study within the wool industry', *Race* (X, 1, 1968).

B2

H. O. Patterson, 'West Indian Migrants Returning Home: Some Observations', *Race* (X, 1, 1968).

Research in Progress, or Completed and Awaiting Publication

Wholly assisted:

Study of the St. Paul's area and of three housing estates in Bristol (Professor Anthony Richmond and Michael Lyon).
Policies for Integration: a study of Bradford (Eric Butterworth).
Study of Pakistanis in Bradford (B. Dahya).
Study of Yemenis in Birmingham (B. Dahya).
Study of Bute Town, Cardiff (Leonard Bloom).
West Indian School leavers in North London (Peter Figueroa).
Survey of attitudes (Research Services Ltd.)
Study of the 1966 Census (Valerie Jackson).
Study of immigrant crime and the relations of the police and immigrants in a division of Birmingham (John Lambert).
Investigation of household budgets among a sample of Indians, Pakistanis, and West Indians in the Midlands (Robert Radburn).
Study of settlement patterns (Michael Lyon).
Study of Sikhs in Southall (Anjali Patnaik).
Social History of Immigration to Britain, 1840–1965 (Sheila Patterson).
Race Relations and the Police (Derrick Sington).

Partially assisted:

Study of Immigrant Workers in London Transport (Acton Society).
Study of Pakistanis in Employment, Bradford (Sheila Allen).
Study of Moss Side (Clive Kinder).
Study of prejudice and discrimination (Ben-Hur Yemeni).
Study of Cypriots (Robin Oakley).
Socio-medical study, Bristol (Dr. J. F. Skone and Dr. R. E. Simpson).

THE FINANCES OF THE SURVEY

The Survey was financed by an initial grant of £70,000 from the Nuffield Foundation which was made to the Institute in 1962 and which was later increased in 1965 by a further grant of £23,500. At the end of 1965, the Home Office made a grant to the Institute of £10,000 for research and this was allocated to the completion of the Survey. The Survey was also allocated £790 from the Joseph Rowntree Memorial Trust, being the unexpended balance of a grant already received by the Institute.

The Survey has thus received grants totalling £104,290 and has spent £103,930 over the five years, as follows:

Headquarters	£	Research	£
Salaries	26,750	41 research projects	61,861
Superannuation, etc.	5,110	Consultants' fees	779
Premises	4,554	Research reports	756
Running costs	4,140		
	£40,554		£63,396

The gearing between the amount spent on running the Survey and the amount spent on research would not have been possible without the services that were provided by the Institute of Race Relations, including the Library, the editorial and publishing department, and accountancy, for which no fee had to be paid.

Appendix I.2. Acknowledgements

Our first debt is to those who agreed to participate in the research programme. Not merely because of the intrinsic value of their work—and we are convinced that the results of the programme, taken as a whole, constitute an important contribution to the body of knowledge on race relations. Nor is our obligation confined to the help and guidance that those who undertook research were able to give us, although in many cases this help far transcended the obligations accepted by the contractual arrangements between us. More than this, nearly all those involved were unstinting in their assistance to us during the course of the drafting of the present Report. Those whose research had already been published were able to provide us with further material and the benefit of their advice; those whose findings are still awaiting publication, willingly consented to their material being employed in the body of this Report. In this connexion, we would particularly like to mention Eric Butterworth, Badr Dahya, John Lambert, Michael Lyon, and Anthony Richmond.

We are also greatly indebted to those who have at various times acted as advisers to the Survey. In the spring of 1964, we invited a small group consisting of Michael Banton, Peter Calvocoressi, Maurice Freedman, Marie Jahoda, Sheila Patterson, and the Director of the Institute to review the research proposals which had been submitted from a number of sources. The discussion with this advisory group proved of great value in clearing our minds about the task in hand. In the following year, the group was reconstituted as an advisory panel by the addition of Michael Caine, Roland Oliver, and Margaret Read from the Institute's Research and Finance Committees (Michael Banton and Maurice Freedman were no longer able to serve). It was with this Panel that we periodically reviewed the Survey's progress and all proposals for additional research projects. Towards the end of 1967, when the outline of the Survey's final volume was being considered, the advisory panel was joined by Mark Abrams, Henri Tajfel, and Richard Rose. We also record our gratitude to Mark Abrams, Julius Gould, Marie Jahoda, and Henri Tajfel for serving on the advisory panel for the survey of attitudes. Michael Banton also served on this advisory panel, thereby putting us further in his debt. Indeed, he was always ready, from the inception of the Survey, to give us the benefit of his unrivalled knowledge and experience in this field. We are most grateful to him.

Our next debt is to our colleagues in the Institute of Race Relations. We were much sustained by the support and encouragement of the Associate Director, Sir Herbert Marchant. A. Sivanandan's help—as Librarian of the Institute—was indispensable, as it is to all those who undertake work in this field. Simon Abbott, as Assistant Director, provided willing support and assistance for an operation that added considerably to his already substantial burdens. Hilary Arnott cheerfully bore the heat of a seemingly endless day as Editorial Assistant responsible for production. For the task of drafting the Report the original central team of two were joined by two additional members of the Institute's staff, Julia Gaitskell and Brian Cohen. Their contribution was crucial to the carrying through of the enterprise. The present Report is therefore the work of several hands; and also contains additional material provided by outside contributors.

The overall responsibility for the Report and its contents rests with the Editor, but individual chapters are in most cases the work of different members of the team. Apart from his editorial responsibilities, E. J. B. Rose is responsible for Chapters 1, 5, 8, 23, and 24. Nicholas Deakin is responsible for Chapters 2, 3, 6, 15, 16, 17, 25, 26, 27, the latter section of 28, 29, and 32. He and Julia Gaitskell drafted Chapters 20, 21, and 22 jointly, except for the sections on the police and the Churches. These were contributed by Paul Ward, who joined the team for three months in the summer of 1968 and also contributed material for Chapter 24. Julia Gaitskell is also responsible for Chapter 18, and Brian Cohen for Chapters 7, 13, and 19. Other Chapters were contributed by Valerie Jackson (9, 10, 11, 12, and 30), Mark Abrams (the first half of Chapter 28), Maurice Peston (Chapter 31), and A. H. Vanags (Chapter 14). Chapter 4 is adapted from the writings of Philip Mason.

The recommendations in Chapter 33 are the responsibility of E. J. B. Rose and Nicholas Deakin, but they owe much to the ideas contributed by all parties to the drafting.

The following specialists in various aspects of race relations or other relevant topics were good enough to help with advice and additional material. However, they have no responsibility for the contents of this Report: Christopher Bagley, Geoffrey Bindman, Trevor Burgin, Elizabeth Burney, Eric Butterworth, June Derrick, John Downing, Paul Foot, Eric Hawkins, Judith Haynes, Bob Hepple, Ronald Goldman, Louis Kushnick, John Lambert, Anthony Lester, John Lyttle, Mavis Maclean, Robert Moore, Dipak Nandy, Sheila Patterson, Nadine Peppard, William Plowden, John Power, John Rex, Richard Rose, Sir Lionel Russell, Andrew Shonfield, Lucy Syson, Donald Tyerman, Roger Warren-Evans, and Priscilla Young.

The graphics which adorn Parts II, III, and VII are the work of Richard Natkiel, of *The Economist*. We are grateful to him and his colleague, Peter Dunbar, for their advice and help in illustrating some of the statistical evidence in the Report.

We should also like to record our thanks to Oxford University Press and particularly to Richard Brain for their willingness to produce this Report in such a short period of time and for their patience in supporting delays which seem to be the inevitable accompaniment of authorship.

Finally, but from the present writers' point of view most important of all, there is the staff of the Survey of Race Relations. Without Lois Anthony the Survey could not have been conducted. Her good-humoured but never-failing reliability have been the cornerstone of the whole enterprise throughout the five years of its existence. For the second half of the study she was joined by Anita Marks who carried responsibilities far beyond those usually allotted to secretaries and discharged them faultlessly.

Appendix III.1.   The Seven Inner London Boroughs

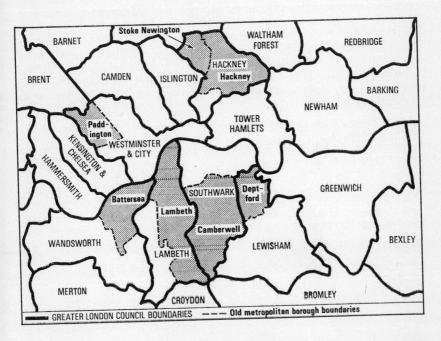

This map shows the seven selected London boroughs at 1961 which were selected for study by R. B. Davison, *Black British* (London, Oxford University Press, for the Institute of Race Relations, 1966). The 1966 Census data was tabulated for the Survey of Race Relations in Britain to be exactly comparable, i.e. observing the same boundaries.

Appendix III.2. Selected Midlands Wards

The wards included in the inner study zone of the West Midlands conurbation are defined in terms of 1961 administrative boundaries. They are as follows:

Birmingham County Borough
All Saints, Aston, Balsall Heath, Deritend, Duddeston, Edgbaston, Gravelly Hill, Handsworth, Ladywood, Lozells, Market Hall, Rotten Park, Saltley, St. Paul's, Sandwell, Small Heath, Soho, and Sparkbrook.

Walsall County Borough
Birchills, Bridge, Caldmore, and Pleck.

West Bromwich County Borough
Sandwell, Spon Lane, Lyng, Tantany, and Town Hall.

Wolverhampton County Borough
Blakemore, Dunstall, Eastfield, East Park, Graisley, Merridale, Parkfield, St. Peter's, and West Park.

Smethwick County Borough
Cape, Sandwell, Soho, Spon Lane, Victoria, and Uplands.

Appendix III.3. Adjustments to Census Estimates

(a) THE WHITE INDIANS AND WHITE PAKISTANIS

The 1961 Census estimated that 75,911 persons born in India but resident in England and Wales were British by birth or descent; the figure for Pakistanis was 5,837 persons; 40,044 of the Indians were women and 2,295 of the Pakistanis. Our problem is to remove the effect of these groups from the national count of Indians and Pakistanis in 1951, in 1961, and in 1966. In particular we need to make some specific estimates about age structure and housing conditions in the London and West Midlands conurbations at this latter date. This note sets out in some detail the procedures adopted to amend information relating to the Indian population; precisely similar techniques were adopted for the Pakistani population. Here we shall only reproduce significant sets of figures in the Pakistani analysis, devoting fuller attention to the more significant Indian minority.

We must first describe our assumptions about the nature and composition of this population. We are not concerned primarily with the Indian Civil Servants who were repatriated following Independence in 1947. It is only children born in India to white parents which concern us. Some of the white Indians and Pakistanis enumerated in 1961 will be children who returned with their parents following Independence, but many others will have migrated between India and the United Kingdom at various stages over a lifetime. In 1961, the 82,000 white Indians and white Pakistanis represent the remnants of a series of migrant streams. Three major sources may be distinguished. There has always been a substantial number of British residents in these countries who chose to send their children back to Britain for their education. After university, some of them would filter into employment in Britain, though before 1947 it was the practice for the colonial elite to replace itself with its own natural increase. Prior to the early 1950s, much of the flow into education establishments was probably of a temporary nature, providing a constant stock of children who would eventually return to their parents.

But there is a second source which would provide a small inwards flow. It has of course been customary for white executive and administrative officers to return to the United Kingdom on retirement. Here again we are concerned not with the total retirement flow, but only with the flow of persons who were initially born abroad. By 1961, the slow progression of years will have provided a significant sector of men and women in their middle 50s and older. Since these were predominantly middle-class people, we would expect them to have favourable mortality rates and quite a lot of them would live into their late 70s.

The repatriation following Indian Independence forms our third major population source. This would be composed of two sectors. In 1947, India contained an estimated 100,000 white persons and almost 50% of these were personnel of the Armed Forces. Clearly there would be a considerable number of children returning with the garrisons. Again, the returning adults interest us only in so far as they were originally recruited from within the white population born in India. We think this is more likely to have applied to professional and business people than to the lower ranks of the serving forces. Our conclusion is that in 1947 the returning white Indian population comprised a considerable proportion of children but also a sizeable number of young and middle-aged adults.

Thus we assume that the white Indian population was composed of three major sections:

(i) school children,
(ii) a retirement population generated over a long period, and
(iii) repatriates from 1947.

On the basis of these hypotheses we have estimated the age structure of the white Indian and Pakistani population in 1961. But our chief aim was to make similar estimates relating in particular to the London and West Midlands conurbations in 1966. On the basis of an estimated age structure and fairly precise information on their regional distribution, it has not been difficult to estimate how many of these people would be alive in 1966 and to allow for further arrivals between these two dates. We have assumed no net distributional changes between the regions during this period. We have further assumed that these people would be predominantly middle class and have estimated their demographic and housing characteristics accordingly.

We estimate that the 1961 age structure would have been roughly as shown in Table III.i.

Appendix Table III.i. Estimated age structure of white Indian and Pakistani populations, 1961

Age	School	Retired	Repatriated	Total
Under 5	—	—	—	—
5-9	3,000	—	—	3,000
10-14	6,000	—	—	6,000
15-19	7,500	—	1,500	9,000
20-24	3,000	—	5,000	8,000
25-44	—	—	18,000	18,000
45-64	—	10,000	15,000	25,000
65+	—	10,000	3,000	13,000
Total	19,500	20,000	42,500	82,000*

* Estimates include white Indians and white Pakistanis.

Source:
Estimated, with reference to Census of Population 1961, Birthplace and Nationality Tables.

Such an age structure would generate a high crude death-rate since quite a high proportion of those in the 65+ age group would be advanced in age. We have thus estimated that the 82,000 persons in 1961 would have been reduced to 74,000 in 1966. On a similar argument, it is assumed that the white Indian population was larger at 86,000 in 1951. Estimates are as shown in Table III.ii.

Appendix Table III.ii. Estimated numbers of white Indians and Pakistanis 1951, 1961, and 1966

	Census 1961	Estimated 1951	Estimated 1966
Indians	76,000 m = 35,900 f = 40,100	80,000 m = 39,200 f = 40,800	68,600 m = 32,400 f = 36,200
Pakistanis	5,840 m = 3,540 f = 2,300	6,130 m = 3,600 f = 2,530	5,400 m = 3,000 f = 2,400

Source:
Estimated, with reference to Census of Population 1961, Birthplace and Nationality Tables.

The regional distribution of white Indians and Pakistanis may be estimated from 1961 Census material. Regional totals are available for the total number of persons born in India but with United Kingdom citizenship; on average 75% of these have this citizenship by virtue of their parents' nationality and we have assumed that this percentage may be applied from region to region. For our purposes the figures in Table III.iii are important.

Appendix Table III.iii. Regional distribution of white Indians and Pakistanis, 1961 and 1966

1961

| Area | Indians | | | Pakistanis | | |
	Males	Females	Total	Males	Females	Total
England and Wales	35,867	40,044	75,911	3,542	2,295	5,837
London conurbation	14,955	16,334	31,289	1,100	850	1,950
Selected London boroughs	1,590	1,630	3,220	130	100	230
West Midlands conurbation	1,722	1,038	2,760	565	72	637
Selected Midlands wards	450	550	1,000	80	60	140

1966

Area	Males	Indians Females	Total	Males	Pakistanis Females	Total
London conurbation	13,000	15,200	28,200	1,000	800	1,800
Selected London boroughs	1,480	1,510	2,990	120	90	210
West Midlands conurbation	1,140	1,370	2,510	340	270	610
Selected Midlands wards	400	510	910	80	60	140

Source:
Estimated, with reference to Census of Population 1961, Birthplace and Nationality Tables.

Demographic characteristics in 1966 have been estimated on the following assumptions:

(i) the age structure at 1961 has been changed marginally by deaths among the elderly and the arrival of a small contingent of new school residents;

(ii) males would have the same propensity to marry as the English population in general;

(iii) females would have a slightly lower propensity to marry than the average English woman, a feature which until the last twenty years has been evident in the higher class even in the United Kingdom.

In Chapter 12 we have assumed that housing conditions among white Indians would be best approximated by a relatively high-class residential area, for example Cheltenham or Reading. In household configuration we have also considered the importance of the fact that white Indian children would have been predominantly in boarding school and average household size among the remainder would be low because of a high proportion of elderly people.

(b) COLOURED CHILDREN BORN IN THE HOST COMMUNITY

The shortfall on the total count of coloured persons derived solely from birthplace tabulations may to some extent be remedied by considering the total number of persons resident in households where the head belongs to a particular ethnic group.

Again we have to ask if this is a valid method likely to give an accurate count of all coloured persons. The answer to this depends on the degree of racial mixture among households. In 1961, we have published information which indicates that over 80% of all West Indian heads of households were married to a spouse of the same or another West Indian group; the Indian and Pakistani groups were more mixed but a large part of this apparent mixture is probably due to marriages where one of the partners was a white Indian.

For our purposes we may assume that all West Indian, Indian, and Pakistani fathers have coloured children. We think that by and large the advantages of getting some form of count of coloured children by far outweighs the disadvantages arising from this system. Recent house-to-house studies have revealed a remarkable amount of racial homogeneity within households and it is likely that relatively few children are wrongly attributed.

Among adults there is, of course, more overlap of various ethnic groups within separate households, particularly where immigrants may be forced to share housing accommodation. We have, therefore, used special census tabulations to arrive at a composite population. Persons under 15 years of age are allocated to a nationality group on the basis of the birthplace of the household head; all other persons were allocated on the basis of their own birthplace. This system more or less accurately upgrades our estimates of the total coloured population so that children born in this country are included.

(c) CENSUS UNDER-ENUMERATION

In 1961, part of the Census was collected from all households, and some only on the basis of a selected 10% of households. It is now common knowledge that the 10% coverage was not entirely random, although this had been intended. An important study (unpublished) for the Survey by Brian Cohen has shown that in the 10% sample, several immigrant groups were severely under-enumerated. But these calculations were based on the full census count and it is highly likely that this itself was deficient. In 1966, we have only the 10% sample for evidence and although the sampling procedure was strengthened by the census office, clearly some immigrants escaped the attention of the enumeration officer. We have shown in Chapter 10 that at least 35% of all Pakistanis resident in England and Wales in 1966 were not enumerated.

We can use supplementary records to amend our estimates of the total coloured population. The central problem with partial enumeration relates to selectivity. How accurately can we describe coloured immigrants from a sample where some sectors of the population are more heavily represented than others? It is necessary to locate the source of bias, estimate its effect in the tabulated results, and make amendments if possible. On the basis of what firm evidence there is, it is likely that enumeration is particularly bad among those whose housing conditions and working hours are unorthodox, and those living in small households. Merely at the probability level there is a greater likelihood that small households are missed by the census enumerator, so it seems likely that single persons and those living alone are under-enumerated. The most expensive census ever launched, that of 1960 in the United States, was under-enumerated by 3%; a careful post-enumeration survey indicated under-enumeration of almost 10% in several minority groups; in particular 17% of non-white males aged 20 to 39 were not enumerated.

It seems inevitable that a similar form of selectivity is present in our own special tabulations. It is clear that the census loses by being selective, but it can be argued that the enumerated group may be regarded as a group worthy of special attention. In terms of some general concept of social integration, one may argue that those who were missed are at the bottom end of the scale. From this it follows that the total picture of housing conditions, a significant indicator of social integration, is almost certainly less favourable than that presented by our special tabulations. Nevertheless, our analysis forms a useful starting point, representing as it does the most detailed body of knowledge currently available.

Appendix III.4. Details of Aspects of the Procedure to Estimate the Total Coloured Population of England and Wales

We have indicated that the Census failed to enumerate 116,000 coloured persons who were resident in England and Wales in 1966. The composition of this estimate by national groups is revealed in Table III.iv below, in which estimates for India and Pakistan have been amended to exclude white Asians.

As explained in the text, we have no record of net arrivals from Census 1951 to January 1955. Thus it is possible for a census estimate in 1961 to exceed one based on a joint estimate of Census 1951 and net arrivals until 1961. Where this is the case, we have rejected the possibility that the census count at 1961 is an over-estimate, preferring to believe that the difference arises from unrecorded net arrivals from 1951 to 1955. On the other hand, where the census estimate at 1961 is less than what would have been derived from the 1951 estimate and arrivals during that period we are assuming that the later census count was under-estimated. Hence, at 1961, the chosen best estimates are those which provide the larger estimates of the immigrant population, either by Census 1961 alone, or from the earlier Census and net arrivals since then. By 1961, we have only clear evidence of under-enumeration of West Indians and Pakistanis. By 1966 there is also some evidence of under-enumeration of Indians and West Africans.

Our total estimate of 924,200 coloured persons resident in England and Wales at census date 1966 is composed of four component parts. In order that the reader may be more able to assess the importance of various assumptions in this total estimate, these component parts are listed below.

The final estimate quoted in the text assumes that children in households which the census failed to enumerate were only 75% as numerous as those in enumerated households; this estimate is reached by taking an average of results from two models set out in Table III.v. At a probability level, there is more likelihood that smaller families are missed by the census enumerator. It seems likely therefore that the number of children in the non-enumerated population will be smaller. Model I assumes that children are just as numerous in unenumerated households as elsewhere; Model II assumes that they are only half as numerous. Our data on children in households referred only to those groups to which we have devoted special attention in this study, Indians and Pakistanis, West Indians and West Africans, and all the estimates in the table below relating to children were derived from these. We realize that these may not be very accurate assumptions. Setting the table out in this way enables the reader to assess the importance of errors. The total number of children added to our population estimate for these poorly documented countries amounts to only about 8% of all children and less than 2% of the total population estimate for 1966.

Appendix Table III.iv. Adjustment of census estimates by reference to net arrivals

	India*	Pakistan†	Ceylon	Jamaica	Rest of Caribbean	British West Africa	Far East	Total
(a) Census 1951	30,800	5,000	5,800	6,400	8,900	5,000	12,000	74,500
(b) Net arrivals, January 1955 to Census 1961	37,900	22,100	n.a.	106,200	71,300	7,900	n.a.	25,400
(c) Joint estimate (a) + (b)	68,700	27,100	n.a.	112,600	80,200	13,500	n.a.	302,100
(d) Census 1961	81,400	24,900	9,000	100,100	71,700	19,800	29,600	336,500
(e) Best estimates, 1961	81,400	27,100	9,000	112,600	80,200	19,800	29,600	359,700
(f) Net arrivals, Census 1961 to Census 1966	99,000	82,500	3,400	75,500	49,600	23,300	6,500	339,800
(g) Joint estimate (e) + (f)	180,400	109,600	12,400	188,100	129,800	43,100	36,400	699,800
(h) Census 1966	163,600	67,700	12,900	151,900	116,000	36,000	47,000	595,100
(i) Best estimates, 1966	180,400	109,600	12,900	188,100	129,800	43,100	47,000	710,900
(j) Estimated census under-enumeration in 1966 (minimum)	16,800	41,900	—	36,200	13,800	7,100	—	115,800

Note. Best estimates (e and i) are arrived at by taking the larger of the two alternatives immediately above.

* Excluding white Indians.
† Excluding white Pakistanis.

Source:
Censuses of Population and Home Office Returns.

Appendix Table III.v. Total estimated coloured population resident in England and Wales,
Census 1966, component parts

Area of origin	Census enumerated		Not enumerated			Totals	
	Born overseas	Children born here	Natives	Children Model I	Children Model II	Model I	Model II
India*	163,600	40,100	16,800	4,100	2,100	224,600	222,600
Pakistan†	67,700	6,900	41,900	4,300	2,100	120,800	118,600
Ceylon	12,900	3,200	—	—	—	16,100	16,100
Jamaica	151,900	72,700	36,200	17,400	8,700	278,200	269,500
Other Caribbean	116,000	46,400	13,800	5,500	2,800	181,700	179,000
British West Africa	36,000	6,600	7,100	1,300	700	51,000	50,400
Far East	47,000	13,000	—	—	—	60,000	60,000
Totals	595,100	188,900	115,800	32,600	16,400	932,400	916,200

Source: Census Population and our own calculations.

* Excluding white Indians.
† Excluding white Pakistanis

Appendix III.5. The percentage of the Population (15 and over) Retired and Students from Selected Birthplace Groups and Total Population, 1966

(a) Males—Greater London conurbation

	India	Pakistan	Jamaica	Rest of Caribbean	All Caribbean	British West Africa	Cyprus	Total population
Total population 15 and over*	41,290	10,500	35,680	32,720	68,400	13,070	20,910	2,875,530
Of whom retired	3·1	0·6	0·4	0·4	0·4	0·6	1·6	8·1
Of whom students	6·4	6·9	2·2	5·2	3·6	32·3	7·0	4·1

(b) Males—West Midlands conurbation

	India	Pakistan	Jamaica	All Caribbean	Total population
Total population 15 and over*	13,590	11,750	13,940	17,400	888,270
Of whom retired	0·8	—	0·1	0·1	7·5
Of whom students	4·0	1·4	1·1	1·1	3·0

* Figures for the total population of 15 and over are multiplied by ten as the size of the sample was 10% of the total population.

Sources:
1966 10% Sample Census, Special Tabulations;
Table 13, Economic Activity Tables, Part I,
H.M.S.O.

Appendix III.6. The Distribution in Major Industries for Selected Birthplace Groups by Percentage,* by Sex, 1966

(a) Males—Greater London conurbation

	India	Pakistan	Jamaica	Rest of Caribbean	All Caribbean	British West Africa	Cyprus	Total Population
Number in employment†	35,470	9,140	32,400	29,340	61,740	7,940	17,940	2,684,980
Selected industries								
VI Engineering and electrical goods	16·1	12·1	11·6	9·3	10·5	9·2	—	10·4
XII Clothing and footwear	—	10·6	—	—	—	—	12·7	1·3
XVII Construction	—	—	17·9	10·8	14·5	—	—	10·3
XIX Transport and communications	14·9	9·0	18·2	26·2	22·0	22·0	—	12·9
701 Railways‡	—	—	8·5	11·6	10·0	—	—	2·6
707 Postal services and tele-communication	—	—	—	—	—	14·2	—	3·5
XX Distributive trades	8·5	7·8	—	—	—	—	11·5	12·4
XXII Professional and scientific services	11·2	9·1	—	—	—	14·6	—	7·1
XXIII Miscellaneous services	9·5	16·0	—	8·9	—	12·0	33·9	10·3
884 Catering, hotels, etc.	—	10·8	—	—	—	—	20·2	2·3
XXIV Public administration and defence	—	—	—	—	—	11·8	—	7·1

Appendix III.6.—cont.

(b) Males—West Midlands conurbation

	India	Pakistan	Jamaica	All Caribbean	Total population
Number in employment	12,450	11,170	13,050	16,340	807,753
Selected industries					
V Metal manufacture	39·9	30·0	24·7	22·2	11·0
VI Engineering and electrical goods	13·2	9·1	9·3	9·9	15·0
VIII Vehicles	—	14·4	9·8	10·6	11·1
IX Metal goods not elsewhere specified	12·0	28·0	14·3	14·3	12·3
XVI Other manufacturing industries	—	—	7·8	—	2·5
XVII Construction	—	—	7·7	7·7	9·3
XIX Transport and communications	—	—	10·3	11·8	5·6

Appendix III.6.—cont.

(c) Females—Greater London conurbation

	India	Jamaica	Rest of Caribbean	All Caribbean	British West Africa	Cyprus	Total population
Number in employment†	15,520	21,940	19,180	41,120	4,760	7,900	1,641,440
Selected industries							
VI Engineering and electrical goods	11·0	9·8	7·6	8·8	8·0	—	7·8
XII Clothing and footwear	—	17·2	11·3	14·3	9·2	60·6	4·5
XX Distributive trades	12·3	—	—	—	8·2	10·6	17·9
XXII Professional and scientific services	22·6	26·0	30·8	28·3	22·9	—	16·6
874 *Medical and Dental Services*	9·3	24·8	27·9	26·3	20·0	—	7·0
XXIII Miscellaneous services	17·3	12·4	12·6	12·5	16·6	12·8	19·0

Appendix III.6.—*cont.*

(d) *Females—West Midlands conurbation*

	Jamaica	All Caribbean	Total population
Number in employment†	7,150	8,930	453,480
Selected industries			
V Metal manufacture	10·1	8·8	4·6
VI Engineering and electrical goods	11·3	11·3	10·8
IX Metal goods not elsewhere specified	23·9	24·1	14·0
XXII Professional and scientific services	24·9	25·1	14·2
874 Medical and dental services	23·8	23·9	5·3

* Percentages have been shown for immigrant groups only in those industries where 7·5% or more of the economically active were enumerated. A dash (—) does not mean no members of that group were in that particular industry but only that less than 7·5% were enumerated.
† Figures for number in employment are multiplied by ten as the size of the sample was 10% of the total population.
‡ Unit groups (identified by three-digit code numbers) are sub-divisions of the industry orders (identified by Roman numerals) directly above them.

Sources:
1966 10% Sample Census, Special Tabulations; figures for total population from Table 16, *Economic Activity Tables*, Part I, H.M.S.O.

APPENDIXES TO PART VII

Appendix VII.1. Method of Sampling

The names and addresses of the people to be interviewed were selected by drawing every *n*th name from the total electoral registers for the five boroughs. The interval between the names was determined by the aim of finishing up with 500 interviews in each borough. To ensure this we started by drawing a little over 4,500 names and addresses. Slightly over 7% of these were discarded when the interviewer found that they belonged to a coloured person, and another 11% of names and addresses were unusable, either because the premises were standing empty or had been demolished, or because the named person had moved or died. For reasons such as these we found ourselves left with only 3,600 eligible respondents; of these, 14% refused to be interviewed and it proved impossible to make contact with another 11% even after four calls. Some inadequately completed forms were rejected at the editing stage, and the analysis finally was based on 2,500 completed interviews spread over the five boroughs.

The age, sex, and social class details of this sample are shown in Appendix VII.3; it slightly over-represents adult women (55% in the sample as against 53% shown in the census) and those aged 65 and over (19% as against 17%); the socio-economic status of the heads of households in the sample would seem to be in line with the findings of other random samples taken in the five boroughs, i.e. one-third white-collar workers, one-third skilled manual workers, and one-third un-skilled and semi-skilled workers.

Appendix VII.2   The Five-Borough Survey

The census contains no enumeration of people by the colour of their skin; it does, however, record place of birth. If we take the numbers born in Commonwealth countries as a crude measure of coloured immigrants, then on the night of the census these Commonwealth-born residents amounted to 1·9% of the total British population. The corresponding ratios were very much higher in Lambeth and Ealing (8·9% and 6·2%, respectively), much higher in Wolverhampton and Bradford (5·2% and 4·6%), and significantly higher in Nottingham (3%). Both the London boroughs also had comparatively high proportions of residents who had been born in Ireland and in foreign countries.

The published census reports do not give any figures of the age composition of immigrants, but the Department of Education and Science's Statistics of Education for 1966 does list those large boroughs in England and Wales where immigrant children exceed 2% of all pupils in maintained primary and secondary schools. All five surveys towns appear in this list, and the proportion of immigrant children ranges from 18% in Lambeth and 14% in Ealing to 7% in Bradford and Nottingham; the Wolverhampton ratio of 10% comes roughly half way between these levels.

There is available one other piece of non-census information about the five towns in 1966. At the general election in March of that year, they contained fifteen Parliamentary constituencies; Labour candidates were successful in thirteen of them; the exceptions were S.W. Wolverhampton and South Ealing, where Conservatives were returned. Even at the 1964 general election, when in the country as a whole Labour M.P.s constituted a bare majority in the House of Commons, the five survey boroughs together were solidly Labour and their fifteen constituencies returned ten Labour M.P.s.

Appendix Table VII.i. Total population, 1966 Census

		Females as % of total
Bradford	290,310	51·5
Ealing	292,750	51·5
Lambeth	320,780	52·3
Nottingham	305,050	51·3
Wolverhampton	262,170	50·1
		(Great Britain 51·6)

Appendix Table VII.ii. Sex and age composition, 1966 Census

	Bradford	Ealing	Lambeth	Notting-ham	Wolver-hampton	Great Britain
Males	%	%	%	%	%	%
0–14	25	20	23	25	25	25
15–34	28	30	30	27	28	27
35–44	14	13	13	14	14	13
45–64	24	28	25	25	25	25
65 and over	9	9	9	9	8	10
Total	100	100	100	100	100	100
Females						
0–14	23	18	20	22	23	22
15–34	24	25	27	25	26	25
35–44	12	12	13	13	14	13
45–64	25	29	25	25	25	25
65 and over	16	16	15	15	12	15
Total	100	100	100	100	100	100

Appendix Tables VII.iii. Proportion of all residents born outside Great Britain, 1966 Census

	Bradford	Ealing	Lambeth	Notting-ham	Wolver-hampton	Great Britain
	%	%	%	%	%	%
Any part of Ireland	1·5	4·8	4·6	1·6	1·5	1·8
Commonwealth	4·6	6·2	8·9	3·0	5·2	1·9
Foreign countries	2·6	4·3	3·6	2·3	1·4	1·7
Total	8·7	15·3	17·1	6·9	8·1	5·4

Appendix Table VII.iv. Proportion of all persons living at densities of over 1 person per room, 1966 Census

	Bradford	Ealing	Lambeth	Notting-ham	Wolver-hampton	Great Britain
	%	%	%	%	%	%
	15·6	12·4	19·1	12·5	13·6	12·8

Appendix Table VII.v. Proportion of households at various tenures, 1966 Census

	Bradford	Ealing	Lambeth	Notting-ham	Wolver-hampton	Great Britain
	%	%	%	%	%	%
Owner-occupied	57	49	20	26	39	46
Municipal-rented	24	14	28	36	42	28
Rented, private, unfurnished	15	26	37	31	14	19
Rented, private, furnished	2	9	12	5	3	5
Other	2	2	3	2	2	5
Total	100	100	100	100	100	100

Appendix Table VII.vi. Plumbing amenities: proportion of households at 1966 Census

	Bradford	Ealing	Lambeth	Notting-ham	Wolver-hampton	Great Britain
	%	%	%	%	%	%
No hot water tap*	13	9	21	19	10	12
No fixed bath*	20	9	17	28	10	15
No exclusive inside w.c.	31	21	33	41	24	23

* Not even shared use.

Appendix Table VII.vii. Proportion of males in each socio-economic group, 1966 Census

	Bradford	Ealing	Lambeth	Notting-ham	Wolver-hampton
	%	%	%	%	%
Professionals	2	6	3	3	4
Employers, managers	9	11	8	8	8
Foremen, skilled manuals	40	38	34	41	48
Non-manual workers	15	22	24	15	13
Personal service, semi-skilled manuals	24	14	16	22	17
Unskilled manual workers	9	7	11	10	8
Others	1	2	4	1	2
Total	100	100	100	100	100

Appendix Table VII.viii. Average unemployment rates, September–November 1966 (%)

Bradford	1·2
Nottingham	1·8
Wolverhampton	1·5
Greater London	1·0
Great Britain	1·9

Appendix VII.3. The Prejudice-Tolerance Scale

The method of scaling was to select those attitudinal questions which provided the respondents with an opportunity to express unconditional hostility to coloured people. Four questions particularly leant themselves to this. They were:

'If you had any choice would you particularly avoid having neighbours from any of these places—West Indies, India, Pakistan?' Those who said they would were then asked if they would still take this line even if the potential coloured neighbours were professional people working at the hospital or university. Those who still objected were given a prejudice score of fifteen points.

'Do you think the authorities should let or refuse to let a Council house or flat to a family born in the West Indies, India, or Pakistan?' Those who said the Council should refuse to have them as tenants were then asked if they thought the refusal should be maintained even if the coloured family had been on the waiting list for the right length of time. Again, those who persisted in their opposition were given a prejudice score of fifteen points.

'Do you think a private landlord should let or refuse to let accommodation to a family born in the West Indies, India, or Pakistan?' Those who said he should refuse to have them as tenants were then asked if he should still exclude them even if he knew that the coloured family would look after the accommodation properly. If, even after this proviso, the respondent said the landlord should refuse to let, then he was given a prejudice score of fifteen points.

'Do you think the majority of coloured people in Britain are superior, equal, or inferior to you?' Those who said that coloured people are inferior, and added that this was because of their colour, were similarly given a prejudice score of fifteen.

Thus, anyone who answered all four of these questions in a consistently hostile way rated a prejudice score of sixty.

In addition to these four key attitude questions there were ten others (scattered throughout the interview) where an unfavourable attitude to coloured people could be expressed. On each of these when the respondent gave a reply that expressed an unfavourable attitude towards coloured people he received a prejudice score of one. The full text of those ten questions is given in the questionnaire (available in the I.R.R.

Library). Some typical replies of respondents assessed as prejudiced were:

Those who said that the neighbourhood in which they lived was changing for the worse and attributed this deterioration to the presence of coloured people.

Those who said that their own personal experience of coloured people made them feel less favourable towards them.

Those who said that if a choice had to be made between declaring a coloured worker redundant or a white worker redundant then the coloured worker, irrespective of his skill or length of service, should be the one to go.

Those who said that coloured people should not be let into Britain to settle on the same basis as other people from abroad.

Similar indicators were obtained from replies to six other questions.

Appendix VII.4. The Questionnaire

On the structure of the questionnaire, Research Services conducted various pilot inquiries, and from these it was decided that the final questionnaire should seek information from each respondent on three main topics:

(i) The respondent's personal circumstances—age, sex, socio-economic class, occupation, terminal education age, housing, proximity to coloured people in neighbourhood and work, etc.

(ii) The respondent's social circumstances—inter-generational social mobility, party politics, trade union membership, etc.

(iii) The respondent's personality traits—as shown by his scores on various scales such as authoritarianism, sense of social potency, feelings of isolation from the local community, etc. Each of these scores was to be derived from a series of attitude and opinion questions.

The final questionnaire ran to eighteen foolscap pages, contained almost 100 questions and sub-questions, and necessitated an interview of approximately three-quarters of an hour. Essentially, the questionnaire used in the national sample aimed to concentrate on half a dozen questions, taken from the five-borough questionnaire, that seemed likely to differentiate prejudiced from non-prejudiced people, and on a dozen or so personal and social variables that were most likely to be associated with differences in degrees of prejudice.

Appendix VII.5. Composition of Authoritarian and Non-Authoritarian Groups

Appendix Table VII.5. Composition of authoritarian and non-authoritarian groups

	Authoritarian	Non-authoritarian	Rest of sample
	%	%	%
Social class:			
Professional, managerial	13	20	13
Lower middle class	20	23	21
Skilled manual working class	32	26	32
Semi and unskilled manual w/c	35	31	34
Total	100	100	100
Age:			
Under 35	20	28	23
35–44	15	17	18
45–54	19	25	22
55–64	23	21	18
65 and over	23	9	19
Total	100	100	100
Politics:			
Conservative	39	38	35
Labour	39	44	43
Liberal	7	4	6
Other and Don't know	15	14	16
Total	100	100	100

Appendix Table VII.5.—*cont.*

	Authoritarian	Non-authoritarian	Rest of sample
	%	%	%
Borough:			
Ealing	21	26	19
Lambeth	17	21	20
Bradford	21	21	20
Nottingham	22	18	20
Wolverhampton	19	14	21
Total	100	100	100
Mobility:			
Up	34	37	35
Down	25	24	27
Stable	41	39	38
Total	100	100	100

Appendix VIII.1.   The Arrival of Further Dependants to Immigrants already in the U.K. by mid-1968*

The number of dependants eligible to join family members already resident in England and Wales is derived from viewing the 1968 resident population in terms of a series of complete and incomplete families. At Census 1966 it is possible to determine the number of married males without resident wives, and a similar estimation has been made in respect of those persons not enumerated by the census. Further to this there are families which still have some of their children in the home land. The precise calculations are complicated and not essential to the argument here. We have reproduced below the numbers which we have estimated in these major categories and our assumptions about how many of these people are likely to arrive in Great Britain. In fact, there will be a few hundred male dependants arriving, though basically this is a problem relating to women and children. We have confined our attention here merely to these two groups. The table on the following page sets out major items in our calculations for each country concerned.

* This section of the analysis draws heavily upon the work of David Eversley and Frederick Sukdeo, *The Dependants of the Coloured Commonwealth Population of England and Wales* (London, I.R.R. Special Series, 1969), to whom the author acknowledges a considerable debt.

Appendix Table VIII.i.

	India		Pakistan		West Africa		Jamaica		Rest of Caribbean	
	Women	Children	Women	Children	Women	Children	Women	Children	Women	Children
Dependants to married men without a spouse in England at 1966 (a)	17,800	35,600	45,300	90,600	4,900	9,800	3,600	7,200	1,700	3,400
Children of families already resident in 1966 (b)		30,700		30,000		11,100		14,500		16,000
Eligible dependants of voucher holders arriving Census 1966–mid-1968 (c)	3,250	6,900	1,200	2,400	80	160	200	500	350	860
Total eligible at mid-1968 (d) (= (a) + (b) + (c))	21,050	73,200	46,400	123,000	5,000	21,100	3,800	22,200	2,050	20,260
Enumerated arrivals, 1966 Census–mid-1968 (e)	13,050	22,200	7,100	22,600	1,800	−1,700	1,400	13,000	1,500	5,900
Still eligible to come to U.K. ((d)−(e))	8,000	51,000	39,300	100,400	3,200	22,800	2,400	9,200	550	14,360
of which:										
Expected to arrive before 1971 Census	6,000	30,000	7,500	15,000	2,000	−2,000	1,500	8,000	500	6,000
Expected to arrive 1971–6	1,000	10,000	7,500	25,000	—	−3,000	500	1,000	—	5,000
Not expected to arrive	1,000	11,000	24,300	60,400	1,200	not applicable	400	200	—	3,360

BIBLIOGRAPHY

Books and Articles

Alderson, S., *Britain in the Sixties, Housing* (Harmondsworth, Penguin Books, 1962).

Aurora, G. S., *The New Frontiersmen* (Bombay, Popula Prakashan, 1967).

Bagley, C., 'The Educational Performance of Immigrant Children', *Race* (Vol. X, no. 1, July 1968).

— 'Relative Deprivation and the Working-Class Racialist', I.R.R. *Newsletter* (June 1968).

Banton, M., *The Coloured Quarter* (London, Cape, 1955).

— *The Police and the Community* (London, Tavistock, 1964).

— *Race Relations* (London, Tavistock, 1967).

— *White and Coloured* (London, Cape, 1959).

Barker, E., *Commonwealth Immigrants: the Work and Attitude of the Church of England* (London, Board for Social Responsibility, 1963).

Barr, J., 'New Towns as Anti-Ghettoes?', *New Society* (No. 131, 1 April 1965).

Bayliss, F. J. and Coates, J. B., 'West Indians at Work in Nottingham', *Race* (Vol. VII, no. 2, October 1965).

Beetham, D., *Immigrant School Leavers and the Youth Employment Service in Birmingham* (London, I.R.R., Special Series, 1968).

Bennett, A. G., *Because They Know Not* (London, Phoenix Press, n.d.).

Bettelheim, B. and Janowitz, M., *Social Change and Prejudice, including dynamics of prejudice* (1st edn.) (New York, Free Press of Glencoe, 1950).

Blake, Judith, *Family Structure in Jamaica* (New York, Free Press of Glencoe, 1961).

Borrie, W. D. (ed.), *The Cultural Integration of Immigrants* (Paris, U.N.E.S.C.O., 1959).

Bouscaron, A. T., *International Migrations since 1945* (New York, Praeger, 1963).

British Medical Association, *Medical Examination of Immigrants: report of the working party* (London, B.M.A., 1965).

Burgin, T and Edson, P., *Spring Grove: the education of immigrant children* (London, O.U.P., for I.R.R., 1967).

Burney, Elizabeth, *Housing on Trial* (London, O.U.P., for I.R.R., 1967).

Burt, R. A., 'Colour Prejudice in Great Britain' (B.A. Thesis, Princeton, 1960).

Butterworth, E. (ed.), *Immigrants in West Yorkshire* (London, I.R.R., Special Series, 1967).

Callaghan, Rt. Hon. James, M.P., Speech to Institute of Race Relations, 8 February 1968, in I.R.R. *Newsletter* (February 1968).

Calley, M. J. C., *God's People* (London, O.U.P., for I.R.R., 1965).

Campaign Against Racial Discrimination, *The White Paper: A Spur to Racialism* (London, C.A.R.D., 1965).

Ciba Foundation, *Immigration, Medical and Social Aspects*, edited by Wolstenholm, G. E. W., and O'Connor, M. (London, Churchill, 1966).

Clarke, Edith, *My Mother who Fathered Me* (2nd edn.) London, Allen & Unwin, 1966).

Cohen, B. and Jenner, P., 'The Employment of Immigrants: a case study within the wool industry', *Race* (Vol. X, no. 1, July 1968).

Collins, Sidney, *Coloured Minorities in Britain* (London, Lutterworth Press, 1957).

Collins, W., *Jamaican Migrant* (London, Routledge & Kegan Paul, 1965).

Conference on Racial Equality in Employment, London, February 1967, *Report* (London, National Committee for Commonwealth Immigrants, 1967).

Cumper, G. E., 'Employment in Barbados', *Social and Economic Studies* (Vol. VIII, no. 2, 1959).

— 'Working Class Emigration from Barbados to the U.K., October 1955', *Social and Economic Studies* (Vol. VI, no. 1, 1957).

Dahya, Z., 'Pakistan Wives in Britain', *Race* (Vol. VI, no. 3, January 1965).

Daniel, W. W., *Racial Discrimination in England* (Harmondsworth, Penguin Books, 1968).

Davison, Betty, 'No Place Back Home: a study of Jamaicans returning to Kingston, Jamaica', *Race* (Vol. IX, no. 4, April 1968).

Davison, R. B., *Black British* (London, O.U.P., for I.R.R., 1966).

— *West Indian Migrants* (London, O.U.P., for I.R.R., 1962).

Deakin, Nicholas (ed.), *Colour and the British Electorate 1964* (London, Pall Mall Press, 1965).

— 'The Politics of the Commonwealth Immigrants Bill', *Political Quarterly* (Vol. 39, no. 1, January–March 1968).

Deedes, W., *Race Without Rancour* (London, Conservative Research Department, 1968).

Derrick, June, *English for the Children of Immigrants*, Schools Council, Working Paper, No. 13 (London, H.M.S.O., 1967).

Desai, R., *Indian Immigrants in Britain* (London, O.U.P., for I.R.R., 1963).

Donnison, D. V., *The Government of Housing* (Harmondsworth, Penguin Books, 1967).

Economist Intelligence Unit, *The Immigrant Community in Southall* (London, E.I.U., 1965).

Economist Intelligence Unit, *Studies on Immigration from the Commonwealth, 1. Basic statistics* (London, E.I.U., 1961).

Eversley, D. and Sukdeo, F., *The Dependants of the Coloured Commonwealth Population of England and Wales* (London, I.R.R., Special Series, 1969).

Fitzherbert, K., *West Indian Children in London* (London, G. Bell, 1967).

Foley, Maurice, Speech given at Leicester, 12 September 1965, reprinted in *Plebs* (December 1965).

Foot, Paul, *Immigration and Race in British Politics* (Harmondsworth, Penguin Books, 1965).

Francis, O. C., 'The Characteristics of Emigrants just prior to Changes in British Commonwealth Immigration Policies', in *The Caribbean in Transition* (University of Puerto Rico, Institute of Caribbean Studies, 1965).

— *The People of Modern Jamaica* (Kingston, Department of Statistics, 1963).

Glass, Ruth, *Newcomers* (London, Allen & Unwin, for Centre for Urban Studies, 1960).

Glass, R. and Westergaard, J., *London's Housing Needs* (London, Centre for Urban Studies, 1965).

Goodall, John, 'Huddersfield', I.R.R. *Newsletter* Supplement (October 1966).

Griffith, J. A. G., *Central Departments and Local Authorities* (London, Allen & Unwin, 1966).

Grigg, Mary, *The White Question* (London, Secker & Warburg, 1967).

Hall, Stuart, *The Young Englanders* (London N.C.C.I., 1967).

Hawkes, N., *Immigrant Children in British Schools* (London, Pall Mall Press, for I.R.R., 1966).

Heineman, Jr., B. W., 'The Politics of Race: a study of the Campaign Against Racial Discrimination' (unpublished B.Litt. thesis, Oxford, 1967).

Henriques, Fernando, *Family and Colour in Jamaica* (London, Eyre & Spottiswoode, 1953).

Hepple, Bob, *Race, Jobs and the Law* (London, Allen Lane, the Penguin Press, 1968).

Hill, Clifford S., *West Indian Migrants and the London Churches* (London, O.U.P., for I.R.R., 1963).

Hill, C. S. and Matthew, D. (eds.), *Race: A Christian Symposium* (London, Gollancz, 1968).

Hindell, K., 'The Genesis of the Race Relations Bill', *Political Quarterly* (Vol. 36, no. 4, October–December 1965).

Hinds, Donald, *Journey to an Illusion* (London, Heinemann, 1966).

Hunte, J. A., *Nigger Hunting in England?* (London, West Indian Standing Conference, London Branch, 1966).

International Social Service, *Immigrants at London Airport and their Settlement in the Community* (London, I.S.S., June 1967).

Israel, W. H., *Colour and Community* (Slough, Council of Social Service, 1964).

James, J., in Campaign Against Racial Discrimination *News Letter* (No. 2, July 1967).

Jenkins, Rt. Hon. Roy, M.P., Address given by the Home Secretary to a meeting of Voluntary Liaison Committees, 23 May 1966 (London, N.C.C.I., 1966).

Jenkins, Roy, *The Labour Case* (Harmondsworth, Penguin Books, 1959).

Jenkins, Rt. Hon. Roy, M.P., 'Speech to Institute of Race Relations', reprinted in *Race* (Vol. VIII, no. 3, January 1967).

John, DeWitt, *Indian Workers' Associations in Britain* (London, O.U.P., for I.R.R., 1969).

Jones, K., 'Immigrants and the Social Services', *National Institute Economic Review* (No. 41, August 1967).

Lester, A. (ed.), *Essays and Speeches by Roy Jenkins* (London, Collins, 1967).

Lester, A., 'The Race Relations Bill', *Venture* (Vol. XX, no. 5, May 1968).

Lester, A. and Deakin, N. (eds.), *Policies for Racial Equality* (London Fabian Society, 1967).

Little, K. L., *Negroes in Britain: a study of race relations in English society* (London, Kegan Paul, 1947).

Lowenthal, David, 'Race and Colour in the West Indies', in *Daedalus* (Spring 1967).

Manchester University Liberal Society, Study Group, *Anti-immigrant Organizations* (London, Union of Liberal Students, 1966).

Marris, P., 'The British Asians in Kenya', *Venture* (Vol. XX, no. 4, April 1968).

Marsh, P., *The Anatomy of a Strike: Unions, Employers, and Punjabi Workers in a Southall Factory* (London, I.R.R., Special Series, 1967).

Maunders, W. F., 'The New Jamaican Emigration', *Social and Economic Studies* (Vol. IV, no. 1).

Maxwell, Neville A., *The Power of Negro Action* (London, The Author, 1965).

Milson, F., *Operation Integration Two: The Coloured Teenager in Birmingham* (Birmingham, Westhill College of Education, September 1966).

Morris, H. S., *The Indians in Uganda* (London, Weidenfeld & Nicolson, 1968).

Nandy, Dipak, *The National Committee for Commonwealth Immigrants* (C.A.R.D. discussion paper, July 1967).

National Committee for Commonwealth Immigrants, *The First Six Months: a report of the National Committee for Commonwealth Immigrants* (London, N.C.C.I., 1966).

National Committee for Commonwealth Immigrants, *Areas of Special Housing Needs* (London, N.C.C.I., May 1967).
— *The Housing of Commonwealth Immigrants* (London, N.C.C.I., April 1967).
— *Practical Suggestions for Teachers of Immigrant Children* (London, N.C.C.I., 1967).
— *Report for 1966* (London, N.C.C.I., 1967).
— *Report for 1967* (London, N.C.C.I., 1968).
National Union of Teachers, *The N.U.T. view on the Education of Immigrants* (London, N.U.T., 1967).
Nevitt, Della, *Housing, Taxation and Subsidies* (London, Nelson, 1966).
Oakley, R., *New Backgrounds* (London, O.U.P., for I.R.R., 1968).
Patterson, Orlando, *The Children of Sisyphus* (London, Hutchinson, 1964).
Patterson, S., *Dark Strangers* (London, Tavistock Publications, 1963).
— *Immigrants in Industry* (London, O.U.P., for I.R.R., 1968).
Peach, G. C. K., 'Factors affecting the Distribution of West Indians in Britain', in *Transactions and Papers 1966* (No. 38, Institute of British Geographers, 1966).
— 'West Indian Migration to Britain: the Economic Factors', in *Race* (Vol. VII, no. 1, July 1965).
— *West Indian Migration to Britain* (London, O.U.P., for I.R.R., 1968).
Political and Economic Planning and Research Services Ltd., *Racial Discrimination* (London, P.E.P., 1967).
Powell, Rt. Hon. J. Enoch, M.P., Text of speech delivered on 20 April 1968 in Birmingham, *Race* (Vol. X, no. 1, July 1968).
Power, J., *Immigrants in School: a survey of administrative policies* (London, Councils and Education Press, 1967).
Race Relations Board, *Report of the Race Relations Board 1966–7* (London, H.M.S.O., 1967).
Radin, B., 'Coloured Workers and British Trade Unions', *Race* (Vol. VIII, no. 2, October 1966).
Report of the National Advisory Commission on Civil Disorders (Kerner Report) (New York, Bantam Books, 1968).
Rex, J., 'The Race Relations Catastrophe', in *Matters of Principle: Labour's Last Chance* (Harmondsworth, Penguin Books, 1968).
Rex, J. and Moore, R., *Race, Community and Conflict: a study of Sparkbrook* (London, O.U.P., for I.R.R., 1967).
Richmond, A. H., *Colour Prejudice in Britain: a study of West Indian workers in Liverpool, 1942–51* (London, Routledge, 1954).
Richmond, A. H., *The Colour Problem* (Harmondsworth, Penguin Books, 1955).
Roberts, G. W. and Abdulah, N., 'Some Observations on the Educational Position of the Caribbean', *Social and Economic Studies* (Vol. XIV, no. 1, March 1965).

Roberts, G. W. and Mills, D. O., 'Study of External Migration affecting Jamaica 1953–55', *Social and Economic Studies* (Vol. VII, no. 2, Supplement, 1958).

Rose, Hilary, *The Housing Problem* (London, Heineman, 1968).

Silver, Eric, 'Maurice Foley', in I.R.R. *Newsletter* (February 1967).

Simpson, G. W. and Yinger, J. M., *Racial and Cultural Minorities: an analysis of prejudice and discrimination* (3rd edn.) (New York, Harper and Row, 1955).

Singh, Kushwant, *A History of the Sikhs 1839–1964*, Vol. 2 (Princeton, Princeton University Press, 1966).

Tajfel, H and Davison, J. L. (eds.), *Disappointed Guests* (London, O.U.P., for I.R.R., 1965).

Times News Team, *Black Man in Search of Power* (London, Nelson, 1968).

Titmuss, R. H., *Commitment to Welfare* (London, Allen & Unwin, 1968).

Townsend, P., *Social Services for All*, Part one and four, Fabian Tracts 382 and 385 (London, Fabian Society, 1968).

Trades Union Congress, *99th Annual Report, 1967* (Cooperative Printing Society, n.d.).

Uberoi, Narindar, 'Sikh Women in Southall', *Race* (Vol. VI, no. 1, July 1965).

U.N.E.S.C.O., *The Positive Contribution by Immigrants* (Paris, U.N.E.S.C.O., 1955).

Waterhouse, J. A. H. and Brabban, D. H., 'Inquiry into fertility of immigrants: preliminary report', *The Eugenics Review* (Vol. 56, no. 1, April 1964).

West Indian Standing Conference, *The Unsquare Deal* (London, W.I.S.C., 1967).

Whitaker, B., *The Police* (Harmondsworth, Penguin Books, 1964).

Wiles, S., 'Children from Overseas' (1) and (2), in I.R.R. *Newsletter* (February and June 1968).

Williams, L. F. Rushbrook, *The State of Pakistan* (rev. edn.) (London, Faber, 1966).

Williams, R. M., *Strangers Next Door: ethnic relations in American communities* (Englewood Cliffs, Prentice Hall, 1964).

Willmott, P. and Young, M., *Family and Kinship in East London* (London, Routledge & Kegan Paul, 1957).

Wood, W. and Downing, J., *Vicious Circle* (London, S.P.C.K., 1968).

Wright, P., *The Coloured Worker in British Industry* (London, O.U.P., for I.R.R., 1968).

Yudkin, S., *The Health and Welfare of the Immigrant Child* (London, N.C.C.I., 1965).

Zander, M., 'The Unused Rent Acts', *New Society* (Vol. 12, no. 311, 12 September 1968).

Official References

Children and their Primary Schools, a Report of the Central Advisory Council for Education (Plowden Report) (London, H.M.S.O., 1967).

Commonwealth Immigrants, Circular No. 15/67 (London, Home Office, February 1967).

Commonwealth Immigrants Act, 1962 (London, H.M.S.O., 1962).

Commonwealth Immigrants Act, 1968 (London, H.M.S.O., 1968).

Commonwealth Immigrants Act 1962: control of immigration statistics 1962/3–1966, Home Office (Cmnd. 2151, 2379, 2658, 2979, 3258) (London, H.M.S.O., 1962–7).

Commonwealth Immigrants Advisory Council, *Report* (Cmnd. 2119) (London, H.M.S.O., July 1963).

— *Second Report* (Cmnd. 2266) (London, H.M.S.O., February 1964).

— *Third Report* (Cmnd. 2458) (London, H.M.S.O., September 1964).

— *Fourth Report* (Cmnd. 2796) (London, H.M.S.O., October 1965).

The Education of Immigrant Pupils in Primary Schools, Report of the Working Party of Members of the Inspectorate and School Psychological Service (London, Inner London Education Authority, 1967).

The Education of Immigrants, Department of Education and Science, Circular No. 7/65 (London, D.E.S., June 1965).

English for Immigrants, Ministry of Education (London, H.M.S.O., 1963).

General Register Office, Census 1961 England and Wales (London, H.M.S.O.).

— Sample Census 1966 Great Britain (London, H.M.S.O.).

Half Our Future, A Report of the Central Advisory Committee for Education, England (Newson Report) (London, H.M.S.O., 1963).

The Housing Programme 1965 to 1970, Minister of Housing and Local Government, White Paper (Cmnd. 2838) (London, H.M.S.O., 1965).

Immigrants and the Youth Service, Report of a Committee of the Youth Service Development Council (Hunt Report) (London, D.E.S., July 1967).

Immigration Appeals Bill 1968, Aliens: Draft Instruction to Immigration Officers, Home Office, White Paper (Cmnd. 3830) (London, H.M.S.O., 1968).

Immigration from the Commonwealth, The Prime Minister, White Paper (Cmnd. 2739) (London, H.M.S.O., August 1965).

Old Houses into New Homes, White Paper (Cmnd. 3602) (London, H.M.S.O., April 1968).

Our Older Homes: A Call for Action, Report of the Sub-Committee on Standards of Housing Fitness (Denington Report) (London, H.M.S.O., 1966).

Race Relations Act 1965 (London, H.M.S.O., 1965).

Race Relations Act 1968 (London, H.M.S.O., 1968).

Report of the Committee on Housing in Greater London (Milner Holland Report) (Cmnd. 2605) (London, H.M.S.O., 1965).

Report of the Committee on Immigration Appeals (Wilson Committee) (Cmnd. 3387) (London, H.M.S.O., 1967).

Report of the Committee on Local Authority and Allied Personal Social Services (Seebohm Report) (Cmnd. 3703) (London, H.M.S.O., 1968).

Royal Commission on Trade Unions and Employers' Associations 1965-1968, *Report* (Donovan Commission) (Cmnd. 3623) (London, H.M.S.O., 1968).

Special But Not Separate, A Report on the Situation of Young Coloured People in Liverpool (Liverpool, Liverpool Youth Organisations Committee, 1968).

The Work of the Youth Employment Service 1965-8, Central Youth Employment Executive (London, H.M.S.O., 1968).

Unpublished Survey Material

Action Society, 'Study of Immigrant Workers in London Transport'.
Allen, Sheila, 'Study of Pakistanis in Employment, Bradford'.
Bloom, Leonard, 'Study of Butetown, Cardiff'.
Butterworth, Eric, 'Policies for Integration: a study of Bradford'.
Craven, Anna, 'Study of West Africans in London'.
Dayha, B., 'Study of Pakistanis in Bradford'.
— 'Study of Yemenis in Birmingham'.
Figueroa, Peter, 'West Indian School Leavers in North London'.
Gaitskell, Julia, 'Study of Employment, Croydon'.
Kinder, Clive, 'Study of Moss Side'.
Lambert, John, 'Study of Immigrant Crime and the Relations of the
    Police and Immigrants in a Division of Birmingham'.
Lyon, Michael, 'Study of Settlement Patterns'.
McPherson, Klim, 'Survey of Immigrants in Industry in East London,
    and in particular their Relations with the Trade Unions'.
Oakley, Robin, 'Study of Cypriots'.
Patnaik, Anjali, 'Study of Sikhs in Southall'.
Patterson, Sheila, 'Social History of Immigration to Britain, 1840–
    1965'.
Radburn, Robert, 'Investigation of Household Budgets among a
    Sample of Indians, Pakistanis, and West Indians in the Midlands'.
Richmond, Anthony and Lyon, Michael, 'Race Relations in Bristol'.
Sington, Derrick, 'Race Relations and the Police'.
Skone, Dr. J. F. and Simpson, Dr. R. E., 'Socio-medical Study,
    Bristol'.
Yemeni, Ben-Hur, 'Study of Prejudice and Discrimination'.

INDEX

accommodation, defined, 25

Alavi, H., joins N.C.C.I., 523; *on* the White Paper, *Immigration from the Commonwealth,* 526

Anglo-American Conference on Employment, *see* Racial Equality in Employment Conference

aliens, numbers in Britain, 72, 73

Aliens Order, 1953, *and* health controls, 331

Allen, Sir K., *on* racial equality in employment, 531

Allison, A., description of a West Indian pupil, 283

anti-discrimination legislation, *see* discrimination and legislation

anti-immigration associations, 217, **393–400**, 619

apprenticeships, 482

Argus Briton's Rights Association, 395

Armed Services, *and* coloured personnel, 305–6

assimilation, defined, 23–4

Association of Teachers of English to Pupils from Overseas, 278–9

attitudes, *and* beliefs, 566–70; *and* beliefs and stereotypes, 570–2; changes in, 1958–68, 592–600; *and* cultural background, 602; *and* employment, 299, 575–8; *and* housing, 578–81; hypotheses, 600–3; measured by personality factors, 565–6; measured by social and demographic characteristics, 554–64; measured on prejudice-tolerance scale, 552–3, 593, 790–1; *and* perceptions of other group attitudes, 583–4; *and* personal contact, 572–5; *and* relative deprivation, 601–2; sample design, 551–2, 785; *and* social distance, 601; *and* status crystallization, 602; survey of, **551–88**, **785–94**; to anti-discrimination legislation, 597; to coloured people, **551–604**; to different ethnic groups, 581–3

Banton, M., *White and Coloured,* 592

Barbados Immigrants Liaison Service, 67

Beddoe, J., *Colour and Race,* 28

Birmingham, Coloured People's Liaison Officer, 247; cost of schools for immigrant children, 648; education of immigrant children, 277–8; housing, 246–51; incidence of T.B., 335; survey of immigrant households, 182–97; *see also* Sparkbrook

Birmingham Corporation Act, 1965, 249

Birmingham Immigration Control Association, 217, 395

Black People's Alliance, 620

Black Power, 732, 755

Bonham Carter, M., appointed Chairman of Race Relations Board, 514

Boyle, Sir E., *on* education of immigrant children, 268

Bradford, coloured workers and trade unions, 313–14; housing, 238, 252–4; incidence of T.B., 334–5; infant mortality rates, 343; provision of hostel facilities, 342

Bristol, West Indian immigrants and housing, 254–7, 426–9

Bristol Committee for the Welfare of Colonial Workers, 383

British Caribbean Association, 214

British Caribbean Welfare Service, 211, 499

British Council of Churches, 377

British Hotels and Restaurants Association, recruitment of skilled labour from Barbados, 68, 78, 86

British Medical Association, *and* health controls, 332–3; *Medical Examination of Immigrants,* 1965, 332–4, 335, 336

British Nationality Act, 1948, 21, 208

British Overseas Socialist Fellowship, 221, 523

British Rail, employment of coloured workers, 309

Brooke, H., *on* race relations policy, 206

Burney, E., *on* size of immigrant households, 123

Butterworth, E., *on* Bradford housing, 238, 253; *on* health patterns in Bradford, 343; *on* immigrant labour, 645–6

Callaghan, J., defines integration, 608; on Race Relations Bill, 1968, 608

Camden Committee for Community Relations, 390

Campaign Against Racial Discrimination, 525–7, 528, 543, 546; Islington branch, 390

Campaign for a Rational Immigration Policy, 228

C.A.R.D., see Campaign Against Racial Discrimination

Cardiff, coloured community, 487–90

Carron, Sir W., on immigrants and welfare services, 316–17

Catholic Institute for International Relations, 377

Census, 1961, 91–5, 769–73

Census, 1966 Sample, 91–5, 769–73; under-enumeration, 95, 98, 774–5

Central Office of Information, attitude survey, 592

Chapman, R. D., and education of immigrant children, 277, 278

child-minders, 346, 478–9, 703

children, coloured, born in U.K., 98–9, 774; see also second generation

Church of England, Board of Social Responsibility, 377

Churches, 370–80; and Asian immigrants, 376–7; attendance, 372–3; community activities, 373; and integration, 371–2; pentecostal, 374–5; publications, 377; and race prejudice, 370; and schools, 379–80, 709–10; Survey recommendations, 732–4; use of buildings, 378–9; in West Indies, 45–6, 62n

Citizens Advice Bureaux, 718

citizenship, 13–25; Survey recommendations, 751–2

Civil Service, and coloured personnel, 306–7

class/colour theory, 5

Cohen, B., on economic aspects of immigration, 646

Collins, W., experience as an immigrant, 434

colour/class theory, 5

coloured immigrants, age structure, 108–12, 636; and crime rates, 357; demographic data, 104–19; distribution in Britain, 80–1, 100–3, 678–83; and employment, 78–80, 149–72, 180–181, 296–327; family structure, 116–19; and housing, 120–48, 187–93, 232–62; income and expenditure, 182–97;

marital status, 106–8; numbers in Britain, 72, 96–100, 629–38, 776–80; remittances and savings, 193–5, 442–3, 644, 649; sex ratio, 104–6, 636; socio-economic status, 172–7; and unemployment, 177–80; see also under countries of origin

Coloured Immigrants in Britain, 8–9

Coloured Peoples' Progressive Association, 500

Commonwealth Immigrants Act 1962, 77, 83, 87; Expiring Laws continuance debates, 512, 514, 539, 546; health controls, 331

Commonwealth Immigrants Act 1968, assessed, 625–7; health controls, 332

Commonwealth Immigrants Advisory Council, 221, 523; and education of immigrant children, 265–7

Commonwealth Immigrants Bill 1962, 220–1

Commonwealth Immigrants Bill 1968, 610–14

Commonwealth Property Owners' Association, 505

Commonwealth Welfare Council for the West Midlands, 385

Communist Party of India, and Indian Workers' Association, 498, 503

community centres, 721

Community Relations Commission, 621; Survey recommendations, 727–31; see also under National Committee for Commonwealth Immigrants

community relations councils, see voluntary liaison committees

community service, 735–6

conciliation, and anti-discrimination legislation, 536–7; Hahn's scheme, 531; in industry, 298–9, 318–19

Confederation of British Industry, and anti-discrimination legislation, 521, 529, 535; non-discrimination policy, 317–19; and voluntary conciliation, 536–7

Confederation of Shipbuilding Engineering Unions, non-discrimination policy, 318

Conservative party, manifesto, Make Life Better, 752

Constantine, Lord, and Overseas Volunteers Scheme, 66

Council of Christians and Jews, 376

crime and delinquency, 357, 430, 486–7

Crossman, R., *and* anti-discrimination legislation, 518; *on* housing, 257

Cypriot immigrants, age structure, 110; employment, 151–71 *passim*; family structure, 117; fertility, 113, 114; housing, 122–47 *passim*; marital status, 106; numbers in Britain (with Maltese), 72, 97; sex ratio, 105

Daniel, W. W., *on* discrimination in employment, 411

Davison, R. B., survey of West Indian living conditions, 92–3, 138, 140

Deakin, N., 9

Deedes, W., *on* R. Jenkins as Home Secretary, 548

de Freitas, M., *and* Coloured Peoples' Progressive Association, 496

demographic policy, Survey recommendations, **752–3**

dependants, analysis of arrivals, 88–90, 795–6

deportation, 213, 750

Derrick, J., *and* Leeds project, 280–1, 287–8

Dines, M., *on* West Indian children in care, 342

discrimination and legislation, 304, **511–533, 534–50**; attitudes towards, 597; extensions to housing and employment, 514–15, 525, 537; and Government contracts, 304, 528, 712; policy aims, 517–18; Survey recommendations, **686–8**; and voluntary conciliation, 536–7; *see also* P.E.P. Report; Race Relations acts and bills; Street Report

dispersal policy, 678–83

Donnison, D. V., *on* housing, 235

Ealing, housing, 245–6; Pathway Further Education Centre, 706

earnings, *see* income

education, **264–93**, 479–81; achievement, 270–1, 286–7, 480–1; Association of Teachers of English to Pupils from Overseas, 278–9; Churches' provision, 379–80, 709–10; cost of schools in Birmingham, 648; dispersal policy, 265–73, 288–93, 678, 699; H.M. Inspectorate, 290–1, 699–700; language classes, 273–8; liaison officers, 707; Leeds project, 280–1, 287–8, 708–9; local authority activities, 273–278, 701–2; N.C.C.I. Education Panel,

279; quotas, 268, 291; Spring Grove primary school, 271; Survey recommendations, **698–710**; teacher training, 279–81, 700–3; West Indian children, 281–6, 709; *see also* children; second generation; school leavers

Education and Science, Department of, circular 7/65, *The Education of Immigrants*, 268; circular 8/67, *Immigrants and the Youth Service*, 698; definition of immigrant children, 269; *Parent/Teacher Relations in Primary Schools*, 707; Survey recommendations, **699–701**

Egbuna, O., *and* U.C.P.A., 546

Empire Windrush, S.S., 66, 208

Employment and Productivity, Department of, *see* Labour, Ministry of

employment and unemployment, **149–181, 296–327**; anti-discrimination legislation, 514–15; *and* armed services, 305–6; attitudes, 299, 575–8; *and* civil service, 306–7; closed shop system, 312–13; company policies, 714–15; *and* discrimination, 297–301, 710–11; economic activity, 150–2; employers' associations, 317–19; exchanges, 302–303, 712–13; Government contracts, 304, 528, 712; Government policies, 301–11; *and* health services, 307–8; *and* immigration, 641–3; industrial distribution, 166–72; industrial status, 152–5; *and* local government, 310; *and* nationalized industries, 307–10; occupational distribution, 155–66, 781–4; *and* P.E.P. Report, 297, 407–11, 534; post-war situation, 78–81; *and* promotion, 301; quotas, 300, 303; record keeping, 711; skills of coloured workers, 319–23; socio-economic status, 172–7; *and* strikes, 315–16; Survey recommendations, **710–17**; *and* trade unions, 311–317, 715–16; training for, 716–17; *see also* apprenticeships; Industrial Relations Commission; Racial Equality in Employment Conference; recruitment schemes; Youth Employment Service

employment vouchers, *see* Labour, Ministry of

Engineering Employers' Federation, non-discrimination policy, 318

Ennals, D., *and* race relations policy, 614–15

Ennals, M., *on* C.A.R.D., 527; joins N.C.C.I., 524; survey of Kenya Asians, 625

Equal Rights, 615, 617, 618
estate agents, 243, 693
European Economic Community, and migrant labour, 78, 751
European Volunteer Workers, 20
Expiring Laws continuance debates, see Commonwealth Immigrants Act 1962

family, size and structure, 106–19
Family Expenditure Survey, 1966, 182
Fanon, F., on colour, 21
fertility statistics, 112–16
Fitzherbert, K., on West Indian children in care, 342
Foley, M., as Co-ordinator of Policy on Integration, 225, 511–12; move to Home Office, 516

Gallup Poll, attitude surveys, 592–3, 602
Gardiner, Lord, on race relations, 206
Georgic, S.S., 66
ghetto, defined, 678
Glass, R., on housing, 235
Government contracts, 304, 528, 712
Government, machinery of, and Survey recommendations, 683–6
Greater London Council, mortgage scheme, 244
Grigg, M., on voluntary liaison committees, 343
Gujarat, 57–8
Gunter, R., and anti-discrimination legislation, 518, 544; on the White Paper, Immigration from the Commonwealth, 512

Hahn, O., scheme for voluntary conciliation, 531
Handlin, O., definition of immigration, 16
Health, Ministry of, advice to general practitioners, 333–4; see also Social Affairs, Department of
Health and Social Security, Department of, see Social Affairs, Department of
Health and Welfare services, 330–49; and child-minders, 346, 478–9; coloured personnel, 307–8; community centres, 721; health controls, 331–4; health education, 344–5; hospital services, 336–9; and immigrants' tax contributions, 647–9; and immigration controls, 348; incidence of T.B. and V.D., 334–6; local authority expenditure, 346–7; local authority provision, 339, 342, 720–1; mental health, 337–8;

and nursery schools, 345–6, 703, 719–720; social workers' problems, 340–1; Survey recommendations, 717–21; Youth Service, 343–4
Heath, E., speech on immigration, September 1968, 623–4
Heineman, B., on anti-discrimination legislation, 514–24 passim, 543; on W.I.S.C., 506
Hepple, B., on Race Relations Board powers, 519–20
Hindus, 57, 468–72
Holland, Milner, see Milner Holland
Home Office, and inter-departmental working party on immigration, 208–9, 212; and research, 685; see also Callaghan; Foley; Jenkins; Soskice
Hornsby-Smith, P., on Indian and Pakistani immigrants, 212
households, Birmingham survey, 182–97; size, 123–5, 127–8, 135, 184
housing, 120–48, 232–62; and attitudes to coloured people, 558–61; changes 1961–66, 138–47; density, 121–5, 135; and estate agents, 243, 693; facilities, 129–32, 136; in Birmingham, 246–51; in Bradford, 238, 252–4; in Ealing and Southall, 245–6, 455; in Lambeth, 239–42; in Wolverhampton, 251–2; landlords, 248; local authority provision, 236–9, 690–2, 693–5; mortgages, 190, 243–4, 691–2, 695; multi-occupation, 235–6, 239, 249, 257; N.C.C.I. Housing Panel, 259, 541–2; New Towns, 696–7; and P.E.P. Report, 411–14; property values, 245–6; rents, 191–3, 690; shared, 125–8, 136; and Sikh immigrants, 454–5; subsidies, 696; supply, 232–4; Survey recommendations, 688–97; tenure, 132–4 137; and West Indian immigrants, 424–9, 430
Housing Act, 1961, 247
housing associations, 260–1, 379, 384, 695–6
Housing Programme 1965–1970, The, White Paper, November 1965, 258
Housing Subsidies Act, 1967, 260
Hunt Report, on Immigrants and the Youth Service, 343–4, 485, 544

illiteracy, see literacy
Immigrants Advisory Committee, see London Council of Social Service, Immigrants Advisory Committee

immigration, **43–62**; arrivals, 1955–67, 82–3; changing proportions, 84; economic aspects, **629–55**; entry refused, on health grounds, 333; estimates, 1952–62, 69; from India, 52–8; from Pakistan, 58–62, 440–1; from West Indies, 43–51; Handlin's definition, 16; health controls, 331–4; Home Office inter-departmental working party, 208–9, 212; host society response, 403–6; Jenkins' formula, 515, 659; policies, **206–30, 605–27**, 657–61; post-war development, **65–73**; sponsorship systems, 70, 441–2; Survey recommendations, **683–4, 744–53**; see also dependants; deportation; migration; and under countries of origin

immigration appeals, Wilson Committee on, 348, 544, 546

immigration controls, 70–1, 209, 211, 219–21; associations, 217, 393–400, 619; and bilateral agreements, 212, 213, 218–19, 227; effect on migration, 68, 77, 82, 104, 444–5, 476; and health checks, 331–4; and illegal entry, 71, 539; and welfare services, 348

Immigration from the Commonwealth, White Paper, August 1965, 511–12; criticisms, 203, 504, 526; and education, 268–9; and health and welfare services, 346; and housing, 232; proposals, 227–8

Immigration Officers' Instructions, 1966, and health controls, 332

income and expenditure, 182–97

income tax, evasion, 446; immigrants' tax contributions, 647–9

Indian immigrants, **52–8, 452–72**; areas of emigration, 52–3; and dispersal, 680; as landlords, 248–9; and leadership, 497–9, 502–4; post-war emigration, 68, 70; white Indians, 94–5, 769–73

Indian Workers' Association, activities, 71, 457–8, 465, 497–9, 502–3, 526; Coventry branch, 497; Southall branch, 620

Industrial Relations Commission, 714

industry, see employment

Inner London Education Authority, *The Education of Immigrant Children in Primary Schools*, 270–1, 292, 480–1

Institute of Race Relations, evidence to Seebohm Committee, 331; see also Mason, P.

integration, 662–5; Callaghan's defini-

tion, 608; Government policy, 199–205; Government policy and Survey recommendations, **683–4**; Jenkins' definition, 25, 514; Labour party policy, 221; and local authorities, 201–2; meanings of, 24; and role of law, 200; see also pluralism

intelligence and race, 38–40

inter-marriage, 448–9, 470

International Social Service, London Airport survey, 88, 348, 719

Irish immigrants, 17–19; age structure, 111; family structure, 117, 118; fertility, 113, 114, 116; housing, 122–46 *passim*; numbers in Britain, 72, 73, 97; sex ratio, 105; socio-economic status, 173–7 *passim*

Isaac, J., on immigration, 660

Jamaica, Colonial Office Report on, 66; migration to United States, 67

Jamaican immigrants, distribution in Britain, 102–3; numbers in Britain, 97–8

Jats, see Sikhs

Jenkins, R., and anti-discrimination legislation, 511–33, 534–50; defines integration, 25, 514; Home Secretaryship assessed, 547–8; immigration formula, 515, 659; personality assessment, 513–14; 'social contract' argument, 539–40; speech to I.R.R., 527; speech to London Labour party, 536; speech to National Co-ordinating Conference, 521

Jenner, P., on economic aspects of immigration, 646

Jewish immigrants, 19–20

Joint Council for the Welfare of Immigrants, 348, 620–1, 750

Jones, J., on anti-discrimination legislation, 530

Jones, K., on immigrants and the social services, 330

Keith, Sir A., on race, 28

Kent, B., on problems of social workers, 340–1

Kenya Asian immigrants, 539, 545, 547, 610–12, 623–6

Kerner Report, 2, 12, 678

Kushnick, L., on complaints against police, 353

Labour, Ministry of, employment exchanges, 302–3, 712–13; employment vouchers, 83–7, 89
Labour party, Home Policy Committee study, 221; National Executive Committee Working Party on race relations, 544–5
Lambeth, housing, 239–42
leadership, **492–510**; Survey recommendations, **731–2**
League of Coloured Peoples, 494
Lester, A., *on* Commonwealth Immigrants Act, 1968, 626
liberalism, 12
literacy, decline in rate for migrants, 49; in Barbados, 46; in Gujarat, 57; in Pakistan, 60; in the Punjab, 57
Liverpool, coloured community, 490
Lloyd-George, G., *on* integration policy, 200
local authorities, coloured personnel, 310; *and* education, 273–8, 701–2; *and* health and welfare services, 339, 342, 346–7, 720–1; *and* housing, 236–9, 690–2, 693–5; *and* voluntary liaison committees, 385
Local Government Act, 1966, *and* local authority expenditure on immigrants, 346; Survey recommendations, **685**
Local Government Bill, 518
Local Government Grants (Social Need) Bill, 685
London Council of Social Service, Immigrants Advisory Committee, 385, 522–3
London and Home Countries Tenants' Association, 397
London Transport, recruitment policies, 67, 78, 86, 308–9
Lyttle, J., joins Race Relations Board, 521

McCarran-Walter Act, 1952, 67
Macleod, I., *on* immigration control, 219
Maltese immigrants, numbers in Britain (with Cypriots), 72, 97
Mancroft, Lord, *on* immigration controls, 211
Marris, P., *on* Kenya Asians, 625
Marshall, R., *and* Equal Rights, 615
Marshall, T. H., *on* citizenship, 17, 27
Marx, K., *on* Irish immigration, 18
Mason, P., 8–9; *on* immigration policy, 658
mass media, 740–4

Maxwell, N., *on* pluralism, 439; *on* West Indian leadership, 506
migrant labour, 78
Migrant Services Division, *see* West Indian Federal High Commission
migration, determinants, 74–7; return, 433
Milner Holland Report, on *Housing in Greater London*, 239
miscegenation, *see* inter-marriage
Moody, H., *and* League of Coloured Peoples, 494
Mosley, Sir O., 215
Muslims, 58, 60–1
Myrdal, G., *An American Dilemma*, 1–2, 602

Nandy, D., *on* C.A.R.D., 543; *on* N.C.C.I., 542; *on* voluntary liaison committees, 387
National Association of Schoolmasters, *The Education of Immigrant Children*, 698
National Committee for Commonwealth Immigrants, *afterwards* Community Relations Commission, **522–5**; advisory panels, 525, 541; *and* Commonwealth Immigrants Bill, 1968, 615; Conference on Racial Equality in Employment, 531; Education Panel, 279; evidence to Seebohm Committee, 331; Housing Panel, 259, 541–2; origins and role, 522–33, 542; *on* White Paper, *Immigration from the Commonwealth*, 524; *and* 'Wood proposals', 621; *see also* voluntary liaison committees
National Federation of Pakistani Associations, 505
N.C.C.I., *see* National Committee for Commonwealth Immigrants
neighbourhood projects, 734; *see also* Sparkbrook Association
Notting Hill Social Council, 389
Nottingham Commonwealth Citizens Consultative Committee, 383–4
Nuffield Foundation, 9
nursery schools, provision, 345–6, 703, 719–20

Old Houses into New Homes, White Paper, 1968, 259–60, 689
Orbach, M., anti-discrimination bill 528–9
Orbita, S.S., 66
Overseas Volunteers Scheme, 66

Oxford Committee for Racial Integration, 391

Page, J., *and* London and Home Counties Tenants' Association, 397
Pakistani immigrants, **58–62, 440–52**; adaptation, 451–2; areas of emigration, 59; attitude to out-groups, 448; contrasts between E. and W. Pakistan, 58; culture conflict, 447; *and* discrimination, 445; *and* dispersal, 680–1; family life, 61; illegal entry, 71, 446, 539; *and* incidence of T.B., 334–5; *and* inter-marriage, 448–9; *and* Islam, 60–1, 446–7; as landlords, 248–9; language differences, 58; literacy, 60; occupational distribution, 60, 449; post-war emigration, 70; social and economic relations, 442–4, 450; sponsorship system, 70, 441–2; *and* tax evasion, 446; white Pakistanis, 94–5, 769–73; women, 72
Parsons, T., *on* the American Negro, 16–17
Pathway Further Education Centre, Ealing, 706
Patterson, S., *on* West Indian immigrants, 422–3
Peach, C., *on* West Indian migration, 74
Pentecostal churches, 45–6, 374–5
Peppard, N., 522, 523
Pitt, D., *and* C.A.R.D., 508; joins N.C.C.I., 523
Plowden Report, on *Children and their Primary Schools*, 704, 706–7
pluralism, 24–5, 439, 663–5
police, **349–66**; complaints against, 353–6, 725–6; in-service training, 362–4, 722–3; liaison officers, 358–61, 724–5; *and* prejudice, 356; recruitment of coloured policemen, 361–2, 723–4; relations with immigrants, 349, 431; relations with public, 352, 726–7; role in society, 350–2, 355; Survey recommendations, **722–7**
Polish immigrants, 20
Political and Economic Planning, *Report on Racial Discrimination*, **406–15**, 534; *and* employment, 297, 407–11, *and* housing, 411–14
Population, Royal Commission on, *and* immigration policy, 207; *see also* demographic policy
Port Advisory and Welfare Service, 348
Powell, E., *on* immigration, 535–6; *on*

Kenya Asians, 545; speech, April 1968, 616, 617–18
prejudice, dimensions of, 589–91; incidence in Britain, 551–604; *see also* attitudes
press, 740–4
Press Council, 741–4
public education, Survey recommendations, **736–44**
Public Health Act, 1936, 331
Public Health Ships and Aircraft Regulations, 1966, 331
Public Order Act, 1936, amended, 520
Punjab, *see* Hindus; Sikhs

race, biological and social aspects of, 34–41
Race Relations Act 1965, deficiencies, 519–20; prosecutions under, 544; Survey recommendations, **687–8**
Race Relations Act 1968, 686, 692, 710
Race Relations Bill 1965, background, 225–6
Race Relations Bill 1968, draft stage, 608–9; passage, 616–18
Race Relations Board, activities, 520–1; M. Bonham Carter, Chairman, 514; powers, 519–20, 686–7, 710; Report, 1966–67, 534
Race Relations Committee, *see* Society of Friends, Race Relations Committee
Rachman, P., 236
Racial Equality in Employment Conference, 531
Racial Preservation Society, 395–6
recruitment schemes, 66, 68, 78, 86, 207
Reid, I., *on* C.A.R.D., 546
remittances and savings, 54, 193–5, 442–3, 644, 649
Rent Act 1957, 234
Rent Act 1965, 690
Research Services Ltd., *see* P.E.P. Report
Rex, J., *on* housing, 236
Richmond, A., *on* migration, 746
Runciman, W. G., *on* relative deprivation, 31–2, 601–2

salaries, *see* income
Salmon, Lord Justice, *on* equal rights, 214
Sandys, D., *on* housing, 240; *on* Hunt Report, 544; *and* immigration policy, 609
savings, *see* remittances and savings
school leavers, *and* employment, 304, 477, 481–4
schools, *see* education

Schools Council, 265, 280, 287, 708–9
Schorr, A., *on* housing, 239
second generation, **476–90**; aspirations, 478; defined, 476, 521; delinquency, 486–7; education, 479–81; employment, 481–4; handicaps, 478; in Cardiff, 487–90; in Liverpool, 490; numbers in schools, 477; social contact, 484–6; *see also* Hunt Report
Seebohm Report, on *Local Authority and Allied Personal Social Services*, 331, 717–718, 721
Select Committee on Race Relations and Immigration, 687
Sikhs, **52–6**, **452–68**; adaptation, 465–8; caste system, 55, 459; childrens' education, 463; family system, 54, 56, 63n.; host community hostility, 464; housing, 454–5; marriage, 458; religion, 54–5, 455–6, 459–61; remittances 54; social and economic relations, 453–4, 461; women, 71–2, 461–2; *and* Woolf's strike, 315–16, 456
Silver, E., *on* Maurice Foley, 512
Simpson, Sir J., *on* police-immigrant relations, 349
slavery, abolition, effects of, 46; legacy of, 47, 48
social services, *see* health and welfare services
Social Affairs, Department of, 684
Social Security, Ministry of, *see* Social Affairs, Department of
Society of Friends, Race Relations Committee, 376, 377, 390–1
Society of Labour Lawyers, *and* anti-discrimination legislation, 545
Soskice, Sir F., retiring Home Secretary, 513
Southall, education of immigrant children, 267–8; housing, 245–6, 455; strike at Woolf's, 315–16, 456
Southall and District Residents' Association, 398
Sparkbrook, Birmingham fertility study, 116
Sparkbrook Association, 389
Stonham, Lord, *on* conciliation, 519; *on* Kenya Asians, 547; *on* race relations policy, 528
'stranger' theory, 5
Street Report, on *Anti-Discrimination Legislation*, 712, 714
strikes, Preston, 315; Queensbury, 316; Southall, 315–16, 456

taxation, *see* income tax
Team Work, on West Indian leadership, 502
Thompson, E. P., *on* Irish immigration, 18
Townsend, P., *on* racial and social equality, 665
trade unions, **311–17**; closed shop system, 312–13; membership, 313–14; *and* strikes, 315–16; Survey recommendations, **715–16**
Trades Union Congress, *and* anti-discrimination legislation, 529–31, 535, 545; non-discrimination policy, 311–312; Survey recommendations, **716**; *and* voluntary conciliation, 536–7

unemployment, *see* employment
United Nations Institute for Training and Research, study of West Indian leadership, 621
United States, National Advisory Commission on Civil Disorders, 2, 12, 678
Universal Coloured Peoples Association, 546
University Council for the Education of Teachers, 702
Urban Programme (1968), 260, 347, 348, 621–3; Survey recommendations, **684–5, 697**

voluntary liaison committees, **380–93**, 541; *and* conciliation, 386; National Co-ordinating Conference, 521; role of liaison officers, 392–3; welfare work, 387

wages, *see* income
Webb, S., *on* race, 29
welfare services, *see* health and welfare services
West Bromwich, hospital services, 336
West Indian Federal High Commission, Migrant Services Division, 499–500
West Indian Gazette, 497
West Indian immigrants, **43–51, 419–40**; adaptation, 422–4, 429–40; areas of emigration, 44; childrens' education, 281–6, 709; class/colour relationships, 47; class distribution, 66; *and* crime rates, 430; cultural background, 45, 420–4; *and* dispersal, 681–2; expectations, 420–2, 434–7; family life, 48, 429, 431–2; *and* housing, 424–9, 430; in Bristol, 255–7, 426–9; in Lambeth,

West Indian immigrants—*cont.*
241–2; leadership, 432, 495–7, 499–502, 505–7, 621; moral standards, 429; *and* newspapers, 433, 497; occupational distribution, 49–51, 63n.; *and* pentecostal churches, 374–5; *and* pluralism, 439; *and* police, 431; post-war emigration, 66–8; qualifications, 49; return migration, 433; use of child care services, 342, 720–1
West Indian Standing Conference, 500–502, 505, 620; *and* police-immigrant relations, 349, 360–1
Westergaard, J., *on* housing, 235
Willesden Friendship Council, 384, 386
Wilson, H., *on* the Urban Programme, 622

Wilson Committee, on *Immigration Appeals*, 348, 544, 546, 750
Wolverhampton, hospital services, 336–337; housing, 251–2
women immigrants, economic activity, 150–1, 152; industrial status, 153, occupation distribution, 155, 157–8, 159, 162–3, 164, 166
Wood, W., *and* 'Wood proposals', 621
Woolf's rubber factory, employment of Sikhs, 454; strike, 315–16, 456

Youth Employment Service, *and* coloured school leavers, 304, 481–4, 713
Youth Service, 343–4; *see also* Hunt Report; community service